France

at its best

BY ROBERT S. KANE

The World at Its Best Travel Series
BRITAIN AT ITS BEST
FRANCE AT ITS BEST
HOLLAND AT ITS BEST
SPAIN AT ITS BEST
GERMANY AT ITS BEST
ITALY AT ITS BEST
SWITZERLAND AT ITS BEST
HAWAII AT ITS BEST
LONDON AT ITS BEST
NEW YORK AT ITS BEST
PARIS AT ITS BEST
WASHINGTON, D.C. AT ITS BEST

A to Z World Travel Guides
GRAND TOUR A TO Z: THE CAPITALS OF EUROPE
EASTERN EUROPE A TO Z
SOUTH PACIFIC A TO Z
CANADA A TO Z
ASIA A TO Z
SOUTH AMERICA A TO Z
AFRICA A TO Z

Robert S. Kane

France at its best

PASSPORT BOOKS
a division of *NTC Publishing Group*
Lincolnwood, Illinois USA

More praise for Robert S. Kane...

"The strength of Kane's books lies in their personal flavor and zestful writing style. He doesn't shy away from expressing opinion, is strong on culture, art, and history, along with dining and shopping."

—Jack Schnedler, *Chicago Sun-Times*

"Kane's books take the reader beyond the expected. His works are carefully researched, succinctly presented and opinionated."

—Jane Abrams, *New York Daily News*

"Kane is a man of perception and taste, with a knowledge of art, architecture and history. He doesn't spare the occasional sharp evaluation if something is less than highest quality."

—Lois Fegan, *Jersey Journal*

"Anyone going should take one of Bob Kane's books."

—Paul Jackson, *New York Post*

"Kane's candor, conciseness and credibility have made his books among the top selling in the travel field—a must for travelers."

—Joel Sleed, *Newhouse News Service*

"Kane does not mince words. His choices, ranked according to price, service, location and ambiance, are selective; he provides opinions."

—Ralph Gardner, *San Antonio Express-News*

"Kane wanders the globe, testing pillows, mattresses and, in some cases, abominable food in order to be a faithful guide, writing his own observations, and leaving nothing to ghost writers or a band of behind-the-scenes reporters; Kane's unafraid to recommend some places and condemn others."

—Maria Lisella, *The Travel Agent*

Published by Passport Books, a division of NTC, Publishing Group
4255 West Touhy Avenue, Lincolnwood, Illinois 60646-1975.

Manufactured in the United States of America.
Library of Congress Catalog Card Number: 89-62583
0 1 2 3 4 5 6 7 8 9 ML 9 8 7 6 5 4 3 2 1

NORTH SEA
ENGLAND
NETHERLANDS
GERMANY
BELGIUM
LUX.
Rhine
La Manche
ENGLISH CHANNEL
Omaha Beach
Arromanches
Cherbourg
Le Havre
Rouen
Bayeux
Honfleur
Trouville
Caen
Deauville
Lille
Amiens
Compiègne
Reims
Chantilly
Versailles
PARIS
Seine
Nancy
Strasbourg
VOSGES
Route du Vin
Colmar
Mulhouse
Basel
St.-Malo
Mont-St.-Michel
Dinard
Dol
Rambouillet
Chartres
Fontainebleau
Fougères
Quimper
Rennes
Vitré
Loctudy
Orléans
Auxerre
Chablis
FRANCE
Angers
Blois
Chambord
Nantes
Tours
Amboise
Semur-en-Auxois
Saumur
Chenonceaux
Vézelay
Dijon
Azay-le-Rideau
Lac Léman
SWITZERLAND
Loire
Beaune
Bourges
Poitiers
Lausanne
Evian-les-Bains
Île de Ré
Mâcon
Genève
La Rochelle
Vichy
Courmayeur
BAY OF BISCAY
Chamonix
Tunnel du Mt. Blanc
Annecy
Mont Blanc
Gironde
Limoges
Clermont-Ferrand
Lyon
Crémieu
Aix-les-Bains
Chambéry
Saône
Voiron
MÉDOC
Périgueux
Grenoble
LES ALPES
ITALY
Bergerac
Les Eyzies-de-Tayac
Sarlat
Bordeaux
St.-Emilion
Rhône
Orange
MONACO
Avignon
Albi
Nimes
CAMARGUE
Les Baux-de-Provence
Vence
Nice
Biarritz
St.-Jean-de-Luz
Montpellier
Arles
Grasse
Antibes
Auch
Toulouse
Cap d'Antibes
Bayonne
Pézenas
Aix-en-Provence
Cannes
Marseille
San Sebastián
Pau
Carcassonne
Cassis
St.-Tropez
Lourdes
Palavas-les-Flots
Stes.-Maries-de-la-Mer
LES PYRÉNÉES
SPAIN
MEDITERRANEAN SEA

For George L. Hern, Jr.

Contents

Foreword

France: La Grande Image

Paris problematical? It is, indeed. As the continent's ranking metropolis—with a name so magical that it has been synonymous over long centuries with the country of which it is capital—Paris has sufficient magnetism to preclude even the well-traveled among us from venturing beyond its core and environs.

Make no mistake. There are reasons. Enough of them for me—admittedly a longtime Paris partisan—to open this expanded and thoroughly revised edition of *France at Its Best* with an in-depth Paris chapter that profiles not only the grand hotels (not everyone can stay at the Bristol or the Crillon), but good-value mid-category and smaller houses in quantity; that counsels not only the occasional splurge meal in glossy restaurants, but recommends a wealth of reasonably priced places for lunching and dining in the style of rank-and-file Parisians themselves; that brings to your attention well over a score of treasure-filled museums to complement the Louvre and the Pompidou; that steers you to quite as many history- and art-filled churches, the better to appreciate that spiritual Paris is infinitely more than Notre-Dame Cathedral; that fills you in on a miscellany of monuments, Sorbonne to City Hall, Invalides to Bois de Boulogne; that appraises an extraordinary shopping scene—*grands magasins* (the department stores) to typically Parisian boutiques; that counsels excursions not only to the obligatory Versailles and Fontainebleau, but to châteaux whose names may be less familiar—Chantilly and Compiègne, St.-Germain-en-Laye and Vaux-le-Vicomte.

Then comes what the non-Parisian French—who constitute, I want to emphasize, some 53 million of the republic's total population of more than 56 million—often call "The Other France": 34 chapters evaluating not only the two areas beyond Paris—Riviera and Loire Valley—where foreigners traditionally fear not to tread, but points France-wide, from Alsace in the northeast, next door to

Germany, where locals speak German about as fluently as they do French, and sauerkraut is the basis of the most famous food specialty, to the Basque country of the southwest, adjacent to Spain, with the Spanish language widely understood, and the bullfight a spectator sport.

You find yourself fascinated, as you move about provincial France, with the way Bretons cling to their folk costumes and, for that matter, their Celtic tongue; the way Normans to this day take pride in the long-ago duke who became king of a conquered England; the way southwesterners in Périgord keep their towns small and their fare rich; and the way citizens of Nice—masses of visitors notwithstanding—preserve as a landmark their city's venerable core.

Even bigger surprises are the cosmopolitan aspects, not to mention cultural resources, of the big provincial cities—Lyon's Gothic cathedral dominating a charming Old Town, the amazing wealth not only of Old Masters, but of Postimpressionists in Grenoble's Musée des Beaux-Arts, the remarkable caliber of the furniture and other antique objects in the opulent town house that serves as Marseille's decorative-arts museum, the world-class opera house that is but one example of the eighteenth-century architectural elegance of Bordeaux, and delightful quarters that are throwbacks to the Renaissance, in such cities as Dijon, Rouen, and Strasbourg.

In no country that I know do smaller places produce bigger treats. Bourges is as notable for its all-Europe ranker of a cathedral as for smart shops. (You soon learn, as you move about, that provincial France's shopping facilities can match those of Paris in quality, if not quantity.) The Riviera offers a veritable network of museums, each devoted to the work of a modern master—Matisse, Chagall, Picasso, to name three. You expect vineyards, of course, in the neighborhood of Bordeaux's St.-Émilion and Burgundy's Beaune—but they are centers of Middle Ages art and architecture, as well. The globally celebrated Loire châteaux? Chambord and Azay-le-Rideau—among many—of course. But they have France-wide competition from, say, Fougères in the north, Meillant in the center, Castries in the south—three of many. Provence's Nîmes remains an architectural outpost of ancient Rome, and so many other superb Roman remnants dot the landscape.

No matter where in France you travel—uncelebrated albeit stimulating cities like Caen and Rennes in the north, Périgueux and Pau in the southwest, Annecy and Vienne in the east, Alpine Chamonix, the Mediterranean's Cannes, lakeside Évian, the port-resort of La Rochelle on the Atlantic, Bayeux near the English Channel's World War II landing beaches—you are engulfed by the culture of France. By that, I mean you find yourself speaking the French language (is there a more beautiful tongue?) even if you've not studied it, relishing the French cuisine (is there a more delicious one?), savoring French wines (are there any finer?), observing French midday closings, staying in French-style hotels, and queueing up to pay cashiers for your purchases in French *supermarchés.* If you afford your hosts a chance to know you, the while giving yourself the opportunity to know them (always remembering the ages-long formality with which strangers greet each other and become acquainted in France), you come to admire a remarkable people who are, at their best—which is often—well educated and well organized, intellectually curious and conversationally loquacious, good fun and good friends.

ROBERT S. KANE

1

France

A Mini A to Z

ADDRESSES: French Government Tourist Office has its American headquarters at 610 Fifth Avenue, New York, NY 10020, with branches at 645 North Michigan Avenue, Chicago, IL 60611; 9454 Wilshire Boulevard, Beverly Hills, CA 90212; and 2305 Cedar Springs Road, Dallas, TX 75201. There are FGTO offices, as well, at 1 Dundas Street, Toronto, Ontario, and 1981 Avenue McGill College, Montreal, Quebec, in Canada; and at 178 Piccadilly, London. These offices—among whose functions is to provide the prospective traveler in France with gratis information and literature—are part of a worldwide network whose headquarters—Maison de la France—is located at 8 Avenue de l'Opéra in Paris. Beyond the capital, throughout France, the traveler's best information source is the local *Office de Tourisme,* upon occasion termed *Syndicat d'Initiative.*

Addresses of these offices appear in chapters following.

AIR FRANCE, France's global carrier—one of the world's largest—has linked Paris with the United States since as long ago as 1946, although it goes back to 1933, when it was created by the merger of four smaller French-flag carriers that dated to the post–World War I period of France's great aviation pioneers.

That innovative tradition continued into our own time. With the advent of the jet age, Air France embraced the Caravelle in 1959, the Boeing 747 in 1970, the Concorde (heralding the supersonic era in 1976) and the Airbuses—310 and A310—in the eighties and nineties.

Contemporarily, the airline's routes—on which celebrated French cuisine, fine French wines, and convivial French bonhomie brighten global skies—span more than half a million miles, linking some 200 destinations in 80 countries on the five continents. Nine of those cities—New York, Los Angeles, Houston, Chicago, Washington, Newark, Philadelphia, San Francisco, and Miami—are U.S. passenger gateways; there are an additional pair—Toronto and

Montreal—in Canada; and Mexico City is served via Houston. Besides Paris, Air France links Nice, Lyon, Bordeaux, Marseille, Montpellier, Nantes, Toulouse, Strasbourg, Lille, and Mulhouse—all in France—with the United States.

What I especially like about Air France is that regardless of whether you fly Concorde, Première (First) Class, Le Club (Business) Class, or popular Economy, you experience the ambience of France from the moment you step aboard. A recent Air France Le Club flight Paris–Kennedy was the occasion of one of the best meals I've had aloft. It opened with a special treat—navarin de lotte—a monkfish casserole accompanied by buttered carrots and deliciously prepared endive; another choice was noisettes of lamb mustard-sauced, in tandem with braised lettuce and sautéed mushrooms. A mix of greens tossed as a salad, vinaigrette-dressed, was next, in preparation for cheese from a platter, and an utterly delicious bavarian cream on raspberry-surfaced pastry, with coffee to conclude and perhaps a digestif of port. Vintage Bordeaux and Burgundies accompanied the meal, and cocktails preceded it. (American, Delta, Pakistan International, and Pan Am are among the other carriers linking the U.S. and France.)

AIR INTER: France's principal domestic airline, Air Inter crisscrosses France with service to 31 destinations, carrying more than 15 million passengers annually. (Inter, incidentally, is pronounced *Ann-tair*.) Air Inter uses both de Gaulle and Orly airports; in the case of departures, be sure and ascertain from which airport you'll be taking off. And arrive in plenty of time to be among the first boarders; seats are not assigned.

BREAKFAST—*petit déjeuner*—is nothing more than the term (translated as "little lunch") implies. Unless you specify otherwise, it will consist of café au lait—a pot of intense black coffee served with an equal-sized jug of hot milk, the idea being that you mix the two, more or less half and half—and a petit pain (crusty roll), a croissant (for some reason or other, these are at their flakiest in Paris), and/or a brioche, along with butter and jam. This is a *café complet* or Continental breakfast, upon occasion served with fruit juice. Where that is not the case, juice, as well as eggs, bacon, and ham may be ordered additionally, at least at better hotels. (If a Frenchman ever has anything more than *café complet,* it is a single boiled egg served *à la coque*—in the shell—with salt, but rarely pepper, which must usually be specially requested. In virtually all cases, no matter how simple the hotel, breakfast is served in bedrooms, as well as in the hotel's dining or special breakfast room. And in certain instances—I indicate these in pages following—hotels offer the option of breakfast buffets; those of the Crillon and Ritz hotels in Paris are quite the grandest such of any that I know in France; links of the Novotel chain serve generous buffet breakfasts, too.

BUSES: Given a choice, I prefer the train—especially in France, where they are so good (see S.N.C.F., below)—to the long-distance bus. Still, for the very occasional town that is not served by rail (Honfleur in the north and St.-Tropez in the south are two such), buses fill the gap. They are, as well, a pleasant way to traverse the Riviera, which is of course served by train, also. The bus system is France-wide and, in my experience, efficient and inexpensive, although drivers—while usually helpful—tend to speak only French. Although you mightn't do so at home, it's considered polite to greet them with a *bonjour* upon boarding; they'll reply in kind, often wishing you *bonne journée,* when you exit. Bus stations—the term is *gare routière*—are often, but not always, near the just plain *gare,* or railway station.

CASINOS: Slot machines are *interdit,* forbidden by law, in France (although you'll find them in independent Monaco, chapter 23). But casinos—with such games of chance as roulette, trente et quarante, and baccarat—are dotted about the republic; I indicate a number of them in chapters following. As a general rule, foreigners are required to show passports upon entering, and gents are expected to wear jacket and tie in the evening.

CHIENS: Although they do not vote (at least, to my knowledge), dogs come close to being full-fledged French citizens. I have no figures, but there simply has to be a higher proportion of dogs—vis-à-vis the human population—in France than in any other country. Certain restaurants deny them entry, but they go shopping with masters and mistresses, and rare is the hotel in France that does not have special rates *pour les animaux*. I have yet to meet a French dog that I did not like (they are invariably friendly and quite prepared to charm the pants off you). Which is not to say they all have been properly trained. *Caveat:* Watch where you walk.

CLIMATE: You are, of course, in a temperate-zone country, but a relatively mild—albeit erratic—temperate-zone country. By that, I mean Paris summers may be gray, nasty-rainy, and Paris winters may be glorious and crystal-clear, with spring and autumn—France-wide—delightful, if you're lucky with respect to rain clouds. In Paris, winter (late November through March) averages in the high thirties and forties, with January and February the coldest months. Spring (April and May) is likely to be in the fifties. Summer (June through early September) averages in the sixties, with July and August the hottest months, averaging in the mid-seventies—but capable of being much hotter. Autumn (late September through October) is apt to be fiftyish. Down south, along the Mediterranean coast, expect temperatures that average 10 degrees above those of the capital, with the Riviera the sunniest sector of the republic year-round (although its winters can be moist and chilly). Brittany and Normandy tend to have the coolest summers, and, not surprisingly, Savoie and the Alpine regions, the coldest—albeit sunniest—winters. Rain can fall at any time of year; don't travel without a collapsible umbrella.

CLOTHES: Although its capital is *couture* capital of the world, France—taken as a whole—is neither as well dressed as Italy nor as clothes-conscious as Britain, which is hardly to imply, however, that you want to pack only jeans. Paris and the principal provincial cities—Lyon, most especially—make a point of looking extremely good on business and more festive social occasions, by which I mean opera, ballet, concerts, and theater, as well as both lunches and dinners in better-category restaurants. Côte d'Azur resorts are smartly casual the day long, but dressier—especially at glossy eateries and casinos—after dark. Throughout France, the best and simplest rule is to clothe yourself informally in the course of daytime explorations, less so in the evenings.

CONFÉRENCIERS are university-educated specialists in art history and architecture—*not,* I want to emphasize, ordinary guides—who lead individuals, as well as groups, on day-long and halfday tours, coordinated by the French government's Caisse Nationale des Monuments Historiques et des Sites, at some 40 of the cities, towns, and châteaux about which I write in later chapters of this book—Paris and environs, of course, included. Upon occasion, they are English-speaking. You learn a lot this way. Local Offices de Tourisme have details.

CREDIT CARDS are accepted in many—but by no means all—restaurants, chain department stores, and shops. But they are not yet as widely accepted as in the United States. Most popular are Visa, American Express, Diners Club, and MasterCard—usually in that order.

CRUISING BY BARGE: You either like the concept of traveling in smallish, hardly luxurious barges along a country's inland waterways, or you do not. I do not, for a number of reasons. First is accommodations: although better companies' boats have private facilities attached to all cabins, space is, of necessity, limited—to understate. A single main cabin usually serves as restaurant, bar, and lounge. Deck space is so tight that there's room only for sit-up chairs—no recliners on which to lie back, as on a proper cruise ship. There is no choice of courses, for the most part, at meals, nor, for that matter, of wine served with lunch and dinner—usually included in the rate. You are bound by the company's prearranged itinerary. A lot of time is spent making small talk with fellow passengers in close quarters. And rates are high. For what a barge tour costs, you can stay in comfortable, first-class hotels with decent beds and full-sized bathroom facilities (large people can have difficulty fitting into barge-cruise shower stalls, and sinks can be the size of a dinner plate), dine in restaurants ordering from multichoice menus and wine lists, and set your own schedule. That said, and if you're still game for a river cruise, ask your travel agent to fill you in on *French Cruise Lines,* whose two relatively recently built vessels each have 100 outside cabins on two decks, with private shower, sink, toilet, TV, and air-conditioning.

CURRENCY: The franc is subdivided into 100 centimes, with coins in 10-franc and lower denominations (always keep a supply of ever-so-handy one-franc coins) and notes in higher denominations. Inquire as to rates from bank and currency-exchange firms before departure; you may want to buy some in advance. In France, best rates are obtained at banks and *bureaux de change*—change offices (you absolutely *must* have your passport with you)—but hotel cashiers also change money. I must point out that rates may vary even on the same day in a single city. If you're exchanging a considerable amount, and you have the time, shop around for the best rate. Take the bulk of your funds in traveler's checks—they're the safest—with plenty in 20- and 50-dollar denominations; they're the most convenient.

CUSTOMS: *Entering France.* Coming from non–Common Market countries such as the United States, you're allowed a carton of cigarettes and a couple of bottles of alcohol, as well as your own personal effects, including, of course, cameras and a reasonable amount of film. Coming from Common Market countries, the ante is raised by a third in the case of cigarettes and doubled in the case of alcohol. French immigration officers tend not to stamp passports, indicating dates of entry into and exit from France, unless you so request.

Returning to the United States. Each individual may bring back $400 worth of purchases duty free. That is allowable once every 30 days, provided you've been out of the country at least 48 hours. If you've spent more than $400, you'll be charged a flat 10 percent duty on the next $1,000 worth of purchases. Remember, too, that antiques, duly certified to be at least 100 years old, are admitted duty free and do not count as part of your $400 quota; neither do paintings, sculptures, and other works of art, of any date, if certified as original; it's advisable that certification, from the seller or other authority, as to their authenticity accompany them. Also exempt from duty, but as a part of the $400 quota: one quart of liquor. And—this is important—there is no restriction on how much one may bring in beyond the $400 limit, so long as the duty is paid.

DEPARTMENT STORES, SHOPS, AND SUPERMARKETS: Paris is a department-store city of consequence: I detail facilities in chapter 2. Its two major *grands magasins—Galeries Lafayette* and *Printemps*—have branches in a number of other cities. There are other chains, exclusively provincial, such as *Nouvelles Galeries* and *Dames de France.* There are nationwide budget-category chains, as well, such as *Monoprix*. Even the British-origin *Marks & Spencer* is on scene, as is the occasional locally owned department store. I make shopping suggestions in some detail, and by category, not only in chapter 2 (Paris) but in chapters on a number of other important cities and towns around the country. The supermarket—*supermarché*—is happily ubiquitous and a source not only of grocery items, but of wines for hotel-room aperitifs.

DRIVING: Take your own car, rent one in advance of arrival or on the scene, or buy a new French car. You need a valid driver's license of your country of residence, as well as the international green card indicating that you are insured. (Home insurance companies can assist in this regard.) Of course, you know that gas is sold by the liter, but it's worth noting that an American gallon equals just over three and three-quarter liters, and an Imperial gallon is four and a half liters. Kilometers? One km = 5/8 of a mile; conversely, one mile = 1.6 km. *Automobile Club de l'Île de France* (8 Place de la Concorde, Paris; phone 4266-43-00) answers questions 24 hours a day. On the road, in case of accident, breakdown, or an empty gas tank, contact the nearest *Gendarmerie* or *Poste de Police.* Rental firms? *Avis, Hertz,* and *Budget-Rent-a-Car* are on scene, as well as a number of French firms. France has some 930,000 miles of roads, of which more than 3000 miles are superhighways. You may, for example, cut through the country by this means, on a north–south route taking you from Burgundy through the Rhône Valley and Provence to the Mediterranean—with rest areas every 10 miles, frequent emergency phones, motels and cafés along the way, and an 80-mile-per-hour speed limit.

ELECTRIC CURRENT: 220 volts AC. Take along a transformer for your shaver or hair dryer and an adapter-plug to be attached to prongs of your appliance, so that it will fit into holes of the French outlet. American department stores sell kits containing a transformer and a variety of variously shaped adapters. Alternatively, you may buy a French-made appliance for use during your journey upon arrival in France—recommended if your stay will be lengthy.

GEOGRAPHY AND GOVERNMENT: Texas is bigger—by a fifth. Still, France's area, exceeding 210,000 miles, is considerable. Bordered on three flanks by water—English Channel (*La Manche,* to the French) on the north, Mediterranean to the southeast, Atlantic to the west—France shares land frontiers with half a dozen countries: Belgium, Luxembourg, Germany, Switzerland, and Italy to the east; and Spain to the south. It lacks neither mountains (Mont Blanc, the Alps's highest peak, with a tunnel cut through it to neighboring Italy; the northeasterly Vosges range; the aptly named Massif Central; and formidable Pyrenees on the frontier with Spain) nor gently rolling plains (extending over its northern and western territory). Each of the Big Four rivers is celebrated: Seine, because it bisects Paris; Loire, because of the châteaux on its shores; Garonne, because it's the core of Bordeaux wine country; and Rhône, which cuts through Burgundy and Lyon into Provence and the Mediterranean, wherein lies Corsica, metropolitan France's sole island of consequence.

There are some 56 million Frenchmen living in a democratic, multiparty republic, led by a president (the term is seven years), premier, and cabinet. The two-house legislature is big—491-seat Assemblée Nationale (terms are five years) and 318-member Sénat (terms are nine years). France is divided into 95 départements (four of them overseas, including Guadeloupe and Martinique in the Caribbean). Départements are grouped into more than a score of administrative régions approximating—but only *approximating*—territory of the ancient provinces that were officially abolished during the Revolution but remain, two centuries later, France's traditional geographic and cultural subdivisions.

HISTORY: Chapter 2 (Paris) deals the most extensively with what has gone before, the better to appreciate what remains today; in succeeding chapters, I capsulize, but sufficiently, I hope, to provide you with perspective for intelligent on-scene exploration. At this point, let me compress the succession of dynasties and other governmental entities that France has known, following the first five centuries of the Christian era when it was Roman-governed *Gaul. Carolingian kings*—the dynasty was named for eighth-century Charlemagne—reigned until the mid-tenth century. There were more than a dozen, with both Louis the Debonair and Louis the Stammerer and both Charles the Bald and Charles the Fat, among them. *Capetians*—named for King Hugh Capet, founder of the line—were quite as numerous as Carolingians; their numbers included the sainted Louis XI, Robert the Pious, and Philippe the Fair; and they were in power until the beginning of the fourteenth century, when the dozen-plus sovereigns of the *Valois* dynasty succeeded, starting with Philippe VI and including the debonair arts patron François I, not to mention Charles the Well Beloved and

Louis XII, the Father of His People. *Bourbons*—to us foreigners, the most celebrated dynasty—took over in the sixteenth century, with the accession of Henri IV, France's all-time favorite sovereign. Henri's successors—Louis XIII, Louis XIV, Louis XV, Louis XVI—are the stuff of familiar history courses. The late eighteenth-century *Revolution* abolished the ancien régime. Following were the *Convention* and, later, the *Directoire.* Then came the *Consulat,* headed by Napoleon Bonaparte, who declared himself *Emperor Napoleon I,* ruling from 1804 to 1815 and twice exiled. Two of Louis XVI's brothers, Louis XVIII and Charles X, followed Napoleon with their reigns (1814–1830) jointly dubbed the *Bourbon Restoration. Louis-Philippe*—Bourbon partly (on his mother's side)—was proclaimed King by the Assemblée Nationale after Charles X was forced to abdicate; Louis-Philippe himself abdicated in 1848. An ambitious nephew of Napoleon I—at first president as Louis Napoleon, later *Emperor Napoleon III*—ruled France from 1848 to 1870, only to be deposed as a consequence of the *Franco-Prussian War.* Ever since (*World War II Nazi occupation* under the puppet Pétain regime excepted), France has been a republic. *Charles de Gaulle* became provisional president for two years in 1944, returning as president for the decade 1959–1969, a momentous period that saw France reemerge as a universally respected world power.

HOLIDAYS: As in every country, they're a pleasure for residents, but major ones can be a bother for visitors, who do well to plan around them, noting the likelihood of closed museums and other places of interest, certain shops, and some restaurants. Besides Christmas and New Year's, take note of Easter Monday, Ascension, Whit Monday, Labor Day (May 1, with parades in the cities), Bastille Day (July 14, joyous celebrations France-wide), Assumption Day (August 15), All Saints' Day (November 1), and Armistice Day (November 11).

HOTELS: *About the hotels in this book.* I have either lived in, dined and drunk in, and/or thoroughly inspected the hotels carefully selected for evaluation in these pages; I disregard the complexities of the official French government star system and, as in all books of my *World at Its Best* series, have divided hotels (and restaurants) into three price groups: *Luxury, First Class,* and *Moderate.* Bear in mind that I am fussy. In towns of any size and cities, I concentrate on *centrally situated* hotels, including country hotels only when they are exceptional and will be of interest to travelers with cars. All hotels in my *Luxury* and virtually all in my *First Class* categories, and many in the *Moderate* category, have television and minibars (stocked with liquor, wine, soft drinks, and sometimes snacks, for purchase) in all rooms, as well, of course, as private baths. Air-conditioning is standard in better modern hotels and many, but not all traditional-style houses, and is, of course, more prevalent along and near the Mediterranean than in the cooler north; inquire when booking. My *Moderate* category hotels are *better*-Moderate, very often with TV and/or minibars and with baths attached to most or all rooms; I indicate the proportion especially with *Moderate* category hotels. The French rank with the very top-run European hoteliers—Germans, Italians, and Swiss. I want to make clear that, by and large, at least in my not inconsiderable experience, they take as much pride in running modest hotels as in running luxury houses. (This is important to note in the case of Paris, which has more budget hotels than any other European city, with relatively few lemons in the lot; of the provincial cities, Nice is No. 2 in this respect.) When a French hotel is well operated, everything works well, reception to room service. I don't know of a hotel in the republic (except perhaps in the Basque country [chapter 9]) without English-speaking personnel or without crackerjack housekeeping; French hotels, by and large, are shipshape. My principal caveat is with respect to showers. Outside of Paris—where they are fairly common, especially in better hotels—expect only hand showers attached to tubs, and no shower curtains for the most part, except in some hotels where single rooms may have stall showers in lieu of tubs. (In a small residue of lower-category French hotels, a "private bath" might consist of only a sink and a tub—with the toilet a public one, down the hall; happily, not many such arrangements remain, but in really modest places it pays to ask in this regard.)

Hotels operated by crack international chains, such as *Inter-Continental* (heaviest represented, with two historic Paris hotels and a third—still another landmark—on the Riviera) will not be unfamiliar to transatlantic visitors. But there are other chains, French and international—with hotels France-wide—for which orientation is warranted. *Hôtels Concorde* is, on the basis of my experience, No. 1 of the lot, beyond any question; it is by no means the biggest, but the best, with half a dozen Paris houses—Crillon and Lutétia are the top rankers—and a dozen additional hotels in provincial France, Nancy's Grand among them. The *Altea* and *Pullman International* chains include some very nice houses, too. There are a number of chains whose hotels are dominantly French Contemporary, upon occasion more functional—they are principally for business travelers on overnight missions and for groups—than charming, albeit with delightful exceptions to the rule in the case of each. This group includes *Arcade, Ibis, Mercure, Novotel,* and *Sofitel.* Britain's *Trusthouse Forte* is on scene, too; and such leading American hotel representatives as *David B. Mitchell & Co., Robert F. Warner, Inc.,* and *Marketing Ahead, Inc.* book French hotels. There are, as well, a number of associations of privately operated hotels, banded together for purposes of promotion and central booking. Of these, in the mostly Moderate category group, I consistently have the most satisfaction with U.S.-based *Best Western.* There remains the First Class/Luxury *Relais et Châteaux.* They're located in the countryside more than in cities, often occupying antique-furnished houses of considerable age—and frequently with distinguished restaurants. They are represented in North America by David B. Mitchell & Co., 200 Madison Avenue, New York, NY 10016. Last—but hardly least—is aptly titled *Leading Hotels of the World* (head office: 747 Third Avenue, New York, NY 10017), an extraordinary association of extraordinary hotels around the planet that become affiliated only by invitation and after careful screening. Its dozen French affiliates number some of the finest hotels in the land; the range, to give you an idea, is Paris's George V and Ritz through Nice's Negresco and Évian's Royal. *A final note:* Especially beyond big cities, French hotels often, if not always, close for *fermeture annuelle*—vacation, usually during their slackest season; check before you go.

LANGUAGE: It's true that many Frenchmen are impatient with the less-than-perfect French spoken by foreign visitors, and that, indeed—more in Paris and on the Riviera than elsewhere—they'll often rudely reply in English (if they speak it) to your French. But it is increasingly true that these same Frenchmen—themselves studying foreign languages more than has been the case and traveling increasingly abroad—realize that speaking a strange tongue is no easy matter. There is, as a consequence, more tolerance with foreigners' pronunciation than there was, say, a decade or so back. What is important to Franco-foreign relationships are the polite niceties of conversation. To say simply, "Thank you," to a woman is enough in English; in French it is not. One says, "Merci, madame" or "Merci, mademoiselle," and, with a man, "Merci, monsieur." It is the same with a *bonjour* or an *au revoir;* you tack on *madame, mademoiselle,* or *monsieur*—no matter how impersonal or brief the exchange has been, and no matter the occupation or station in life of the person with whom you are speaking. It helps, believe me. And one more point: By no means everyone in France speaks even *un petit peu d'anglais.* Your French will be very useful with this vast majority; don't be bashful about using it. Conversely, don't hesitate about venturing forth without French. After all, English is France's most popular language, after the native tongue; 80 percent of the country's secondary and college language students are studying it. *Tip:* Before you go, pick up a copy of *Just Enough French,* one of Passport Books' excellent *Just Enough* phrase-books; or study the language in advance of departure, with Passport's *Just Listen 'n Learn French*—a three-cassette-and-textbook kit.

OPEN HOURS: Quite sensible. *Museums* operated by the French government traditionally close on Tuesdays and major holidays; many other—*but by no means all*—museums operate similarly. For example, the considerable clutch of museums operated by the City of Paris (Carnavalet, Petit Palais, Cognacq-Jay are but three) close on Mondays. Many—again, not all—museums close for approximately two hours at midday, as do *historic houses* and *palaces* operated as museums, *cathedrals,* and *churches,* especially beyond Paris. *Department stores* have the longest hours, usually Monday through Saturday from 9:00 A.M. to 6:30 P.M., with one or two late-opening nights in Paris and major provincial cities. *Other stores* generally open between 9:00 and 10:00 A.M., shuttering (especially outside Paris) between noon and 2:00 P.M., and reopening until 6:30 or 7:00 P.M., Tuesday through Saturday. *Banks* are exceptionally generous with open hours: 9:00 A.M. to 4:30 P.M., Monday through Friday, closing at noon the day before a holiday. *Hairdressers and barbers* close on Monday.

OPERA, BALLET, CONCERTS, AND FESTIVALS: France and the performing arts have been synonymous these many centuries. I make a point of bringing particulars to your attention in chapters following, but I want at this point to emphasize that quality remains high beyond the capital and that settings for performances can be positively opulent. Festivals take place year-round but are most prevalent in summer. Be on the lookout for them as you move about, noting such festivals of consequence as those of *Paris* (Festival du Marais, Festival d'Été—summer), *Aix-en-Provence* (July), *Antibes* (late April and May), *Avignon* (July), *Bordeaux* (May), *Dijon* (July), *Île de France* (mid-May through mid-July, at many points), *Lyon* (Berlioz Festival, September), *Marseille* (August), *Montpellier* (June–July), *Orange* (July), *Périgueux* (August), *Poitiers* (May), *Strasbourg* (June), *Tours* (late June–early July), and *Vienne* (July).

PASSPORTS: Necessary for admittance to France and to be presented to U.S. Immigration upon your return. Apply at Department of State passport offices in a dozen-plus cities (look under U.S. Government in the phone book) or—in smaller towns—at the office of the clerk of a federal court and at certain post offices. Allow four weeks, especially for a first passport (valid for 10 years), for which you'll need a pair of two-inch-square photos and birth certificate or other proof of citizenship. There's a $42 fee (subject to change) for first passports; renewals are cheaper. If you're in a hurry when you apply, say so; Uncle Sam will usually try to expedite if you can show documentation indicating imminent departure. Upon receipt of your passport, sign your name where indicated, fill in the address of next of kin, and keep this valuable document with you—*not packed in a suitcase*—as you travel. In case of loss, contact local police, nearest U.S. embassy or consulate, or Passport Office, Department of State, Washington, D.C.

RATES for selected hotels (where I've stayed or which I've inspected) and restaurants (where I've eaten) are categorized as *Luxury, First Class,* and *Moderate;* these translate pretty much into what they would mean in the United States, adjusted, of course, to the purchasing power of the dollar with respect to the French franc at the time of your visit.

RESTAURANTS/CUISINE—TRADITIONAL VS. CONTEMPORARY: France's nouvelle cuisine, emulated transatlantic, north of the English Channel, in much else of Europe and at other points planetwide, has given up its maiden name—the term *nouvelle* is rarely applied any longer, at least in France—and grown up. A better term is contemporary. By that I mean that ambitious young chefs—cooks who name restaurants after themselves, hire publicists, compile cookbooks, demonstrate on the telly, and charge high tabs—still are an intrinsic part of the French restaurant scene.

But they are, by and large, no longer wild-eyed radicals of the kitchen. They remain creative—and more power to them, in this respect. Still, they have come to appreciate that diners paying enormous sums (there are no *Moderate*-category and few *First Class* restaurants with contemporary cuisine) want the dishes set before them to be recognizable, not without familiar ingredients (the potato, historically France's most popular and most-consumed vegetable, has blessedly returned from banishment to contemporary restaurants) served in decent-sized portions (the old nouvelle invariably appeared in skimpy servings), and—while not without welcome innovations, even surprises—devoid of absurd and bizarre combinations that focused on oddball mixes of sweet and savory.

The influence of nouvelle has been stronger than some of us like to admit. Presentation of cuisine, always important to nouvelle chefs, has become more sophisticated—surely there are influences of artfully arranged Japanese dishes—in restaurants of all persuasions, in France and abroad. Desserts, again emulating early nouvelle sweets, are often served on near-dinner-size plates in precise symmetrical designs. Vegetables—still too often, for this diner—arrive sliced and wrapped in spherical shapes, even to being tied in knots, awaiting demolition by the diner's fork. Bread (still somewhat suspect) instead of being produced by the basket, is served a tiny roll at a time so that, often, you must ask for seconds.

Withal, we must—it seems to this devotee of what is, when all is said and done, the world's greatest cuisine—be glad that its classic and traditional influences again are accorded the respect they deserve. French sauciers—whose output, when skilled, was never "heavy," despite old nouvelle criticisms—again are acclaimed. French ingredients again are respected. French appetites again are being satisfied in posher places; although it must be emphasized that even during the nouvelle vogue's flightiest years, traditional restaurants—wherein the overwhelming majority of French men and French women dine, Paris-wide and nationwide—never stopped producing dishes that made their national cuisine celebrated. And still do.

A glory of French food is that it has never been necessary, even in the most diehard brasserie, to overindulge. France has never neglected foods that are today standbys of healthy eating: salads (who does them more justice?) and seafood (where are fish and mollusks prepared in more infinite variety, from bivalves on the half shell in tandem with lemon slices, through to simply broiled fish?), poultry (the roasted chicken is a French masterwork) and green vegetables (who knows better than the French how to simply cook, say, string beans or broccoli?). For that matter in what land did fresh fruit gain currency as a dessert? In which cuisine (certainly not American) is bread served without butter—except in distinctly pricey temples of gastronomy? Again, where (certainly not in the United States) is coffee never served with rich cream, and even with milk only at breakfast?

You will find some of the outstanding contemporary-cuisine restaurants on pages following. By and large, though, I make a special point of concentrating on restaurants easier to reserve for, with more realistic prices, and that serve the kind of food that the great bulk of visitors from across the Atlantic have crossed over to experience on its home ground.

A typical meal will open with hors d'œuvres or soup, go on to an entrée of meat or fish or a seafood dish, with a green salad dressed with oil, vinegar, salt, and pepper following; thence, cheese selected from a platter, fresh fruit or dessert, and postmeal coffee. If the meal is unfestive, one wine will accompany it—red, if with meat; white, if with fish. The French have far less aversion to the consumption of water than do, say, the British; feel free to request it.

Meal hours are sensible; lunch service in restaurants starts between noon and 12:30 P.M., continuing until about 2:00 P.M.; between 8:00 and 9:00 P.M. (often as late as 10:00 P.M. in Paris, in other big cities, and on the Riviera) is the preferred time for dinner, although restaurants begin serving between 7:00 and 7:30 P.M. It's advisable to *reserve in advance,* except in simpler places (hotel concierges will do this for you, or phone yourself), noting that many restaurants observe a weekly closing day as well as a *fermeture annuelle,* or annual vacation.

Menu specifics: Hors d'œuvres might include relishes like scallions and radishes, black and green olives, and celery rémoulade. There might be, as well, eggs-mayonnaise, lentils or beans, tiny shrimp or other shellfish, and snails served piping hot in their shells, with a parsley-butter and garlic sauce; various pâtés and terrines, and, the supreme opener, foie gras—poached fattened duck or goose liver. *French soups*—the widely exported onion, of course, but even simple potages du jour—are invariably delicious, as, indeed, are creamy bisques based on lobster or crab. *Meats* are masterfully prepared. Beef appears as steak (entrecôte, châteaubriand), roasted on skewers, and in stews as ragoûts and daubes. Blanquette de veau is the veal stew par excellence. But look also for veal escalopes, as well as chops (côtelettes), sweetbreads (ris de veau) and brains (cervelle). Lamb appearing roasted, as gigot d'agneau avec flageolet-type beans is a favorite. Pork specialties are no less good, from charcuterie (sausage and specialty pork products) to jambon (ham) and roasts. *Fish and seafood:* If simply grilled with a squeeze of lemon or accompanied by a delicate sauce, fish in France is a winner. Likewise, such seafood as crab, crayfish, lobster, and oysters. Nowhere is *poultry* more imaginatively prepared; chicken, of course, but duck and goose, as well. If you haven't tried frog's legs (grenouilles), you're missing a treat. In non-nouvelle restaurants, fresh *vegetables* still are served in decent-sized portions and never are overcooked. The *cheese* course is important in France. You know camembert, brie, and Roquefort, but try pont-l'évêque, reblochon, port-salut, chèvre (goat cheese, several species of which often appear on a single tray), and any number of others, varying by region, not unlike wine. *Pastries* are at their most enjoyable mid-morning or mid-afternoon, with coffee or tea in a *pâtisserie* that doubles as a *salon de thé,* or simply purchased by the bag from shops whose windows prove irresistible. They're always available as *desserts,* along with gargantuan *ice cream* sundaes, called bombes or coupes, hot soufflés—chocolate, lemon, vanilla, Grand Marnier—and so are crêpes, the thin pancakes of Breton origin. Feel free to ask for tap water (une carafe d'eau) and if you prefer bottled water, rather than ordering Perrier (which the French tend to regard as too effervescent to drink with food), select their favorite mealtime eau gazeuse: Badoit; Évian leads the bottled nonbubblies.

SALES OR VAT TAXES of 13 or 20 percent can be refunded, if you buy a minimum of 1,200 francs worth of merchandise from any given shop. Department stores are experts at explaining intricacies of an operation that involves filling out a long form at point of purchase, presenting it upon your departure from France to customs officers based at special airport counters signposted *Détaxe,* who rubber-stamp it and return it to you along with the stamped envelope the merchant has given you, so that you may drop it in a mailbox adjacent to the counter. It is thus returned to the seller, who only then draws a French-franc check for the amount of the tax (known as TVA in French) and posts it to your home address. Upon receipt of these foreign funds, you take them to your bank, where—unless you have a very friendly banker—charges for conversion to dollars may equal (or exceed) the amount of the check. Unless—and this "unless" is important—you make your purchase with a credit card, in which case request that the refund be credited to the card, obviating the return to you in francs. Note, too, that in certain cases—ask on the spot—refund can take place at the time of purchase. Complicated? You bet, but I've never known it not to work. *Bonne chance!*

SENIORS: There are, to be sure, conditions, limitations, and qualifications. But seniors—generally, in France that means women who are 60 and older, men who are 62 and older—do well to take passports with them to places where they might serve as money-savers. In the case of French trains, apply for the document known as Carte Vermeil 50, which allows for the purchase of half-off tickets, First or Second Class. Air Inter affords reductions to seniors on certain flights, and there are reductions by as much as half at certain museums, cinemas, and other attractions.

SHAKING HANDS: Everybody does it, toddlers onward; don't hesitate—it's appreciated. Bear in mind, too, that nonromantic kissing in France—in the nature of a greeting or a farewell—is on both cheeks. And note that the French are positively compulsive wipers of shod feet on doormats, even in fair-weather, slush-free situations; follow suit.

S.N.C.F.: *Société Nationale de Chemins de Fer Français* = FrenchRail, Inc. You're not going to ride any better trains in any country; in Europe those of Germany and Switzerland come close. But the French distinguish themselves on the rails because they are such innovators. TGV—the world's fastest trains (with speeds up to 186 miles per hour, cutting travel time by as much as a third)—are theirs. Easy-to-use advance-purchase Rail and Drive and Fly passes and Rail and Drive passes (available for varying durations) are theirs. Daylong Franceshrinker excursions—escorted tours out of Paris with English-speaking guides that are essentially by train but also make use of buses, visiting points in Burgundy and Normandy (and including lunch)—are theirs. So are smartly updated stations (Paris's Gare Montparnasse the most spectacular of the lot), restaurant cars and casual buffets, polite conductors, an amazingly comprehensive network, and—hardly to be underestimated—trains that run on time (in my not-inconsiderable experience, at least) easily 95 percent of the time.

TGV—Train à Grande Vitesse—translates, in effect, as Very High Speed. The TGV network connects Paris with such southeastern points as Dijon, Lyon, and Grenoble (with connections to Savoie ski resorts), to Provençal cities down south like Avignon, Marseille, Nîmes, and also Montpellier, to Rennes in Brittany and nearby Nantes—with TGV routes all the time expanding France-wide. All seats for premium-fare TGV trains must be reserved in advance, in both First and Second Class (TGV Second is very nice, indeed), through your home travel agent, by means of a trip to a TGV reservations counter in a French train station in advance of your TGV departure, or from FrenchRail offices at 610 Fifth Avenue, New York, NY 10020; 360 Post Street, San Francisco, CA 94102; 100 Wilshire Boulevard, Santa Monica, CA 90401; 11 East Adams Street, Chicago, IL 60603; 2121 Ponce de Leon Boulevard, Coral Gables, FL 33134; 1500 Rue Stanley, Montreal, Quebec; 409 Granville Street, Vancouver, British Columbia; and 178 Piccadilly, London, WI.

Besides Franceshrinker Tours, Rail and Drive and Fly Passes and Rail and Drive Passes, FranceRail collaborates with BritRail with the BritFrance Railpass, for travel in Britain as well as France, and including trans-English Channel passage via Hovercraft.

Train Travel tips: Travel overnight, on a sleeper or *couchette,* and you save the cost of a hotel room. It's good practice to carry snack food with you, as the French do. Reserve seats in advance, even in First Class, particularly on popular fast trains (not only TGV) en route to major cities—Paris most especially.

SON ET LUMIÈRE: The French invented *Son et Lumière*—sound and light—at Château de Chambord in the Loire Valley (chapter 20). The idea was to tell its story to an audience seated in the shadow of the castle by means of the play of lights on features of the building and its grounds, coordinated with a spoken, dramatized commentary. The technique spread like wildfire, not only to neighboring Loire châteaux, but to points that stand out architecturally, scenically, and historically throughout France. When well done, it effortlessly blends entertainment with education. Summer only.

STEAMSHIP SERVICE, transatlantic, is almost—but not quite—ancient history. Cunard Line's luxurious flagship, *Queen Elizabeth 2,* valiantly maintains scheduled sailings—about two dozen per year—between New York and the English Channel port of Southampton (see *Britain at Its Best*), with calls, as well, at the French port of Cherbourg—across the Channel—on selected westbound sailings. For France-bound passengers, Cunard arranges charter flights Southampton-Paris; alternatively, there is the option of crossing the Channel by the ferry service linking Southampton and Le Havre in France.

TELEPHONES: I include phone numbers of hotels and restaurants selected for evaluation in each chapter, under Settling In and Daily Bread, respectively. If you are calling from Paris to anywhere else in the country, you need to first dial 16 and then the eight-digit number. By and large, when calling from telephone booths, or kiosks, you use a *Télécarte,* which can be bought at post offices and tobacconists. The cards have a specific number of "bits" that expire as you speak, with the remaining amount of credit available indicated on the phone. Throw away used-in-full cards, but retain those that still have unused portions.

TIPPING is relatively effortless, thanks to the French system of adding a service charge—usually 15 percent—to restaurant bills and to café tabs as well. (*Service compris* on menus translates as service included; so does *prix net*.) There's no need to tip a hotel concierge unless he has performed special services beyond handing you your key. Hotel porters who carry your bags to and from your room expect the franc equivalent of half a dollar per bag, more if the hotel is especially grand. Tip moderately to theater ushers if they escort you to your seat, 10 percent to barbers and hairdressers. Tip Paris and Riviera taxi drivers 10 to 15 percent of what's on the meter; elsewhere, they don't expect tips. In all events, tips are for cordial, efficient service. At no time are they obligatory in France—or anywhere.

TOURS, TOUR OPERATORS, TRAVEL AGENTS: Agents, first: Select one who is affiliated with the *American Society of Travel Agents* (ASTA) and, ideally, who knows France firsthand. For a first trip, some travelers are happy with a package; tour operators making a specialty of France—whose packages may be booked through travel agents—include (among many) *Abercrombie & Kent, American Express, Auto Venture, B & D Vogue Travel Services, Caravan Tours, Cityrama, Extra Value Vacations, France Tourisme, Inc., The French Experience, Globus-Gateway, H.S. & Associates, Jet Vacations, David B. Mitchell & Co., Olson Travelworld, Paris-Vision, Solrep International, Travel Bound, Wagons-Lits International, World of Oz, XO Travel Consultants* (food, wine, garden tours), as well as tours operated by *Air France* and other transatlantic carriers. In studying brochures, note *location* of hotels—in cities, you want to be *central*—not out in the boonies; places *actually visited* (not simply passed by, on the bus); *free time* at your disposal, especially in cities; and—in the case of meals—whether they're prix fixe or à la carte. An introductory package behind you, you're ready for return visits on your own—to where *you want to go,* at *your* speed.

WINES OF FRANCE, by Max Drechsler: Wine in France is, traditionally, a facet of daily living—the natural accompaniment to food. As such—except for rarefied vintages sought out by connoisseurs—it is not something to be reverenced with awe. It is true, of course, that some of France's wines are the greatest and most noble in the world. But it is by no means necessary to be an expert to enjoy drinking wine in the course of a French journey. Although some wines are drunk as aperitifs, by and large they augment and enhance meals. My maxim, while traveling in France—and my advice to you—is to be inquisitive and try, whenever possible, the regional wines, so often a part of experiencing the regional cuisine itself. There are hundreds of delightful wines encountered in the course of provincial wandering that are not ordinarily come upon in Paris. Discover them!

Always ask to see the wine list; read it over. You learn a lot from these carefully prepared compilations as you go from restaurant to restaurant. Conscientious restaurateurs—even in smaller places—give a great deal of thought, attention, and consideration to their wine lists. And lists of bigger restaurants are frequently publications deserving of far more careful reading than can usually be devoted to them in advance of a restaurant meal. If your interest in wine is such that you would like one of these lists, don't hesitate to ask, offering to pay for it if it appears to have been costly to produce.

As far back as the Middle Ages, the French recognized the need for legal controls to offer guarantees of origin and method of production. But it was not until 1935 that the government created the world's first comprehensive wine legislation. Termed *Appelation d'Origine Contrôlée* (A.O.C.), or Controlled Place of Origin, it covers every aspect of wine-making from soil and vine to bottle. Though not necessarily a guarantee of quality, A.O.C. regulations ensure that the consumer knows what goes into the bottle he or she may purchase, where it came from, and how to identify it; there are some 400 A.O.C. wines. In addition, there are two categories of wines that meet less rigid classifications: *Vins Délimités de Qualité Supérieure* (V.D.Q.S.)—developed in 1945—and the even more recent *Vin de Pays.* Wines in these two last-mentioned categories are worth trying and can be very good value. There remains *vin de table*—not officially designated—made in vast quantities around the Mediterranean and often with little but its low price as a plus. In all events, it's the label that tells the story. Don't hesitate, in a restaurant of any quality, to ask to see several different bottles before making a decision; when in doubt, pose questions to the waiter, captain, or *sommelier*—the specialist wine-server (wearing a silver necklace containing a *tastevin,* or wine-tasting minicup), to be found in better spots. Invariably they're happy to be helpful. French table wines—reds and whites in quantity, fewer rosés—are usually dry, fruity, or flowery, but never sweet. Here's a breakdown by principal areas:

Alsace's wines are almost entirely white. Alsace (chapters 15 and 35) is unique among French wine regions in that all of its wines are sold under the name of the grape from which they're made and with but one A.O.C. (Alsace), albeit broken down as *Riesling* (dry, clean taste, rich bouquet); *Gewürztraminer* (spicy, fruity, pungent, with a flowery bouquet); *Sylvaner* (agreeable, fruity, and dry); and *Tokay* (not to be confused with the sweetish Hungarian Tokay, dry and full bodied).

Bordeaux (chapter 10) has been a wine center since the beginning of the Christian era. It's regarded as the area of the planet that produces the greatest wines (although Burgundy partisans might quarrel with this). This southwestern region, dominated by the city of Bordeaux and bisected by the Garonne River, divides itself into sectors that have given their names to the various types of Bordeaux. The *four major areas* are *Graves, St.-Émilion, Médoc,* and *Pomerol;* from these come the most noted red and white table wines. A fifth, *Sauternes,* produces the most celebrated of the French sweet whites. There are two additional types of Bordeaux. One, named for an area called *Entre-Deux-Mers,* is a type of dry white wine. The last is *Bordeaux Rouge*—moderate-priced reds that come from throughout the Bordeaux area.

There are two broad types of bottled Bordeaux: château-bottled and regional-bottled. Château designates wine produced on the estate of a specific château or grower (a real castle may or may not be part of the grower's estate). *Château-bottled* wine is entirely a product of that vineyard—the grapes have been grown and tended there, then harvested and processed into wine, and finally bottled and labeled on the premises. Among the most expensive and famous are Château Latour, Château Margaux, Château Lafite, and Château Mouton Rothschild, but there are 84, all told. *Regional-bottled* wine comes from a broader area rather than a single vineyard; they include Graves and St.-Émilion. Wines are taken to various shippers' cellars in the city of Bordeaux, processed, and bottled. Besides the name of the area of production on the label, that of the shipper is indicated (rather than the individual vintner or château owner-grower). Quality tends to be good—and consistent.

Bordeaux *reds* are usually firm and delicate, yet sturdy when young, and mellow and full bodied when mature. They grow better as they age—traditionally 10 years, sometimes sooner. At their best, they are subtle, with elegant flavor and brilliant color, the while being generous but neither heavy nor strong. Among the more important reds from the Left Bank of the Garonne River are Médoc, Haut Médoc, Moulis, Listrac, St.-Julien, St.-Estèphe, Pauillac (home of three of the five Premier Grands Crus—or top rankers—Château Lafite, Château Latour, and Château Mouton Rothschild), Margaux (noted for Château Margaux), and Graves Rouges (noted for Château Haut-Brion). Important Right Bank reds include St.-Émilion, Pomerol (smallest of the leading Bordeaux districts), Fronsac, Côtes de Blaye, Côtes de Bourg, and Premières Côtes de Bordeaux.

Bordeaux *whites*—constituting about half the region's total output—include Graves, Entre-Deux-Mers, noted for light, crisp vintages; and—continuing south, where wines are less dry and more mellow—Premières Côtes de Bordeaux, Graves de Vayres, and St.-Macaire. The sweet Sauternes dessert wines (Château d'Yquem is the most noted) and those of Barsac are the most southerly; these last double as aperitif wines and go well with *foie gras frais*.

Burgundy (chapters 8 and 17), southeast of Paris, produces some of the greatest of the world's wines, with its reds full, elegant, vigorous, big, and complex. Geographically, from north to south, it embraces *Chablis* (with France's most celebrated whites), *Côte d'Or* (divided into northerly *Côte de Nuits* and southerly *Côte de Beaune*), *Mâcon*, and *Beaujolais*. Originally attached to monasteries, the region's vineyards were secularized after the French Revolution and subdivided; the system of small owners prevails. In the Côte de Nuits-Côte d'Or area, they include Fixin, Gevrey-Chambertin (with eight Grand Cru vineyards), Morey St.-Denis (with four Grand Crus), Chambolle-Musigny, Clos Vougeot, Vosne-Romanée (with the ranking Romanée-Conti, La Tache, and Richebourg), and Nuits St.-Georges. Some of the best-known Côte de Beaune wines are Aloxe Corton (only Grand Cru of Côte de Beaune), Savigny, Pommard, Meursault, and Chassagne-Montrachet (lighter reds); Santenay and Côte de Beaune-Villages. Mâcon produces some light reds but is known mainly for whites. Beaujolais, at Burgundy's southern tip, produces one of the best-known red wines—light and fruity and at its best when young and slightly cooled. Beaujolais Nouveau is drunk in the fall just after being made; the better Beaujolais include Brouilly, Chénas, Chiroubles, Côte de Brouilly, Fleurie, Morgon, and Moulin-à-Vent. Beaujolais is the favorite wine of Lyon (chapter 21)—France's gastronomically reputed No. 2 city.

Best Burgundy whites? Those of Chablis—crisp, fruity, extremely dry, with a refreshing acidity—embrace four categories: Petit Chablis (drunk young), Chablis (green-tinged, fruity), Chablis Premier Cru, and Grands Crus (with such labels as Blanchots, Les Preuses, and Valmur). Côte de Beaune ranking whites include Aloxe-Corton (Grand Cru Corton-Charlemagne), Meursault, Puligny-Montrachet, Bâtard-Montrachet, and Montrachet (considered one of the best dry whites extant). Mâcon whites—Mâcon, Mâcon Supérieur, Mâcon Villages, Pinot-Chardonnay-Mâcon—are invariably light, crisp, and good value. The best-known Mâcons are Pouilly-Fuissé (slightly green-tinged, very dry), Pouilly Vinzelles, and St.-Véran.

Champagne—from the region based in Reims (chapter 2) that constitutes the most northerly of France's A.O.C. areas—produced still wines until, in the seventeenth century, a Benedictine monk (of course, you will have heard of Dom Perignon) began corking bottles, the better to keep the bubbles therein for an indefinite period. All Champagne is blended wine, and most of it is nonvintage. Each of the firms in the area has created its particular *cuvée,* or characteristic blend, and knowledgeable Champagne drinkers choose by the producer's name. Champagne may be called Champagne—in France, at least—only if it's from Champagne (otherwise, if made in the same manner, it is *vin mousseux,* created by the *méthode champenoise);* the French are sticky about this. According to how dry it is, it is categorized Brut (driest of the lot, and for most Champagne drinkers the preferred type), extra dry (next to the driest, despite its always-in-English designation), sec (medium sweet), demi-sec (even sweeter), and doux (the sweetest). Champagne is the all-occasion wine, and Brut champagne is the one wine that is good served throughout a meal, with each and every course (omitting the salad, with which no wine is preferable). There are close to a score of top-rank Champagne firms, with Moët et Chandon, Mumm, Piper-Heidsieck, Taittinger, and Veuve Clicquot among the best known; all adhere to rigid standards set by Comité Interprofessional du Vin de Champagne (C.I.V.C.).

Languedoc-Roussillon—the Mediterranean area around Montpellier (chapter 24)—produces red, white, and rosé, but the best are reds—Corbières, Minervois, Côtes du Roussillon, Fitou, and Costières. There is an exceptional white—Clairette du Languedoc.

Loire Valley (chapters 4 and 20) output includes white wines (both still and sparkling and accounting for three-quarters of the production), reds, and rosés. Better-known wines include such whites as Muscadet, Quincy, Sancerre, Saumur, Pouilly Fumé—clean, dry, crisp, and occasionally fresh and fruity; such sparkling whites as Vouvray and Saumur; such reds as Chinon, Bourgueil, Sancerre, and Saumur-Champigny; and two pleasant rosés: Rosé d'Anjou and Rosé de Cabernet.

Provence (chapters 3, 6, 7, 22, and 27) provides a fascinating array of white, rosé, and red wines—with rosés especially celebrated and including Bandol (of which there are reds and whites, as well), Cassis (not to be confused with the black currant liqueur of Burgundy and a good white wine, as well), and Bellet (red and white, as well as rosé). Also worth trying (and not widely available beyond the area of production): Côtes de Provence, a red wine with rosé characteristics.

Southwest (chapters 9, 28, 34, and 36): Beyond Bordeaux is a less famous wine region, but one that produces large quantities of very drinkable wines, especially well suited to the local cuisine. Reds include Bergerac, Côtes de Bergerac, Côtes de Duras, Pechermant, Madiran, and Cahors—the excellent "black" wine, so called because of its dark hue. Southwest whites of consequence include

Montravel, Côtes de Haut-Montravel, Bergerac, Rosette, and Montbazillac—an excellent Sauternes-like sweet wine, good with dessert.

Savoie and Jura (chapters 5 and 14)—the Alpine regions: Savoie wines have the tang of their bracing environment. They are mainly whites, which can be excellent—such as Crépy and Seysel (both still and sparkling). Reds and rosés include Arbin and Cruet. Jura is famous for its *vin jaune,* or yellow wine; as well as Château-Chalon—reminiscent of sherry; L'Étoile—a sparkling white; and the sweet, highly alcoholic *vins de paille,* or straw wines.

Côtes du Rhône may well have been the very first region of France in which grapes were cultivated for wine, and production was spurred by the medieval popes' seat in Avignon (chapter 7); indeed, the most famous Rhône red—Châteauneuf-du-Pape, the Pope's New Castle—celebrates the Provence papacy. That wine—strong and pungent—is the best known of the area's southern vineyards, along with Côtes du Rhône and Côtes du Rhône Villages (both red and white) and Tavel and Lirac (fine rosés). From the region's northern vineyards come Côte Rôtie (red, white, and rosé), Hermitage and St.-Joseph (red and white), Cornas (red), and Condrieu (white).

Cognac and Armagnac are the most noted of French brandies, which is to say, the best extant. Like Champagne—which may be so called only if from Champagne—Cognac may be so designated only if it is from the well-defined Cognac region, based on the little town of Cognac, north of Bordeaux. Cognac is made in traditional stills from Charentes wine and matured in oaken casks. There are several categories, designated by stars, and in the case of the finest, with initials VSOP for Very Special Old Pale. Armagnac comes from the Gascony region of the southwest around Auch (chapter 36); like Cognac, it is protected by government controls. Best type is Bas-Armagnac. But all Armagnacs are made from distilled grapes by an ancient process that continues largely to ignore the machine. To experience it is to enjoy it. *Marc,* less known abroad, is a robust brandy, emanating principally from Burgundy and—somewhat more refined—from Champagne. It takes getting used to.

Eaux-de-Vie are highly distilled brandies made, by and large, from fruits of Alsatian orchards. They are clear and colorless and served icy cold as digestifs—after meals—with positively irresistible aromas redolent of the fruits from which they derive. Not unlike ice cream, they come in a variety of flavors, including framboise (raspberry), poire (pear), fraise (strawberry), mirabelle (plum), and kirsch (cherry).

Aperitif wines—nowhere better than in France—are worth becoming acquainted with, particularly if one is to follow the cocktail hour with a meal that will include wine and that may be followed by still additional variations on the alcoholic theme. It is not for nothing that Europeans prefer them to the transatlantic custom of more potent premeal cocktails. Best known is *vermouth*—excellent on the rocks with a twist of lemon. Popular, too, is *vermouth cassis*—the cassis being black currant syrup out of Burgundy. Noilly Prat, Boissière, and Martini are among the leading vermouth brands. (Note: *un Martini* means simply a glass of vermouth; *martini-gin* is what you ask for when you want a dry martini cocktail—and then only in better-category hotel bars accustomed to American and British tastes.) *Kir*—the most popular aperitif with the French—blends the earlier-mentioned cassis syrup with white wine; *Kir Royal*—esteemed by those French with higher drink budgets—substitutes Champagne for the white wine. *Pastis* is the French national café drink—a Gallic variation of the Turks' raki and the Greeks' ouzo, anisette in flavor and so constituted that it turns cloudy when diluted with water; Pernod and Ricard are leading makes. *Dubonnet, Byrrh, St.-Raphaël,* and *Lillet* are aperitif wines of the vermouth family—sweetish but not cloyingly so, and good on the rocks and/or with soda.

Liqueurs: Orange-based *Grand Marnier,* widely exported, is known to many visitors in advance of arrival, as are *Bénédictine* and less-sweet *B & B*—brandy and Bénédictine combined; it emanates from the Norman town of Fécamp (chapter 31). *Chartreuse,* which comes in two colors (green and yellow), is the only liqueur still made by monks (chapter 18).

Bière: Foreigners are often surprised to learn that beer is popular with the French. Draft is cheaper than bottled; to order it, specify *à la pression.* Top brands, mostly out of Alsace, are Kronenbourg, Mutzig, Champigneulles, and Kanterbrau. Imports, too.

2

Paris

The Continent's Great Capital

BACKGROUND BRIEFING

The surprise of Paris is that it asks the visitor to meet it halfway. It presupposes a special kind of familiarity even though, as Continental Europe's premier city, it is by no means an unknown quantity. We grow up with Notre-Dame and the Eiffel Tower. Even the basic geography—division by the Seine into Right and Left banks—is a schoolchild commonplace. Many of us have studied the French language and acquired a taste for the masterful French style of cooking and of France's wines.

But once the basics of the usually abbreviated initial stay are completed, we are likely to say ho-hum and want to move right along, even though the encounter to date has been only with the tip of the iceberg. I very much suspect that Paris deserves a much better break than seven or eight out of ten transatlantic visitors afford it. This may or may not be because their orientation has been superficial, if not downright ooh-la-la stereotyped. Whatever, a few tightly scheduled days are not enough. Paris unravels only for the tourist who unwinds.

So often, the trouble with the visitor new to this city is that he or she knows so much less about it—and the country of which it is the capital—than he or she thinks. We know Jeanne d'Arc and Chanel No. 5 and Napoleon and the Folies-Bergère, of course. But we are hard put, without a little research, to distinguish between Louis XV and Louis XVI (the monarchs, not the furniture styles, although they can put us off, too). It has to do with our schools. We have been taught disproportionately much about Queen Victoria and Oliver Cromwell. We are sadly weak on, say, the Second Empire of Napoleon Bonaparte's nephew, and on King François I, who rebuilt the oldest part of the ancient Louvre to use as his palace.

All those Merovingians and Carolingians and Capetians: Is it because Shakespeare didn't get around to writing plays about the

French dynasties that they remain mostly beyond our pale? The only fairly early sovereign of whom we have some knowledge is Mary Queen of Scots, although I suspect many fewer of us realize that she was a Queen of France and married her first husband in Notre-Dame-de-Paris, than that she was imprisoned the second half of her life by Elizabeth I in a series of drafty English castles.

It is entirely possible to have the holiday of a lifetime in Paris without the faintest idea of what transpired before Charles de Gaulle. But not every country can also boast a King Clodion the Hairy (so called because he ordered his Frankish subjects to wear their hair long) or a Queen Clotilda (who was sainted because she converted her husband—King Clovis, the sovereign who designated Paris as France's capital—to Christianity) or a King Pepin the Short (his son was Charlemagne) or a King Charles the Fat or sovereigns of such distinctive dispositions that they are remembered as Louis the Quarreler and Charles the Affable.

THE PARIS BEFORE CHRIST

Early Paris goes back to the century before Christ, when Caesar conquered it and its residents—a tribe called the *Parisii,* whose name gradually replaced the earlier Lutetia. But before that happened, Lutetia, with its Seine location, became the tie-up point for ships sailing past, toward Rouen, which it gradually passed in importance, thanks to the ingenuity of transplanted Romans, who cleared its swampy environs. These same Romans built a temple to their deities on Île de la Cité, and later the area developed as the town center. But in 451, Attila's Huns might well have taken the town had not a young woman named Geneviève inspired the people to resist, to the point where the Huns were driven away, and the young heroine of the battle is the same Ste.-Geneviève who has been the patron saint of Paris down through the centuries.

Charlemagne, who in 800 went to Rome to be crowned the first Holy Roman Emperor by Pope Leo III, is known as a military-minded monarch and as a much-married one. (He does not quite measure up to England's Henry VIII, but four wives is a record not to be lightly dismissed.) Between spouses and battles, Charlemagne made Paris a seat of learning to be reckoned with.

At the end of the tenth century, with the start of King Hugh Capet's Capetian dynasty, Paris had become a handsome, substantial city. This was the era of the founding of the University of Paris, the paving of streets, the founding of a police force, the first city wall, and substantial progress in the building of Notre-Dame by another very military and much-married monarch, Philip Augustus.

Louis IX—later to become St. Louis—embellished Paris with the exquisite Ste.-Chapelle, and by the time Philip the Fair added even more to its beauty, Paris had become the biggest and richest of medieval cities. Albertus Magnus and St. Thomas More contributed theological eminence to the Sorbonne's already-established intellectual reputation. The rich merchants and guilds set up their own municipal government, with the provosts on an equal footing with the provost of Paris, who was the king's own man.

JEANNE D'ARC AND THE RENAISSANCE

The Hundred Years War—that near-interminable series of struggles waged by the French to drive the English from their shores—saw the burning of Jeanne d'Arc at the stake two years after her unsuccessful siege of Paris, an English-occupied Paris in which the English Henry VI had been crowned king in Notre-Dame. The Renaissance came in with a bang with François I, who substantially rebuilt the Louvre, founded the Collège de France, started the first royal printing press, and set the stage for continued royal patronage of architecture and the fine arts as well.

Under Louis XIII, Cardinal Richelieu made Paris the intellectual, as well as the political, center of Europe. The succeeding Louis—the Fourteenth—began his reign in 1643 and moved his court to the palace he built at suburban Versailles, a palace that was to be copied by monarchs all over Europe for the next two centuries.

Louis XIV reigned an astonishingly long time—seventy-two years. It was a period of tremendous cultural, political, and military accomplishment for France. It was, after all, Louis XIV who stated—apocryphally, if not in fact—*"L'état, c'est moi"* ("I am the state"). The move to Versailles benefited Parisian industry immeasurably; indeed, it was from that period that Paris became a world center for luxury goods, which it remains to this day. Architects like Hardouin-Mansart, under Louis XIV, and Soufflot, under Louis XV, created works that added to the splendor of Paris. This was the period, too, of the plays of Molière and Racine, of scientists like Lavoisier and Buffon, of brilliant salons, of Gluck operas, and of powdered wigs.

"L'ÉTAT, C'EST MOI"—AND THE REVOLUTION

But the poor were getting poorer. If isolating his courtiers from the people was politically expedient for Louis XIV, it was also the beginning of the estrangement of the sovereign from his subjects. The succeeding reigns of Louis XV and Louis XVI culminated in the Revolution. Mobs forced the Royal Family from Versailles to Paris and stormed the Bastille. One may still visit the cell in the gloomy Conciergerie in which Marie-Antoinette, the excessively extravagant Austrian-born wife of Louis XVI, lived just before being guillotined at a public execution on what is now Place de la Concorde.

Paris was a turbulent city in the years that followed. The Reign of Terror, as the Revolutionary period was called, was followed by the

First Republic, proclaimed in 1792. In 1795, the stormy Directory began its rule. There was a sweeping change in matters aesthetic—from the elaborate Louis XIV, Louis XV, and Louis XVI decor of the monarchy to a neoclassic simplicity in architecture, furniture, and even clothes, with women in severe high-waisted dresses and men—the *incroyables*, or "unbelievables"—in tight trousers.

Politically, the severity was equally *incroyable*. The Directory was bankrupt, and its personnel were at such odds with each other and so intrigue-laden that on November 9, 1799—a fateful day in French history—a bright young Corsican army officer, who had distinguished himself in foreign engagements, played a major role in a *coup d'état*.

THE CORSICAN NAMED BONAPARTE

The Consulate replaced the Directory. It was actually a dictatorship, with Napoleon Bonaparte the No. 1 of the three consuls. In 1802, he was made first consul "for life." In 1804, we are back in historic Notre-Dame for the coronation of Emperor Napoleon I. As he set about conquering Europe and brilliantly reforming French domestic institutions, he found time to begin the Arc de Triomphe and to erect the Arc du Carrousel in the Tuileries, the arcaded Rue de Rivoli, and the splendid column in Place Vendôme. Most important, he expanded the collection of the recently founded Louvre with loot that his troops had gathered in military campaigns. Those artistic spoils had to be returned to their rightful owners after the Congress of Vienna in 1815, but no matter. The concept of great public museums had been popularized. The Congress of Vienna was, of course, the aftermath of Napoleon's earlier and final defeat by Wellington at the Battle of Waterloo.

LITTLE-KNOWN KINGS AND LOUIS-PHILIPPE

The Bourbon dynasty restored itself rather briefly after Napoleon's exile, in the persons of two monarchs we hear little about these days—Louis XVIII and Charles X. (Louis XVII, if you are wondering, was the son of Louis XVI and died in prison at the age of ten in 1795.) Charles X was forced, as a result of the so-called July Revolution, to abdicate in 1830, and in came Louis-Philippe, who was proclaimed king, in a rather complex run of affairs, by the National Assembly. His "July Monarchy" (called after the revolution that brought him to the throne) was a big-business reign. He even dressed like a businessman, walking the boulevards, umbrella in hand. He had no comprehension of the working class's plight, though, and was attacked from both right and left.

All the same, France prospered materially (the Arc de Triomphe was completed), and the Romantic movement flowered. Victor

Hugo made his reputation as a writer. Delacroix painted. Berlioz composed. Still, Louis-Philippe went out as had Charles X before him, by abdicating. The Second Republic followed—but only for four years. Louis Bonaparte (an ambitious nephew of Napoleon Bonaparte), who had been elected president, managed to get his title changed. In 1852, he was proclaimed Napoleon III, although he was also known as Louis Napoleon. (Napoleon II, the first Bonaparte's son, was better known as the King of Rome; he never reigned and died at the age of 21 at Schoenbrunn Palace, Vienna.)

THE LATER NAPOLEON—AND HAUSSMANN

The 18-year reign of Napoleon III (who was emperor for precisely as long as Louis-Philippe was king) proved a significant period for Paris. The emperor appointed Baron Eugène Haussmann to convert Paris into a modern city. With the authority of the imperial command behind him, Haussmann was ruthless in the changes he made. Indeed, there are students of art, architecture, and town planning who still have not forgiven him. In order to build the wide arterial boulevards and the great squares that typify Paris today, he had to destroy much that dated back to medieval times. Notre-Dame, for example, was fronted by a cluster of venerable houses, all of which were razed to make way for the broad open space that Haussmann considered an improvement. Much of the facade of the Paris we are so accustomed to today—the grandiose Opéra/Garnier is a prime example—dates from the Second Empire.

That epoch came to a dreary culmination with the siege of Paris, which was a consequence of the Franco-Prussian War, and the Commune of Paris. The Third Republic saw recovery. Paris escaped damage during World War I, after which the victorious Allies met in the palace that Louis XIV had built in Versailles. They imposed harsh terms on the vanquished Germans, who—never forgiving—invaded Paris and the rest of France in 1940.

THE TWO WORLD WARS—AND DE GAULLE

The government temporarily left the capital for the thermal resort of Vichy, where the quisling Pétain regime was a Nazi puppet until 1944. That was when Paris was liberated by France's own remarkable Resistance force. American troops entered the city thereafter, and the city—though austere and hungry in the early days of peace—quickly regained its brilliance.

The postwar years saw Charles de Gaulle as president in 1945 and 1946 and later from 1958 to 1969 under a new, strong-executive constitution. France voluntarily relinquished its vast Black African empire, as well as Tunisia and Morocco, and eventually—after much blood was shed—Algeria. The great student-worker uprisings of 1968 alerted France to the need to update its institutions even more rapidly than it already had. Under de Gaulle's Fifth Republic successors, Georges Pompidou, Valéry Giscard d'Estaing, and François Mitterrand—the modern era's builder-president—this has been happening.

ON SCENE

Lay of the Land: No great city is easier to find one's way about in than Paris. We may regret that Baron Haussmann destroyed much of the medieval Paris when Napoleon III commissioned him to redesign the city—with the installation of the wide boulevards and great squares. But there is no gainsaying that Haussmann's Paris is sensible and practical—and supremely walkable, despite its considerable size. Let me try to orient you by delineating what I consider the thoroughfares and landmarks that are essential to a basic geographical understanding of Paris.

Start with the *Rive Droite/Right Bank* circle that was for long *Place de l'Étoile* but is now officially *Place Charles de Gaulle.* (Like New York's Avenue of the Americas—still Sixth Avenue to natives—Place Charles de Gaulle remains "Étoile" to many who have so known it.) No less than twelve streets radiate from the Étoile (thus the name *étoile*—star), whose anchor is the Arc de Triomphe. The most important of these is *Avenue des Champs-Élysées*—broad but no longer the class act it had been (it's packed with auto showrooms and fast-food joints, although some cafés, boutiques, and restaurants remain, with a sidewalk widening and general sprucing-up at long last planned for the nineties)—which (with the name *Avenue de la Grande Armée)* continues west to Neuilly and the monumental *Grande Arche* of *La Défense* skyscraper complex, and which leads east into the square that is the most beautiful in the world and the most difficult to negotiate in traffic: *Place de la Concorde.* Continue around Concorde, and you are in the heart-of-Paris park that is the *Jardin des Tuileries,* with *Palais du Louvre*—the onetime royal residence turned museum. Tuileries and Louvre are bordered on the south by the *Seine River* and on the north by arcaded *Rue de Rivoli.*

One may leave this Concorde-Tuileries-Louvre area for *Place de l'Opéra*—heart of the Right Bank—by any one of three routes. The *first:* From the Concorde, take Rue Royale directly north to the Parthenon-like *Church of the Madeleine,* turn right at the Madeleine on the *Grands Boulevards* (comprising Boulevards de la Madeleine, des Capucines, and des Italiens—one street with three successive names). Walk, then, for a few blocks to Place de l'Opéra and the Opéra/Garnier, for which it is named. *Two:* Walk from Rue de Rivoli, bordering the Tuileries, onto short, shop-lined, *Rue de Castiglione,* and a couple of moments later emerge into extraordinarily

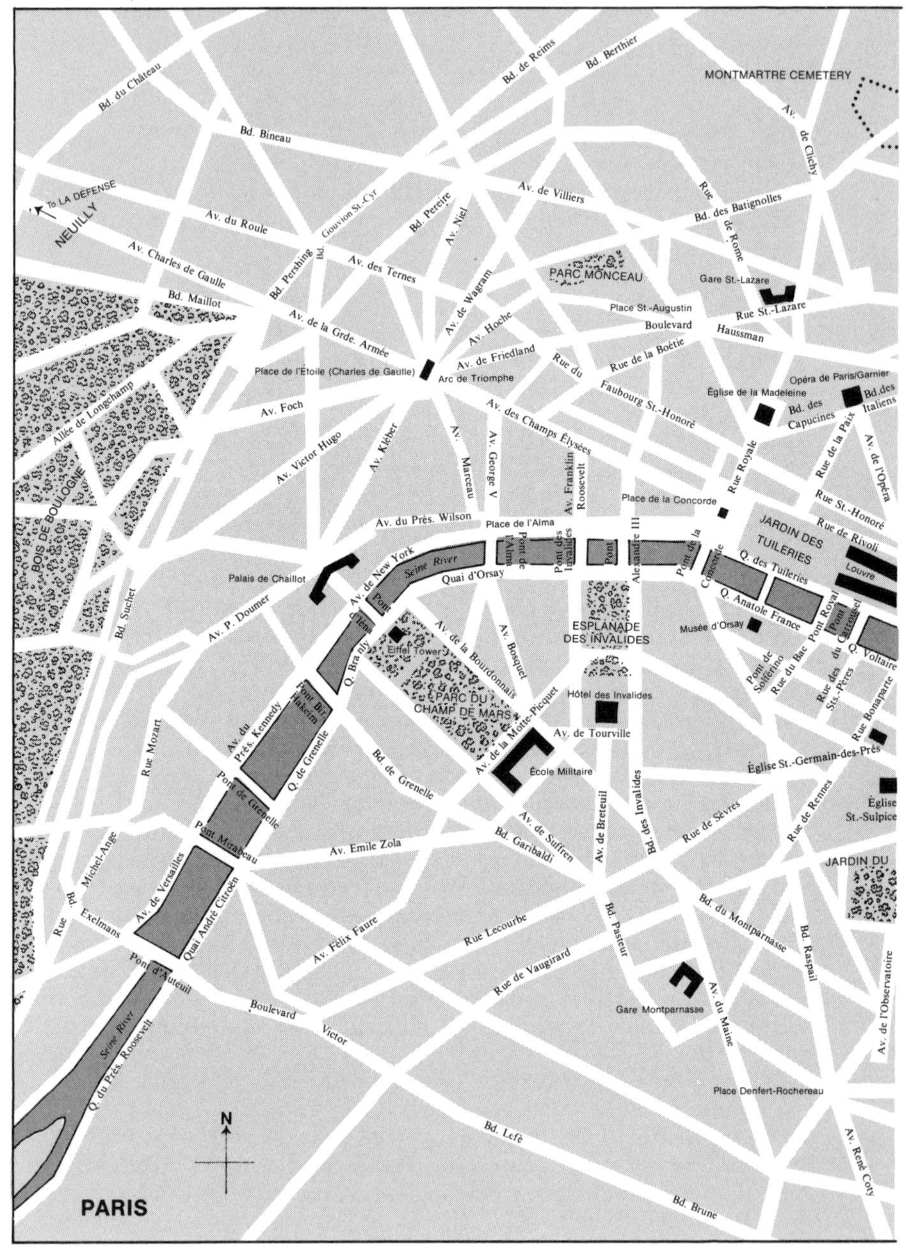

MONTMARTRE CEMETERY
Bd. du Château
Bd. de Reims
Bd. Berthier
Av. de Clichy
Bd. Bineau
To LA DEFENSE
NEUILLY
Av. de Villiers
Rue de Rome
Bd. des Batignolles
Av. du Roule
Bd. Gouvion St.-Cyr
Bd. Pereire
Av. Niel
Av. Charles de Gaulle
Bd. Pershing
Av. des Ternes
PARC MONCEAU
Gare St.-Lazare
Bd. Maillot
Av. de Wagram
Place St.-Augustin
Rue St.-Lazare
Av. de la Grde. Armée
Av. Hoche
Boulevard Haussman
Av. de Friedland
Rue de la Boétie
Place de l'Étoile (Charles de Gaulle)
Arc de Triomphe
Rue du Faubourg St.-Honoré
Opéra de Paris/Garnier
Église de la Madeleine
Bd. des Capucines
Bd. des Italiens
Allée de Longchamp
Av. Foch
Av. des Champs Élysées
Av. Victor Hugo
Av. Kléber
Av. Marceau
Av. George V
Av. Franklin Roosevelt
Rue Royale
Rue de la Paix
Av. de l'Opéra
BOIS DE BOULOGNE
Place de la Concorde
Rue St.-Honoré
Av. du Prés. Wilson
Place de l'Alma
JARDIN DES TUILERIES
Rue de Rivoli
Pont de l'Alma
Pont des Invalides
Pont Alexandre III
Pont de la Concorde
Av. de New York
Seine River
Louvre
Q. des Tuileries
Palais de Chaillot
Quai d'Orsay
Pont d'Iena
Q. Anatole France
Pont Royal
Pont du Carrousel
Av. P. Doumer
Bd. Suchet
ESPLANADE DES INVALIDES
Musée d'Orsay
Q. Voltaire
Av. de la Bourdonnais
Av. Bosquet
Q. Branly
Eiffel Tower
Pont de Solférino
Rue du Bac
Rue des Sts.-Pères
PARC DU CHAMP DE MARS
Hôtel des Invalides
Pont Bir-Hakeim
Rue Bonaparte
Av. du Prés. Kennedy
Av. de la Motte-Picquet
Av. de Tourville
Rue Mozart
Q. de Grenelle
École Militaire
Église St.-Germain-des-Prés
Bd. de Grenelle
Pont de Grenelle
Av. de Breteuil
Bd. des Invalides
Église St.-Sulpice
Rue de Sèvres
Rue de Rennes
Av. de Suffren
Pont Mirabeau
Av. Emile Zola
Bd. Garibaldi
Michel-Ange
JARDIN DU
Av. de Versailles
Bd. Pasteur
Bd. du Montparnasse
Bd. Exelmans
Rue
Quai André Citroën
Av. Félix Faure
Rue Lecourbe
Bd. Raspail
Pont d'Auteuil
Rue de Vaugirard
Av. du Maine
Av. de l'Observatoire
Boulevard Victor
Gare Montparnasse
Q. du Prés. Roosevelt
Place Denfert-Rochereau
N
Bd. Lefè
Av. René Coty
PARIS
Bd. Brune

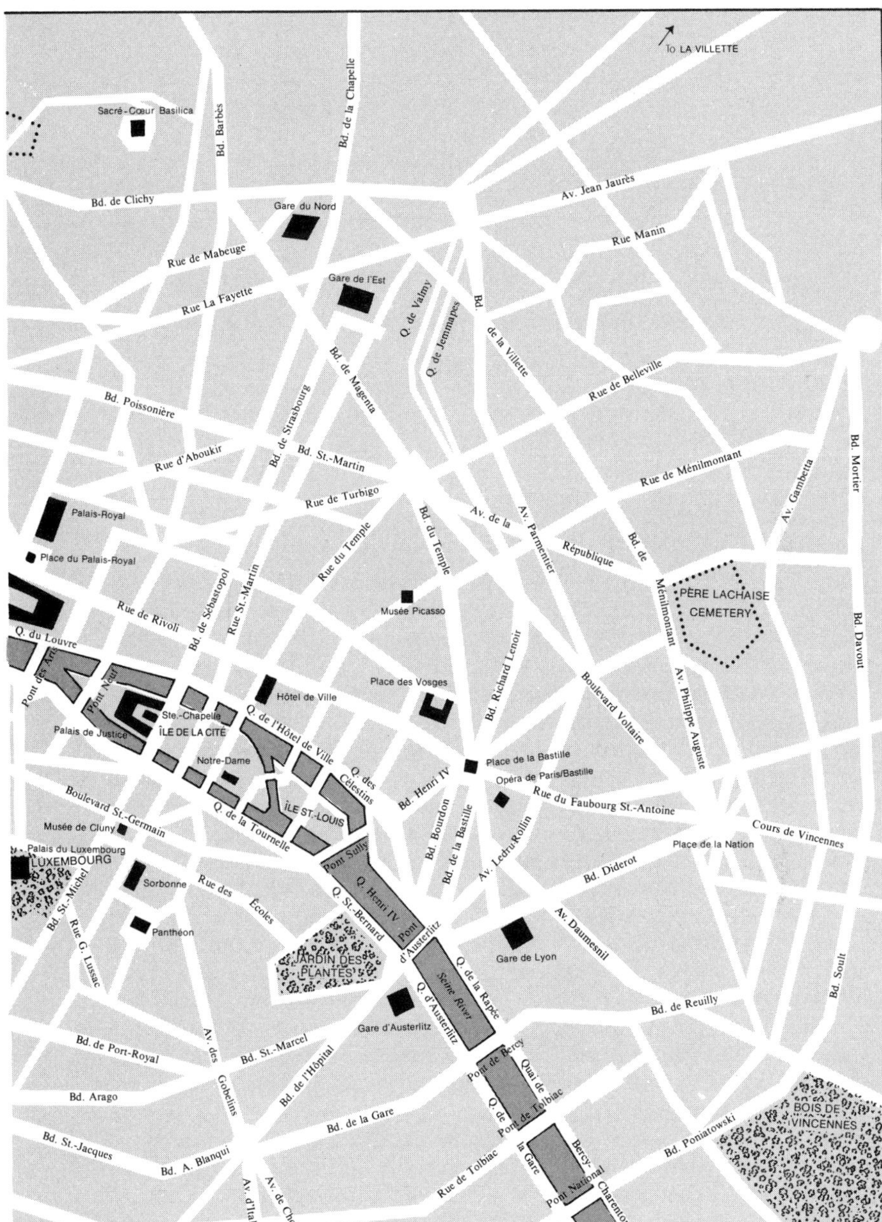

To LA VILLETTE
Sacré-Cœur Basilica
Bd. Barbès
Bd. de la Chapelle
Bd. de Clichy
Gare du Nord
Av. Jean Jaurès
Rue Manin
Rue de Mabeuge
Gare de l'Est
Rue La Fayette
Q. de Valmy
Q. de Jemmapes
Bd. de la Villette
Bd. de Magenta
Rue de Belleville
Bd. Poissonière
Bd. de Strasbourg
Bd. St.-Martin
Rue d'Aboukir
Rue de Ménilmontant
Bd. Mortier
Rue de Turbigo
Av. Gambetta
Palais-Royal
Bd. du Temple
Av. de la République
Av. Parmentier
Bd. de Ménilmontant
Place du Palais-Royal
Rue du Temple
PÈRE LACHAISE CEMETERY
Musée Picasso
Rue de Rivoli
Bd. de Sébastopol
Rue St.-Martin
Bd. Davout
Q. du Louvre
Pont des Arts
Pont Neuf
Hôtel de Ville
Place des Vosges
Bd. Richard Lenoir
Boulevard Voltaire
Av. Philippe Auguste
Ste.-Chapelle
Palais de Justice
ÎLE DE LA CITÉ
Q. de l'Hôtel de Ville
Notre-Dame
Q. des Célestins
Place de la Bastille
Opéra de Paris/Bastille
Bd. Henri IV
Rue du Faubourg St.-Antoine
ÎLE ST.-LOUIS
Boulevard St.-Germain
Q. de la Tournelle
Musée de Cluny
Palais du Luxembourg
LUXEMBOURG
Bd. Bourdon
Bd. de la Bastille
Av. Ledru-Rollin
Cours de Vincennes
Place de la Nation
Pont Sully
Q. Henri IV
Bd. Diderot
Sorbonne
Rue des Écoles
Bd. St.-Michel
Q. St.-Bernard
Pont d'Austerlitz
Av. Daumesnil
Rue G. Lussac
Panthéon
JARDIN DES PLANTES
Q. de la Rapée
Gare de Lyon
Seine River
Q. d'Austerlitz
Bd. Soult
Gare d'Austerlitz
Bd. de Reuilly
Bd. de Port-Royal
Av. des Gobelins
Bd. St.-Marcel
Pont de Bercy
Quai de Bercy-Charenton
Bd. de l'Hôpital
Bd. Arago
Pont de Tolbiac
Q. de la Gare
BOIS DE VINCENNES
Bd. de la Gare
Bd. St.-Jacques
Bd. A. Blanqui
Bd. Poniatowski
Rue de Tolbiac
Pont National
Av. d'Italie
Av. de Choisy

beautiful *Place Vendôme,* easily identifiable because of the column in the center—erected by Napoleon and with a statue of none other than himself at its summit. Pass through Vendôme to celebrated *Rue de la Paix,* and within a few moments you have reached Place de l'Opéra by a second route. *Three:* Continue walking down Rue de Rivoli, bordering the Louvre, until reaching broad *Avenue de l'Opéra.* Turn left on that thoroughfare, walking north to the Opéra/Garnier at its far end.

Now to the *Rive Gauche/Left Bank* via the greatest landmark of them all, *Notre-Dame,* which is situated on an island—*Île de la Cité*—in the Seine. Return to the Louvre—flanking Rue de Rivoli. Pass Avenue de l'Opéra and continue east on Rivoli, beyond the entrance to the *Palais Royal,* until you reach *Rue du Pont Neuf.* Turn right here; this street leads directly onto the famous bridge for which it is named. Over the bridge and there you are: on *Île de la Cité,* with the twin towers of Notre-Dame just beyond. An even smaller island, *Île St.-Louis,* is directly to the rear of Notre-Dame, gained by little *Pont St.-Louis.* But you want to continue from Île de la Cité to the Left Bank. The most direct way is to proceed via the same Pont Neuf you took from the Right Bank to the island; it continues to the Rive Gauche.

Or, if you would rather orient yourself on main thoroughfares, go this way: After arriving on Île de la Cité, walk toward Notre-Dame to the first broad thoroughfare you hit. It will be *Boulevard du Palais.* Turn right across narrow *Pont St.-Michel,* and voilà! Boulevard du Palais has changed names to become *Boulevard St.-Michel*—a principal Left Bank street. Spires of *Ste.-Chapelle*—another landmark—are to your right. But continue south on Boulevard St.-Michel—"Boule Meesh"—to the first principal cross street. This will be *Boulevard St.-Germain.* Turn right on it, and you are in the core of *Quartier Latin,* with the landmark *St.-Germain-des-Prés Church,* shops, and cafés nearby. If you like, return to the Rive Droite in roughly circular fashion. Continue along Boulevard St.-Germain, past St.-Germain-des Prés, following the boulevard's curves. Before long, you will reach *Palais-Bourbon,* the colonnaded neoclassic landmark that is the National Assembly, facing the Seine, and the bridge that is *Pont de la Concorde.*

Before crossing, look up to your left at the Eiffel Tower. Make a note of it at this point, so you will realize its Left Bank situation. Behind it is the broad green called *Champ-de-Mars,* at whose other extremity is the *École Militaire,* or Military Academy. Still another Left Bank landmark—not at all far from where you are standing at Pont de la Concorde—is the complex of *Hôtel des Invalides,* with the domed church where Napoleon is buried. Back you go now to the Right Bank—over Pont de la Concorde to familiar Place de la Concorde.

CHOICE DESTINATIONS, OR THE ESSENTIAL PARIS

Notre-Dame and the river islands. Notre-Dame, along with Westminster Abbey in London and St. Peter's in Rome, is the church we grew up with. It is part of our life—from history-book illustrations and travel posters and old movies—long before we ever see it. And when we do, it does not disappoint. Begun in the mid-twelfth century, it was not completed until the mid-thirteenth. It is one of the great Gothic cathedrals of Europe—conveniently placed smack in the heart of one of the great capitals—with its twin bell towers (you may climb up, as did Victor Hugo's hunchbacked *jongleur,* Quasimodo), its trio of arched portals, its exquisite rose window, its famed flying buttresses along the sides, and its needlelike spire over the transept. The apse, or altar area, behind the choir is perhaps the loveliest part of the always-crowded interior. The time to go—regardless of one's religious faith—is on Sunday for the 10:00 A.M. High Mass. Visitors from everywhere join Parisians in the packed pews. Celebrants of the Mass swing incense lamps from the high altar. The white-robed children's choir sings beautifully, organ music is richly sonorous, and Japanese observers record it all with ever-clicking cameras. Outside, take note of two other visitable destinations: *Musée de Notre-Dame-de-Paris* (10 Rue du Cloître Notre-Dame)—crammed with paintings, prints, reliquaries, and historic documents associated with the cathedral; and *Crypte Archéologique de Notre-Dame,* entered by a not-easy-to-locate stairway on Place du Parvis, in front of the cathedral, which leads to a series of remarkable underground spaces, some dating to Roman-era Paris, others medieval.

The island in the Seine on which Notre-Dame is located—Île de la Cité—is the core of Paris, historically as well as spiritually, and has been from medieval times onward. It was only about a century and a quarter back that Napoleon III's Baron Haussmann removed the maze of house-lined streets from the front of the cathedral and otherwise altered the island, evacuating thousands from their homes. The island's other principal monuments are the Conciergerie and its Ste.-Chapelle church, dealt with in later pages. Suffice it to say at this point that Île de la Cité is explorable walking territory, as is its smaller neighbor island, St.-Louis—essentially a Renaissance quarter, whose streets are lined with graceful houses of that architecturally rich epoch, and whose main thoroughfare, Rue St.-Louis-en-l'Île, has become, in recent seasons, a veritable Restaurant Row (chapter 5).

Musée du Louvre (Cour Napoléon, Jardin de Tuileries): Not another visitor destination—on any visitor's list of requisites—more reflects late-twentieth-century Paris than the Louvre. (See *Grands Travaux:*

Late-Twentieth-Century Paris, below.) Call it what you will: Musée National du Louvre (its old name), Musée du Louvre (the name currently used in its printed materials), or Le Grand Louvre—the immodest but certainly accurate label used by the government for the massive $850 million redesign that resulted, after six years, in a largely (if not entirely) reopened Louvre in 1989 that changed the face of central Paris, by means of a new entrance punctuated by a giant glass pyramid in the Renaissance-style courtyard of the architecturally cohesive, history-rich Tuileries Gardens.

The idea for new access that would take visitors from street level to a capacious subterranean lobby—a mix of restaurants and cafés, (reviewed on later pages) generous-size shopping area, first-ever auditorium of 420 seats (for concerts, lectures, and other museum-related programs), and three distinct wings of exhibits—was intelligent and commendable. And although I was never, over a period of regular visits extending through three decades, a critic of the old Louvre (it has become fashionable to term it the world's worst-equipped museum of consequence and with the nastiest guards, pre-facelift), I did, of course, recognize its eccentricities, always got lost, was always set in the right direction by a kindly guard, and thoroughly enjoyed myself on each and every bout of exploration. I adored the old Louvre. It was French. It was Parisian. It was unique. It is still all the foregoing—but with an American accent. Architect I. M. Pei was obviously selected for the makeover, which resulted in his inappropriately placed pyramid, because he had done a creditable job with the East Building of the National Gallery of Art in Washington, linked to the original museum structure by an underground area that works very well, and is topped by a decorative clutch of very low (perhaps 10 feet or less) stylized pyramids.

Despite commendable worldwide opposition, the immense Louvre pyramid was accorded seals of approval by major French *(Le Figaro)* and major American *(The New York Times)* newspapers when it opened, and with such international Establishment approbation, it has come to attract visitors who have never before entered an art museum, and no doubt—after interminable waits in long lines—never will again. (Sundays, traditionally admission-free, are the worst, but weekdays are not so bad if you go early in the day.)

Think what you will of the Pei pyramid and the trio of mini-pyramids that flank it (adding unnecessary glitz to Cour Napoléon), there is the newly reorganized museum to evaluate. Despite the cold, clean lines of its big new basement entrance hall, and the Yank-inspired logic of its newly organized galleries, there's nothing for it but to praise Pei for the tremendous additional space that's been acquired. The *Pavillon Richelieu* of the Louvre palace complex—fronting on Rue de Rivoli and for long occupied by a government ministry that was moved to new quarters elsewhere in town—is now part of the new museum, one of three principal exhibit wings, each with its own subterranean entrance. The others are *Pavillon Denon*—with sculptures; paintings; Greek, Etruscan, and Roman antiquities and graphic art (and with the top two Louvre treasures: Leonardo da Vinci's *Mona Lisa* and the *Winged Victory of Samothrace* sculpture)—and *Pavillon Sully*, home to Asian and Egyptian antiquities, Renaissance and Baroque French paintings and objets d'art, and exciting sections that were created after excavations in Cour Napoléon—for the new basement lobby—which resulted in quite marvelous discoveries. Many are displayed in the Louvre History galleries, based on the thirteenth-century foundations of the fortress built by King Philippe Auguste.

Decor has been enhanced (new marble cases, newly surfaced walls, new molding and woodwork). Egyptian Galleries are strikingly good-looking and rooms with small French Renaissance portraits—by greats like Clouet and Corneille de Lyon—are elegant. The principal area for paintings, the Grande Galerie, remains as it was albeit repainted, still with works by Fragonard and Greuze, Oudry and Chardin, not to mention Hubert Robert's painting of the space, executed during the eighteenth-century period when he was the Louvre's director. The adjacent Grande Salle still exhibits Veronese, Titian, and Leonardo. And as you wander, you will find Poussin and Lorrain, Le Nain and Le Brun, and you'll delight in seeing old palace spaces—Chambre du Roi and Galerie d'Apollon—quite as splendid as they had been.

Museum aspects of the Louvre date to the same François I who razed the old Louvre in the early sixteenth century and started building the new. His collection of Old Masters was the nucleus of the royal collection that never stopped expanding through all the later Louis—XIII to Louis-Philippe—as well as Napoleon I. It's not easy to highlight a collection of 400,000-plus objects. But besides the painters I mention above, look for Fra Angelico's *Coronation of the Virgin*, Raphael's *Virgin with a Veil*, Vermeer's *Lace Maker*, and works by France's Ingres, David, Delacroix, and Corot. You'll encounter, as well, Tintoretto and Botticelli. Not to mention Van Cleve and Van Eyck, Hals and Rembrandt, Velázquez and Zurburán, Turner and Constable. Sculpture is a Louvre specialty: Greece's *Venus de Milo* complementing *Winged Victory of Samothrace*, and later works—Michelangelo's *Slave*, Goujon's Diana of *Anet*, and an unknown Tuscan genius's painted, carved-wood head of a fifteenth-century lady. Period rooms compete with those of neighboring Musée des Arts Décoratifs (below)—full of furniture and accessories of the periods Louis XIII, Louis XIV, Louis XV, Louis XVI, the Directorate, and the Restoration era of Louis XVIII and Charles X. An entire chamber is pure Napoleon—with his throne from St.-Cloud and his incredibly elaborate toilet kit, or *nécessaire*, and the majestic cradle of his son, the King of Rome. There is a rolltop desk that was Marie-Antoinette's, a bed with a red and white velvet canopy slept in by a marshall of Louis XIII, masterful Louis XV chairs, tapestries and tables, carpets and cupboards.

Once inside the updated Louvre, your attitude toward its pyramid—pro or anti—becomes insignificant. The exhibits take over; they're the winners.

Tour Eiffel (Quai Branly): The Eiffel Tower was completed in 1889; weighs some 7000 tons; was almost razed in 1909; is dramatically illuminated every evening by 292 upward-pointing interior floodlights that replaced almost 1,300 external floodlights in 1986; is 984 feet high; draws some 5 million visitors annually; contains 15,000 different kinds of parts including 2.5 million rivets; has three observation levels; and, when reproduced in miniature, continues year after year as the most popular Paris souvenir. (I was given this intelligence by Galeries Lafayette department store.) The level of the tower to head for is the top one, from whose platform, given a clear day, one can see for many miles. Even in winter, when the top level can be closed, the views from the lower platforms are hardly to be despised: No. 2 at under 400 feet, No. 1 about half that high. There is, of course, an elevator, but if you want to shed some weight, you may walk; there are 1,652 steps to the summit. I evaluate the tower's restaurants on later pages.

Arc de Triomphe (Place Charles de Gaulle/Étoile) was begun by Napoleon I and finished by Louis-Philippe. Baron Haussmann, whom Napoleon III commissioned to make drastic changes in the city, added nine to the three existing avenues that lead from Place Charles de Gaulle/Étoile—of which the arch is the centerpiece—making the total a magnificent, if rather confusing, twelve traffic arteries leading from the circle. (The chief of these is, of course, Champs-Élysées, which extends east from the arch to Place de la Concorde; going westward from the arch, it becomes Avenue de la Grande-Armée, leading toward the Grande Arche of La Défense. The remaining eleven avenues radiating from L'Étoile are a blend of residences, shops, hotels, restaurants, and cafés, the lot comprising one of the most fashionable quarters of Paris.) There's a little museum relating to the monument upstairs in the arch, whose major attribute is the fine vista it affords (in many ways better than the one from the Eiffel Tower). It's fun being up there above the traffic.

Les Invalides (Rue de Grenelle): If you are wondering why Napoleon is buried in a place called Les Invalides, it is because the church with his tomb is but a part of an enormous veterans' hospital—probably the world's first—built by Louis XIV and with a 7,000-patient capacity, of which not even a handful remains today. (English King Charles II's also-big Chelsea Royal Hospital went up contemporarily in London and remains in operation.) Les Invalides, today, embraces a pair of churches and a trio of museums. *Musée de l'Armée,* largest of the three, constitutes one of the major collections of arms, from the medieval period onward. *Musée de l'Ordre National de la Libération* tells the story of World War II anti-Nazi Resistance forces and is not unlike similarly commendable museums in Copenhagen and Oslo, not to mention others throughout France. *Musée des Deux Guerres Mondiales*'s exhibits relate to both world wars. The relatively uncelebrated *Church of St.-Louis-des-Invalides* is architecturally severe. In its chapel is the carriage on which Napoleon's remains started their long journey from the exile-island of St. Helena to the next-door Hardouin-Mansart–designed *Church of the Dome,* where they repose under a top-heavy cupola in an ambience at once overblown, graceless, and ostentatious. Whether or not you are taken with the aesthetics of the Church of the Dome, there is no denying the strength of its architecture. The dome—rising just over 350 feet from the floor to the top of its spire—is supported by 40 columns. Its intricate gilding, picking out reliefs of its surface, was restored most recently in 1989.

Place Vendôme is an almost completely enclosed square that is the work of a single architect—Hardouin-Mansart. It has but two entrances, one on Rue St.-Honoré, the other on Rue de Castiglione. The shape is square, but with the charm of chopped-off corners. Palaces of the square are all early eighteenth century; one is now the Ritz Hôtel, and its next-door neighbor—with a near identical facade—is the Ministry of Justice. The towering column in the center is a shaft of stone decorated with a spiral of bronze that is a souvenir of the Battle of Austerlitz. It was erected by that battle's victor, Napoleon, with a statue of himself atop it. This is rather a pity because the Bonaparte likeness replaces an earlier statue of Louis XIV, the original builder of the sublimely beautiful square, to which not a few visitors make return pilgrimages within moments of arrival in Paris.

Place de la Concorde: Thank Louis XV for Place de la Concorde; it was begun during his reign and named for him—until Revolutionists tore down the central statue of him, named the square for their insurrection, and proceeded to set up their guillotine in its midst. When you try to cross today, as hundreds of cars block your way, think of earlier days. Louis XVI, his queen, Marie-Antoinette, and Madame du Barry—successor to Madame de Pompadour as mistress to Louis XV—were among those whose heads were chopped off in this beautiful spot. Indeed, the reputation of Place de la Révolution was so bloody that the Directory, when it took over the government, gave it its present name. The square, with its myriad black wrought-iron lampposts, an Egyptian obelisk more than 3,000 years old as a centerpiece, a pair of fountains, and eight statues dedicated to as many French cities, is fronted on the river side by the bridge that takes its name. On the opposite side are twin structures, each a part of the original eighteenth-century design of the square. The palace on your left as you look inward from the Seine is Hôtel de Crillon, while the twin palace to the right is the Navy Ministry. Directly to the left of the Crillon, but not directly on the square, is the newer, albeit classic-style, American Embassy; like its counterparts in virtually every capital around the world that I have visited, it has one of the most enviable locations in town. In this case it has views of the Concorde, the Tuileries, and the Seine from its front windows; to the rear and a hop and a skip away is Palais de l'Élysée, official residence of the President, not to mention the house in which the U.S. envoy resides, as distinct from the main Embassy building, known as the Chancellery. But I have not quite finished with Place de la Concorde. As if views, toward and away from the Seine, are not enough, the other two are quite as spectacular—one looking way beyond, up the wide Champs-Élysées to Place Charles de Gaulle and the Arc de Triomphe, and the other toward the formal gardens of the Tuileries and the little *Arc du Carrousel,* a kind of mini-Triomphe that is—you will see for yourself when you look from one to the other—perfectly aligned with the Arc de Triomphe; with the decidedly contemporary pyramid-entrance to the Louvre.

Opéra de Paris/Garnier (a.k.a. Opéra/Garnier, Place de l'Opéra) is the great neobaroque structure that dominates the square that takes its name. Ever since it opened in 1875, Opéra-Garnier—simply l'Opéra or Théâtre de l'Opéra until 1989 when the change of name was necessitated—has been the embodiment of Belle Époque Paris. "Garnier" in its present title refers to the architect, the same Charles Garnier who designed a similarly brilliant theater in the Casino of Monte Carlo. Since 1989—with the opening of Opéra de Paris/Bastille, now the seat of the Paris Opera—it has been home base for Ballet de l'Opéra—as well as dance by visiting companies. Opéra/Garnier is remarkable for its splendid red and gold auditorium.

There is an enormous backstage area (decades ahead of its time) and a promenade area above the sumptuous grand staircase that must have been a perfect foil for Second Empire audiences. Even with today's relatively casual audiences, the Promenade Salon and its adjacent refreshment rooms are quite the classiest of any theater in Europe. It is, of course, sad that this world-class theater, designed for the presentation of grand opera and so named, is no longer used for its original purpose. Its successor, the state-of-the-art theater on Place de la Bastille (detailed, along with more on Opéra/Garnier, on later pages focusing on the performing arts) is a worthy structure, certainly in my view. Still, visitors who have known Paris over a sustained period (including this one) must be forgiven their regret at Garnier's reduced function (time was when both ballet *and* opera were performed on its stage), and at the same time grateful—to paraphrase a statement by an opera official in an interview—that Garnier was neither razed nor sold to the Japanese.

Musée National des Thermes et de l'Hôtel de Cluny (6 Place Paul-Painlévé): The Cluny is, along with the Louvre, the most Parisian of museums, embracing both Roman-era and Medieval-era Paris. Its building is part Gallo-Roman baths, part Middle Ages monastery. You see the immense, high-ceilinged and extravagantly arched Frigidarium—Roman-built in the second century. And you visit, as well, the later monks' chapel and a couple of dozen additional chambers rich with medieval art, the most noted piece of which is the *Dame à la Licorne* tapestry. Take your time as you go through, noting sculpture and stained glass, altars and paintings, and exquisitely detailed rooms of the period—the brilliantly vaulted chapel, dating to 1500, most especially. The Cluny is one of all France's loveliest museum experiences.

Place des Vosges is the most celebrated treasure of the Renaissance-era Marais district, the Right Bank area near Place de la Bastille that has recovered from a long period of neglect and is the subject of additional comment on later pages. Henri IV had the square built in the early seventeenth century. Houses surrounding it are basically of uniform design. No. 6 is where Victor Hugo lived and is now a Hugo museum. But the Place des Vosges is at its nicest on a sunny day in spring, when the old trees have their new leaves, and you have time to sit back in a café or on one of the benches and relax with the neighborhood locals—early enough in the day so that the kids are still in school, and this remarkably unspoiled, authentically Parisian antique is still quiet enough to savor and be grateful for.

Montmartre, way up in a detached area of town in the shadow of Sacré-Coeur, is the romanticist's Paris. No visitor who knows Utrillo's paintings will rest until he or she has had a walk through it. Montmartre, even today, is hilly, narrow streets, with very paintable old houses, funny little squares, and broad vistas. Remove the blinking signs, the mod clothing, and vendors of mostly tacky, embarrassingly poor "art" in and around *Place du Tertre,* and Utrillo could go right back to work. What I suggest you do is take the Métro up to *Place Pigalle,* or a nearby stop, and amble about. You will move via funicular up to that absurdly designed old chestnut of a landmark, Sacré-Cœur (see Ecclesiastical Paris, on later pages of this chapter), and after taking in the view of the town from its terrace, you'll walk over to Place du Tertre, populated primarily by

German tourists. Pop your head into lovely old *St.-Pierre-de-Montmartre* (see Ecclesiastical Paris), look at the delicious food shops of *Rue Lépic,* lunch in a local restaurant, work your way down the steep streets to *Place des Abbesses,* gradually gaining broad *Boulevard de Clichy* and Place Pigalle. Memories of such past Montmartre folk heroes as Toulouse-Lautrec and the people he immortalized in his paintings—like Yvette Guilbert, Jane Avril, and La Gouloue—die hard. But today's sadly overcommercial Montmartre, despite remaining pockets of charm, does not do them justice.

HISTORIC PARIS

Bridging the Seine: By my count, the river that flows through Paris is crossed by some thirty bridges—representing a mix of the city's epochs. Most significant: *Pont Alexandre III,* my favorite—with wrought-iron lampposts evoking its Second Empire origin—traverses the Seine at the point where Grand and Petit palaces face Les Invalides. *Pont Neuf,* way to the east, is the oldest bridge—early seventeenth century. It's the first bridge on Île de la Cité, as you approach from the west, and is worth crossing slowly to savor the views—in all directions. *Pont de la Concorde,* joining Place de la Concorde with the Left Bank frontage of Assemblée Nationale, is eighteenth-century and rewards with memorable vistas. *Pont d'Iéna* links the Eiffel Tower on the Left Bank with Palais de Chaillot on the Right; sightseeing boats depart from its Left Bank extremity. *Pont de Grenelle,* noteworthy for its miniature Statue of Liberty, a thank-you in kind from New York City to the French, in appreciation of the French gift of the original Miss Liberty, is west of Palais de Chaillot, near the circular O.R.T.F. building—headquarters of French TV. *Pont Marie,* way east, makes for a pleasant approach—amidships, so to speak—to Île St.-Louis, when you come from the Right Bank. To gain the Left Bank, the bridge continues, renamed *Pont de la Tournelle.*

Château de Vincennes: Take the Métro often enough, and the names of the lines—bearing the destinations at either end—become familiar to you. One that had long intrigued me was Neuilly-Vincennes. I knew Neuilly—a suburb to the north of the Bois de Boulogne. And, on a recent visit, I took the Métro all the way in the opposite direction to Bois de Vincennes (see Verdant Paris, on a later page) and the château for which it is named. The castle is the only medieval royal palace in the Paris area. It goes back to the fourteenth century; so there is no question but that it is respectable. What it is not is beautiful. The most impressive of the remaining structures is the Dungeon, a gawky medieval skyscraper that had known royal tenants, then took to boarding the more respectable of the kingdom's prisoners, with the nastier of the lot reserved for the

Bastille. The interior is what might be termed Grim Gothic, not terribly unlike much vaster chambers of the Conciergerie. Opposite the Dungeon and in great contrast to it is a church with a lovely, lacy Gothic exterior, Ste.-Chapelle. Its interior is in somber contrast, for it is completely without furnishings. The other principal buildings are the newer, Renaissance-era King's and Queen's pavilions, partially restored from earlier desecrations. Someday—not too long off, one hopes—enough skilled restoration of the entire Vincennes Château complex will have been achieved so that we will have a less depressing, fuller, more joyous, and more lifelike idea of what the medieval royal courts of France were all about.

Conciergerie (Quai de l'Horloge)—the vast Île de la Cité palace, with its matchless round towers themselves a Paris landmark—is the one ancient building in Paris—with which I am familiar, at least, that is more interesting outside than within. Guides take groups through darkish, depressing spaces of cavernous size, the only exception being the simple little cell—now a chapel—where Marie-Antoinette lived before she was carted to her death on Place de la Concorde. She was by no means the only prisoner of the Revolution. The old Conciergerie—originally a part of the royal palace when kings lived on Île de la Cité and named for the palace caretaker—had served as a prison before the Revolution and was pressed into service for that purpose during the Terror. More than 2500 enemies of the Revolution were incarcerated in its Gothic depths, most passing from there to the Tribunal, which heard their cases and then sent most to their execution. Of the Conciergerie's toured chambers, the Men-at-Arms' Hall is the least depressing. There are, as well, an enormous kitchen, guards' quarters, and courtyards of both men and women prisoners. The place served as a prison long after the Revolution for a succession of monarchs—the murderer of a nephew of Louis XVIII, a pesky bomber of the Louis-Philippe era, and still another, who attempted to take Napoleon III's life. Cheery place, this. Adjoining it is *Palais de Justice,* all of whose law courts (save Juvenile and Divorce) are open to the public. This massive maze embraces a variety of epochs, much eighteenth- and nineteenth-century, some considerably older. There are gowned, briefcase-bearing, scurrying *avocats* all about, to liven the place up. And there is the treasure of the complex, Ste.-Chapelle, dealt with on a later page.

Le Marais: We are creatures of habit, even in strange cities. Take Rue de Rivoli. We walk it, and upon return visits rewalk it, but only between Place de la Concorde, where it begins, and as far in the other direction as theater-flanked Place du Chatelet, where we invariably turn toward the Seine, Notre-Dame, and the Rive Gauche. By staying right on Rivoli, though, walking past the landmark ruin that is Tour St.-Jacques and the marvelously neo-Gothic Hôtel de Ville, Paris's City Hall, we come to the beginnings of the Marais, the heart of fashionable Paris in medieval and Renaissance times.

Toward the end of the sixteenth century, aristocrats put up grand mansions—*hôtels particuliers,* as they still are called—which became the prototype of the French town house, in an area that had long been a center of artisanship and commerce. But, after a century, the smart set gravitated toward the other side of the river. The posh Marais once again became the artisans' Marais. Aesthetics of the great houses were forgotten by shopkeepers and craftsmen, who altered them for their own purposes.

After World War II, a civic group that translates as the Association for the Preservation and Enhancement of Historic Paris went to work to right matters. Legislation was enacted to encourage rehabilitation. Upwardly mobile Parisians have moved into the old houses. Nonprofit organizations lease others. Specially trained guide-scholars—*conférenciers,* as they are called—offer visitors detailed commentaries. *Hôtel de Sully,* an early seventeenth-century masterwork with a magnificent courtyard through which you may pass right into Place des Vosges, has beautifully restored interiors; do have a look.

Hôtel de Marle (1 Rue Payenne) is also easy of access, at least on afternoons; it houses the Swedish Cultural Center. *Théâtre Sylvia Montfort* occupies an immense old palace—modernized, to be sure—at 8 Rue de Thorigny. There are two Marais churches of special interest: *St.-Gervais-St.-Protais* (Place St.-Gervais) and *St.-Paul-St.-Louis* (Rue St.-Antoine). Three Marais houses shelter museums and are included in the Museums section, following: *Hôtel Carnavalet* (23 Rue de Sévigné, with a recently acquired annex), *Hôtel de Soubise* (60 Rue des Francs-Bourgeois), and *Hôtel de Guénégaud* (60 Rue des Archives).

Palais-Royal is a tranquil oasis of striking beauty smack in the heart of town—at the Louvre-Tuileries end of Avenue de l'Opéra, next to the Comédie-Française. Originally built by Louis XIII's prime minister, Cardinal Richelieu, the palais was actually royal for only two brief periods—when Louis XIV lived in it as a youthful monarch and later when it was inhabited by Philippe II of Orléans, Regent of France during the minority of Louis XV. Palais-Royal looks today much as it did in the late eighteenth century, when it was converted from a relatively intimate residence to a great, quadrangular mass of buildings that must surely have been one of Europe's first apartment houses of consequence. There have been more downs than ups in the Palais-Royal's history (the most recent "down" has been the placement, in the late 1980s, of an ugly network of tree-stump-like "sculpture" on its grounds), but for much of the past century its flats have been a very good address, indeed, with the novelist Colette among the more celebrated of its tenants. The gardens of the quadrangle are open to the public. On a sunny day, in between sightseeing or shopping, there is no pleasanter respite than a pause on a bench in the odd seclusion of a palace lived in by the very same king who built Versailles—long before it was even a gleam in his eye.

Panthéon (Rue Soufflot, near Jardins du Luxembourg) is a good deal more recent than that of Rome—about 1,700 years. It is the somber, neoclassic, domed structure that Louis XV commissioned the noted architect Soufflot to design; it was finished in 1789. There is more to the building than at first meets the eye. Detail work—Corinthian columns, ceilings, arches, and cupolas—is superb. And in the basement is a crypt containing tombs of such French immortals as Zola, Hugo, Rousseau, and Voltaire. You may see the crypt only in the company of a guide who takes groups as they collect. Because French civil servants have a way of staying on their jobs, it is conceivable that you will have the same guide who has been in the crypt these many seasons. No matter how elementary one's French, his repartee results in the funniest running show in Paris.

Duke and Duchess of Windsor's house (4 Route du Champ d'Entraînement) is the turn-of-century Bois de Boulogne mansion to which the late Duke and Duchess of Windsor (Britain's former King Edward VIII and his American wife, née Wallis Warfield Simpson) moved in 1953, twenty-seven years after the duke abdicated in 1936 to marry Mrs. Simpson. Following the duchess's death in the house in 1986 (her husband died there in 1972), an Egyptian—the same Mohammed al-Gayed who owns London's Harrod's department store and Paris's Ritz Hôtel—took it over and spent nearly $15 million on a restoration. Formally reopened in late 1989, the house now looks as it did in its Windsor heyday. Open only on application—and then principally to historians and VIPs (Queen Elizabeth II and her son and heir, Prince Charles, have been visitors)—the house's restoration embraces ground-and upper-floor salons, dining room, library, ducal couple's bedrooms and clothes-filled closets (the duchess's shoes, handbags, and hats are in original storage spaces). Single most historic object is the table at which the king signed papers declaring his abdication official. But there are tapestries and paintings, furniture and books, and photos of the couple on tables dotted about the house.

Cimetière du Père Lachaise (Avenue du Père Lachaise, near Place Gambetta): Cemeteries, even when their occupants are celebrated, are not to every sightseer's taste. This one, Paris's largest, in eastern Paris away from the action, is named for the Jesuit priest who was a chaplain of Louis XIV. It has all sorts of historic associations, but it is best known for the personalities buried within: Molière, Chopin, Corot, Delacroix, Balzac, Bizet, Bernhardt, Proust, and Oscar Wilde, to name some from earlier periods and—more recently—Colette and Édith Piaf.

OFFICIAL PARIS

Hôtel de Ville (Place de l'Hôtel de Ville) is City Hall, fronting a square named for it, with Rue de Rivoli on one side, a Seine-front street—with Notre-Dame just beyond—on the other, and the Marais just beyond. English-speaking visitors would call Hôtel de Ville Victorian—giddy Victorian, at that. The French prefer the more appropriate Belle Époque label, an equally evocative description. The interior is quite as grand as the exterior leads one to believe it will be. The room to head for is the vast, high-ceilinged Salon Principal, in which no aspect of the decorative arts is absent; if anything, quite the reverse is the case.

Palais de l'Élysée (Rue du Faubourg St.-Honoré): You cannot go in, but it is worth passing by Palais de l'Élysée on modish Rue du Faubourg St.-Honoré; this is, after all, the President's official home. Guards and police on duty are used to people peering into the courtyard to see what they can see. When one considers that the Élysée was taken over by Madame de Pompadour not long after it went up in the early eighteenth century, it is not difficult to appreciate how beautiful it must be. Madame de Pompadour—longtime mistress of Louis XV—was a woman of keen intelligence and considerable taste in the fine and applied arts. Ever since her tenancy, the palace has known occupants of note. Napoleon abdicated there—for the second and final time; the third Napoleon—nephew to the first—lived there, and so have all subsequent presidents of France. You can get an idea of the size of the palace's gardens by walking past walls that enclose them, either on Avenue de Marigny, leading to Champs-Élysées, or Rue de l'Élysée, running parallel to it. Back on Rue du Faubourg St.-Honoré, don't confuse the also-impressive—and neighboring—British Embassy with the Élysée, nor indeed the similarly designed minipalace (No. 41) that serves as the residence of the American ambassador, whose offices are in the embassy's chancellery, just off Place de la Concorde, opposite the west facade of Hôtel de Crillon.

Palais du Luxembourg (Rue de Vaugirard): It is a measure of the admirable flexibility of the French that the home of one of the grandest of all French queens—Italian-born Marie de Médicis—now houses a chamber of republican France's legislature. Queen Marie, after becoming the widow of Henri IV in the early seventeenth century, yearned for a new home that would evoke her childhood.

Luxembourg is rather loosely based on Florence's Palazzo Pitti and has had a multitude of alterations over the centuries, right through to the middle of the nineteenth. Still, one wants to see the Senate Chamber, the reception rooms, and the Delacroix paintings in the elaborate library. The Senate president's official residence is next door in the house that preceded Queen Marie's palace as the original Luxembourg. The setting is a park worthy of space on its own, in pages following.

Palais-Bourbon (Quai-d'Orsay)—facing the Seine at Pont de la Concorde—is the home of Assemblée Nationale, the 491-member lower chamber of Parliament. Palais-Bourbon has a colonnaded, neoclassic facade not dissimilar to that of the Church of the Madeleine way over on the Right Bank. It was planned that way by Napoleon, so that you could look from one harmonious facade to the other and enjoy the way the two complement each other. Palais-Bourbon takes its name from a daughter of Louis XIV—the Duchess of Bourbon. Her early-eighteenth-century townhouse got its present look in the early nineteenth century. To see the Assembly in session in its great half-circle of a hall is, indeed, a special Paris experience.

Palais du Quai-d'Orsay (Quai-d'Orsay): Foreign offices in capitals around the world habitually occupy handsome old houses. (The State Department in Washington, in a modern, specially constructed building, is an exception to the rule.) The French Ministry of Foreign Affairs headquarters in a venerable villa conveniently next door to the earlier-described Palais-Bourbon. Chief lures are Louis-Philippe and Second Empire salons and the chamber where the Congress of Paris met and the Kellogg Pact was signed.

Maison de l'UNESCO (Place de Fontenoy on the Left Bank, near École Militaire) is the Y-shaped, glass-and-reinforced-concrete world headquarters of the United Nations Educational, Scientific and Cultural Organization and is among the more imaginative pieces of contemporary architecture in town. It was a joint international collaboration, and displays works of art by Picasso, Mexico's Tamayo, Japan's Isamu Noguchi, and America's Alexander Calder, to name a few. Visitors are welcome.

SCHOLAR'S PARIS

Académie Française (23 Quai de Conti) is the august body founded in the seventeenth century by Cardinal Richelieu. It is best known for the French-language dictionary it has compiled and revised eight times over the centuries. But it is, as well, a body of 40 elected leaders from various fields of endeavor—engineering and diplomacy, as well as writing and painting. The academy's headquarters are in the Institut de France, a building only some decades younger. The Institut embraces half a dozen additional academies of various arts and sciences; one must make advance arrangements for admission. Rooms to see are the chambers in which the Académie Française and its fellow bodies deliberate and the Great Hall, where members of the academy are installed.

Bibliothèque Nationale (58 Rue Richelieu) occupies a substantial eighteenth-century complex, just behind Palais-Royal. A descendant of an earlier Royal Library, the National Library is at once a repository of books (some 7 million of them, including—like Washington's Library of Congress and London's British Library—a copy of every new book printed in the country) and of rare old manuscripts, coins, and other antiquities. To see: short-term art exhibitions in the Mazarin Gallery and Salle Labrouste—the vast and exquisitely arched main *salle de lecture,* or reading room.

Going up is the state-of-the-art *Bibliothèque de France,* budgeted at a billion dollars when its construction was announced by the "builder president," François Mitterrand, in 1989. Location is Tolbiac, in southeastern Paris not far from the also-new Ministère des Finances, the government department for which a new headquarters was built when it was forced to move from a wing in the old Louvre Palace that has been taken over by the Louvre Museum. Happily, lovely old Bibliothèque Nationale is slated to remain in operation as a repository for books published before 1945; books that have appeared since that year will be stored in the new library.

École Militaire (Place Joffre)—on the Left Bank and separated from the Eiffel Tower by the broad, formal expanse of green called Champ-de-Mars—albeit deteriorating when last I passed by, is substantially as it was when Louis XV founded it in the eighteenth century.

La Sorbonne (Rue des Écoles) is the University of Paris. It is France's preeminent university and, academically, one of the great ones of the world, which is not to say that it is without the scruffy look that is inevitable in so aged and overtrafficked a facility. Location is Left Bank, between the Cluny Museum and the Panthéon. If you are tempted to enter, as many visitors are, on Place de la Sorbonne, don't. The gate you want is on Rue des Écoles, around the corner. There's a concierge there, and I suggest you request that someone lead you to the classical-style seventeenth-century University Church (it is usually kept locked) and the Main Hall. Otherwise, the university is a largely nondescript, mostly nineteenth-century maze of classroom and lab blocks interspersed by student-filled courtyards, their entrance passages adorned with the myriad bulletin boards that no university—in any land—can apparently survive without. Almost next door, on Rue St.-Jacques, is the *Collège de France,* whose roots go back to the Middle Ages and which functions today as an exclusive center of research, not unlike the Institute for Advanced Study in Princeton. Some distance away, at the Left Bank's extreme edge fronting Montsouris Park, is the remarkable *Cité Universitaire,* a campus full of dormitories—more than 35—housing 7000 Sorbonne students. There is an International House, not unlike the similarly named dorm at New York's Columbia University, but a good many of the halls are for students of a single country. The grounds are green, extensive, and attractive, and the buildings—dating from the 1920s to the present—comprise an architecturally diverse melange.

GRANDS TRAVAUX: LATE-TWENTIETH-CENTURY PARIS

The presidency of Socialist President François Mitterrand was expected to effect changes in the operation of government, national through to regions and departments. And so, to an extent, it did, although not so much that the visitor from abroad would notice. What the visitors to Paris *do,* however, encounter, in the decade constituting the eve of the twenty-first century, is a network of major construction projects which, given the caliber of design, boldness, and imagination inherent in their intuition, has caused the rest of the world to take notice—considerable notice.

Les Grands Travaux have not come about without criticism, mostly, albeit not entirely, French. Not a few citizens of the republic have objected when architects have been foreign, rather than French. (I must say that they have a point. If it's the greater glory of France that's the *raison d'être,* why not have it realized by French brainpower?) Not a few non-French Paris enthusiasts have joined a substantial number of Parisians and fellow French in criticism of the most ambitious of the new constructions—a giant American-designed pyramidal structure that serves as entrance to the Louvre, emerging as a kind of sore thumb (in objectors' opinions) from a core-of-Paris garden none of whose traditional architecture is newer than nineteenth century.

When it was announced, in the late 1980s, there were outcries against the planned new Bibliothèque de France (above) to augment Paris's admittedly aged and outdated but lovely Bibliothèque Nationale. Conversion of the long-disused Orsay train station into a museum of nineteenth-century art whose anchor is the paintings collection of the now out-of-business Musée de Jeu de Paume, has met mostly with public approbation—but not entirely. The Grande Arche, completed in time for a 1989 meeting of leaders of western summit nations, appears to be quite—if not entirely—universally admired. La Villette, an away-from-the-center complex—too distant for most foreign visitors—is terra incognita for many non-French who come to town, despite its attributes.

And l'Institut du Monde Arabe, a Franco-Arab cultural center on the Left Bank, remains underappreciated—as one of the great new buildings in Europe. Which leaves still another controversial structure: the Canadian-designed Opéra de Paris/Bastille, on a historic square nobody had paid much attention to since the Revolution. There are naysayers with respect to its contemporary design (an opera house without chandeliers!) and the transfer to it of the Opéra de Paris from its Belle Époque quarters on Place de l'Opéra—now the seat only of Ballet de l'Opéra and visiting dance troupes. Today's visitor—if he or she is a repeater—may or may not like these aspects of the new Paris. The first-timer—without memories clouding his or her objectivity—is likely to be fascinated with these departures from the norm. There is, after all, no logical reason the metropolis of western Europe's largest nation should not evolve from stereotypes implanted by earlier architects, designers, rulers, painters, and writers into an innovative world capital leading—not nostalgically following—into the twenty-first century.

Of the buildings often included in the Grands Travaux category, I place three of those in operation elsewhere in this book. The enlarged *Louvre,* officially part of a project labeled Grand Louvre, is included in the section Choice Destinations, or the Essential Paris. *Musée d'Orsay* is a part of the section headed Museumgoer's Paris: After the Louvre and the Cluny. *Opéra de Paris/Bastille* is under the heading After Dark. Here are the others:

Grande Arche de la Défense (Parvis de la Défense): When construction began in the late sixties (completed in the late eighties), not a pleasure visitor of my acquaintance bothered with an excursion west of the center to the clutch of sleek office towers embracing a new Buck Rogers-like area called La Défense. The attitude amongst foreigners, especially those from across the Atlantic, was that we have our share of skyscrapers at home. Fair enough. Then, though, in the spring of 1989, word spread that the structure built to serve as an anchor for the complex would be completed in time for a western summit meeting in conjunction with observance of the two-hundredth anniversary of the French Revolution. And so it did. A steady stream of visitors—ever since—has been a consequence.

No one appears disappointed, certainly not me. I was fascinated, to start, with the business complex—devoid of motor transport; La Défense is a station on the R.E.R. underground network. Interesting buildings line its main Esplanade—including that of IBM, with its elegantly positioned mass of windows; imposing Tour Fiat; and headquarters of such firms as Mobil, Rhone-Poulenc, Hoechst-France—a total of 40 towers, housing 55,000 workers, and an underground shopping mall, Les Quatre Temps, that's one of France's largest.

Still, when all is said and done, it's the Grande Arche and its observation space, or *Belvédère,* that knocks your socks off. The late Johann Otto von Spreckelsen (who died of cancer before the building opened) created a quite marvelous 35-story, white marble-surfaced cube with sides nearly 330 feet long, an inside space into which the Cathedral of Notre-Dame would fit, which is 230 feet wide and just under 300 feet high. Positioning is in the axis that unites the Louvre, Place de la Concorde, and the Arc de Triomphe with this new masterwork. You'll see what I mean when you ascend the fabulous free-standing glass elevators for a vista of Paris easily as exciting as that from the Eiffel tower.

Institut du Monde Arabe (23 Quai St.-Bernard at Rue des Fosses St.-Bernard) is the Left Bank's sleeper—arguably one of the most outstanding contemporary buildings in Europe. It edges the Seine, at Pont de Sully, with Île St.-Louis just opposite. A joint project of France and twenty-two Arab nations that pays tribute, through its museum, library, and special-events calendar, to Arab culture and Franco-Arab amity, the Arab World Institute (often simply IMA, its initials in the French language) was designed by Jean Nouvel, a justifiably celebrated French architect, in collaboration with Pierre Soria, Gilbert Lezenes, and a firm called Architecture Studio. We are all in their debt.

You want to peruse the museum at the institute. Occupying five floors, its exhibits are mostly from the rich stores of Arab art—ceramics, metal objects, decorative works—of the Louvre, from which they are on permanent loan, along with treasures from other museums, including Arts Décoratifs. But you go to IMA principally to take in its architectural beauty. Single most breathtaking aspect is an entire facade whose windows appear as moving metallic mosaics, their intricate parts' constant openings and closings ingeniously regulated by photoelectric cells in accordance with the available light.

But detailing throughout is extraordinary—a mass of stairways, as if out of a child's metal construction set, is set against glass walls. Another floor's windows are offset, within, by a network of severe metallic pillars. Decorative, pipelike balconies create still another facade. Volumes of the 40,000-book library are stored on circular shelves of a transparent tower, with readers' chairs and tables made of designed-for-the-library aluminum. The staff—mostly young Arab women in Western dress who speak fluent French if not English—smiles. Views, from the institute's northern side, of the Right Bank (especially from the terrace of the restaurant) are brilliant. But that is as it should be; this is a brilliant building.

La Villette (Avenue Corentin-Cariou, northeast of Gare du Nord and between Porte de Pantin and Porte de la Villette Métro stations): To term La Villette a multipurpose 136-acre park is to understate. Evolving over the last decade and planned by a number of talented architects, it is based on a onetime meatpacking plant and it's ringed by a no-two-alike network of modular constructions—the lot painted in bright red enamel—some of them restaurants, cafés, or bars, one a belvedere with an observation platform, another for children's play, another a computer station. Called Les Folies, these are the work of Bernard Tschumi, chief La Villette architect. But there's more: the immense Grande Halle, a site for concerts and variety and trade shows; La Géode, an extraordinary spherical cinema surfaced with mirrorlike stainless steel; Le Zénith, a concert hall with the appearance of a handful of giant connected balloons—and a capacity of 6400; Cité des Sciences et de l'Industrie—a seven-and-a-half acre mix of museum exhibits and special shows about science that packs in kids (adults are also welcome)—and is illuminated by a pair of mobile cupolas controlled by a computer, with its interior a marvelous meld of steel and glass and the movement of centrally situated escalators. Cité de la Musique, La Villette's newest component part, lies beneath a roof of undulating curves and is home to France's National Music Conservatory, with a large open-to-the-public concert hall and a viewable collection of musical instruments.

VERDANT PARIS

Bois de Boulogne is not very far from Arc de Triomphe, at the city's western flank. It is bordered by good residential neighborhoods, and within its 2500 acres are a multitude of attractions. There are a pair of racetracks—better-known Longchamp (the noted Grand Prix de Paris is an annual spring event—France's answer to Britain's Ascot) and Auteuil, a steeplechase track. There are, as well, a lake for rowboating; Jardin d'Acclimatation, which is at once amusement park (with a Paris-traditional marionette theater *pour les enfants*) and zoo; riding trails; picnic glades; ultramodern Musée National des Arts et Traditions Populaires (below); and, not surprisingly, good restaurants.

Bois de Vincennes fringes eastern Paris. Its landmark and namesake is earlier-described Château de Vincennes, but it has other lures; most recent is Jardin Floral. A broad expanse of gardens encircles a central lake. There's a restaurant-café and display areas for special exhibitions as well as something called the Exotarium (what does the Académie Française think of that word?), with displays of tropical fish and reptiles. Better known and more fun is the park's big zoo, which is No. 1 in France and, like many of its contemporary counterparts around the world, has its residents living cageless lives in open terrain.

Champ-de-Mars is the front yard of École Militaire, or the backyard of the Eiffel Tower, whichever you prefer. Begun in the eighteenth century, along with the military school, this so-called Field of Mars is a formal garden in the French tradition. Proportions are extravagant; its fountains, arbors, benches, and paths are inviting. It's pleasant for a stroll in conjunction with an Eiffel Tower visit or a morning or afternoon at the Palais de Chaillot museums, just across the Seine.

Jardin du Luxembourg, the Left Bank's favorite playground, takes the name of the earlier-described palace originally built for Queen Marie de Médicis in the seventeenth century. Not all of the park's 60 acres are as formally Franco-Italian as they were when it was laid out, but there are still a central allée; a great fountain; vivid, carefully manicured patches of flowers; and a popular marionette show, Théâtre du Luxembourg.

Jardin des Plantes (57 Rue Cuvier): I first visited the Jardin des Plantes when I had time to kill before departing on a train from nearby Gare d'Austerlitz, way at the eastern end of the Left Bank. This is at once a spacious and beautiful botanical garden and a zoo, with the latter—elephants, lions, tigers, and monkeys are resident—perhaps more diverting than the former. The whole complex is an agreeable way to brush elbows, on a balmy day, with Paris at its leisure.

Jardin des Tuileries: Until the inappropriate placement, in 1989, of a 71-foot-high glass and steel pyramid in Cour Napoléon—over the subterranean entrance to the Musée du Louvre (above)—the Tuileries Gardens constituted an architecturally cohesive essence of the city—big and bold and precise and elegant and ravishing in their beauty. Even with the addition of the jarring modern pyramid, the siting remains matchless, with the Seine on the south, arcades of Rue de Rivoli on the north, Louvre Palace to the east, and Arc de Triomphe perfectly aligned with smaller Arc du Carrousel to the west. The gardens were begun in the sixteenth century by Queen Catherine de Médicis, but the great Le Nôtre—of Vaux le Vicomte and Versailles—redesigned them a century later. With their reflecting pools, sculpture, clipped lawns, and brilliant, multicolored flowerbeds, they cry out for walks—to remove the kinks, say, of a long Louvre afternoon or an expensive morning in the shops. And there are the youngsters to be observed, sailing bathtub-boats in a great circle of a pond, watching Guignol and Gnafron in a marionette show, or cavorting on gaily painted merry-go-round chargers.

ECCLESIASTICAL PARIS: BEYOND NOTRE-DAME

Chapelle Expiatoire (Square Louis XVI, off Boulevard Haussmann, near Place St.-Augustin): With the Bourbon Restoration, King Louis XVIII moved the bodies of his ancestors, Louis XVI and Marie-Antoinette, from a Paris cemetery to Basilica of St.-Denis, on the outskirts of town. To mark the site of their city resting place, he began erection of this severe neoclassic chapel; it was completed by Charles X. Under its dome are somewhat fanciful statues of Louis XVI and his Austrian wife. Setting is an engaging little park, whose benches are frequented by neighborhood locals. Go at midday and savor the delicious odors of lunch being cooked by the wife of the concierge in their apartment adjacent to the ticket office.

Notre-Dame-des-Victoires (Place des Petits-Pères, a couple of steps north of Place des Victoires) fronts a minisquare bearing the nickname of the Augustinian monks whose monastery was, in centuries past, adjacent to it. This is an imposing baroque building that goes back to the reign of Louis XIII, who ordered its construction and who is portrayed in one of the half-dozen-odd paintings by Van Loo, within. The many thousands of ex-votos you'll note affixed to walls are souvenirs left by the faithful in the course of pilgrimages to the Virgin Mary, annual events in the church since 1836.

St.-Augustin (Place St.-Augustin, not far north of Place de la Madeleine) is included here for much the same reason as Église Polonaise—the Polish Church; lots of visitors pass by and are curious. St.-Augustin is mid-nineteenth century, and its exterior—with an oversized central dome surrounded by four towers—makes the interior anticlimactic.

Ste.-Chapelle (Île de la Cité), after Notre-Dame, is the most important church in town. Tucked into the vast Palais de Justice complex, it is a thirteenth-century masterwork built by Louis IX—later St. Louis. The slimness and elegance of its exterior proportions would be enough to make it a standout for the centuries, but its immense stained-glass windows are easily the finest in Paris and among the best in Europe. I only wish it did not close for lunch and, moreover, that there were no admission charge for what is, stained glass or no, a place of worship.

St.-Denis, 10 miles north of town on Route A1, is much-restored Romanesque. The present basilica was built in the twelfth century, but five centuries before, in an earlier St.-Denis, Dagobert I became the first of a long line of French monarchs to be accorded a St.-Denis burial. Since he was interred there, every one of his successors has been, save a few monarchs of the medieval Capetian dynasty and successors to the post-Napoleonic era's Louis XVIII—Charles X, Louis-Philippe, and Napoleon III. The solitude of the St.-Denis crypts was interrupted by the Revolution, when coffins were removed and remains within unceremoniously disposed of. Tombs themselves were saved, though, and later returned. One sees them today empty but hardly unimpressive. They total 79—kings, queens, princes, and princesses.

St.-Étienne-du-Mont (Place Ste.-Geneviève and Rue Clovis, near the Panthéon, on the Left Bank) is very important to Paris, for it contains a shrine to Sainte Geneviève, the city's patron saint. Beyond that, however, it is an exceptional Gothic structure, with the only rood screen of any church in town, handsome vaulting, fine stained glass, and splendid proportions.

St.-Eustache (Rue du Jour) is a welcome and familiar landmark of yesteryear in the Halles quarter, for long the produce center of town until those operations were removed to the drearily dull Rungis sector, beyond the city, and the market was largely replaced by a stark and forbidding shopping mall. St.-Eustache is big and beautiful, a meld of Gothic and Renaissance, with a rich history and an equally rich decor. Ceilings are high, with fine vaulting and elaborate columns in support. Much of the stained glass is good, and there are side chapels, one with a painting by Rubens.

St.-Germain-l'Auxerrois (Place du Louvre) is so overshadowed by its across-the-street neighbor, the Louvre, that it is more often than not ignored. This is a Gothic church that is among the loveliest in the city, which is not surprising when one considers that it had been the parish church of the Royal Family during periods when the Louvre was a royal residence. Bits and pieces of it are Romanesque and Renaissance, but it is essentially Gothic, with a pair of rose windows of that era and a handsome choir. Like St.-Eustache, this church is noted for its concerts.

St.-Germain-des-Prés (Boulevard St.-Germain at Rue Bonaparte) goes all the way back to the sixth century, but is mostly more recent; the bulk of it is eleventh-century. Within, the Gothic sanctuary and choir are attractive, even if the unfortunate late-nineteenth-century stained glass is not. This church's concerts are of higher caliber.

St.-Gervais (Place St.-Gervais, behind Hôtel de Ville, in the Marais) rather oddly combines a Gothic interior with a baroque facade—and gets away with it. There are surprises within—a long and beautiful nave, art objects, an organ said to be the oldest in Paris, and lovely glass vaulting. But it's open-hours that make this church especially distinctive. Though barely illuminated (candles, mostly), it welcomes visitors well into the evening; since 1975 it has been operated by resident contemplative orders of monks and nuns.

St.-Julien-le-Pauvre (Rue St.-Julien-le-Pauvre, on the Left Bank) is so literally in the shadow of Notre-Dame that you find yourself sitting in its garden to have a look at Big Brother; from nowhere is Notre-Dame seen in finer perspective. From still another angle, the view is of nearby St.-Séverin Church, later described. But you must go inside St.-Julien-le-Pauvre; it is a millennium old, with a high, high nave, and an unusual-for-Paris inconostasis (the church is Malachite, an Eastern rite), from which hang paintings of saints and over which is suspended a great cross. Go for the Sunday morning service to hear the first-rate choir and smell the incense.

St.-Louis-en-l'Île (Rue St.-Louis-en-l'Île, Île St.-Louis) is a richly embellished Renaissance church, with a slim steeple and—of interest if you are from Missouri—a tablet from that state's St. Louisans paying tribute to the American city's namesake.

La Madeleine (Place de la Madeleine) is an enormous, late-eighteenth-century neoclassic landmark that started out to be all manner of things, none of them a place of worship, and was almost a railroad station before the final decision was reached (one of the few we hear about, of the reign of Louis XVIII). It is the scene today of *haut monde* weddings. There are flower stalls in the surrounding square, whose food shops are in many ways more inviting than the austere interior of this church.

St.-Merri (Rue St.-Martin, just north of Tour St.-Jacques, near Hôtel de Ville) is an opulent Gothic church that has known some unfortunate tampering over the centuries, but there are stained-glass windows, handsome vaulting, and a honey of a choir.

St.-Nicolas-des-Champs (Rue St.-Martin, near Place de la République) is about 900 years old and holding up very well, thank you. The interior appears a beautiful sea of pillars, and there are lots of paintings. While you are about it, go next door and visit *St.-Martin-des-Champs,* smaller, equally venerable, and reminiscent only in name of the considerably more recent St. Martin-in-the-Fields, on London's Trafalgar Square.

St.-Nicolas-de-Chardonnet (Rue des Bernardins, just off Boulevard St.-Germain) is essentially late Renaissance, with a good deal of charm and exemplary paintings. It's rather a nice contrast to the cafés of St.-Germain when you're exploring the neighborhood.

St.-Philippe-de-Roule (Rue du Faubourg St.-Honoré at Place Chassaigne-Goyon) is included here only because you might well pass it in the course of shopping the Faubourg St.-Honoré. The church is originally late eighteenth century—neoclassic, with a colonnaded portico that is at least as meritorious as any of the architectural or decorative aspects within.

St.-Pierre-de-Montmartre (Place du Tertre) is just the aesthetic relief you are looking for after a pilgrimage to Sacré-Cœur, its near neighbor way up in the mountains of Montmartre. St.-Pierre is the genuine architectural article—Gothic, with bits and pieces that are even older Romanesque. This church goes back to the twelfth century, so that whoever was inspired to implant striking contemporary stained glass in its windows had courage. And taste: the combination is pleasing.

Église Polonaise (Place Maurice Barrès at Rue St.-Honoré) is a domed, Italianate-looking structure that shoppers frequently pass by and are curious about. It is seventeenth-century and not nearly as impressive inside as out, despite frescoes lining its dome. The name derives from the national origin of most parishioners—Polish—in which language Masses are said.

St.-Roch (269 Rue St.-Honoré) is here included, first because it is in the heart of tourist Paris, and you might want to know what's inside. Second, its priests say Masses in English. This is a beauty of a baroque church, with fine sculptures and paintings.

Sacré-Coeur (Square Willette, Montmartre): The world is full of churches built as acts of thanksgiving to God. Sacré-Cœur is quite the opposite: It was conceived as an act of contrition after France's emergence as the loser in the Franco-Prussian War, which was such a disaster that it led to the abdication of Napoleon III. It was not, however, until after still another conflict, World War I, that this enormous basilica finally opened. There is little one can appreciate as regards its aesthetics. The best that can be said for it is that its white domed facade and its high Montmartre elevation make it stand out as a landmark of the Paris skyline, and that the view from its dome is excellent.

St.-Séverin (Rue des Prêtres-St.-Séverin) is a near- neighbor of earlier recommended St.-Julien-le-Pauvre, on the Left Bank. You begin liking St.-Séverin because of the garden that sets off its substantial Romanesque facade so well. And you like what you see inside, too: a mostly Gothic church of fine proportions and detailing not the least of which are the stained glass and the unusually capacious, strikingly decorated area behind the altar.

Église de la Sorbonne (Rue des Écoles) is the University of Paris chapel and the only one of its buildings that is quite as it was when Cardinal Richelieu had it constructed four centuries ago. It contains the cardinal's tomb. Get the key from the concierge inside the gate on Rue des Écoles.

St.-Sulpice (Place St.-Sulpice, between Palais du Luxembourg and Boulevard St.-Germain) is still another Left Bank standout, with ancient origins, but with baroque rebuilding, a twin-tower facade, and an absolutely immense interior, full of splendid art and artisanship, mostly eighteenth-century. The surprise, in one of the chapels, is a clutch of mid-nineteenth-century murals by Delacroix.

Val-de-Grace (Rue du Val-de-Grace at Place Alphonse-Laurent, near Boulevard du Montparnasse) had its origins with Anne of Austria, mother of Louis XIV. She ordered it built (it is domed baroque and so Italian that you pinch yourself to make sure you are not in Rome) after giving birth to her son, having been unable to conceive during the first 23 years of her marriage. Young Louis laid the cornerstone when he was still a tot, in 1641. The Italian motif continues within, with a St. Peter's-like baldachin—twisted columns and all—sheltering the altar. Then look up: The inside of the great dome is frescoed.

Some non-Catholic places of worship: *American Cathedral,* Avenue George V; *American Church of Paris,* Quai d'Orsay; *British Embassy Church* (Anglican), 6 Rue d'Aguesseau, near the embassy on Rue du Faubourg St.-Honoré; *Église Grecque* (Greek Orthodox), 5 Rue Georges-Bizet; *Église Russe* (Russian Orthodox), Rue Daru; *Institut Musulman et Mosquée* (Moslem—and in beautiful Moroccan style, with a pretty inner courtyard that is worth inspecting), Place du Puits-de-l'Ermite; *Temple Israélite* (known as Synagogue Rothschild—for its benefactors), 44 Rue de la Victoire; *Temple Protestant de l'Oratoire,* 147 Rue St.-Honoré; *Temple Protestant de Ste.-Marie,* 17 Rue St.-Antoine.

MUSEUMGOERS PARIS: AFTER THE LOUVRE AND THE CLUNY

Atelier de la Manufacture Nationale des Gobelins, de Beauvais et de la Savonnerie (42 Avenue des Gobelins) has royal origins—Louis XIV, to be precise, who appointed the Versailles designer-decorator-artist, Charles Le Brun, as its head. Ever since, skilled artisans have been at work, one generation after the other, laboriously, slowly, and tediously creating tapestries that represent the time-honored techniques of their forebears. And there are completed specimens of their work displayed, museum-style.

Centre International de l'Automobile (Porte de Pantin) is Paris's car museum. There are 120 significant models on display at any given time, with a cast change every six months—vintage Buggatis, Delahayes, and Ferraris are typical. Near La Villette (see Grands Travaux, above).

Centre National d'Art et de Culture Georges Pompidou, a.k.a. Le Beaubourg (Rue Beaubourg): Ask Parisian friends for an opinion, and by and large they mostly appear no happier with the look of the Beaubourg—a brutally stark, six-level rectangle of unadorned glass and steel that is positively aggressive in its oil-refinery ugliness—than with its location. Opened in 1976, it's on the site of razed buildings in the beloved ex-produce center of Les Halles, adjacent to Hôtel de Ville, the city hall. Still, in the company of foreign and provincial-French visitors, locals mob the center's stadium-sized lobby-cum-bookshop, whose only decoration is a stylized portrait of the late president for whom it is named. As many as 25,000 visitors per day queue to ride its messy, glass-enclosed exterior escalators (similar to—but not as frequently cleaned, it would appear—as those at De Gaulle Airport) to the fourth-level exhibition area, wherein are hung contents of *Musée National d'Art Moderne*—the national modern art museum for long housed in what is now dubbed Musée du Palais de Tokyo (below). This area of the Beaubourg proved to be so aesthetically unsuccessful as an exhibit space that it was subjected to a major redesign in 1985, for which, praise be. On display at all times are a thousand works out of a total of 20,000 by some 3000 artists. This is an undeniably exemplary collection, by contemporary greats like Picasso, Bonnard, Braque, Vlaminck, Rouault, Gris, Modigliani, Chagall, Kandinsky, Matisse, Mondrian, Magritte, Duchamp, Klee, and Brancusi, with solid American representation including works by Stella, De Kooning, Pollock, Rauschenburg, and Calder. Paintings and sculpture—some of it massive—by contemporary French artists occupies main-floor galleries. There's an externally jammed café on the top level (affording views of Notre-Dame and the next-door Church of St.-Merri); and street entertainers perform frequently in the broad square outside, called La Piazza.

Cité des Sciences et de l'Industrie: See Grands-Travaux: Late-Twentieth-Century Paris, above.

Galeries Nationales du Grand-Palais (Avenue de Selves off Champs-Élysées, near Place de la Concorde): The Grand-Palais, with its neighbor, the Petit-Palais, are among the more maligned of Paris's public buildings, at least architecturally. I would surely rather have them than what might well go up today in their place, the Beaubourg (above), for example. They are relics of a turn-of-century world's fair, and I like their monumental scale. The Grand-Palais is put to intelligent use for special exhibitions, frequently world-class and arranged with skill and imagination. Consult papers for the current show.

Maison de Victor Hugo (6 Place des Vosges, in the Marais district): Memories of Charles Laughton as the *jongleur* of Notre-Dame notwithstanding, this seventeenth-century house, inhabited by Victor Hugo between 1821 and 1848, should be of interest, if only for its advanced age, inspired Place des Vosges situation, and sumptuously furnished rooms. But there are bonuses—manuscripts of the author's works, letters, pictures, and all manner of Hugo memorabilia.

Musée d'Art Moderne de la Ville de Paris (11 Avenue du Président Wilson) is the next-door neighbor of Musée du Palais de Tokyo (below) and, like it, attractive Art Deco. (They are wings of a building constructed for the Paris Exhibition of 1937.) In the old days, when the Tokyo housed the national modern art collection (now at the Beaubourg, above), visitors took in both at a single clip. Contemporarily, this excellent city-owned cache is not as appreciated as it might be. Matisse, Dufy, and Sonia and Robert Delauney are but a quartet of painters in the permanent collection, and there are frequent temporary exhibitions.

Musée des Arts Africains et Océaniens (293 Avenue Daumesnil) is well worth the longish Métro ride. Housed in a thirties-modern pavilion is a sumptuous collection that the French—always appreciative of the cultures of peoples whom they governed during the days of empire—acquired during the colonial period. The African masks, headdresses, and other ceremonial pieces are among the finest extant.

Musée des Arts Décoratifs (107 Rue de Rivoli, in the separately entered Marsan Pavilion of the Louvre complex)—closed for a major refurbishing for a full two years before reopening in 1985—does justice to the Catherine de Médicis-era palace it occupies. There are four treasure-filled floors of exhibits relating to the arts of decoration—a fifteenth-century wood canopied bed from Auvergne; the collapsible desk that traveled with Napoleon in the field, with lines so clean it could have been designed at the end of the twentieth century instead of the end of the eighteenth; and chairs of the three Louis periods, so that once and for all—if this trio of styles confuses you—you can sort them out to your satisfaction. There are, as well, porcelains, silver, jewelry, tapestries, sculpture, and painting—from Asia, as well as from Europe. Best of all, though, are the period rooms. They evoke the look of French interiors from the seventeenth century through Art Deco of the twentieth, with the boudoir and bath of couturière Jeanne Lanvin an especial dazzler. Along with London's Victoria and Albert and Copenhagen's Decorative Arts, this is one of the Continent's great repositories relating to the decorative arts, well complemented by French counterparts in Bordeaux, Lyon, and Marseille. There's a bookstore and a shop selling pricey reproductions of museum objects.

Musée des Arts de la Mode (107 Rue de Rivoli—on different floors of the building also sheltering the Musée des Arts Décoratifs, above) opened in 1986, half a decade after the French government budgeted the equivalent of $5 million for its creation. The museum's collection comprises several thousand articles of clothing, accessories, and fashion designs on paper, with the span eighteenth century through to this very moment, and including costumes worn by personages as disparate as Sarah Bernhardt, Empress Eugénie, and Brigitte Bardot. There are nearly a hundred dresses by Elsa Schiaperelli and half that many by Paul Poiret. Selections, arranged thematically as exhibitions that extend over some months, are on view in galleries extending from the building's fifth through ninth floors. Not surprisingly, there's a shop featuring fashion accessories based on designs from the collection. Two fashion museums in the world's fashion capital is not too many; this national repository nicely complements the City of Paris's Musée de la Mode et du Costume (below).

Musée National des Arts et Traditions Populaires (6 Avenue du Mahatma-Gandhi, near the kids' Jardin d'Acclimatation in Bois de Boulogne) occupies striking modern quarters. Besides sections on French folk and other costumes, there are exhibits concerning literature, music, dance, theater, and farm and city life. Objects on display are old and contemporary, fine and folk, rare and commonplace: the French museum profession putting its boldest foot forward.

Musée Balzac (47 Rue Raynouard, in the Passy area, not far from Palais de Chaillot): Honoré de Balzac's novels had not been especially popular in the United States until a British dramatization of *La Cousine Bette* made its way across the water to American TV screens, sparking something of a renewal of interest in Balzac's extensive fictional series, *La Comédie Humaine,* a sharply delineated picture of French society during the reign of the bourgeois businessman king, Louis-Philippe, in the mid-nineteenth century. Balzac lived and wrote in this atmospheric house for nearly two decades.

Musée Carnavalet (23 Rue de Sévigné)—earlier recommended as a major monument of the Marais district—is the museum of the history of Paris, one of a number operated by the city government with great finesse. Its main building—the splendid sixteenth-century mansion of no less a personality than Madame de Sévigné, where she wrote her famous letters of social commentary—was supplemented, in time for the two-hundredth anniversary of the French Revolution in 1989—with a neighboring second building, the *hôtel particulier,* or mansion, called Peletier de St.-Fargeau, with which it is connected by a passage (up a flight from the street). The addition doubles the Carnavalet's space, with pre-Revolutionary Paris in the first building, post-Revolutionary Paris (with a dozen fascinating galleries devoted to the years of the Revolution) in the addition, continuing with exhibits from the Consulat through to, say, last month. Choicest part of the museum is a group of rooms—the Henriette Vouvier Collection—furnished in the Louis XV and XVI styles of the eighteenth century. Elsewhere, you see what Paris was like in earlier eras, from specimens of citizens' clothes, documents, etchings, paintings, and all manner of bibelots—even including personal possessions left by Louis XVI and the extravagant Marie-Antoinette before they were beheaded. Take your time here, making sure to have a look around the often-neglected courtyards and gardens; and not missing the noteworthy facades. Special.

Musée Cernuschi (7 Avenue Velásquez) is recommendable on three counts. First, its contents are Chinese works of art collected by a rich turn-of-century Parisian, who bequeathed them to the City of Paris, along with his house, to be utilized for their display. Second, the house itself is a mansion in the grand style, on a block of similarly opulent houses. And third, the museum is near a smallish park relatively unknown to visitors—*Parc Monceau.* On a sunny day, a walk here is a pleasurable Paris experience. Of the museum's exhibits, the most memorable is an enormous Japanese Buddha in bronze; it dominates the main gallery, whose other standouts include spectacular screens and ceramics, of which a very ancient and sad-looking pottery pig is particularly appealing.

Musée de la Chasse et de la Nature (60 Rue des Archives) occupies an *hôtel particulier* of especial grace in the Marais, and has been earlier recommended for that reason alone. As a museum, it is perhaps more limited in its appeal. Still, there is no denying the beauty of the paintings and tapestries—mostly eighteenth-century—of hounds, with other hunting motifs, not to mention other art objects with the same theme. But it is the architecture of this house, its courtyard, and its interiors (be sure to go upstairs) that make it visit-worthy.

Musée Clemenceau (8 Rue Franklin, near Palais de Chaillot) is the apartment of Georges Clemenceau, who held the premiership of France immediately before and during World War I and whom we remember from history books as France's vocal representative—and an antagonist of President Wilson—at the Versailles Conference. The irony of Clemenceau is that he criticized Wilson because he considered the Wilson-inspired peace treaty too moderate to assure France's security; yet he was defeated in the postwar elections for being too mild in his attitude toward Germany. His apartment is hardly without interest, for this man was his country's most important early-twentieth-century politician.

Musée Cognacq-Jay (25 Boulevard des Capucines): It is the location of this museum that makes it a sleeper. You just don't expect this sort of treasure trove to be located upstairs in an otherwise unexceptional building in the heart of the busy Grands Boulevards area. Downstairs, Parisians and their visitors go about their business. But within the quiet confines of the Cognacq-Jay, the matter at hand is France's eighteenth century and its art—a gift of the founder of the Samaritaine department store to the City of Paris. In a series of furnished rooms of the period, one finds some of the finest pieces of furniture and other objects of the era to be seen in Paris, with a bonus of paintings by such renowned masters as Fragonard, Chardin, Greuze, Boucher, Tiepolo, and Watteau. Special.

Musée Guimet (6 Place d'Iéna, off Avenue du Président Wilson, near Palais de Chaillot), severe and gloomy despite partial refurbishing, comes to life only when you concentrate on its collection. It embraces choice works not only from big Asian countries—Indian sculpture, Chinese jade, Japanese scrolls—but from smaller lands, as well, with rare pieces from Indonesia, Cambodia, Korea, Nepal, and Tibet. Allow yourself time; this is a much bigger collection than, say, that of Musée Cernuschi (above).

Musée de l'Histoire de France (60 Rue des Francs-Bourgeois III, in the Marais district) occupies the very grand and very beautiful Hôtel de Soubise (earlier described), whose interiors—a magnificent stairway and sumptuously decorated rooms—are in themselves reasons for a visit. But the subject matter of the museum—the history of the country as recorded in the National Archives' most precious documents, such as seals, treaties, manuscripts, and even marriage contracts—is absorbing on its own.

Musée de l'Homme (Palais de Chaillot, Place du Trocadéro) is the most important of the trio of Palais de Chaillot museums. The idea is to show us how anthropologists can dramatize the excitement of variations in the human condition. There are two floors of galleries.

The Black African section is one of the better collections of African art and artifacts. There are Bambara headpieces from Mali, sculpture from Baoule in the Ivory Coast, and some of the finest bronzework of the ancient Benin civilization in Nigeria. There are good North African pieces, as well—jewelry, metalwork, ceramics. See, too, galleries devoted to the folk art of Europe—a Lithuanian *St. George and the Dragon*, esoteric Swiss dance masks, processional figures from Flanders, and costumes from Iceland and Wales, Romania and Spain, Holland and Italy. There are, as well, exceptional works from India, Burma, Tibet—indeed, all of Asia—as well as the South Pacific, with a carved-wood Maori tomb from New Zealand. Surprises for North Americans are remarkable collections devoted to the folk art of the Indians and Eskimos of the New World.

Musée de l'Institut du Monde Arabe: See Grands Travaux: Late-Twentieth-Century Paris, above.

Musée Jacquemart-André (158 Boulevard Haussmann, some blocks west of the big-domed Church of St.-Augustin) is still another example—along with others, like the Cernuschi, Cognacq-Jay, and Nissim de Camondo—of the legacy of a single wealthy Parisian family. In this case, founder-donors were a remarkable couple—Edouard André, son of a banker, and his wife, Nélie Jacquemart, a painter. They spent much of their life collecting antiques, with certain of them destined for their Boulevard Haussmann mansion. Monsieur André died in 1894, his wife in 1912, by which time the Haussmann house had become a repository of two types of art: eighteenth-century French and Italian Renaissance. House and collection were left to the Institut de France to be administered as a museum; Président Poincaré officiated at the opening in 1913. There are fabulous treasures here. Downstairs is mostly French, and upstairs is mostly Italian. French paintings alone are memorable, with works by Fragonard, Chardin, Proud'hon, and Greuze among them. Tapestries are rare and beautiful. Eighteenth-century furniture is choice, too. Uccello's *Saint George Slaying the Dragon* is perhaps the most celebrated of the Italian works. But there are pieces by Botticelli, Mantegna, Carpaccio, and Titian as well, with sculpture by Donatello, ceramics by Della Robbia, furniture, and accessories.

Musée National de la Légion d'Honneur et des Ordres de Chevalerie (2 Rue de Bellechasse): A special one, this, for history buffs. It tells the story not only of France's Legion of Honor and its various subdivisions, but of foreign orders of chivalry, as well. (More than 300,000 Frenchmen hold the Legion of Honor, while some 75,000 have been awarded the lesser Order of Merit.) Displays are not only of orders, medals, and ribbons. There are a considerable number of historic paintings, some good, some of historical interest; not to mention sculpture, etchings, drawings, and costumes. And the location is convenient: right opposite Musée d'Orsay (below).

Musée de la Marine (Palais de Chaillot, Place du Trocadéro) offers perhaps more than a layperson can absorb on matters maritime. Still, going at one's own pace, judiciously skipping here and there, it makes for a diverting visit. Ship models of all eras and ages are minor treasures. There are decorative objects taken from old ships, not to mention paintings, drawings, documents, and flags, evoking the romance of the high seas during the presteam era. Other sections are devoted to later periods; models of the ill-fated, pre-World War II *Normandie* indicate what a masterwork that ship was.

Musée Marmottan (2 Rue Louis-Boilly) had always been a worthy enough destination—a fine home filled with the collection of its late owner, including Empire furniture and Renaissance tapestries. In later years, though, came two groups of paintings by Claude Monet. The second group was so large—65 works—that a special subterranean gallery was built to house it, along with paintings by Monet's contemporaries, including Pissarro, Renoir, and Berthe Morisot. Subject matter is mostly the flowers for which this first of the Impressionists is celebrated, but there is a good deal else: a Trouville beach scene with Monet's wife and cousin, sunset in the harbor of Le Havre, a Tuileries landscape, and, in contrast, smoky Gare St.-Lazare. Among the second group of Monets are many of the water lilies painted at his Giverny home (later counseled as an excursion destination), as well as such diverse subjects as a Dutch tulip field and Rouen Cathedral. A brilliant collection.

Musée de la Mode et du Costume (10 Avenue Pierre 1er de Serbie, just off Place d'Iéna, south of Champs-Élysées) occupies a sumptuous Belle Époque town house that's the ideal foil for its celebrated temporary exhibitions—most extend over a period of some months—which are usually retrospectives of the great Paris-based couturiers, with the *œuvre* of the designers (Lucien Lelong and Pierre Balmain were relatively recent subjects, to give you an idea) displayed on mannequins chronologically, earliest clothes through to later models. Fashion buffs, in this preeminent fashion capital, will be happy here.

Musée de la Monnaie (11 Quai de Conti): You don't have to be a coin collector to enjoy this one, but it helps. For those of us who simply like to spend the stuff, the kicker is the setting—a splendid Baroque mansion entered only after you pass through its Cour d'Honneur. Situation is riverfront, on the Left Bank. There are two floors of galleries with displays of French currency from the early

Gauls onward, into our own era—at the end of the money trail on the upper floor.

Musée des Monuments Français (Palais de Chaillot, Place du Trocadéro) is an absolutely fabulous put-on; it is surely the only museum—serious museum, that is (I exclude waxworks)—that consists of nothing but fakes. Its exhibits are reproductions of sculpture and painting in the great cathedrals and churches of France. The main floor embraces one enormous arch, doorway, window frame, and saint-in-plaster after another. The museum is late nineteenth century, and the idea was to see it as a teaching tool for students who were unable to get around their country as easily as they can now to see monumental art and sculpture. Anyone who has traveled France will see favorites, Amiens to Vézelay.

Musée National de la Renaissance (Château d'Écouen, Écouen, not far north of Paris, via Métro to Porte de la Chapelle station, thence via Bus No. 268-C) is a case of taking the city to the country. By that I mean that this double-winged castle, dating to the early sixteenth century—and one of the great Renaissance-era structures of northern France—was put to good use, starting in the 1970s, a decade after a school that had long occupied it moved to another site. The idea—well executed—was to restore it as a museum of Renaissance objects that had long been stored away in Musée de Cluny (The Essential Paris, above) for lack of display space. The ground floor looks once again as it might have when Catherine de Médicis accompanied her husband, King Henri II, on state visits. Completed only in 1988, Écouen lures—aside from the great building itself—are frescoes surfacing a dozen massive ground-floor chimneys, their themes a mix of the biblical and mythological; a series of ten Brussels tapestries from the same era as the castle—they tell the story of David and Bathsheba—woven with gold and silver thread; and a series of painted leather smaller objects, clocks through locks. Closed for lunch.

Musée National des Techniques (292 Rue St.-Martin): A technology museum in an originally Gothic church complex? You bet. And that's what makes this oddball, oddly underappreciated museum (on scene since a priest founded it in the eighteenth century) so unusual. Exhibits are fun because they're so aged, with subject matter running from physics and optics to robots, turbines, and a mechanical puppet purported owned by Marie-Antoinette. Equally aged *Church of St.-Nicolas-des-Champs* is next door, with a lovely interior whose main altar painting is by the Baroque master Simon Vouet. Note that the Techniques is traditionally open only in the afternoon from 1 to 5:30 P.M. on weekdays, longer on Sunday. Check in advance. Near Place de la République.

Musée Nissim de Camondo (63 Rue de Monceau, near Parc Monceau, northeast of the Arc de Triomphe) occupies the mansion—always beautiful, but with its interiors relatively recently restored and refurbished—of the parents of a young man who died while serving as a lieutenant in the French Air Force in World War I. His father and mother left the house as a museum in their son's memory. Though the structure itself is relatively modern, albeit in colonnaded Louis XVI style, interiors are of the eighteenth century. Aside from mostly Louis XVI furniture and accessories, there are exceptional paintings (Guardi, Oudry, Dupléssis, Vigée-Lebrun), gilded bronzework, porcelain, Beauvais and Aubusson tapestries. The most dazzling room is the rectangular Grand Salon—with gold and beige classic-style paneling and a suite of a dozen-odd chairs, all of whose seats are tapestry covered, and a blue-and-gray Savonnerie carpet. Special.

Musée de l'Orangerie des Tuileries (Place de la Concorde)—the elongated, classic-style pavilion at the western edge of the Tuileries—served for many years as the site of short-term exhibitions, much like the Grand-Palais (above). Recent seasons have seen it transformed—after a thorough refurbishing—into the repository of a brilliant collection bequeathed to the French government by Madame Jean Walter, who put it all together over a long period, in collaboration with her first husband, dealer-collector Paul Guillaume, and her second husband, a wealthy architect. It comprises 144 paintings covering the period beginning with the Impressionists and continuing through 1930, either by French nationalists or foreigners who worked in France. It is difficult to fault the collecting trio's taste. There are a full two dozen Renoirs, 14 Cézannes, a dozen Picassos, and almost as many Matisses and Utrillos, with even heavier representation of André Derain. Specifics? How about *Blonde à la Rose* by Renoir, *Odalisque à la Culotte Grise* by Matisse, *Pommes et Biscuits* by Cézanne, *Femmes au Chien* by Marie Laurencin, a Rousseau wedding party, the harbor of Argenteuil by Manet, and Chaim Soutine's *pâtissier*? Lovely.

Musée d'Orsay (Rue de Bellechasse) occupies the onetime main hall and adjacent hotel of Gare d'Orsay, the Seine-front railway station on the Left Bank that went up at the height of the Belle Époque era, in 1900. It came about as a consequence of a decision in the 1970s, when the administration of President Valéry Giscard d'Estaing—looking for a cultural project of consequence that would serve as a monument of the Giscard presidency, in the manner of President Pompidou's Centre Beaubourg and President Mitterrand's subterranean entry to the Louvre—earmarked the station as site of a museum of mid-nineteenth to early-twentieth century art, spanning the period 1848 to 1914. The idea was to transfer exhibits of that era from the overcrowded Louvre and its dependencies, and obtain still other works from other French museums. The space is magnificent and monumental: a 453-foot-long room, barrel-vaulted, glass-roofed, and comprising three exhibit levels created in the refurbishing by a team of six French government-commissioned architects. Exhibits run a broad and beautiful gamut. Take your time at the Orsay, allowing a good half day. Stars of the Orsay show are great Impressionist paintings that had long been exhibited at Galerie du Jeu de Paume in the Tuileries and now are on display in galleries on the top—or third—floor. They include a Van Gogh self-portrait, Renoir's *Le Moulin de la Galette,* Manet's *Déjeuner sur l'Herbe,* Monet's *Rouen Cathedral* and *Tour d'Abane,* Pissaro's *Red Roofs,* Cézanne's *The Blue Vase,* and paintings, as well, by Gauguin, Sisley, Toulouse-Lautrec, Mary Cassatt, Rousseau, and Degas—to name some. Postimpressionists like Seurat, Signac, Toulouse-Lautrec, and Henri-Edmond Cross are on hand, too, as well as Bonnard and Vuillard. But there are also sculpture, graphics, posters, and photographs, with architecture and applied arts of the era represented too. Sequence? The museum suggests you start with Second Empire displays on the ground floor (don't miss the detailed scale model of Opéra Garnier), moving then via hard-to-find escalators to the top-floor paintings, concluding with art nouveau—among much else—on the second level. The noteworthy restaurant and café are evaluated on a later page. Bravo, Orsay!

Musée du Palais de Tokyo (13 Avenue du Président Wilson): Paris visitors who first knew the city a decade or so back and have pleasant memories of the old Musée National d'Art Moderne will recognize this pleasing Art Deco structure. Alas, when much of the building's collection was transferred to the harsh quarters of Centre Pompidou (above), authorities rechristened this building and displayed a cache of works long in storage. Works by Paul Signac and H. E. Cross and a goodly group of paintings by Vuillard are among them. These are all on the main floor. But don't leave without a trip to the basement, chock-full of masterworks by the likes of Braque, Picasso, Rouault, and Henry Laurent, whose original donors forbade their being transferred to the Beaubourg.

Musée Picasso (5 Rue de Thorigny): Picasso is hardly a stranger to museums in Paris or the French provinces, for that matter; indeed, the château where he once lived in Antibes, on the Riviera, displays a choice cache of his output. And Museo Picasso in Barcelona (see *Spain at Its Best*), with more than a thousand of his works, embraces major Picasso periods. Still, Paris's Musée Picasso, opened in late 1985, is hardly to be ignored. Occupying space in Hôtel Salé, an opulent seventeenth-century mansion in the Marais quarter, which has been brilliantly restored (and which is not without an interesting history, having served variously as the Venetian Embassy and as the residence of Archbishops of Paris), the museum's nucleus is an extraordinary collection of works from Picasso's estate. It embraces well over 300 of his paintings and sculptures (a riveting 1901 self-portrait is the museum's trademark, but there are memorable works from principal Picasso periods, including *Les Deux Frères* [1906], *Violon* [1915], *La Flûte de Pan* [1923], *Tête de Femme* [1931], *L'Homme au Mouton* [1943], and *Vieil Homme Assis* [1971—two years before his death]), some 3,000 drawings and prints, as well as ceramics and paper collages. On display, too, is a clutch of paintings by other masters that Picasso had collected—Seurat, Cézanne, Degas, Matisse, Derain, and Rousseau among them. You go as much for the setting—sculpture-embellished facades, courtyard, grand stairway, splendidly stuccoed Salon de Jupiter, wrought-iron furniture and lighting fixtures designed for the various galleries by Diego Giacometti—as you do for the five levels of art treasures. And the restaurant is worthy of evaluation on another page.

Musée du Petit-Palais (Avenue Winston Churchill, off the Champs-Élysées) is the fine arts museum of the City of Paris and is, as well, the site of frequent special shows. Like its bigger sister, across-the-street Grand-Palais, it's a souvenir of a turn-of-century World's Fair, elaborate Belle Époque. Special shows get more public play than the permanent collection, although this is an eminently inspectable hodgepodge. Range extends from Etruscan and Egyptian through the Middle Ages and Renaissance, up to the romantics and impressionists of the last century. There are Maillol and Rodin sculptures; paintings by Toulouse-Lautrec and Cézanne, Courbet, and Delacroix; Beauvais tapestries and Louis XV furniture; Limoges china and medieval manuscripts. Eclectic. *Good* eclectic.

Musée Rodin (77 Rue de Varenne) has one subject: Auguste Rodin and his sculpture. A rendering of *The Thinker,* his best-known work, is in the garden. Smaller pieces are up a flight, with the ground floor devoted to medium-sized works. What makes this museum at least as inviting as its exhibits is the building itself—a honey of an early eighteenth century *hôtel particulier*.

Pavillon des Arts (Terrasse Rambuteau, Les Halles) serves as a venue for temporary cultural exhibitions presented by the City of Paris. You'll recognize it by its several-story-high glass walls. Newspapers and *L'Officiel des Spectacles* announce current shows.

EXCURSIONIST'S PARIS: A SELECTION OF DAY TOURS

Chantilly (23 miles north of town, via Route A1) is the site of a pair of connected castles—originally Renaissance but rebuilt—in the bigger of which are the painting collections of the Condé family. Raphael, Titian, Clouet, Lippi, and Perugino are among artists represented. There is a room full of antique jewels, not to mention ancient illuminated manuscripts and other treasures, as well as a stable that cared for several hundred horses two centuries ago. Grounds and artificial lake are splendid—surprising when one considers that they were laid out by the same Le Nôtre who played a major role in the design of the gardens of Versailles. Lunch is indicated at *Relais du Coq Chantant* (21 Route de Creil; phone 4457-01-28; *First Class*). A visit to nearby *Senlis* combines well with Chantilly. Special lure is Notre-Dame Cathedral, a twelfth-century masterwork with a soaring steeple that dominates the main square and is among France's finer Gothic specimens—from the sculpted facade through transept, choir, and side chapels of the interior. Senlis is not without other monuments of a rich past (it was a royal seat in medieval times)—remains of a onetime king's castle, a bishop's palace, a fifteenth-century town hall, Rue Vieille de Paris (filled with aged houses), and nearby Maison Haubergier, now the surprise-packed local museum.

Chartres (50 miles southwest of Paris) is for many visitors to France the first great out-of-Paris cathedral town. It does not disappoint. I suspect this is because, tourist traffic notwithstanding, the town itself remains the same provincial capital it was long before the advent of day-trippers out of Paris. Approached from the front, with low-slung houses setting it off, the Cathedral of Notre-Dame reveals its proportions without any pretense. The vastness of the cathedral is immediately apparent. Two steeples—one Romanesque, one Gothic—flank a magnificent rose window. Length of the building is almost 400 feet, and the transept is almost half that in width.

Then one goes indoors to see the globally celebrated windows. There is no finer stained glass in France; peers of Chartres are the Cathedral of Bourges and Paris's much smaller Sts.-Chapelle. Chartres's rose windows flanking the facade and the transept are only starters; windows of the long nave are equally lovely. Special, also, are sculptures of the choir: 40 groups and 200 statues portraying great moments in the life of Christ and the Virgin Mary.

Beyond, fronting a quiet garden, is the Bishop's Palace; it shelters *Musée de Chartres,* rich with Renaissance tapestries and medieval ivories and enamels; and paintings and drawings by such French masters as Teniers, Hugo Robert, Rigaud, Boucher, and Fragonard, as well as foreign greats like Holbein and Zurbarán. Art-rich *Church of St.-Pierre* is nearby, with fine stained glass and a dozen enamels of the Apostles. Old Chartres is of interest, particularly houses on streets like Du Bourg, Du Pont, St.-Hilaire, and Des Écuyers. Lunch is lovely at *La Vieille Maison* (5 Rue au Lait; phone 3734-10-67; near the cathedral; *First Class*); or stop for pastries-cum-tea at *A. Gilbert* on Rue du Cygne.

Compiègne (47 miles north of Paris), given its pedigree, is strangely incognito to most foreign visitors. It has not, to be sure, the beauty of other excursion destinations out of Paris—it is not and never has been Versailles or Fontainebleau—but it remains a place of considerable importance in the history of France: a touristic sleeper of no little interest. At journey's end is a château that knew many medieval and Renaissance kings of France. Charles V built a palace on the site in the fourteenth century. Jeanne d'Arc was taken prisoner nearby in the fifteenth. In the mid-eighteenth century, Louis XV commissioned the very same Gabriel whom he had design Paris's Place de la Concorde to rebuild the Compiègne castle. Its facade is the same today as it was from that time: a great neoclassic expanse with a colonnaded central portico. The whole, viewed from the formal garden it dominates, is not unlike a vastly widened White House.

Compiègne is the last—and newest—of the French royal palaces. From the time of its builders through to the third Napoleon and his empress, a century and a quarter back, considerable use was made of it. All manner of historic events have taken place within its walls. Louis XV and his grandson, the future Louis XVI, welcomed the young Austrian princess and future queen, Marie-Antoinette, to Compiègne upon her arrival in France in 1770. Napoleon I did likewise, with still another Austrian lady—his second wife-to-be, Marie-Louise, in 1810, concurrently redecorating the sovereigns' apartments in the style of the period. The later Napoleon—the third—and his empress, Eugénie, made Compiègne synonymous with fashion, with their annual autumnal "Series" of house parties. Several generations later, Marshal Foch signed the World War I Armistice on behalf of his country in a nearby wood; he used the castle as his headquarters.

A great part of the palace is given over to *Musée du Second Empire,* an era that the French know—and appreciate—more than does the outer world, particularly the English-speaking outer world, which concentrates on contemporary events across the Channel and calls the age Victorian. The Second Empire of Napoleon III and Eugénie was replete with overdecorated salons and bedchambers and portraits of royalty and beautiful ladies by the very same Winterhalter who painted Victoria.

There are a number of state rooms. Marie-Antoinette's game room is the most charming (along with Empress Eugénie's giddy bedroom). But I like the Napoleon rooms, too—the ballroom, with its crystal chandeliers; and the library, with its Empire-style furnishings and fittings. The castle's biggest draw, with French youngsters at least, is a museum of old cars and carriages. But if your visit is for only a day, skip the antique autos and move on into town. *Hôtel de Ville* is a Renaissance city hall. It contains a museum of toy soldiers—90,000 of them—portraying melodramatic moments in French history. More requisite is *Musée Vivenel.* It occupies a beauty of an early-nineteenth-century house set in a serene garden. Within is a catchall of exhibits—Old Masters drawings, eighteenth-century furniture, ancient Greek pottery, medieval wood carvings, Renaissance enamels, and Limoges china. Lunch is excellent at Hôtel du Nord's *La Rôtisserie,* Place de la Gare (phone 4488-22-30; *First Class*).

Fontainebleau (40 miles south of Paris), although on an equal historical footing with Versailles, is considerably less visited, thanks to a situation that places it farther from the capital than the Sun King's masterwork. This helps make a visit less enervating than a tour of visitor-jammed Versailles, especially in summer. No one would call Fontainebleau intimate. But in contrast to the competition—which was precisely what Versailles turned out to be—it is positively minuscule. It is, after all, the country palace that long preceded Versailles. But it was used concurrently with it. It had been a royal palace since the twelfth century. Louis IX—the same king who built the Ste.-Chapelle in Paris and was later canonized, becoming St. Louis—lived there. Louis XIII was born there. François I, the same who rebuilt the Louvre, largely rebuilt Fontainebleau, with the help of Italian artists and artisans. Succeeding monarchs—including Louis XV, who built an entire wing, and Napoleon I, who created apartments for himself and his empress—made contributions. Today's Fontainebleau, with its darkish, largely Renaissance facade, appears somber to the arriving visitor. But interiors—surrounding several magnificent courtyards—offer glittering surprises, with such rooms as the chapel, theater, François I Gallery, and ballroom (with a parquet floor to end all parquet floors). No soldiers could have clicked their heels in a more elaborate Guard Room. The chamber in which Bonaparte abdicated is among the more memorable. And the Queens' Apartments housed such illustrious royals as Catherine de Médicis, Mary Queen of Scots, and Marie-Antoinette. For lunch, choose *Hôtel Aigle Noir* (Place Napoléon, Fontainebleau; phone 6422-32-65; *First Class*) or the excellent and elegant *Hôtellerie du Bas-Bréau,* at nearby Barbizon (phone 6066-40-05; *Luxury*).

Giverny (45 miles north of Paris): You've seen the monumental collection of the Impressionist painter, Claude Monet, at Musée Marmottan in Paris; you've followed that up with Monet's matchless *Les Nymphées,* at Musée de l'Orangerie. Now, appetite whetted, you want to make a pilgrimage to Monet's lovely house at Giverny to the north, midway between Paris and Rouen. Monet's home from 1883 to 1926, this classic-style house was opened to the public after a masterful restoration in 1980; it was an overnight success. The house, with a pale pink and white facade—complemented by green shutters at the windows—is at its best in the rooms hung with the painter's collection of Japanese engravings. His studio, in its own building, is visitable, as are the gardens that inspired so much of his work, most especially the Water Garden, whose weeping willows and pink-blossomed lilies became the subject matter of his best-loved paintings. You may go via commercial bus tour, but it's more fun on your own, via train from Gare St.-Lazare to the station of the little Seine River town of Vernon, a taxi ride from the Monet house. Restaurant *Beau Rivage* (13 Avenue Maréchal Leclerc, in Vernon; phone 3251-17-27), is a satisfactory and *Moderate* choice for lunch.

Reims (78 miles northeast of Paris) is the city in whose cathedral Charles VII was crowned in the presence of Jeanne d'Arc, five and a half centuries back—at the conclusion of the Hundred Years War and following Joan's successful defense of Orléans from the English enemy. This is the city, as well, where a full two dozen kings of France were crowned, from an early Louis (the eighth) in 1223 to the final Charles (the tenth) in 1824. Depart early enough so that you have the bulk of the morning for an inspection of the *Cathedral* (Place de Six Dadrans). But tarry a bit before entering. This Gothic work, created between the thirteenth and fifteenth centuries, is at its most spectacular from without. The deepset trio of portals—beneath a rose window surmounted by a friezelike gallery of sculpted kings, surmounted by a pair of square towers—makes for one of the most impressive of cathedral entries in France. The apse is flanked by broad flying buttresses and delicate pinnacles delineating them. Only after entering do proportions seem skimpy; Reims Cathedral appears narrow, which is hardly to carp, given the quality of the stained glass (including some by this century's Marc Chagall). The adjacent ex-archbishop's residence, *Palais du Tau*—operated as a museum—displays half a hundred rich medieval tapestries and other treasures of the cathedral proper and boasts an exquisitely scaled Great Hall. Move, then, to *Basilique de St.-Rémi,* a Romanesque-Gothic meld taking the name of the saint after which the city is called and dating to the eleventh and twelfth centuries; vaulting of both nave and altar stands out. Pause for lunch in the exemplary restaurant of *Boyer-Crayères Hôtel* (64 Boulevard Vasnier; phone 2682-80-80), a decidedly *Luxury* category restaurant in a charming, park-encircled, 16-room hotel affiliated with Relais et Châteaux; the owner-chef's roast baby squab and fish specialties are delicious. In the afternoon, work off lunch by pacing the galleries of *Musée des Beaux-Arts* (a.k.a. Musée St.-Denis), with a group of portrait-drawings by Cranach and a collection of paintings by such masters as Philippe de Champaigne (who was, alas, not a local but from Flanders), Poussin, Boucher, Daumier, Daubigny, Renoir, Monet, Gauguin, Dufy, and—special treat—a substantial clutch of works by Corot. And note that Reims's champagne-producing firms—Krug, Mumm, Pommery, Piper-Heidsieck, Roederer, Ruinart, and Taittinger, among them—cordially welcome visitors to their *caves*. Still other champagne houses in the not-far-distant town of *Épernay* also are open to the public; these include Martel, Moët & Chandon, Perrier-Jouet, and Pol-Roger. *Royal Champagne Hôtel* (in Champillon; phone 2652-87-11), between Épernay and Reims, is a good *First Class* overnight selection, with an excellent restaurant.

Malmaison (10 miles west of Paris) is the country house Napoleon built for his first empress, Josephine, who came from the still-French Caribbean island of Martinique (her Martinique birthplace is a popular visitor attraction). There is nothing *mal* about the sumptuously furnished, pure Empire-style *maison,* except its excessive expense. Josephine remained after her husband, wanting a male heir, divorced her to marry Austrian Archduchess Marie-Louise. Though left well off by her husband, Josephine still found it difficult to manage. Despite a settlement of more than three and a half million francs from the emperor, she was in debt after two years. But seeing what she spent her money on is easy on the eye. Malmaison is low-slung and set in a flower-garnished formal park. You enter a marble vestibule, full of busts, Roman style. The gilded salon is a maze of Empire-style armchairs. The dining room is simpler, with a black-and-white-checkerboard marble floor and Pompeian decor wall designs. The imperial couple's bedrooms are the most original interiors in the house. Josephine's resembles a luxurious desert chieftain's tent, an exception being her canopied bed topped with a gold eagle. Napoleon's room is the simplest and the handsomest in the house; beige moiré covers the walls and is draped over an unpretentious bed and a half-dozen-odd chairs, as well. Throughout the house, the paintings are knockouts, most especially one of Josephine by Gérard; another of Napoleon as First Consul, arm in vest; and a third of the emperor on horseback, by David—the very same one you've seen in Courvoisier cognac ads. Book lunch at appropriately named (and aptly addressed) *Restaurant Pavillon Joséphine,* 19 Avenue Bonaparte (phone 1751-01-62). *First Class.* Go by R.E.R., an extension of the Paris subway.

Rambouillet (35 miles southwest of Paris) is a little forest-surrounded town whose drawing card is the properly turreted and ever so venerable castle—a part of it dates to the eighth century—

that has, since the reign of Napoleon III, belonged to the French government, becoming, at the turn of this century, official summer house of presidents of the republic. When they're not on scene, Rambouillet keeps open hours. Thank Louis XIV, a onetime resident, for the opulent paneling of the series of Assembly Rooms within and his successor twice removed, Louis XVI, for a pair of unusual buildings in the surrounding park—a mock dairy and a house surfaced in shells—that were constructed as gifts for Queen Marie-Antoinette. Oddly unfamiliar to foreign visitors—not many remember that then-President Valéry Giscard d'Estaing hosted a major summit conference in Rambouillet—the château has known historic moments. François I died there. It was from Rambouillet that Napoleon was taken to his initial exile on St. Helena. Charles I abdicated there and—to jump a few centuries—it was from this castle that General de Gaulle directed the liberation of Paris in 1944. *Restaurant Cheval Rouge* (78 Rue Général de Gaulle; phone 3485-80-61) is a reliable lunch choice. *First Class.*

St.-Germain-en-Laye (13 miles west of Paris)—like the earlier recommended Malmaison—is easily reached via the R.E.R. suburban line of the Paris Métro. It's attractive, with a charming core. What brings one to St.-Germain-en-Laye, though, is its castle—a formidable, if substantial, pile, dating to the mid-sixteenth century and largely the work of king, François I. There is, as well, a pre-François Gothic chapel of uncommon beauty, a park (grand and formal, as how could it not be, what with Versailles's Le Nôtre its designer?), and, as a surprise package, an unusual museum within the château. The exhibits at *Musée des Antiquités Nationales* are very antique, indeed, going back to the medieval Merovingian dynasty and earlier. The museum was originally a project of Napoleon III, but it was completely redesigned in 1968 and is one of the handsomest in the land, with exhibits set off to advantage in rough-finished plaster-walled galleries. On display are pottery and metalwork objects. Louis XIV was born at St.-Germain-en-Laye, in a room of *Pavillon Henri IV* that had been the oratory of his mother, Anne of Austria, and that is now the smart, 42-room luxury *Hôtel Pavillon Henri IV,* where I suggest you have lunch (phone 3451-62-62).

Sèvres (five miles southwest of Paris): Porcelain has been keeping this town busy since the eighteenth century, when the Crown-sponsored china factory that had been at suburban Vincennes was moved. The visitor's Sèvres breaks down into two parts. *Musée de Sèvres* is an eye-opener for the porcelain-wise traveler. On display are specimens from the best-known factories of Europe—England, the Continent, both east and west—and Asia, as well, including Japan and China, where it all started. There is, also, the Sèvres factory, where visitors get a start-to-finish tour.

Vaux-le-Vicomte (30 miles southeast of Paris, near Melun) is the French country house at its pinnacle: grand in scale but not so large that it is dizzying to comprehend; brilliant in decor but never overtly so; splendidly sited—set off by gardens at once formal and capacious—but not so extensive that they create a feeling of isolation; and, most important, stylish, elegant, and—to this very day—livable.

Its very construction can be said to have altered the course of history. The man behind the château was Nicolas Fouquet (a contemporary of the young Louis XIV), who, after becoming the king's finance minister, set about building a house befitting his exalted rank. Fouquet was bright and rich and a friend not only of royalty but of such luminaries as Molière (who performed his plays at Vaux-le-Vicomte) and La Fontaine. To build his house, Fouquet brought together three young geniuses: architect Louis Le Vau, painter-interior designer Charles Le Brun, and landscapist André Le Nôtre. They razed an older house on the site and put up what one sees today: a château in a formal garden that was the inspiration for the Versailles of Louis XIV—the palace that took the court of France out of the capital, isolating it from the people for most of three long reigns, during which time a court style developed that engendered a revolution.

Moreover, the builders of Versailles were the very same who created Vaux-le-Vicomte: the Le Vau–Le Brun–Le Nôtre trio. A visit to Vaux in 1661—the year he attained his majority—inspired Louis to outdo his finance minister. He not only built Versailles as his answer to Vaux, he had Fouquet arrested for embezzlement, to die two decades later in prison. In 1875, the rich Sommier family bought the place and began to restore it.

Vaux is an enchantment—from the moment one steps into the oval, high-ceilinged great hall. Each room—dining room, with its half-timbered Louis XIII ceiling; Muses' Room, with sumptuous Le Brun decor; gilded Games Room; Louis XIV-style King's Chamber-Cabinet-Library—is breathtaking. And the sculpture-dotted gardens are no less so. *Auberge Vaugrain* (1 Rue Amyot, in nearby Melun; phone 6452-08-23; *First Class*), with four-century-old quarters, is a good lunch stop; build your meal around the house veal-stew specialty.

Versailles (a dozen miles southwest of Paris and easily accessible by train [a good, cheap way to go] or bus tour) was the residence of Louis XIV, Louis XV, and Louis XVI and is essential for an understanding of France's history and culture. Go first to Vaux-le-Vicomte (above), which, as I explain, was the inspiration for Versailles.

Louis XIV visited it and lost no time in hiring its designers—architect Le Vau, landscapist Le Nôtre, and interior designer Le Brun—to build a castle that would make Vaux, the country house of Fouquet, his finance minister, appear inconsequential in contrast. A half-century went into the building of Versailles. Louis XIV changed architects in midstream, hiring the noted Hardouin-Mansart to replace Le Vau. At one point, more than 35,000 artisans and laborers were at work on the palace and its gardens. Moving-in day meant a lot more than the royal family and servants; something like a thousand courtiers came to call Versailles home, with as many additional settling in the area, the better to be near the powerful Sun King, his favorites, and his patronage. Louis played the divide-and-conquer game. He kept nobles and their wives and families living to the hilt, emulating his elaborate way of life and expensive tastes in food, furnishings, and fashion. And, by concentrating them all in and around Versailles, he could keep his eyes on intra-court intrigues and diversions, the while governing France with minimal interference, if not always maximum wisdom.

A full day is by no means too much time to devote to Versailles. Two days or at least part of two days is even better. Pick midweek days; there will be fewer visitors. Versailles is enormous. Getting about the château complex can be confusing; it is not well sign-posted, and in warm weather months it is mobbed. I suggest you begin with a *Visite Libre* ticket which will allow you to follow the crowds to and through *Galerie des Glaces*—the very same Hall of Mirrors where the World War I peace treaty was signed; the colonnaded *Chapelle Royale,* where royals and courtiers worshiped; and a number of other seventeenth- and eighteenth-century rooms; *Musée de l'Histoire de France* (pictorial documentation of the seventeenth to nineteenth centuries); and—a fair-sized walk away—*Grand and Petit Trianons,* smaller mansions to which kings and their mistresses got away from the hubbub of the main palace. The Grand Trianon dates to Louis XIV and housed monarchs through to Louis-Philippe. Restored in the 1960s, it shelters official state guests now, much like Blair House in Washington; furniture is essentially Empire. The Petit Trianon is mid-eighteenth century, dating from the reign of Louis XV, and was a project of his first mistress, Madame de Pompadour, with her successor, Madame du Barry, the first tenant; Louis XVI's queen, Marie-Antoinette, was still another. The restoration—with superb furniture—is Louis XVI. Marie-Antoinette's exquisite theater, made of papier-mâché, is nearby, as is the 10-building complex called the *Hamlet*—a mock Norman village where Marie-Antoinette retreated for rustic respite.

Your second, separately purchased ticket will take you on an expertly guided visit (in French or English, as you choose) to rooms of the château that have been refurbished by the French government in recent years at staggering expense and with meticulous attention to historical accuracy—as part of a commendable, ongoing project. These include the king's and queen's private apartments; Madame du Barry's, Madame de Pompadour's, Madame de Maintenon's, and Madame Adelaide's apartments; and Louis XVI's library, the lot constituting interiors of the period—ceilings, mirrors, stucco-work, marble, gilding, paintings, sculpture, furniture, textiles—unsurpassed anywhere in Europe. Allow time for sculptures and fountains of the vast formal gardens. Lunch is recommended in the delightful restaurant of lovely old-school *Trianon Palace Hôtel* (1 Boulevard de la Reine; phone 3950-34-12; *First Class*)—and a splendid overnight spot as well. *Restaurant des Trois Marchés*(3 Rue Colbert; phone 3950-21-21; *Luxury*) is also an excellent choice for a meal—at once atmospheric (it's an eighteenth-century mansion) and delicious (build your meal around braised duck).

Loire Valley Châteaux (a hundred-plus miles south of Paris): See chapter 20.

Amiens (74 miles north of Paris) is visitable primarily because its *Cathedral of Notre-Dame* (Rue Henri IV) is not only the largest in France, but one of the most extraordinary; a ravishingly beautiful masterwork, begun in the early thirteenth century and completed more than two centuries later. Pause before entering at the entrance, itself reason enough for an Amiens excursion. Its dazzlers are a trio of portals, their deep frames a veritable museum of sculpture; stone-carved biblical stories appear in rich abundance. Go inside, then. Amiens visitors do not forget their first glance down an exquisitely Gothic-vaulted nave that is 336 feet in length, flanked by rows of elegant columns, 63 on each side. There are three sumptuous rose windows, a pair flanking the transept, another—you must look back—over the entry. The choir is Renaissance, a mind-boggling mass of carved small figures—lay, as well as biblical—several thousand strong. And don't neglect the Treasury. Amiens's *Musée de Picardie* (not far from the cathedral, on Rue de la République) is at its loveliest, for me, at least, with a clutch of eighteenth-century portraits by the likes of Fragonard and Chardin, but there is notable sculpture, as well, and contemporary paintings, too. A good lunch spot is the First Class *Nord-Sud Hôtel Restaurant* (11 Rue Gresset, phone 2291-59-03)—heart of town, near the cathedral, with prix-fixe menus, and a couple of dozen rooms, should you opt to stay overnight.

AFTER DARK

Opéra de Paris/Garnier (Place de l'Opéra) is the Second Empire theater, one of the half-dozen world greats, that is earlier recommended architecturally and brought to your attention herewith as home base for Ballet de l'Opéra de Paris—a major European company—that presents performances, as well, by visiting dance troupes, many from abroad. The ballet-only function of this 1,991-seat house, which had been home to the Paris Opéra since it opened in 1875, came about during the administration of President François Mitterrand when it was determined that a new structure would be built (Opéra de Paris/Bastille, below) for the opera, and that this international landmark would have its function limited to ballet.

Dance—and I speak as an enthusiast—is, to be sure, among the more estimable of the performing arts. And the Mitterrand administration must be praised for neither razing nor otherwise disposing of this Charles Garnier–designed masterwork. Still, Paris is not without citizens—nor, for that matter, visitors—saddened by the transfer of opera to Place de la Bastille, from a theater that gave its name to the busy square, the major Métro station, and the broad avenue it backs.

Withal, Ballet de l'Opéra is a company hardly to be despised. It dates to 1713, with would-be dancers entering its school between the ages of eight and twelve (at that early stage, they're known as *les rats*—the rats), eventually climbing the company's ladder, first becoming members of the Corps de Ballet (they must be no younger than 16) and then moving along (after a three-year minimum period) to higher-level categories—quadrille, coryphée, sujet, premier danseur, and—top-of-the-line (for a select few)—étoile, or star.

It is, of course *les étoiles* whose dancing you want to concentrate on, in the course of a performance—Patrick Dupond, superstar of the lot; Claude de Vulpian, Monique Loudières, Sylvie Guillem, and Isabelle Guérin—among the ballerinas; Patrice Bart, Laurent Hilaire, Jean Guizerix, and Jean-Yves Lormeau among the *premiers danseurs*.

Repertory is nothing if not eclectic, the range of works set to music of the seventeenth century by Jean-Baptiste Lulli through Serge Lifar's *Les Mirages* and Petipas's late-nineteenth-century *Raymonda,* in a contemporary version by Rudolf Nureyev (who served during much of the decade of the eighties as the company's *directeur de la danse*), with dances as well by America's Balanchine and Robbins, France's Roland Petit, and beloved classics like *Swan Lake.*

For the first-timer who has never experienced this masterful theater, an evening is an adventure; it should include a stroll in the Promenade Salon, with a pause at a banister of the Grand Stairway to take in comings and goings in the equally spectacular Grand Foyer. The auditorium—multimarbled, and illuminated principally by a three-ton chandelier, with an inappropriate ceiling painted by Marc Chagall—embraces orchestra, boxes (*baignoires*), balcony (*balcon*), three higher balconies (called *loges*), the topside *amphithéâtre,* and the even-higher-altitude *stalles de côté.* And English is spoken at the box office.

Opéra de Paris/Bastille (Place de la Bastille): Don't underestimate Opéra de Paris/Bastille—the ever-so-contemporary successor to Opéra de Paris/Garnier as seat of the Paris Opéra. Attention must be paid to a building costing $350 million, occupying a historic square that had not known prominence (except for erection, in the middle of the last century, of the 171-foot-high July column, topped by a statue known as Liberté) since the fourteenth-century fortress-prison whose name it takes was toppled by Revolutionaries in 1789.

Now the core of an art-gallery- and restaurant-dotted quarter with a new populace of young professionals, Opéra Bastille was designed by an Uruguay-born Canadian architect based in Toronto, named Carlos Ott, who set out to design a state-of-the-art structure that would be—and indeed, is—the complete antithesis of traditions of architecture and decor embodied in the Garnier building. Bastille's pale-gray facade—based on a motif of curves, whose only ornament is a pattern of squares—is too often photographed from the side, not as flattering as its directly-on-the-square main entrance, which is like nothing so much as walking through a giant picture frame. Even Ott's restraint, in terms of color, is striking. Lounges leading from the well-proportioned foyer are furnished in black leather. Gray and white, combined with wood trim that emerges as terra-cotta in tone, are the only other hues.

Bulk of the 2700 seats—and note the exquisite detail of their design—is in the orchestra, with the remainder in two balconies; additional seating is in side boxes and galleries that appear more decorative than functional. Pre- and postperformance and intermission lighting is bright, from fixtures concealed in a glass ceiling, and there are no chandeliers. The drama of the interior results from its splendid scale and contours of the balconies—conveying the impression of giant waves protruding over a sea of faces. The Bastille's second theater is the striking 600-seat Amphithéâtre, blue its dominant color.

There are weak points: Lounges leading from foyer and balconies might be larger. The theater is contemporary enough for there to be escalators (they would not strike an odd note) to supplement steep stairways and invariably crowded elevators connecting various levels. And had I been Ott, I would have razed the next-door building whose ground-floor restaurant's oversized sign fights with the theater's low-key facade. No opera house has had more contentious beginnings.

Indeed, this building's early days constituted a modern-day storming of the Bastille. The first music director is a young Korean-born American (who had been conducting an orchestra in Germany) named Myung-Whun Chung. He replaced earlier-hired (and subsequently fired) Daniel Barenboim at the conclusion of a chain of events that had both the international music and the French political worlds taking sides, either for or against—often vehemently—

the dictums of the Opéra's fearless president, Pierre Bergé, head of the Yves St.-Laurent fashion firm. It no longer shares performance time with Ballet de l'Opéra—which has remained at Opéra de Paris/Garnier, where the opera troupe had been based since the Charles Garnier-designed theater opened in 1875.

Repertory range has been from such favorites as *Madama Butterfly, La Traviata,* and *Cosi Fan Tutti,* to such lesser-known works as Lulli's *Alceste,* Gluck's *Iphigenia in Taurus,* Berg's *Wozzek, Les Troyens* by Berlioz, and Janacek's *Kata Kabanova.* In addition, there are concerts by both Parisian and visiting symphonies and recitals by noted soloists. A technological feature of the new theater—made possible by a network of secondary performing and rehearsing areas that allow constant use of the main stage—makes a wide-ranging repertory possible. The main stage is surrounded by five identically sized secondary stages that permit quick changes of scenery. And the stage frame, proscenium, and orchestra pit are modular to meet varying specifications, production by production, French or foreign, including orchestral concerts. The main auditorium of this new opera house is the largest such in France built for the performance of opera. Even for longtime fans of Garnier's opera house, this successor to it is at once significant and *sympatique.*

Opéra de Paris/Opéra Comique (a.k.a. Salle Favart, Rue de Marivaux), though by no means as grandiose or splendid as Opéra de Paris/Garnier, is a treasure of a turn-of-century, 1,200-seat theater with a lavish interior that has, traditionally, been the city's principal venue for operetta.

Opéra de Versailles (in the gardens of Château de Versailles): Recent summers have seen the Versailles Opera Festival become a popular tradition during the second half of July. Two operas with internationally recognized directors and casts are usually presented—*Aïda and La Traviata,* for example, with such stars as Placido Domingo, Sherill Milnes, Natalia Troitskaya, and Nelly Miricioiu.

Theater: There are several score legitimate theaters, albeit with appeal limited to visitors with enough command of the French language to understand offerings—the range Molière through musical comedy. Most significant is the *Comédie Française* (Place du Théâtre-Français, at the foot of Avenue de l'Opéra)—France's most historic theater. Although the present home is *fin de siècle*—and on the button, having opened in 1900—the company itself goes back to the reign of Louis XIV. Napoleon subsidized the troupe, and it remains government-funded, with a repertory based upon classics: Racine, Corneille, Molière, as well as productions, in French, of plays by Shakespeare, Congreve, and Bertold Brecht. The 892-seat house is one of the most beautiful in Europe and reminds me, rather sadly, of the old Metropolitan House—R.I.P.—on New York's Broadway. Productions are styled with considerable panache and, it is surely worth noting, tickets are considerably cheaper than those of the Opéra. Other major theaters include the 1,042-seat *Théâtre National de l'Odéon* (Place Paul-Claudel, on the Left Bank), a nineteenth-century building that enjoyed contemporary fame during the post–World War II decades, when its company was led by the gifted husband-wife team of Jean-Louis Barrault and Madeleine Renaud; *Théâtre Musical de Paris* (Place du Châtelet, on the Right Bank near the Seine), an elaborate house specializing in operettas and musicals; *Théâtre de la Ville* (another Place du Châtelet old-timer, with a thousand seats, often used for concerts); *Théâtre du Palais-Royal* (Rue de Montpensier), at the rear of the quadrangular Palais-Royal, with a handsome eighteenth-century interior, its principal fare variety and musicals; and the thousand-seat *Théâtre National de Chaillot,* which shares the Art Deco–era Palais de Chaillot with a trio of museums (above) and gained fame in recent decades as home base of the *Théâtre National Populaire.*

What's-on publications: Hotels give away *Allo Paris*—of limited value. It's well worth going to any news kiosk and purchasing the inexpensive but extraordinarily comprehensive weekly, *L'Officiel des Spectacles.*

Concerts and Recitals: *Orchestre de Paris* and *Orchestre National de France,* the principal Paris symphonies, are both world-class—and usually perform in 1,900-seat *Théâtre des Champs Élysées,* a charmer of an Art Deco house that is not—take note—on Champs-Élysées, but on a street leading from it, Avenue de Montaigne. It hosts ballet, too. Concerts are played in several other halls, including 2,300-seat *Salle Pleyel* (252 Rue du Faubourg St.-Honoré) and *Salle Gaveau* (54 Rue de la Boëtie). *Orchestre Philharmonique de Radio France* plays at Théâtre des Champs-Élysées. And *Ensemble Orchestral's* concerts take place at Salle Pleyel and Salle Gavreau. *Olympia* (28 Boulevard de Capucines) is home to rock concerts and other pop programs, as is huge, 5,000-seat *Palais des Sports* (Porte de Versailles) at the southwest edge of the city. *La Cité de la Musique* and *Le Zénith* (Avenue Corentin-Cariou) in the La Villette complex in the northeast corner of town, beyond Gare de l'Est—are venues for concerts, classical and pop. Note, too, that many concerts and recitals take place in beautiful churches—including *Notre-Dame Cathedral* (Île de la Cité), *St.-Germain-des-Prés* (Place St. Germain-des-Prés), St.-Sulpice (Place St.-Sulpice), and *St.-Eustache* (Rue Rambuteau), whose fine organ has been completely reconstructed and is used for annual organ festivals.

Movies: Parisians adore movies; they line up for hits, just like the rest of us. There are three principal movie sectors: Champs-Élysées, Quartier Latin (in and about Boulevard St.-Michel), and Grands Boulevards (Boulevard de la Madeleine, Boulevard des Capucines, Boulevard des Italiens). When movies are foreign-made, they are sometimes shown with original sound tracks. When that is the case, ads and marquees say "V.O.," for *Version Originale.* This is worth bearing in mind if you've a yen for a movie from home or across the Channel, in its original English.

Music halls and cabarets: Music halls are places in which you watch a show from a theater-type auditorium, neither eating nor drinking, except at intermissions; cabarets are nightclubs in which you are obliged to eat and/or drink—paying dearly for the privilege—while you watch. Give one or two of the better places a go; shows are, indeed, spectacles—smashing costumes, perfectly beautiful women in the chorus (often with breasts exposed), and productions so elaborate that Las Vegas annually imports several. *Les Folies-Bergère* (32 Rue Richer; phone 4246-77-11) remains the all-time favorite, with good reason—atmospherically Belle Époque—with long-legged, high-kicking dancers carrying on, elaborate act after elaborate act, each more gorgeously costumed than the last. If you limit yourself to one such evening, this should be it; top-balcony seats are inexpensive. *Le Moulin Rouge* (Place Blanche, in Montmartre; phone 4606-00-19) is hardly what it was when Toulouse-Lautrec immortalized it with his paintings, but the can-can still is danced and the show—performed in a Nevada-style showroom, with visibility excellent from all over—is probably the best of all the cabaret offerings; sit at the bar and you've found yourself a bargain. *Le Lido* (116-bis Avenue des Champs-Élysées; phone 4563-11-61) is still another cabaret leader—and pricey. *Crazy Horse* (12 Avenue George V; phone 4223-32-32), also a cabaret, is the Wild West, or at least a rather fanciful—and amusing—Paris concept of the Wild West; as at the Moulin Rouge, it's cheaper sitting at the bar. *Alcazar* (62 Rue Mazarine; phone 4329-02-20) offers both dinner (8 P.M.) and 10 P.M. shows. *Au Lapin Agile* (16 Rue de Saules; phone 4606-85-87) must surely have been around since the Renaissance reign of François I; it has unlimited staying power, thanks to the surefire formula of unpretentious Montmartre entertainment that's good-natured, fun, and less costly than the competition.

SETTLING IN

SELECTED RIVE DROITE/RIGHT BANK HOTELS

Ambassador Concorde Hôtel (16 Boulevard Haussmann; phone 4246-92-63): Consider this attractive, full-facility house, especially if you're a music buff (the Opéra/Garnier is a hop and a skip distant) or a dedicated shopper (top department stores are just down the street). The Ambassador Concorde has 300 rooms, traditional-style, and was relatively recently renovated. There's a credible restaurant and friendly bar-lounge. Hôtels Concorde. *First Class.*

Arcade Bastille Hôtel (15 Rue Bréguet; phone 4338-65-65) is a good-size link (305 rooms) of the Arcade chain, with Arcade's usual clean-lined rooms (some with double-decker beds) and stall showers sensibly substituting for tubs in each room's bath. The restaurant features buffets at all meals and there's a bar. Just off Place de la Bastille and not far from Place des Vosges and the Marais. *Moderate.*

Astra Hôtel (29 Rue Caumartin; phone 4266-15-15) is middle-sized, elderly, and modernized to the point where every one of its rooms has a bath. Equally commendable is the convenient location—on a street between Boulevard des Capucines and Boulevard Haussmann, with the Opéra/Garnier to the east and the Madeleine to the west. Restaurant. *Moderate.*

Balzac Hôtel (6 Rue Balzac; phone 4561-97-22) is strategically situated between Faubourg St.-Honoré and the Champs-Élysées. Its aces in the hole are that it's not overlarge (there are 56 rooms and suites with fine baths) and that it's good-looking and professionally staffed. Its Restaurant Sallambier is exemplary and there's a relaxing bar. *Luxury.*

Bastille Speria Hôtel (1 Rue de la Bastille; phone 4272-04-01) is neat as a pin, with contemporary public spaces (including a welcoming breakfast room—there is no restaurant) and lounge. There are 42 okay rooms, and you're a near-neighbor of Opéra/Bastille. *Moderate.*

Bradford Hôtel (10 Rue St.-Philippe-de-Roule; phone 4359-24-20) is worth knowing about because it's good value—all 46 rooms have bath—and well located, on a short street just off Rue du Faubourg St.-Honoré, with Champs-Élysées nearby. Breakfast only. *Moderate.*

Brighton Hôtel (218 Rue de Rivoli; phone 4260-30-03) is a comfortable, smallish, smartly located hotel. All 69 rooms have baths, although doubles can be smallish. Breakfast only. *Moderate.*

Bristol Hôtel (112 Rue du Faubourg St.-Honoré; phone 4266-91-45) comes closer to seeming like a palatial town house than any other luxury hotel in town. Public rooms are eighteenth-century; crystal chandeliers illuminate spaces furnished with Louis XV and Louis XVI pieces, some of museum caliber. The Winter Restaurant is an exquisite oval, its oak panels hand-carved in Hungary for the hotel, when it opened in 1924. In summer, the restaurant—recommended on a later page—moves to an airy, rattan-furnished pavilion, whose glass walls give onto a capacious garden. The bar is dark-paneled, with striped Louis XVI chairs flanking its tables. There are 220 rooms and suites in two buildings, the more recent a onetime convent overlooking the garden and smartly traditional in look, with super marble baths. Remaining is the Bristol's special treat: a honey of a swimming pool on the roof, glass-walled and with a sauna and solarium adjacent. Location, on the smartest shopping street in town, just steps from Palais de l'Élysée, the presidential residence, is inspired. Member, Leading Hotels of the World. *Luxury.*

Britannique Hôtel (20 Avenue Victoria; phone 42-33-7459) has an easy-to-remember situation: just behind Théâtre du Chatelet, about midway between the Louvre and the Hôtel de Ville. Relatively recently refurbished—there are 40 bath-equipped rooms and breakfast but no restaurant—it had its moment of glory during World War I, when it was headquarters for American relief operations. *Moderate.*

Burgundy Hôtel (8 Rue Duphot; phone 4260-34-12) is fortunate in its location (between Boulevard de la Madeleine and Rue St.-Honoré), its agreeable middling size, and its 90 good-looking rooms, all with bath and in traditional style. There is a restaurant-grill-bar in connection and a capacious lobby. Conscientious owner-management. *First Class.*

Calais Hôtel (5 Rue des Capucines; phone 4261-50-28) is at the corner of Place Vendôme and Rue de la Paix and has been a favorite of mine these many years. The bigger of the 59 rooms, with their own bath, are comfortable and attractive. Breakfast only. *Moderate.*

Cambon Hôtel (3 Rue Cambon; phone 4261-55-20), long popular because of its location on the street distinguished by the rear entrance of the Ritz Hôtel, has upgraded in recent seasons—and tastefully. Public spaces include an inviting bar-lounge and agreeable breakfast room (there is no restaurant), and the 44 rooms have been brightened, too, with the larger among them noteworthy. *First Class.*

Castiglione Hôtel (38 Rue du Faubourg St.-Honorê; phone 4265-07-50) is enviably well situated on the city's smartest shopping street, diagonally opposite the British Embassy. This is an attractive 120-room house whose public spaces include Le Callione Restaurant and a bar-lounge. Proportion of suites is high, but double rooms, some with balconies, can be very nice, too. *First Class.*

Castille Hôtel (37 Rue Cambon; phone 4261-55-20)—recommended in earlier editions of this book—is no longer counseled. On my most recent inspection visit, I was rudely received at reception, and ultimately shown but one of the 100 rooms—a duplex suite that wanted refurbishing—after an appeal to management. Readers have reported similarly substandard accommodations. Despite its being restaurant-equipped and with a good location just opposite the rear entrance of the Ritz, I do not suggest staying here. *First Class.*

Caumartin Hôtel (27 Rue Caumartin; phone 4742-95-95): Enviably well positioned between Opéra/Garnier and Madeleine, this is a worth-knowing-about house in contemporary style, with brown leather sofas in the lobby-lounge and light and airy looks to the 40 rooms, all with bath. Breakfast only. *Moderate.*

Centre Ville Matignon Hôtel (3 Rue de Ponthieu; phone 4387-55-77) is indeed *centre ville,* or heart of the city, on a street that parallels Champs-Élysées at its lower end, near Rond-Point, so that you can do a great deal by foot in every direction. This is a well-equipped house with 23 bath-attached, nicely maintained rooms; restaurant and bar. *Moderate.*

Choiseul-Opéra Hôtel (1 Rue Daunou; phone 4261-70-41) has location as a major plus; it's on a short street just off Avenue de l'Opéra near Place de l'Opéra. There are 42 well-maintained, bath-equipped rooms. Breakfast only. *Moderate.*

Concorde-Lafayette Hôtel (Place du Général Koenig; phone 4758-12-84) occupies a strikingly designed, 34-story tower adjacent not only to Palais des Congrès—Paris's principal convention center—but, of more immediate interest, also next door to Porte Maillot Air Terminal, from which buses depart for and arrive from de Gaulle Airport quarter-hourly. A kingpin of France-wide Hôtels Concorde, along with the landmark Crillon on Place de la Concorde, the Concorde-Lafayette embraces a thousand pastel-colored rooms and suites, agreeably contemporary, full-facility and many with absolutely fabulous views, especially those at the summit embracing the Top Club—premium-tabbed with extra amenities. There's a trio of restaurants (the range is from haute-cuisine L'Étoile d'Or to casual Les Saisons), and as many bars, with that on the picture-windowed roof—all Paris lies below—an especial treat. And there's a bonus of shops—60, all told—adjacent. *Luxury.*

Continent Hôtel (30 Rue du Mont Thabor; phone 4260-75-32) bases its decor motif on the style of Louis XVI. There are 28 rooms of varying sizes, the lot with okay baths or showers. Location is super;

you're on a street leading from Rue de Castiglione, just below Place Vendôme, with the Tuileries also a hop and a skip. Breakfast only. *Moderate.*

Crillon Hôtel (10 Place de la Concorde; phone 4265-24-24) is an intrinsic and original component of a monumental Paris square, with its next-door twin housing a ministry of the French government. It is surely the only hotel extant with one of its original rooms—a rococo boudoir—moved in toto for permanent display in a world-class museum (New York's Metropolitan Museum). Like Place de la Concorde, both hotel and Ministère de la Marine date to the eighteenth century when, in 1758, King Louis XV commissioned architect Jacques-Anges Gabriel to design the north facade of the square; along with Place Vendôme and Place des Vosges, it is the loveliest such in Paris. Some years after its construction, the building served as a residence of the Spanish ambassador. In 1788, it was purchased by Comte de Crillon, whose name it took and in whose family it remained until the turn of the present century. In 1909, along with two adjacent buildings, it became a hotel, passing relatively recently to control of the Taittinger family, producers of the esteemed champagne bearing their name and proprietors of Hôtels Concorde, of which the Crillon is flagship. The Taittingers have invested more than $10 million in a splendid refurbishing. Walls of the lobby, Grand Salon (a smart venue for tea and cocktails), and Restaurant Les Ambassadeurs (an appropriate name, what with the American Embassy just next door) are sheathed in gold-hued marble, a perfect foil for illumination provided by a network of crystal chandeliers and sconces. There's a snappy cocktail lounge paneled in warm walnut, its chairs covered in the same red velvet as those of the adjacent Obélisque, an informal grill with quick but stylish service. (I evaluate both Crillon restaurants on later pages, but at this point let me urge you to try the buffet breakfast at Les Ambassadeurs, even if you're staying in another hotel.)

Rooms? A brilliantly proportioned formal staircase leads up a flight to the quartet of Grands Apartements—high-ceilinged and with broad terraces giving onto Place de la Concorde. They have been painstakingly refurbished—Louis XV and XVI furniture, Aubusson carpets, Flemish tapestries, original stuccowork and sculpture; there is nothing else quite like them in France and if you're a guest in the hotel with a special interest in interior design, furniture and accessories of the rococo era, I suggest you ask the head concierge if at some point during your stay, when one or more of these suites—each a national treasure—is between occupants, you may have a peek. The group includes Salon des Aigles with Bohemian crystal chandeliers and extraordinary gold leaf, Salon Marie-Antoinette, in which the queen whose name it takes is believed to have taken music lessons and with a terrace framed by Corinthian columns; Salon des Bâtailles, with exceptional parquet flooring and Louis XV furnishings; the Imperial and Royal suites (Rooms 101 and 158), with painted panels after originals now on display in Paris's Chilean Embassy, Vermont's Middlebury College and, as I note above, Manhattan's Metropolitan Museum; and the space that was for long the Crillon family's chapel, again as it was in the eighteenth century. Smaller suites—all told, there are 40—are hardly to be despised; with 140 bedrooms, no two quite alike, that are stunning in their simplicity: eighteenth-century-style furniture is set against pale-hued, paneled walls; high windows are hung with sumptuous draperies, and baths are elaborately equipped and marble-walled. The Crillon is one of a kind: a unique experience. Member, Leading Hotels of the World and Relais et Châteaux. *Luxury.*

Duminy-Vendôme Hôtel (3 Rue du Mont Thabor; phone 4260-32-80) is nicely situated on a convenient street a step or two from Place Vendôme. There are just under 80 traditional-style rooms with brass beds and marble baths, and a friendly bar. Breakfast only. *Moderate.*

Edouard-VII Hôtel (39 Avenue de l'Opéra; phone 4261-56-90): Paris abounds in hotels named for British royals. I counsel on other pages hostelries called after George V, his son Edward VIII (when Prince of Wales), and George's wife, Queen Mary. The Edouard-VII, whose title honors George V's papa, occupies a building dating to the Edwardian—or early twentieth century—era, with just a hundred tastefully mod-look rooms, popular-with-Parisians Restaurant Delmonico, busy bar, and strategic situation just down the avenue from Opéra/Garnier, corner of Rue d'Antin. *First Class.*

Élysée-Park Hôtel (5 Rue de Ponthieu; phone 4359-70-36) is positioned on a street that parallels the Champs-Élysées; besides its convenient location, it offers 30 well-kept rooms with bath. Breakfast only. *Moderate.*

Étoile-Maillot Hôtel (10 Rue du Bois de Boulogne; phone 4500-42-60) is a winner, just off Avenue de la Grande-Armée, which is Champs-Élysées with a new name, substituted when it goes beyond Étoile. Rooms, all with bath, are spacious and tasteful, and there are some suites, good to know about if your Paris stay will be for some time and will involve entertaining. Breakfast only. *Moderate.*

Excelsior-Opéra Hôtel (5 Rue La Fayette; phone 4874-99-30) is a near-neighbor to the Opéra, for which it is partially named. Behind its busy Belle-Époque facade are half a hundred mod-look rooms, all with bath, and a bar-equipped lobby-lounge. Friendly. Only breakfast is served. *Moderate.*

Family Hôtel (35 Rue Cambon; phone 4261-54-84) is, as far as I can tell, the least expensive of the Rue Cambon hotels that more or less cluster across from the rear entrance of the Ritz. This is a long-admired, heavily repeat-clientele old-timer, with baths attached to 18 of its functional rooms, and showers in the case of the remaining 8. Friendly and good value. Breakfast only. *Moderate.*

France et Choiseul Hôtel (239 Rue St.-Honoré; phone 4261-54-60) is a heart-of-town oldie near Place Vendôme. There are 135 rooms, all with bath, although some appear smaller than one might like in a hotel of this caliber. Public rooms are traditional, Louis XV mostly. There's a bar-lounge, and an agreeable patio. *First Class.*

George V Hôtel (31 Avenue George V, just off Champs-Élysées; phone 4723-54-00) is a grand hotel in the grand manner, handsomely furnished (and recently, extensively, and superbly refurbished) in eighteenth-century style, with the genuine articles—tapestries, paintings, sculptures, clocks, boiserie—scattered about to add authenticity to the ambience. The restaurant moves to the lovely courtyard in summer. The bar is one of the most engaging in Paris, particularly at day's end, when it's time for an aperitif—or a scotch or dry martini. But what really makes the George V, when all is said and done, is service: skilled and quick, and that includes concierges, room-service waiters, chambermaids, doormen, and bellmen. The George V is a part of Trusthouse Forte's Exclusive Division and a member of Leading Hotels of the World. *Luxury.*

Le Grand Hôtel (2 Rue Scribe, with entrances also on Boulevard des Capucines and Place de l'Opéra; phone 4268-12-13) is, to understate, accurately named. It was a key part of the master plan for the reconstruction of Paris during the reign of Napoleon III, in the mid-nineteenth century, by the innovative architect Baron Haussmann. An immense Belle-Époque triangle, whose three sides surround a court the size of a football stadium, it is quite the oldest of the city's landmark luxury hotels, constructed as such. Work began in the spring of 1861, and in July 1862 Empress Eugénie toured the completed building, remarking at the time that its splendor put her in mind of the pair of palaces she called home. *("C'est absolument comme chez moi, je me soie crue à Fontainebleau ou à Compiègne.")* Alas, a succession of managements over the succeeding years did not do justice to the Grand's interiors. We must be grateful that the original, brilliantly decorated restaurant, now called Salon Opéra and used for private parties, has mercifully been left intact; the same

Charles Garnier who would later create the next-door opera house was one of its designers. And we must appreciate, as well, that the relatively recent landlord, Inter-Continental Hotels, which realizes that it has a national treasure on its hands, undertook an intelligently conceived program of restoration and refurbishing. This is a big house, but as the eighties became the nineties all 515 rooms and suites had been refurbished albeit in traditional style (when booking, request a room overlooking Opéra/Garnier; the view is fabulous, and public spaces—main lobby, bar, glass-roofed Cour d'Honneur with stylishly re-created restaurant—were tastefully renewed as well. The Grand's celebrated Café de la Paix, a history-laden Paris institution (about which I write more in a later paragraph), thrives as always, but the hotel's Restaurant Opéra, one of the ranking luxury-hotel eateries in town (and reviewed on a subsequent page) is underappreciated. *First Class/Luxury.*

Inter-Continental Paris Hôtel (3 Rue de Castiglione; phone 4260-37-80): Talk about felicitous name changes: If your Paris experience extends back a couple of decades, you'll remember the Continental Hotel—one of the great Second Empire houses. When Inter-Continental took over in the 1970s, all they had to do was add the prefix *Inter* to the original title. Not unlike the same chain's Le Grand Hôtel (above), the Inter-Continental dates to the Belle Époque, when Napoleon III and Empress Eugénie reigned. Its architect, Paul Blondel, was a son-in-law of Charles Garnier, designer of the nearby opera house taking his name. The hotel opened in 1878 to immediate plaudits. In 1883, it was the site of a banquet to honor Victor Hugo, turned 80. Come 1887, and it was advertising in magazines as *''le plus confortable, le plus vaste et le plus élégant des hotels du continent,''* with room tabs beginning at four francs per night. By 1892, it was a favorite of guidebook authors, with *Guide Joanne* lauding its five-franc lunches, 600 bedrooms, and the elevators connecting the bedrooms to a lavish lobby. Empress Eugénie liked the Continental well enough to settle in for an entire month in the spring of 1898, occupying a suite overlooking the Tuileries. By the time of World War I there were 300 bathrooms for the 600 rooms—an exceptionally high proportion. During World War II, playwright Jean Giraudoux was based in the hotel, heading the government's information office. The early 1960s saw the first of several extensive refurbishings, the most recent of which, in the early 1990s, was coordinated by general manager Fred de Roode—U.S.-born, French-speaking, Swiss-trained—who, when I first met him, was at the helm of the Inter-Continental on Maui (see *Hawaii at Its Best*). The current $65 million facelift had as highlights reduction of the room total (long since reduced from the original 600 to 450) to 365 (with small rooms considerably enlarged), and a restyled La Terrasse Fleurie Restaurant (reviewed on a later page) occupying space in the fountain-centered courtyard—to which horse-drawn carriages pulled up in the early decades. But the hotel's trio of historic public rooms remain as officially protected monuments, in all their nineteenth-century glory—Salon Imperial, the frescoes of its ceiling gilt-framed; Salon Napoléon, Corinthian columns surrounding its crystal chandeliers; and Salon Aiglon, richly carved and ornamented. They're used today for private parties and meetings, but management is proud of them, and I'm sure that if, as a guest, you express an interest in seeing them, the concierge will see that you have a peek. The traditional look and contemporary amenities of rooms and suites are top-of-the-line, and there are a pair of additional restaurants, busy bar, staff at once alert, skilled, and congenial. Location is heart-of-town. *Luxury.*

Lancaster Hôtel (7 Rue de Berri, just off Champs-Élysées; phone 4361-59-43) is surely among the more engaging of the deluxe hotels—bathrooms are mostly as big as the hotel is small; ditto, the baths. There is a cozy bar and *First-class* restaurant that in summer is transferred to what may well be Paris's prettiest courtyard-garden. And public spaces are old-school handsome. Skilled management, too, which is not surprising; the lovely, century-old Lancaster is a part of the London-based Savoy Hotels group. *Luxury.*

London Palace Hôtel (32 Boulevard des Italiens; phone 4824-54-64) has no discernible connection to the British capital (except that there are Brits among its guests) and it is hardly a palace. Still, this is a functionally updated house—I wish that the favored color was not orange—with comfortable lounge and 50 clean-lined rooms each with bath or shower. Situation is exemplary; you're on one of the *grands boulevards* within shouting distance of Place de l'Opéra and with the Boulevard Haussmann department stores perhaps almost too close to your quarters, at least if you're a compulsive shopper. *Moderate.*

Lotti Hôtel (7 Rue de Castiglione; phone 4260-37-34) is a long-on-scene neighbor of centrally situated Rue de Castiglione hotels like the Inter-Continental Paris, Meurice, and Vendôme. Recent seasons have seen it tastefully and thoroughly refurbished by its current landlord, Italy-based Jolly Hotels, a chain I have come to know through research for *Italy at Its Best.* The Jolly people have wisely retained the quietly traditional look of the Lotti, starting with its attractive lobby-lounge and small but reliable restaurant, beyond to the 131 rooms and suites, many of them good-sized and the nicest with views of Rue de Castiglione and the Tuileries beyond. *First Class.*

Louvre Hôtel (Plaza André-Malraux; phone 4261-56-01): Talk about being heart-of-Paris: the Louvre Concorde is just opposite the Comédie Française, just down the avenue from Opéra/Garnier, adjacent to the Palais-Royal, and an immediate neighbor to the Tuileries and the Louvre. There are 220 rooms, a chatty cocktail lounge, and the commendable Brasserie Tuileries, whose terrace-café lies under arcades of the Palais-Royal. *Historical note:* This is a hotel with roots to New York Harbor's Statue of Liberty, because it was at an 1875 banquet in the Louvre Hôtel that the Franco-American Union was created, for the purpose of presenting the statue to the United States on the hundredth anniversary of its independence in 1886. Members of the committee included the Colmar-based sculptor of the statue, Bartoldi, and a chap named Gaget, whose company manufactured miniatures of the statue, which were sold to raise funds for its construction; Monsieur Gaget's name was the inspiration for the word *gadget,* in both the French and English languages. Hôtels Concorde. *First Class.*

Lys Hôtel (23 Rue Serpente; phone 4326-97-57) is venerable seventeenth-century, furnished with old French Provençal pieces and loaded with atmosphere. All 18 of its rooms have baths. Breakfast only. *Moderate.*

Madeleine-Palace Hôtel (8 Rue Cambon; phone 4260-37-82) is a fair-sized oldie that has been, as its management succinctly put it, *entièrement rénové.* That means all of the 116 rooms have their own baths, and there is a bar. Location is middle-of-everything. Breakfast only. *First Class.*

Marriott Prince de Galles Hôtel (33 Avenue George V; phone 4723-55-11) began life as the just plain Prince de Galles (doesn't *Prince of Wales* sound nice in French?) in 1929, as a next-door neighbor of the hotel (above) named for the father (George V) of the then Prince of Wales, who was to reign so briefly as Edward VIII. Though the Prince de Galles is considerably smaller than the George V (it has just over 170 rooms and suites, in contrast to its neighbor's near 300), their facades are both of the Art Deco era, and both have gracious inner courts. The Marriott chain, which purchased the "Prince" in 1984, completed an extensive and masterful renovation the following year. The look of the hotel is now essentially early nineteenth century, Directoire and Empire, with careful attention paid to luxurious textiles, wall-coverings, and lighting fixtures. (Bravo, interior designer Robert Lush, who also directed renovation of the Carlton Inter-Continental in Cannes.) Amenities include a striking-looking peach- and ivory-hued, marble-accented restaurant (which moves to the flowering courtyard in summer and which is evaluated on a later page) and a bar-lounge beloved by Parisians and visitors over the years, refurbished to be sure, but still with its original handsome paneling. *Luxury.*

Mayfair Hôtel (3 Rue Rouget-de-Lisle; phone 4260-38-14) has an inspired location on a tiny street between Rue de Rivoli and Rue du Mont-Thabor just below Place Vendôme. This is a lovely 53-room house, with a capacious lobby, handsome bar-breakfast room, accommodations mostly based on Louis XVI-style furnishings, decor in tones of gray, excellent baths. The staff is delightful. There's no restaurant, but the Mayfair is otherwise *First Class.*

Mercure Montmartre Hôtel (1 Rue Caulaincourt; phone 4294-17-17)—not far from Place de Clichy—adheres to the Mercure chain's formula: compact but nicely fitted-out modern rooms with good baths (there are 308 all told), copious buffet breakfasts, and a bar. Montmartre's landmark Sacré Cœur Basilica is not far north. *Moderate.*

Mercure Paris Étoile Hôtel (267 Avenue des Ternes; phone 4766-49-18) pleases visitors who enjoy the Étoile–Arc de Triomphe area at the termination of Champs-Élysées. It's a block north of the arch, occupying a modern building, with 56 smallish but well-planned rooms with plenty of surface space, good baths (as is customary in hotels of the Mercure chain), and—also typically Mercure—breakfasts (no other meals) from a generous buffet. Cocktail lounge. *Moderate.*

Meurice Hôtel (228 Rue de Rivoli; phone 4260-38-60), with its inspired locale—as beautiful as it is convenient—at the intersection of Rue de Castiglione and Rue de Rivoli, steps from Place Vendôme and the Tuileries, was built the year Napoleon abdicated, and the ambience remains at once elegant and low-key, so meticulously have Italy-based Ciga Hotels (famous as the chain that includes such houses as Rome's Excelsior, Venice's Gritti Palace, and others I evaluate in *Italy at Its Best*) carried out a major restoration. The lobby and its most spectacular lounge, Salon Pompadour—still with original gilded paneling strikingly patterned and crystal chandeliers—remains one of the great Paris public spaces, and a smart choice for a drink or afternoon tea. Accommodations are super, carefully and authentically refurbished by Ciga, along with upper-floor corridors. Suites, mostly overlooking the Tuileries, are Louis XV and Louis XVI with antiques of that era among their furnishings. Standard rooms are smart, too, often generous-size with excellent baths, and overlooking Rue de Castiglione or an inner court; you must specify preference. Ciga very wisely moved the restaurant from the basement to the high-ceilinged, chandelier-hung, gilt-embellished Salon Tuileries, facing arcaded Rue de

Rivoli; and the hotel's main entrance (formerly on Rue du Mont-Thabor) is now on Rue de Rivoli, adjacent to the restaurant. The Meurice takes its name from its founder, whose aim, in the early decades of the last century, was to establish a hotel that would meet standards of the upper-class English, then the dominant upscale travelers on the Continent. By 1819, but three years after opening, Monsieur Meurice advertised "his sincere thanks to the English who have kindly honoured him with their patronage [and for whom he opened] four new apartments in front of the Tuileries Garden." The original Meurice was succeeded by a second hotel in the mid-nineteenth century (Queen Victoria was among guests) and a later third (Spain's Alfonso XIII stayed, as a young man—bringing his own furniture—and again years later, after he abdicated, pre–World War II). *Luxury.*

Ministère Hôtel (31 Rue de Surène; phone 4266-21-43) is a pleasant selection in the central Madeleine quarter. Rooms can be smallish, but those with bath (24 of 32) are comfortable. Management is accommodating; service, personal. Breakfast only. *Moderate.*

Molière Hôtel (21 Rue Molière; phone 4296-22-01): A hotel named for the playwright simply has to have something going for it, and the Molière does. It has an excellent location near the Opéra/Garnier and good-looking rooms, all with bath, be they single, twin, or suite. Breakfast only. *Moderate.*

Montana Tuileries Hôtel (12 Rue Saint-Roch; phone 4260-35-10) has location as a secret weapon. Rue Saint-Roch, taking its name from a landmark church situated where it intersects Rue St.-Honoré, leads into Avenue de l'Opéra, but is, as well, a hop and a skip from Rue de Rivoli and the Louvre. Those of the 25 rooms I have either inhabited or inspected are generous in size, all with bath—and, in some cases, relatively recently refurbished. The lounge opposite reception doubles as breakfast room, and service is sprightly. A good deal. *Moderate.*

Mont-Thabor Hôtel (4 Rue du Mont-Thabor; phone 4260-32-77) is smack in the heart of things on a street that lies between Rue de Rivoli and Rue St.-Honoré, near Place Vendôme. The lobby and bar are agreeable; and those bedrooms I've inspected, likewise. Clientele is an interesting mix of South and North Americans and Japanese. *First Class.*

Normandy Hôtel 7 (7 Rue de l'Échelle; phone 4260-30-21) is situated on a short thoroughfare leading from Avenue de l'Opéra to Rue de Rivoli and the Tuileries. It's a fine, traditional-style house that's well-maintained, with 140 no-two-alike rooms with good baths; attractive restaurant in Louis XVI style; paneled cocktail lounge with leather chairs encircling well-spaced tables. *First Class.*

Novotel Paris–Les Halles (8 Place Marguerite-de-Navarre; phone 4221-31-31) is a contemporary high-rise (gained by Rue des Halles) that's part of the international, French-origin Novotel chain. I wish the link in New York (see *New York at Its Best*) was as good-looking. Lobby is clean-lined and high-ceilinged, there's a rambling cocktail lounge, a high-tech restaurant under a glass roof, and 285 ever-so-contemporary rooms with good baths. To be happy, you have to want to be this far east—near vast Forum des Halles shopping center and the Beaubourg. *First Class.*

Orion Paris-Les Halles (4 Rue des Innocents; phone 4508-00-33) is a kind of apartment-hotel, modern as can be, in the Halles area, near the Beaubourg. All the accommodations are kitchen-equipped (including dishes and utensils), with bath, and rates by day, week (cheaper), or four-weeks-plus (cheapest). Take your choice of studios (of which there are 134, accommodating one to three persons) or one-bedroom suites (of which there are 55, accommodation 1 to 5 persons). *First Class.*

Pavillon de la Reine Hôtel (28 Place des Vosges; phone 4277-96-40): If you've longed to stay directly on beautiful Places des Vosges—and in style—this might well be your hotel choice. Half of its 50 handsome rooms overlook a garden, the others a courtyard. The look is essentially seventeenth-century, what with a beamed lobby, paneled, fireplace-centered lounge, and handsome rooms (alas, doubles can be smallish) with excellent marble-counter baths. With a full-service restaurant (there is limited-menu room service) and bar, this hotel could be Luxury category, but it's *First Class.*

Place du Louvre Hôtel (21 Rue des Prêtres Saint-Germain-L'Auxerrois; phone 4233-78-68) is on a street that you wouldn't normally pass by, but that's convenient and easy to locate: directly behind the eastern facade of the Louvre in the direction of Hôtel de Ville and paralleling the Seine. There are 20 neat rooms with bath. Breakfast only. *Moderate.*

Plaza-Athénée Hôtel (25 Avenue Montaigne; phone 4723-78-33) is, not unlike the George V, a relatively modern building with a fashionable off-Champs-Élysées location, perfectly beautiful eighteenth-century interiors (Relais Grill and the Bar Anglais are contemporary-look exceptions), and an inner patio that becomes a restaurant in summer. A special feature is Les Gobelins, a long gallery connecting the extraordinarily handsome Restaurant Régence with the lobby, which sees service as a tea lounge in the afternoon.

Suites are sumptuous, but ordinary guest rooms are attractive, too; all are in the style of Louis XV or Louis XVI, with luxurious baths, and face either the quiet street or the courtyard; specify preference. Lavish attention to detail is evident throughout, with the budget for fresh flowers in excess of that for electricity—to give you an idea. A Trusthouse Forte Exclusive Division hotel that's also a member of Leading Hotels of the World. *Luxury.*

Princesse Caroline Hôtel (1-bis Rue Troyon; phone 4380-62-20) is named for the sister of Napoleon who married Joachin Murat, King of Naples. But I digress. This hotel, just north of the Étoile, on a street leading from Avenue Wagram, has a nice sense of style, with a paneled Louis XVI–inspired lobby, Bar Le Murat—named for Caroline's husband—and 63 rooms some of whose baths have double sinks set into side counters. Breakfast only. *Moderate.*

Pullman Windsor Hôtel (14 Rue Beaujon; phone 4561-04-04) occupies a turn-of-century building in a tranquil quarter between Étoile and Parc Monceau and is among the more comfortable links of the Pullman chain at which I've stayed, France-wide. Public spaces—generous-sized lobby, cozy bar, excellent, weekdays-only Restaurant Clovis—are a deft meld of contemporary and Belle Époque, while those of the 135 rooms I've seen, including some big ones, are gracious old-school. Lovely service. *First Class.*

Queen Mary Hôtel (9 Rue Greffulhe; phone 4266-40-55) could have been named for Mary Queen of Scots, who was, after all, queen of France before she was queen of Scotland. But I suspect it was named after the more recent wife of the late George V. The only royal picture in the lobby is of none of these sovereigns, but of Edward VII, instead. At any rate, this is a smallish, nicely managed and located hotel (the Madeleine is nearby) that has been recently refurbished with a Louis XVI salon off the lobby. All 16 rooms have bath. Breakfast is served, but there is no restaurant. *Moderate.*

Regina Hôtel (2 Place des Pyramides; phone 4260-31-10) is *fin de siècle,* albeit updated as regards baths and the like, but has retained its original decor. There is a long gallery of a lobby, cozy restaurant-bar, which extends into a patio in summer, and some of the best-looking bedrooms and suites in town. (The bedsteads are inevitably old-fashioned brass.) Those with a view of the Tuileries are special (and more costly, of course). Location is noteworthy on a square bisected by Rue de Rivoli, almost opposite the Louvre. *First Class.*

Résidence du Bois Hôtel (16 Rue Chalgrin; phone 4500-50-59) is a town-house kind of hotel on a residential street just off fashionable Avenue Foch, which is one of the arteries leading from the Étoile.

The 20 suites and rooms and public rooms are period style and luxurious; you have the feeling that you're in the country. *First Class.*

Résidence St.-Honoré Hôtel (214 Rue du Faubourg St.-Honoré; phone 4225-26-27): You might not think of this fashionable shopping street as the site of a well-priced hotel (admittedly, near its western end). But the Residence St.-Honoré is worth knowing about, what with 91 comfortable, bath-equipped rooms and a bar-lounge. Breakfast only. *Moderate.*

Ritz Hôtel (15 Place Vendôme, with an entrance, as well, on Rue Cambon; phone 4260-38-30) has not, to its great credit, been content to rest on the laurels of a global reputation; it's the "original" Ritz, founded by the legendary César Ritz in 1898. Acquired by a new management team in the late 1970s, it has undergone a long-range multimillion-dollar renovation—undertaken with extraordinary imagination, taste, and skill—that has been more a case of renewing and enhancing original decorative elements than of replacing them. The Ritz occupies one of the original eighteenth-century Place Vendôme palaces and extends through to an early-twentieth-century Rue Cambon addition. The opulent Vendôme-side bar-lounge is a splendid choice for afternoon tea or cocktails. But then you walk through the arcade that connects Vendôme with Cambon buildings, alongside a block-long series of windows displaying luxury goods from Paris shops (with a *vendeuse* on hand during daytime hours to take orders), and there is still another bar, the Hemingway, intimate, named for a one-time resident, and with black leather surfacing stools and chairs surrounding the tables. Restaurant Espadon (which I review on a later page) moves from Louis XV-inspired winter quarters to the sculpture-accented, lantern-hung garden in summer. The relatively recently created Ritz Health Club is a capacious subterranean installation of especial beauty. Its swimming pool, edged by a full-meal-service café on its balcony, just has to be the handsomest in France, and is supplemented by not one but a pair of gyms (men's and women's), squash court, saunas, Turkish baths, and a health center and facial service that are open evenings. Noteworthy, too, are the Ritz Club, softly lighted and good-looking, which welcomes hotel guests for traditional-cuisine meals, drinks, and dancing into the wee hours; and École de Gastronomie Française Ritz-Escoffier, a somewhat unwieldy monicker for the hotel's cooking school, with wine, pastry, and table-setting among specialties, and course durations ranging from two hours to three months. Accommodations? There are just 200 suites and rooms. The suites—including one with a bed that was Marie-Antoinette's, and with museum-caliber eighteenth- and early-nineteenth-century furniture and accessories in most—constitute, in my view, the most beautiful of any that I know of in any hotel in Europe. But ordinary rooms, minimum singles as well as standard doubles—at least those I have stayed in or inspected—are superbly appointed as well. Member, Leading Hotels of the World. *Luxury.*

Royal Monceau Hôtel (37 Avenue Hoche; phone 4561-98-00): Long reputed as one of Paris's smarter hotels—it is located on one of the very grand avenues that radiate, like spokes, from Place Charles de Gaulle—the Royal Monceau joined the crack Italian luxury chain, Ciga, a few seasons back and has emerged handsomer than ever as a consequence of a $15 million renovation. There are close to 200 rooms and nearly 30 suites—decorated in the style of the Empire and the Directoire—good-looking lobby, welcoming bar-lounge, and pair of noteworthy restaurants. One, Le Jardin, is surmounted by a glass dome in the hotel's garden; the other, Carpaccio, is authentically—and deliciously—Italian. You may work out, too; there are both a swimming pool and a gym-cum-sauna. *Luxury.*

Royal St.-Honoré Hôtel (13 Rue d'Alger; phone 4260-32-79) is a satisfactory smaller house, with a situation that is nothing if not convenient—on a short street between Rues St.-Honoré and Rivoli, just east of Place Vendôme. There are 78 traditional-style rooms with good baths, a pleasant lobby and lounge. Breakfast only. *First Class.*

St. James et Albany Hôtel (202 Rue de Rivoli; phone 4268-31-60) went up, in part, toward the end of the seventeenth century as the *hôtel particulier* of Duc de Noailles. Half a century later, Marquis de Lafayette married a daughter of the Noailles clan, on premises; and not long thereafter, Queen Marie-Antoinette welcomed Lafayette at Château de Noailles upon his return from America. Later dubbed Hôtel St. James, the earlier structure was combined with the adjacent Hôtel d'Albany in the mid-nineteenth century, to open as a commercial hotel, which it has been ever since. The early 1980s saw refurbishing—traditional interiors, alas, became acceptable, if undistinguished, contemporary (each of the 145 units—some two-room suites, some duplex suites—has a fridge and electric plate, should you want to make coffee or tea). The restaurant moves to a pretty courtyard in summer, and there's a bar. But, in the process of renovation, there was a name change. The longtime stubbornly plural Hôtels St.-James et d'Albany became the singular Hôtel St. James et Albany, and the preposition preceding Albany disappeared in the process. *Alors,* such is *le progrès. First Class.*

St. James's Club (5 Place Chancelier Adenauer; phone 4704-29-29) is a counterpart of the London original (see *London at Its Best*), where I've enjoyed staying. But the Paris club is far less central and far posher than the original north of the Channel. (Its vice-president, Jane Eland, told the American magazine *Architectural Digest* that "the key to turning Paris's 'little Fontainebleu' into Paris's finest club is to make sure the right sort of people come." Tut, tut. I do not devote space to private clubs in my books and make mention of this one for the same reason that I do of the London cousin: you may stay the first time without being a member, as you would at any hotel, deciding after that if you'd like to join.) The Paris St. James's occupies a restored mansion way out near Bois de Boulogne, with a fountain in the garden and interiors by the same Andrée Putnam responsible for the severe black-and-white Morgans Hotel in New York (see *New York at Its Best*). Madame Putnam relaxes a little here—beige, with green plants in the lobby, a bit of warmth in the bar, graceless upholstered chairs in rooms and suites that are, to their credit, Art Deco–patterned; and a salmon-draped restaurant, perhaps the handsomest room in the house. *Luxury.*

St.-Paul le Marais Hôtel (8 Rue de Sévigné; phone 4804-97-27) is an aged house that has been deftly transformed into a contemporary hotel of considerable style and is nicely located between Places des Vosges and Musée Carnavalet. There's a nifty main-floor lounge, breakfast room in the barrel-vaulted cellar, and 27 beamed-ceiling rooms that are otherwise pale-hued and contemporary with good baths. There is no restaurant. *Moderate.*

St.-Petersbourg Hôtel (33 Rue de Caumartin; phone 4266-60-38) is no more Old Russian—the name notwithstanding—than it is Old English. It is, however, an elderly house that has been spruced up to the point where all 120 rooms have baths. There is a neat little lobby, a convenient restaurant, and a dark-paneled bar that calls itself Anglais, perhaps because it sports a framed photo of Queen Elizabeth II and Prince Philip. The location, between the Madeleine and the Opéra, is good. *Moderate.*

St.-Romain Hôtel (5 Rue Saint-Roch; phone 4260-31-70) charms with its good looks. Relatively recently refurbished, it offers 33 rooms with marble baths, bar-lounge, and breakfast in the old cellar—whose stone walls are barrel-vaulted. I should add that—unusual in Moderate-category French hotels—there's a printed breakfast menu from which you may order not only the usual boiled egg, but fried eggs with bacon, cereals, cheeses, and yogurt, all as à la carte extras. Location is a convenient street between Rue St.-Honoré and Rue de Rivoli. *Moderate.*

San Regis Hôtel (12 Rue Jean Goujon; phone 4359-41-90)—on a street leading from Avenue Franklin Roosevelt, near the Étoile—is a looker, as smartly furnished and accessorized in its 33 rooms (including 4 suites—all with fine baths) as in public spaces, which include a stained-glass-ceilinged restaurant and bar. *First Class.*

Scribe Hôtel (1 Rue Scribe; phone 4742-03-40) is in the heart of the busy Opéra area. It's a big, comfortable old-timer that has been intelligently, expensively, and tastefully refurbished in appropriate Louis XVI style, in the course of recent seasons. The high-ceilinged bedrooms are a highlight. There's a congenial bar-lounge and reputed restaurant in the basement. *Luxury.*

Sydney-Opéra Hôtel (50 Rue des Mathurins; phone 4265-35-48) is a honey—smallish, with a convenient Madeleine-Opéra location and 40 rooms, no two alike, each delightfully decorated and with bath. Breakfast, but no restaurant. *Moderate.*

Touraine Opéra Hôtel (73 Rue Taitbout; phone 4874-50-49) is aptly named. It is indeed in the neighborhood of Opéra/Garnier, north of Boulevard des Italiens. There are 38 well-equipped rooms with bath. Breakfast only. *Moderate.*

Trémoille Hôtel (14 Rue de la Trémoille; phone 4723-34-20) is intimate and quiet—on the serene street for which it is named, off Champs-Élysées, parallel with Avenue Montaigne. Public rooms are Louis XV and furnished with elaborate boiserie and tapestries. There is a dining room–bar-lounge, and the 112 bedrooms are capacious and comfortable. A Trusthouse Forte Exclusive Division hotel, affiliated with Leading Hotels of the World. *Luxury.*

Tuileries Hôtel (10 Rue St.-Hyacinthe; phone 4261-06-94): The Tuileries is on a tiny street that gives onto more-substantial Rue Marché St.-Honoré, lying midway between Place Vendôme (to the west) and Avenue de l'Opéra (to the east), with Rue St.-Honoré a bit south. This is a gracious, late-eighteenth-century mansion converted with panache, in the style of the epoch when it was built, into a 30-room hotel. Breakfast only. *Moderate.*

Vendôme Hôtel (1 Place Vendôme at Rue de Castiglione; phone 4260-32-84) occupies a house designed by Hardouin-Mansart, the architect who took over Versailles from Le Vau at midpoint and completed it for Louis XIV. The front facade of the Vendôme is original; the rest of the building, although less venerable, is hardly unimpressive. This is a smallish hotel. The intimate bar-café doubles as a restaurant, making a specialty of full-meal service in the 40 high-ceilinged bedrooms (all of whose beds are super brass ones). And location is A-1. *First Class.*

Warwick Hôtel (5 Rue de Berri; phone 4563-14-11): A step or two off Champs-Élysées, the Warwick is decorated in contemporary tones, with traditional accents adding warmth. There are just under 150 rooms and suites, including a suite-cum-garden-terrace that looks out on the city, La Couronne Restaurant, bar-lounge, and a bountiful breakfast buffet. *Luxury.*

Westminster Hôtel (13 Rue de la Paix; phone 4261-57-46) went up a couple of centuries back as a convent and became a hotel in the nineteenth century. Located on a legendary, heart-of-town street (Cartier adjoins its entrance), it has been extensively remodeled by its owners, Warwick Hotels. A fifth of its hundred units are suites, and bedrooms are antiques-accented, with updated baths. Neighborhood locals keep the hotel's Le Céladon Restaurant humming (it's evaluated on a later page), and the bar-lounge (go for afternoon tea or a wee-hours' drink) is mock-Renaissance, with a fireplace as high as its two-story ceiling. *Luxury.*

SELECTED RIVE GAUCHE/LEFT BANK AND ÎLE ST.-LOUIS HOTELS

Abbaye St.-Germain Hôtel (a.k.a. Hôtel de l'Abbaye; 10 Rue Cassette; 4544-38-11) occupies what had been a convent, not far east of Boulevard Raspail, with Boulevard St.-Germain-des-Prés a fairish walk north. Relatively out-of-the-way situation notwithstanding, the Abbaye has built up a loyal following, thanks to the good looks of its lobby, bar, and garden and the marble baths of its 45 smartly traditional rooms. Breakfast only. No credit cards accepted. *Moderate.*

Académie Hôtel (32 Rues des Saints-Pères; phone 4548-36-22) boasts a location on a Rive Gauche mini Hotel Row. There are 32 rooms with bath and pleasant public spaces. *Moderate.*

Angleterre Hôtel (44 Rue Jacob; phone 4260-34-72) is no more English than the Quartier Latin street on which it is situated. It is a typical Parisian inn; all rooms have bath or shower. Breakfast only. *Moderate.*

Arcade Montparnasse Hôtel (71 Boulevard de Vaurigard; phone 4320-89-12) embodies major aspects of the successful formula of the national chain of which it's a link: small but contemporary rooms (with as many as four beds, some double-decker, but with standard doubles available as well), restaurants featuring copious buffets for all three meals, and bar. This one's smaller than most with just over 30 rooms. Near skyscraping Tour Main-Montparnasse and Gare Montparnasse as well. *Moderate.*

Beaugency Hôtel (21 Rue Duvivier; phone 4705-01-63) has the dubious distinction of having the smallest-in-size rooms (30 all told) of any hotel of its category with which I am familiar in all France; it was obviously designed for French business travelers on quick overnight stays, with little more than a briefcase for baggage. Staff is minimally cordial and the location near École Militaire some blocks south of Tour Eiffel, is inconvenient. Breakfast only. I can't recommend this one. *Moderate.*

Bellechasse Hôtel (8 Rue de Bellechasse; phone 4551-52-36) is core-of-Rive Gauche on a street that intersects Boulevard St.-Germain. Lobby is clean-lined and appealing, rooms—relatively recently renovated—likewise. There are 32, all with bath. Breakfast only. *Moderate.*

Bersoly's St.-Germain Hôtel (28 Rue de Lille; phone 4296-32-34) is nicely located on the same street as the Musée d'Orsay and convenient to the Right Bank. The lobby is unprepossessing, but those of the 16 rooms I've inspected, though small and with narrow twin beds, are otherwise agreeable. Breakfast only. *Moderate.*

Bonaparte Hôtel (61 Rue Bonaparte; phone 4326-97-37) is an unpretentious, worth-knowing-about oldie on a core-of-St.-Germain street that leads to the Seine. All 29 rooms are bath-equipped (the smaller ones have showers instead of tubs). Breakfast only. *Moderate.*

Bradford Hôtel (10 Rue Saint-Philippe-du-Roule; phone 4359-24-20) is good value—all 46 rooms have bath—and well located, on a short street just off Rue du Faubourg St.-Honoré and near Champs-Élysées as well. *Moderate.*

Claude-Bernard Hôtel (43 Rue des Écoles; phone 4326-32-52) is a neighbor of the Sorbonne and Collège de France. It is simple but adequate; most rooms have private baths. Breakfast only. *Moderate.*

Colbert Hôtel (7 Rue de l'Hôtel-Colbert; phone 4325-85-65) lies on the short street taking its name, between Boulevard St.-Germain and the Seine. It's a charmer, with 40 no-two-alike rooms in the style of Louis XV and Louis XVI (including a honey of a suite with views of Notre-Dame), bar-lounge, and atmospheric breakfast rooms in a basement *cave.* There's no restaurant, but Moderate-category Le Cour Colbert is just opposite. *Moderate.*

Danube St.-Germain Hôtel (58 Rue Jacob; phone 4260-34-70), strategically situated at the intersection of Rues Jacob and Sts.-Pères, boasts a winsome inner patio and lounge. Management is pleasant;

30 of the 45 rooms have baths. Breakfast, but no restaurant. *Moderate.*

Derby Hôtel (5 Avenue Duquesne; phone 4705-12-05) has a fin-de-siècle facade—and ambience within as well—on an attractive street near the École Militaire, the Invalides, and UNESCO, from whose global membership it draws much of its clientele. Virtually all of the 36 good-looking rooms have baths. Breakfast only. *Moderate.*

Deux-Îles Hôtel (59 Rue St.-Louis-en-l'Île, on Île St.-Louis; phone 4326-13-35) is center of the Île St.-Louis action, on its principal street. The lobby is attractively antique-accented, and although no two of the 17 rooms are quite alike, they're pleasant, and all with bath. Breakfast only. *Moderate.*

Fleurie Hôtel (32 Rue Grégoire-de-Tours; phone 4329-59-81) occupies quarters in an eighteenth-century house splendidly facaded. The 29 rooms tend to be small (although there are a few pricier larger-size chambers) but all have marble-accented baths. Situation is half a block from Boulevard St.-Germain. This is an attractive, relatively recently renovated house. Breakfast only. *Moderate.*

Grand Hôtel des Balcons (3 Rue Casimir-Delavigne; phone 4634-78-50): A hotel with ten of its 55 rooms without private baths is not grand in the accepted sense. Withal, if you land a room *with* bath you can be happy indeed. Near Place de l'Odéon and Jardin de Luxembourg. Breakfast only. *Moderate.*

Grands Hommes Hôtel (17 Place du Panthéon; phone 4634-19-60) Use the dome of the neighboring Panthéon as a landmark and you'll have no difficulty in locating the Grands Hommes, a pleasant house with 32 bath-equipped rooms. Breakfast only. *Moderate.*

Hilton International Paris Hôtel (18 Avenue de Suffren; phone 4273-92-00) was considered a sassy Yank upstart by the locals when I covered its opening. It was the first completely new hotel in Paris for decades. At first, the French tended to be patronizing about the *Eel-tohn,* but they soon realized that it represented contemporary luxury hotelkeeping. And so this hotel has thrived, despite a location that is more romantic than convenient (its next-door neighbor is the Eiffel Tower) and a look that is more functional than beautiful. There are fine views from riverside rooms; a restaurant called Le Western beloved of the Parisians for its U.S.-style steaks; and a Gallic-accented coffeeshop. And I'll say this for the location: During my first visit, I made up my mind to take no taxis; I wanted to master the Métro. With the system map in hand, I took it everywhere; and have been a Métro fan ever since. *Luxury.*

L'Hôtel Guy-Louis-Duboucher (13 Rue des Beaux-Arts; phone 4325-27-22)—despite, or possibly because of, small capacity (there are but 27 no-two-alike, antique-accented rooms, each with a marble-surfaced bath)—has achieved a certain snob status. There is no denying its good looks, convenient location, or interesting past (Oscar Wilde died on the premises). Still, I have found its reception staff unwelcoming and its restaurant more attractive than delicious. *Luxury.*

Jeu de Paume Hôtel (54 Rue St.-Louis-en-l'Île, on Île St.-Louis; phone 4326-14-18) went up as a tennis court (its name, in the French language) in the eighteenth century and, relatively recently, was transformed, with considerable style, into a honey of a 32-room-with-bath, antique-accented hotel, with inviting public spaces (including a bar). Location is Île St.-Louis's principal thoroughfare, abounding in restaurants. Breakfast only.

Latitudes St.-Germain Hôtel (7 Rue St.-Benoît; phone 4261-53-53), situated between Boulevard Saint-Germain and the Seine is at once good-size (117 bath-equipped rooms in a variety of color schemes) and good-looking, with wood-paneled, marble-accented lounges, *fin-de-siècle* bar-lounge Art Deco reading room, and a greenhouse in which breakfast is served. *Moderate/First Class.*

Left Bank Hôtel (9 Rue de l'Ancienne Comédie; phone 4354-01-70) is, despite its English-language name, authentically Rive Gauche, occupying a seventeenth-century house, with antiques and tapestries dotted about, 31 beamed-ceiling rooms with modern baths sporting marble-counter sinks, and an agreeable breakfast room. Location is core of the area for which the hotel is named. Best Western. *Moderate.*

Lenox Hôtel (9 Rue de l'Université; phone 4296-10-95) successfully employs a traditional-contemporary mix, with respect to decor; there's a convenient bar and all 34 rooms are bath-equipped. Quartier Latin location is convenient. *Moderate.*

Lutèce Hôtel (65 Rue St.-Louis-en-l'Île; phone 4326-23-52) is not far behind the flying buttresses and apse of Notre-Dame, on neighboring Île de la Cité. To stay on Île St.-Louis in this charming house—there are but 31 pleasant rooms—is to live in a small community surrounded by the larger city. Breakfast only. No credit cards. *Moderate.*

Lutétia Hôtel (46 Boulevard Raspail, at Rue de Sèvres; phone 4544-38-10), with its brilliant, carved-stone facade, is an Art Nouveau landmark of Paris and has been since it went up in 1910. Hôtels

Concorde, its proprietors, have refurbished it stem to stern, and, to their great credit, they illuminate that one-of-a-kind facade every evening. There are 315 rooms and suites, with the ones to ask for those with views of Les Invalides and the Eiffel Tower. There are a pair of restaurants; I am partial to the popularly priced Brasserie, reviewed on a later page. The bar is congenial. And the situation is super. *First Class.*

Madison Hôtel (143 Boulevard St.-Germain; phone 4329-72-50) is not only fully air-conditioned but also has a good location opposite the Church of St.-Germain-des-Prés, with a view of it from the front. All 55 rooms have baths. Breakfast only. *Moderate.*

Marronniers Hôtel (21 Rue Jacob; phone 4325-30-60) is strategically situated on an atmospheric Quartier Latin street about midpoint between the Seine and Boulevard St.-Germain. There are 37 neat rooms with bath. Breakfast only. *Moderate.*

Montalembert Hôtel (3 Rue Montalembert; phone 4548-68-11) is an old-school house of fairish size, with an equally agreeable core-of-Left Bank situation. All 60 rooms have been modernized and have baths. Breakfast only. *First Class.*

Notre-Dame Hôtel (1 Quai Saint-Michel; phone 4354-20-43) is, to be sure, accurately titled. By that I mean there are views of the great Paris cathedral from all 26 of its bath-equipped rooms, relatively recently refurbished. Breakfast only. *Moderate.*

Pas-de-Calais Hôtel (59 Rue des Saints-Pères; phone 4548-78-74) is conveniently situated in the heart of the Left Bank, on one of its most attractive streets. It is smallish, spotless, and inviting. All 41 rooms have baths. There's a spacious lounge, congenial management, and breakfast (but no restaurant). *Moderate.*

Pont-Royal Hôtel (7 Rue de Montalembert; phone 4544-92-07) is located on a pleasant Quartier Latin street just off Boulevard St.-Germain. The look is spiffy traditional—lobby, paneled bar with green leather chairs, terraced Les Antiquaires Restaurant—as well as 80 comfortable rooms and suites with good baths. Very nice, indeed. *First Class.*

Quai Voltaire Hôtel (19 Quai Voltaire; phone 4261-50-91) has a location that is nothing less than inspired, on the Seine, right across from the Louvre, between Pont Royal and Pont du Carrousel. This is a nicely freshened-up old building. There are fewer than 35 rooms, a good proportion with private baths. Breakfast only. *Moderate.*

Relais St.-Germain Hôtel (9 Carrefour de l'Odéon; phone 4329-12-05) is, in a nutshell, small but smart. By that I mean 9 rooms only, each with a fabulous marble bath with double sinks, plus an antique-accented suite. Location is between Place de l'Odéon and Boulevard St.-Germain. Breakfast only. *First Class.*

Ste.-Beuve Hôtel (9 Rue Ste.-Beuve; phone 4548-20-07) has but 22 rooms, but they're attractive, not unlike the rest of the house—and popular. Only breakfast is served, but you're only a hop and a skip from the celebrated La Coupole Restaurant (below). *Moderate.*

St.-Germain-des-Prés Hôtel (36 Rue Bonaparte; phone 4326-00-19) is an aged building that has been imaginatively refurbished, with a paneled lobby, Louis XIII-style lounge, fresh flowers at every turn, beamed ceilings, tapestried walls, and 30 rooms, mostly with papered walls, all with bath, and for the most part good-sized. Location is super—steps from the church of St.-Germain des Prés and the boulevard taking its name. Breakfast only. *Moderate.*

St.-Grégoire Hôtel (43 Rue de l'Abbé Grégoire; phone 4548-23-23): I don't know of a hotel the interior designer David Hicks has created in his native Britain. But he is responsible for the decor—beige, pale rose, yellow in a setting of beamed ceilings and abundant jumbo-size vases of flowers—of the St.-Grégoire. There are just 20 rooms, each with touches unique to it and a good bath, and one with its own terrace. Only breakfast is served, but the hotel's management owns the neighboring La Marlotte Restaurant, which provides room service. Near Rue de Rennes and Boulevard Raspail. *Moderate/First Class.*

St.-Louis Hôtel (75 Rue St.-Louis-en-l'Île; phone 4634-04-80)—on Île St.-Louis's busy main drag—shelters 21 bath-equipped rooms and serves breakfast (no other meals) in its medieval cellar. Nice. *Moderate.*

St.-Simon Hôtel (14 Rue St.-Simon; phone 4548-35-66), flanking a short street just off Boulevard St.-Germain, is a case of good things in small packages—just under 30 rooms, all with bath, and a welcoming management. Breakfast only. *Moderate.*

Solferino Hôtel (91 Rue de Lille; phone 4705-85-54) is a long-on-scene favorite with considerable repeat clientele, thanks to its convenient location (near Musée d'Orsay), and functional rooms, most of which (27 of 33) have baths. Breakfast only. *Moderate.*

Splendid Hôtel (29 Avenue de Trouville; phone 4551-24-77) is a neighbor of École Militaire, UNESCO, and the Invalides. 45 simple but pleasant rooms have bath. There's an inviting lobby-lounge with a bar but no restaurant, although breakfast is served. *Moderate.*

Tour Notre-Dame Hôtel (36 Rue St.-Jacques; phone 4354-47-60) is an interestingly restored *hôtel particulier* that's a neighbor of Musée de Cluny (above), at the corner of Boulevard St.-Germain. There are just under half a hundred ultramod rooms with marble baths and, in some cases, balconies, from which there can be views of Notre-Dame. There's a cozy bar and breakfast, but no restaurant. Nice. *Moderate.*

Trianon Palace Hôtel (1-bis Rue de Vaugirard; phone 4329-88-10) is fair-sized—120 rooms—and situated near Boulevard St.-Michel and the Jardin du Luxembourg. Most rooms have baths, and breakfast is served. *Moderate.*

Université Hôtel (22 Rue de l'Université; phone 4261-09-39) is a long-popular, attractively furnished charmer, with 27 no-two-alike, bath-equipped rooms and convenient situation. Breakfast only. *Moderate.*

Verneuil St.-Germain Hôtel (8 Rue de Verneuil; phone 4260-82-14) is a pleasure. It's a tastefully updated eighteenth-century house between Rue du Bac and Rue des Sts.-Pères, with 26 attractive, bath-equipped rooms, two of which are living-room-attached suites. Breakfast only. *Moderate.*

La Villa Hôtel (29 Rue Jacob; phone 4326-60-00): Starkly contemporary hi-tech design—once you leave major monuments like the Beaubourg—are the departure rather than the rule in Paris, and when, relatively recently, the former Hôtel d'Isly, in a centuries-old house core-of-Quartier-Latin, was gutted and replaced with a decidedly contemporary interior—well, Parisians took notice. The look is leather and unembellished wood, and all 35 rooms sport ultramod baths. Bar in the basement (the music is jazz) and breakfast. *Moderate.*

STAYING AT THE AIRPORTS

Paris Orly Airport Hilton Hôtel (phone 4687-33-88) has the great advantage of being directly opposite Orly's main entrance. It is, of course, soundproofed and air-conditioned, with 366 comfortable French-modern rooms, moderate-tab coffee shop, smart La Louisiane Restaurant, bar-lounge, and amenities, including business center, dozen-plus meeting rooms, barber and beauty parlor, and gratis bus service to and from the terminal. *Luxury.*

Holiday Inn Roissy Hôtel (Allée du Verger, Roissy; phone 3429-30-00) is typically Holiday Inn functional, with 250 rooms, each with a shower-equipped bath; convenient restaurant, comfortable bar-lounge, and a location adjacent to de Gaulle Airport. *First Class.*

Altéa Paris-Roissy Hôtel (Zone Hôtelière, Allée du Verger, Roissy; phone 3429-40-00), among the newer hostelries serving de Gaulle, is low-slung and well-appointed, with just over 200 pleasant rooms (including 8 suites and a good-sized clutch of premium-tab, extra-amenity Club rooms). There are both dressy and brasserie-style restaurants, congenial bar, and business services including fax and telex, as well as meeting rooms. *First Class.*

SELECTED RIVE DROITE/RIGHT BANK RESTAURANTS AND CAFÉS

Ambassade d'Auvergne (22 Rue du Grenier-St.-Lazare; phone 4272-31-22) offers specialties of south-central Auvergne, rarely encountered in Paris. The prix-fixe dinner, to give you an idea, might embrace soupe aux choux (a cabbage potage), petit salé aux lentilles (a hearty pork dish), and the difficult-to-describe but delicious aligot—with a mashed-potato base. Mousse au chocolat is a favored dessert. *First Class.*

Les Ambassadeurs (Crillon Hôtel, 10 Place de la Concorde; phone 4625-24-24): The approach to this restaurant—an all-Paris leader—is hardly to be despised. Place de la Concorde for starters, with the Crillon lobby following. You pass, then, up a couple of steps, to the hotel's high-ceilinged Grand Salon, where you could do worse, if it's evening, than to pause for a predinner drink in one of the city's handsomest environments. The salon leads to Les Ambassadeurs: marble-walled, hung with crystal chandeliers, massed with great bouquets of flowers, its tables flanked by black-upholstered armchairs, with the staff swift, skilled, and tuxedo-clad. Splurge with foie gras or smoked salmon to start. Seafood is special at Les Ambassadeurs—sole meunière or, more spectacular, a whole lobster in a coriander-infused bouillon. Beef entrées are top of the line; ditto breast of chicken, crisp-skinned in a light ginger-honey sauce. And so are braised sweetbreads. Chocolate desserts are irresistible, none more so than one termed Dôme Chocolat Noisettes Croquantes et Nectar de Cacao—alone worth a pilgrimage to this restaurant. Don't fail to peruse the eighteen-page wine list, outstanding not only for Bordeaux (how about a $2,500 Château Mouton-Rothschild '61?) but for a selection of Burgundies that's one of the most extensive I've encountered, with no less than three dozen types of Champagne (half a dozen from the House of Taittinger, the Crillon's proprietors), and—among digestifs for post-meal relaxation—two dozen cognacs and Armagnacs. Note that there's a multicourse menu at lunch and that the Crillon's own chocolates offered at meal's end (I think, the best in town) may be purchased by the box through the captain, or in the hotel's shop. *Luxury.*

L'Ambroisie (9 Places des Vosges; phone 4278-51-45) is surely the smallest (there are just a dozen tables in a compact, cozy space) and least pretentious (principal decor is a giant vase of flowers and a tapestry-surfaced wall) of Paris's costly ranking restaurants. Time to go is midday for the prix-fixe lunch, which might open with chef-propriétaire Bernard Pacaud's jellied duck terrine or lobster minestrone, followed by, say, braised turbot, basil-scented lamb, or game in season, with a Pacaud-created sweet to conclude—his fig melba, perhaps. Apple strudel as you've not had it previously, or a fabulous frozen concoction based on pear sherbet. Dinner—à la carte only—is considerably pricier. Wines are ordered from a relatively small but top-of-the-line list, staff is cordial, and no location in town—setting is a venerable Place des Vosges *hôtel particulier*—is more romantic. *Luxury.*

André Faure (40 Rue du Mont-Thabor; phone 4260-74-28): You are not going to lose weight as a consequence of an André Faure meal. But it will have been worthwhile. This is a smallish place on a street leading from Rue de Castiglione, near Place Vendôme. You go for the warmth of the welcome and the satisfying à la carte, composing a meal that might, to give you an idea, start with a dozen snails, continue with coq au vin or a rich duck confit in the style of the southwest, and conclude with a Norman-origin tarte tatin. *Moderate.*

Androuet (41 Rue d'Amsterdam, near Gare St.-Lazare; phone 4874-26-93). The name of the Androuet game is cheese, glorious cheese. Its ground floor is a shop selling nothing but, in infinite variety. Up a flight you go—for a meal; I suggest you order "Le Grand Plateau." A hundred and fifty types of cheese are presented (they take up space on seven trays), with wine and bread to accompany. I know of no better introduction to the cheeses of the world's No. 1 cheese country. *First Class.*

Angelina (226 Rue de Rivoli) is for afternoon tea deluxe. China is fine Limoges. Decor is Belle Époque. Clientele is an amusing mix of ancien régime and younger Parisians. Irresistible pastries. *First Class.*

Auberge de France (1 Rue du Mont-Thabor; phone 4260-60-26) is worth knowing about when you seek a core-of-Rive-Droit restaurant. The prix-fixe meal centered on grilled entrecôte nicely garnished, with dessert, is tasty and fairly tabbed. Pleasant service. *Moderate/First Class.*

Au Chien Qui Fume (33 Rue du Point Neuf; phone 4236-07-42) had been a mainstay of sustenance in the old days when the area in which it's situated was the site of Les Halles produce markets. Alas, the markets have moved, but this restaurant, on scene for something like three-quarters of a century albeit updated, stays on. A shellfish shucker is on duty at the entrance (oysters are a specialty). Or open with the house's own smoked salmon or duck foie gras. Entrées include roast lamb, thyme-scented. A don't-miss sweet is profiteroles au chocolat. Traditionally open until 2 A.M. *First Class.*

Au Dauphin (167 Rue St.-Honoré, phone 4260-40-11) An upstairs table by the windows affords a view of the Comédie Française, the staff is cordial, and the price is right, but there's not too much that can be said in favor of the food. The menu might open with house terrine and feature roast pork with mustard sauce as an entrée. *Moderate.*

Au Lyonnais (32 Rue St.-Marc; phone 4296-69-04), with cozy, *fin-de-siècle* dining rooms on two floors, is proficient at preparing the fare of Lyon. Start with hot sausages, go on to lamb with flageolet-type beans or coq au Beaujolais, making certain that you do not fail to order a portion of gratin Dauphinois, the tastiest of potato casseroles. Drink Beaujolais—the wine of Lyon. *First Class.*

Au Petit Riche (25 Rue le Peletier; phone 4770-68-68) observed its hundred-tenth birthday in 1990. It's a lively atmospheric brasserie, with good things to eat and drink, peppy service with a *sourire,* and an enviable location just north of Boulevard Haussmann not far from Opéra/Garnier. The three-course menu offers a choice of six oysters on the half-shell or nine Burgundy-style snails to open, lamb fricassée or beef filet among entrées, and delicious pastry among desserts. Grilled sole is a good à la carte choice, and a bottle of the house's Vin Bistrot is sound value, with a big list to supplement it. *First Class.*

Aux Petits Pères (8 Rue Notre-Dame-des-Victoires; phone 4260-91-73) is not, at first glance, prepossessing. What attracts you is the address: a street named for the neighboring church of Notre-Dame-des-Victoires (see Ecclesiastical Paris, above), just off a similarly titled—and fashionable—square. The staff out front is feminine and charming, the chefs are gents and talented. Walls are half-timbered, with postcards received from *copains* of the *direction* tucked neatly into edges of mirrors. You order from the à la carte, opening, perhaps, with eggs delicately poached in a Bordeaux sauce, continue with an exquisite duckling, prepared Rouen style, or a sautéed veal chop served with braised endives. The house Bordeaux is sound and well-priced; have assorted cheeses with what remains of it. Or a house-created sweet. *First Class.*

Au Trou Normand (9 Rue Jean-Pierre Timbaud; phone 4805-80-23): In Normandy, a trou Normand refers to the opening in one's face—the mouth—into which is ingested, between courses of a traditional meal—a snort of Norman-origin Calvados. This restaurant is something else again: a source of entrecôte and other grills (a dozen entrées, all told) teamed with socko frites, preceded by a wide choice of tasty openers, the lot exceptional value, albeit à la carte. Near Place de la République, northeast of the Beaubourg. *Moderate.*

Bistro de la Gare (38 Boulevard des Italiens; phone 4828-49-61) is a Parisian success story, thanks to its ingenious simplicity: an inexpensive menu embracing but a handful of combinations, that of steak (or broiled chicken) with frites, preceded by a salad, the most popular. Setting is bright, welcoming, and cordial; service, efficient. (A competing operation, *Hippopotamus,* which also has several Paris outlets and is in the provinces, too, is diagonally opposite, and Bistro de la Gare has several other locations.) *Moderate.*

Brasserie Bastille (14 Place de la Bastille; phone 4343-42-76)—though without the excitement, exceptional looks, or celebrated cuisine of Brasserie Bofinger, below—is worth knowing about, given its location on a square shared with Opéra/Bastille. Go for lunch in connection with a matinee or pre- or postperformance in the evening. Fare is traditional—oysters and terrines, substantial beef and other entrées, wicked sweets. *Moderate/First Class.*

Brasserie Bofinger (5 Rue de la Bastille at Place de la Bastille; phone 4272-87-82) calls itself the oldest brasserie in town, dates to 1864, and can well be proud of its smashing good looks—stained-glass ceilings, elaborate marquetry, oversized turn-of-century ceramic sculptures, paintings dating to the restaurant's founding years, and quick-as-a-wink waiters. Choucroute garnie, the classic Alsatian dish wherein a mound of sauerkraut is topped by assorted meats, sausages, and boiled potatoes, is, with reason, the most noted specialty, but there's a good-value three-course menu (embracing oysters on the half shell, navarin d'agneau—France's famed lamb stew—with floating island for dessert) to supplement the à la carte. *First Class.*

Brasserie Flo (7 Cour des Petites-Écuries; phone 4770-13-59) is worth a detour from the visitor-trafficked part of town around Opéra/Garnier to a street midway between it and Gare de l'Est.

Lure is an authentic *fin-de-siècle* brasserie—Art Nouveau carved wood, lavish oil paintings, exuberant stained glass, and stick-to-the-ribs fare, including oysters by the dozen served on elegantly elevated metal stands, foie gras frais, and choucroute garnie, Alsace's sauerkraut masterwork. Convivial. *First Class.*

Brasserie Vaudeville (29 Rue Vivienne, not far east of Avenue de l'Opéra; phone 4271-90-75) is not a whit less atmospheric—agreeably high decibel count, massive proportions, waiters in long, white aprons, carved-wood-cum-stained-glass decor—than Flo (above). Seafood is excellent, but you do at least as well with a dinner that might run to onion soup and steak with sauce Bordelaise accompanied by frites, with cheese to conclude, washed down by what remains of a bottle of the house's Côtes du Rhône. Swift and smiling service. *First Class.*

Bristol Hôtel Restaurant (112 Rue du Faubourg St.-Honoré; phone 4266-91-45): Go in winter, and the setting is an oval room superbly paneled and chandelier-hung. Go in summer, and you'll be seated in a rattan-furnished pavilion giving onto the Bristol's capacious garden. The menu blends traditional with contemporary. You may, for example, begin with smoked Norwegian salmon or lobster bisque, among the familiar starters, or a more innovative salad built around duck breasts and crayfish; continuing with roast lamb or filet of beef, among old-school type entrées, in contrast to, say, escalope of turbot cooked with sauternes or confit of sweetbreads prepared with wild mushrooms. Desserts rate a separate card. And you need not go thirsty: 70,000 bottles are stored in the Bristol's cellar. Splendid service. *Luxury.*

Cafés: Of the Right Bank cafés, most requisite is *Café de la Paix* (Place de l'Opéra), which has been a Paris institution for nearly a century and a quarter—from the time when Le Grand Hôtel went up alongside the Opéra, as part of Baron Haussmann's reconstruction of Paris. Nary a visitor, celebrated or not, who has passed through Paris over that long period has missed stopping for coffee, a drink, or a bite to eat, the better to take in action on the square. (Relais Capucines, adjacent to the café, is a proper restaurant counseled in a later paragraph.) *Café Royal Concorde* (7 Rue Royale) is a super spot to sit for a spell, observing broad Place de la Concorde, just beyond. *Café Pény* (3 Place de la Madeleine) is strategically situated, with the colonnaded Church of the Madeleine and the square's pedestrians as subject matter. If you're hungry, order salade Niçoise or an assiette froide while seated at an outdoor table. *Fouquet's* (99 Avenue des Champs-Élysées) is as much restaurant as café, but it's to the tables out front, spilling around onto Avenue George V, that I direct you for observation of ambulatory action in this quarter. *Café Les Tours de Notre-Dame* (23 Rue d'Aréole): Take a table in the shadow of the cathedral's gargoyles; splendid views. *Café Wepler* (Place de Clichy) and *La Mère Catherine* (Place du Tertre and later recommended as a restaurant) are for people-watching in Montmartre. *Café Royal Vosges* and *Café Ma Bourgogne* are well situated on beautiful Place des Vosges. And *Café Flore en l'Île* (42 Quai d'Orléans) doubles as a creditable restaurant, but its ace-in-the-hole is an Île St.-Louis location affording extraordinary vistas of Notre-Dame's flying buttresses and apse. *Café de la Plage* (Rue de Charonne near Place de la Bastille) is the ideal spot to become acquainted with the newly popular Bastille quarter, now heavily populated with artists, art-gallery entrepreneurs, and architects. All the foregoing, when utilized as cafés, are *Moderate.*

Café Tuileries (Inter-Continental Paris Hotel, 3 Rue de Castiglione; phone 4260-37-80) is called to your attention as a source of tasty, well-priced sustenance, breakfast into the evening; menus at lunch and dinner are good buys; onion soup is always a good bet; and there's an entrance on Rue de Rivoli. *Moderate/First Class.*

Capucine (39 Boulevard des Capucines; phone 4261-14-71) makes for a perfect mid- or late-afternoon pause, with your object tea accompanied either by pastry or one of the house's irresistible coupes, or sundaes. You'll be in the company of neighborhood regulars, mostly mature—and gossipy—ladies. Pleasant. *Moderate.*

Cartet (62 Rue de Malte, north of Place des Vosges; phone 4805-17-65) is a smallish, narrowish place with tables packed together. You go for the food. Order a bottle of Côtes du Rhône and start with a selection of house terrines and sausages. There are half a dozen fish choices. Main courses? If you're two, order gigot d'agneau and wait for the arrival of an entire leg of lamb perfectly roasted, with pommes de terre gratinées in tandem. Or try saucisson de Lyon chaud or daube of beef. You'll be in no shape for a sweet, but persevere. Your options include profiterole aux fraises, a choco-strawberry sensation; tarte au citron; or gâteau au chocolat, with pears in its central regions. Memorable. *Luxury.*

Caveau des Chevillards (1 Rue St.-Hyacinthe; phone 4261-19-74): Down you go, to the vaulted seventeenth-century cellar of an elegant house a bit north of Rue St.-Honoré and due east of Place Vendôme. Time to go is evening, when candles illuminate smartly set tables, and you sit on Louis XIII chairs, feasting on such traditional dishes as seafood mousse or a salad based on confit of duck, trout prepared the house's way, half a dozen beef dishes, or roast lamb, garlic-scented. Menu at lunch is *First Class*; dinner, à la carte, comes closer to *Luxury.*

Le Céladon (Westminster Hôtel, 13 Rue de la Paix, with its own entrance on Rue Daunou; phone 4261-57-46) is—not surprisingly—decorated in pale celadon green. Ambience is intimate; fare, a sensible traditional-contemporary mix (open with an extravagant lobster-caviar salad, if you're flush, opting for entrées of, say, grilled salmon or roast lamb, concluding with a coffee-sauced sundae); and location conveniently central. Prix-fixe menus are well priced. *First Class/Luxury.*

Charcuterie St.-Roch and ***Pâtisserie St.-Roch*** (Rue St.-Honoré neighbors at Rue St.-Roch) are brought to your attention as examples of satisfying sources of the makings of a picnic (or hotel-room) meal. Select from a big selection of salads, sliced meats, and other victuals, which might be termed French deli, at the charcuterie, following with sandwiches if you like, but certainly cake and/or pastry, from the pâtisserie. Depending, of course, on what you order, and how much of it: *Moderate/First Class.* (I selected these two places for this entry because they're so central—and neighbors. But you may duplicate this kind of scene all over town, especially at such charcuteries as *Chedeville* (12 Rue Marché St.-Honoré) and the charcuterie section of *Fauchon* (26 Place de la Madeleine—with pastries, as well.)

Chartier (7 Rue du Faubourg Montmartre; phone 4740-86-29) has Folies Bergère as a neighbor and is nicely combined with the Folies, of an evening. This is a big turn-of-century place with a small army of white-aproned waiters darting about with trays full of good things to eat—as for example Burgundy-style snails or steak tartare as openers, hearty beef or poultry entrées, perhaps fresh strawberries with crème chantilly for dessert. *Moderate.*

La Chaumière (38 Rue du Mont-Thabor, near Place Vendôme; phone 4544-67-91) is mobbed at lunch with workers of the area, tucking into its good-value menus. Three courses typically include such entrées as chicken and steak. Cheerful service. *Moderate.*

Chez Gabriel (123 Rue St.-Honoré; phone 4233-02-99) comes through with flying colors by means of a three-course menu with a grilled veal chop and a mound of crisp frites indicated as the entrée choice. Old-fashioned in look; ditto, the smiling service. *Moderate.*

Chez La Vieille (a.k.a. Chez Adrienne, 37 Rue de l'Arbre Sec; phone 4260-15-78) is, to summarize in three words, eccentric albeit exceptional. It's not going to win a beauty contest, given a setting that consists of but two plain rooms, the larger main floor adjacent to an entry passage dividing it from the kitchen, the smaller annex up a flight. It does not serve as the setting for a leisurely dinner because it serves only lunch. It has no business card, as do most restaurants in most countries, the better for you to retain name, address, and phone. And more significant, it has neither menu nor posted prices. You take what you're served (there's a choice of entrée) and pay, in cash, what you're asked, at meal's end. Madame Adrienne, the chef-propriétaire, speaks only French, pops in from the kitchen only if she's curious about an arriving party, or is already familiar with its personnel (the restaurant draws smart, sometimes celebrated Parisians), and appears more interested in cooking well for you than charming you with chitchat. Her sister, Madeleine, the chief waitress/hostess (who also speaks only French), is, however, cordial, and the third visible member of the enterprise is a woman who serves but neither speaks (except when addressed) nor smiles. The drill here (location is a street running north from the Seine, near Pont Neuf) is Adrienne's old-fashioned food, starting with generous-size portions of the day's hors-d'œuvre, ladled on your plate one selection at a time, and including, on one visit, rillettes (chunky pork pâté from the Loire valley), poultry-based pâté de volaille, deliciously stuffed tomatoes, pickled beets (rarely encountered in France's restaurants, or those of any country, for that matter), superbly sauced mussels, the best celery rémoulade you will have consumed, and Adrienne's masterful version of ratatouille, Provence's eggplant-onion-tomato meld bound in olive oil. Entrées can be anticlimactic after the gargantuan first course; they include roasts of pork and lamb, sautéed veal chop (the only less-than-spectacular dish that I have tasted), and superbly prepared duckling. Chocolate mousse is a winner among desserts, Beaujolais popular as a wine choice. As for mineral water, Chez la Vieille is the only restaurant of consequence I recall encountering in France that does not stock the mildly *gazeuse* Badoit (the country's No. 1 mealtime water); you must be content with nonbubbly Évian, hardly a sacrifice, given the extraordinary flavor and excitement of your lunch. *First Class.*

Chez Marcel (7 Rue St.-Nicholas; phone 4343-49-40) is a Bastille-area institution—a no-nonsense bistro with delicious country pâté and sausages, fresh fruits (strawberries in season are super), and fruit pastries, with old-fashioned bistro cooking—steak/frites, bœuf bourguignon, coq au vin—in between, and a fine selection of wines, aperitifs and digestifs. Lots of neighborhood regulars. *First Class.*

Chez Pauline (5 Rue Villedo; phone 4296-20-70) straddles a short street just east of Avenue de l'Opéra, just north of the Comédie Française. It is at once small and smart, with paneled walls and silk-shaded table lamps. You are heartily welcomed and well fed; a dinner might run to jambon persillé (one of the best such I've had in France) or bisque de homard, continuing with bœuf bourguignon or the house's deservedly reputed stuffed cabbage. Super sweets. *First Class.*

Chicago Meatpackers (8 Rue Coquillière; phone 4028-01-83) is the very same you may recall from London or Glasgow (see *Britain at Its Best*). It's indicated at the onset of a sinking spell—when you're a little homesick for, say, baby back ribs, a bowl of chili, or a bacon cheeseburger. Don't neglect side dishes: coleslaw, baked potatoes, onion loaf, or the desserts: mud and pecan pies, cheese and carrot cakes. You may begin with a dry martini, Harvey Wallbanger, piña colada, or Scotch; and Michelob is among the beers. There are California as well as French wines. And where else on the Continent are you going to find Diet Coke? Location is Les Halles, near the Church of St.-Eustache (above). *Moderate.*

La Chope des Puces (122 Rue des Rosiers) is just the ticket on a day when you're exploring Marché aux Puces (Flea Market) and you crave a seat and some sustenance. Build your lunch around moules marinières—mussels in white wine—the specialty of the quarter, and be prepared for live musical accompaniment from an ensemble of long-on-scene gypsy guitarists. *Moderate.*

La Chope des Vosges (22 Place des Vosges, phone 4232-64-04): You've been touring the Marais of a morning and have just come from, say, Musée Victor Hugo. You're ready for lunch. At La Chope, it might consist of soupe du jour (usually a vegetable potage), a nicely grilled brace of lamb chops with frites, and a glass or carafe of the house red. With a view of the square as a bonus. *Moderate.*

Cochon d'Or (31 Rue du Jour; phone 4236-38-31) is about midway between Palais Royal and the Beaubourg, in the shadow of St.-Eustache Church. Stop in after a Beaubourg morning for a hearty—and delicious—lunch that might open with jambon persillé or a snail casserole. Filet of pork and roast lamb are indicated entrées. Very small, very friendly. *First Class.*

Coconnas (2-bis Place des Vosges; phone 4278-58-16) pleases first with its location—in a centuries-old house fronting one of the city's great squares, and with outdoor tables for warm weather—and is satisfactory, as well, when your meal arrives. The three-course menu might open with rabbit terrine, proceed with sautéed veal, and conclude with chocolate mousse. *Moderate-First Class.*

Le Coin de Caviar (62 Rue Bastille at Rue des Tournelles; phone 4272-32-39) translates—accurately—as Caviar Corner. It is just that. You're seated at pink-linen-covered tables—set against teal velvet walls—for a Russian-accented meal that, if you order à la carte, might open with the four-caviar platter. There are well-priced lunches, seafood-accented, with blinis or fish-based rillettes among openers, the day's fish as entrée, pastry or sherbet to conclude. Fun. *First Class.*

Coupe d'Or (316 Rue St.-Honoré at Rue 29 Juillet) is accorded valuable space in this book only because it typifies many modest-appearing cafés with outdoor tables where, to order anything to eat as an accompaniment to say, coffee or tea, can result in an astonishing *addition.* Two teas with two pieces of pastry and service can add up to the price of a prix-fixe lunch (admittedly for one) in an unassuming restaurant. Better to enjoy your tarte au citron as the concluding course of a meal, or purchased from a pâtisserie for consumption on the street as you move along, or in your hotel room. *First Class.*

La Cour St.-Germain (19 Rue Marbeuf, off Avenue George V near Champs-Élysées; phone 4723-84-25—with other locations at 156 Boulevard St.-Germain, phone 4726-85-49, and Gare de Lyon, phone 4343-35-48) is a good-value chain that has made its fame with a two-course *formule,* or menu, centered on a substantial entrée, usually of beef and well garnished. *Moderate.*

La Crémaillère (15 Place du Tertre, phone 4335-43-88) is a Montmartre old-timer that could, at least in the course of my most recent sampling, do with a sprucing up and a new chef. Even a standard menu embracing onion soup and bœuf bourguignon was disappointing. But service proved engaging. *Moderate/First Class.*

Le Drouot (103 Rue Richelieu, just off Boulevard des Italiens; phone 4296-68-73): There's a neon sign on the corner to guide you to the Drouot's unimpressive entrance, which leads to an equally unimpressive stairway, which you ascend, to find yourself in a noisy, cavernous, utterly unpretentious space. I don't know if this restaurant dates to the turn of the century, when Toulouse-Lautrec painted. Had it, he would surely have been on scene to record this panorama of working-class Paris. The lure is so-so bistro food (the standard is nothing like what it was a few years back) at rock-bottom prices—the lowest such of any I know in Paris. Open with céleri rémoulade, tomato or cucumber salad, a dozen snails, mayonnaise-dressed avocado, or an omelet. Your entrée might be roast chicken, choucroute garnie (which I counsel), or beef any number of ways. Cheeses are okay; so are pastries and ice cream. Ditto the house wine. Service may—or may not—be cordial. Caveat: No credit cards. *Moderate.*

La Durée (10 Rue Royale) has been baking cakes and pastries—the while creating tempting chocolates—for some nine decades. If your hotel is near Place de la Madeleine, it's ideal for a croissants-and-coffee breakfast. Later in the day, stop in for something sweeter. Attractive. *Moderate.*

L'Écluse (64 Rue François 1er, near Champs-Élysées; 15 Place de la Madeleine; and several other locations) just has to be the definitive Paris wine bar. Decor varies according to locale, but in each case tables are tight; decibel count, high; waiters, more efficient than you would dare hope, given the impression of turmoil at mealtime; and food, tasty. Bar signs identify principal wine choices; order *au verre* (by the glass), *à la bouteille* (by the bottle), or *en carafe.* Accompany with the assiette charcutière, a delicious cold meat platter; and a generous order of smoked salmon, cold roast beef, or the house's pâté. End with cheese—preferable to L'Écluse's chocolate cake. *First Class.*

Entracte Opéra (1 Rue Auber; phone 4742-26-25) is easy to pass by, hovering, as it does, in the shadow of the Opéra/Garnier. But locals working in the neighborhood patronize it with good reason: tasty food at good prices, with service on its two floors smiling and snappy. In summer, consider a range of salads and cold platters. At any time, onion soup is the indicated starter; then zero in on saucisson chaud, grilled sausages-cum-potatoes, with a coupe—or sundae—to conclude. *Moderate.*

Espadon (Ritz Hôtel, 15 Place Vendôme; phone 4260-38-39) has been a personal favorite since the occasion of a long-ago summer lunch, hosted by the late Charles Ritz, in the garden. At other seasons, Espadon occupies high-ceilinged quarters within, its arched walls the palest green and tables pink-napped, with red roses and gleaming crystal. Franco, Espadon's Italian-born director, rarely removes his eye from a vividly animated scene—tuxedoed captains and waiters and white-jacketed busmen looking after a clientele that's a marvelous mix of dark-suited Paris execs, modishly attired Parisiennes, affluent gentry in from the provinces, Ritz guests, and transient diners from around the world. It works beautifully. So, indeed, does the kitchen. Classics like foie gras, caviar, and smoked salmon are among starters—with the house's own lobster and artichoke salads as well. The Ritz has never stopped serving gratinée à l'oignon, Paris's beloved onion soup. Fish are fabulous, as for example grilled turbot in tandem with sauce Béarnaise. Red meats tempt, too—rack of lamb, tournedos, sautéed veal médaillons. Ask for the dessert cart to be wheeled to your table. If you've any interest in wine, request the full—not the abbreviated—*liste des vins;* it constitutes a course in oenology. And note that there's a multi-course menu to supplement the à la carte. *Luxury.*

Fauchon (26 Place de la Madeleine): The city's most reputed fancy-food shop is a lunchtime magnet for Parisians who pack its self-service buffet. There are hot dishes—the moussaka is as savory as it is in its native Greece—along with sandwiches, salads, the celebrated Fauchon pastries, and sublime chocolate sodas. To order: Decide what you want, pay the cashier, *then* take the cashier's receipt to present to the counter attendant in exchange for your grub. And expect crowds. *Moderate/First Class.*

La Fermette du Sud-Ouest (31 Rue Coquillière; phone 4236-73-55)—not far from Pont Neuf—charms from the moment of entry. You find yourself in a venerable stone-walled house, with blanched-wood tables set with white linen on two levels, a bar at the rear. Chef-propriétaire Jacky Mayer serves up what his restaurant's title suggests: cuisine of the southwest. You order à la carte from a limited bill of fare, opening perhaps with chunky, tarragon-accented terrine of rabbit, smoked ham, Monsieur Mayer's own terrine of foie gras frais or—exceptional, this—the stuffed-snail specialty called cassolette de petits gris charentaise. Entrées please, too; cassoulet, the bean-based casserole with southwest origins, is as good as I've had it anywhere in France. Confit de canard aux cèpes, preserved duck-cum-mushrooms—is delicious. And there are memorable pork and quail specialties, with floating island and tarte Tatin the dessert rankers, and Cahors, a southwest red, among vintages. A ranking restaurant. *First Class.*

Galeries Lafayette (Boulevard Haussmann): Lunch is invariably a pleasure at this department store. No. 1 locale is the handsome *Lafayette Grill* on the sixth floor—a proper restaurant with a well-priced menu (salad, entrée, cheese, or help-yourself dessert buffet). The same floor's *Relais des Galeries* is a good-value cafeteria. And in the separate building housing Galfa Club (the men's store) is the up-a-flight *Le Pub,* with steaks the specialty and *plats du jour,* as well. *Moderate/First Class.*

Garnier (111 Rue St.-Lazare; phone 4387-50-40): It's odd how rarely visitors venture north of Boulevard Haussmann to the Gare St.-Lazare quarter—unless they're catching a train. Garnier, just below the station, is smart, its banquettes a mix of tan leather and chrome, its staff expert and cordial, its prix-fixe menu—oysters or snails, grilled sole (or other fish) with beurre fondu or Béarnaise sauce, with dessert following—the ideal way to become acquainted with the offerings of a premier seafood house. *First Class.*

La Grande Cascade (Bois de Boulogne; phone 4506-33-51): It's a glorious day, with the sun bright and clouds billowy. Why not lunch in the park, on the terrace of this delightfully Belle Époque restaurant? Open with a refreshing salad, concentrate on tournedos or roast partridge as entrées, and end with one of the Cascade's made-on-premises sherbets. *First Class.*

Le Grand Louvre (Musée du Louvre; phone 4020-53-41) takes its name from the expanded and refurbished art museum in which it is located—at the foot of the spectacular stairway leading to the subterranean lobby from which visitors take off to inspect collections in the various wings. Look of the restaurant—priciest and most formal of the museum's eateries—is severe, albeit not unattractive, with gray walls setting off tables whose white napery is accented by bowls of orchids. Cuisine, with commendable southwest inspiration, is selected from a relatively limited choice, available as either a main course and dessert menu, or a costlier three-course prix-fixe. Smoked trout and an unusual leg of goose ballottine combined with foie gras are among openers; grilled half duck, tournedos, and lamb specialties are examples of entrées. Pavé au chocolat sauce café—a chocolate-and-coffee masterwork—is counseled to conclude, but other sweets are satisfying, too. Southwest wines—Jurançon among the whites, Cahors among the reds—are worth a try, but there are others. Even though you're in a jam-packed museum, service is smiling. And it is worth noting that this part of the Louvre (including shops) is open evenings, so that you may go for dinner as well as lunch, afternoon snacks (terrines, cheese platters, salads, ice cream) or a set afternoon tea. *First Class/Luxury.* (There are considerably less costly sources of sustenance in the Louvre, including *Cafeteria du Musée*—plats du jour self-service, with salads, hors d'œuvres, burgers or franks with frites, pastries including a mean tarte aux pommes—with the chairs at the tables copies of the metal seats you rent to sit upon in parks: *Café Richelieu,* for sandwiches, coffee, and ice cream; and *Café du Louvre,* the smallest. This aforementioned trio is *Moderate.*)

Le Grand Véfour (17 Rue Beaujolais; phone 4296-56-27): Louis XV was king when Le Grand Véfour opened in 1760. Its location then—fronting gardens at the rear of Palais-Royal—was one of the choicest in town; two centuries later, it still is. The walk across the quadrangular garden is a joy at midday or in the evening, with myriad lamps lighting the way. For long, bailiwick of the celebrated restaurateur Raymond Oliver—whose faded sign on the windows, "Sherry Cobblers, Lemon Squash, English Spoken," was an amusing put-on—the restaurant in recent seasons was acquired by the Taittinger champagne interests and exquisitely refurbished. (Alas, my only quarrel with the decor is the elimination of M. Oliver's window sign.) The menu, formerly grandly traditional, is now a happy mix of the conventional and the creative. Beneath the painted glass panels of the ceiling and from tables set with cut glass and old Limoges, you lunch or dine exceedingly well, opening with vichysoisse, mushroom-flecked poached eggs, a foie gras terrine, or escalope of salmon in aspic. Roast duck or tournedos—among traditional entrées—are super, but there are contemporary veal and sweetbread dishes that go down very well, indeed. Conclude with either hot apricot tart or chocolate mousse. *Luxury.*

La Guirlande de Julie (25 Place des Vosges; phone 4887-94-07) is indicated for midday sustenance in the course of Marais exploration. The three-course menu—which includes wine—is good value and features an unusual duck ragoût among entrées, another of which is a tasty filet de bœuf. Attractive. *First Class.*

Hippopotamus (Boulevard des Italiens et Rue Louis-le-Grand; Avenue Franklin-Roosevelt near Champs-Élysées; Place de la Bastille at Rue Bastille, other locations) is an estimable chain whose success is based on attractive interiors, efficient and sometimes even smiling service (a plus considering the crowds), and well-priced steaks, lamb and pork chops appropriately sauced (Béarnaise with the beef), and accompanied by good-sized portions of frites, and, extra of course, inexpensive wines. *Moderate.*

L'Incroyable (26 Rue de Richelieu; phone 4296-24-64) is, indeed—to translate its title—unbelievable, or at least its prices seem so, for what you get: a three-course menu that might run to soup or escalope of veal or grilled pork chop, nicely garnished, as well as cheese or pastry. Just east of Avenue de l'Opéra. *Moderate.*

Juvenile's (47 Rue de Richelieu; phone 4297-46-49)—on a street extending from Avenue de l'Opéra is nothing if not memorably titled. Its game is wine by the glass in copious variety, with minimum-tabbed labels inexpensive, substantial sandwiches, steak especially, to accompany. If your wine is among the less costly: *Moderate.*

Lasserre (17 Avenue Franklin-Roosevelt; phone 4359-53-43): Time was, not so many seasons back, that when you wanted to dine at this gala and gorgeous spot, you picked up the phone and booked a day or two ahead. Recent seasons have seen the matter of booking become so complex and long-range that one wonders if it's worth it; there are, after all, countless outstanding restaurants in Paris, most of them considerably less pricey than Lasserre and willing to let you pay for a high-priced meal with a credit card. That is not the case here. Should you be among the chosen, you'll be impressed by the show, although the attitude toward foreigners, in my experience, can be patronizing and the atmosphere distinctly chilling. Setting is a sumptuous town house. You have a drink in one of the ground-floor lounges. When the table is ready, poof! You're escorted upstairs to the dining room, whose roof—in summer at least—slides open to reveal the heavens. Food can be anticlimactic after all of this splendidly staged drama. Which is not to say it is not creditable; such classic standbys as foie gras, rich terrines, grilled lobster, and game birds are elaborately prepared. Remember now, have a wad of franc notes or traveler's checks; no credit cards. *Luxury.*

La Main à la Pâte (35 Rue St.-Honoré; phone 4236-64-73): French cuisine is so masterful, distinguished, and distinctive that when foreign-cuisine restaurants open in the French capital, like it or not, they tend to take on Gallic characteristics, whereas in other countries—America and Britain, for example—they retain the flavor of their country of origin. La Main à la Pâte was recommended to me by an Italian who really knows both his own and French cuisine—Franco, the director of L'Espadon in the Ritz Hotel. If you forget the decor—the restaurant proper is a flight up from a street-level bar and is an outrageously corny, and plastic, reproduction of a massive grape arbor—you can be reasonably content here. Despite French headings on the menu and translations into French of Italian dishes (not considered necessary in Italian restaurants of the major American and British cities), fare is reasonably authentic. You do okay with pasta, cannelloni, and lasagne through agnolotti and maccheroni quattro formaggi. Osso bucco is creditable, as can be veal chops variously prepared. And note that prices are surprisingly high. *Luxury.*

Marriott Prince de Galles Hôtel Restaurant (33 Avenue George V; phone 3723-55-11)—though no less elegant than the handsome hotel (see Settling In, above) in which it is situated, and with summer service in the hotel's courtyard—is the venue of an exceptionally well-priced menu. It's available at dinner only (expense-account execs fill the restaurant midday). The meal might open with the egg masterwork from the southwest called piperade, feature roast loin of lamb, herb-scented, as an entrée, completing the meal with the dessert you choose from a trolley wheeled to table. Super service. At any time other than dinner with this menu (which is *First Class*), the Marriott's restaurant is *Luxury.*

Maxim's (3 Rue Royale; phone 4265-27-94) is hardly without attributes. Staying power is No. 1; it goes back to the turn of the century when *Le Tout Paris* populated it. Decor is No. 2; its original Art Nouveau environment—splendidly carved wood, elegant brass, superb stained glass, richly hued paintings—is so special that the French government has declared it a protected historic site. No. 3 is the enormous staff—by and large (forgetting the occasional lemon), cordial and fluent in English. Fare—stubbornly classic style, albeit with contemporary options—can be competent but, in my experience, hardly more so than that of any number of *brasseries* that are similarly aged (see Flo and Vaudeville, Right Bank, above, and Lutétia, Left, below), albeit with tabs easily a third that of Maxim's. Still, if the present *patron*, Pierre Cardin, should invite you to be his guest for, say, a meal embracing terrine de canard, médaillons de veau, pommes Maxim's and tarte Tatin—when he's not off opening a clone-Maxim's in such unlikely spots as Peking, Mexico City, or Singapore (not to mention Manhattan's Madison Avenue)—well, of course, accept. If you're on your own, though, note that those bottles of champagne in ice-filled buckets, on each table, are for sale; they're not offered with Pierre's compliments. Though à la carte only, like dinner, lunch is somewhat less costly. *Luxury.*

La Mère Catherine (6 Place du Tertre; phone 4606-37-69), a Montmartre institution for generations, shows no sign of slacking. It remains a congenial locale for a dinner up on the hill. A pastis in the forward room—all red-and-white-checked cloths and lampshades—is for premeal. Dinner out back is served to musical accompaniment and embraces an unchanging menu: appetizer, chicken or steak, cheese, dessert, and wine. *First Class.*

Monoprix (21 Avenue d l'Opéra): The up-a-flight eatery of this outlet of the nationwide budget-price department-store chain is a good bet for lunch on the run. (And note that the *Monoprix* on Boulevard Haussmann—tucked into the facade of Galeries Lafayette, the department store whose management owns both chains—has a main-floor take-away counter that's convenient when you're hungry and on the run, featuring satisfactory sandwiches and cold drinks. *Moderate.*

Le Moulin du Village (Cité Berryer—a tiny street tucked between Rue Royale and Rue Boissy d'Anglas, just off Rue du Faubourg St.-Honoré; phone 4265-08-47) is a neat little exercise in white, with walls and linen of that hue set off by good contemporary art, and tables surrounded by bentwood chairs. There's a cozy bar at the entrance (the restaurant is operated by wine importers who also operate the Blue Fox wine bar in the next building) and a tasty three-course menu, which might open with the day's potage (soup au pistou is good) or mushroom-stuffed ravioli, with such entrées as braised beef accompanied by Yorkshire pudding (the latter is a manifestation of the propriétaires' British origins); and a choice of sweets to conclude. If one of the bosses is on hand and you're a wine buff, talk over the interesting cellar before ordering your bottle. *First Class.*

Mövenpick (12 Boulevard de la Madeleine; phone 4742-47-93) is accorded space here only because it's traditionally open until midnight, and because you may have encountered outlets of this chain in Switzerland, its nation of origin, as have I, with satisfaction. The Paris version is something else again: a garish succession of connected basement spaces that makes an attempt at standard dishes like chicken, steak, and paillard de veau, without success. Environment and fare are coffee-shop caliber, albeit with steepish tabs and service that can be disagreeable. *First Class.*

Musée Picasso Café (5 Rue de Thorigny) is no less handsome than the museum (above) of which it is a part. Look is smartly severe—white walls hung with framed museum posters, black-metal tables and chairs. You may go for as little as a cup of coffee or a glass of wine. But the food is good enough to consider starting—or concluding—your museum visit with a lunch that might embrace a seafood terrine or the day's soup; a hot spinach, chicken, ham, or chicken-liver tart, or the day's meat entrée; and pastry or cheese. Service is swift and smiling. *Moderate.*

Les Noces de Jeannette (14 Rue Favert; phone 4296-36-89) teams up well with a performance at the just-opposite Opéra Comique. This is an upstairs spot with somewhat excessive Second Empire décor. It's popular with groups and has reliable fare—coquilles St.-Jacques or a pot of rillettes (pork pâté) to begin, a chicken entrée or steak marchand de vin following, served as part of a prix-fixe menu that is sound value. *First Class.*

L'Obélisque (Crillon Hôtel, 10 Place de la Concorde, with its own entrance on Rue Boissy d'Anglas; phone 4265-24-24) is the less expensive—and more recent—of the Crillon's restaurant pair. This is a snappy grill room, all red velvet chairs and Lalique-like chandeliers, with wines offered by the glass or bottle and delicious comestibles, the lot of them speedily—and cheerily—served; the range salads and omelets, pasta and *poisson* (there's always a fish of the day), smoked salmon and steak, with gratin Dauphinois the potato specialty, a super cheese board, and luscious desserts. Lots of locals and staff members from the next-door American Embassy are regulars. *First Class.*

L'Œuf à la Neige (16 Rue Salneuve; phone 4763-45-43) is, in a word, Alsace transported—gastronomically, at least—to the Arc de Triomphe. There are lovely things to eat here, as you may remember them from Strasbourg. By that I mean a meal that might embrace a savory hot tarte to commence, bäckoffe—an Alsatian masterwork with a preserved-duck base—or the pork entrée known as pâté Lorrain; and rich desserts to conclude. And of course there are Alsatian whites in the cellar. The prix-fixe is good value. *First Class.*

Opéra (Le Grand Hôtel, 2 Rue Scribe; phone 4268-12-13) is so overshadowed in the public mind by the same hotel's historic Café de la Paix (above) that its premium restaurant—beautifully paneled and chandeliered, with a crackerjack kitchen and serving staff—is perhaps the least appreciated of the important hotel restaurants. Pity, this. You want to book for a dinner that might embrace the best vichyssoise in town or smoked Norwegian salmon served with Russian blinis, roast lamb, the house's chicken-breast specialty, with poached pears in a Poire William-flavored sabayon sauce as a festive finale. *Luxury.*

Opéra de Paris/Bastille (Place de la Bastille): Because it's relatively new, I make mention at this point of the stand-up bars at this sleekly contemporary theater (see After Dark, above) should you wonder if you may have something to eat before or during the performance. Of course, the answer is in the affirmative: rather skimpy sandwiches at prices less expensive than you might expect for the republic's most talked-about theater. Coke, Perrier, wine, and champagne by the glass. Fare and facilities are similar at *Opéra de Paris/Garnier* (Place de l'Opéra). *Moderate/First Class.*

Patachou (9 Place du Tertre; phone 4251-06-06): A smart and stylish restaurant in tourist-trod Montmartre? Don't fight it. Relatively recently installed Patachou—despite its location on a square packed with vendors of souvenirs being grabbed up by mostly German customers—is a class act. Its principal space, tile-floored and furnished in Louis XV style, has three walls of paneled wood, with the fourth—overlooking Paris below and beyond to the Eiffel and Montparnasse towers—a massive pane of glass. And just beneath it is a capacious terrace, an enviable spot for a warm-weather lunch or dinner. Go at midday for the good-value menu, based on the day's catch, nicely prepared poultry or a meat entrée, with ice cream or pastry (a specialty here) as dessert. *First Class.*

Paul (15 Place Dauphine with another entrance at 52 Quai des Orfèvres; phone 4354-21-48) lies in the shadow of Paris's Palais de Justice on a quiet square—the site of its front door; its back door is on a quai edging the Seine. Locals are bowling on the green as you enter for a meal—everything is à la carte—that might open with a tomato salad dressed with a perfect vinaigrette or a platter of super sausages that go well with the house's excellent bread. The plat du jour may or may not please (sautéed veal chop, for example, can disappoint) but always-available roast chicken is a winner. *First Class.*

Le Petit Ramoneur (74 Rue St.-Denis; phone 4236-39-24) has the solitary Tour St.-Jacques, edging the Seine, as its nearest landmark. Lamb, with France's (and my) beloved flageolet beans, and beef are among entrées on the bargain-tabbed menu, which includes half a carafe of wine and pastry. Expect crowds. *Moderate.*

Pharamond (24 Rue de la Grande Truanderie; phone 4233-06-72)—in a house of yore that exudes ambience, near Le Beaubourg—is a touch of Normandy in the capital. You may not want to go so far as to order the Norman standby, tripe à la mode de Caen, but there are such satisfactory dishes as duck terrine and marinated salmon salad, scallops prepared with Norman cider, filet of veal in a rich sauce, and roast lamb. Pear charlotte, bathed in raspberry sauce, is the indicated sweet. *First Class.*

Pierre Traiteur (10 Rue de Richelieu; phone 4296-09-17; a hop and a skip from Palais-Royal) is intimate in scale, unspectacular—paintings of no special discipline punctuate pinky-buff walls—and staffed by a team of congenial waitresses uniformed in neat black and white. The menu is limited, but everything I have tasted is commendable. Starters include asparagus sauce mousseline, poached eggs in a piquant sauce, or a delicious soup à l'ail glacée, which is Pierre's answer to Spain's gazpacho. Steak au poivre and gigot d'agneau are favored entrées, and, in all events, you must order the house's potato winner, gratin Dauphinois. Baked-on-premises fresh grapefruit tart is, to understate, unforgettable. *First Class.*

La Poularde Landaise (4 Rue St.-Philippe-du-Roulle; phone 4359-20-25) is a charming spot between Champs-Élysées and Boulevard Haussmann, with a homely, chintzy look and kind waitresses in attendance. Specialties are of the southwest—confit de canard (preserved roast duck) especially. It's served with sautéed potatoes and a salad, but it is not, I caution you, as good as you'll get in the area of origin. *First Class.*

Printemps (Boulevard Haussmann, diagonally to the east of the Opéra/Garnier), one of the preeminent department stores, is a spectacular setting for lunch, thanks to the situation of its complex of eateries—restaurant, grill, *salon de thé*—on the sixth floor of its Nouveau Magasin building (one of a trio that's closest to the Opéra), beneath an absolutely fabulous (and immense) stained-glass dome. *Moderate.*

Relais Capucines (Le Grand Hôtel, Place de l'Opéra entrance; phone 4268-12-13) is the often neglected restaurant section of the Grand's celebrated Café de la Paix (above). It's a Belle Époque space adjacent to the outer café, with an extensive brasserie menu; the range from oysters, soups, fish, and meat entrées to cold plates, hamburgers, and a selection of coupes, or sundaes; not to mention a half-dozen changed-daily *plats du jour. Moderate/First Class.*

Le Roi du Pot au Feu (34 Rue Vignon; phone 4742-37-10): Any number of national cuisines have a boiled beef dish in star position. None surpasses France's pot au feu, a soup that's a meal (or vice versa). In this restaurant, which translates as King of Pot au Feu, it's the specialty you want to order—nicely served at tables laid with red-checked cloths, in an agreeable setting not far from the Madeleine. But there are other options on the à la carte, roast chicken and grilled steak among them. *Moderate/First Class.*

La Samaritaine (Rue du Pont Neuf, between Rue de Rivoli and Quai du Louvre) is a multibuilding, budget department store that has put its riverfront location to good use with *Restaurant Terrasse* on the tenth floor of Building No. 1. Lures are cold-plate lunches offered in combination with truly spectacular vistas of Paris. *Moderate.*

Self-Tuileries (205 Rue de Rivoli, east of the Meurice Hôtel) is a long-on-scene cafeteria, adequate for a snack or casual meal on the run. No credit cards. *Moderate.*

La Table de Jeannette (12 Rue Duphot, entered through a courtyard just south of Place de la Madeleine; phone 4260-05-64) is comfortably Louis XIII in look—brass chandeliers, wood-burning fireplace that's put to use in winter, draperies matching the upholstery of high-back chairs surrounding generously spaced tables. Perfectly delicious food comes served on Haviland Limoges porcelain. The rich cuisine of the southwest is the name of Madame Jeannette's game. And she plays it well. Build your meal around entrées either of confit de canard accompanied by pommes Sarladaise or an authentically hearty cassoulet, making sure you conclude with the apple tart, doused with crème fraîche. *First Class.*

Taillevent (15 Rue Lamennais; phone 4563-39-94) has had so much praise quite literally heaped upon it in recent years that prospective customers must set to work weeks in advance to gain entry, only to have to lay out considerable cash (or traveler's checks) for the privilege. When innumerable other restaurants of good repute are so glad of one's credit-card business, it's questionable if the effort is worthwhile. In a setting of oak-paneled walls, crystal chandeliers, and caned Louis XVI chairs, the ambience, to be sure, is engaging. Food is taken very seriously, indeed, and there's no denying that service can be impeccable, with the menu a meld of contemporary and traditional. A Taillevent lunch or dinner might embrace foie gras or truffled seafood sausage, a guinea-hen pot-au-feu, and a dessert representing the handiwork of the house's *pâtissier. Luxury.*

Tartempion (15-bis Rue du Mont-Denis; phone 4606-10-40) is an agreeable alternative to La Mère Catherine (above) for a Montmartre meal. Setting is a charming old house; lure is a well-priced menu based on beef and poultry entrées. *Moderate.*

Terrasse Fleurie (Inter-Continental Paris Hôtel, 3 Rue de Castiglione; phone 4260-37-80) is a pavilion sheathed in glass—the better to take in the playing fountain and greenery of the Inter-Continental's splendid courtyard—that's become one of the smartest—and tastiest—restaurants in town. There is an extensive à la carte at both lunch and dinner, with caviar and crayfish among hors-d'œuvre, filet of sole and pan-fried char among fish, Aberdeen Angus beef and breast of pigeon among meats, wild strawberry soufflé among sweets. And there is, as well, an excellent five-course-and-coffee menu, which might run to a salad embracing foie gras, string beans, shallots and mushrooms, or bisque de homard; filet of beef or champagne-sauced sweetbreads; a selection of cheeses from an enormous tray and a likewise generous choice of sweets from a chariot wheeled to table; with coffee to conclude. Wines are from a ranker of a cellar (Inter-Continental knows its vintages). And service is at once congenial and professional. *Luxury.*

Le Train Bleu (Gare de Lyon; phone 4343-09-06): Wow! That's what you say when you climb the steep flight from Gare de Lyon's main floor to this turn-of-century restaurant that is surely among the great Belle Époque environments in the republic. A series of ravishing circular murals, framed in heavy gold, embellish the ceiling. Additional paintings are embedded in the walls, elaborate frames setting them off. You are not surprised to learn that it was the president of France who inaugurated this restaurant in 1901, nor that it is still going strong. Start with potage cressonière or smoked filet of mackerel and continue with gigot d'agneau, duckling à l'orange, or braised Provençal beef. Don't skip the cheese platter, nor, for that matter, a fruit tart to conclude. And turn the menu over; an excellent wine list is on the reverse. *First Class.*

Le Vieil Écu (166 Rue St.-Honoré, phone 4260-20-14): There are times, in Paris as elsewhere, where that old bromide—You Get What You Pay For—holds true. Le Vieil Écu is a case in point. It packs in neighborhood workers seeking a filling lunch bargain-tabbed. And if you get a table—even with a reservation—on one of the two nondescript floors, consider yourself lucky and make an effort to command the cheaper of the two menus, grateful for a reasonably competant meal of the day's soup, steak/frites, a wedge of cheese, or a simple sweet. Service is neither kind nor smiling. I can't recommend this one. *Moderate.*

SELECTED RIVE GAUCHE/LEFT BANK AND ÎLE ST.-LOUIS RESTAURANTS AND CAFÉS

Allard (41 Rue St.-André-des-Arts, off Place St.-Michel; phone 4326-48-23) is an old-timer with staying power. The look is Congested Quartier Latin; you enter a cramped barroom; there are low-ceilinged dining rooms on either side, with tables at close quarters. Old-school waiters are gracious. Fare is unpretentious—Paris bistro cooking at its delicious best, including the casserole that is cassoulet, an estimable coq au vin, a masterfully prepared gigot d'agneau aux flageolets, beef and lamb stews. What you start off with—terrine de canard, escargots, salade de concombre, or radishes with butter—is excellent, too. Desserts are few but satisfying, with tarte aux fraises and fresh orange salad as house specialties. *First Class.*

L'Assiette au Beurre (34 Rue St.-Benoît; phone 4222-49-76) is at once atmospheric and delicious—a salute to the glory of the turn-of-the-century Art Nouveau period—with a loyal following. There's a reasonably priced menu centered on such entrées as côtes d'agneau (lamb chops) and maigret de canard (duck breasts), with profiteroles au chocolat a favored dessert. *First Class.*

Auberge Comtoise (a.k.a. Le Chevert, 34 Rue Chevert; phone 4705-51-09): Talk about silk purses from sow's ears. I was, in the course of a recent Paris visit, staying at a hotel in the École Militaire quarter, with which I was not at all happy. In the course of an evening walk, though, I came upon Auberge Comtoise, unpretentious and unassuming, but heartily welcoming—and with utterly delicious specialties from the Jura mountains of the Franche-Comté region of the northeast. Madame Laroche, who served as hostess and sole waitress of this small establishment, insisted that she would soon retire. I hope she has been dissuaded by her partners (her husband and son), but even if she kept to her promise, you want to have a meal, selecting from the well-priced menu. Open with either the day's soup (hope that it will be puréed vegetable served with grated cheese) or a platter of sausages. The chicken casserole, or gratin volaille, served with rice—is tasty, but so are the grilled sausages, presented in tandem with lentils. Conclude with either cheese or one of the made-on-premises desserts, gâteau comtois or apple charlotte buried under apricot sauce. And if it's not too late, stay on for a digestif of marc de Jura—clear-as-crystal firewater imported from the mountains. *Moderate.*

Au Gourmet de l'Île (42 Rue St.-Louis-en-l'Île; phone 4326-79-27) occupies ancient quarters on the pretty island to the rear of Notre-Dame and operates a first-rate kitchen. Pâté or stuffed mussels are ideal starters. Entrées are specialties of the Auvergne region—chicken with lentils, for example. You may order à la carte, but the menu is a better bet. *Moderate.*

Au Monde des Chimères (69 Rue St.-Louis-en-l'Île, Île St.-Louis; phone 4354-45-27): There are, to be sure, better-value, lower-priced, albeit satisfactory restaurants on this Restaurant Row of a thoroughfare. But Madame Ibane runs her restaurant well. There's good modern art on the stone and brick walls and service is cordial. Go at dinner and you order from the à la carte, starting perhaps with œufs meurettes, wine-sauced as you remember them with pleasure from Burgundy, or leeks vinaigrette. Garlicky chicken and braised veal are entrée specialties—and tasty. Warm apple tart is indicated as a sweet. And you do well with a carafe of the house red. *First Class.*

Au Quai d'Orsay (49 Quai-d'Orsay; phone 4551-58-58) is convenient to Les Invalides and Tour Eiffel, not to mention the Foreign Ministry. Snag a window table and you've views—through starched lace curtains—of Pont Alexandre and the Grand Palais across the Seine. Quai-d'Orsay is a compact maze of shiny black banquettes that complement tables so tightly packed that you are very close to being in your neighbor's lap. The resulting discomfort is of the kind you put up with in a budget eatery with good grub. But here, hoity-toity serving staff notwithstanding, the seafood soup and capon galantine are okay, if unexceptional, and the cassoulet aux trois viandes, while adequate, does not do justice to this southwest specialty. All told, in my view, overpriced. *Luxury.*

La Belle France (Tour Eiffel, first floor; phone 4555-20-04): I like the name—France is indeed beautiful. I like the Eiffel Tower. And I like the Jules Verne Restaurant, up a level, and evaluated in a later paragraph. But this place, in my experience at least, is disappointing, with neither the traditional fare nor the service commendable. I can't recommend it. *Moderate/First Class.*

Bistrot de Paris (33 Rue de Lille; phone 4261-16-83) is the bourgeois bistro at its smartest, most convivial, and most delicious, with such stick-to-the-ribs dishes as coarse and tasty house pâtés, among starters; entrées like sauté de veau à l'estragon and bœuf Bourguignon. Desserts run to favorites like apple tart and chocolate mousse. *First Class.*

Blanc (26 Avenue de Tourville; phone 4421-38-82) is a sensible choice for a sensibly priced lunch when you're in the neighborhood of the Eiffel Tower; there's a wide variety of set menus, both midday and at dinner. Plain in look, but welcoming. *Moderate.*

Les Bouquinistes (53 Quai des Grands Augustins; phone 4325-45-91) takes its name from the book-, print-, and old-postcard-sellers' stalls across the road, flanking the Seine. This is a smallish restaurant, with a light, bright look, paper cloths on its tables, and two good-value menus, the least costly of which might open with the house's terrine or avocado salad, to be followed by gigot d'agneau, or roast lamb, served with the super potato casserole, gratin Dauphinois. Nice. *First Class.*

Brasserie Lipp (151 Boulevard St.-Germain; phone 4548-53-91) has been a Quartier Latin institution these many years. The fin-de-siècle interior, with superb stained and cut glass and dark woods, is among the more engaging in Paris. Fare is Alsatian. Not surprisingly, choucroute garnie is No. 1 entrée. But consider also the specially prepared Baltic herring, pigs' feet, and sweetbreads, ending with tarte maison. No credit cards. *First Class.*

Brasserie Lutétia (Lutétia Hôtel, 45 Boulevard Raspail; phone 4544-38-10): I don't know of a hotel restaurant in town with a larger proportion of neighborhood regulars among its clientele. Big and bright and humming, it works like a charm. By that, I mean the food is as satisfying as the service is kindly and swift. The menu, or *formule,* embraces thyme-scented gigot (roast lamb) garnished and served with a salad, wine or beer, and coffee. But the à la carte is extensive—omelets and terrines, snails and soups, with such entrées as coq au vin, châteaubriand, and steak tartare. And the chocolate mousse is justifiably celebrated. *First Class.*

Cafés: The Left Bank's best-known are *Café des Deux Magots* (170 Boulevard St.-Germain) and *Café de Flore* (172 Boulevard St.-Germain): They're always packed with visitors as well as Quartier Latin types, but they are considerably costlier than nearby but less-celebrated spots, as for example *Café Rouquet* (Boulevard St.-Germain at Rue des Sts.-Pères)—where a coffee is less than half the price than at the Big Two, a few blocks distant on the same boulevard. *Café-Select-Latin* (Boulevard St.-Michel at Rue des Écoles) is ideal for observation of the Sorbonne student populace, while *Café Quartier Latin* (6 Place Edmond Rostand) offers a fine view of the Jardins de Luxembourg. *Café Notre Dame* (Rue la Grange at Parc la

Grange) affords breathtaking views of Notre-Dame Cathedral from its outdoor tables. Beyond, in Montparnasse, position yourself at *Café la Coupole* (Boulevard Montparnasse at Boulevard Raspail, below recommended as a restaurant, and *First Class*.) All of the other cafés in this paragraph are *Moderate.*

La Cagouille (10 Place Constantin Brancusi; phone 4322-09-01)—a near neighbor of Tour Montparnasse, just up Avenue de Maine—makes a specialty of seafood: tuna salad (not often encountered in France and not at all like U.S. counterparts) and assorted mollusk openers, premium-species fish as entrées, including red mullet, sole, and turbot, as well as less well known types that may be unfamiliar to you and that are grilled, sautéed, poached, or otherwise prepared. Not surprisingly, there's a copious selection of well-chosen white wines. *First Class.*

Chez Dumonet (117 Rue du Cherche-Midi; phone 4222-81-19) is unpretentiously traditional, with a menu to match. This is a honey of a Montparnasse dinner spot. Consider a meal that might consist of salade paysanne; entrecôte grilled on an open wood fire and served with the potato masterwork, gratin Dauphinois; and crème caramel or poire belle Hélène to conclude. *First Class.*

Chez Maître Paul (12 Rue Monsieur le Prince; phone 4354-74-59) is located on a not-necessarily-easy-to-find little street near Place de l'Odéon and the theater taking its name. It's a tiny, neat-as-a-pin place, with Monsieur Gaugain the expert chef, Madame Gaugain the charming hostess, service expert, and fare perfectly delicious. I counsel starting with snails, opting for one of several chicken entrées, entrecôte, or veal chop. They come with tasty pommes Pont-Neuf and a well-dressed salad. *First Class.*

Chez Toutoune (5 Rue de Pointoise; phone 4326-56-81) is an ever-reliable bistro on a street near the Seine, with a popular three-course menu that might open with the day's soup or salad, preserved (confit) goose or duck, or a roast, with the fruit flans the favored sweets. Friendly. *Moderate.*

Christian Constant (26 Rue du Bac) is an inviting salon de thé, white-walled with brocaded chairs, that is indicated for a midafternoon break of, say, a pot of tea (you choose the type of leaf) with delicious pastry in tandem. Near the Seine. *Moderate.*

La Coupole (102 Boulevard Montparnasse; phone 4320-14-20)—closed for several years after it was purchased by the man who might well be termed Roi des Brasseries, Jean-Paul Bucher, a one-time Maxim's chef—reemerged as the most spectacular of its genre in town. As well it might; M. Bucher is reported to have spent $10 million to buy the place and $3 million to refurbish it, carefully preserving the Art Deco ambience of its 600-seat, 60-year-old interior, whose chefs-d'œuvre are 32 pillars painted by a clutch of artist-customers—as payment for meals—in the early years. Named for its great beige dome, La Coupole has again become the Montparnasse landmark it was in its initial heyday. Go for a mug of beer (à la pression), a sausage- and potato-topped plate of sauerkraut (choucroute garnie), oysters, onion soup, or for that matter, a prix-fixe meal (there's a whopping six-course menu) with wines from an extensive list and lighter modern dishes to complement the classics. M. Bucher's other brasseries include Vaudeville and Flo (Right Bank Restaurants, above) but La Coupole is one of a kind. *First Class.*

Le Divellec (107 Rue de l'Université; phone 4551-91-96)—named for its congenial and talented chef-propriétaire—looks as good as it tastes. On a street running parallel with the Seine, near the Assemblée Nationale at Pont Alexandre III, it embraces a stylish mix of blue-upholstered Louis XV chairs set against walls of the same hue, with tables set in pink linen complemented by bowls of red roses. A native of Brittany, M. Divellec is as expert at preparing fish and shellfish as at creating sauces to accompany his fruits de mer. Time to go is midday, when there are a pair of set menus. Pricier of the two might open with an amusing-tasting platter of half a dozen house specialties, continue with saffron-sauced mussels or cassolette of oysters, basil-flavored, with a choice of the day's fish specials—again, superbly sauced—as entrées, and pastries from a *chariot* wheeled to table. The à la carte represents seafood in Paris at its most sublime—half a dozen kinds of oysters, lobster salad, and caviar among openers; fish soup à la rouille as you remember it from the Midi, but Spain's chilled gazpacho as well; and such fish as St. Pierre, salmon, and sole prepared as you direct. The cellar is first-rate and so are the waiters. Member, Relais et Châteaux. *Luxury.*

Dodin Bouffant (25 Rue Frédéric Sauton; phone 4325-25-14) is here accorded precious space only because its name is known to transatlantic visitors. Alas, success seems to have had a not very pleasant effect. A recent lunch was a disappointment—grim service throughout, a hot soup served cold; flat, overchilled rillettes, bland poularde de Bresse, the lot served in the company of an oddly unprepossessing clientele. *First Class.*

La Ferme St.-Germain (5 Rue du Dragon; phone 4548-94-40)—on a restaurant-dotted street leading from Boulevard St.-Germain—has an agreeable bistro look, and offers an agreeably priced menu with a choice of openers (salads are good here) and such entrées as poulet sauté, a tasty chicken dish. Wines are reasonable. *Moderate.*

Les Fous de l'Île (39 Rue des Deux Ponts, Île St.-Louis; phone 4325-76-67): Brunch is a transatlantic creation that still has not found substantial favor in France, but Les Fous is an exception. Go Sunday morning for a menu that opens with nothing less than a Yank-style Bloody Mary and features scrambled eggs among entrées. Of course, you may opt for more conventional lunches and dinners as well. *Moderate.*

La Grosse Horloge (22 Rue St.-Benoît; phone 4548-28-12) comes close to being the prototypical Rive Gauche bistro. By that I mean you go for a convivial dinner with good friends, sticking to hearty standbys. If it's the season, begin with asperges sauce mousseline (I have had neither the vegetables nor the sauce any better prepared) and continue with steak-frites accompanied by a big *pichet* of the house red; fruit tarts are indicated for dessert. *First Class.*

L'Îlot Vaché (35 Rue St.-Louis-en-l'Île, Île St.-Louis; phone 4633-55-16) is atmospherically stone-walled, with tables nicely set off in white linen and a tasty menu that might commence with the house's own crêpes or a chicken terrine, preparatory to châteaubriand accompanied by sauce Béarnaise (my favorite) or grilled shoulder of lamb, with cheese or sweets as finales. *Moderate.*

Jardin de la Mouff (75 Rue Mouffetard, near the Panthéon; phone 4326-56-31) offers lunchers or diners a picture-window view of its neat rear garden and a value-packed set menu, with a choice of seven hors-d'œuvres and the same number of entrées. And everything that I've tried tastes good. *Moderate.*

Les Jardins de St.-Germain (14 Rue du Dragon; phone 4544-72-82) is a reliable budget eatery. The lower priced of two menus starts you off with a salad or duck mousse, preparatory to an entrée of sole meunière, sautéed chicken, or entrecôte. Busy at dinner. *Moderate.*

Jules Verne (Tour Eiffel, second floor; phone 4555-20-04): You want to book in advance for this one, and, when you approach the tower, look for signs that will direct you to its Pilier Sud, or South Column. There you'll find the restaurant's private elevator. Its attendant phones up to confirm your reservation and then whisks you to a sleek, gray, black, and white environment, picture-windowed, which is, in my view, the single best-looking example of modern interior design that I have come upon in France. It carries through to the glassware (black-stemmed), porcelain (black and white), soap in the washrooms (in black plastic boxes), and silk flowers on the tables (black-stemmed in black vases). Not surprisingly, staff is in tuxedos. The meal you'll be served from an extensive à la carte is contemporary accented, but hearty and tasty. Start with mussel soup, puff-pastry topped (considering also smoked salmon, lobster salad, duck terrine, or half a dozen oysters). Entrées run a wide gamut—filet of salmon, filet of beef, a chicken-crayfish stew, and a delicious veal specialty, tomato- and basil-flavored. Desserts are spectacular to look upon—and taste. I counsel accurately named Le Grand Dessert Jules Verne. Lovely service. (And with a bonus: If your meal has been lunch, walk down a flight to the bottom observation deck; you won't be charged the usual admission.) *Luxury.*

Lapérouse (51 Quai des Grands Augustins; phone 4326-68-04) is an old-timer occupying a handsome house of considerable vintage on a Seine-view street. It has had ups and downs over the years that I have known it. The same people who operate Bofinger (above) with style and skill are now its proprietors, and they do it proud. Smartly refurbished, this is among the city's better-looking restaurants. Up you go from the street-floor bar to a table on either of two higher levels, preferably one at a window allowing for a vista of the river. Fare is not without contemporary touches, but remains essentially traditional. The three-course menu includes such luxurious first courses as foie gras de canard naturel or an herb-accented smoked salmon. Entrées run to inventively prepared fish or the duck-breast favorite, magret de canard. You skip profiteroles au chocolat for dessert at your peril. Wines are first-rate, service professional and polite. *First Class.*

Lous Landès (157 Avenue du Maine, Montparnasse; phone 4543-08-04) makes a specialty of southwest cuisine. Open your meal with coupe de garbure, which could be an entire meal, if you let it. The cassoulet is one of the best in Paris. For dessert: tourtière—a meld of puff pastry, prunes, and Armagnac. Gracious service. *Luxury.*

Les Ministères (30 Rue du Bac; phone 4261-22-37) sports a delightful turn-of-century ambience on a street close to Boulevard St.-Germain, core of Quartier Latin. Best buy is the lower-priced of two lunchtime menus, with œuf en gelée or the house's own terrine as appetizers, and brochette of lamb as entrée. But the à la carte is extensive, with côte de bœuf and escalope de veau—Normandy-style veal—among specialties. The menu is *Moderate;* otherwise, *First Class.*

Musée d'Orsay Restaurant (Rue de Bellechasse; phone 4549-42-33) opened as a dining room of the hotel that had for long been an appendage of the old Gare d'Orsay before it became one of Paris's most popular museums. Be grateful to the museum's architects for leaving this spectacular Belle Époque interior intact. Gilded and sculpted and frescoed and high-ceilinged, this is one of the city's memorable interiors. Best buy is the utterly delicious buffet, at which you help yourself to assorted cold comestibles, salads, and sliced meats that will tide you through the afternoon, especially when taken in tandem with a glass of house wine and the good bread that accompanies. *Caveat:* only one trip to the buffet is allowed; pile your plate high. The restaurant is on the museum's middle level and is *First Class.* (Note, too, that there's a smartly styled, less pricey café on the upper level, with views memorable and tabs. *Moderate.)*

Le Petit Boulé (16 Avenue de la Motte-Piquet; phone 4551-77-48) is an especially appealing salon de thé. You're served on any number of patterns of antique porcelain, the cakes are delicious, the neighborhood regulars at surrounding tables loquacious (the quartier is that surrounding École Militaire), and there are a few outdoor tables. *Moderate.*

La Petite Chaise (36 Rue de Grenelle; phone 4222-33-84; near Boulevard St.-Germain) occupies two floors of a seventeenth-century house. Look is brocaded walls, brass chandeliers, paintings in original frames. Lure is one of the best set menus in town, both as regards taste and price. Entrecôte aux frites, for example, is first rate. *Moderate.*

Le Petit Zinc (25 Rue de Buci; phone 4354-79-34) is a good bet for a mid-category seafood repast, opening with oysters on the half shell or deliciously stuffed mussels, with any of a number of fish entrées, simply grilled or prepared house-style. This is a busy spot, but for that reason can be amusing. Near Boulevard St.-Germain. *First Class.*

Le Port Saint-Germain (155 Boulevard St.-Germain; phone 4548-22-66)—stucco-walled, with a beamed ceiling—is indicated for a reasonably priced seafood repast, with assorted mollusks served on stilted platters. But there are meat dishes as well. Not a few of your fellow diners will be tucking into lamb or beef accompanied by mounds of crispy frites. Solid value. *First Class.*

Le Procope (13 Rue de l'Ancienne Comédie; phone 4326-99-20) made a comeback during the 1989 celebration of the two-hundredth anniversary of the French Revolution. It was during the revolution that it knew such Americans as Benjamin Franklin, Thomas Jefferson, and John Paul Jones, not to mention such

Frenchmen as Pierre Beaumarchais, Georges Danton, and Jean-Paul Marat. Relatively recently restored in period style—it's good-looking—Le Procope occupies two floors, both invariably humming. Go at lunch for the well-priced menu, which gives you a choice of sweet or salad, with hearty beef (tartare de bœuf/pommes allumettes) and other entrées. Between courses have a look around, not missing the portraits and other paintings punctuating the wine, gold, and ivory decor. Celebrity notwithstanding, service is cordial. And location is on a street just off Boulevard St.-Germain. *First Class.*

Le Récamier (4 Rue Récamier; phone 4548-86-58): You're welcomed with a smile in this good-looking restaurant (tables spill into Rue Récamier in warm weather). And, if you're attached to the rich cuisine of Burgundy, this is the place—œufs meurettes (poached and served in a wine sauce) and bœuf Bourguignon are but two stellar specialties. With a wide choice of Burgundy wines to accompany. Very pleasant. *First Class.*

Le Relais de l'Isle (37 Rue St.-Louis-en-l'Île, Île St.-Louis; phone 4634-72-34) is a case of many good things in a small package. There are just ten tables by my count, but the menu is memorable, opening perhaps with hot sausages in a pastry crust or tomato soup, following with côte de bœuf or confit de canard as entrées, with warm tarte tatin served with cream or floating island as desserts. *Moderate.*

La Taverne du Sergent Recruteur (41 Rue St.-Louis-en-l'Île, Île St.-Louis; phone 4354-75-42): I have not come across a restaurant operated by an ex–recruiting sergeant in the United States, but this one packs them in, thanks to a romantic environment of stone walls and candle-lit tables, and a tasty, well-priced menu including wine, along with openers like house terrine or sliced sausages, entrées including bœuf bourgignon and steak-frites, and a choice of cheese, chocolate mousse, or ice cream for dessert. *Moderate.*

Tea Caddy (7 Rue St.-Julien-le-Pauvre) is the perfect respite spot when sightseeing Quartier Latin, Notre-Dame, or the neighboring church of St.-Julien-le-Pauvre. Stop in, midmorning or midafternoon, for coffee or tea served with a slice of the Caddy's own cake or pastry. Setting is a *very* old house, all beamed ceilings and paneled walls. *Moderate.*

Le Télégraphe (44 Rue de Lille; phone 4011-06-65) is at once convenient to Musée d'Orsay (and for that matter the just-across-the-bridge Right Bank) and big, seating a couple of hundred usually satisfied lunchers or diners. You go for the three-course menus and the sprightly service, starting, perhaps, with leeks vinaigrette or smoked salmon interestingly garnished, selecting an entrée no doubt based on poultry or fish, and concluding with a rich dessert, ideally one of those that glorifies chocolate. Well-priced wines. *First Class.*

Tour d'Argent (15 Quai de la Tournelle; phone 4354-23-31): If you're on an initial Paris foray, nothing is going to stop you from booking eons in advance for a meal in this Paris institution, which appears quite as tourist-populated as the Beaubourg, though it's considerably pricier. You enter a venerable riverfront structure and, reservation or not, are led into a ground-floor bar to while away time (awaiting your table upstairs) over a costly drink. A lift operated by a very small boy with a very big smile (which must net him an enormous nightly take-home in *pourboires*) then transports you to the rooftop dining room, whose picture windows, with vistas of the river and Notre-Dame, are used to good advantage. Serving staff, because moneybags Americans constitute a heavy proportion of its stock in trade, is English-speaking and—especially if they sense this is your first experience in a snazzy Paris eatery—patronizing. Order the satisfactory pressed duck, making sure that souffléed potatoes accompany it. Insist on seeing the wine list so that you may, if you like, select a relatively reasonably priced bottle (rather than simply following the unpriced verbal suggestion that may be proferred by the *sommelier*). Chocolate cake is a sensible dessert choice. And if you depart wondering what all the fuss was about, you will not have been the first. *Luxury.*

La Truffière (4 Rue Blainville; phone 4633-29-82), as its name suggests, specializes in truffled dishes from Périgord. Escargots stuffed with truffles and ham are a fine opener, as is the more traditional Périgordine specialty, foie d'oie frais à la gelée—fresh goose liver in aspic. Brochette de truffes or cassoulet are counseled for entrées. *First Class.*

Vagenende (142 Boulevard St.-Germain; phone 4548-44-96) is absolutely super-looking Belle Époque. But dark paneling, intricate mirrors, and brass fixtures are only a part of its appeal. Prime lure is sound-value prix-fixe lunches and dinners; steak grillé, liver and bacon, stuffed eggplant, coquilles St.-Jacques, for example, are one day's entrées. Although Vagenende is invariably packed, service is invariably swift and polite. *Moderate.*

La Vigneraie (14 Rue du Dragon; phone 4548-57-04) offers menus both at lunch (lower-priced) and dinner. You are seated either at a ground-floor table in front of the open kitchen or on the balcony. The kitchen is skilled, but an evening meal can be curious in that the appetizers—chicken liver and spinach salad as well as salade Niçoise—are so large as to constitute entrées, so that you have relatively little appetite remaining for main courses like gigot d'agneau or an excellent tuna preparation. Both midday and evening menus include a glass of Bordeaux on the house, and service is pleasant. *Moderate.*

SHOPPER'S PARIS

Parisians are the world's most glamorous shopkeepers. In no city are merchants—large or small, expensive or modest—able to display wares more alluringly or make them appear more desirable. The French know how to market, how to display, and how to sell, and the visitor to Paris, no matter how parsimonious, does well to savor the mercantile scene, if only as a looker or window-shopper.

Perfumes, colognes, and soaps remain the best Paris bargains and, for that matter, are as typically French as any gift can be. Women's accessories—scarves, bags, gloves, lingerie, shoes, blouses, hats, costume jewelry, compacts—can be very smart. Men's clothes, in better places, are attractive and smartly cut, but not inexpensive and often with no more style than clothes from Rome, London, or the principal American cities. Neckties can be good-looking, but they are at least as pricey as those in the United States and England and often do not tie as well. Housewares—the inimitable Limoges porcelain, the matchless Baccarat crystal and Christofle silver, kitchen equipment, and gadgets—are sensible buys in this most gastronomic of capitals. Antiques can be superb, for Paris remains one of the leading international markets for them. And last, food and wines; in no city are they more temptingly presented or of better quality.

SHOPPING AREAS: RIGHT AND LEFT BANKS

On *Rive Droite/Right Bank,* my candidate for the all-around smartest street is *Rue du Faubourg St.-Honoré,* with its extension, *Rue St.-Honoré* (somewhat less fashionable); ever-so-posh *Rue Royale* is the dividing line between these two. Also browseworthy are certain streets leading from the Champs-Élysées, such as *Avenue Montaigne, Rue François 1er* and *Avenue George V.* Avenues proceeding from the Étoile—*Wagram, Friedland, Kléber, Marceau, Iéna*—cater mainly to affluent Parisians and are not without interest. Relatively short *Rue de la Paix* has noteworthy shops, as do *Place Vendôme* (where the emphasis is on precious jewelry) and *Rue de Passy* (near Palais de Chaillot). *Place de la Madeleine*'s forte is food emporiums and flower stalls, and *Boulevard de la Madeleine* is middle category. *Boulevard Haussmann,* behind the Opéra/Garnier, is the site of two leading department stores. *Rue de Rivoli* is smartest at *Place de la Concorde* and becomes more popular as it extends east, becoming a center of low-priced schlock after it passes the Louvre and extends to the *Marais*—a venerable quarter centered by *Place des Vosges,* now filled with trendy clothes, in both men's and women's shops. *Place des Victoires,* a long-neglected Baroque beauty, a bit northeast of Palais-Royal, has in recent seasons become a center of avant-garde fashions. Streets in the area of Place de la Bastille, site of the new Opéra/Bastille, have become trendy, with not a few galleries of contemporary art on *Rue de Lappe, Rue de Charonne,* and *Rue de la Roquette.* Streets in the vicinity of the Beaubourg are dotted with art galleries, too. *Le Louvre des Antiquaires,* just east of Palais-Royal, is a multilevel mall with some 250 high-quality antique dealers. *Galeries Vivienne,* also near Palais-Royal, embraces a mix of fashion and gift boutiques. *Galerie du Claridge* is a onetime Champs-Élysées hotel transformed into a 36-shop emporium, with blue-chip names—*Cacherel* through *Xavier Danaud. Forum des Halles,* near the Beaubourg, massive, monolithic—anything but inviting—shelters some 250 shops. *Tour Montparnasse*'s lower level shelters 80 shops anchored on a department store. There's an additional mass of shops in *Palais des Congrès* (Porte Maillot); and some 260 shops, cafés, fast-food joints, and even a branch of New York–based Citibank at *Les Quatres Temps* in the futuristic La Défense complex.

On *Rive Gauche/Left Bank, Boulevard St.-Germain* is Main Street—with wares ranging from old books to *haute* clothes and superb antiques. Equally significant is *Rue de Rennes,* running south from St.-Germain and with fine shops, at least until it reaches *Boulevard Raspail. Boulevard St.-Michel* is another major Left Bank artery, with popular-priced shops, many dealing in books and shoes. A number of other Left Bank streets constitute a major antique area—quality is invariably superb—including *Rue des Sts.-Pères, Rue Jacob, Rue du Bac,* and river-front *Quai Voltaire.*

PROFILING THE DEPARTMENT STORES

DEPARTMENT STORES are a glory of Paris, quite on a par with those of big American cities, London, Copenhagen, and Tokyo and—given a pricing policy geared to a French clientele—constitute ideal shopping territory for the visitor, in contrast to pricey boutiques catering heavily to foreigners. The Big Two are both on Boulevard Haussmann, just behind the Opéra/Garnier. Of these, *Galeries Lafayette,* the better known, and with a big New York branch, is a three-building complex: the center building is the main one, with multilingual interpreters, money exchange, travel agency, men's and women's hairdressers, watch repair; two of four restaurants, as well as several upper floors of women's and children's clothes, housewares, and kitchen equipment on five; and on main an immense perfume section, souvenirs, gifts, and leather goods. Men's clothes and accessories have a building of their own, with

Galfa Club (the store's house-label) and wares of ranking designers, as well, occupying three floors. A final building contains additional departments. *Printemps,* directly west, is another three-building complex, with its Welcome Service, hostesses, and women's and children's clothing and accessories in the building labeled Nouveau Magasin; home furnishings and kitchenware in Magasin Havre; and men's duds in a building to the rear of the Havre pavilion, called Brummel. Printemps is known for its fashion shows, traditionally Tuesdays and Fridays, March through October, at 10 A.M. And there are three restaurants. (Branches of both Printemps and Galeries Lafayette—whose second Paris location is at Tour Montparnasse on the Left Bank—can be found in cities throughout France.) Another chain—this one low-budget—called *Prisunic,* has an outlet on Rue Caumartin to the rear of Printemps and still another branch on the Champs-Élysées; both have supermarkets. Still another France-wide cheapie chain, *Monoprix,* has two central outlets; one (with a giant supermarket) is a part of the Galeries Lafayette complex (above); another is on Avenue de l'Opéra, several blocks below the Opéra/Garnier. *Aux Trois Quartiers* (Boulevard de la Madeleine) is a thoroughly refurbished old-timer, central as can be, with all departments in its main building except men's clothing and accessories—in a detached building with its own name, *Madelios.* Across the river, again in a two-building complex, is the Left Bank's principal department store, *Au Bon Marché,* with the main entrance on Rue de Sèvres; don't miss the mouthwatering food department in Building No. 2. It is worth noting that Galeries Lafayette, Printemps, and Au Bon Marché—the first two of these especially—feature merchandise (men's and women's fashions, accessories, cosmetics, perfume, jewelry, china, crystal) by top designers and manufacturers, often in shoplike areas or at counters of their own; diversity is extraordinary. *La Samaritaine* (75 Rue de Rivoli) occupies no less than a quartet of buildings in a cluster east of the Louvre, with emphasis on lower-cost goods (have a look around for bargains); and, a chief lure for visitors, with an on-high restaurant called to your attention in Daily Bread, above.

SHOPS BY CATEGORY

ANTIQUES: You are in a world-class antique city. Ranking dealers—often with museum-caliber French seventeenth-, eighteenth-, and nineteenth-century furniture, accessories, and paintings—include *Didier Aaron* (31 Avenue Raymond Poincaré), *Aveline* (20 Rue du Faubourg St.-Honoré), *Étienne Levy* (178 Rue du Faubourg St.-Honoré), *Jacques Pérrin* (3 Quai Voltaire), and *Bernard Steinmitz* (4 Rue Drouot). Consider also such dealers in the 250-shop *Louvre des Antiquaires* (2 Place du Palais-Royal) as *Aubinière* (seventeenth- through nineteenth-century furniture), *Colanne* (Art Nouveau),

Avedis (antique carpets), *Appollon* (bronzes), and *Martin de Bazine* (eighteenth-century furniture). And browse in shops like these as you amble about town: *J. Armengaud* (19 Rue du Bac), seventeenth- and eighteenth-century furniture and paintings; *Annamel* (26 Place des Vosges), African masks; *Bresset* (196 Boulevard St.-Germain), seventeenth- and eighteenth-century French furniture; *Nina Borowski* (40 Rue du Bac)—ancient Greek, Roman, and Etruscan terra cotta figurines, reliefs, and gold work, including gem-studded jewelry; *Camoin* (9 Quai Voltaire), fine Louis XV and Louis XVI furniture; *Compagnie Parisienne d'Antiquités* (22 Rue de Bellechasse)—antique porcelain, small objects, porcelain; *Philippe Delpierre* (3 Rue du Bac)—seventeenth-, eighteenth-, and early nineteenth-century (Directoire, Consulat, early Empire) furniture, mirrors, and other objects; *Emery* (157 Rue St.-Honoré)—Asian antiques; *Jacques Kugel* (135 Rue St.-Honoré)—Louis XV and XVI; *André Mancel* (42 Rue du Bac)—Directoire, Consulat, Empire furniture and accessories; *Michel Mathounet* (17 Rue du Bac)—Oriental antiques; *Mythes and Légendes* (16 Place des Vosges)—tapestries and Baroque furnishings; *Ors et Arts* (44 Rue des Sts.-Pères)—antique silver; *Janette Ostier* (26 Place des Vosges)—antique Japanese screens and scrolls; *Pinault* (27 and 36 Rue Bonaparte)—antique autographs and books; *Antoine Perpitch* (240 Boulevard St.-Germain)—Gothic, Renaissance, Louis XIII, and Louis XIV tapestries, sculptures, furniture, and other objects; *Jean Sarfati* (220 Boulevard St.-Germain)—Italian and German antiques, mostly eighteenth-century; *Saurine* (23 Rue du Bac)—antique paneling as well as furniture and paintings; *Lucien Vigneau* (5 Rue des Sts.-Pères)—antique porcelain.

ANTIQUE AUCTIONS: *Drouot Richelieu* (9 Rue Drouot) is the city's best-known auction house; it's enormous, and excellent buys are possible, what with a thousand sales each year, in which some 400,000 objects are sold. *Drouot Montaigne,* a branch, specializes in blockbuster sales, taking place in Théâtre des Champs-Élysées (Avenue Montaigne). Sales take place Monday through Friday between 2:00 P.M. and 6:00 P.M., but you may inspect the merchandise in advance daily from 11:00 A.M. to 6:00 P.M. About half the auctions are cataloged (including all the big-money sales at Drouot-Montaigne) and the 100 auctioneers are accorded the title *maître.*

ART GALLERIES: With New York, London, and Rome, Paris is a world leader in the complex business of vending works of art. General rule of thumb had for long been the Right Bank's Rue du Faubourg St.-Honoré, Avenue Matignon, and Boulevard Haussmann, along with the Left Bank's Boulevard St.-Germain and streets leading from it, as principal art-gallery areas. To these must now be added streets in the shadow of the Beaubourg in Les Halles, the Marais/Place des Vosges quarter, and thoroughfares leading from

Place de la Bastille, site of Opéra/Bastille. Pop into any gallery with works that appeal, considering also this relative handful of specifics: *Jacques Barrère* (13 and 36 Rue Mazine)—ancient works, Chinese and Greek especially; *Claire Burrus* (3 Rue de Lappe)—moderns in a socko setting; *Révillon d'Apreval* (23 Quai Voltaire)—Baroque and rococo paintings and with furniture of those periods; *Michèle Chomette* (24 Rue Beaubourg)—photography a specialty; *Crousel-Robelin-Bama* (40 Rue Quincampoix)—worthy group shows; *Delaville* (15 Rue de Beaune)—eighteenth-century paintings, with furniture of that era; *Galerie K* (19 Rue Guenégaud)—Miró and Picasso; *Keller* (15 Rue Keller)—contemporary, of-this-moment output; *Gismondi* (20 Rue Royale)—old Dutch, French, and Italian paintings as well as eighteenth-century furniture; *Lavignes-Bastille* (27 Rue de Charonne)—stellar moderns; *Boudoin Lebon* (34 Rue des Archives)—Americans like Rauschenberg and Mapplethorpe, but French and other works, too, including sculpture; *J. O. Leegenhoek* (23 Quai Voltaire)—old masters; *Marcus* (20 Rue Chauchat)—seventeenth- and eighteenth-century paintings; *Maeght* (42 Rue du Bac)— big-bucks works, with branches in Barcelona, Milan, and Tokyo; *Bruno Meissner* (23 Quai Voltaire)—top-rankers; *Mermoz* (9 Rue du Cirque)—pre-Columbian art; *Melki* (55 Rue de Seine)—name moderns like Gris and Miró; *Nane Stern* (26 Rue de Charonne)—a leader of the Bastille-area group for contemporary works; *Enrico Navarra* (75 Rue du Faubourg St.-Honoré)—works by such stars as Roy Lichtenstein; *Gilbert et Paul Petrides* (63 Rue du Faubourg St.-Honoré)—Impressionists and onward, including Chagall, Dufy, Léger, Albert Marquet, Renoir, Utrillo, and Van Dongen; *Claude Samuel* (18 Place des Vosges)—interesting new names; *Urban* (22 Avenue Matignon)—aspiring painters and sculptors; *Natalie Seroussi* (34 Rue de Seine)—Cristo, Dubuffet, and Soulages are in its stable; *Wigersma Fine Art* (75 Rue du Faubourg St.-Honoré)—leading masters of this century.

BARBERS AND HAIRDRESSERS: *Galeries Lafayette* department store (Boulevard Haussmann) has a staff of half a hundred, so that chances are you won't have to wait; no need to book ahead. Next-door *Printemps* department store is similarly good. If you're up to shooting the works, consider such glitter spots as *Alexandre* (3 Avenue Matignon)—on scene a quarter century-plus; *Carita* (1 Rue du Faubourg St.-Honoré); and *Jacques Dessange* (37 Avenue Franklin-Roosevelt). *Henri Courant* (61 Avenue Franklin-Roosevelt; phone 4359-14-40) is reliable for men. *Julie* (180 Boulevard St.-Germain; phone 4548-98-37) is unisex.

BOOKS: *Brentano's* (37 Avenue de l'Opéra), *W. H. Smith* (248 Rue de Rivoli), and *Galignani* (224 Rue de Rivoli)—which bills itself as the "oldest English bookshop established on the Continent"—all have English-language books—huge stocks—as specialties. *Librairie Hachette* (20 Boulevard St.-Michel) has enormous stocks of French books on all subjects. *Opéra Hachette* (Place de l'Opéra at Boulevard des Capucines) is heavy on imported newspapers and magazines, including American. *Librairie Gourmande* (4 Rue Dante) deals in cookbooks, contemporary and aged—and mostly in French. Bear in mind books on the fine arts in the *Librairies* of the *Musée du Louvre* (Tuileries) and the *Musée d'Orsay* (Rue de Bellechasse) and on the decorative arts in the *Librairie* of the *Musée des Arts Décoratifs* (Rue de Rivoli).

CHILDREN'S CLOTHES: Biggest selections are in department stores (above); also consider *Jones* (Avenue Victor Hugo) and—for marvelous toys, as well—*Au Nain Bleu* (406 Rue St.-Honoré).

CHOCOLATES: *Godiva* (11 Rue de Castiglione), *Marquise de Sévigné* (32 Place de la Madeleine), *Maison du Chocolat* (225 Rue du Faubourg St.-Honoré), *Au Duc de Praslin* (44 Avenue Montaigne), *Jadis et Gourmand* (27 Rue Boissy d'Anglas), and *Lenôtre* (44 Rue du Bac, 49 Avenue Victor Hugo, and additional branches) are tempting chocolate sources.

COOKING LESSONS: You will have heard of *Le Cordon Bleu* (8-bis Rue Léon Delhomme; phone 4555-02-77), easily booked on relatively short notice for a sample lesson—conducted in French; other cooking schools include *La Varenne* (34 Rue St.-Dominique; phone 4705-10-16) and *Chef Hubert* (48 Rue de Sèvres; phone 4056-91-20).

CRYSTAL: Department stores (above), of course; *Baccarat* (30-bis Rue du Paradis) and *Lalique* (11 Rue Royale). But for choice selections of Baccarat, along with Daum and Lalique, head for *Limoges Unic* (12 Rue du Paradis); and investigate *Christofle* (24 Rue de la Paix).

DUTY-FREE SHOPPING: Allow plenty of time upon departure for duty-free shops at *Aéroport Charles de Gaulle.* Besides a supermarket-type store with a big selection of French wines in varying categories and price ranges—as well as liqueurs, eaux-de-vie, liquor, chocolates, and tobacco—there are other shops selling French foodstuffs (remember that, if you're bound for the United States, meat products—even canned—are *interdit,* more's the pity), silk scarves and neckties, perfumes and colognes, jewelry, leather, and other gifts.

FOOD AND WINE: They're everywhere: *boulangeries* (bread bakeries), *charcuteries* (French counterpart of our delicatessen, with cold meats, sausages, pâtés, terrines, salads), *pâtisseries* (wherein pastries are baked; when they have tables at which you may order, they double as *salons de thé*), *épiceries* (groceries), *fromageries* (cheese stores), and *supermarchés* (supermarkets, at which wines—nice for hotel-room aperitifs—are also sold). Have a look at the fabulous concentration of food shops on *Rue Lépic* (Montmartre) and *Rue de Seine* (Quartier Latin), also taking in the old-style open-air market—*Marché de la Mouffe* on Rue Mouffetard, near the Panthéon, on the Left Bank. And note these shops: *Fauchon* (26 Place de la Madeleine), the greatest retail food show in town, with a café (above) that's fun for lunch; *Hédiard* (21 Place de la Madeleine), a smaller-scale Fauchon, with vast varieties of tea, an excellent wine department, and a reliable restaurant; *Caviar Kaspia* (17 Place de la Madeleine, with its own restaurant, where you might enjoy caviar served with blinis); *Petrossian* (18 Boulevard La Tour-Maubourg), celebrated for caviar and with its own pricey caviar restaurant in New York; *La Maison de Truffe* (19 Place de la Madeleine), for truffle addicts, but a full-fledged *charcuterie* as well; *Androuet* (41 Rue d'Amsterdam) is at once a restaurant (evaluated above) and cheese shop—with 150 species. *Chedeville* (12 Rue du Marché St.-Honoré), perhaps the prototypical Parisian *charcuterie*—old-fashioned and mouth-watering; *Poilane* (8 Rue du Cherche-Midi)—arguably the quintessential *boulangerie,* or bread bakery; *Berthillon* (31 Rue St.-Louis-en-l'Île, Île St.-Louis)—celebrated for its ice cream; *Lenôtre,* called to your attention above for its chocolates, but equally skilled at pastries and charcuterie, with shops at 44 Rue du Bac on the Left Bank, 49 Avenue Victor Hugo, and other locations; *A. Lerch* (4 Rue Cardinal-Lemoine on the Left Bank)—masterful fruit tarts in near-limitless variety, along with so many other scrumptious pastries that you end wanting to sample the lot; and, to conclude this paragraph, a trio of retail wine specialists. You no doubt know *George DuBœuf* (9 Rue Marbeuf) for exported Beaujolais bottled with his label; he sells them here, with wines from adjacent Burgundy as well. Both *Caves de la Madeleine* (25 Rue Royale) and *Galerie des Vins* (201 Rue St.-Honoré) sell wines from throughout France.

FRENCH LESSONS: Long-established *Alliance Française* (101 Boulevard Raspail) teaches privately and in classes.

JEWELRY: Paris is one of the world's great jewelry cities, and it doesn't cost a sou to look at, for example *Cartier* (12 Rue de la Paix)—with *Le Must de Cartier* on Place Vendôme; *Fred* (6 Rue Royale); *H. Stern* (17 Rue de la Paix); *Jean Dinh Van* (24 Rue de la Paix); and the fabulous shops on Place Vendôme—*Aldebert, Boucheron, Gianmaria Buccellati, Chaumet, Van Cleef & Arpels,* and *J.A.R.'s* (in the arcade at No. 7).

KITCHENWARE AND TABLEWARE: *Déhillerin* (18 Rue Coquillière) is the great kitchen-equipment shop, an old-timer with copper pots (which they will ship) a specialty, and a great deal else to tempt serious cooks. Also visit *Au Bain Marie* (20 Rue Hérold)—tableware, table linens, cooking equipment; *Christofle* (24 Rue de la Paix) with its own celebrated silver flatware, plus Crystal and Limoges porcelain; *Culinarion* (99 Rue de Rennes), a link of a mod-look chain—clean-lined accessories for cooking, serving, dining; *Haviland et Parlon* (47 Rue du Paradis), for big stocks of Limoges china; *P. Nicholas* (27 Rue Marbeuf), with lovely patterns of fine china and crystal; *Porcelaine Blanche* (108 Rue St.-Honoré; 112-bis Rue de Rennes, and other locations) with well-priced white china the name of its game. (See also Crystal above, and inspect housewares floors of such department stores as Galeries Lafayette, Printemps, and Au Bon Marché.

LINEN: *Porthault* (48 Avenue Montaigne)—for table, bed, and bath, with a branch in New York.

LUGGAGE AND WOMEN'S HANDBAGS: I've had good luck at the big luggage department in *Printemps; Galeries Lafayette*'s good, too. Consider also *Aux États-Unis* (229 Rue St.-Honoré) with dog collars and dog bowls with French legends for your Fido—*mais seulement s'il comprend le français; Morabito* (1 Place Vendôme)—very posh, indeed; and *Schilz* (30 Rue Caumartin), from which I purchased a handsome leather carry-on bag that wears and wears and wears. For pricey women's handbags, consider *Étienne Aigner* (3 Rue du Faubourg St.-Honoré; *Hermès* (24 Rue du Faubourg St.-Honoré) and *Lancel* (8 Place de l'Opéra)—with U.S. branches; *Peau de Porc* (240 Boulevard St.-Germain)—pigskin specialists; and *Shizuka* (49 Avenue de l'Opéra)—elegant and expensive Japanese leather and other accessories.

MARKETS: *Marché aux Puces* is the French for flea market. It's open Saturday, Sunday, and Monday each week from 7:30 A.M. to 7 P.M.; and it's a *long* Metro ride. Get off at Porte de Clignancourt and allow yourself a good half-day, as the market sprawls, there being some 2000 dealers in seven individually named sections. Much of the stuff is new or elderly rather than antique. You must search diligently, and if your time is limited, you do well to appreciate that you're dealing with a 75-acre area patronized each week by close to 200,000 shoppers. Consider shopping in just a few of the big market areas; *Marché Bert* and *Marché Serpette* are two such. And mind, you are expected to bargain over prices. *Marché aux Timbres* is French for stamp market, but note that old postcards are also on sale at this one. Location could not be more fashionable—corner of Avenue Marigny and Avenue Gabriel, just off Champs-Élysées,

Thursday, Saturday, and Sunday, from 10:00 A.M. *Marchè aux Fleurs* is the flower market lining the curbs of Place de la Madeleine on Tuesday, Wednesday, Thursday, Saturday, and holidays. And, on any day, take a walk on *Quai de la Mégisserie,* fronting the Seine just east of the Louvre, for a remarkable sidewalk market embracing birds, tropical fish, monkeys, and heaven knows what other lower-order representation.

MEN'S CLOTHING: I check out *Brummel,* the big, multifloor men's store at Printemps, and the also capacious *Galfa Club* at Galeries Lafayette on each Paris visit; each stocks wares of a generous variety of name couturiers, but best buys are their house-label merchandise. *Alain Figaret* is a smart France-wide men's chain, in Paris at 32 Rue de la Paix. *Daniel Crémieux,* a nationwide chain, is strongly influenced by classic American clothes and accessories; its Paris outlets are at 6 Boulevard Malesherbes, 24 Rue Marbeuf, and 2 Place St.-Sulpice. *Façonnable* (whose principal Paris shop is at 1 Rue Royale) has classy stores France-wide. *Cerruti* (3 Place de la Madeleine and 27 Rue Royale) sells its own-design clothes—smart, conservative, costly. *Arnys* (14 Rue de Sèvres) is known for custom-made suits. *Emilio Batchi* (115 Boulevard St.-Germain) is, in a word, elegant; *Celio* (79 Champs-Élysées, 122 Boulevard St.-Germain, and in the big shopping malls) is a national chain, with nice, well-priced clothes, women's as well as men's; *Comme Ça* (127 Boulevard St.-Germain) is pricey but stylish; *Cravatterie Nazionali* (249 Rue St.-Honoré)—neckties; and *Hartwood* (123 Rue du Faubourg St.-Honoré and 40 Rue du Bac) is conveniently located on both banks and serves women as well as gents—and very smartly. *Marks & Spencer* (45 Boulevard Haussmann) is the very same you know from Britain—its sweaters and accessories can be good value (and there's an on-premises supermarket). *Hilditch & Key* (252 Rue de Rivoli) is from across the Channel, too—London's Jermyn Street—and sells elegant haberdashery; so is *Burberry* (8 Boulevard des Malesherbes); *Old England* (12 Boulevard des Capucines) seems English—but was Paris-founded a century ago. *Lacoste* (8 Boulevard des Malesherbes) features the Lacoste line—sportshirts through jogging gear. *Charvet* (28 Place Vendôme) is very conservative and very costly, with custom-made shirts and striking neckties its specialties; sold by stores like New York's Bergdorf Goodman in the United States. *Lanvin 2* (244 Rue de Rivoli) is quite possibly the smartest of the French-origin men's shops. *Charles Jourdan Monsieur* (12 Rue du Faubourg St.-Honoré) sells clothes, as well as shoes. *Yves St.-Laurent Homme* (38 Rue du Faubourg St.-Honoré) offers fashions not unlike those in foreign branches. *Hermès* (24 Rue du Faubourg St.-Honoré) has the most beautiful—and expensive—ties in town; other menswear, too. *Courrèges* (49 Rue de Rennes) is very trendy and pricey. *Givenchy Gentlemen* (3 Avenue George V) is smart and stylish, year in, year out. *Rodier Monsieur* (8 Rue Babylone and other locations) has sensibly priced shirts and sweaters. *J. C. d'Ahetze* (250 Rue de Rivoli) has sold good-value neckties for as many years as I can remember.

Which leaves men's discount clothing stores. Prestigious French and Italian labels (more of the former than of the latter) go at usually substantial reductions at *Club des Dix* (58 Rue du Faubourg St.-Honoré), *David Shiff* (4 Rue Marbeuf), *Frank Beral* (7 Rue de la Boëtie and 141 Avenue de Wagram), and *Depôt des Grandes Marques* (DGM—on the second floor at 15 Rue de la Banque).

PERFUME AND COLOGNE: At every turn in this, the planetary perfume capital. Department stores and certain shops sell at list prices, albeit offering exemption from the government's 15 percent VAT tax if your purchases meet the legal minimum of the moment. At *de Gaulle Airport's* duty-free shop, you pay list, but obtain VAT exemption regardless of the amount you buy—although variety of labels and bottle sizes can be limited. Trick, if your order will be at all substantial, is to buy at an in-town discount shop, offering diverse stocks, 20 percent to 25 percent discounts from list prices, *and*—if you purchase the legal minimum amount—VAT exemption, as well, in which case savings are around 40 percent. *Michel Swiss* (16 Rue de la Paix, up a flight) fills this bill, with huge selections; smiling, bilingual staff with time to take; mail-order service (they publish a catalog); flight-type canvas bags gratis with bulky orders; and a manager—loquacious and omnipresent Max Cohen—who knows the scent scene, Balenciaga and Balmain through Weil and Worth. (If you want any of the Guerlain scents, you may buy them in Paris only at *Guerlain*'s own retail shops; those at 2 Place Vendôme and 68 Avenue des Champs-Élysées are the most central.)

SHOES: Among the leading outlets are *Carel* (22 Rue Royale and other locations); *Céline* (24 Rue François 1er, other locations), unisex; *John Lobb* (at Hermès, 24 Rue du Faubourg St.-Honoré), custom-made, as in the same firm's London store; *Alaine Harel* (64 Rue François 1er), lizard, ostrich, and crocodile specialties; *Walter Steiger* (49 Rue du Faubourg St.-Honoré), very smart, and with a New York branch; and the ubiquitous *Charles Jourdan* (5 Boulevard de la Madeleine is its main address). But if you're *really* into shoes, stroll the Left Bank's Rue de Sèvres; it's Paris's Shoe Street—with *Ellen, Valmont,* and *Jet Set* among numerous shops.

SILVER: *Christofle* (31 Boulevard des Italiens, 12 Rue Royale) is the most esteemed; beautiful and expensive. *Puiforcat* (134 Boulevard Haussmann) is justifiably noted for its own designs in sterling. (Both have New York branches.)

STATIONERY: *Armorial* (98 Rue du Faubourg St.-Honoré) sells engraved note paper, personal and business cards, and invitations to your wedding.

TUXEDO RENTAL: *Au Cor de Chasse* (40 Rue de Buci) also rents top hats, tails, and morning suits. Rental fitting hours, traditionally, are 9 to 11 A.M. and 1:30 to 5 P.M. This firm, dating to 1875, asks that you phone (4326-51-89) for a fitting appointment.

WOMEN'S CLOTHING: Women's clothes in the couture capital of the world? Where begin? Where stop? Department stores devote by far the greater part of their selling space to female fashions; you want to check out *Galeries Lafayette, Printemps,* and London-origin, good-value, unisex *Marks & Spencer*—just opposite the Big Two on Boulevard Haussmann. But, to give you an idea of how easy it is to pop into the outlets of celebrated designers, I walked down Rue du Faubourg St.-Honoré with a notebook, and these are the shop names I noted: *Pierre Cardin, Louis Férraud, Karl Lagerfeld, Chloë, Courrèges, Yves St.-Laurent, Ungaro, Léonard, Hermès, Christian la Croix,* and *Lanvin.* To these, add *Christian Dior, Nina Ricci, Chanel, Jean-Louis Scherrer, Guy Laroche,* and *Valentino* on Avenue Montaigne; the original *Chanel* shop on Rue Cambon; *Balenciaga, Givenchy,* and *Per Spook* on Avenue George V, *Ted Lapidus* on Avenue François 1er; *Maud Frizon* (shoes) on Rue des Sts.-Pères; *Lancel* and *Samantha* on Rue de Rennes; and *Daniel Hechter* on Boulevard St.-Germain (and at other locations). *Kenzo, Thierry Mugler, Stéphane Kelian, Victoire,* and *France Andrevie* are among the avant-garde unisex fashion and shoe shops on Place des Victoires. *Au Bon Marché* (with its main entrance on Rue de Sèvres) is the Left Bank's No. 1 department store and features a number of haute-couture designers' clothes as well as less costly labels. In and around Boulevard St.-Germain are many more fine shops that many transatlantic newcomers appreciate. For example: *Agnès B.* (13 Rue Michelet)—youthful designs; has New York branches; *Biba* (18 Rue de Sèvres)—noted sportswear; *Iris 4* (4 Rue de Babylone)—with a mix of trendy labels; *Emmanuelle Khanh* (10 Rue de Grenelle)—among the top-rankers. *Women's Clothing at a Discount?* Paris has a number of cut-rate outlets, including *Courrèges* (7 Rue de Turbigo), *Mendès* (65 Rue de Montmartre)—for Yves St.-Laurent discounts; *Nina Ricci* (39 Avenue Montaigne)—with reduced garments in the *sous-sol,* or basement; *Cacherel Stock* (114 Rue d'Alésia), with men's as well as women's bargains; *Dorothée Bis Stock* (79 Rue d'Alésia); *Emmanuelle Khanh* (6 Rue Pierre-Lescot), on the second floor; *Stock Austerlitz* (16 Boulevard de l'Hôpital), with Daniel Hechter duds for gents as well as the ladies; and *Mic-Mac* (13 Rue Laugier), with buys for both women and men.

INCIDENTAL INTELLIGENCE

Airports/air terminals: Air France and other transatlantic carriers use *Aéroport Charles de Gaulle,* at Roissy, 15 miles north of Paris. (Air France has its own terminal—No. 2—at de Gaulle.) Efficiently operated buses that depart approximately quarter-hourly connect de Gaulle with *Porte Maillot Air Terminal* in the basement of the Palais des Congrès (Paris Convention Center), not far northwest of Arc de Triomphe. From there, you may take a taxi to your hotel, or vice versa. Certain domestic flights take off from and land at *Aéroport d'Orly,* connected with bus service to *Invalides Air Terminal* on the Left Bank. Additionally, there is bus service between de Gaulle and Orly airports for passengers with connections, one to the other.

Boat tours: *Bateaux Mouches* are the Seine River sightseeing vessels that first-timers often enjoy; they depart approximately half-hourly from Pont de l'Alma, at the foot of Avenue George V; they have both open and glass-roofed decks. Departures at 1:00 P.M. and 8:30 P.M. are restaurant-equipped. Competition includes *Vedettes du Pont Neuf,* departing from its pier on Pont Neuf, at Île de la Cité; and *Vedettes Paris-Tour Eiffel,* which departs from Pont d'Iéna on the Left Bank, just below the Eiffel Tower.

Buses and bus tours: Métro tickets are valid on buses, but it is worth noting that bus routes are divided into fare stages, or *sections.* One ticket covers up to two sections; two tickets are valid for three or more sections. *Buses* take a lot more getting used to than the Métro. Worth knowing about routes include No. 21, which takes you from Gare St.-Lazare, on the northern fringe of the Right Bank, through cores of both Right and Left banks, to Cité Universitaire, on the Left Bank's southern edge; No. 73, connecting Place de la Concorde with the futuristic quarter of La Défense; and No. 82, which begins at Jardin du Luxembourg, passing one notable monument after another on both Left and Right banks, terminating at the American Hospital in the suburb of Neuilly. *Bus tours* with varying itineraries are operated by such firms as *American Express* (11 Rue Scribe; phone 4266-09-99), *Cityrama* (4 Place des Pyramides; phone 4260-30-14), and *Paris-Vision* (214 Rue de Rivoli; phone 4260-31-25). An introductory half-day or day-long jaunt is never a bad idea, but before going off on longer, pricier tours, consider on-your-own excursions by train or rented car—of the kind I outline earlier in this book.

Car hire: Many firms provide sightseeing by guide-driven car; one that I can recommend from experience is *Service 3000,* whose president, Sylvain Deschamps, knows Paris—and, indeed, all of France—very well; address is 31 Rue Sauffroy; phone 4563-99-11.

There are many car-rental options, among them *Avis* (phone 4609-92-12), *Hertz* (phone 4788-51-51), *Citer* (phone 4341-45-45), and *Serval* (phone 4504-22-13).

Local literature: The skillfully edited English-language *International Herald Tribune* is published as a joint venture of *The Washington Post* and *The New York Times;* its news content is more international than Parisian, except in weekend editions. Whether you are fluent in French or not, consult the leading dailies, *Le Monde* and *Le Figaro.* And pick up the inexpensive—but amazingly comprehensive—what's-on weekly, *L'Officiel des Spectacles* at news kiosks.

Le Métro:—Paris's subway system—ranks with London's Underground, in my view, at least, as the world's best. I use taxis in Paris only for arrival to and departure from the air terminal, with baggage; otherwise, when not walking, I travel the Métro. Pick up a map of the system, gratis, at any station. There are some 15 routes, each with terminus stations, identified by the key word, *Direction,* at their extremities. If you want to go from Place de la Concorde to Place Charles de Gaulle/Étoile, enter the Concorde station, buy a ticket specifying the class—first or second (difference in cost is minimal and facilities identical, but at rush hour first class is less crowded). Having studied your pocket map or wall maps, you know that you are to proceed to the platform of Neuilly-Vincennes line; you'll have noted on the map that your stop—De Gaulle/Étoile—is en route to the Neuilly end of the line, so you look for the track marked "Direction Neuilly," board the appropriate train, and exit at your station. Métro cars are equipped with maps of the route they travel, and sign-posting throughout the system is superb. Note, too, that some trips may involve a change of trains, or transfer. Key French word in this case is *correspondance;* by plotting out your route on a map in advance, you easily determine where to transfer.

Automatic machines at each station admit you to the Métro by ticket—but neither token nor coin. You may buy single tickets at Métro stations. There are two classes, first and second—with the former offering identical albeit less crowded cars identified by yellow horizontal stripes extending their length above the doors—and I counsel second. You may also buy packs of ten tickets (at any station's ticket window—the term is *carnet*) in either class, at a considerable savings over individual fares. Still another money-saver is the *Carte Orange* (also good on Paris buses); it's obtainable Mondays at Métro stations, for durations of a week or a month (the weekly card is popular with many visitors), for as many rides as you like, but to obtain it *you must have a passport-type photo* to present when purchasing. Convenient, too—especially so since you may purchase it before departing the United States—is the Métro ticket called *Paris Sésame,* for two-, four-, or seven-day durations (from Marketing Challenges International, 10 East 21st Street, New York, NY 10010; phone 212-529-8484; available also in Paris at airports and railway stations). *R.E.R.*, which stands for *Réseau Express Régional,* is a suburban/exurban extension of the Métro and ideal for trips to such points as Malmaison and St.-Germain-en-Laye.

Museum pass: It's called *La Carte* when you buy it in advance of departure from the United States, and its name in France is *Carte Musée.* A rose by any other name...; it's a good deal, in that it not only admits you, as many times as you like during the period of validity (one, three, or five days), to sixty museums and places of interest—such as Versailles—in the Paris area, but (and this is important in the case of crowded museums like the Louvre and the Beaubourg) with this card, you may bypass whatever queue there may be and go right to the admission gate of most museums for instant entry without waiting in line. And since some museums close for lunch, the card is additionally valuable as it permits unlimited visits and reentries for as long as it's valid. To buy the card in advance, contact Marketing Challenges International, 10 East 21st Street, New York, NY 10010; phone 212-529-8484. In Paris the card is available at major museums and at the Office de Tourisme de la Ville de Paris, 127 Avenue des Champs-Élysées.

Restrooms: There are modern, unisex public restrooms, strategically situated on streets of central Paris. They're automatically cleaned upon each customer's departure, and I say customer advisedly; there is a charge. Let me point out, too, that restrooms in railway stations charge for entrance; possibly for this reason, they are generally clean and decent. Station restrooms are well signposted and generally lead from areas directly adjacent to tracks, rather than from inner waiting rooms. And don't hesitate to use off-lobby restrooms in hotels.

Train stations: There are half a dozen, and it's important to ascertain the correct one, especially for departures. Four are on the Right Bank—*Gare du Nord, Gare de l'Est, Gare St.-Lazare,* and *Gare de Lyon;* while *Gare d'Austerlitz* and *Gare Montparnasse* are on the Left Bank. Note—especially if you're traveling first class—that first class coaches—or sections of coaches—are indicated not only by the numeral "1" on their sides, but by horizontal yellow stripes edging their roofs.

Visites-Conférences: *Visites-Conférences* translates as guided walking tours conducted by extraordinarily well-educated specialists called *conférenciers* (who are not ordinary guides) to areas where they are experts, coordinated by the government's Caisse Nationale des

Monuments Historiques; for information: *Hôtel de Sully,* 62 Rue St.-Antoine (in the Marais quarter); phone 4887-24-14. Tours are listed in issues of the what's-on weekly, *L'Officiel des Spectacles,* and in the newspaper *Le Figaro.*

Paris addenda: *Police* emergency phone is 17; Police headquarters is at 9 Boulevard du Palais. Paris *Lost and Found* is at 32 Rue Morillons; phone 4531-14-80. *Main Post Office* (52 Rue du Louvre) is open 24 hours for postage, phone calls, telegrams, . . . Other post offices are open 8 A.M. to 7 P.M. daily and 8 A.M. to noon Saturdays. Remember, too, that you may purchase stamps at tobacconists; the word *Tabac* will be above the door. *To obtain a physician at night,* phone 4578-15-00; *day or night physicians:* phone 4542-37-00. *Pharmacie Dhéry* (84 Champs-Élysées; phone 4256-02-41) is open 24 hours. . . . For an *ambulance,* phone 4887-27-50. . . . *United States Embassy* is at 2 Avenue Gabriel (phone 4296-12-02); *British Embassy:* 35 Rue du Faubourg St.-Honoré (phone 4266-91-42). *American Hospital* is at 63 Boulevard Victor Hugo, in the suburb of Neuilly (phone 4747-53-00). . . . *British Hospital* is at 48 Rue de Villiers, in the suburb of Le Valois (phone 4758-13-12). *Agence Vendôme* (Rue de Castiglione at Place Vendôme) is a long-established ticket agency—worth knowing about for opera, ballet, concert, and theater seats that even hotel concierges might not be able to obtain.

3

Aix-en-Provence

The Quintessential Provence

BACKGROUND BRIEFING

It may perhaps be exaggerating to term Aix the quintessential Provence. But not by much. Arles (chapter 6) is immediately associated with a foreign artist—Van Gogh. Nîmes (chapter 27) technically—if not traditionally—in Languedoc, brings to mind memorable monuments of its ancient Roman period. Avignon (chapter 7) has built its reputation on the palace of a succession of seven medieval popes. Marseille (chapter 22), as a major metropolis, belongs as much to the entire south as to Provence.

Aix, though, is Provençal through and through, evoking the beauty of the region in a fountain-centered, boulevardlike main street and the Romanesque cloister of its cathedral, than which there is no lovelier in France. As seat of the counts of Provence, it was the Provençal capital for much of the period embracing the formative twelfth through fifteenth centuries; toward the end of that period, the multititled René—variously King of Naples, Duke of Anjou, *Bon Roi* René de Provence—passed his final years in Aix, where his courtiers were writers and musicians; his pastimes, painting and poetry.

Post-René centuries saw Aix evolve as cultural center of Provence, even as it remained seat of the provincial *Parlement* until the *ancien régime* was no more, upon the advent of the Revolution. More recently, painters have replaced politicians. The most reputed was Aix-born Paul Cézanne, whose paintings of the neighborhood and its people motivate the Aix-bound visitor at least as much as the sculpture-embellished palaces lining Cours Mirabeau and the aromatic herbs—rosemary, thyme, marjoram—that distinguish Provençal cuisine.

Musée du Vieil-Aix (17 Rue Saporta) is set in a baroque mansion on a principal street that will lead you to the center of town. Halt, though, for lovingly tended memorabilia of Old Aix—paintings and prints, clothes and certificates, and, among much else, an exemplary collection of the carved-wood Provence figures called *Santons.*

Musée d'Histoire Naturelle (6 Rue Esparist): I'm not bringing this museum's collection to your attention, but rather its smashing baroque facade, with a stone gate enclosing the courtyard and, within, original ceilings and carved-wood doorways and window frames.

Atelier de Cézanne (Avenue Paul-Cézanne): Cézanne was born in Aix and died here in 1906. You must visit Musée Granet (below) to see paintings by this major Impressionist in his hometown. Here, you'll find his studio carefully re-created, with a good bit of Cézanneiana exhibited, as well.

Musée Granet (Place St.-Jean-de-Malte) is, the cathedral and its cloister (above) excepted, a case of saving best for last. First things first: Cézanne paintings. By my count, there are five of that Aix-born artist's works here, all small in size: *Bathsheba, Nature Morte, Madame Cézanne, Baigneuses,* and *Femme Nue.* Still another Granet painting, *Les Joueurs de Cartes*—a work of the Le Nain brothers dating to the seventeenth century—was used by Cézanne as a basis for his painting of the same name, at the Metropolitan Museum in New York. This museum is named for a nineteenth-century Aixois painter and contains a number of his works, none of them as good as a portrait of him, black-cloaked, by no less a master than Ingres. It's with Italians that the Granet starts you off—fine works by the likes of Vivarini, Giordano, and Guercino. Then comes a Rembrandt self-portrait to introduce the Dutch, with a De Hooch in this group, along with Seaghers and Paul Bril. Van Cleve and Rubens (the latter with handsome man-and-wife portraits) are the stellar Flemings. Cézanne aside, it is the late-seventeenth-century and eighteenth-century French masters at which the Granet excels; Largillière and Philippe de Champaigne, Fragonard and Hugo Robert, Rigaud and Jacques Louis David. Take your time; this is one of the best art museums in provincial France.

Musée Arbaud (24 Rue du Quatre-Septembre): A visit to this museum—with its theme antique Provençal pottery, paintings, and prints, supplemented by antique books bound in leather—is killing two birds with one stone. You see the handsome Arbaud, occupying a Baroque mansion in the architecturally rich Quartier Mazarin. And, en route to it, you pass by facades of landmark neighboring houses.

ON SCENE

Lay of the Land: The landmark thoroughfare, *Cours Mirabeau,* cuts a horizontal swath through the city on a west–east axis, from a circle of a square called *La Rotonde* (a.k.a. Place du Général de Gaulle), flanked by the municipal casino, eastward to more modest *Place Forbin,* off which *Rue de l'Opéra* leads the Théâtre Municipal. The *railway station* is south of La Rotonde on *Avenue Victor-Hugo.* Mansion-bordered *Rue du Quatre-Septembre* leads from Mirabeau past Musée Arbaud to *Place des Quatres-Dauphins,* named for sculpted dolphins of its baroque fountain and flanked by rococo mansions. Otherwise, most of what you will want to visit in Aix is a walk north from Mirabeau on *Rue Clemenceau* to *Place St.-Honoré* and the boutiques of the *Rue Marius-Reinaud.* Or go north on *Rue Nazareth* from Mirabeau to reach *Rue Aude,* smartest of the pedestrian shopping streets, which leads into shop-lined *Rue du Maréchal-Foch,* whose northerly terminus is *Place Richelme* just south of *Hôtel de Ville*—massively Baroque, but with a graceful Gothic clock tower. That square will take you into *Rue Saporta* which, as it continues north, becomes—when bisected by *Place des Martyrs de la Résistance*—*Rue Laroque,* locale of the cathedral and former archbishop's palace, now sheltering a museum.

Cathedral of Saint-Sauveur (Rue Laroque) spans a dozen centuries, with its oldest component part a sublimely beautiful octagon of a tower. The portal is Gothic; it frames a treasure: a pair of sixteenth-century carved-wood doors. Inside, beeline to a triptych, *The Burning Bush,* painted by the fifteenth-century artist Nicholas Froment. The nave's Flemish tapestries are standouts, too. But I've saved loveliest for last: the Romanesque cloister, each of its arches supported by a pair of pillars, no two of whose exquisite carvings are alike.

Musée des Tapisseries (Place des Martyrs de la Résistance) occupies a seventeenth-century palace that long served as residence of the archbishops whose seat was the next-door cathedral (above). Now, its second floor displays a collection of tapestries gathered by long-ago clerics. They occupy walls of a suite of high-ceilinged rooms, with the most arresting the series called *Les Grotesques,* a seventeenth-century Beauvais group that could be stage sets, peopled with dancers, musicians, and animals.

Pavillon Vendôme (Rue Vendôme, not far from Musée des Tapisseries) dominates a charming park and is the very model of a nobleman's town house, circa late seventeenth century; it bears the name of the Duc de Vendôme, a grandson of King Henri IV. There are two floors, with plasterwork walls and ceilings, paintings, and what furniture there is of high quality.

Church of St.-Jean-de-Malte (Place St.-Jean-de-Malte), built by Knights of Malta in the thirteenth century, is distinguished by an extraordinarily wide nave. The high-altar painting is exceptional, and there are nineteenth-century replacements of original tombs of a pair of ancient Comtes de Provence.

SETTLING IN

Cézanne Hôtel (40 Avenue Victor-Hugo; phone 4226-34-73) is Aix's surprise package: a relatively recently refurbished house whose interiors are an exceptionally creative—and successful—mix of antique and contemporary furniture and accessories, teamed with an eclectic range of textiles and wallpapers. Even corridors are smashing: doors of each of the 44 rooms leading from them are taken from eighteenth-century armoires. Decor of each room is distinctive. One, for example, embraces a pair of canopied beds, plaid-spreaded, with beige club chairs; in another room, green-and-white wallpaper is complemented by white woodwork and crocheted white bedspreads, with furniture a mix of Directoire and modern. There's no restaurant, but both breakfast and a range of drinks—available at any hour—are served in rooms. And the staff is at once professional and cordial. *First Class.*

Nègre Coste Hôtel (33 Cours Mirabeau; phone 4227-74-22) has more than a central location going for it. This fine eighteenth-century mansion on the city's landmark street has been transformed into an exceptionally agreeable hotel with just three dozen no-two-alike rooms, accented with antiques of the period of construction. Breakfast only. *Moderate.*

Roi René Hôtel (14 Boulevard du Roi René; phone 4226-03-01) is a gracious old-timer with a welcoming staff, a capacious series of main-floor lounges, attractively Art Deco, a restaurant (cuisine is traditional style, with regional specialties featured) overlooking a terrace (to which it moves in summer), and a good-sized swimming pool. There are 64 rooms; nicest are period style, with toile fabrics, balconies overlooking the pool, and stall showers supplementing tubs in the baths. At the other extreme are smallish rooms on the top floor. The Roi René is not heart-of-town; you're a quarter-hour's walk south of Cours Mirabeau. *First Class.*

Des Augustins Hôtel (3 Rue de la Masse; phone 4227-28-59) is well worth knowing about; location is a pleasant street just off Cours Mirabeau. Setting is a onetime Augustinian monastery, still stone-walled, with soaring arches in public spaces. Original architectural details remain, as well, in certain of the 29 rooms. *Moderate.*

St.-Christophe Hôtel (2 Avenue Victor-Hugo; phone 4226-01-24) is neat as a pin, with a friendly reception area, mod-look bar-lounge, and half a hundred brightly contemporary rooms. Central as can be—edging Cours Mirabeau at La Rotonde—and good value. *Moderate.*

Moderne Hôtel (34 Avenue Victor-Hugo) is small, efficiently run, and just down Avenue Victor-Hugo from La Rotonde; 22 rooms. Breakfast only. *Moderate.*

Le Pigonnet Hôtel (Avenue du Pigonnet; phone 4259-02-90): Were it central, Le Pigonnet would top my Aix grouping. With a car, you can be very happy in this park-encircled good-looker of a hotel—a ten-minute drive from the center. Those rooms and suites I've inspected are antique-accented, with traditional design fabrics and wallpapers and, very often, big baths. Public spaces—lounge, bar, gardens, swimming pool—are a pleasure. So, indeed, is the restaurant, which moves to a terrace in summer and is evaluated on a later page. *First Class.*

Mas d'Entremont Hôtel (Route d'Avignon, several miles north of Avignon; phone 4223-45-32) is an attractive country house—rough walls, beamed ceilings, reproduction furniture in period style—with a restaurant and just 8 rooms that, according to the proprietor-manager, are booked a year in advance by his French clientele. I received the distinct impression, in the course of my brief visit, that transatlantic guests are not welcome. *First Class.*

DAILY BREAD

Le Vendôme (Place du Général de Gaulle; phone 4226-01-00) is just the ticket for a gala Aix dinner (it's adjacent to the casino). Dine in the main salon, with a mural-topped fireplace; in an adjacent room highlighted by a stained-glass ceiling; or, in warm weather, on the terrace. Game is the specialty. There are three prix-fixe menus, with such openers as salmon rillettes or vegetable terrine, a fish course, médaillon of veal or filet of beef as entrées, cheese to follow, and a choice of desserts. *First Class/Luxury.*

Clos de la Violette (10 Avenue de la Violette; phone 4223-30-71)—just north of the cathedral—is at once comfortable and compact, with its best bet a multicourse menu that might open with the house's mussel specialty, continue with roast lamb, and conclude with a chocolate dessert. Nice. *Luxury.*

L'Abbaye des Cordeliers (21 Rue Lieutaud; phone 4227-29-47) is especially inviting on a sunny day, when your table is set under shady trees in the garden, whose residents include two dogs, a cat, and an itinerant rooster. Order either of the prix-fixe menus, opening perhaps with foie gras de canard or a beautifully presented platter of crudités-cum-dips. Brochettes d'agneau—grilled cubed lamb on a skewer—is a favored entrée, one of a number. Super sweets. Charming. *First Class.*

Flambée des Bourras (22 Rue Lieutaud; phone 4227-69-69) is rustic stone-walled in look, with grills the specialties. Smoked salmon makes a nice opener. Choose filet de bœuf, brochette Provençale, or lamb chops; for dessert, the house's own sherbet. *First Class.*

Le Bouchon (19 Rue des Tanneurs; phone 4227-92-66): The open kitchen at the rear is appetite-producing. Well-priced menus might open with piperade, the masterful omelet of the Basque country; continue with escalope de porc, nicely garnished; and then conclude with crème caramel. *Moderate.*

Le Picotin (16 Rue de la Paix; phone 4227-95-44) makes a specialty of confits—the preserved meats and poultry of the Southwest. They come off only fairly well; highlight of a meal here is its conclusion: utterly delicious baked-on-premises sweets, including mousse au chocolat served with a fresh-orange salad; tarte Tatin, the Norman upside-down cake; and a chocolate cake smothered with the irresistible sauce called crème anglaise. Small and friendly. *First Class.*

La Gousse d'Ail (15 Rue des Tanneurs; phone 4227-94-25) is a happy choice for a modestly tabbed meal. The prix-fixe might open with sautéed shrimp, garlic-accented, leeks and turnips puréed and baked in a deliciously crusted casserole; steak or gigot d'agneau, both served with frites, are entrées; sweets follow. Cordial service. *Moderate.*

Malta (28 Place des Tanneurs; phone 4225-15-43) prides itself on being Aix's first pizzeria. The pies are indeed tasty, but you may have entrecôte or poulet aux frites, if you prefer. Take a table on the terrace. *Moderate.*

Le Pigonnet Hôtel-Restaurant (Avenue du Pigonnet; phone 4259-02-90)—though away from the center—is worth the drive from town on a moonlit evening, when dinner is served al fresco. Prix-fixe menus are based on traditional specialties, and don't skip the cheese platter or, for that matter, dessert. *First Class.*

Arbaud (19 Cours Mirabeau; phone 4226-66-88) is up a flight, in a sumptuous Cours Mirabeau mansion dating back two centuries, with decor (brocaded walls hung with fine paintings and illuminated by crystal chandeliers) of the period. At lunch, salads are tasty. Go for afternoon tea. Or pop in for a dinner centered on maigret de canard (breast of duck) or filet de bœuf. *First Class.*

Café des Deux Garcons (27 Cours Mirabeau) is Aix's preeminent see-and-be-seen watering hole and has been since Émile Zola was an habitué. Take an outdoor table; order coffee, pastis, or a snack; and watch the passing parade. *Moderate.*

Palatino (1-bis Cours Mirabeau) is deservedly popular as a salon de thé with super ice cream a specialty, and a bar as well. *Moderate.*

SHOPPER'S AIX

Printemps (Avenue des Belges) and *Monoprix* (Cours Mirabeau) are principal department stores. *Souleïado,* which makes a specialty of typically Provençal hand-blocked cottons (which are sold in the United States) is on Place des Tanneurs. Rue Aude is chock-full of fine shops, including *Les Olivades* (5 Rue des Choudronniers) for Provençal-designed cotton textiles and accessories; *Geneviève Lethu* (housewares, including Provençal linens, with china in matching patterns), *La Layette* (kids' clothes), and *Comptoir Anglais du Thé* (jams and other food gifts). Rue Marius Renaud is another chic street, with *Yves St.-Laurent, Charles Jourdan, Daniel Hechter, Lasserre,* and *MicMac*—essentially for women—all represented; and such men's shops as *Daniel Crémieux*. Rue du Maréchal Foch is strollable, too, with *Rodier* and *Georges Rech* but a pair of smart shops. *Paradox* is the name of an English-language book and periodical shop at 2 Rue Reine Jeanne.

SOUND OF MUSIC

Théâtre Municipal (Rue de l'Opéra) is Aix's eye-filling, four-tier opera house, still with original nineteenth-century decor. Besides opera, there are concerts, ballet, and plays. (The last three weeks of July is the traditional time for Aix's renowned summer music festival, with events scheduled at a number of sites, including the interior and the cloister of Cathedral Saint-Saveur and Hôtel de Ville's courtyard.)

INCIDENTAL INTELLIGENCE

This is a region well served by long-distance buses, as well, of course, as by train. Avignon (chapter 7), for example, is less than an hour and a half from Aix by bus, and there are sightseeing bus tours—half-day and day-long—to regional points. *Further information:* Office de Tourisme, Place du Général de Gaulle, Aix-en-Provence.

4

Angers

Evoking the Plantagenets

BACKGROUND BRIEFING

Consider a visit to this humming, handsome, history-rich city—at the western edge of the Loire Château country—and you must, at the same time, consider the Plantagenets. The extraordinary Anglo-French dynasty—whose early nickname, a derivative of *planta Genista*, a species of bush, bits of which the clan's progenitor wore as a part of his headdress—is more properly named Angevin, connoting Angers origins. Angevin is to this day what you are called if you are fortunate enough to live here, as, indeed, did Counts of Anjou, starting in the tenth century.

One of those counts, the very same Geoffrey who wore twigs of *planta Genista* in his hats, unwittingly commenced an English relationship of consequence when he married Matilda, daughter of English King Henry I. Their son became Henry II, first of a considerable clutch of Plantagenet rulers (Richard I, John, Henry III, Edward I, Edward II, Edward III, and Richard II). But more to the point of this chapter, Henry II took as his wife no less formidable a personage than Eleanor of Aquitaine, at once daughter of the powerful Duke of Aquitaine and divorced wife of the French king, Louis VII. These first Plantagenets, whose remarkable realm came to include much of France, as well as England, not only based themselves in Angers, but lived in and expanded the castle that remains today this city's principal—and most visited—landmark. Later centuries saw dukes of Anjou, successors to the counts, rule from an increasingly wealthy Angers, with the fifteenth-century's learned, militarily cunning, and well-liked René, the last of the line.

ON SCENE

Lay of the Land: The *Maine River* flows through Angers, north to south, but does not bisect it evenly, in the manner of, say, the Seine with respect to Paris. Bulk of the city—its core—is on the east, or

Right Bank, in a quadrangular area bounded by the river to the west, *Boulevard du Général-de-Gaulle* (which becomes *Boulevard de Roi-René)* to the south, and *Boulevard Carnot* to the north. *Rue des Lices*—midships in this area—is Main Street, with big department stores like Nouvelles Galeries and Dames de France. It leads into *Place du Ralliement,* ideal starting point for a leisurely walk through *Vieux-Angers*—along atmospheric streets, lined by Renaissance and medieval houses. Still another square—this one distinguished by a half-timbered sculpture-embellished, fifteenth-century house, Maison d'Adam—is *Place Ste.-Croix.* The landmark cathedral is adjacent, and the city's multitower château is nearby, edging the river.

Château d'Angers (Place du Président-Kennedy) is the catchall name for a thirteenth-century complex flanking the Maine River, whose walls are punctuated by seventeen perfectly splendid towers, some nearly 200 feet high, and surrounded by moats, partially surfaced as formal gardens, partially the venue for a herd of deer. This longtime seat of the Counts of Anjou—almost razed in the sixteenth century, but mercifully spared—is one of the great French fortresses. There are a number of visitable interiors—a minichâteau where King René of Anjou was born half a millennium back; a charming chapel of the same era; royal apartments; and, most spectacularly, *La Tenture de l'Apocalypse,* commissioned by Duke Louis of Anjou in the fourteenth century and to this day a record holder: largest tapestry extant—551 feet long, 16 feet high. With its theme the Apocalypse—it embraces seven sections, each with a dozen subdivisions—this masterwork, in shades of red, blue, and gold, was woven in Paris over a half-decade period, beginning in 1375. It reposes in a modern pavilion constructed for the purpose, some 350 feet long. But the Apocalypse tapestry has company. Others, only somewhat more recent, are on display in the chapel and other castle spaces.

Cathedral of Saint-Maurice (Place Freppel) has a smashing situation atop stone steps that climb a fair-sized hill, ascent of which brings into perspective a building of impressive symmetry. Two bold steeples of this essentially twelfth- and thirteenth-century church flank an incongruous third, added several centuries later. The cruciform-shaped interior makes much of a splendid transept bordered by superb rose windows. The Gothic nave is handsomely vaulted and the colonnaded and gilded altar—though as recent as the eighteenth century—manages to fit well into its surroundings. Observe the stained glass created over a four-century span, starting with the twelfth. Departing the cathedral, pop into *L'Ancien Évêché* (2 Rue de l'Oisellerie), a nineteenth-century rebuilding—for the most part—of the medieval bishop's palace, still with a twelfth-century chapel, chapter room, and sixteenth-century staircase.

Musée des Beaux Arts (10 Rue du Musée) is headquartered in Logis Barrault, a turreted palace erected five centuries ago by the man whose name it takes—a rich noble who was thrice mayor of the city. Beeline for the French eighteenth-century work. Watteau's *Les Concerts Champêtres* is the most celebrated single painting. But such masters as Chardin, Boucher, Greuze, Van Loo, and Lancret are represented, too.

Hôtel Pince (a.k.a. Musée Turnin de Crisse; 12-bis Rue Lenépeveu, near Place du Ralliement) is a knockout of a Renaissance palace fronted by a formal garden that had for long been seat of a distinguished Angers family. Within, architectural and decorative features—coffered ceilings, massive fireplaces, well-proportioned staircases—are at least as interesting, to me, as displays of Oriental art.

Hôpital St.-Jean (4 Boulevard Arago): You cross the river to visit this hospital, dating to the twelfth century and used for the purpose for which it was built, to care for some 200 patients—half men (on one bay of the main ward), half women (on the other)—until as recently as 1865. There are a cloister, a chapel still with original stained glass, a wine museum in the basement, and—star of the St.-Jean show—a set of tapestries by a contemporary weaver, Jean Lurçat, collectively titled *Le Chant du Monde.*

Church of St.-Serge (Avenue Marie-Talet) is an Angers treasure—visitable principally because of the magnificent Gothic nave and pair of side aisles, an also-venerable choir, and stained glass as old as the twelfth century.

Église Réformée (12 Rue du Musée) was not, of course, a Protestant church when it went up in the twelfth century. Happily, the original architecture—that of a small, severe chapel built during the transition period between Romanesque and Gothic—remains, the capitals of columns supporting vaults the only embellishments.

Musée David d'Angers (34 Rue Toussaint): This thirteenth-century church, no longer sanctified and with a decidedly contemporary glass roof, houses works by the nineteenth-century local sculptor whose name it takes. The architectural mix of the building—opened by President Mitterrand in 1984—is decidedly striking; you will have to decide for yourself whether David's sculpture was worth all the effort.

Saumur (25 miles southeast of Angers) is a pretty Loire River town dominated by *Château de Saumur* (Place du Château) whose profile of towers, turrets, slate roofs, and chimneys has been the subject of paintings—and later photographs—ever since it was erected five centuries ago by Duke Louis I of Anjou. There have been alterations over the years, none of them seriously damaging, and the castle was put to varying uses—prison, army barracks, military arsenal. At the turn of this century, the city of Saumur bought the place, set it to rights, and installed within a pair of delightful museums. The more important—*Musée des Arts Décoratifs*—embraces an entire floor filled with furniture, art objects, porcelain, and tapestries, with the range a thirteenth-century enameled crucifix through *fauteuils* (armchairs) of the Louis XV period of the eighteenth century; the Medieval Hall—chock-filled with tapestries, furnishings, and monochrome sculpture of the Middle Ages—is perhaps the loveliest room. An upper story is for equestrians—a veritable international museum of the horse.

A quartet of Anjou châteaux: The Anjou region surrounding Angers is rich in still-inhabited châteaux, none as celebrated as the Loire châteaux to the east (chapter 20), but hardly to be passed by. Here are a selected quartet, each about a half-hour's drive east of Angers. *Château de Brissac* (Route N-748) is a veritable Renaissance skyscraper. Building seven stories skyward at the turn of the sixteenth century was by no means common. Its pair of formidable towers makes this a fortress as well as a residence. Still, state rooms are not without amenities; the range is from Gobelin tapestries, Limoges porcelain, and frescoed walls to gilded ceilings, eighteenth-century furniture, and an amusing mid-nineteenth-century theater. Your hostess is the Marquise de Brissac. *Château de Montgeoffrey* (Route D-74) is a celebration of the late eighteenth century, although it's flanked on one side by a medieval church and on the other by dramatic towers of the same period. The grand salon, within, is a felicitous mix of Louis XV furniture with Louis XVI paneling. And there are paintings by such artists as Poussin, Rigaud, Desportes, and Van Loo. La Famille Contades are your hosts. *Château de Montreuil-Bellay* (Route N-38) is surrounded by a high wall punctuated by circular towers, its inner precincts containing a splendid church and arcaded subterranean passages. Decor is based on furniture of the seventeenth and eighteenth centuries. And there is a fabulous kitchen. *Château du Plessis-Bourré* (Route N-23) is formidable from without—a veritable fortress, high-walled and with a conical tower at each of its four corners. Go inside, then, crossing the wide moat, and you'll note that this originally fifteenth-century construction is very comfortable as you pass through antique-furnished library, drawing room, and—most impressive—the intricately painted ceiling of its guard room.

SETTLING IN

Concorde Hôtel (18 Boulevard Foch; phone 4187-37-20) is a crackerjack modern house, core of town, that is one of the best equipped and best operated that I know in provincial France. There are 75 rooms and suites, each of whose baths has a proper shower-cum-curtain attached to the tub, along with plenty of soap and towels. There are thoughtful touches in the rooms, like makeup mirrors over combination desk-vanities. Staff—reception, concierges, chambermaids—is quick, bright, and smiling. And the restaurant, about which I write more on a subsequent page, is an all-Angers leader. Hôtels Concorde. *First Class.*

D'Anjou Hôtel (1 Boulevard Foch; phone 4188-24-82) is meticulously owner-managed, with half a hundred attractive rooms, Louis XV-style bar-lounge, Louis XIV-style Restaurant La Salamandre, and central situation. Very nice. Best Western. *First Class.*

Mercure Hôtel (Place Pierre-Mendès-France; phone 4160-34-81), abutting the city's modern convention center complex and Jardin des Plantes, is itself contemporary. If it will not win a beauty contest, it is neat and functional, with 86 rooms, rust-hued bar-lounge, and pink and white restaurant whose picture windows give onto the Botanical Garden. Chaîne Mercure. *First Class.*

De France Hôtel (8 Place de la Gare; phone 4188-49-42) is elderly but has been thoroughly updated; there are 62 rooms with bath or shower, reputable restaurant, and pub-bar. Near the station. *Moderate.*

Du Progrès Hôtel (26 Rue Dénis-Papin; phone 4188-10-14): This 42-room house's interior designer felt no restraint with respect to the use of primary colors, nor any inhibitions with respect to restraint in the selection of wallpapers. Withal, it is spotless, welcoming, and convenient to the railway station. Breakfast only. *Moderate.*

Le Prieuré Hôtel (Chênehutte-les-Tuffeaux, near Gennes, which is four miles west of Saumur; phone 4167-90-14) is a pristine white château—dating to the fifteenth century—in its own 60-acre park, elevated from the Loire. Public spaces are handsome, and the 40 rooms and suites are partly in the main building, partly in detached pavilions, with the higher-up riverview accommodations the choicest. The restaurant—its cuisine is traditional, albeit with contemporary accents—is exceptional; there are tennis courts and a swimming pool, and service is warm and welcoming. Member, Relais et Châteaux. *Luxury.*

DAILY BREAD

Le Toussaint (7 Place Kennedy; phone 4187-46-20) is agreeably traditional—rillettes de porc to start and entrées of beef, chicken, or local fish deliciously prepared. Unusual sweets. *Luxury.*

Le Logis (17 Rue St.-Laud; phone 4187-46-15) has made a reputation on seafood; you will not regret ordering sole prepared Logis style or any of a number of specialties, including crab-stuffed mushrooms as a starter. Very pleasant. Central. *First Class.*

Le Grand Cercle (Concorde Hôtel, 18 Boulevard Foch; phone 4188-52-37) is big, bustling, and welcoming, with a pleasant buzz, especially at lunch, when Angers business types come in to help themselves from the huge—and delicious—buffet, an Angers institution. You do well, too, with soupe à l'oignon to start, entrées like brochette or filet of beef, and grilled lamb chops. And don't skip the gratin potatoes. *First Class.*

Belle Rive (25-bis Rue Haute Reculée; phone 4148-18-70) is well named, given a situation overlooking the Maine River, a few minutes' drive from the center of town. Start with soupe au poisson, continue with entrecôte Roquefort, and conclude with the house's own profiteroles au chocolat—a rich, puff-pastry-and-chocolate confection. Friendly. *Moderate.*

Le Blé Noir (43 Rue Delâge; phone 4187-03-81): You're just next door to Brittany—whence French crêpes originated. There's a big choice of them here, savory and sweet. *Moderate.*

Pâtisserie/Salon de Thé du Château (55 Rue Toussaint) is just the spot for a midmorning or midafternoon pick-me-up; made-on-premises pastries accompany your tea or coffee. *Moderate.*

AFTER DARK

Théâtre Municipal (Place du Ralliement), elaborately Second Empire, with a frescoed ceiling, is the site of concerts, drama, and ballet.

INCIDENTAL INTELLIGENCE

Further information: Office de Tourisme, Place du Président-Kennedy, Angers.

5

Annecy

and Savoie: Aix, Chambéry, Évian

BACKGROUND BRIEFING

Alpine peaks? They're for mountain climbers, skiers, and, of course, the rest of us who enjoy cable-car rides to their summits-cum-views (chapter 14). But what of history-laden towns in Alpine valleys? In the case of France's Savoie region, they constitute treasure troves of art and architecture complemented by lakes that are inland seas and by backdrop mountains that have assured centuries-long insularity. Only in relatively recent years have outlanders like ourselves popped in to partake of their spectacular beauty.

The point about urban Savoie, if that it may be called, is that, unlike the winter resorts—which are a modern phenomenon—it considerably predates the mountaineers. Though it is compact—French Savoie is bordered on the north by Lake Geneva, on the west by the Rhône, on the south by France's Dauphiné country (which is centered on Grenoble—chapter 18), and on the east by the massif along which lie its borders with Italy and Switzerland—it is not lacking in the patina that is a concomitant of advanced age. The range has been Julius Caesar through Burgundians, Holy Roman emperors, and later Savoy kings in power through the middle of the last century.

In common with lesser nobles, the church, and a long-wealthy mercantile class, Savoie's governors have left their mark in these towns. None of them is big or of special contemporary significance. But they combine to present a dimension of France like no other in the republic. And Annecy—its castle out of the Brothers Grimm, its canals overhung with flowers and swan-populated, its lake a shimmering jewel—takes pride of place.

ON SCENE

Lay of the Land: Dominant landmarks make Annecy geographically quick to comprehend. *Lac d'Annecy*—nine miles long, two miles wide, and third-largest in France—edges its core to the east, with jagged, snow-dusted peaks backing it. *Thiou Canal,* flowing on a west–east axis into the lake, is flanked by a jumble of pedestrian streets like *rues Ste.-Claire, Perrière,* and *Filaterie,* the lot of them lined by fine old houses, Renaissance through rococo, with outdoor cafés at intersecting squares. *Jardin Public,* a public park occupying a peninsula jutting into the lake, is the point from which lake steamers depart. The railway station is northwest of the center on *Place de la Gare.*

Château d'Annecy (Place du Château) was home to counts of Geneva for most of the thirteenth century, until the last of the family line became Pope Clement VII and made his home in Avignon (chapter 7). Dukes of Savoie were their successors through the mid-eighteenth century. You go to see it not only to appreciate its architecture—it is a maze of square towers with high-ceilinged inner spaces and a broad terrace affording panoramas of peaks, lake, and city—but also to take in *Musée d'Annecy.* Relatively recent—and utilizing contemporary museum presentation techniques—this is a compendium of Annecy history, at its best in the section relating to the town's Roman origins, with some superb sculpture; but with a plethora of antique furniture, pewter, and pottery as well.

Cathedral of St.-Pierre (Rue Jean-Jacques Rousseau), originally a Franciscan church, severely facaded, is mellow within—boasting a fine Gothic nave and exuberantly Baroque altar, pulpit, and organ. St. François de Sales, Annecy-born and canonized for his accomplishments in converting Protestants to Catholicism during the Counter-Reformation of the seventeenth century, lived across the street while he was bishop of Annecy.

Church of St.-Maurice (Rue Granette), originally the chapel of a Dominican convent and enlarged in the fifteenth century, has as its prime lures a pair of Renaissance frescoes discovered quite by accident as recently as 1953, as well as a striking interpretation by the eighteenth-century painter Pieter Purbus, *The Descent from the Cross.*

Mont Veyrier, Lac d'Annecy, and Talloires: Mont Veyrier, some 4,000 feet over town, is easily ascended by cable car—departures are frequent; views, unforgettable. When you come down, allow time—several leisurely hours—for a boat tour of the lake. You may go for lunch or dinner on the water or on a boat sans restaurant. There are stops at villages along the way; if you've time to go ashore, select pretty little *Talloires,* with exceptional hotels and fare (below). Better yet, budget time for a stay of a night or two in Talloires—to completely unwind.

Aix-les-Bains (21 miles south of Annecy), though by no means out of business—everything's up to date in its popular thermal spa—just has to be a shadow of what it must have been a century and more back, when moneybags Victorians (including Victoria herself, with Avenue Victoria commemorating the royal visit) and even Americans (Boulevard Pierpont-Morgan is north of the core) came to take the waters, first put to therapeutic use by rheumatic Romans. But that is hardly to suggest that you not visit Aix. Taken as a period piece—alas, its grand hotels are no longer—it is not without interest. And Aix's setting—edging Lac de Bourget at the foot of Mont-Revard—remains spectacular. Indeed, a cable-car ascent of the mountain—for an overall view of town and lake—makes for a proper introduction. Amble about the center of its pedestrian shopping area. *Palais de Savoie* (Rue du Casino) is the casino; you might like to try your hand at roulette, and there's a restaurant (with dinner-dancing) on the premises—fin de siècle, with a mosaic ceiling embellishing the lobby. *Thermes Nationaux* (Place des Thermes) is the spa. It was built in the last century, but it's gone through contemporary updating; you might be given a tour if you express interest at the reception desk. *Musée Lapidaire,* located in Hôtel de Ville, the town hall, is smallish but with choice sculpted remnants of Roman Aix. *Musée Faure* (Boulevard des Côtes) has as its trademark a Degas painting of a pair of tutu-clad ballerinas, but there are a number of other distinguished works, mostly nineteenth century, by the likes of Cézanne, Sisley, and Pissarro. Move along, then, to Boulevard du Lac, to take in small craft bobbing in the waters of *Petit Port,* which has both a public swimming pool and a bathing beach. Conclude with an excursion by lake steamer—there are frequent departures—of *Lac du Bourget,* zeroing in on a single destination like the pretty village of *Le Bourget du Lac* (whose originally eleventh-century *Prieuré,* a onetime cloistered monastery-cum-garden, welcomes visitors) or opting for the Grand Tour du Lac, an overall view of a beautiful segment of Savoie.

Chambéry (14 miles from Annecy), smallish and uncelebrated contemporarily, knew eminence in earlier centuries. As early as the fifth, it was the seat of a bishop. From the early thirteenth through the mid-sixteenth, its castle was home to dukes of Savoy. It remained rich enough to have built, in the early nineteenth century, the elegantly arcaded street, *Rue de Boigné,* which cuts through town—passing *Place St.-Léger,* core of the pedestrian shopping precinct—from one principal monument to a second. The first is *Château des Ducs de Savoie* (Place du Château), a still splendid complex and locale of both *Cathedral of St. François de Sales* (Gothic with a lovely apse and cloister) and *Ste.-Chapelle* (Gothic, as well, with its kicker a painted *trompe l'oeil* ceiling that looks stone-carved but isn't) and fine stained glass. The second, at the opposite end of porticoed Rue de Boigné, is *Fontaine des Éléphants* (Place Octagone), a nineteenth-century tribute to the same wealthy and generous local whose name was given to Rue de Boigné and who struck it rich in Asia; thus, its standout feature—life-sized, sculpted elephants peering out at pedestrians from each of the monument's four sides. *Musée des Beaux-Arts* (Place du Palais de Justice) surprises with its estimable collection. Italians are especially strong—Titian, Giordano, Guercino, and Uccello, whose *Portrait of a Young Man* is the star of the show. *Musée Savoisien's* (Boulevard du Théâtre) ranking exhibits are a clutch of medieval paintings—so-called Savoie Primitives—and sculptures; the setting is super: a onetime Franciscan monastery-cum-cloister.

Évian, an unassuming little spa town on the south shore of the Lake of Geneva (a.k.a. Lac Léman), just opposite the Swiss city of Lausanne (with which it is linked by frequent and fast—45-minute—ferry service), bases itself on *Rue Nationale,* a pedestrian-shopping core that parallels the lake, with adjacent and handsomely maintained public beaches and swimming pool. In a flower-embellished, parklike setting, you'll find a modern spa building where visitors drink the therapeutic water (not the same as the Évian bottled table water, a staple throughout France) and a surprisingly small, mod-look casino, without so much as a whiff of grandeur. Less costly hotels are in this area, with the two best atop the hill that backs the town. Excitement? Aside from the casino, there's a cable car at nearby *Thollon* (several miles east) that ascends to the summit of *Plateau des Mémises* (4,800 feet). And there's lots of golf, tennis, and sailing on the lake. You go to Évian to relax.

SETTLING IN

ANNECY

Carlton Hôtel (Rue des Glières at Rue St.-François; phone 5045-47-75) is at once central and agreeable, with half a hundred traditional-style rooms in tones of brown and gold, bar-lounge, and inviting lobby. Breakfast only. *First Class.*

Au Faisan Doré Hôtel (34 Avenue d'Albigny; phone 5023-02-46) is lakefront and attractive, with just over 40 rooms—those I've seen are pleasant, although beds can be narrow—a flower-filled lobby, and a reliable restaurant, counseled below. *Moderate.*

La Réserve Hôtel (21 Avenue d'Albigny; phone 5023-50-24) is a deftly converted residence of some years, with just a dozen inviting rooms in shades of rose and beige, nicely wallpapered; a bar-lounge; and, in a modern wing, a picture-window restaurant. Lakefront. *Moderate.*

Ibis Hôtel (12 Rue de la Gare; phone 5045-43-21) is heart-of-town, in the pedestrian shopping zone, with 83 rooms, which are functional, if hardly fancy; a restaurant; and a bar. *Moderate.*

Alp Hôtel (26 Rue Vaugélas; phone 5045-59-80) has as its plus a core-of-the-city situation. This is a plainly modernized elderly house with 40 minimally furnished rooms, whose beds are the narrowest I have encountered in France. Breakfast only. *Moderate.*

TALLOIRES, LAC D'ANNECY

L'Abbaye Hôtel (phone 5060-77-33) is precisely what its name implies, a seventeenth-century Benedictine abbey—lakefront and cloistered. Monks' cells have been deftly converted into guest rooms—just 31, no two alike, each (of those I inspected) antique-accented and with good paintings. Rooms lead from either the cloister or a two-story-high gallery; their windows give onto the lake. Public spaces, including a bar-lounge in the monks' *cave* and a restaurant about which I write in a later paragraph, are a pleasure; management and staff are delightful. This is certainly one of France's most beautiful hotels. Member, Relais et Châteaux. *Luxury.*

Auberge du Père Bise (phone 5060-72-01) is the only luxury hotel I know of whose glass-walled kitchen is just opposite the reception desk in the lobby, a reflection of the significance management wisely accords the justifiably celebrated on-premises restaurant, evaluated in a later paragraph. The hotel itself—there are 34 suites and rooms—spreads itself around its own lakefront park, occupying several pavilions, with decor of accommodations varying, from Louis XIII with beamed ceilings to quite grand Louis XV. There's a congenial bar-lounge with a player piano (it doesn't need a pianist) that's fun. The third generation of the founding family is in charge of a skilled and friendly staff. Member, Relais et Châteaux. *Luxury.*

L'Hermitage Hôtel (phone 5060-71-17), straddling a Talloires summit, is a contemporary house with a good-sized swimming pool, congenial bar-lounge, 40 terraced rooms, a picture-window restaurant serving traditional cuisine, and absolutely fabulous views. *First Class.*

AIX-LES-BAINS

Ariana Hôtel (Avenue de Marlioz; phone 7988-08-00)—set back in an away-from-the-center park adjacent to Marlioz Spa, which is No. 2 in Aix after that in the core of town—is modern, with 60 terraced and tasteful rooms, swimming pool, and both bar-lounge and restaurant attractively Art Deco. Impersonal service. *First Class.*

Le Manoir Hôtel (37 Rue George 1er; phone 7961-44-00) is an old-timer with a look of flowered wallpaper and upholstery, and just over 70 rooms, some good-sized and with terraces. Restaurant. Situation is the summit of a veritable mountain overlooking town; you need a car. *Moderate.*

CHAMBÉRY

Le Grand Hôtel (8 Place de la Gare; phone 7969-54-54) would be even more desirable if it were more into the center, which is, however, easily walkable. This is a gracious, good-looking house, with high-ceilinged public spaces and 55 suites and rooms; those I have seen are traditional-style, smart, comfortable. And don't neglect its reliable restaurant, La Vanoise. *First Class.*

Des Princes Hôtel (4 Rue de Boigné; phone 7933-45-36) is nicely situated on Chambéry's snazziest street. The lobby is welcoming, those of the 50 rooms I have inspected—decor varies—are agreeable, and the restaurant is worthy of space in a later paragraph. *Moderate.*

ÉVIAN-LES-BAINS

Royal Hôtel (phone 5075-14-00) has the best location in town: high above the hill overlooking Évian and the Lake of Geneva (when the atmosphere is clear, you can see Lausanne), in its own 28-acre deer-filled park. The building went up at the turn of the century, when ceilings were high, proportions grandiose, decorative detail extravagant. A few years back, the current owners—the Pomméry champagne people—set aside a multimillion-franc budget, hired architects and interior designers from Paris, and set about restoring this grande dame stylishly, but retaining the atmosphere of the era in which it was constructed. They succeeded. A series of extraordinarily handsome lounges lead from the lobby, along with a kicky cocktail lounge and an enormous formal restaurant. Upstairs, there are 200 suites and rooms; those I have inhabited or inspected are smashers—capacious and terraced (you want to specify lakefront) with decor luxuriously low-key. There's a swimming pool in the garden (around which barbecue lunches are served in summer), tennis courts-cum-pro, eighteen-hole golf course, a health club with attached dietetic restaurant, shuttle-bus service to the casino in town, and skilled concierges. Affiliated with both Leading Hotels of the World and Hôtels Concorde. *Luxury.*

La Verniaz Hôtel (phone 5075-04-90) embraces an impeccably maintained garden complex up in the hills behind town, with suites, chalets, and rooms—no two alike, but those I have inspected, comfortable—located in a mix of pavilions dotted about the swimming-pool-centered grounds. Lounges are stone-walled, with a country look; the cocktail bar could be a mountain chalet; and the restaurant, which moves outdoors in summer, is exemplary enough to warrant later comment. Management is friendly; staff, professional. Member, Relais et Châteaux. *First Class.*

Bellevue Hôtel (Rue Nationale; phone 5075-01-13) is a lovely, old-fashioned house, heart-of-town, with capacious public areas, corking good restaurant, pretty garden, and half a hundred rooms, with lake-front ones the nicest. *Moderate.*

La Bourgogne Hôtel (Rue Nationale; phone 5075-01-05) belies its advanced age with exceptionally good-looking rooms (two dozen all told) and phone-equipped baths. The reputed restaurant is well worth a visit, even if you're staying elsewhere. It's *First Class,* but the hotel is *Moderate.*

De La Plage Hôtel (Avenue Général-Dupas; phone 5075-29-50) is indicated for swimmers; it's opposite the municipal pool and adjacent beach. Some rooms are lakeview, some face the garden; those I've seen are smart. Restaurant and bar. *Moderate.*

DAILY BREAD

ANNECY

Auberge du Lyonnais (Quai de l'Évêché at Rue de la République, phone 5051-26-10) is congenial, canal-bordering, and heart-of-town, with perfectly delicious things to eat. From the well-priced menu, a meal might run to smoked Savoie ham, a slice of the house's own terrine de petits légumes, or grilled trout, followed by roast lamb or roast duck, the latter served with gratin Dauphinois; both cheese and dessert courses are included. Friendly. *First Class.*

Auberge de Savoie (1 Place St.-François, adjacent to the landmark Annecy church for which the square is named; phone 5045-03-05) is intimate and nicely appointed, with a competent kitchen. Order from the good-value menu, choosing perhaps a fish soup, filet of veal, deliciously sauced, with tartes aux fraises—buried under an avalanche of whipped cream—to conclude. *First Class.*

Auberge de l'Éridan (7 Avenue de Chavoires, in Annecy-le-Vieux, northwest of the center; phone 5066-22-04) is, if you're flush and in the market for a luxurious meal, worth the trip from the core of town. This is an attractive restaurant, with such tempters among specialties on its multicourse menus as garlic-scented foie gras, lake fish prepared house style, and crème brûlée as I'm sure you haven't had it before. Deft service, fine wines. *Luxury.*

Au Faisan Doré Hôtel Restaurant (34 Avenue d'Albigny; phone 5023-02-46) is a source of lake fish, skillfully prepared, with meat entrées as well, the lot served in conjunction with well-tabbed menus. It is lakefront and *Moderate.*

Le Crocodile (Place Ste.-Claire; phone 5045-31-30) bases its reputation on specialties of the Savoie: the hot cheese and kirsch dip called fondue; raclette, a cheese dish you may know from Switzerland; and super Savoie sausages. *Moderate.*

MS. Libellule (reservations, phone 5051-08-40) is the sleek white lake steamer that sails each evening at eight o'clock from its heart-of-town pier on a two-and-a-half hour Lac d'Annecy dinner excursion. A traditional multicourse meal is served on white linen in a candlelit, picture-windowed dining room. Entertainment follows dinner, and there's a piano-bar aboard. Lunchtime sailings, too. Fun. *First Class.*

Le Fidèle Berger (Rue Royale) is in the heart of the pedestrian shopping area and indicated for a coffee/tea and pastry stop. *Moderate.*

Pub Cheltenham (Passage de l'Évêché) is a waterfront café. Pause for something to drink, the while taking in the beauty of Annecy—and its crowds. *Moderate.*

TALLOIRES, LAC D'ANNECY

Auberge du Père Bise (phone 5060-72-01): As I indicate when evaluating the hotel part of this lakefront operation (above), the open-to-view kitchen is just opposite reception as you enter—an indication of the importance attached to a well-regarded restaurant. You may order from an extensive à la carte, but there are three prix-fixe menus, too. The least pricey might include oysters prepared the house's own way or pigeon casserole, followed by cheese and méli-mélo—a fabulous mélange of fruits and ice cream—with baked-on-premises petits-fours to accompany coffee. Tarragon-flavored or truffled chicken, lobster grilled or as the basis of a Breton-origin stew; roast shoulder or saddle of lamb, a goose-liver masterwork (escalope de foie d'oie Richelieu)—these are a handful of other memorable entrées. Breakfast is special here, too, with the best croissants I have had outside of Paris, except for those at De La Poste Hôtel in Beaune. And service is as skilled as it is smiling. In my experience, one of France's best restaurants. *Luxury.*

L'Abbaye Hôtel Restaurant (phone 5067-40-88) presents a pair of four-course, prix-fixe menus. You might commence with a terrine of foie gras de canard served in tandem with a salad, continue with an unusual escalope of lake trout served with a confit of onions, follow with cheese from an oversized platter, and conclude with choice of desserts. *First Class.*

AIX-LES-BAINS

Lille (Grand-Port; phone 7935-04-22)—not surprisingly, given its garden-backed, lakefront setting—does very well by fish. There are well-priced menus and an à la carte as well. Consider a meal that would open with omble (char—a type of salmon), champagne-sauced; continue with the house's sautéed chicken specialty; and conclude with a mouthwatering raspberry soufflé. Congenial. *First Class.*

Brasserie de la Poste (32 Avenue Victoria; phone 7935-00-65) is old-reliable, heart-of-town, and satisfactory for a lunch of, say, entrecôte aux frites or salade Niçoise. If it's sunny, take an outdoor table. *Moderate.*

La Verre d'Eau (Place de l'Hôtel de Ville): You're determined to be the first on your block to taste Aix's long-celebrated thermal water. As the title suggests, this café is the place. Outdoor tables. *Moderate.*

CHAMBÉRY

Des Princes Hôtel Restaurant (4 Rue de Boigné; phone 7933-45-36) makes its home in a delightful, traditional-style room and serves up essentially traditional-style fare. Open with foie gras or a salad based on smoked breast of goose and choose grilled filet of beef—deliciously garnished and sauced—as your entrée. Very nice, indeed. *First Class.*

Roubatcheff (6 Rue du Théâtre; phone 7933-24-01): There are three prix-fixe menus and an à la carte, including such specialties as smoked-trout salad; brochette of grilled fish, a kind of marine shishkebab; fricasee of chicken, Roquefort-sauced; and a luxuriant Grand Marnier soufflé. Attractive. *First Class/Luxury.*

La Venoise (44 Rue Pierre-Lanfrey; phone 7969-02-78) is tiny, cramped, and overdecorated, but food can be satisfactory, as, for example, a meal embracing fish soup or a casserole of baked mussels, filet of red snapper, basil-scented, or a competently sauced filet de bœuf accompanied by pommes Dauphiné. *First Class.*

Taverne (Place St.-Léger) is heart-of-the-action, on the square that anchors the pedestrian shopping zone. Take an outside table. *Moderate.*

ÉVIAN-LES-BAINS

La Verniaz Hôtel Restaurant (phone 5075-04-90) is at its best in summer, when tables are set in the garden. But the indoor restaurant—tables set in pink linen, with Louis XV chairs—is attractive, too. The two menus are both good value. A meal might commence with the house's own hot trout terrine or fresh foie gras, continue with saffron-scented steamed turbot or aiguillettes de canard, with cheese and dessert following. And note that grilled meats are a specialty—the filet of Charolais beef for two and grilled lamb chops especially. *First Class/Luxury.*

SOUND OF MUSIC

Théâtre Charles-Dullin (Rue du Théâtre, Chambéry) is a regional showplace—nineteenth-century, and based on the design of Teatro alla Scala in Milan. Go for opera, ballet, concerts.

INCIDENTAL INTELLIGENCE

Aéroport de Chambéry-Aix-les-Bains, is at Le Bourget-du-Lac, five miles north of Chambéry; scheduled domestic flights. *Further information:* Office de Tourisme, 1 Rue Jean-Jaurès, Annecy; Place Mollard, Aix-les-Bains; 24 Boulevard de la Colonne, Chambéry; Place d'Allinges, Évian-les-Bains.

6

Arles

Caesar's Legions and Van Gogh

BACKGROUND BRIEFING

The irony of this small Provençal town is that despite early eminence as a Roman colonial city founded by no less an emperor than Julius Caesar—with still-standing Caesar-commissioned constructions—it was not until after a prolific Dutch-born artist came for a 15-month sojourn some 900 years later that it achieved a measure of global repute.

And the irony is compounded when one considers that even though Vincent Van Gogh created some 200 paintings, drawings, and watercolors during his Arles stay, not a single one of his works hangs in its art museum. The painter's association with the town is evident today only in postcard reproductions of works in distant galleries, for sale at the occasional news kiosk. A multilingual brochure, *Arles et Van Gogh,* published by the city tourist office, acknowledges the "hostile attitude of the Arlesian people" toward Van Gogh, but concludes that Arles "feels thankful to Van Gogh for having placed the name of the city in all the greatest museums of the world." As well it might.

The point of an Arles visit today is not, then, association with Van Gogh (of what he painted, only a rural road flanked by stone sarcophagi and a rebuilt out-of-town bridge, *Le Pont de Langlois,* remain), but, rather, the heritage of the Romans. They followed earlier Phoenicians and Greeks who had been attracted to this town's strategic situation at the mouth of the Rhône. Caesar's town dates to 49 B.C., and was heaped with perquisites accorded only those colonies in whose establishment he had a personal hand. Later emperors, like Constantine and Honorius, saw Arles only as the hub of the early Christian world, and it became the seat of regional archbishops. Now, though, its onetime cathedral is but a parish church.

ON SCENE

Lay of the Land: Although the Rhône flows through Arles, you've only to concern yourself with the larger right bank of town, whose core is marked by *Place de la République,* seat of a pair of landmarks: Hôtel de Ville, or city hall, and Church of St.-Trophime, the one-time cathedral. Commercial *Rue de la République* runs east-west, just below the square taking its name. What remains of the Roman theater edges *Place Pomme,* to the west, while the massive amphitheater is centered on *Rond-Point des Arènes,* directly to Place Pomme's north. *Boulevard des Lices* runs east-west and constitutes the southern edge of the city center; the railway station is at its northern tip.

Les Arènes (Rond-Point des Arènes): Some 1,900 years young, this amphitheater remains in use—not unlike its Nîmes counterpart—for the Provençal species of bullfighting, and you're in luck if your visit coincides with one of these spectacles. In any event, have a look at this remarkable monument, embracing 60 arches in its two remaining levels and built to accommodate 20,000 Roman-era Arlésiens, who came for the excitement of contests pitting gladiators against savage animals. The Middle Ages saw the amphitheater put to use as an enclosure for houses and shops, and the three towers built at that period—to fortify it—remain.

Théâtre Antique (Rue de la Calade): When they weren't watching gladiators at Les Arènes (above), ancient Arlésiens went to the theater, as, indeed, their descendants do many centuries later. Alas, much less of this theater remains than of the bigger amphitheater. A solitary pair of columns behind the stage—nicknamed Deux Veuves (Two Widows)—are reminders of what had been a fine portico, enclosed by a three-tiered arcade that surrounded a space large enough to accommodate 12,000 spectators. Arrive in Arles during July, and chances are the theater will be in use for a play or pageant.

Les Alyscamps (Avenue des Alyscamps, southeast of the center) is what, over long centuries, Arles has come to call this unusual cemetery originally named Champs Élysées—Elysian Fields. It is nothing more than an elongated thoroughfare on either side of which residents, from the early Christian era through the Middle Ages, ordered elaborate sarcophagi containing their dead to be placed. Over the centuries, most of the best tombs disappeared; some, however, are now to be seen in the Musée d'Art Chrétien (below), while some—of lesser quality—remain in Les Alyscamps (not all that different today from when Van Gogh painted it). A ruined Romanesque Church, *St.-Honorat,* is at its terminus.

Musée Lapidaire (Place de la République) has as its inspired location the desanctified seventeenth-century Church of Ste.-Anne, its high and splendid Gothic-inspired vaults a fine foil for mint-condition Roman-era mosaics that line what had been the nave. The latter are flanked by other early Arles pieces—strikingly carved sarcophagi, fine busts, and full-length statues as well.

Musée d'Art Chrétien (Rue Balze) is still another desanctified church seeing contemporary service as a repository of ancient art. Beautifully Baroque, originally built by Jesuits, it brims with lovely objects, most of them early Christian sarcophagi—many from Les Alyscamps (above)—with biblical scenes replacing those relating to Roman mythology in the sarcophagi at Musée Lapidaire (above). Take your time studying these; workmanship is exceptional. Before exiting, descend to the cellars—a 300 × 500-foot space built approximately 2,000 years ago as a granary of superb proportions.

Church and Cloister of St.-Trophime (Place de la République): A cathedral until the eighteenth century, St.-Trophime had a great deal of art lavished upon it, more than would appear from its modest-sized facade. Indeed, its portal, framed by a pediment, occupies easily half of that otherwise simple exterior. Pause before entering to get an idea of the way sculptors set to work in the twelfth century, portraying the Old Testament for largely illiterate worshipers. The lunette above the door is Christ as the judge of the Last Judgment, with the angel of St. Matthew, the eagle of St. John, the ox of St. Luke, and a legendary St. Mark's lion being blessed. The frieze directly below is a representation of the twelve apostles, while an assortment of saints stand in niches, between columns, on either side of the door. Inside, concentrate on finely worked sarcophagi dotted about an otherwise unexciting space. I save best for last: a separately entered Romanesque cloister (the cathedral was originally staffed by resident monks), which is the single most outstanding monument of Arles, along with Les Arènes (above). Give time not only to capitals above columns supporting arches ringing the cloisters, but to statues of saints at each of the four corners—especially on the east and north sides, which are twelfth-century—some 200 years older than the remaining work.

Musée Réattu (Rue du Grande Prieuré) is as good a reason as any for a walk through atmospheric older sections of the city to this utterly beautiful fifteenth-century palace, for long the Arles seat of the Knights of Malta and, since the early decades of the last century, repository not only of works—some of them interesting—by the Arles-born artist for whom it is named (and who became its owner), but of eighteenth-century furniture dotted about, in rooms graced by beamed ceilings and massive fireplaces; a onetime chapel is the handsomest. Paintings are mostly French, with a Simon Vouet self-portrait outstanding. There are works, as well, by the likes of Gauguin and Dufy, Marquet and Vlaminck, with the kicker of the collection a clutch of 57 Picasso drawings, many of them portraying clowns.

Musée Arlaten (Rue de la République) makes its home in a sixteenth-century palace. Its theme is the Arles life-style over the centuries. There are a couple score galleries, the best of which are period rooms, meticulously furnished and accessorized, even to mannequins appropriately costumed; a dining room set for a traditional feast and a kitchen are standouts.

Camargue is the name given to marshland flanking the Rhône delta as the river flows south from Arles to the Mediterranean; much of it is cultivated, principally with good-quality rice. There is, as well, a not inconsiderable population of horses and bulls, kept in check by what have come to be called Camargue cowboys. I can understand the fascination of French visitors with these wide, open, albeit somewhat soggy, spaces, but it has always seemed to me that France has points of considerably more interest, at least for transatlantic visitors familiar with the American West. Excursion boats make daily trips from Arles during the summer. There are bus tours as well, and of course you may go on your own. Essentials include *Musée Camarguais*—all that you wanted to know about the area, its people, animals, and agriculture—at Mas du Pont de Rousty; and the charmingly named village of *Stes.-Maries-de-la-Mer,* whose lure is a fortified Romanesque church with walkable ramparts.

Les-Baux-de-Provence (13 miles north of Arles) is the name of a village, half atop a tablelike stone mountain, half at the mountain's base. And, thanks to smart hotels, reputable restaurants, and trendy shops, the elevated portion of Les Baux has become a destination of consequence for travelers in Provence and an easy excursion—ideally for lunch, if not overnight—from Arles, or from Avignon (chapter 7) to the north. A part of the rocky mountain range known as the Alpilles, Les Baux (which, incidentally, gave its name to the mineral bauxite, mined nearby—has medieval origins, with both a castle and a village (eerily called La Ville Morte) to prove its age. What you especially want to visit, though, are the shops of *Grande Rue; Musée d'Art Moderne* in a Renaissance mansion; contemporary murals in *Chapelle des Pénitents-Blancs;* and, more impressive and much older, *Church of St.-Vincent,* a mini-Romanesque marvel.

SETTLING IN

Jules César Hôtel (Boulevard des Lices; phone 9093-43-20) was built as a Carmelite convent in the seventeenth century and converted with panache into a perfectly lovely 61-room hotel. The cloister has been glassed in, and the rooms are capacious, with excellent baths, and no two rooms are alike in their traditional good looks. The lobby-lounge is one of the biggest and best-looking of any such that I know in France. Management is astute, staff is blessed with sunny Provençal dispositions, and restaurant is worthy of comment in a later paragraph. Member, Relais et Châteaux. *First Class.*

D'Arlatan Hôtel (26 Rue du Sauvage, near Place du Forum; phone 9093-56-66) went up as the château of Comtes d'Arlatan de Beaumont. Credit them with building a substantial sixteenth-century house on an even older base. Stone-walled public rooms are atmospheric and welcoming, and there's a pretty garden that's pleasant for drinks. The hotel has just under a half a hundred rooms; those I've seen are charming. Friendly owner-management. Breakfast only. *First Class.*

L'Atrium Hôtel (1 Rue Fassini, phone 9049-92-92) is a modern, atrium-centered hostelry, with a pair of restaurants (the Brasserie is good-value) and 91 nicely designed rooms with good baths. *First Class.*

Reginel Hôtel (45 Avenue Sadi-Carnot; phone 9093-93-93) is not as central as the also contemporary L'Atrium (above) but it's an agreeable, full-facility house with nearly 70 pleasant rooms, restaurant, bar, and indoor pool. *First Class.*

Forum Hôtel (10 Place Forum; phone 9093-48-95) makes good use of wallpapers, textiles, and antique accents in the decor of its public spaces and 43 bedrooms. Bar-lounge is cozy, and there's a swimming pool out back. *Moderate.*

Calendal Hôtel (22 Place Pomme; phone 9096-11-89) is a near-neighbor of the Roman theater. There are 17 neat rooms, a bar, and a welcoming garden. *Moderate.*

Cloître Hôtel (18 Rue Cloître; phone 9096-29-50) and the street on which it's situated take their names from the nearby cloister of St.-Trophime Church; you're heart-of-town in this 31-room-cum-bar house; breakfast only. *Moderate.*

Oustau de Baumanière Hôtel (Les-Baux-de-Provence; phone 9097-33-07) is an aged Les Baux dwelling in the shadow of the village's also ancient château, with stone-walled public spaces, antique-accented accommodations (there's a high percentage of suites—11, in contrast to 15 regular rooms), panoramic terrace and swimming pool, pair of tennis courts, and restaurant worthy of comment on a later page. Member, Relais et Châteaux. *Luxury.*

Cabro d'Or Hôtel (Les-Baux-de-Provence; phone 9097-33-21) is owned and operated by the Oustau management (above). It, too, occupies venerable quarters, agreeably updated in traditional style: 22 rooms, delightful restaurant and bar, swimming and tennis. Member, Relais et Châteaux. *First Class.*

Auberge la Fenière (a few miles east of Arles on Route N-453; phone 9098-47-44) is—if you have a car—an indicated overnight stop. Each of its 25 rooms is individually decorated, the garden is pretty, and the restaurant reliable, with multicourse menus that can be good value midday. *First Class.*

DAILY BREAD

Lou Marques Restaurant (Jules César Hôtel, Boulevard des Lices; phone 9093-43-20) sports classy, old-school good looks and gives onto a terrace where meals are served in warm weather, on tables set with pink linen. There is a pair of prix-fixe menus—sweetbread salad, a remarkable chicken stew, a homemade pasta, and cheese and desserts from a wagon might be the order of battle—and an extensive à la carte that includes fish soup, fresh foie gras, and a reputable filet mignon. Super service. *Luxury.*

Côté Cour (Rue André Pichot; phone 9049-77-76) is among Arles's newer esteemed restaurants, and with good-value—and tasty—multicourse menus. *First Class.*

Vaccarès Restaurant (Place du Forum; phone 9096-06-07): I retain pleasant memories of a delicious navarin d'agneau—old-fashioned lamb stew—at this long-on-scene restaurant. It has, since then, become more *nouvelle*-accented but with the beef entrées and desserts quite special. No credit cards. *First Class.*

Tourne Broche (6 Rue Balze; phone 9096-16-03) is indicated for lunch after touring Musée d'Art Chrétien just opposite. Walk through a courtyard and you're in an elongated *cave*-like room, where the chef-owner serves up a prix-fixe menu that might run to fish soup with a dollop of hot rouille sauce atop it, pork filet teamed with endives, cheese, and a sweet. *Moderate.*

Arlésienne (Boulevard des Lices; phone 9096-40-72) terms itself a *grande brasserie,* which means you may order anything from coffee or a simple snack to a roast chicken with frites. Outside tables. *Moderate.*

Hippocampe (Rue Charles-Pelletan, Stes.-Maries-de-la-Mer; phone 9091-80-91): a reliable choice for a lunch based on seafood in the course of a Camargue outing. *First Class.*

Ostau de Baumanière Hôtel Restaurant (Les-Baux-de-Provence; phone 9097-33-07) is the celebrated dining room of a celebrated hotel; you lunch or dine beneath massive electrified lanterns seated on Louis XIII chairs beneath stone arches. Open with foie gras, bisque de homard, crayfish salad, or filet of red mullet in an unusual red-wine sauce; cream-sauced chicken with mushrooms and the house's celebrated gigot d'agneau in a light pastry shell are indicated entrées. And you'll not have an easy time with dessert choice, although the house's gâteau au chocolat is a classic choice. The cellar is arguably the best in southern France. *Luxury.*

Riboto de Taven (Les-Baux-de-Provence; phone 9097-34-23) occupies a centuries-old stone house, antique-filled and with a honey of a terrace. Fare is exceptional. Seafood openers are indicated here. Entrées of roast quail, rabbit, and shoulder of lamb are exemplary; so are sweets. Gracious service. *Luxury.*

Le Mas d'Aigret (Les-Baux-de-Provence; phone 9054-33-54) is at once a smartly decorated First Class hotel with fabulous views of the countryside from many of its 14 good-sized rooms and a restaurant of consequence. The solid-value-for-category lunch menu might open with a mushroom-in-pastry specialty, continue with a stellar specimen of Provence's beloved brandade de morue—salted cod puréed with olive oil and garlic-scented—or the house's own version of tournedos, this richly sauced; with chocolate tart understandably a favored sweet. Wines are special. *Luxury.*

AFTER DARK

Théâtre Antique (Rue de la Calade) is a beautiful Arles setting for plays and folklore performances: summer only. Also in summer, *Les Arènes*—the amphitheater—becomes *una plaza de toros,* with bullfights; your hotel or the tourist office (below) will have schedules.

INCIDENTAL INTELLIGENCE

Further information: Office de Tourisme, Boulevard des Lices, Arles; Office de Tourisme, Avenue Van Gogh, Stes.-Maries-de-la-Mer; Office de Tourisme, Grande Rue, Les-Baux-de-Provence.

7

Avignon

Medieval Papal Stronghold

BACKGROUND BRIEFING

Sur le pont d'Avignon, on y danse, on y danse...—Traditional song

The point about Avignon is not its long-sung-about, now-in-ruins—albeit still visitable—bridge, but popes.

After thirteen centuries of Roman residence, an unlikely fluke of history—having to do with the especially prickly Italian political scene of the moment and the coincidence of there being a bit of papal-owned territory in southern France—saw His Holiness, Clement V, a Frenchman who had been archbishop of Bordeaux, take himself and the papal entourage to oddly named Comtat Venaissin—a compact area centered on the little town of Venasque, northeast of Avignon. Facilities for the elaborate court were so limited there that Clement accepted an invitation to settle in at bigger Avignon, then within the realm of the counts of Provence. The year was 1309.

John XXII, still another Frenchman—all seven Avignon-based popes were French-born—remained in Avignon. But it remained for his immediate successors, Benedict XII (originally a Cistercian monk) and Clement VI (an extravagant patron of the arts) to build the Palais des Papes—actually a joined pair of palaces, one Benedict's, the other Clement's—that we see today, either as casual visitors or, believe it or not, as conventioneers. The City of Avignon, owners of the palace, have annexed a Centre des Congrès to it, utilizing original palace halls—that had been, in the Middle Ages when Avignon was center of the Christian world, the scene of brilliant banquets—for contemporary badge-wearers' receptions beneath Gothic vaults of what is surely France's most curious historic site. It was that site—and the presence of not only popes in Avignon for most of the fourteenth century, but their successors, the Cardinal Legates, and *their* successors, the Vice Legates, who were in charge until 1790, when the city became a part of France—that shaped Avignon's destiny. It not only fostered culture (there was an Avignon school of Renaissance painting), but encouraged construction of churches and chapels, convents and monasteries, elegant town houses and formidable fortifications, in across-the-Rhône Villeneuve-lès-Avignon, as well as in the city proper, the while creating an ambience of vitality and sophistication that are Avignon hallmarks to this day.

ON SCENE

Lay of the Land: Observed from Villeneuve-lès-Avignon, the satellite town across the Rhône, Avignon retains its matchless medieval profile: towers of irregularly contoured Palais des Papes coupled with the dome of its cathedral and the ruins of its legendary bridge, ending abruptly at midpoint in the river. But once one sets foot and ambles about, it is immediately clear that Avignon has known the hand of a good town planner; its layout is one of the easiest to master of the smaller French cities. Still surrounded by medieval ramparts, Avignon begins at the *railway station.* It is situated at the foot of the north–south thoroughfare that delineates the core of town—called *Cours Jean-Jaurès* in its southerly reaches, later becoming *Rue de la République* before it concludes at the nerve center called *Place de l'Horloge.* This square is flanked by the pair of nineteenth-century focal points, Hôtel de Ville and next-door Théâtre Municipal, with cafés spilling into its center. Go north a hop and a skip, and you're at *Place du Palais,* named, I need hardly point out, for the medieval papal residence dominating it. *Rocher des Doms,* directly to its north, is a rocky eminence serving as a city park that affords views of the Rhône, the city's celebrated bridge, and bastions of Villeneuve-lès-Avignon beyond. Avignon's cathedral borders this park, and the so-called Petit Palais, now an art museum of consequence, is just beyond. Shopping? It's good in Avignon. *Rue Joseph-Vernet*—entered from Cours Jean-Jaurès and with its landmark the eighteenth-century palace housing one of the most beautiful art museums of the republic—has the smartest shops. Other streets, leading west from central Place de l'Horloge, constitute shopping territory as well; they are *Rue des Marchands* and *Rue de la Bonneterie.* Try to find time for strolls along central streets—*Rue du Roi-René* and *Rue du Four* are two such—lined with town houses that attest to Avignon's centuries-long eminence.

Palais des Papes (Place du Palais): You are apprehensive as you climb steep stone steps at the entrance. Suppose the magneticism of Rome was not strong enough to have lured the popes back at just about the time when the Middle Ages were evolving into the Renaissance? What would the Italian capital be like today without the cachet of the Vatican? Would this smallish Mediterranean city, now simply the seat of one of 95 *départements* of the French Republic, have evolved into a metropolis, as headquarters of the globe-girdling Catholic church? Although it is not without disappointments—alas, its somberly gray and unfurnished interiors lack warmth, if not an extraordinary sense of proportion and scale—the palace is a history book, a century-long chapter in the affairs of a church whose evolution in the medieval epoch was intertwined with that of temporal powers like Italy, France, and the far-flung Holy Roman Empire. The palace is at its best when it is massive—the 135 × 30-foot *Grand Tinel,* where the papal court entertained state visitors at banquets, and the 166 × 45-foot *Chapelle Grande,* site of papal worship—both on the upper floor; and *Salle des Audiences,* similar in size to the chapel (just above it) and with Matteo Giovanetti's frescoes—the subject is a group of bearded prophets—among the palace's art treasures. There is, to be sure, other admirable art. In the ground floor's *Chapelle de St.-Jean,* Giovanetti has interpreted feats of the two most eminent of the sainted Johns, Evangelist and Baptist. The upper level's *Chapelle St.-Martial,* just above St.-Jean, is graced by still another clutch of Giovanetti works. *Chambre du Pape*—the pope's bedrooms, upstairs and relatively intimate as rooms go in this complex—retains its decoration, an overall painted wall design that might well be the predecessor of wallpaper. Save the best for last: *Chambre du Cerf,* called the Deer Room, after exquisite—and still exquisitely colored—murals, again by Giovanetti, surprisingly secular in theme, that of hunters-cum-dogs, against a lovely, leafy background.

Cathedral of Notre-Dame-des-Doms (Place du Palais) is, not surprisingly, the palace's next-door neighbor. It is relatively small for a church of its status, but it's of a respectable age, with Romanesque portions dating to the twelfth century. There are features of note, most particularly an archbishop's throne in dramatic white marble and tombs of a pair of popes—John XXII, the second of the Avignon pontiffs, and his builder-successor, Benedict XII.

Musée du Petit Palais (Place du Palais)—originally a kind of satellite space, supplementing Palais des Papes, used to house VIP guests (King François I was reputedly among them)—saw architectural changes during the Renaissance. Centuries later, in the 1970s, the building was brilliantly refurbished to serve as setting for the nucleus of its exhibits—some 300 medieval Italian masterworks gathered by a sixteenth-century Roman nobleman named Campana. These are supplemented by a selection of works, many of the fifteenth-century Avignon school, from Musée Calvet (below). But it's the Campana paintings that make Petit Palais one of the best small-city museums in France. I would be a wealthy man if I had a

20-centime piece for each postcard sold in the museum's shop of Botticelli's luminous *Virgin* robed in red and blue and framed by an arch, with a chubby baby Jesus before her. There are a Carpaccio *Sacred Conversation,* a Giorgione *Madonna and Child,* a Giovanni di Paolo *Nativity,* an *Annunciation* believed to be by Perugino, a Simone Martini *David,* and the museum's mascot painting—a hunter with his dog. The setting—there are 19 no-two-alike galleries—is as sumptuous as the art.

Musée Calvet (Rue Joseph-Vernet) is one of the most beautiful museum environments in France, an enchanter of an eighteenth-century palace, with peacocks in its garden; superb furniture in high-ceilinged, exquisitely detailed galleries (including a set of eight Régence chairs in the crystal-chandeliered library); and lovely paintings. A view of Avignon from the Rhône by a local master named Robert Bonnart in 1700 is memorable; no less so is an eighteenth-century procession in Place du Palais. With works, as well, by the likes of Bourdon, Robert, Mignard, and le Nain, and an unexpected oil of England's King Henry VII by an unknown Renaissance portraitist.

Musée Lapidaire (Rue de la République) is quartered in a handsomely Baroque church, originally Jesuit, now desanctified, with the exhibits of sculpture embracing Avignon's Roman period—the capitals of columns are special—through the later periods of the popes and their successors.

Musée Louis Vouland (17 Rue Victor-Hugo) is the handsome nineteenth-century town house, or *hôtel particulier,* of a twentieth-century grocery magnate, whose hobby was collecting decorative-arts objects, mostly of the eighteenth century. Monsieur Vouland had taste as well as wherewithal, as this exhibit—in 8 galleries of his two-story house—indicates. There are some paintings of note—by Avignon's own Joseph Vernet and the Low Countries' Jan Gossaert especially. But you go, principally, for the beautiful furniture and porcelain, bronzes and mirrors, objects of gold and silver, tapestries and carpets.

A quartet of churches: *St.-Agricole* (Rue de la Petite-Fusterie) stuns with its enormous porch and Gothic portal, exceptionally wide nave, and charmer of a chapel under its side cupola. *St.-Didier* (Rue de la République) has a fifteenth-century fresco by the Sienese painter Simone Martini and a joyous, angel-studded Baroque altar. *St.-Pierre* (Rue de la République) greets you with a pair of engaging mini-steeples framing a Gothic facade. The interior is art-embellished Renaissance. *Chapelle des Pénitents-Noirs* (Rue Banasterie) represents rococo Avignon, with exuberance typical of the eighteenth century, and the street on which it's located is a scenic one.

Villeneuve-lès-Avignon, the town across the Rhône that developed handsomely as a consequence of the thirteenth-century papal period, warrants the inspection it is all too often denied by Avignon visitors. If you have the strength or the youth—or both—I would begin at *Fort St.-André* (Rue Montée du Fort St.-André), the very same medieval battlement whose fabulous twin towers you see from Avignon; a view of the city opposite is obtainable in exchange for your having ascended a considerable expanse of steps. Proceed, then, to . . .

Chartreuse du Val de Bénédiction (Rue de la République), a former Carthusian monastery of the same order as the closed-to-visitors motherhouse outside of Grenoble (chapter 18). This is the only charterhouse in France where you may see the relatively capacious, two-room-cells-cum-gardens in which the Carthusians lead solitary lives. The cells open off a trio of cloisters; their chapel is visitable, too. *Église Paroissiale* (Place Meissonier) is a visit-worthy church, if only because of a pair of sculpted Virgins, one in marble—beautiful enough, to be sure—the other in ivory. End at *Musée Municipal* (Rue de la Foire, near the church), brimming with antique furniture, but with its masterwork a painting, *Couronnement de la Vierge,* by a fifteenth-century local—Charanton by name.

Orange (18 miles north of Avignon) is a small town big in remnants of Roman Provence. Head first, upon arrival, to *Théâtre Antique* (Rue St.-Florent). You'll find it difficult to believe that this amphitheater, built 21 centuries ago (and still in use), remains in near-mint condition—the best preserved Roman theater extant, with the stone wall backing its stage graced by a statue of the building emperor, Augustus, and with elegantly contoured rows of seats (capacity 10,000) climbing a hillside. The theater edges a dramatically hilly park, *Colline St.-Eutrope;* a ruined temple is nearby, as is *Musée Municipal,* whose exhibits are of Orange-area Roman sculpture and fragments. And don't leave town without glimpsing a Roman-built *Arc de Triomphe,* on the avenue taking its name; not unlike the amphitheater, it's the best preserved of its kind in Europe.

SETTLING IN

D'Europe Hôtel (12 Place Crillon; phone 9082-66-92): In a town that lures the curious anxious to see what had been the popes' only non-Italian seat, it is odd that the D'Europe is the only in-town hostelry with a government four-star rating. Such, though, has been the case for many years, and this no doubt at least partly explains why such an indisputably handsome seventeenth-century mansion packs in customers, the while lacking up-to-the-minute bathrooms (no shower curtains, no hair dryers), not to mention solid mattresses on beds, or even the in-room minibars that are such a commonplace even in lower-rated French hotels. What lures guests is the look of the place. You enter through a capacious courtyard to which the pricey restaurant is transferred on summer evenings, continuing to public spaces under whose beamed ceilings furniture is a mix of seventeenth-century through the Directoire and Empire periods of the nineteenth, with just over half a hundred rooms; those I've inhabited or inspected are hardly overlarge. And reception and staff, in my experience, have been more foreign (expatriate Britons and Dutchmen) than French, so that you're not at all times sure what country you're in while at the D'Europe. Still, there's nothing really the matter that a generous management with a multimillion-franc refurbishing budget couldn't right. But without city-center competition in its category, that doesn't seem likely. A pity, this. *First Class.*

Mercure Palais des Papes Hôtel (Rue Ferruce; phone 9085-91-23): Arrive by car, and you enter from a motor entrance to the rear, facing the town ramparts. Approach on foot and there's a conventional front door. In either event, you must not expect an aesthetic treat. Advantages here are kind staff as well as a central location. There are rooms in mock-traditional style, and a bar. Breakfast only. *First Class.*

Cité des Papes Hôtel (1 Rue Jean-Vilar; phone 9086-22-45) is the building with the striking modern facade, just below Palais des Papes, that you cannot help but notice, given the divergence in architectural styles. There are just over 60 neat but graceless rooms, with the twins smallish—palace views from some. The hotel serves breakfast only, although there's a reliable restaurant—Le Bristol—adjacent. *Moderate.*

Du Midi Hôtel (33 Rue de la République; phone 9082-15-56) has its central location and the cleanliness of its nearly 60 plain rooms to recommend it. *Moderate.*

Bristol-Terminus Hôtel (44 Cours Jean-Jaurès; phone 9082-21-21), long on scene and central, offers the highest room capacity—91—of the in-town hotels, which makes it of interest to groups. *Moderate.*

Blauvac Hôtel (11 Rue de la Bancasse; phone 9086-34-11) occupies restored and refurbished space in a venerable heart-of-town structure just off Place de l'Horloge. Rooms, with bath, are attractive and there's a restaurant-bar. *Moderate.*

Primotel Horloge (1 Rue David; phone 9086-88-61) is relatively recent, is central (near Place de l'Horloge), and has 71 bath-equipped rooms albeit no restaurant. Breakfast only. *Moderate.*

Hostellerie Le Prieuré (7 Place du Chapitre, Villeneuve-lès-Avignon; phone 9025-18-20) was the palace of a cardinal in the court of John XXII, second of the Avignon popes. John had part of his palace converted into a priory—thus the hotel's name—and only in this century did it become a charming hotel, in its own park. There are two dozen handsome rooms and 10 suites; antique-accented public spaces, including a restaurant (which moves to a terrace in summer) exceptional enough to warrant comment on a later page; and a good-sized swimming pool in the garden. Member, Relais et Châteaux. *First Class.*

La Magnaneraie Hôtel (37 Rue Camp-de-Bataille, Villeneuve-lès-Avignon; phone 9025-11-11), built in the fifteenth century, ivy-walled, and on a hill overlooking the town, welcomes with 20 pleasant rooms, bar-lounge, swimming pool in the garden, and a restaurant commendable enough for comment on a later page. *First Class.*

Les Frênes Hôtel (Avenue des Vertes-Rives, Montfavet; phone 9031-17-93) is just the ticket for a relaxing overnight, a honey of a nineteenth-century country house, set in its own garden-cum-swimming pool, with 18 elaborately decorated rooms and suites and an exceptional restaurant, where a meal is indicated even if you're not in residence. Avignon is six miles west. Member, Relais et Châteaux. *First Class.*

L'Auberge de Noves (Noves; phone 9094-19-21) is an oasis in a sea of vineyards, just eight miles south of Avignon. This is a rambling country mansion, with 20 traditionally furnished, good-sized rooms, charming lounges and bar, swimming pool in the garden that's covered with a plastic bubble in cool weather, and a commendable restaurant, al fresco in summer. Member, Relais et Châteaux. *First Class.*

DAILY BREAD

Hiely-Lucullus (5 Rue de la République; phone 9086-17-07) belies its eminence with a decidedly unpretentious setting: up a flight in a nondescript building on Avignon's main street. Bowls of flowers and tables meticulously set with pale pink linen are the only bright touches in an otherwise plain decor. But you're received with smiles, service is professional, and fare—happily based on traditional Provençal specialties—is excellent. You do well to order the carefully created prix-fixe menu. Openers might be fresh asparagus or artichokes, deliciously sauced. Entrées run to escalope de saumon, maigret de canard, or a typically Provençal estouffade d'agneau. Cheese platter is next, preparatory to a choice of the house's memorable desserts. Member, Relais et Châteaux. *Luxury.*

Les Domaines (28 Place de l'Horloge; phone 9082-58-86) is at once handsome (contemporary touches in an antique setting), cheerful (welcome is warm; service, a delight), and delicious. The prix-fixe is indicated, commencing with the likes of a terrine de foie de canard and continuing with salmon-trout soufflé or the house's rabbit specialty, with dessert either pastries from a trolley or a choice of ice-cream concoctions. *First Class.*

Les Trois Clefs (26 Rue Trois Faucons; phone 9086-51-53): Smartly set tables are framed by pink-and-ivory murals in this inviting restaurant, where there are three good-value prix-fixe menus, with chicken specialties counseled. *First Class.*

Le Vernet (58 Rue Joseph-Vernet; phone 9086-64-53) lures first with good looks (it occupies an eighteenth-century house, with warm-weather tables in its walled garden). Go for lunch (value is better) with such openers as quail mousse, such entrées as sautéed rabbit, with a choice of sweets and coffee. Dinner is pricier, location is central, service is cordial. *First Class.*

La Fourchette II (17 Rue Racine; phone 9085-20-93) is a kind of Gallic *Mildred Pierce* (my reference is to an old Joan Crawford classic in which the star is a no-nonsense restaurant operator), except that the decor is ditsy (Mildred acquired good taste), with the boss in firm command of a timid staff of ladies who speak in hushed tones only when addressed. Fare is okay, though; you order from a menu that might open with grilled sausage and lentils and includes a beef specialty or roast pork among entrées. Central. *Moderate.*

Le Saint-Didier (41 Rue de la Saraillerie; phone 9086-16-50) is agreeable enough to look upon, with peach-hued draperies and linen and antique prints of horses on the walls. But the prix-fixe menu can be slim pickings—a green salad or fish pâté to start, skimpy beef fillet or seafood platter as entrées, and cheese or the dessert of the day. The dinner menu offers more choice. *First Class/Luxury.*

Chantegril (24 Place d'Horloge; phone 9082-76-10)—a link of a national chain—has an attractive garden decor and makes a specialty of a buffet embracing all the crudités you can eat; ditto, desserts. With a slightly pricier and more conventional prix-fixe menu and an à la carte of grills. Good value. *Moderate.*

Crêperie l'Aveline (3 Rue des Corps Saints; phone 9085-09-28) is the genuine Breton article; crêpes savory (order a pair to start), and crêpes sweet (order one for dessert). Satisfying and *Moderate.*

Simple Simon (26 Rue Petite Fusterie; phone 9086-62-70, and pronounced sam-ple-see-*mohn*) bills itself as *Le Salon de Thé Anglais d'Avignon,* but you'll need your best French to order its delicious cakes with a cup of tea or, for that matter, breakfast or a casual lunch. Attractive and central. *Moderate.*

Lou Mistrau (13 Place de l'Horloge; phone 9082-40-98) is at once a *brasserie* (order a simple, but satisfying, meal of, say, entrecôte aux frites) and a café with its tables spilling onto the square (for coffee or a drink). *Moderate.*

Hostellerie Le Prieuré Restaurant (7 Place du Chapitre, Villeneuve-lès-Avignon; phone 9025-18-20). If your visit is during the cool weather months, the setting for a meal will be a dark-beamed room, with country Provençal chairs surrounding tables set with great bowls of flowers to contrast with yellow linen. In summer, you're al fresco. A nibble served with your aperitif might well be canapés tapinade—the so-called caviar du pauvre—which is a pâté of black olives, anchovies, and capers bound with olive oil and garlic-seasoned. A shrimp-and-spinach salad might follow, with one of the house's poultry, beef, or lamb specialties as entrées, well garnished. The cheese platter is a requisite here. So are the chef's pastries. *Luxury.*

La Magnaneraie Hôtel Restaurant (37 Rue Camp-de-Bataille, Villeneuve-lès-Avignon; phone 9025-11-11): Tables are set in the garden in summer. Select one of the two well-priced menus, building your meal around a seafood or poultry entrée, with the house's own crêpes fourrées to conclude. *First Class.*

La Maison (1 Rue Montée du Fort St.-André, Villeneuve-lès-Avignon; phone 9025-20-81) is as tasty as it is good-looking, traditional-style, with its celebrated specialty—maigret de canard au beurre rouge, a duck delight—counseled. *First Class.*

Le Pigraillet (Chemin Colline St.-Eutrope, Orange; phone 9034-44-25) is strategically situated on the hill facing the amphitheater, an ideal spot for a lunch pause in connection with an Orange excursion; prix-fixe menus center on chicken and lamb with port-infused foie gras a treat among the openers. *First Class.*

SHOPPER'S AVIGNON

Department stores—*Galeries Lafayette, Dames de France, Monoprix*—are on Rue de la République. Rue Joseph-Vernet's classy boutiques include *Jean Christophe* (men's and women's accessories), *Jacques Hiely* (women's haute couture), *J. P. Palun* (classic-design men's clothes); *Henry Doux* (jewelry); *Alex Bretinière* (men's and women's shoes), and *Idées Formes-Fonctions* (leather, watches, jewelry). *Les Olivades* on shop-filled Rue des Marchands is a source of Provençal products, especially hand-blocked cottons by the bolt and fashioned into bags, skirts, aprons, place mats, and sachets. *Souleïado,* a link of a chain with similar specialties, is on Rue Joseph-Vernet. And *La Taste* (Rue de la Balance) vends Provençal foods and wines.

SOUND OF MUSIC

Théâtre Municipal (Place de la Horloge) is the city's principal theater—opera, ballet, concerts, plays; there are others. (And in summer, July usually, the Avignon Music Festival takes place in historic sites—Palais des Papes included—all around town.)

INCIDENTAL INTELLIGENCE

This is a good point of departure for excursions—many of them day-long—to points throughout Provence: The tourist office (below) has details. *Further information:* Office de Tourisme, 41 Cours Jean-Jaurès, Avignon; Office de Tourisme, 1 Place Charles-David, Villeneuve-lès-Avignon; Office de Tourisme, Cours Aristide-Briand, Orange.

8

Beaune

Burgundy's Wine Center, South to Mâcon

BACKGROUND BRIEFING

You go to Beaune—small, congenial, and fortuitously situated in east-central France—for three reasons: Burgundy wines, first. (In no French city of my acquaintance is tasting, purchasing, and—most important—*understanding* more effortless.) Art and architecture share second billing. (However, in the case of non-wine buffs, they move up to first place.) And the classic cuisine of Burgundy is No. 3. Beaune is strong in restaurants serving regional specialties in tandem with wines that, with those of Bordeaux (chapter 10) constitute the most esteemed on the planet.

Medieval dukes of Burgundy favored Beaune. Until Louis XIV revoked the Edict of Nantes, which had guaranteed religious freedom, Beaune's big Protestant community enriched it, as weavers whose textiles were coveted throughout Europe. Simultaneously, the town thrived as a shipping point for area vintners; Burgundy wine was hardly less sought after than Beaune-made cloth. All this occurred while Beaune developed as a cultural crossroads between France to the west and easterly Teutonic territories. Handiwork of these rich centuries remains—ramparts-cum-watchtowers that could be sets for adventure films; town houses somberly stone-faced and town houses ebulliently Baroque; a plethora of cloistered convents, some now put to clever secular use; and, not to be overlooked, centuries-old *caves* lined with casks of the wine that affords Beaune its livelihood and its celebrity.

ON SCENE

Lay of the Land: Beaune bases itself on a pair of central squares, southerly *Place Carnot* and northerly *Place Monge*—dominated by a fourteenth-century bell tower—which are joined by the principal pedestrian shopping street, *Rue Carnot. Rue de Lorraine,* leading north from Place Monge, is flanked by fine old houses and the visitable *Chapelle de l'Oratoire,* with *Porte St.-Nicolas,* an eighteenth-century ceremonial gateway, at its terminus. Place Carnot is almost contiguous with *Place de la Halle* and neighboring *Place Fleury,* both due west and focal points of a quarter redolent of *Vieux-Beaune.* Major monuments (below) are in this core and easily accessible on foot. The *railway station* is beyond the center, at the eastern end of *Avenue du 8 Septembre.* Although Beaune is principal trading center for wines of the entire Burgundy region, the vineyards surrounding it—some northerly, most to the south—comprise the area called *Côte de Beaune,* including such celebrated townships as *Savigny-lès-Beaune, Pommard, Meursault,* and *Puligny-Montrachet,* with the *Mâcon* and *Beaujolais* vineyards south of Côte de Beaune. These are conveniently visited on excursions from Beaune, while Burgundy's northerly vineyards are best inspected on tours out of Dijon (chapter 17).

L'Hôtel-Dieu (Rue de l'Hôtel-Dieu) represents a mix of superlative Renaissance architecture and great Renaissance art. What happened was that in the fifteenth century, a local bigwig—Nicolas Rolin, by name—endowed the town with a paupers' hospital, the likes of which were unknown in the Europe of the period, or since, for that matter. (In my trans-Europe travels, I have encountered nothing comparable, with the exception of Hostel de los Reyes Católicos in the northwestern Spanish city of Santiago de Compostela; it was built by Ferdinand and Isabella for pilgrims arriving sick, after the long pilgrimage-trek to the tomb of St. James the Apostle, and is now a luxury hotel, which I recommend highly in *Spain at Its Best.*) L'Hôtel-Dieu—a Sisters of Charity-operated hospital to this day, albeit with its patients now in detached modern quarters—is a dazzler even from without. You start in a stadium-size courtyard whose steeply pitched roofs are tiled in a diamond pattern in shades of green, beige, and black, with a near-limitless maze of pinnacles surmounting a sea of turrets and gracefully framed windows. Eventually, it's your turn to go inside (crowds are such that batches of visitors are taken through on guided-in-French tours, with explanatory leaflets in major foreign languages passed around to non-French-speakers). The hospital's sole ward, 236×48 feet, could be a ballroom, with its vaulted ceiling—the shape of a ship turned upside down—measuring 66 vertical feet. And patients were not doubled up in beds—as they were, for example, in Lyon (chapter 21), where a typical bed that accommodated four is on exhibit in that city's hospital-museum. Beaune's beds were canopied and curtained, and Beaune's ward doubled as a chapel, with the altar at the far end visible from all beds, so that patients could worship while confined; prayers were led by the nuns, whose no-longer-worn blue and white habits are displayed in an adjacent museum. Best comes last at L'Hôtel-Dieu; the altarpiece. Builder

Rolin commissioned Roger Van der Weyden to paint for the ward a nine-panel interpretation of *The Last Judgment,* centered by a somber-visaged, white-robed Archangel St. Michael, exquisitely detailed and recognized as the most brilliant masterwork by a Flemish master who painted many such.

Basilique de Notre-Dame (Place Notre-Dame) is Beaune's showplace church, a Romanesque beauty begun in the thirteenth century, as handsome from out back (the three-level apse-cum-flying buttresses is exceptional) as from within, where the severe barrel vault of its nave frames architectural features—the range, capitals of columns supporting it to a serene cloister. But standouts here are the tapestries, a series lining walls behind the choir, that date to the fifteenth century and are believed to have been woven in what is now the Belgian city of Tournai. Theme of the series—17 all told—is *La Vie de la Vierge.* You have, of course, seen many representations of the Virgin's life. But these panels—each in still-luminous color, framed by borders with overall designs embracing birds and flowers—will stay with you. *Presentation at the Temple, Marriage, Annunciation, Nativity, Visitation, Adoration of the Magi, Flight into Egypt, Dormition and Crowning*—I wager you'll buy postcard reproductions of the lot as you exit.

Musée des Beaux-Arts (in Hôtel de Ville, the town hall, on Rue Oudot) is small and unexceptional, as such museums go in France. But there are some noteworthy paintings, especially a batch by Beaune-born Félix Zeim, a talented nineteenth-century master whose works are in the same vein as England's brilliant J. M. Turner, a contemporary. There are, as well, Flemish Primitives to complement the Van der Weyden in Hôtel-Dieu; and eighteenth-century charmers by the likes of Greuze, Lancret, and Boucher.

Musée du Vin (Rue Paradis) makes its home in a multiroomed mansion that goes back half a millennium and had been the Beaune residence of the dukes of Burgundy. Exhibits may well tell you—if you give them enough time—more than you want to know about the history of wine, by means of considerable documentation and a vast array of implements.

Marché aux Vins (Rue Nicolas-Rolin, a street named for the builder of l'Hôtel-Dieu, nearby) is without doubt the best-organized regional wine-tasting/orientation/sales enterprise of any that I have come across in France, or in all Europe, for that matter. Setting first: The main hall is a stunner of a desanctified Gothic church—Des Cordeliers, by name. And it is supplemented by extensive *caves.* Look at the exhibit of wines from throughout Burgundy (not just Côte de Beaune)—from Chablis up north through Mâcon and

Beaujolais to the south. Then move about, sampling whichever wines you like, as many as you like, with you yourself doing the pouring into glasses available at each display. Close to 40 wines are on hand, ranging in age from three to ten years old. (The trick is not to get tipsy.) It's all free, and you are under no obligation to buy, but you may if you like: pick up whatever bottles interest you from their shelves (prices are indicated, and there are printed order forms), taking them in supermarket-type baskets to the cashier at the exit. The market ships overseas.

Visits to individual Beaune caves: Besides Marché aux Vins (above), you may visit any of a number of prominent Beaune wine firms' cellars. One that I have enjoyed is *Calvet* (6 Boulevard Perpreuil), whose *caves* are below atmospheric medieval ramparts, and which invites its guests to taste representative vintages. Other open-to-visitors *caves* include *Léonce Bocquet* (29 Boulevard Clemenceau) and *Patriarche Père et Fils* (Rue du Collège).

La Rochepot (12 miles southwest of Beaune): Regional vineyards and *caves* excepted, La Rochepot is the requisite Beaune excursion destination—a picture-book village in the hills, surrounded by vineyards, based on a single-steeple Romanesque church and dominated by a Middle Ages château on which patterned tile roofs are at least as intricate as those of L'Hôtel-Dieu (above). Of the state rooms within the castle, the Salle à Manger stands out, not so much for its dining table and chairs, but because of its marvelously painted beamed ceiling and a monster of a fireplace.

Côte de Beaune—the southern tier of Burgundy's Côte d'Or—makes for an agreeable excursion. A region of both red and white wines, its *vignobles*—smaller and less pretentious than the châteaux of Bordeaux—welcome visitors to their *caves,* where tasting is invited, and purchases may, or may not, be made, quite as you like. A nice routing might take in *Pommard* (whose reds are among the region's most prestigious and whose eighteenth-century *Château de Pommard cave*-vineyard is traditionally open daily the year round); *Meursault,* with world-class white wines and an eminently visitable Gothic parish church; *Puligny-Montrachet,* perhaps the most charming of the villages of this group and noted for its whites as well as its reds; *Santenay,* whose Church of St.-Jean is a Romanesque-Gothic mix; and—en route back to Beaune—*Auxey-Duresses,* near La Rochepot and its château (above) and a good lunch stop. *Mâcon,* the neat-as-a-pin Saône River town, has given its name to the celebrated Burgundy wine region south of Côte de Beaune and just north of the Beaujolais area. *Musée Municipal* (Rue *des Ursulines*) has as its setting a mellow seventeenth-century convent, and its ace-in-the-hole is a clutch of mostly French paintings by such artists as Greuze, Courbet, and Monet, with a Titian as a bonus. The nearby *Hôtel-Dieu* (Square de la Paix) is an eighteenth-century hospital with charming antique porcelain and furnishings in an open-to-visitors pharmacy. Note the detailed Renaissance facade of *Maison de Bois* (Place aux Herbes). *Maison Mâconnaise des Vins* is for tasting as well as purchases and is at 484 Avenue de Lattre-de-Tassigny. Just beyond town, any number of *caves* welcome visitors: *Les Vignerons des Côtes Mâconnaises et Beaujolaises* at nearby *Cavaye* has representative vintages of a region whose wines include Pouilly-Fuissé and Chardonnay, both reputable whites, as well as Mâcon rouge.

SETTLING IN

De la Poste Hôtel (1 Boulevard Clemenceau; phone 8022-08-11) has been operated by several generations of the same family since the turn of the present century. I like the old-fashioned, high-ceilinged lobby-floor lounges, agreeable for drinks prior to a meal in the hotel's capacious restaurant—worthy of comment in a later paragraph. There are just 23 rooms and suites, no two alike, and those that I have either inhabited or inspected are delightful in period decor, with imaginative wallpapers and textiles, not to mention antique accents. Breakfasts are the most thoroughly satisfactory of any I have experienced in any French hotel. Taken either in your room or in one of the lounges, the first meal of the day comes on a big tray covered with a linen placemat and matching napkin of the same material, a vase of fresh flowers, a basket containing warmed-for-you brioches and croissants of the highest quality (hardly to be taken for granted in contemporary France, alas), generous-sized crocks of jam, honey, and butter, and a really jumbo pot of coffee. The hotel is a five-minute stroll from the core, and management is at once skilled and friendly. Demi-pension only; you must have lunch or dinner. *First Class.*

Le Cep Hôtel (27 Rue Maufoux; phgone 8022-35-48) is an originally Renaissance mansion, core-of-town, that, with also-renovated contiguous houses, has been converted with considerable panache into a 46-room hotel. No two rooms are alike, but each—at least, those I have inspected—is furnished with superb antiques (Louis XV, Louis XVI, and Directoire), is stylishly accessorized, and has a modern bath attached. Breakfast is served in a stone-walled *cave* (or, of course, in your room) and drinks in a lovely lobby-lounge. And the commendable Restaurant Bernard Morillon occupies sixteenth-century quarters, atmospherically beamed. *First Class.*

L'Auberge Bourguignonne (4 Place Madeleine; phone 8022-23-53) is aptly named. It is, indeed, an inn, of advanced age, although nicely—and traditionally—updated. There are just 8 rooms; those I have seen are very pleasant, indeed. And the Auberge's restaurant—featuring Burgundy specialties, both à la carte and with a choice of two prix-fixe menus—is good value, good-tasting, and *First Class,* but the hotel proper is *Moderate.*

Central Hôtel (2 Rue Victor-Millot; phone 8024-77-24) is accurately titled. There are just under two dozen satisfactorily equipped rooms but no elevator, and a nice-looking restaurant. *Moderate.*

Henri II Hôtel (12 Faubourg St.-Nicolas; phone 8022-83-84) is just north of the town center, with half a hundred period-style rooms with bath, and a bar in the lobby-lounge. Breakfast only. *Moderate.*

Le Home Hôtel (138 Route de Dijon; phone 8022-16-43) is not, to be sure, central. But it's pleasant—a garden-encircled house with 22 neat rooms and an inviting bar-lounge. Madame Jacquet, the patronne, makes everyone feel at—dare I use the word?—home. Breakfast only. *Moderate.*

La Closerie Hôtel (61 Route d'Autun, a few miles south of Beaune; phone 8022-15-07) is ultra modern, with 32 comfortable rooms, all more or less alike, and an outdoor swimming pool. Breakfast only. *Moderate.*

Samotel (Route de Pommard, a few miles south of Beaune; phone 8022-35-55) is plop in the center of a vineyard. Its plus is an attractive restaurant. The 66 rooms—good-sized and modern, like the rest of the hotel—are comfortable enough, but, mind, mattresses are soft. *Moderate.*

Bellevue Hôtel (416 Quai Lamartine, Mâcon; phone 8538-05-07) is just south of the core, with 32 period-style rooms with bath, reliable and inexpensive restaurant, and bar-lounge. Best Western. *Moderate.*

Château d'Igé Hôtel (Igé; phone 8533-33-99) is a derring-do castle, dating to the Middle Ages when counts of Mâcon fortified it. (Today's town of Mâcon is less than 10 miles distant.) There are a dozen accommodations—half of them rooms, half suites; and a reliable restaurant ideally sampled at lunch when tabs for the multicourse menu are considerably less than in the evening. Member, Relais et Châteaux; *First Class.*

Altéa Mâcon Hôtel (26 Rue de Coubertin, Mâcon; phone 8038-28-06) is not central, but it's nicely situated on the banks of the Saône, with 63 similarly decorated, contemporary-style rooms, bar-lounge (which expands to a river view terrace in summer), and convenient restaurant. Nicely operated. *First Class.*

DAILY BREAD

De la Poste Hôtel Restaurant (1 Boulevard Clemenceau; phone 8022-08-11): You appreciate the significance of this dining room in relation to the rest of the hotel when you see how much space is accorded it. It's high-ceilinged, with plenty of space between handsomely set tables; a staff that smiles but at the same time knows its business; and a kitchen that turns out the Burgundy dishes we cross oceans for. Open, for example, with a dozen escargots à la Bourguignonne, expertly sauced, delicious tranche of jambon persillé, or an unusual veal terrine. Entrées, accompanied by a masterful gratin Dauphinois, include filet mignon, shallot-accented shoulder of lamb, chicken with a Beaujolais-laced stuffing and the mushrooms called morilles, and traditional coq au vin. Cheeses are accorded care; desserts wheeled over on a chariot are the handiwork of a master *pâtissier.* There are always a hundred-plus of *grands crus* Burgundies to choose from, and you may order à la carte or from either of two prix-fixe menus. *Luxury.*

Le Relais de Saulx (16 Rue Louis-Very; phone 8022-01-35) comprises a pair of formal and contiguous rooms—Louis XV style in front, Louis XVI to the rear, both framed by Burgundy velvet walls and matching draperies. Every table is adorned with silver candelabra and a bowl of flowers. I suggest you order one of the three prix-fixe menus—traditional, but with the distinctive touch of a talented chef. Choose a Beaune-style cassolette of snails or a more unusual salad of marinated and minced sea bass and salmon, as openers. Entrées run a gamut—grilled lamb chops, sautéed pork, confit of rabbit with a mustard sauce, seafood fricassee. As you proceed, bear in mind that not one, but a pair of trolleys will be rolled up, each groaning with desserts. Choose samplings of two or three—not missing the gâteau au chocolat, hot tarte Tatin, and génoise aux fraises. *First Class.*

Auberge St.-Vincent (Place de la Halle; phone 8022-42-34): Restaurants just opposite tourist-trod monuments of consequence tend to aim for mass markets; rarely are they top-category. St. Vincent, in an aged mansion opposite l'Hôtel-Dieu, is an exception. Brass chandeliers illuminate a room whose tables are set with gold linen. Order à la carte such tempters as smoked trout, crayfish, and string bean salad, with seafood pot-au-feu a reputable entrée. Or select the good-value menu of four courses, with poultry or beef the entrées and sweets from a wheeled-to-table cart. *First Class.*

Jacques Lainé (10 Boulevard Foch; phone 8024-76-10) edges the core of town, just west of Porte St.-Nicolas. Its quarters are a nineteenth-century mansion, with walls graced by Louis XVI paneling. You lunch or dine in one of a suite of connected rooms or, if it's summer, in the garden. I counsel the prix-fixe menu—with starters like pâté of scallops in a lobster sauce, escalope of trout as the fish course, a pigeon sauté or the house's ham specialty, choice of cheeses *and* of Lainé-prepared desserts. Go for the good-value menu midday; dinner is costlier. *First Class/Luxury.*

Le Bistrot du Marché (11 Place Carnot; phone 8022-12-00) is indicated for a low-tabbed meal of, say, œufs en meurette—eggs poached in a red-wine sauce, with entrecôte aux frites following. Central. *Moderate.*

Bouché (12 Place Monge): Make your selections from the main-floor counter of this *pâtisserie* before moving along to the upstairs *salon de thé,* where you may have coffee or tea to accompany. Ice cream, too. Central. *Moderate.*

Ouvrée Hôtel Restaurant (Savigny-lès-Beaune; phone 8021-51-52): The 17-room hotel, first: It's simple and unpretentious but worth remembering if you're in the area and can't find space in Beaune, four miles distant. If you've a car, the capacious restaurant is worthy of the drive out, for a hearty lunch. Œufs en meurette are the best such I have enjoyed; ditto, expertly prepared trout, meunière style. Beef is good, too. Cheeses are Burgundian, sweets are made by the Ouvrée's chef, and wines are from the *patron*'s vineyard constituting the backyard, and bearing the Savigny-lès-Beaune appellation. *First Class.*

Hostellerie de Levernois (Route de Verdun-sur-le-Doubs, at Levernois, three miles east of Beaune; phone 8024-73-58) is—in its main building—a comfortable 12-room *First Class* hotel, and in its addition (glass-walled and looking out to gardens and the pool) a restaurant of consequence, where the emphasis is on traditional Burgundian cuisine, including the region's globally emulated style of snails, fish specialties including red mullet in foil, and entrées among which sautéed pigeon with foie gras is memorable. Desserts are delightful and, not surprisingly, the cache of Burgundies in the cellar is exemplary. Go for the good-value menu at lunch; dinner is costlier. *Luxury.*

André Parra (a.k.a. Ermitage de Corton, Route 74, two miles north of Beaune, at Chorey-lès-Beaune; phone 8022-05-28) makes for an appropriate lunch pause in the course of a drive through vineyard country north of town, in the direction of Dijon. Red-upholstered

Louis XVI–style chairs surround carefully set tables in a formal room. Prix-fixe menus are good buys; fare is based on traditional specialties. Filet of beef in a Corton wine sauce and roast duckling whose sauce is cassis-based are entrée favorites. *First Class.*

La Crémaillère (Route 73, Auxey-Duresses; phone 8021-22-60) is a long-on-scene and sensible choice for lunch in the course of a half-day exploration of wine towns south of Beaune; base your meal on coq au vin or bœuf Bourguignon; your wine will come from an adjacent vineyard. *First Class.*

Georges Blanc (Vonnas, 10 miles southeast of Beaune; phone 7450-00-10) appears, as you approach, to be a comfortable country house on a canal, and, indeed, it is—an attractive hotel (with duplex suites, as well as conventional rooms and a swimming pool) but, more to the point, an exceptional restaurant, now in the third generation of operation by the Blanc family. You are expected to order a premeal drink in one of the lounges, the while perusing a menu that embraces a pair of table d'hôtes and an à la carte. To select the cheaper of the two menus is hardly to skimp; it might include wine-sauced snails and the house's specialty entrées, a cream-sauced breast of chicken, garnished with a rainbow of vegetables and followed by cheese and an extraordinary choice of desserts. Setting is a capacious room, its well-spaced tables illuminated by silk-shaded lamps and flanked by Louis XIII chairs. Service is at once impeccable and congenial. Member, Relais et Châteaux. *Luxury.*

Rocher de Cancale (393 Quai Jean-Jaurès, Mâcon; phone 8538-07-50) has the advantage of edging the Saône River albeit with a heart-of-town situation. You do very well with the traditional Burgundian menu at lunch; dinner is pricier. *Moderate.*

Au Chapon Fin (Thoissey, edging the Saône River, 10 miles south of Mâcon; phone 7404-04-74) occupies a contemporary, three-story pavilion in its own garden (it is a looker of a 25-room hotel, as well as a restaurant of consequence). A capon—the kind of poultry for which the establishment is named—is the subject of a painting above the fireplace in the paneled dining room, whose tables are surrounded by caned Louis XV chairs. Order over a drink in the cocktail lounge. And go with an appetite. A meal—either à la carte or from the prix-fixe menu—might open with poached perch, accompanied by a superb sauce Hollandaise; continue with the No. 1 specialty: chicken fricasseed with morille-type mushrooms. Charolais beef in a marchand de vin sauce is satisfying, too. Continue with local cheeses. For dessert: Grand Marnier–doused chocolate cake or raspberry sherbet under a blanket of fresh raspberries. If it's summer, you'll lunch or dine in the garden. Member, Relais et Châteaux. *First Class.*

INCIDENTAL INTELLIGENCE

Further information: Office de Tourisme, Rue de l'Hôtel-Dieu, Beaune; Office de Tourisme, 187 Rue Carnot, Mâcon.

9

Biarritz

and the Basque Country: Bayonne, St.-Jean-de-Luz

BACKGROUND BRIEFING

The point to be made about the southern tip of the French Atlantic—delineating the relatively compact stretch constituting France's Basque country—is not so much the exoticism of a people with their own consonant-packed, not-all-that-widely-spoken language, but rather the exoticism of non-Latin visitors in their midst. What I mean to say is that the English-speaking visitor in Biarritz, the once-fashionable resort that is the most widely reputed Basque town, sticks out like a sore thumb. The overwhelming majority of visitors in France's distant southeast corner appear to be either *citoyens français* or Spaniards from just over the border. (See *Spain at Its Best.*) Indeed, I don't know of any other quarter of the republic where English is less widely spoken; muster all the French and/or Spanish at your command for Côte Basque exploration.

It was not always so. After Empress Eugénie, the Spanish-born consort of Napoleon III, created a vogue for Biarritz in the middle of the last century (much like she did for still another coastal watering-hole, the English Channel's Trouville [chapter 16]), north-of-the-Channel royalty joined Eugénie and her imperial husband in Biarritz, as today's visitor is reminded, by streets named for such onetime holiday-makers as Queen Victoria and her son, Edward VII. White, white sand beaches and spectacular coastal vistas, a hearty cuisine and royal patronage of yore notwithstanding, Biarritz and neighboring Côte Basque points have not been able to compete with the easier-of-access Côte d'Azur, to which this volume devotes four chapters (13, 23, 26, and 33). Which is hardly to say you don't want to have a look around, if you're in the neighborhood.

ON SCENE

Lay of the Land: A fishing village fronted by a still-magnificent beach—*Grande Plage*—Biarritz, prior to its discovery by Empress Eugénie, was known primarily to residents of adjacent Bayonne (the coast's art and cultural center [below]). Ideally, you position yourself in a central Biarritz hotel, the better to absorb whatever action emanates from the quarter surrounding *Place Clemenceau*—café- and shop-lined, just inland from *Boulevard du Général de Gaulle,* which flanks Grande Plage and is the site of *Casino Municipal*—one of two such; and leading to shop-filled *Avenue Édouard VII. Place Bellevue,* with *Casino Bellevue,* is a hop and a skip west. To experience Biarritz at its most scenic, head west of the center to *Plage du Port-Vieux,* from which I suggest a stroll to the edge of a narrow promontory at whose terminus lies a rock formation, *Rocher de la Vierge,* high above swirling surf, affording coastal panoramas, and named for a statue of the Virgin Mary erected by Napoleon III in 1865. Biarritz's landmark *Phare,* or lighthouse (erected in 1834), is north of town, on a minipeninsula at the end of *Avenue de l'Impératrice,* overlooking *Plage Miramar.* Still other beaches—*Plage de la Côte des Basques, Plage Marbella,* and charmingly named *Plage de Milady*—are south of the center. The railway station is quite central, on *Avenue de la Gare.*

Musée de la Mer (Esplanade du Port-Vieux), easily visited in tandem with Rocher de la Vierge (above), houses an aquarium whose most amusing exhibit is a clutch of loquacious sea lions in a pool of their own; it is, otherwise, unexceptional.

Church of St.-Martin (Rue St.-Martin)— is Biarritz's solitary venerable monument—a mix of styles, Middle Ages onward, with an impressive Gothic choir the best aesthetic reason for a visit.

Bayonne—in effect, Biarritz's next-door neighbor to the east—is the Côte Basque's surprise package: a substantial small city just inland from the Atlantic, with the Adour River to its east, and a monument-filled core based on Rue des Gouverneurs, whose landmark is atmospheric and aptly-named *Château Vieux,* or Old Castle, whose inhabitants—now army officers—have included kings Louis XI, François I, Charles IX, and Louis XIV, an entrance plaque advises. Pedestrians-only *Rue Victor-Hugo* is the big shopping street, with *Printemps* department store nearby. The grandest square, *Place de la Liberté,* edges the Adour and is flanked by a rather grand multipurpose structure at once the city hall and the opera house.

Cathedral of Ste.-Marie (Square Dubarat): Bayonne's cathedral—erected between the twelfth and the sixteenth centuries—is a Gothic structure of no little beauty. Twin steeples frame a felicitous stone porch. The long, high nave is exquisitely vaulted; the high altar, with its graceful baldechin, hardly anticlimactic. Gothic tracery of the galleries of the cloister—separately entered—is extraordinary. So, for that matter, is the perspective of the cathedral from the rear—flying buttresses of the apse, most especially.

Musée Bonnat (5 Rue Jacques-Laffitte)—not unlike the cathedral—is another Bayonne sleeper, in turn-of-century quarters that have been smartly renovated, and with a corking good collection of paintings—the best such that I know of in a town so small, anywhere in France, save for those of its counterpart in Pau (chapter 28). Smashers of this collection are a clutch of canvasses by Rubens in a room of their own—as well they might be, given the total: 16. But there is, as well, work by the likes of Leonardo and Rembrandt, Michelangelo and Dürer, El Greco and Goya, with later painters on scene, too, including Géricault and Delacroix, Ingres and Degas. And there's a superb cache of Old Masters drawings, the lot a gift to the town by native-son Léon Bonnat, a nineteenth-century portraitist-teacher.

Musée Basque (1 Rue Marengo) has quarters in a pretty riverfront house architecturally typical of the region, maroon shutters complementing white walls. Subject matter is the Basque people and their culture, with exhibits running a delightfully diverse gamut—the Basque-created game, jai alai (*pélote,* on home ground), and Basque country furniture, Basque custumes, and Basque art. With exhibits relating to the history of Bayonne, as a bonus.

St.-Jean-de-Luz (10 miles south of Biarritz) played a not unimportant role in French history, and compensates with a plethora of good seafood restaurants for its lack of a solitary in-town, first-class hotel. Nature ordained that this town—flanking the wide, white sands of perfectly crescent-shaped *Baie de St.-Jean-de-Luz*—would be a beach resort. And geography is uncomplicated. *Rue Gambetta*—the main shopping street—runs parallel with the beach's flanking street, *Promenade de la Plage,* site of *Casino de la Pergola. Rue de la République* is Restaurant Row; it runs perpendicular to Rue Gambetta and leads directly to the sands. And *Place Louis XIV* edges the harbor; you want to position yourself at a café table in early evening when the town's fishing fleet returns, its boats brimming with the day's catch—for sale from the decks—of sardines and tuna.

Maison de l'Enfante (Place Louis XIV) is the charming Baroque mansion—inhabited by descendants of the original owners and operated as a museum by them—where Louis XIV and his Spanish bride, Infanta María Teresa, spent their wedding night on June 9, 1660, after the knot was tied in a nearby church (below), after an elaborate procession through the town. You see several authentically furnished rooms, the wedding chamber, of course, but salon and kitchen as well.

Church of St.-Jean-Baptiste (Rue Garat): Pause before entering to read the plaque affixed to the somber facade of this late Renaissance-early Baroque, sixteenth-century church. It advises that after Louis XIV was married within—and France gained as a queen a daughter of Spain's King Felipe IV, born in the Escorial, outside of Madrid—the door through which the royal couple passed was *murée,* or walled, after the ceremony conducted by the then bishop of Bayonne. And it still is. You enter alongside, dazzled by the gilded splendor of the high altar, impressed with unusual dark-wood balconies on either side of the aisle, traditionally occupied only by Basque men. If you've not had a chance to acquaint yourself with the Basque language, this is the place: Have a look at prayerbooks in the pews.

SETTLING IN

BIARRITZ

Du Palais Hôtel (1 Avenue de l'Impératrice; phone 5924-09-40) is accurately titled. It was, indeed, a palace. Napoleon III built it in 1854 for Empress Eugénie, and it served for some years thereafter as an imperial summer residence. In 1893—more than two decades after the demise of the Second Empire—it was converted into a hotel, and rebuilt following a 1903 fire. Setting is core-of-town, in a park of its own, with the Grande Plage just out front. Beneath severe, steeply pitched mansard roofs that were so dear to Belle Époque architects is an anything-but-severe interior that represents, more than that of any other hotel that I know in provincial France, what the turn-of-century grand hotel was all about. Proportions—high ceilings, immense windows, grandiose spaces—are in themselves extraordinary. Decorative details—original crystal chandeliers, bronze sconces, marble mantels, massive French doors, intricate stuccowork of ceilings, capitals of columns, gilded window frames—dazzle. It's difficult to believe that in this capacious environment there are no more than 120 rooms and suites. Seaview accommodations are the loveliest, but the standard rooms on upper floors are hardly to be despised. The formal restaurant, off the lobby, is worthy of an evaluation on a later page. A second, contemporary, with scrumptious buffet lunches, faces the swimming pool, itself flanked by a vast sun deck, at the Atlantic's edge. There is a pair of bars. And service is skilled and smiling. Hôtels Concorde. *Luxury.*

Miramar Hôtel (Avenue de l'Impératrice; phone 5924-85-20) is an undistinguished contemporary house, with capacious public areas, 126 smallish but well-equipped rooms, swimming pool, elaborate health spa in the basement, bar-lounge, and a pair of restaurants, one standard and of good quality, the other for spa customers on diets. *Luxury.*

Régina et Golf Hôtel (52 Avenue de l'Impératrice; phone 5924-09-60) is dramatically situated, agreeably traditional in style, with 45 rooms, reliable restaurant, and Miramar Beach just below. *First Class.*

Carolina Hôtel (Boulevard Prince-de-Galles, phone 5923-03-86) is worth knowing about because of its central beachfront situation; there are just over 30 full-facility rooms, but no restaurant. Breakfast only. *Moderate.*

Eurotel (19 Avenue de la Perspective; phone 5924-32-33): You're away from the center, out at Plage du Port-Vieux, here—near Rocher de la Vierge (above). But if you've a car, you might find this house worthwhile, with smashing views from high-up rooms, kitchenettes attached to all 60 of them, and a closed-weekends restaurant. Contemporary. *First Class.*

Plaza Hôtel (Avenue Édouard VII; phone 5924-74-00) You're a bit inland from the beach here, but core of the shopping district. This is a comfortable, 60-room-cum-restaurant house. *Moderate.*

BAYONNE

Capagorry Hôtel (14 Rue Thiers; phone 5925-48-22) is traditional-style, agreeably situated core of town. There are close to 50 well-equipped rooms, no two identical, bar and breakfast, but no restaurant. Best Western. *Moderate.*

Aux Deux Rivières Hôtel (21 Rue Thiers; phone 5959-14-61) is a near-neighbor of the Capagorry (above), attractive in the traditional manner, with 63 functional rooms and pleasant public spaces. Breakfast only. *Moderate.*

ST.-JEAN-DE-LUZ

Chantaco Hôtel (Golf [course] de Chantaco, a mile and a half east of town; phone 5926-14-76): I rarely begin town hotel evaluations with a noncentral hotel, but this is a standout. Of course, you need a car, and if you're a golfer—18 holes are adjacent—you'll be especially content in this lovely country-house-type hotel. There's a strong—and delightful—Spanish influence in decor of the public spaces, which include capacious lounges, bar, and a fine restaurant that moves to a patio in warm weather. The 20 rooms are lovely, each of them distinctively decorated. And management is delightfully welcoming. Pity there's no swimming pool. Very nice, withal. *Luxury.*

Helianthal Hôtel (Place Maurice-Ravel; phone 5951-51-51) is at once smart and contemporary, with an interesting restaurant, congenial bar, up-to-the-minute fitness center, pool, and 100 nicely equipped rooms and baths. On the beach. *Luxury.*

De la Plage Hôtel (33 Rue Garat; phone 5951-03-44): This is a modest house, but it is, indeed, *sur la plage* and has a reliable restaurant. Ask for an oceanfront room; 30 all told. *Moderate.*

Bel Air Hôtel (Promenade Thibaut; phone 5926-04-86) is a near-neighbor of both the casino and the beach. There are just 16 adequate rooms, and a dinner-only, summer-only restaurant, as well, of course, as breakfast. *Moderate.*

Madison Hôtel (25 Boulevard Thiers; phone 5926-35-02) is a little in from the beach, with 25 neat rooms. Breakfast only. *Moderate.*

DAILY BREAD

BIARRITZ

La Rotonde (Du Palais Hôtel, 1 Avenue de l'Impératrice; phone 5924-09-40): I can't conceive of a visitor coming all the way to Biarritz and missing the experience of a classic dinner in this very grand environment. Precede your meal with an aperitif in the Palais's positively palatial cocktail lounge—through which you pass en route to this room, flanked by mirrored marble fireplaces, illuminated by crystal chandeliers, with the great windows of a half-moon-shaped wall giving on to the sea. A massive flower arrangement atop it draws your eye to the hors d'œuvres table as you enter. You begin with half a lobster mayonnaise or foie gras frais, proceed with a fish course, as a prelude to such classic entrées as châteaubriand—beef is nowhere more succulent in southwest France—one of the house's lamb specialties, or the duck-breast masterwork, maigret de canard. Desserts come wheeled over on a two-level trolley, and the wine list is one of the most extensive in the Basque country. Lovely service. *Luxury.*

Chez Albert (Port des Pêcheurs; phone 5924-43-84) is as essential to an understanding of maritime Biarritz as is La Rotonde (above), for the Biarritz of Empress Eugénie. This big, busy, waterfront house reflects the gregarious hospitality of its *propriétaire,* M. Albert, who darts about, invariably making menu suggestions for newcomers—and good ones. Take his advice and open with the definitive French seafood platter—a gargantuan assemblage of crustaceans: crayfish and oysters through octopus and mussels. Order grilled fish or boiled lobster as an entrée, or take advantage of Biarritz's proximity to Spain and opt for M. Albert's saffron rice–based paella—deliciously enough garnished so as to put it on a level with the Iberian peninsula's best such. Summer only. *First Class.*

Café de Paris (5 Place Bellevue; phone 5924-19-53) puts you in mind of the similarly named establishment on the Place du Casino in Monte Carlo (chapter 23). But they're not related. The Biarritz café is very smart and with traditional specialties, including a mean seafood soup, varied fish dishes, and roast lamb with the chef's own accents. *Luxury.*

L'Operne (17 Avenue Édouard VII; phone 5924-30-30) is stylishly contemporary, with tables on a terrace over the Grande Plage, for summer meals. You will have heard of pipérade, the Basque scrambled-egg meld—onions, green peppers, tomatoes are major ingredients—and, with the obligatory accompaniment of sliced Bayonne ham; you'll not find it more deliciously prepared elsewhere. Open with it, following with grilled salmon or filet of sole meuniére. Friendly. *First Class.*

Atlantic (10 Rue du Port-Vieux; phone 5924-34-08) lures mussel fans, myself certainly included. If you're one of us, open with a giant bowl of moules marinières, served with plenty of bread for dunking. Poulet au vinaigre et à l'estragon—the house's chicken specialty—is indicated as an entrée. Fun. Summer only. *First Class.*

Miremont (5 Rue Mazagran) seems unexceptional, as you enter from a heart-of-town shopping street. Look, then, at the caliber of its pastries in main-floor counters. Proceed up the rear stairway, and poof! You're in a *salon de thé* whose entire far wall is a picture window giving on to the Grande Plage. And the Miremont's pastries are as sumptuous as the view. *Moderate.*

Café Royalty (Place Clemenceau). I can't guarantee crowned heads among the clientele, but it's fun to take a table in this core-of-Biarritz location and watch the passing parade. *Moderate.*

BAYONNE

Victor Hugo (Quai-Amiral-Dubourdieu at Rue Victor-Hugo; phone 5925-62-26) is a throwback to the last century, still with original furnishings, and a smashing situation, riverfront, just beyond landmark Place de la Liberté. Order the seafood-based prix-fixe menu. *First Class.*

L'Escabos (4 Rue Saubiole; phone 5959-70-17) is agreeable for a midday meal following a morning in nearby Musée Basque (above). Open with the house terrine, making sure you select either the lobster-based zarzuela—a casserole with origins in just-over-the-frontier Spain—or the platter of grilled assorted seafood. *First Class.*

Café du Théâtre (Place de la Liberté; phone 5955-19-92) is named for the opera house/city hall building in which it's situated. Take an outdoor table on a sunny day, for a casual lunch, coffee, or a cold drink. Delightful. *Moderate.*

Cazenave (19 Arceaux Port-Neuf): A pity, while you're in this city that pioneered centuries back in the preparation and presentation of then-novel chocolate, not to sample it at Cazenave, both in its *salon de thé* and by the bag or box, from its counter. *Moderate/First Class.*

ST.-JEAN-DE-LUZ

Kaïku (17 Rue de la République; phone 5926-13-20) agreeably typifies the St.-Jean-de-Luz seafood restaurant—stone-walled, beam-ceilinged, with lamps fashioned of local wood-cum-checked shades illuminating tables, and an open kitchen, the better to watch your meal being prepared. Open with cream of crab soup, following with expertly grilled catch of the day or a tasty specialty—gratin de moules aux courgettes, a mussel masterwork. *First Class.*

La Ruelle (27 Rue de la République; phone 5926-45-47) offers a good-value prix-fixe in pleasant surroundings; open with the area's esteemed fish soup or nicely garnished Bayonne ham and continue with a faux-filet steak or breast of duck, with a choice of desserts to conclude. *Moderate/First Class.*

De la Plage Hôtel Restaurant (33 Rue Garat; phone 5951-03-44) is indicated for an ocean view meal that might embrace pipérade to begin, poulet Basquais—the region's premier chicken preparation—or grilled local tuna or sardines, with gâteau Basque to conclude. If you have the prix-fixe menu, *Moderate;* à la carte, *First Class.*

Taverne Basque (5 Rue de la République; phone 5926-01-26) is indicated for regional dishes—pipérade, for example—and—especially at lunch—a good-value menu. Location is central, not far from the beach. *Moderate.*

Dodin (17 Rue Gambetta) is both *pâtisserie* and *salon de thé;* stop in for a cuppa with a slice of cake, perhaps purchasing a bag of their chocolate-cherry candy specialty. *Moderate.*

Le Madrid (Place Louis XIV) is a café on the ground floor of Maison Louis XIV (above) and named for the city of origin of King Louis's bride, on the historic square that overlooks the port, and is the site, as well, of the city hall; that term in French—hôtel de ville—is translated into Basque—Herriko Etchea—on its facade. For drinks or a snack. *Moderate.*

SHOPPER'S BIARRITZ

Nouvelles Galeries department store is on Place Clemenceau, as are *Cartier* (jewelry, leather), *Artéon* (diamonds, watches), *Bord* (still another pricey jeweler), and *Fancy,* with smart duds, men's as well as women's. *Hermès* (Avenue Édouard VII) is a branch of the Paris leather-silk-accessories house. *Silva* (Avenue Édouard VII) features haute couturiers' clothes—Guy Laroche, Ungaro, St. Laurent, among others. *Formen* (aptly named), *Lacaze* (super swimsuits, male and female), *Déclic's* (women's clothes), *L'Île au Trésor* (antique furniture), and *Bernadette Malaganne* (nineteenth-century paintings) are among Place Bellevue's shops.

SOUND OF MUSIC

Théâtre Municipal (Place de la Liberté, Bayonne) is the region's opera house—and a classy one, at that; concerts and ballet, as well. (And check with area tourist offices [address below] for dates and locales of bullfights prevalent in summer.)

INCIDENTAL INTELLIGENCE

Men wear jackets and ties to both Biarritz casinos (addresses above); foreigners must present passports to disagreeable guards, for admission. You may rent umbrellas on the Grande Plage, but bring your own towels. Biarritz abounds in golf courses and tennis courts; the tourist office has details. *Aéroport de Biarritz-Parme* is a mile and a half southeast of town, with flights to and from a number of domestic points. *Further information:* Office de Tourisme, Square d'Ixelles, Biarritz; Office de Tourisme, Place de la Liberté, Bayonne; Office de Tourisme, Place Maréchal-Foch, St.-Jean-de-Luz.

10

Bordeaux

City behind the Wine Label

BACKGROUND BRIEFING

It's the core of the most prestigious wine-producing region in the world, with the magically named quartet of principal vineyard districts—Graves, Médoc, Pomerol, and St.-Émilion—encircling it, in the core of southwest France.

Each year ships bearing five million bottles sail from its Gironde River docks into the nearby Atlantic, the better to please palates of discerning drinkers planetwide.

But what of the city behind the labels on the bottles? Long centuries of development—since the Romans settled in the ancient town they dubbed *Burdigala*—have seen Bordeaux evolve into one of the most elegant cities in Europe.

This sixth-largest of the French Republic's cities was, after all, seat of the early dukes of Aquitaine. Its soaring Gothic cathedral was where strong-willed Eleanor of Aquitaine—later to become Queen of England as the consort of Henry II—married her first husband, France's Louis VII.

That was eight and a half centuries back. But, even then, wine was a Bordeaux staple, as, indeed, it had been since Roman colonists first planted vines in the neighborhood.

English control of the city, through the period of Queen Eleanor and King Henry's reign, coincided with its emergence as an international wine-shipping center, with the English major customers then, as now.

By the time Montaigne, the essayist, and Montesquieu, the philosopher—locals both—had given Bordeaux intellectual cachet in the Baroque centuries, it had become rich. Indeed, the architectural heritage of its greatest century, the eighteenth, remains of consuming interest, which is hardly to suggest a preoccupation with the past. Indeed, perhaps because of its grandeur rather than despite it, contemporary Bordeaux typifies urban France at its most diverting, animated, amusing, and good-tasting, with respect, I should make clear, to solid, as well as liquid, nourishment.

ON SCENE

Lay of the Land: This city of broad boulevards and monumental squares is a walker's town, with its overwhelming bulk on the west bank of the Gironde River, and its railway station flanked by a number of hotels—inconveniently detached from the center, a good 10-minute drive south of the core. Ideally, you want to headquarter in the heart of the city near *Place de la Comédie,* backed by the colonnade of *Grand Théâtre* (below), the landmark opera house. *Cours du 30-Juillet* leads east from the square to nearby *Esplanade des Quinconces,* one of Europe's largest—and most beautiful—squares, from which *Quai Maréchal Liautey* proceeds south to multiwinged *Palais de la Bourse*—the stock-exchange complex that is the eighteenth century's outstanding contribution to the city's neoclassic good looks. Mercantile Bordeaux is centered on one of France's longest pedestrian shopping streets—*Rue Ste.-Catherine,* which cuts across the core, north from the triumphal arch on *Place de la Victoire* to central Place de la Comédie. *Cours de l'Intendance,* leading north from that square, is Bordeaux's answer to Paris's Rue du Faubourg St.-Honoré; it's lined with classy boutiques. And it ends at *Place Gambetta,* on the northern fringe of a venerable sector of town, dotted with landmarks and based on *Hôtel de Ville,* a neoclassic eighteenth-century quadrangle on *Rue des Ramparts.* There's a charming little park out back, enclosed by extensions, that houses a pair of major museums, with the soldier-attended pillbox fronting formidable walls of the *Préfecture* on *Rue Jean-Fleuret,* just beyond the *Cathedral* (below), another near-neighbor.

Grand Théâtre (Place de la Comédie), without peer in France—Paris's Opéra/Garnier excepted—is outstanding enough to warrant attention at this point. Late-eighteenth-century, its magnificent colonnade not only fronts it but flanks its sides. Interiors—foyer-cum-grand staircase; opulent salons for intermission refreshment; cupola-topped, ceiling-frescoed, six-level auditorium illuminated by a massive crystal chandelier—are among the most dazzling of any opera house in Europe. Pop in during the day to see the lobbies; better yet, snag a ticket for a performance, there being no daytime open hours for public inspection.

Cathedral of St.-André (Place Pey Berland) was built over a sustained half-millennium period, with the consequence a felicitous Romanesque-Gothic mix. Unlike most, though, it's not the west—or principal—entrance that's the most art embellished. Here, you want to study Porte Royale, on the southern facade, for the tympanum—or sculpted overdoor—at its best in an interpretation of the Last Supper. The interior is immense, with the fine rose windows flanking the transcept and an especially lovely chapel behind the high altar.

Musée des Arts Décoratifs (39 Rue Bouffard) is a walled palace displaying work of Bordeaux artists and artisans—paintings, sculpture, silver, china—and furnished quite as it might have been two centuries ago, at the apex of the city's Golden Age. Indeed, no other open-to-the-public interior space in town, save the Grand Théâtre, provides the visitor with so graphic a portrait of what rococo Bordeaux was like. And in all of France only this museum's counterparts in Paris, Lyon, and Marseille are its peers. You go from one ravishing room to another—a Louis XV salon in pale gray and blue with gilded *boiserie,* furniture-filled with pieces of that epoch; a dining room whose armoire is packed with period porcelain; Louis XVI-furnished drawing room in delicate green; a severe Directoire sitting room; a walnut-paneled study. Scattered about are glass cases filled with decorative objects—miniature paintings and watercolors, bronzes and busts in marble, amusing antique posters and drawings (including some of the Grand Théâtre), silver tea services and clean-lined wine glasses, cameos and keys.

Musée des Beaux-Arts (Jardin de l'Hôtel de Ville), in an atmospheric and aged pavilion edging the tranquil garden behind the city hall, opens with a bang—you are greeted with Veronese's masterful *Madonna and Child,* along with a Titian of *La Madeleine*—and does not become anticlimactic as you move along. The Italians continue—an immense Perugino *Virgin Mary,* Palma il Vecchio's *Holy Family,* another Titian, and another Veronese. Rubens, Van Ruysdael, Snyders, and Brueghel are among the Low Countries artists, as is Van Dyck, whose *Marie de Medicis* is in a black gown relieved only by stark white collar and cuffs. The eighteenth century—as always, in this, of all French cities—charms with portraits by Largillière and Nattier, among the French; and Hoppner and Reynolds, among the British, with a study by F. J. Konson of the then duc d'Angoulême against a background of Bordeaux. And so you progress—Delacroix, Corot, and Félix Zeim, as the nineteenth century evolved, beyond to Renoir and Boudin, Matisse and Marquet (with a painting of the port of Bordeaux), Soutine and Vlaminck. Nearby *Galerie des Beaux-Arts* on Place du Colonel Raynal houses special short-term exhibitions; the museum's desk or the tourist office (address below) can apprise you of what's on.

Musée d'Aquitaine (20 Cours Pasteur), in well-organized, relatively new quarters, is a worth-perusing repository of the lore of the Aquitaine region (of which Bordeaux is the seat), with sculpture from Roman Burdigala, furniture and costumes, documents and

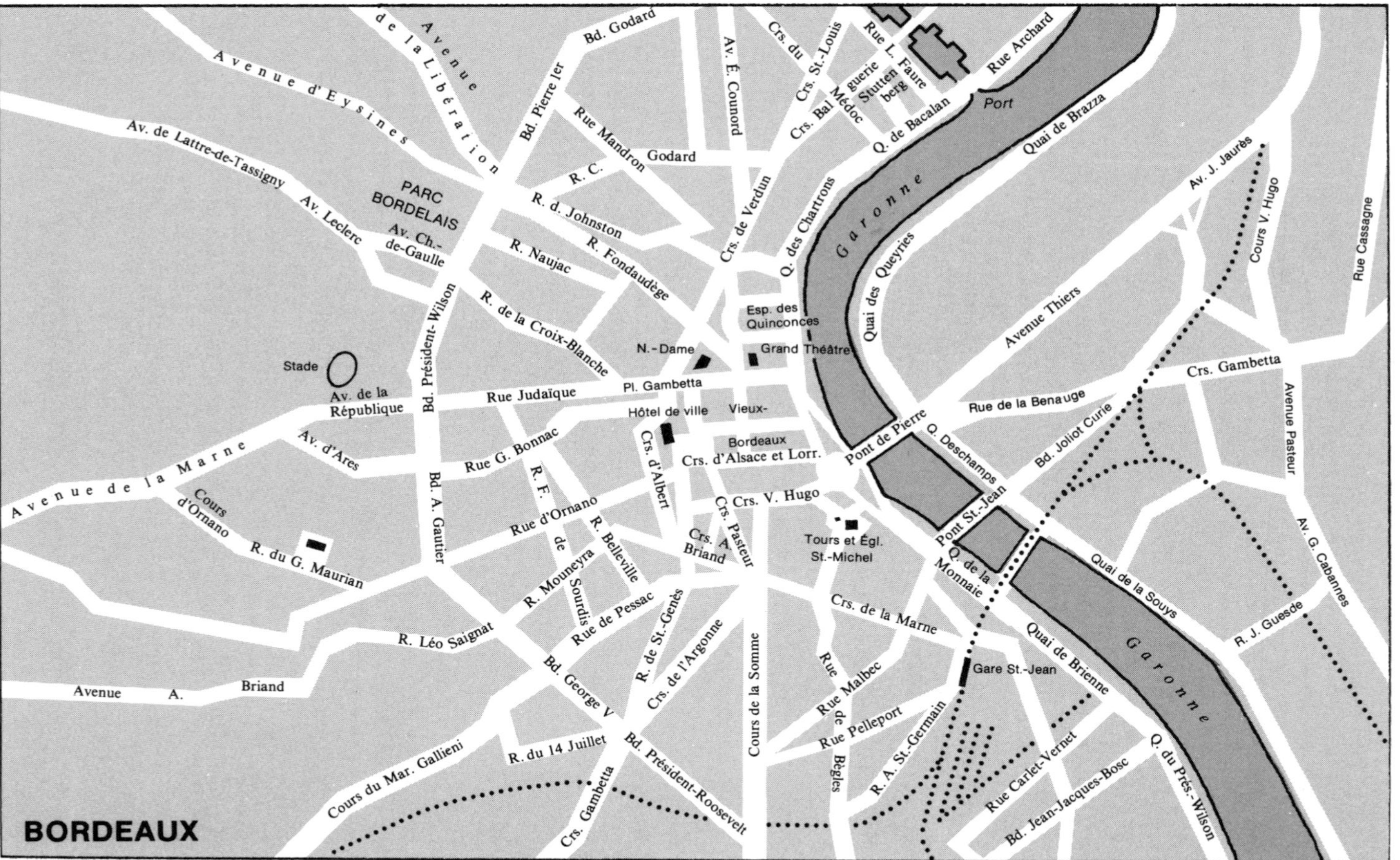

BORDEAUX
Garonne
Port
Rue Archard
Rue L. Faure
Stuttenberg
Crs. Balguerie
Médoc
Q. de Bacalan
Quai de Brazza
Crs. du
Crs. St.-Louis
Av. É. Counord
Bd. Godard
Bd. Pierre Ier
Rue Mandron
Godard
R. C.
R. d. Johnston
R. Fondaudège
R. Naujac
Crs. de Verdun
Q. des Chartrons
Quai des Queyries
Avenue de la Libération
Avenue d'Eysines
Av. de Lattre-de-Tassigny
PARC BORDELAIS
Av. Leclerc
Av. Ch.-de-Gaulle
Bd. Président- Wilson
R. de la Croix-Blanche
Esp. des Quinconces
Grand Théâtre
N.-Dame
Stade
Av. de la République
Rue Judaïque
Pl. Gambetta
Hôtel de ville
Vieux-Bordeaux
Crs. d'Alsace et Lorr.
Crs. d'Albert
Av. d'Ares
Avenue de la Marne
Rue G. Bonnac
Bd. A. Gautier
R. F. de Sourdis
Rue d'Ornano
R. Belleville
Crs. A. Briand
Crs. Pasteur
Crs. V. Hugo
Tours et Égl. St.-Michel
Cours d'Ornano
R. du G. Maurian
R. Mouneyra
Rue de Pessac
R. Léo Saignat
R. de St.-Genès
Crs. de l'Argonne
Cours de la Somme
Crs. de la Marne
Rue de Bègles
Rue Malbec
Rue Pelleport
R. A. St.-Germain
Gare St.-Jean
Quai de Brienne
Rue Carlet-Vernet
Bd. Jean-Jacques-Bosc
Q. du Prés.-Wilson
Avenue A. Briand
Bd. George V
R. du 14 Juillet
Cours du Mar. Gallieni
Crs. Gambetta
Bd. Président-Roosevelt
Pont de Pierre
Q. Deschamps
Pont St.-Jean
Q. de la Monnaie
Quai de la Souys
R. J. Guesde
Av. G. Cabannes
Bd. Joliot Curie
Rue de la Benauge
Crs. Gambetta
Avenue Pasteur
Avenue Thiers
Av. J. Jaurès
Cours V. Hugo
Rue Cassagne

weapons, the lot painting a picture of life in the region to this very day.

Centre National Jean-Moulin (Place Jean-Moulin at Rue des Frères Bonies) is Bordeaux's World War II Resistance Museum, named for a Resistance hero, and portraying—often movingly—the ways in which the underground worked against the Nazis; principal displays are of clandestine printing presses and the illegal broadsides that came from them. Do pay your respects.

Espace Goya (57 Cours de l'Intendance) The great early nineteenth-century Spanish painter Goya in Bordeaux? Well, yes. The artist lived in Bordeaux beginning in 1827, until he died there—in this apartment—on April 16, 1828. Restored to the appearance it had during the Goya tenancy by an organization called Amis de la Casa de Goya, the four-room apartment—living room, dining room, kitchen, and bedroom—is furnished with antique pieces of the period, with some original Goya drawings a special treat. As, indeed, is the view of St.-André Cathedral (above) from the windows. I suggest you ask the Bordeaux Tourist Office (address below) for current open-hours.

Church of Ste.-Croix (Rue Savageau)—a souvenir of Romanesque Bordeaux—is most stunning before you step inside, with facade dating to the twelfth and thirteenth centuries. There is a pair of square towers flanked by a fine central portal and a severely impressive nave.

Basilica of St.-Michel (Rue des Faures, not far from Ste.-Croix (above) is a Gothic treasure, impeccably restored after World War II damage. Have a look at its uncommonly high—and detached—bell tower (ascendable, if you're up to it) and, again, if you're up to it, at mummylike corpses in its crypt.

Church of Notre-Dame (Place du Chapelet) is a seventeenth-century treasure of which Bordeaux is proud. After its roof collapsed in 1975, it was meticulously restored as part of a cooperative project undertaken by city authorities in collaboration with National Historic Monuments Commission architects and the Ministry of Culture. The interior is a felicitous mix of late Renaissance and Baroque, barrel-vaulted, its altar backed by a trio of paintings, with details of the decor throughout—wrought iron, carved wood, sculpted marble—exceptional. And a one-time Dominican monastery (that in earlier times had been united with the church) next door is now a looker of a public library.

Maison du Vin (1 Cours du 30-Juillet, just north of Place de la Comédie) is a wine information center operated by the Bordeaux producers through their Conseil Interprofessional du Vin de Bordeaux, the umbrella that joins together both producers and shippers of wine from more than 7,000—yes, 7,000—châteaux in the Bordeaux region. Stop in for excellent free literature. Ask to see the upstairs tasters' laboratory, where professional *tastevins* ply their trade. Make arrangements—and, where necessary, appointments—for visits to châteaux in the region.

Wine country: You're in the area that is the world's largest producer of fine wines. Bordeaux's vineyards encircle the city in an area of some 250,000 acres with a radius of 35 miles. Growing areas edge three rivers. Best-known, the Gironde, has given its name to the department of the republic that delineates the Bordeaux wine country. Wines, with the appellation d'origine contrôlée Bordeaux or Bordeaux Supérieur may originate anywhere in the department. Other appellations pinpoint smaller areas within the Bordeaux region that can be as large as, say, Entre-Deux-Mers or as small as Pomerol.

Major areas are *Médoc,* extending 50 miles along the Gironde's left bank, and from which come the most blue-chip Bordeaux—including Médoc, Haut-Médoc, St.-Estèphe, Pauillac, St.-Julien, Listrac, and Margaux—all reds; *Graves,* flanking the left bank of the Garonne River, from which come red and white Graves, and generally semisweet and sweet Graves Supérieur whites; *Dordogne Right Bank,* with appellations including St.-Émilion, St.-Émilion Grand Cru, and Pomerol, among others; *Blayais and Bourgeais,* north of St.-Émilion and across the Gironde from Médoc, including such appellations as Côtes de Bourg and Premières Côtes de Blaye; *Entre-Deux-Mers,* between the Dordogne and Garonne rivers, producing the largest quantity of Bordeaux and Bordeaux Supérieurs, including Côtes de Bordeaux and Entre-Deux-Mers whites, Premières Côtes de Bordeaux and Ste.-Foy Bordeaux reds and whites; and *Sauternes,* the area along the Garonne from which comes Sauternes, Barsac, and other famous sweet whites. (See also Wines of France in chapter 1.)

St.-Émilion, one of the four principal Bordeaux wine-growing regions, is, as well, an enchanting medieval village—still walled—in the center of the vineyards that take its name. If you are going to visit a single area wine town, this one—high in the hills 25 miles east of Bordeaux—should be it. Allow a day, or even overnight, for St.-Émilion, especially if you're interested in visiting a château or two. A pair that I have thoroughly enjoyed are *Château Soutard* and *Château Pavié;* hosts at both provide tours of the vineyards and the *caves,* and, of course, there are tastings. But, as I indicate above, château visits are by appointment only, ideally made in advance through Maison du Vin in Bordeaux, but it's possible that *Maison du Vin de St.-Émilion* (Place Mayrat) can be helpful on the spot. And you will find, driving about, small châteaux selling their own wines and offering samples to prospective purchasers. The town itself, as handsome as it is hilly, is based on central *Place du Marché.* It is named for a wandering eighth-century monk, later sainted, who founded a hermitage around which the town eventually developed. It was fortified in the twelfth century, and its walls—punctuated with Gothic gates—remain, as do a number of monuments. Start with the most extraordinary *Monolithic Church* (Place du Clocher), a Romanesque chapel in the nether reaches of a rocky cliff, created by the Benedictine successors of St.-Émilion, probably using preexisting *caves,* beginning in the ninth century—with substantial proportions—more than 100 feet long, 60 feet wide, 32 feet high, and gracefully vaulted. St. Émilion's subterranean hermitage and a maze of catacombs are adjacent. Proceed to the *Collégiale Church,* a Romanesque-Gothic mix (Place Pinceau), with a not-to-be-missed cloister. *Cordeliers' Cloister* (a.k.a. Franciscan Friary, on Rue des Cordeliers) dates to the fourteenth century and is now put to sensible use as a café for the consumption of sparkling wine by the bottle. This leaves little *Musée Archéologique* (Rue du Clocher); it's skippable. But you'll want to allow time for aimless wandering in this pretty environment.

Médoc: The Bordeaux region producing the most glamorous wines—a high proportion of which are *crus classés,* as classified at the request of Emperor Napoleon III in 1855—is immediately north of Bordeaux city, its west flank on the Gironde River estuary. Though embracing eight famous *appellations d'origine contrôlées*—St.-Estèphe, Pauillac, St.-Julien, and Margaux are perhaps the most prestigious—and despite production of some of the planet's priciest vintages, it has nothing to compete with the Middle Ages village of St.-Émilion (above). As in St.-Émilion, smaller châteaux post signs on the road if they're interested in selling to the public. A few of the important châteaux keep regular open hours, including *Château le Bourdieu* (near Vertheuil), *Château Prieuré Lichine,* and *Château Lanessan* (the main feature of which is Musée du Cheval, whose subject is horses—all you ever wanted to know about horses). Other principal châteaux are open only by appointment. Of these, star of the show—usually open only on weekday mornings (and not in August)—is *Château Mouton-Rothschild,* where the kicker, if one dare employ so frivolous a noun, is a collection of art objects based on the theme—you guessed it—of wine, the lot amassed by resident Rothschilds. A cool multilingual hostess receives visitors in a lobby in which postcards (costing twice what they do in French museums) and also-pricey books about the owning family, the château, and its wine are sold in an effort, one supposes, to gain a bit of revenue as compensation for what may well be a misguided policy of gratis admissions. On display are a series of amusing Château Mouton wine-bottle labels designed by such artists as Chagall, Kandinsky, Henry Moore, and Robert Motherwell. There are, as well, quite lovely silver pieces (flagons and the like), antique glassware, Renaissance tapestries (their subject the harvesting of grapes), as well as Delft pottery, Oriental porcelain, and wine-related paintings by Old Masters like Nicolas Maes and David Teniers and such moderns as Gris and Picasso. Afterward, the group is led to a *chais*—Médoc's own word for *cave,* or cellar—where 100,000 bottles are stored, their corks changed every 25 years. A peep is permitted of still another *chais* in which, beneath august portraits of the clan's rulers, a thousand barrels are aging, to be transferred at the proper time to 300,000 bottles. Needless to say, no samples.

SETTLING IN

Majestic Hôtel (2 Rue de Condé; phone 5652-60-44), a gracious old-timer felicitously updated in traditional style, welcomes with a smart lobby and friendly reception staff. There are just 50 rooms, no two identical but those I have inspected are tastefully decorated, with attention paid to textiles, wallpapers, accessories—and bathrooms. Central. Breakfast only. *First Class.*

Normandie Hôtel (7 Cours du 30-Juillet; phone 5652-16-80) is quite obviously proud of the facade of the dignified turn-of-century building it occupies; maintenance is first-rate. There are a hundred agreeable rooms and a helpful staff. Central. Breakfast only. *Moderate.*

Français Hôtel (12 Rue du Temple; phone 5648-10-35) is an eighteenth-century *hôtel particulier,* superbly facaded, that has, in recent seasons, been transformed into an intimate hotel of considerable charm. The main floor's lounges are crystal-chandeliered, with breakfast room—its furniture stark white—adjacent. The 35 rooms vary in size (insist on a decent-sized one), are smartly furnished and with good baths. And location could not be more central. Breakfast only. Friendly. *Moderate.*

Ste.-Catherine Hôtel (32 Rue Ste.-Catherine; phone 4225-11-64) is a contemporary house—it opened as the 1980s became the 1990s—fashioned out of an earlier structure, with 85 bath-equipped rooms, convenient restaurant, bar-lounge, and a location on Bordeaux's main shopping street. *Moderate.*

Des Quatre Soeurs Hôtel (16 Cours du 30-Juillet; phone 5648-16-00). I can't help you in identification of the quarter of siblings for whom the hotel is called. But it's central, has the name of composer Richard Wagner on its guest rolls, and offers 35 rooms—decor is fairly modern blond wood—5 of which are really oversized. Good value. Central. Breakfast only. *Moderate.*

Royal Médoc Hôtel (3 Rue de Sèze; phone 5681-72-42) sports a spiffy black-leather and pale-wood lobby, smiles at reception, and shelters 45 small but otherwise satisfactory rooms (almost all with bath) in a conveniently central location. *Moderate.*

De Sèze Hôtel (23 Allées de Tourny; phone 5652-65-54) is a small (25-room) but satisfactory house, a major plus its location on one of the city's most beautiful thoroughfares. Most rooms have baths. Breakfast only. *Moderate.*

Burdigala Hôtel (115 Rue Georges-Bonnac; phone 5960-16-60) would head my Bordeaux group were it central. Still, it is the only hotel in the nondescript modern business quarter—Mériadeck, by name and a ten- to twelve-minute walk west of the core—that I recommend. This is a relatively recent house with a traditional albeit stylish look—in the lobby, glass-domed restaurant, woodsy cocktail lounge. And in those of the 71 rooms I've inspected—some Directoire, some lighter-look wicker—are interesting textiles and good baths with counter-sinks, separate toilets, glass shower enclosures (a rarity in France), and terry robes. This is a professionally managed, nicely staffed hotel, affiliated with Chaîne Concord. And if you've read the Background Briefing section of this chapter, you'll have noted that its name—Burdigala—was the Roman designation from which the French *Bordeaux* ultimately derived. *First Class.*

Terminus Hôtel (Gare St.-Jean; phone 5692-71-58) is convenient to the railway station to which it is attached, but not to central Bordeaux, which is a 10-minute taxi ride distant. A pity, because this is an attractive, originally Belle Époque house that has been modernized with a sense of style—main-floor lounge off the lobby in red-and-gold Empire style, Provençal-style restaurant, and, hardly unimportant, 80 rooms; those I have lived in or inspected are as attractive as they are comfortable. Best Western. *First Class.*

Arcade Hôtel (Rue Eugène-le-Roy; phone 5690-92-40) has the same inconvenient railway-station location as the Terminus (above) but is lesser-category, albeit adequate, with 140 clean-lined rooms—typical of the Arcade chain of which it's a part—equipped with baths (showers replace tubs) as well as the convenience of a restaurant and bar. *Moderate.*

Bordeaux-Le Lac is not a hotel but rather an architecturally undistinguished quarter, twenty minutes drive north of the city—near Palais des Congrès, the convention center—in which is clustered a group of contemporary hotels, links of national chains for conventioneers or business travelers without any interest in absorbing the flavor of the city. But if you're on your own, intent on enjoying Bordeaux, you want to be in town. Withal, should you find yourself billeted in this area, here's how it breaks down: There are, confusingly, two Mercure hotels. *Hôtel Mercure Bordeaux-Le Lac* (phone 5650-90-30) has 100 okay rooms with bath, 8 suites, restaurant, bar-lounge; *Hôtel Mercure* (phone 5650-90-14) is a 100-room, restaurant-equipped house. There are, as well, *Sofitel Aquitaia* (phone 5650-83-80)—with 210 rooms and suites, two restaurants, bar; and *Novotel Bordeaux-Le Lac* (phone 5650-99-70)—the only one of the quartet without an outdoor swimming pool, and with 170 rooms and a restaurant. All except Sofitel (*First Class*) are *Moderate.*

De Plaisance Hostellerie (Place du Clocher, St.-Émilion; phone 5724-72-32): Overnight in charming St.-Émilion? Why not, with a honey of a hotel like the Plaisance? This aged mansion affords smashing views of vineyards and encircling the town from each of its dozen rooms, none quite like any of its neighbors, but all with fabulous marble baths and inventive antique-accented decor. Pretty public spaces, bar and terrace among them, not to mention a restaurant, later counseled. Friendly. *First Class.*

Château Cordeillan-Bages Hôtel (Pauillac, in the wine country 30 miles northwest of Bordeaux; phone 5659-24-24) is among the more beautiful of France's country hotels—stone-walled, white-shuttered, and overlooking the Pauillac vineyards whose wines take its name. Indeed, a oenophiles can't be more strategically situated. You're dead center in the Médoc, with 34 classified vintages—Châteaux Latour, Lynch-Bages, and Pichonville among them—within six miles. Notes taken as I inspected the hotel brim with exclamation points—lovely lounges with toile-print fabrics surfacing walls, a honey of a bar, handsome terraced restaurant (later evaluated), bright, light, wickery breakfast room, and 18 rooms all giving onto a central lawn. Those I have inspected are good-sized, stylishly furnished, delightfully papered, and with good baths. From here, you may sign up for wine-country tours as well as courses in the art and techniques of wine-tasting, by means of which pupils become familiar with the region, and with growers and other wine personalities. An exceptional hotel. *First Class.*

Relais de Margaux Hôtel (Margaux, 12 miles northwest of Bordeaux, in the wine country; phone 5688-38-30) is centered on a pedimented two-story pavilion in the classic style, whose public spaces including bar, lounges, and restaurant (later evaluated) are formal and attractive. Those of the 31 rooms and suites in the newer wing tend to be larger than the others, and are air-conditioned. Decor ranges from clean-lined contemporary to graceful Louis XVI, with the taste sophisticated albeit with the ambience throughout distinctly chilly. There's a swimming pool and a tennis court. Relais et Châteaux. *Luxury.*

DAILY BREAD

La Tupina (6 Rue Porte-de-la-Monnaie, an easy taxi ride from central hotels, just off Quai Ste.-Croix; phone 5691-56-37): Bordelais cuisine—indeed, much of the cuisine of the southwest—is considerably less celebrated abroad than that of, say, Burgundy, to name another noted wine region. La Tupina—occupying attractive quarters redolent of earlier centuries, in an aged house on an aged street—makes a specialty of regional cooking. Congenial waiters start you out with marvelous coarse pain de campagne setting a basket on your table, which is covered in red, white, and blue striped linen. You look over to the kitchen—cooking is being undertaken in immense copper kettles on an open grill—and you order from an extensive à la carte. Foie gras à la fondue d'oignon, hot and in a pipéradelike sauce, is delicious. A seafood salad—heavy on the crayfish—is, too. Likewise, a starter of garlic-scented smoked breast of duck; ditto, a cubed roast duck salad dressed with a shallot-accented vinaigrette. Entrées are hardly less memorable: cassoulet, the baked-bean dish based on confits of duck; time-honored entrecôte Bordelaise, its sauce rich with the wine whose name it takes; a pot-au-feu combining vegetables with braised duck. La Tupina's made-on-premises sweets are hardly to be ignored: prune and Armagnac ice cream, a giant poached peach bathed in caramel sauce, rich chocolate cake. Needless to say, wine plays a major role in a meal here. In my experience, one of France's best restaurants. *Luxury.*

Le Bistrot de Bordeaux (10 Rue des Pilliers du Tutelle; phone 5681-35-94) makes no pretense of being anything more than its name indicates: simple and clean-lined; with pink linens on tables; long, white aprons on the waiters. The name of the game is wine sampling, so that with the well-priced prix-fixe, a glass of wine—you choose from a dozen available—comes with each course. Select, say, a Domaine de Fussignac to accompany your duck terrine and a Château Conilh to be consumed with your richly sauced chicken breast. Foie gras or lentil salad, grilled lamb or beefsteak are another pairing of courses. Dessert wine or no, you will have done well to open with vin de pêche as an offbeat aperitif and to conclude with the bistrot's celebrated chocolate cake, unfrosted but served in a soup bowl, the better to accommodate the crème Anglaise with which it is heaped. Central. *First Class.*

Le Rouzic (34 Cours du Chapeau Rouge; phone 5644-39-11): In a setting of massed flowers, Louis XV seating, faux-marble placeplates over paisley-patterned linen—you do very well here ordering one of the menus, perhaps starting with terrine of duck liver with morilles—a noted house specialty as entrée—the eellike fish called lamprey in a Bordelaise sauce, or grilled lamb chops sauced with minced-olive tapinade. Desserts are delicious. As in all of this city's leading restaurants, wine choice is generous. And service is smiling. Location is heart-of-town—opposite the Grand Théâtre. *Luxury.*

Le Pavillon des Boulevards (120 Rue Croix-de-Seguey; phone 5681-51-02) is good-looking (there's a garden for summer meals) and good-tasting. The less expensive of two pricey menus might lead off with foie-gras-dotted duck consommé, preparatory to roast lobster or red mullet teamed with bacon (a house specialty that tastes better than it sounds), with cheese and a frozen fruit-based sweet to conclude. *Luxury.*

Bistro Romain (65 Cours de l'Intendance; phone 5644-93-33) is indicated after a morning in the shops. If the day is sunny, position yourself at an outdoor table, ordering the well-priced menu that might comprise carpaccio as a starter, maigret de canard—France's beloved breast of duck—in tandem with pommes allumettes following, with a sweet to conclude. *Moderate.*

Chantegril (37 Cours Clemenceau; phone 5651-19-64)—part of a national chain that made its name on good-value menus and agreeable settings—offers what might be called a loss-leader: opening with as many salads, cold meats, and the like as you can pile on your plate from the appetizer buffet; this to accompany steaks or lamb chops nicely garnished. Alternatively, if you're a buffet nut, another menu embraces all you can pile on a plate, first from the appetizer buffet, then (on another plate), from the dessert buffet. You will not depart hungry. *Moderate.*

Burdigala Hôtel Restaurant (11 Rue Georges-Bonnac; phone 5690-16-16) is at once attractive and—if you select a weekday at lunchtime—good value, with a menu opening with crayfish-stuffed ravioli, a deliciously sauced steak as an entrée, and coffee. There are pricier menus at both lunch and dinner, and an à la carte. Pleasant. *First Class.*

Chapon Fin (5 Rue Montesquieu; phone 5679-10-10) has been in business for a considerable period, so that there is no question but that there's a market for its excessive decor—one wall is of jagged rock, others are mirrored; stained-glass abounds, and there is a veritable forest of plants—to the point where what the French call *accueil,* or welcome, can be cool and unsmiling, with service patronizing. There are several menus. You might open with foie gras teamed with apples and artichokes, continuing with boned pigeon rolled up and roasted in a red-wine sauce, with tiny Russian pancakes, or blini, accompanying. Tournedos, topped with warm foie gras and accompanied by an uncomplicated mushroom dish and sautéed potatoes, is a better choice. Still, so offputting for me is the garish decor and the chilly service that, cuisine notwithstanding one way or the other, this is not a restaurant I can counsel. *Moderate.*

Dubern (42 Allées Tourny; phone 5648-03-44) is a smart town house on a landmark Bordeaux street. Fare served as part of the less pricey of two prix-fixe menus—asparagus soup with oysters, escalope of salmon, turkey entrée, cheese, house-selected dessert—is competent. Gilded Louis XV paneling and crystal chandeliers of the upstairs dining rooms are attractive. *Luxury.*

La Chamade (20 Rue des Pilliers de Tutelle; phone 5648-13-74) is, to be sure, in a basement, but a basement gained via a marble stairway and with tapestry-surfaced walls. There are also tasty victuals: foie gras, oyster stew, filet of sole, roast lamb, super sweets. Congenial. Central. *First Class.*

L'Entrecôte (4 Cours du 30-Juillet; phone 5681-76-10): The name of Entrecôte's game is what the title implies: the steak called entrecôte, scrumptiously Bordelaise-sauced and served with a heap of crispy frites. Nothing else on the menu. Upstairs. Central. *Moderate.*

L'Imprévu (11 Rue des Ramparts; phone 5648-55-43) serves up creditable fare as part of two prix-fixe menus. The less expensive might include a nicely presented plate of crudités; grilled steak, cassoulet, or confit of pork; and dessert. Cordial. Central. *Moderate.*

Aliénor (Quai Louis-XVIII; phone 5681-27-90) is nothing less than a Gironde River steamer, attractively fitted out for evening dinner-dances the while traversing the waterway that—passing villages and vineyards—connects Bordeaux with the Atlantic. Fare is regional—and hearty: ham or seafood terrines, roast lamb, entrecôte, or sole in champagne; and what the menu terms "super-choix de desserts." Board by 8:30; you're back at the pier before midnight. *First Class.*

Café Français (Place Pey-Berland): Take an outdoor table here for vistas of the cathedral and Hôtel de Ville. *Moderate.*

Le Régent (Cours Georges-Clemenceau at Cours de l'Intendance) is an inviting café at an interesting intersection. Relax and observe the shoppers. *Moderate.*

De Plaisance Hostellerie Restaurant (Place du Clocher, St.-Émilion; phone 5724-72-32) is no less handsome than other sections of the hotel in which it's situated (above). And it offers tasty prix-fixe menus, which might include crayfish and asparagus salad to open, sautéed veal filet or roast lamb as entrées, and flaky fruit tarte among the sweets. *First Class.*

L'Emiliano (Rue Portrail Brunet, St.-Émilion; phone 5774-44-64) is an old St.-Émilion favorite, with hearty prix-fixe menus. Begin with a mushroom omelet or snails, and continue with confit of duck or pork, saving some of your wine (it had just better be St.-Émilion!) to accompany cheese; with dessert following. *Moderate/First Class.*

Château Cordeillan-Bages Hôtel Restaurant (Pauillac; phone 5659-24-24) is the handsome terraced restaurant of a handsome hotel (above), with an uncomplicated bill of fare comprising a pair of menus and a relatively limited à la carte. The less expensive menu might open with a warm salad of young rabbit and string beans in a foie-gras-flecked cream sauce. A favored French fish, lotte, roasted in red Bordeaux is the unusual—but tasty—entrée, and an irresistible marquise au chocolat is the sweet. The costlier menu offers a choice of a duo of marinated fish or—super, this—oyster stew, its sauce herb-infused, followed by roast breast of duck or mixed grill of fish accompanied by baby vegetables. Cheese from a generous platter is next, with a choice of sweets, one being (I hope, for your sake!) warm apple tart. Special suggestion: If you don't drink at midday, and you're a wine buff, consider dinner here. The wine list is 25 pages long, with 13 of those devoted to—what else?—Bordeaux, subdivided into a baker's dozen categories, whites to start, with reds running alphabetically from Côtes de Bordeaux through St.-Julien. Friendly. *First Class/Luxury.*

Relais de Margaux Hôtel Restaurant (Margaux; phone 5688-38-30) is imposing—a vast stone-walled space, with white linen, brass-and-glass lanterns overhead, and dramatic draperies framing high windows. The à la carte is extensive, and there are a pair of menus; one the so-called déjeuner léger, or light lunch, is weekday only and includes amuse-bouches (the tidbit you're given while you study the menu or drink an aperitif), appetizer, entrée, dessert, coffee, and petits-fours. On days when the main course is beef Bordelais or maigret de canard, following an opener of duck carpaccio or marinated salmon, this can be quite a repast. Order from the pricier menu and the range is wider—with boned roast quail in a pastry case, truffle-sauced, or veal medaillons lightly breaded under an almond-lime sauce among entrées. Desserts are rich—the cold chocolate soufflé, coconut-topped, for example. And, hardly surprising, the wine list is extensive. The problem is service. In my experience it has been unsmiling and slow as molasses in Janvier. *Luxury.*

Le Savoie (Margaux village, opposite the Office de Tourisme; phone 5688-31-76) is an elderly house transformed into the neighborhood's busiest restaurant, with tables occupying several ground-floor rooms and a pair of generous prix-fixe menus. Open with coarse pâté de campagne, continue with a Béarnaise-sauced filet de boeuf, accompanied by deliciously prepared carrots, and conclude with a rich sweet, with a château-bottled Margaux—from the house's capacious *cave*—to accompany. *First Class.*

SHOPPER'S BORDEAUX

Wine, first: *L'Intendant* (2 Allées de Tourny opposite Grand Théâtre) has 15,000 bottles stored in an air-conditioned tower (the levels are connected by spiral staircase), with something like 500 labels from which to make your choice, grands crus to this week's big bargain. *Bordeaux Magnum* (3 Rue Gobineau) has tastings, with five different wines a month, to sample. *Department stores—Nouvelles Galeries Monoprix, Prisunic,* and *Grand Quartier*—are on Rue Ste.-Catherine, boutique-dotted, with *Yves St.-Laurent—Rive Gauche, Jacques Dessange* (link of a hairdressing chain also in New York), *Fancy* (men's and women's shoes), *Men in Vogue, Geneviève Léthu* (glass and china), and *Brigitte Perot* (classic-style women's clothing). *Cours de l'Intendance* is classy, too—with such shops as *Rodier* (men's and women's clothing), *Daniel Crémieux* (smart men's wear), *Weinberg* (haute women's), *Parfumerie Clemenceau, Carina* (lingerie), *Convent Garden* (women's knitwear), *Louis Féraud* (women's haute couture), *Céline* (smart women's clothing and accessories, with other French and U.S. outlets), *Bally* (men's and women's shoes), *Thomas Burberry* (men's and women's cashmere), next-door *Burberry* (the raincoat house), *Daniel Hechter* (upscale clothing, a chain), *Alain Figairet* (a mens' and women's wear clothing and accessories chain), *Emanuelle Khan* (women's haute couture). Rue Porte Dijeux supplements Rue Ste.-Catherine as a pedestrian street, with shops including *Ted Lapidus* (men's and women's clothing—a chain), *Lothaire* (Hugo Boss and other men's labels), *Stéphane Kélian* (pricey women's shoes—a chain), *Georges Rech* (expensive women's things), *Cacherel* (men's and women's clothing—a chain, with U.S. branches), *Hédiard* (a branch of the Paris fancy-food store), and the Bordeaux outpost of *Galeries Lafayette,* with perfume on main, men's wear on 1, women's clothing on 2, porcelain, crystal, and restrooms on 3. Rue Bouffard's antique shops include *Patrick Marot* (with porcelain and paintings among specialties) and *Xavier Pariente* (with, among other things, fine eighteenth-century mirrors).

AFTER DARK

Grand Théâtre (Place de la Comédie) is not only a principal Bordeaux landmark, but one of France's outstanding theaters, as I try to make clear above. Go for opera by its own fine company (performing works like *Aïda, Elektra, Manon,* and *The Abduction from the Seraglio* November through June), concerts, ballets.

Conservatoire André-Malraux (Rue Peyronnet) is the site of concerts by the esteemed *Orchestre National Bordeaux Aquitaine,* which performs also in the Grand Théâtre above and at points throughout the southwest region of Aquitaine, including Bayonne and Pau. Other musical events, too.

INCIDENTAL INTELLIGENCE

Aéroport de Bordeaux-Mérignac, seven miles north of town, is linked with Newark, U.S.A., via Air France. There is frequent scheduled service to Paris and other domestic points. *Further information:* Office de Tourisme, Place Créneaux, St.-Émilion.

11

Bourges

Heartland of France

BACKGROUND BRIEFING

Is it conceivable that a city can be *too* central? In earlier centuries, Bourges's smack-in-the-heartland location (the precise geographical center of France is but 20 miles distant) served it very well, indeed. Contemporarily, though, trans-France travelers tend to give it short shrift, concentrating instead on the Loire châteaux to the northwest, Bordeaux to the southwest, or Burgundy to the northeast.

A pity, this. Too much remains of a rich past—a Gothic cathedral that's an all-Europe ranker, most significantly—to pass by the town that the Romans made capital of the northern segment of their Aquitanian colony and that later became capital of the medieval province of Berry, during which time it was nothing less than a royal seat.

Charles VII—the very same who, with Jeanne d'Arc's support, forced the English to retreat from France in the mid-fifteenth century—headquartered in Bourges. His son, Louis XI, who organized France's first post office, brought printing to France, and founded an esteemed local university that thrived for three centuries (until the Revolution), was Bourges-born. So, indeed, was the fabulously rich medieval super-merchant called Jacques Cœur—financial brain in the reign of Charles VII, pioneer French trader in the Middle East, owner of factories and mines, and monetary backer of campaigns against the English in the Hundred Years War. Cœur, alas, died ingloriously on a Turkish island, having escaped after enemies falsely arrested him on a charge of having poisoned Agnès Sorel, the bright and beautiful mistress of his employer, Charles VII. But the house that Cœur built—one of the most startlingly prototypical examples of nonreligious Gothic architecture extant—still stands in Bourges, there for us to visit.

ON SCENE

Lay of the Land: Aptly named *Rue Moyenne* (which translates as Middle Street) cuts through the center of this essentially oval-shaped town, from *Place André-Malraux*—honoring one of this century's great French writers—at its south edge, to *Place Cujas,* named for the seventeenth-century teacher who is considered the father of modern jurisprudence and who taught at Bourges's late lamented university. The city's principal landmark, its cathedral, is due east of Place Malraux. *Rue d'Auron,* perpendicular to Rue Moyenne, is the sprightly nucleus of a pedestrian shopping zone (*Nouvelles Galeries* is the top department store, and there are smart boutiques in surprising abundance). Several streets—*Rue Branly, Rue Coursarlon, Rue Mirabeau*—make for lovely strolls, the better to take in an extraordinary residue of medieval houses, many of them half-timbered—*colombage* is the French architectural term. These streets more or less surround the handsomest of the city's squares, *Place Gordaine,* with its cafés the ideal relaxation venue between hours of exploration.

Cathedral of St.-Étienne (Rue du Guichet): French cathedrals—even celebrated ones like Rouen and Reims, to name a pair—are rarely set apart in parks of their own, like most English counterparts. The cities in which they are situated have been built up around them, sometimes allowing open space for perspective, sometimes not. Bourges Cathedral is fortunate in that a venerable formal garden edges it to one side and frames the onetime Palais de l'Archevêque, a Baroque mansion that housed long-ago archbishops and that is now the Hôtel de Ville. The perspective of the cathedral from the park is ravishing. While there, take in its proportions: flying buttresses supporting a pyramidal-shaped apse and, around the side, buttresses, each pinnacle-topped, the while serving as dividers between windows whose stained glass ranks with that of the Cathedral of Chartres—no modest attainment. Still, the approach to the cathedral from narrow Rue du Guichet—itself ancient, as houses flanking it attest—is hardly to be despised. At the street's end, you are faced with the cathedral's west or main facade. Tarry here; the artisans who erected this church (completed about 1350) did not stint at the entrance; worshipers have a choice of entry through five portals. In the tympanum—or recessed arch—above each door, sculptors have interpreted biblical chapter and verse so forcefully that Bourges's entrance these many centuries later is still called *La Bible des Pauvres,* the Bible of the then largely illiterate poor. That designation has even more meaning within. Walk first down the 350-foot-long nave to the high altar. (Bourges has no transept.) Then patrol the aisles, the better to take in the stained glass; that illustrating the Apocalypse, portraying Christ with a two-edged sword between his teeth, is a standout; so are scenes in the life of St. Stephen, for whom the cathedral is named.

Palais Jacques-Cœur (Rue Jacques-Cœur): If politics was the undoing of King Charles VII's finance minister—he died in foreign exile—it was also the means through which he achieved great wealth in the dynamic fifteenth century. The house he built is, indeed, a palace, with a fancifully gabled and many-chimneyed facade, stone walls intricately carved, and windows of its four stories mullioned. There are no furnishings. You go, rather, to appreciate what medieval civil architecture was all about—stunningly proportioned rooms, superb fireplaces (the one in the dining room is two stories high), as well as a masterful kitchen, a running-water system, a sauna, a bathroom, and a lavatory with the same contours as contemporary successors.

Musée de l'Hôtel Lallemant (Rue Bourbonnoux): As compensation for empty interiors of the Palais Jacques-Cœur (above), this *hôtel particulier*, or town house, of a canny Renaissance cloth merchant, is furnished and accessorized so beautifully—and extensively—that it is a veritable museum of decorative arts extending over three centuries, sixteenth through eighteenth. Collections of smaller objects—porcelain, enamels, figurines, and paintings—is exemplary enough. But it is period rooms—one Régence, with walls of blue brocade and a brass chandelier; one Louis XIII, with a coffered ceiling and heavy oak furniture; one Louis XIV, with tapestried walls and tapestry-covered chairs; and one Louis XV, with a magnificent suite of furniture of that era—that especially captivate.

Musée du Berry (Rue des Arènes) occupies still another *hôtel particulier*—Hôtel Cujas, dating to the sixteenth century, double-towered and with a courtyard. It runs a considerable gamut, with respect to the span of time represented in two floors of exhibits, some prehistoric, some the folklore of recent epochs, the most interesting those relating to Gallo-Roman Bourges—busts and sculpted fragments, especially.

Church of St.-Pierre-le-Guillard (Rue des Arènes) is of the same period as the cathedral—begun in the thirteenth century. In one of the chapels of its graceful Gothic interior—the nave is especially lovely—you'll find the tomb of Bourges's honored Renaissance professor, Jacques Cujas.

Château de Meillant and Route Jacques-Cœur: Smaller, less spectacular, and certainly less well known than the châteaux of the Loire to the north, ten castles—most of them inhabited and furnished in period—of the so-called Route Jacques-Cœur, all in the neighborhood of Bourges, are eminently visitable. *Château Meillant,* the biggest, is a Renaissance beauty; its skyscraper of a tower extends to seven stories. The grand salon is tapestry-hung, its furniture Louis XIV and Louis XV. *Château Ainay le Vieil* is surrounded by a wall punctuated with half a dozen towers; *Château Culan*—parts of it are as old as the tenth century—sheltered Jeanne d'Arc in the course of her military travels. Others in the neighborhood include *Châteaux de la Verrerie, Boucard, Menetou-Salon, Chapelle l'Anguillon,* and *Jussy-Champagne.* Bourges's Office de Tourisme (address below) can route you.

SETTLING IN

Angleterre Hôtel (1 Place des Quatre-Pilliers; phone 4824-68-51) is a comfortable old-timer, tastefully updated and professionally operated, with just over 30 well-equipped rooms with bath, an attractive restaurant—Louis XVI–style in blue and white—and a cozy bar. Location is heart-of-town. *Moderate.*

D'Artagnan Hôtel (19 Place Seraucourt; phone 4821-51-51) is more functional than charming, with its chief advantage a good-sized room capacity (73 all told). Restaurant and bar-lounge. Away from the core. *Moderate.*

Christina Hôtel (5 Rue du Halle; phone 4870-56-50) is so-so, neither central nor engaging, but with 75 rooms. Breakfast only is served. *Moderate.*

Tilleuls Hôtel (7 Place de la Pyrotechnie; phone 4824-49-04) is just outside of town, occupying a renovated house of yore, with 29 rooms—some really spacious. Agreeable management. Breakfast only. *Moderate.*

Château de Thaumiers (20 miles south of Bourges, at Thaumiers near Charenton-du-Cher; phone 4860-87-62) looks older—thanks to half a dozen medieval-style conical towers—but is eighteenth-century and inhabited, with 10 rooms-cum-bath for paying guests; breakfast only. Château Meillant (above) is a near neighbor. *Moderate.*

DAILY BREAD

Jacques-Cœur (Place Jacques-Cœur; phone 4870-12-72): Talk about staying power: I enjoyed the Jacques-Cœur for the first time on a visit some two decades back, reporting favorably, at the time, on a dinner embracing snails, roast lamb with flageolet beans, cheese, and a poached whole peach. More recently, I ate equally deliciously; my meal commenced with a salmon terrine and continued with the same escargots I had remembered fondly. These were followed by steak Jacques-Cœur, served with a tarragon-scented mustard sauce and accompanied by Provence-style tomatoes; a sampling of the house's own pastries followed. Setting is opposite Palais Jacques-Cœur (above), and service remains delightful. *First Class.*

Le Sénat (8 Rue de la Poissonnerie; phone 4824-02-56): A restaurant on what translates as Fish Market Street had just better serve good seafood. Le Sénat does. Beef and veal entrées, too. Central. *Moderate.*

Le Bouffetard (Place Gordaine; phone 4824-19-68) is strategically situated at the edge of the city's most picturesque square. Consider entrecôte aux frites or a snack. No credit cards. *Moderate.*

INCIDENTAL INTELLIGENCE

Further information: Office de Tourisme, 21 Rue Victor-Hugo, Bourges.

12

Caen

Bayeux and the D-Day Landing Beaches

BACKGROUND BRIEFING

It is little wonder that so much English is spoken in Caen. The interchange between this ancient Norman port and England began nine centuries ago, when the then-resident duke of Normandy departed his Caen château, crossed the Channel with his legions, won the Battle of Hastings, and became sovereign of the land he vanquished, as William I—the Conqueror.

That was in 1066. In 1984, a successor of William—many generations removed—also crossed the Channel, albeit in a southerly direction, on a mission of joyous commemoration. Queen Elizabeth II worshiped in Caen's Abbaye aux Hommes—built by William. The irony of the occasion was not missed: It was the fortieth anniversary of the World War II, British-led liberation of Caen from the Nazis.

Love-hate relationship? If you like. Caen benefited from William's Hastings victory with a marked increase in commerce—it is just inland from the sea with which it is linked by canal—with England. Later—it was the early fourteenth century, by which time the Duchy of Normandy had become part of the kingdom of France—pro-English sentiment soured when, on two occasions in the course of the interminable Anglo-French Hundred Years War, English forces subdued Caen. On the second, in 1417, they remained as occupiers for more than three decades.

Even in that role, there were positive aspects. King Henry VI—who had been crowned in both London and Paris and founded England's Eton College and King's College, Cambridge, before he was murdered in the Tower of London—created the University of Caen. It thrives these many centuries later, although it was rebuilt, as was so much of Caen, 80 percent of which was destroyed by World War II bombs.

The city's most spectacular historic monuments—including the pair of abbeys built by William the Conqueror and his consort, Matilda, as acts of contrition for having married, even though cousins—were spared. And the immediate region of Caen is a study in stark contrasts, from venerable little Bayeux, with its extraordinary tapestries depicting William's conquest, to the English Channel beaches, on which Allied soldiers struck the invasion of Nazi-held Europe on D-Day, June 6, 1944.

ON SCENE

Lay of the Land: Caen is among the more attractively reconstructed of the European cities heavily damaged during World War II. It is based on its historic Big Three complexes. William the Conqueror's *Abbaye aux Hommes* on the street named for him—*Rue Guillaume-le Conquérant*—marks the western edge of town, while *Abbaye aux Dames,* built by William's wife, is terminus of the core at its eastern extremity on appropriately named *Place Reine-Mathilde.* Between the two—near the city's southern apex—is what remains of William's once-glorious château, with still-splendid ramparts enclosing a mix of cultural institutions housed in recycled structures of the castle complex. *Avenue du 6 Juin*—bearing the date of D-Day—cuts through Caen from the château through central *Place de la Résistance,* flanked by venerable *Church of St.-Jean,* to the railway station on *Rue de la Gare. Boulevard du Maréchal Leclerc* is focal point of the pedestrian shopping precinct (with both *Galeries Lafayette* and *Nouvelles Galeries* department stores) in the core of town, southwest of the château, terminating at *Place Gambetta.*

The château complex—elevated and enclosed by original eleventh-century ramparts—is not all that it once was, but comes off handsomely, with its mix of manicured lawns, museums, and monuments. Still to be observed are formidable foundations of the onetime dungeon; a deftly proportioned little Gothic chapel, *St.-Georges,* by name, which now serves as a memorial to World War II Resistance fighters; also-Gothic *Échiquier* (it's used for conferences and private parties, but you may peep in), and the Baroque-era *Logis du Gouverneur,* an official residence cleverly adapted to house *Musée de Normandie*—an absorbing ethnological mix—with regional lore. I intentionally save best for last: a completely contemporary pavilion that was opened in 1970 to house exemplary collections of the city's *Musée des Beaux-Arts.* There are, to be sure, bigger French provincial art museums, but none, in my experience, with a higher proportion of beautiful paintings. I don't think anyone would not concede that the trademark work is Roger Van der Weyden's ravishing *Virgin and Child*—Mary red-robed, with a breast exposed for presumably imminent feeding of the naked baby Jesus, gently held in her lap. An arresting Rubens, *Abraham and Melchissedech*—vibrant with people and animals, color and movement—is a ranker, too, along with Perugino's *Marriage of the Virgin* and Veronese's *Temptation of St. Anthony,* as much for its melodrama as for its anatomy. Move along, then, to Strozzi and Giordano, Van Dyck and Jordaens, Poussin and Vouet, Panini and Tiepolo, Boucher and Rigaud, Courbet and Delacroix, Impressionists including Boudin and Monet, and later painters like Bonnard and Dufy.

The royal abbeys: What happened was that William the Conqueror—then Duke William (a.k.a. Guillaume le Bâtard, for he was illegitimate)—wooed and won the Flemish Princess Mathilde, a descendant of Charlemagne. But there was a hitch. Though not first cousins, they were related, and the pope of the moment excommunicated them. To achieve papal forgiveness, William erected a Benedictine monastery, while his wife, equally contrite, put up a convent for Benedictine nuns. If you are a gallant traveler, it will be a question of Ladies First, and you will start at the *Abbaye aux Dames* (Place Reine-Mathilde). The convent part of the complex, to the rear, was inhabited by nuns until the Revolution, later became a hospital, and since has been carefully restored—slowly and carefully. You want to see the abbey church, Trinité by name, twin-towered Romanesque, with a fine nave, a crypt made beautiful by the sixteen splendid pillars framing it, and Mathilde's black marble tomb in the choir. *Abbaye aux Hommes* (Rue Guillaume-le-Conquérant), by far the more elaborate of the pair, will take more time. Its Church of St.-Étienne stuns, right off, with a pair of needlelike spires framing a severely beautiful Romanesque facade. Go on in, first, to pay your respects (as Queen Elizabeth II did on her D-Day Anniversary visit) at the simple black-and-white marble tomb, inscribed in Latin, of *Guillelmus Conquestor Normannis Dux et Angliae Rex,* taking in the misericords—the stand-up seats of the choir—with scenes, both lay and secular, of the seventeenth-century period when they were carved, and the portrait of a shrewd-visaged William in the transept. Move, then, to the newer part of the complex, the monastery, which was reconstructed in the eighteenth century, put to use as a school by Napoleon in the nineteenth century, and refurbished after World War II to serve as Caen's Hôtel de Ville, or town hall. The formal garden out front is more palatial than monasterial. Within, it's interesting to see how city fathers have assigned secular functions to interiors built for monks. The priors' reception hall is the city council chamber. The mayor hosts official receptions in the refectory. Civil marriages take place—chances are you'll observe a wedding in progress—in the onetime monks' chapter house. But other rooms—art-filled sacristy, monks' parlor for guests, and superb cloister—happily remain quite as they were, to be admired by visitors.

Memorial de la Bataille de Normandie (Esplanade Dwight Eisenhower): The presence of France's president at the dedication of a building—especially beyond Paris—signifies its importance. It was François Mitterrand who officially opened this structure in 1988, as "a museum of peace," appropriately situated in the city anchoring the decisive World War II Battle of Normandy. The museum—edging an esplanade named for the late American president, who as a general commanded the battle's Allied forces, dramatically utilizing state-of-the-art museum presentation and exhibition techniques—takes visitors on a graphic and moving journey through twentieth-century history, World War I onwards. The route unfolds in five principal sequences: the era of uneasy peace between the world wars, the Nazi occupation of France commencing in June of 1940; the Normandy landings on June 6, 1944; through defeat of the Germans on May 8, 1945; and the post–World War II decades leading into the twenty-first century.

Designed by Jean Millet, a Caen architect, the memorial comprises three levels. You're guided, as you follow the indicated route, by a continuous historical descriptive strip, with the option to read maps and documents, observe equipment, uniforms, and arms, and, by means of what is called a teletext service, project questions to the Memorial's Research and Documentation Center, with answers forthcoming in a jiffy on video discs in the form of animated scenarios—and in the language of the questioner. There are both restaurant and café, as well as a shop. And unless hours change, the memorial is open every day of the year. Go.

Church of St.-Pierre (Place St.-Pierre) is a reminder of how rich Caen's medieval merchants were; they built this single-steeple Gothic beauty, and you want to head down the strikingly vaulted nave to observe the exquisitely carved frieze above the altar.

Château de Fontaine-Henry (seven miles northwest of Caen): The fireplaces—massive and magnificent—of its Renaissance rooms are reason enough for a visit, but the stairways are no less so, in a series of chambers rich with antique furniture, accessories, and paintings. A bonus: the Romanesque chapel in the backyard.

Château de Lantheuil (nine miles northwest of Caen) is the seat of a family whose most illustrious ancestor was a minister of Louis XVI and whose descendants still are resident. It is charmingly furnished in period.

Château de Creuilly (12 miles northwest of Caen) is more a case of history and architecture (it's as much fortress as residence and, at its eldest, dates to the eleventh century) than of art-filled interiors. It had been inhabited by Louis XIV's minister, Colbert, and his family well into the eighteenth century. In June 1944, a resourceful BBC crew moved into one of its towers to broadcast the Battle of Normandy.

Bayeux (18 miles northwest of Caen) is surely, along with Honfleur (chapter 19), the most charming of Norman towns, but with considerably more than cachet to recommend it. Geography is not complicated. The cathedral towers over the town and is dead center. A sleeper of a town museum is just next door; the globally celebrated tapestries—your principal reason for coming—are a short walk east. And there's a pedestrian shopping center on Place du Général de Gaulle—where General de Gaulle made his first speech on liberated French soil (Bayeux was the first town to be freed by Allied troops on June 14, 1944).

Cathedral of Notre-Dame, mostly twelfth- and thirteenth-century Gothic, packs an esthetic—and usually unexpected—wallop. The facade is graced by a trio of portals, two of them richly sculpted, but hardly less so than the smasher of a nave or, for that matter, the transept. Take your time wandering, noting art-filled side chapels, richly embellished high altar, and extraordinary Romanesque crypt—among France's loveliest.

Musée Baron-Gérard, the cathedral's next-door neighbor, shelters a mixed bag collection of uncommon delights. A Clouet portrait of a Renaissance noble is its star painting, but there are works, as well, by Philippe de Champaigne, Boucher, and Boudin; a cache of priceless Bayeux-made porcelain; displays of also-Bayeux-created lace; and a Louis XV salon furnished in period.

Tapisserie de Bayeux (Centre Guillaume le Conquérant) is not, properly, a tapestry, but rather a massive embroidery—when I say "massive," I mean some 230 feet long, with a height of not quite 20 inches—that is believed to have been made in England to decorate Bayeux's cathedral. Created while memories of the Battle of Hastings were still fresh, it relates—in 58 panels, wool-embroidered on a linen ground, with captions for each graphic episode in Latin—not only to the battle events, but also to the political, military, and civil events leading to it. You may rent a portable tape recorder, with a commentary on the tapestry to carry with you as you move along—and I recommend that you do so. Little has been left out by the embroiderers, from historic events like the death of King Edward the Confessor (William's predecessor on the English throne) to mundane matters like loading wine and weapons onto vessels making the Channel crossing. And take your time; it's the details of the tapestry that make it a medieval masterpiece.

Musée Mémorial de la Bataille de Normandie (Boulevard Fabian Ware, a short drive southwest of the center) is good preparation for a trip to the landing beaches (below): a graphic presentation of the Battle of Normandy embracing the 76 days between June 6 and August

22, 1944, by means of dioramas, displays of military equipment and weapons, and even mannequins wearing uniforms, both Allied and German.

Normandy Landing Beaches (Plages du Débarquement): The so-called longest day—D-Day, June 6, 1944—was the start of the World War II campaign by Allied forces that liberated France and the rest of occupied Europe from the Nazis—and paved the way to victory in Europe. General Dwight D. Eisenhower, later to become president of the United States, was supreme allied commander, with British Field Marshal Bernard Montgomery serving as commander of land forces. There were five principal landing beaches. From west to east, these were *Utah* (4th U.S. Infantry Division), *Omaha* (1st U.S. Infantry Division—and the most difficult of the lot), *Gold* (50th British Infantry Division), *Juno* (3rd Canadian Infantry Division), and *Sword* (3rd British Infantry Division). Many lives were lost, as the area's military cemeteries attest. There are 2 American cemeteries, as many Canadian, a Polish cemetery, no less than 16 British cemeteries, and even half a dozen German cemeteries. And there are a number of museums and memorials relating to the campaign.

The American Battle Monuments Commission operates the *Normandy American Cemetery and Memorial* (Memorial du Cimetière Militaire Américain) atop a cliff overlooking Omaha Beach. There are 9,387 American war dead; the remains of 14,000 others originally buried in the region were returned home at the request of their families. Graves—their headstones are of white marble, a Star of David for those of Jewish faith, a Latin cross for all others—are set in 10 plots, on smooth green lawns edging the beach. Walls of the semicircular colonnade of the memorial contain maps detailing the landings. I have noted the legend inscribed on the frieze between the maps: "This embattled shore, portal of freedom, is forever hallowed by the ideals, the valor and the sacrifices of our fellow countrymen. In proud remembrance of the achievements of her sons and in humble tribute to their sacrifice, this memorial is erected by the United States of America."

Musée du Débarquement (a.k.a. Museum of the Landings, in the village of Arromanches, in what was the area of Gold Beach) faces the sea, clean-lined and glistening white, with flags of all the Allied nations flying from it and a simple brass marker with the legend *D-Day—6 Juin 1944* on its black entry doors. The museum's site is where, over a seven-month period, Allied convoys landed supplies used in the invasion. René Coty, then the French president, opened the museum in 1954. Films, dioramas, documents, equipment, uniformed mannequins tell the D-Day story. But, for visitors of a certain age, it is the photos on a lobby wall that are as memorable as any of the exhibits. France's de Gaulle, Britain's Churchill, America's FDR, and Canada's Mackenzie King are on the top row, with military leaders—including Ike, "Monty" Montgomery, and General Omar Bradley—below. Quite a show.

SETTLING IN

Relais des Gourmets Hôtel (15 Rue de Geôle; phone 3186-06-01): You like the location, just below the château. You like the warm welcome at reception. And you fall, at once, for the smart look of this 32-room house, a successful mix of the antique and the contemporary, with attention paid to textiles and wallpapers. All of the rooms I have inspected—no two are alike—are delightful. *First Class.*

Moderne Hôtel (116 Boulevard Maréchal-Leclerc; phone 3186-04-23) is heart-of-town, on Caen's main pedestrian street. This is a bright and lively house, with 57 rooms. Those I have inspected are comfortable and traditional-style, with good baths. And there's an attractive restaurant, popular with locals. Friendly. *Moderate/First Class.*

Mercure Hôtel (1 Rue Couronne; phone 3193-07-62) is reasonably central, just east of the core of town, and it's modern—with 100 well-equipped rooms, good-value menus in its restaurant, and the super buffet breakfasts typical of hotels in this invariably reliable national chain. *Moderate/First Class.*

Malherbe Hôtel (Place Foche; phone 3184-40-06) occupies substantial quarters on a central square. Reception is alert, and there are just half a hundred rooms; those I have inspected are comfortable. Breakfast only. *Moderate.*

Royal Hôtel (1 Place de la République; phone 3186-55-33) is strategically located on a square at once central and attractive. There are just 45 neat rooms. Breakfast only. *Moderate.*

Dauphin Hôtel (29 Rue Gemare; phone 3186-22-26) comprises a score of rooms in a nondescript converted house southwest of the château and an easy walk to the center. It is, however, in my not inconsiderable experience of French hotels, quite the gloomiest I have encountered. My room—one of 21—reminded me of nothing so much as a railway sleeping compartment. Cheerless restaurant. I can't recommend this one. *Moderate.*

Métropole Hôtel (16 Place de la Gare; phone 3182-26-76): You're way over by the railway station if you put up here; however, there are 70 functional rooms. Breakfast only. *Moderate.*

Château d'Audrieu Hôtel (Audrieu, 12 miles west of Caen, 7 miles east of Bayeux; phone 3180-21-52) is a looker of an eighteenth-century château, set in its own park, with 22 no-two-alike antique-accented rooms and suites, public spaces that include a wood-paneled salon, intimate restaurant, bar-lounge, and a swimming pool in the garden. I had a delightful sojourn and delicious meals on one occasion, but a disappointingly ungracious welcome in the course of an inspection visit several years later. There was no denying, even then, however, that the château still *looked* great. Member, Relais et Châteaux. *First Class.*

Manoir du Chêne Hôtel (Nonant, 15 miles from Caen, 3 miles from Bayeux; phone 3192-58-81) is a stone-walled country house that's far less smartly furnished than its neighbor, Château d'Audrieu (above); but it's agreeable, with 19 rooms, restaurant, bar, and tennis. *Moderate.*

Lion d'Or Hôtel (71 Rue St.-Jean, Bayeux; phone 3192-06-90) is Bayeux's chief charm spot—a gracious old house, agreeably updated, with cordial management and staff, 30 traditional-style rooms (those I have seen are handsome), and a restaurant of good repute reviewed in a later paragraph. Central. *First Class.*

Luxembourg Hôtel (25 Rue des Bouchers, Bayeux; phone 3192-00-04) has two dozen rooms; those I inspected are neat as a pin and have showers in their baths. There are, as well, a cozy bar-lounge and a reliable restaurant, attractively Louis XIII in style. Very nice. *Moderate.*

Arrouges Hôtel (21 Rue St.-Patrice, Bayeux; phone 3192-88-86) is away from the center, with 29 bath-equipped rooms. Breakfast only. So-so. *Moderate.*

Altéa Omaha Beach Hôtel (Port-en-Bessen, near Omaha Beach, northwest of Bayeux; phone 3122-44-44) is a contemporary link of a national chain, with 50 pleasant, well-equipped rooms with bath, restaurant overlooking the 27-hole golf course in whose territory the hotel is built, and bar-lounge. *First Class.*

Marine Hôtel (Quai du Canada, Arromanches; phone 3122-34-19) is indicated should you be contemplating an overnight stay in connection with visits to the landing beaches. It's long-established and seafront, with 22 bath-equipped rooms and a restaurant that does well by traditional-style Normandy seafood specialties. *Moderate.*

DAILY BREAD

Bourride (15 Rue Vaugueux; phone 3193-50-76) is a near-neighbor of the château; it's agreeable for lunch after a morning of exploration in the neighborhood or for a candlelit dinner, with the setting an atmospheric house of yore. Open with the house's warm-oyster specialty, soup of the day—seafood bisque, perhaps—or the house's crayfish salad. Fish entrées are reliable; roast pigeon, too. Super sweets are comprehensively sampled by means of a platter, or assiette, of the day's desserts. *Luxury.*

St.-Andrew's (9 Quai de Juillet; phone 3186-26-80) does not, to be sure, sound very *Caennais*. But it is, indeed, strategically—and attractively—situated on the waterfront, with starters and entrées built around seafood. *First Class.*

Relais Normandy (Place de la Gare; phone 3182-24-58) serves traditional favorites: duck Rouen style through tarte Normande. Well-priced prix-fixe menus. *First Class.*

Café des Touristes (3 Boulevard Maréchal-Leclerc; phone 3186-11-56): Don't let the name put you off; situation is heart of the shopping area, so you can have coffee or a snack and take in the crowds. *Moderate.*

Lion d'Or Hôtel Restaurant (71 Rue St.-Jean, Bayeux; phone 3192-06-90) is the Old Bayeux restaurant you're seeking—beamed ceilings, ladderback chairs, reproductions of the Bayeux tapestry on the walls. Open with oysters, fish soup, or the house's own duck pâté. The chicken fricassee is hearty; filet of sole, more delicate but no less tasty. Lovely desserts; ditto, the service. *First Class.*

Rapière (53 Rue St.-Jean, Bayeux; phone 3192-94-97) occupies quarters in a Renaissance town house, with grilled steaks and lamb chops entrée specialties, and tarte Normande the indicated dessert. You're core-of-town, so that lunch is convenient; at dinner, tables are candlelit. *First Class.*

Dentellière (Impasse Prud'homme, Bayeux; phone 3192-16-59): You're in crêpe territory; stop here for a lunch composed of one or two savory crêpes as your main course, with a sweet one to conclude. Omelets, too. Central. *Moderate.*

SOUND OF MUSIC

Théâtre Municipal (Place de l'Ancienne Comédie) is the well-equipped modern house at which are presented opera, ballet, concerts.

INCIDENTAL INTELLIGENCE

Aéroport de Carpiquet is four miles west of Caen; service to London, domestic points. *Further information:* Office de Tourisme, Place St.-Pierre, Caen; Office de Tourisme, 1 Rue des Cuisiniers, Bayeux; Office de Tourisme, Rue Maréchal-Joffre, Arromanches.

13

Cannes

and Beyond to Grasse, Antibes, Juan-les-Pins

BACKGROUND BRIEFING

The kind of public recognition given the English for their role in establishing Nice (chapter 26) as a resort—the sea-girdling Promenade des Anglais—is, alas, absent in this smaller city 20 miles to Nice's west. But Cannes, too, owes England a debt for the cachet that accrued to it as a consequence of an 1834 visit—accidental, as an unplanned pause in the course of a journey to Italy—by Lord Brougham, the British Lord Chancellor, who was so pleased he promptly built himself a villa, impelling winter visits by friends among the British aristocracy.

Unlike Nice—a substantial city before its beaches were discovered by holidaymakers—Cannes, though ancient, was a small fishing port. Named for a reed called *cannae* that grew in nearby marshes, it long predated the Romans who occupied it, to be followed by invading Moors, long-ruling monks, Spanish soldiers, Revolutionary troops, and—in 1815—Napoleon himself, en route from Elba at the start of the One Hundred Days interval before his second exile.

But it was the British invasion set off by Lord Brougham that provided Cannes with its true vocation: tourism. The Second Empire of Napoleon III saw Cannes's crescent-shaped, oceanfront artery, La Croisette—its counterpart of Nice's Promenade des Anglais—lined with palatial hotels. Somewhat later houses, turn-of-century, like the Carlton and the Majestic, continue to thrive. In the 1920s, north-of-the-Channel visitors were joined by continental Europeans, Parisians and other northerly Frenchmen, and the species of wealthy American chronicled in novels by Fitzgerald and Hemingway. Post-World War II decades have seen a democratization of Cannes's clientele—you have your choice, now, of well over a hundred hotels in every category—and newfound celebrity as the venue each spring with the planet's premier film festival.

But the visitor must not expect a duplication of bigger Nice, where tourism is but an aspect of a multifaceted economy. Cannes makes no pretense of being anything other than a tourist town. If it lacks Nice's vitality and diversity, it compensates—at least for sun worshipers and swimmers—with the wide, white-sand beaches replaced in Nice by a narrow, pebble-surfaced strand. Unlike skyscraper-packed Monte Carlo (chapter 23), its core remains horizontal. And it is distinct from ultracasual St.-Tropez (chapter 33) in that it is neither barefoot nor big-city, but rather a compromise between the two—and a happy one, at that.

ON SCENE

Lay of the Land: Thank nature for the crescent-shaped beach on which Cannes is based. And thank the *Cannois* themselves for having had the good sense to base the city's Main Street, *La Croisette,* on the beach's contours, extending from *Pointe Croisette*—western extremity and site of the summer-only *Palm Beach Casino* across the sands, subdivided into hotel-operated and public beaches, with lunch-only restaurants and rentable cabanas and beach chairs—to the area of town where it all began: *Vieux-Port,* the ancient harbor. This is the site of *Gare Maritime,* from where boats depart for the nearby *Îles de Lérins* (below). Above Vieux-Port's *Place de l'Hôtel de Ville* and *Quai St.-Pierre* is the oldest part of town: high-on-a-cliff *Le Suquet,* with a pair of key Cannes destinations (below), and *Rue St.-Antoine,* lined with dinner-only restaurants. Overlooking Vieux-Port to its west is *Palais des Festivals et des Congrès,* futuristic convention center–winter casino–theater complex. Shopping? La Croisette, to be sure. But you want to explore, as well, *Rue d'Antibes,* running parallel and gained by a number of northbound streets, *Rue des États-Unis* and *Rue du Canada,* among them. Center-of-the-action hotels line La Croisette, but others are on interior streets, *Rue Hoche* particularly. The railway station is west of the core, just off *Avenue Docteur-Raymond-Picaud.* And Cannes is a center for excursions to such nearby points as *Antibes/Juan-les-Pins* (six and a half miles east), *Mougins* (six and a half miles north), *Grasse* (ten miles north), and *Vallauris* (four and a half miles east), all evaluated in later pages of this chapter.

Le Suquet, Cannes's dramatically elevated Old Town, is at its most spectacular on *Place de la Castre*—from which there are breathtaking views of the city below and the sea. Go inside *Church of Notre-Dame-de-l'Espérance,* representing a mix of epochs—originally twelfth-century Romanesque, with a later Renaissance portal, and a simple Gothic interior. Nearby *Musée de la Castre* will take more time. This medieval tower houses an unexpected jumble of lovely old objects—an antique Cypriot bust; an early Egyptian-Coptic gravestone; Greek kraters and vases, their terra cotta–hued designs in mint condition; and pieces from Iran to the east (a painted princess) and Peru to the west (pre-Columbian pottery).

Marché Forville (Rue du Marché) is so easy of access, a few blocks inland from Vieux-Port, that it's a pity not to make an early morning stroll through its aromatic stalls, wherein farmers sell fresh herbs—rosemary and basil, dill and thyme—so typical of the south of France. Look, too, at fish and crustaceans on sparkling beds of ice, along with fruits and vegetables arranged as though by artists for still-life paintings.

Île de Lérins: Earmark half a day for a swift excursion by boat to the pretty pair of Lérins Islands. On bigger *Ste.-Marguerite,* walk from the pier, upon arrival, to Fort Vauban, named for a prolific seventeenth-century military architect, to see a prison from that era, with cells not only of recalcitrant Protestants incarcerated after Louis XIV's Revocation of the Edict of Nantes, but of that same king's mysterious *Homme du Masque de Fer*—the Man in the Iron Mask—who was held for 16 years, with his identity never revealed. (Louis Hayward played him in a forties movie that you may have seen on TV.) To inspect as well: a museum of local archeological finds (Greeks and Romans were early settlers), an aquarium, and the flora (including eucalyptus trees) and fauna (including pheasants) of a pretty island. Catch a boat, then, to the smaller island, *St.-Honorat,* but a mile long and part of the Cistercians' Abbaye de Lérins, successor to a monastery that was opened sixteen centuries ago by the saint whose name the island takes. You're welcome to the monks' museum, noted for its antique sculptures, and to their church as well. Then, walk over to the much older *Fortified Monastery* to see its Romanesque chapels and smashing double-decker of a cloister.

Antibes/Juan-les-Pins—a pair of disparate towns east of Cannes, with beautiful *Cap d'Antibes* between them—may be regarded as vacation destinations in and of themselves or taken in, in the course of excursions from Cannes. *Juan-les-Pins* is modern and essentially a case of hotels, restaurants, cafés, and discos; it revolves around a summer-only casino on Square Gould, just in from the wide, white-sand beach flanked by Promenade du Soleil. *Antibes*—the ancient Greeks' *Antipolis,* then a Roman colony, later the seat both of bishops and of rulers related to the Grimaldis of Monaco (chapter 23)—is more substantial, which is not surprising, given its advanced age, and has a charming, centuries-old core that warrants on-foot exploration. Begin at *Place Nationale* and wander the adjacent pedestrian area between it and ramparts edging the sea, along such streets as *Rue Glose, Rue Sade,* and *Rue Aubernon,* taking in *Marché Provençal*—the market brimming with herbs, olives, produce, and fish and stands selling slices of tasty *pissaladière,* southern France's version of Neapolitan pizza. Stop into the so-called *Cathedral of Antibes* (actually a parish church and not the seat of a bishop these many centuries)—multiepoch, with a neoclassic facade, Romanesque choir, and Renaissance altar. Move along, then, to the next-door Château de Grimaldi, the rulers' originally medieval castle edging the ramparts. Severe and squarish, it is now *Musée Picasso,* with two floors of works by the master for whom it is named (and who was, for a time, in residence). The range is from 1935 *Minotaur* to 1970s tapestries, with a considerable cache of Picasso-designed pottery and such standout paintings as *Joie de Vivre, Satyre et Faune,* and *La Femmes aux Oursins,* augmented by a number of sculptures (including a larger-than-life goat) and drawings; many photos of Picasso; paintings by other artists (the most gawked-at is by David Hockney, portraying a nude Hockney at a table with a clothed Picasso); and an herb-planted, sea-view sculpture garden. Deftly tucked into nearby *Bastion St.-André* at the end of the ramparts is *Musée Archéologique,* exhibiting bits and pieces of ancient Antibes. Antibes's medieval, four-pointed *Fort Carré* is now a theater/sports center. And beyond town, on *Boulevard John-F.-Kennedy at Cap d'Antibes,* is *Musée Naval et Napoléonien*—invariably popular with avid Napoleon buffs.

Grasse, as hilly as it is handsome, is Perfumeville—center of France's scent industry for three centuries, surrounded by fields of lavender, roses, and jasmine, with a number of perfume factories open to visitors (*Molinard,* at 60 Boulevard Victor Hugo, and *Fragonard,* at 20 Boulevard Fragonard, have museums in connection). Grasse's monuments attest to its wealth over long centuries, ever since the twelfth, when it operated as an independent republic. Though no longer seat of a bishop, the handsomely Gothic and handsomely situated *Cathedral of Notre-Dame* (Place de Petite Puy) retains its original name and boasts not only a trio of paintings by Rubens, but another by Fragonard, Grasse-born in the eighteenth century. *Villa Musée Fragonard* (Boulevard Fragonard) is a honey of a rococo mansion, with a number of copies of the native son's works, and the distinction of having had one of its paneled rooms moved, in toto, to the Metropolitan Museum of Art in New York, where it is on display. *Musée d'Art et d'Histoire de Provence* (Rue Mirabeau), another fine old house, displays quite the oldest perfume bottles you are likely to encounter and a range of objects relating to Provençal life, costumes through china.

Musée International de la Parfumerie (8 Place du Cours) offers a survey of scent through the ages, with its most interesting exhibits antique perfume containers and contemporary bottles created by firms like Baccarat and Lalique, with a piece of luggage of Marie Antoinette's as a bonus.

Vallauris (two miles west of Antibes) is a pleasant enough little town that would be unexceptional were it not that a chap named Pablo Picasso was a ten-year resident. He impelled locals to restore their once-thriving production of ceramics and left some of his own handiwork. At *Musée National Picasso,* in the chapel of the village's château on Place de la Libération, hangs "La Guerre et la Paix," the master's enormous and highly charged mural on the theme of war and peace; the town's *Musée Municipal,* with prize-winning ceramics from competitions it sponsors, is adjacent. On *Place Isnard* is Picasso's eye-catcher of a bronze sculpture depicting a shepherd with one of his flock. In and about *Avenue Georges-Clemenceau*—for better or for worse—are myriad Picasso-inspired pottery shops, whereas pottery by the instigator of all this enterprise is displayed at Musée Picasso in Antibes (above).

SETTLING IN

Carlton Inter-Continental Hôtel (58 La Croisette; phone 9368-91-68): Pre-World War I years saw Cannes well established, but the time appeared propitious for a new and palatial Croisette hotel. The Carlton—with a hundred-yard facade flanked by conical towers, which is among Europe's most impressive such—opened in 1913 and, it would appear, not a moment too soon, with crowned heads of Belgium, Greece, Italy, Portugal, Spain, and Yugoslavia among its guests during the early years. Later, in 1939, the very first Cannes Film Festival opened with a slambang party at the Carlton; Tyrone Power, George Raft, and the film crowd arrived to compete with the royals on the Carlton guest register. Recent years have seen Inter-Continental Hotels undertake a meticulous, multimillion-dollar, stem-to-stern refurbishing—and, indeed, expansion—of this extraordinarily beautiful hotel, retaining the marble, gold-leaf plasterwork, and original frescoes; installing Le Petit Bar with 2,000 gold-leaf rosettes on its ceiling, off the very grand lobby; re-creating the grill in Louis XIII style; opening an intimate haute cuisine restaurant (La Côte, reviewed on a later page); renewing the 355 suites (Louis XV in style—and sumptuous) and traditional-decor rooms; the while retaining the vast drinks terrace and the lunchtime buffet-restaurant on the Carlton's private beach across La Croisette. Most exciting, though, has been the creation of a brand new floor—the seventh—which from without retains the look of the building's early-twentieth-century facade (the Carlton is a national historic monument), but within is the site, among much else, of what is arguably the most spectacular hotel suite extant: the twelve-room Imperial Suite, whose standout features include a 135-foot-square, Louis XVI-style living-dining-room-cum-kitchen, four big bedrooms (each with its own bath), private passenger and service elevators, and, for occupants, services of full-time butler, helicopter rides to and from Nice Airport at arrival and departure, fruit, flowers, champagne, and daily breakfast. Are you ready? *Luxury.*

Majestic Hôtel (La Croisette; phone 9368-91-00) is a meticulously maintained old-timer—warm, friendly, gracious—with high-ceilinged public spaces, 300 traditional-style rooms and suites of varying sizes, congenial cocktail lounge, trio of restaurants, and palm-shaded garden based on an umbrella-bordered swimming pool. Proprietors are Chaîne Lucien-Barrière, three of whose hotels I recommend in Deauville (chapter 16), as well as others in La Baule (chapter 30). *Luxury.*

Gray d'Albion Hôtel (38 Rue des Serbes; phone 9368-54-54), although not directly on La Croisette, is well situated in a shopping-residential complex between it and Rue d'Antibes. One of the town's newest houses, it is clean-lined contemporary, with 173 rooms (alas, they are small) and a dozen-plus suites (there are phones in all the baths), as well as a trio of restaurants—one quite grand and reviewed on a later page; a second, good value and casual; and a third, for super buffet lunches on the Gray d'Albion's private beach. Service is smiling; management, astute. *Luxury.*

Pullman Beach Hôtel (13 Rue du Canada; phone 9394-50-50) is but a block inland from La Croisette, just across Rue du Canada from the Carlton (above). It's one of the more attractive links of the Pullman chain, with public spaces modified Persian, their walls surfaced in blue and yellow tile. There are 95 rooms—by no means overlarge, but functional—bar-lounge, swimming pool, and restaurant open only to groups staying in the hotel. *First Class.*

Grand Hôtel (45 La Croisette; phone 9338-15-45): Given its enviable location—beyond an enormous lawn (not always neatly clipped) in the core of La Croisette—the Grand really *should* be grand. As it is, the look is inoffensive, albeit nondescript, modern. There are 75 rooms, restaurant, bar, and private beach. To me, disappointing. *First Class.*

Univers Hôtel (2 Rue Maréchal-Foch; phone 9339-59-19) is conveniently located at the corner of a street that is perpendicular with Rue d'Antibes, the thoroughfare that runs parallel with La Croisette. The lobby is small but this hotel gets better as you move along. Those of the 68 rooms I've inspected are light and bright, with either showers or tubs with overhead showers—and rare-in-France shower curtains—and with some rooms bigger than others.

The restaurant (featuring temptingly tabbed menus at lunch and dinner) and bar-lounge are up on the roof, and the views are fabulous. Kindly management. *Moderate.*

Ligure Hôtel (5 Rue Jean-Jaurès; phone 9339-03-11) is a neighbor of the train station, a couple of blocks in from the sea, but still central. Those of the three dozen rooms I've inspected are small but—praise be—with firm mattresses, rare in France in hotels lower than First Class category. All have okay baths with tubs and showers, and the breakfast room is pleasant. There is no restaurant. *Moderate.*

Regina Hôtel (31 Rue Pasteur; phone 9394-05-43) is central (on a street just off La Croisette), and agreeable, with substantial mattresses on brass beds of the rooms (23 all told) I have inspected. Smiling staff. Breakfast only. *Moderate.*

Palma Hôtel (77 La Croisette; phone 9394-22-16) is, to be sure, away from the central portion of La Croisette, at the Palm Beach Casino end. But it has half a hundred neat rooms (book ahead for an oceanview one—they have terraces). Breakfast only. *Moderate.*

Mondial Hôtel (77 Rue d'Antibes; phone 9339-28-70) is well located on the main shopping street, an easy walk from the beach. There are 65 compact rooms. Breakfast only. *Moderate.*

Splendid Hôtel (4 Rue Félix-Faure; phone 9399-53-11): The title exaggerates, but there is no denying the lovely location of this old-fashioned house that overlooks scenic Vieux-Port. There are 64 rooms, some with kitchenettes. Breakfast only. *Moderate.*

Sofitel-Méditerranée (2 Boulevard Jean-Hibert; phone 9399-22-75): You're at the far (by that I mean west) end of Vieux-Port in this pink-facade hotel, a fair walk from the core of town. Still, views can be striking from the best-placed of the 145 modern rooms, and, besides a restaurant and cocktail lounge, there's a swimming pool-sundeck on the roof. *First Class.*

Novotel Montfleury (25 Avenue Beauséjour; phone 9368-91-50) would be higher up in my Cannes hotel evaluations, were it only closer to La Croisette. Location is atop a steepish hill, which makes views of town and sea possible, but it's quite a trek by foot. This is a clean-lined contemporary house (it was originally operated by Inter-Continental Hotels) with 235 comfortable rooms, a trio of restaurants (one haute cuisine, one casual, one al fresco), bar-lounge, and—the hotel at its best—a honey of a pool in a lushly landscaped garden. *First Class.*

Du Cap-Eden Roc Hôtel (Boulevard John-F.-Kennedy, Cap d'Antibes; phone 9361-39-01) comes in two parts. Part one is the main building, a Second Empire mansion with exquisitely furnished and accessorized public spaces and a hundred equally sumptuous, no-two-quite-alike rooms and suites furnished in period, with antique accents and extravagant textiles, not to mention terraces-cum-views. Breakfast comes to you via room service. But, for lunch and dinner, you descend to the considerably detached Pavillon Eden smack on the sea—the hotel occupies an enormous park of its own—and with two levels; upper is the restaurant, evaluated in a later paragraph; a bar (at which casual lunches are served) and pool-cum-terrace flank the rugged shore below, with swimming possible in the sea as well, via an approach along a specially built cement path that cuts through rocks. The Du Cap appears to make a point of catering especially to an international repeat clientele, with bookings made as much as a year in advance. Service is efficient and correct, but cool. This hotel—one of the most beautiful in Europe—takes itself very seriously and, moreover, does not accept credit cards. Member, Leading Hotels of the World. *Luxury.*

Tananarive Hôtel (Route de Nice, Antibes; phone 9333-29-49): If you've a car, this is not a bad spot to alight for a night or two; half a hundred contemporary-design rooms, swimming pool, tennis. Okay restaurant, too. *Moderate.*

Belles Rives Hôtel (Boulevard du Littoral, Juan-les-Pins; phone 9361-02-79) has location as a plus; beachfront and convenient both to the core of Juan-les-Pins, as well as Cap d'Antibes. Public spaces are high-ceilinged, light, and airy; bedrooms (there are 42 and you want to book a seaview one) likewise. The cocktail lounge is handsome, and so is the picture-windowed restaurant, at its best when it moves to a broad terrace for candlelit summer dinners at the edge of the Mediterranean. Very nice, indeed. *Luxury.*

Juana Hôtel (Avenue Gallice, Juan-les-Pins; phone 9361-08-70) was taken over by the Barache family in 1931, shortly after it was built—and is still a distinctively Barache operation, with a staff of 70 on hand to operate a 50-room-and-suite hostelry and a 28-member chef-team for the restaurant, reviewed on a later page. The Juana, it should be apparent, is a class act. There's no denying that its proportions could be more generous—the lobby is compact and rooms can be small. But they're balconied and some have capacious terraces; baths, though without shower curtains, are luxurious. There's a honey of a swimming pool, as well as a private beach at which the Juana provides chaises and umbrellas, with facilities including changing cabins, bar, and restaurant. Very nice, indeed. *Luxury.*

Garden Beach Hôtel (15 Boulevard Édouard-Baudoin, Juan-les-Pins; phone 9367-25-25) has the great advantage of a beachside situation. This is a contemporary house with 163 terraced rooms and nearly a score of junior suites and suites, as well as a dressy restaurant and two casual terraced eateries. The only problems relate to aesthetics. Though highly functional (showers, for example, have glass doors, not often encountered in France), this is not an attractive hotel. It lacks, in the opinion of this inspector, grace and charm and good looks. *First Class.*

Sainte Valerie Hôtel (Rue de l'Oratoire, Juan-les-Pins; phone 9361-07-15), a few blocks in from the beach, is center-of-the-action, a worth-knowing-about small house. Those of the 30 rooms I've inspected are pleasant and have nice baths, the garden is a plus and so, for that matter, is the well-priced restaurant. *Moderate.*

Hôtel du Park (Avenue Guy-de-Maupassant, Juan-les-Pins; phone 9361-61-00) is well situated, edging the beaches, with a handsome, swimming-pool-centered garden, welcoming bar, a restaurant with seafood specialties and multicourse menus, and 28 balconied rooms; those facing the sea are the priciest. *Moderate/First Class.*

Petit Castel Hôtel (22 Chemin des Sables, Antibes; phone 9361-59-37) is, to be sure, petit but not, despite what its name might imply, a castle. This is a small 16-room-with-bath house that's clean, bar-equipped, and convenient to the beaches of both Antibes and Juan-les-Pins. Breakfast only. So-so. *Moderate.*

Club Med Opio (Opio, 900 feet above Cannes) is one of the first outposts of the French-founded, globally scattered vacation clubs that for long have emphasized no-frills holidays. Opio is a departure—designed for vacationers who have thought the club was not for them. Set in a 125-acre plot embracing pine trees, olive groves, and the flowers used to make perfumes at nearby Grasse (above), it has 500 rooms rented on a double-occupancy basis, with hotel features including private baths with tub/shower, phones and TV, five restaurants, fitness centers, two pools, and organized excursions to Riviera points. But you must be a Club Med member and book in advance; call the club (800-CLUB MED) or a travel agent for details. *First Class.*

Des Parfums Hôtel (Boulevard Charabot, Grasse; phone 9336-10-10) just has to be the only hotel extant so named. It's central and modern with 71 bath-equipped rooms, restaurant-bar, pool, and views of the sea. Best Western. *Moderate.*

Beachotel (Avenue Alexandre-III, Juan-les-Pins; phone 9361-81-85): The title might better be *Near the Beachotel;* the sands are a full block distant. Still, this is an agreeable house—contemporary, with just under 30 kitchenette-equipped terraced rooms and a friendly staff. *Moderate.*

DAILY BREAD

Le Royal Gray (Gray d'Albion Hôtel, 38 Rue des Serbes; phone 9368-54-54) starts with smiles. You are cordially welcomed to a relatively intimate space, contemporary and in tones of aubergine and pink, with great bowls of flowers at strategic points. Order from either a five-course menu or a *menu de dégustation* embracing no fewer than 10 courses served in smallish portions. Fare is essentially contemporary—sensible and, by and large, delicious. Your meal might open with a warm oyster-and-caviar salad, continue with shrimp-and-lima-bean casserole and follow with escalope de foie gras de canard poêlée croustillante aux pétales d'artichaut, a wordy way of describing a foie gras, duck, and artichoke dish. Pastries are memorable—a millefeuille de pommes sauce caramel, especially. Fine wines. *Luxury.*

La Côte (Carlton Inter-Continental Hôtel, 58 La Croisette; phone 9368-91-68): You don't expect the leading restaurant of this grand hotel to be so intimate. The smallish scale appeals, as do the good looks—striped Louis XVI chairs surround flower-centered tables under a glass-domed ceiling. The à la carte is what might be termed creative-traditional, with favored openers including foie gras frais, duck terrine, shrimp bisque, lobster salad, sautéed crayfish, or Provençal-style scrambled eggs; a seafood platter served with a basil-scented sauce, grilled sole, broiled lamb chops, and steak au poivre are among the entrées, as is a memorable house specialty—roast duckling en deux services—breast first, then the rest of the bird, deliciously garnished. The cheese selection stands out; ditto wines. Desserts justifiably rate a card of their own. And service is unsurpassed in any restaurant that I know of on the Riviera. *Luxury.*

La Mirabelle (24 Rue St.-Antoine in Le Suquet; phone 9338-72-75) is indicated for a festive dinner in Vieux-Cannes under the beamed ceiling of an aged town house. Open with fresh asparagus served with the chef's special sauce, continuing with grilled salmon, filet of Charolais beef, or roast lamb. Luscious sweets. *Luxury.*

Le Bistingo (Palais des Festivals, Jetée Albert-Édouard; phone 9338-78-38): It's a starry night and you fancy a dinner al fresco, overlooking Vieux-Cannes. Book here, in this convention center restaurant, ordering the good-value prix-fixe menu, based on such entrées as grilled turbot, mustard sauced, or an unusual duck casserole. And wait till the trolley of desserts is wheeled over! *First Class.*

La Mère Besson (13 Rue des Frères-Pradignac; phone 9339-51-24): I don't know who the Pradignac brothers were—other than that they gave their name to the street on which this restaurant is located—but La Mère Besson is female-operated, front and back. Try for a table on the terrace in nice weather. Inside, movie posters line walls in recognition of the annual film festival. Fare has a Provençal accent, with the prix-fixe running to a garlicky green salad with croutons or sautéed mushrooms to start and delicious frog's legs or a not-very-Provençal osso bucco among entrées. Skip the rum-and-chocolate génoise for dessert at your peril. *First Class.*

Carlton Grill and Bar Terrasse (Carlton Inter-Continental Hôtel, 58 La Croisette; phone 9368-91-68) is an indoor/outdoor situation. The former is indicated for a proper dinner, ordered from an extensive à la carte, the range tapenade-sauced crudités, smoked salmon, and onion soup through sole meunière and filet of sea bass to steak au poivre and the plat du jour. If the weather is fine, it's fun to sit outside on the town's most see-and-be-seen terrace, ordering un répas rapide—spaghetti Bolognese or an omelet, a club sandwich, or a croque-monsieur. Or simply pastry or ice cream, coffee or a drink. *First Class/Luxury.*

Le Caveau des Années 30 (45 Rue Félix-Faure; phone 9339-06-33): Within, the look of this restaurant celebrates—as the title suggests—the glory of the 1930s. But if you've picked a sunny day or a moonlit evening, take a table on the terrace, ordering from among many choices on the three-course menu, with a super salade Niçoise, fish soupe rouille-sauced, quiche Lorraine, and mussels marinière among openers; grilled fish of the day, veal piccata, poached salmon sauce béarnaise, or entrecôte among entrées; and a choice of super sweets. Everything I have had is delicious, and service is a pleasure. Central *First Class.*

Astoux et Brun (27 Rue Félix-Faure; phone 9339-39-21—on the same Restaurant Row, Rue Félix-Faure, as Le Caveau des Années 30, above) provides worthy competition, with outdoor tables the most fun, and the menu, accenting seafood, the best bet, with noteworthy oysters, grilled fish of the day, and ice cream desserts. *First Class.*

Le Bistrot de la Galerie (4 Rue St.-Antoine; phone 9339-99-38) is on a street whose restaurants draw crowds in the evening. Go with the reasonably tabbed menu here, perhaps starting with tomato-mushroom salad or the house's terrine de foie, selecting grilled fish of the day or lasagne as an entrée, with cheese or a sweet to conclude. *Moderate.*

Univers Hôtel Restaurant (2 Rue Maréchal-Foch; phone 9339-59-59): Take the lift to the roof, where the fabulous view is for free and the Menu Vacance—available only at midday—is one of the best buys in town, with your choice of pâté de campagne, eggs mayonnaise, or tomato salad to start; grilled pork chop vegetable-garnished or the plat du jour among entrées; with cheese, fresh fruit, ice cream, or chocolate mousse for dessert. There are several menus, all pricier, at dinner. Go for lunch and the Univers is *Moderate.*

Le Galion (3 Rue Félix-Faure; phone 9339-74-00) is indicated if you hanker after pizza (it's good here) or are hungry enough to tuck into the three-course menu. Outdoor tables. *Moderate.*

Le Mesclun (16 Rue St.-Antoine; phone 9339-45-19) has looks going for it. It's softly lit by wrought-iron chandeliers and sconces, intimate in size, and with its staff delightful. Problem is the food. Selecting from a decently priced menu, a party of two—one basing the meal on poultry, the other on pork—could report positively on nothing save the good bread: pain de campagne, delivered only when requested after arrival of a basket of rolls soft and rubbery enough to have come from a U.S. supermarket. I can't recommend this one. *First Class.*

Le Comptoir de la Mer (54 La Croisette; phone 9338-15-37) is a worth-knowing-about café/snack, what with outdoor tables on La Croisette, heart-of-town, and service the day and evening long, breakfast through salads, sandwiches and omelets, and whatever you would like to drink. *Moderate.*

La Terrasse (Juana Hôtel, Avenue Gallice, Juan-les-Pins; phone 9361-08-70): You want a sunny day or a mild evening for lunch or dinner al fresco here, perhaps after preceding your meal with the house's champagne-framboise accompanied, in the bar, by sunny-side quail-egg canapés, foie gras, or smoked salmon. If it's midday during the week, tuck into the menu entitled Carte Affaires. Appetizers run to a coriander-scented fresh-vegetable platter, the chef's tagliatelli with crab in a turtle sauce, with seafood entrées—again in the style of the chef—or such other main-course options as rosemary-seasoned saddle of lamb, wild duck in two services (the second with sautéed foie gras), or, if you prefer, roast hare in two services. The cheese platter—with a generous selection of goat cheeses among others—follows, after which you make a dessert choice; I would opt for the raspberry pastry doused with a warm fruit sauce, anointed with bourbon-infused vanilla ice cream. But you're not finished: the tiny pastries called gourmandises are subsequently served with house chocolates and coffee. Two additional menus and the à la carte are presented at dinner, after which a digestif (the selection is excellent) is indicated in the bar. Lovely service. *Luxury.*

L'Auberge Provençale (61 Place Nationale, Antibes; phone 9334-13-24)—beamed ceilings and stone walls within, a pretty garden as well—might fill the bill for a seafood lunch or dinner, with good-value menus that open with grilled sardines or a mussel and frog-leg casserole, preparatory to such entrées as grilled fish of the day, as well as coq au vin or entrecôte, if you prefer, with pastries, the house's ice-cream coupe, or sundae, or crème caramel for dessert. Friendly. *First Class.*

Au Régal (5 Rue Sade, Antibes; phone 9334-11-69) is good-looking, with brick walls framing tables backed by ladderback chairs and set with red and pink linen. The menu dubbed Marché Provençal is a winner. Open, perhaps, with zucchini stuffed with crayfish, or the house's mussel appetizer. A fish course is next, with a sorbet to refresh the palate preparatory to a lamb entrée—thyme-, garlic-, and olive-accented. The way is paved for dessert by an interestingly dressed salad. Only then comes your sweet, with almond mousse, champagne-sauced fruit salad, or Calvados-spiked warm apple tart as choices. Satisfying. *First Class.*

Il Giardino (21 Rue Thuret, Antibes; phone 9334-56-58): The name is a clue. You miss Italian food, and the Garden comes to your rescue, with a wide choice of seafood-sauced pasta—tagliatelli with crab most memorably. Ravioli with cèpes-type mushrooms is tasty, too. French standbys as well. *Moderate.*

Le Teapot (47 Boulevard Albert 1er, Antibes) is, not surprisingly, given its title, a salon de thé. But quiches and Provençal specialties are served midday and, with wine by the glass, make a good lunch. *Moderate.*

Vesuvio (65 La Croisette; phone 9394-08-28) has as its drawing card a selection of pizzas. But there are steaks and grilled fish as well. The coarse-textured bread is a treat, and there are outdoor tables. *Moderate.*

Gaston et Gastonnette (7 Quai St.-Pierre; phone 9339-99-34) is agreeable for lunch at an outdoor table overlooking Vieux-Port; the menu, embracing mussels marinière style, roast duck, and cheese or dessert, is a good buy. *First Class.*

Lunch on the beach: There are two dozen lunch-only, summer-only restaurants, with justifiably celebrated buffets (including hot entrées and a variety of salads, as well as a choice of desserts), and à la carte choices, like entrecôte, grilled lobster, burgers, or club sandwiches, with ice-cream desserts featured. They range from those operated by leading hotels—*d'Albion,* for example—to those on public beaches like Esterel, which are less costly. Wear what you like, including, of course, swimsuits. *Moderate* through *Luxury.*

Rohr (63 Rue d'Antibes) is No. 1 *Pâtisserie/salon de thé,* ideal for sustenance in the course of a morning in Rue d'Antibes's shops. *Moderate.*

Moulin de Mougins (a mile and a half south of Mougins village, on Avenue Notre-Dame-de-Vie; phone 9375-78-24) is an atmospheric and ancient olive-oil mill converted into a charming, rustic-look restaurant in the late sixties by chef-patron Roger Vergé and his wife, Denise. Over the years—as much because of M. Vergé's skill at promotion, as well as at cooking—it has become one of the best known of France's country restaurants and is agreeable as a lunch or dinner excursion destination from nearby Cannes—but four miles distant. Order à la carte or from a prix-fixe menu embracing half a dozen courses, opening, to give you an idea, with an escalope of salmon; continuing with crayfish fricassee, grapefruit sherbet to freshen the palate, an entrée of basil-sauced noisettes of lamb served with stuffed zucchini and a Vergé potato specialty, and following with cheese, in advance of a strawberry-and-pineapple dessert accompanied by petits-fours. Lovely service. *Luxury.* (Note that M. Vergé operates a *second* Mougins restaurant, *Amandier de Mougins,* edging the village; phone 9390-00-91, also located in a looker of an old house, but about a third less pricey than the Moulin; very nice, indeed, and *First Class.*)

Le Relais à Mougins (Place de la Mairie, core of the village; Mougins; phone 9390-03-47), operated by chef-patron André Surmain in an attractive and aged Mougins house, gives M. Vergé (above) a good run for his money, offering a pair of well-priced, prix-fixe, lunch-only menus that include house wine. The less pricey might open with smoked-salmon rillettes, continue with M. Surmain's popular three-part salad, with breast of duck or sole with a foie-gras flecked cream sauce as entrées, house dessert, and made-on-premises chocolate truffles as a bonus. Dinner is more costly. Friendly and delightful. Member, Relais et Châteaux. *First Class.*

Pavillon Eden Roc (Du Cap-Eden Roc Hôtel, Boulevard John-F.-Kennedy, Cap d'Antibes; phone 9361-39-01) occupies a detached pavilion edging the rockbound shore, in the Du Cap's parklike grounds. White rattan chairs, cushioned in green, surround tables laid with white linen, within the spacious, picture-windowed dining room and on an open deck adjacent. If you go for but one meal, it should be lunch, for two reasons: Smashing views along the coast is the first, and hors d'œuvres—salads in immense variety, cold meats, and relishes—which you yourself select from a groaning buffet, is the second. You order the rest of your meal from an extensive à la carte, with roasts and grills—paillard of veal, lamb chops, duck with sauce béarnaise, sole, or turbot—counseled. Desserts rate a card of their own—and they are elaborate. Service is professional, albeit impersonal. *Luxury.*

Le Cameo (Place Nationale, Antibes; phone 9334-24-17) is a sensible choice for lunch at an outdoor table on this vibrant square. Order fish or entrecôte aux frites. *Moderate.*

Le Sorrento (67 Promenade du Soleil, Juan-les-Pins; phone 9361-18-34) is long-on-scene, central, seaview, and with a terrace from which you might enjoy a seafood repast. Fun. *Moderate.*

Amphitryon (16 Boulevard Victor-Hugo, Grasse; phone 9336-58-73) is reasonably close to the center and pleasant for a lunch pause in the course of Grasse exploration. Well-priced prix-fixe menus. *First Class.*

SHOPPER'S CANNES

Dames de France and *Monoprix* department stores are on Rue Maréchal Foch. Stroll La Croisette and you'll come across blue-chip establishments like *Hermès, Lanvin, Gucci, Léonard, Chloë, Yves St.-Laurent, Christian Dior, Karl Lagerfeld,* and *Valentino* (clothes and accessories); *Bruno, Cartier, Fred, Boucheron, Mappin & Webb* (jewelry); *D. Porthault* (linens); *Select* (shoes); and *Souleîado* (Provençal textiles). On Rue d'Antibes you'll find such stores as *Charles Jourdan* (shoes), *Céline* (women's clothes and accessories), *Giorgio Armani* (women's and men's clothes), and *Le Jardin* (Limoges porcelain). *Cannes English Bookshop* is at 14 Square Merimée. *Cannolive* (16 Rue Venizelos) has cloth sacks of Provençal herbs, other Provençal specialties. And *Marché Forville* (Rue Meynadier) is the public produce/seafood market. Go before it closes at 1 P.M. daily.

SOUND OF MUSIC

The two halls of Cannes's *Palais des Festivals et des Congrès*—the convention center–casino complex—smaller *Théâtre Claude-Debussy* and *Lumière Grand Auditorium,* are venues for winter concerts (especially those of *Orchestre Régional de Cannes*) and musicals. In summer, there are varied entertainments at *Casino Palm Beach.* And ballet and concerts are performed at *Palais Croisette.* (To enter the casinos, men need tie and jacket in the evening; passports are required of all foreigners; games are roulette, blackjack, and *vingt-et-un.*)

INCIDENTAL INTELLIGENCE

Further information: Office de Tourisme, Palais des Festivals et des Congrès, La Croisette, Cannes; Office de Tourisme, 11 Place Général de Gaulle, Antibes; Office de Tourisme, Boulevard Charles Guillaumont, Juan-les-Pins; Office de Tourisme, Place Foux, Grasse; Office de Tourisme, Square 8-Mai-1945, Vallauris.

14

Chamonix

Mont Blanc, Courchevel, and Albertville

BACKGROUND BRIEFING

Means of access can be important. You may—or may not—remember arrival in a new place by train or plane or even sleek superhighway. But I'll not forget my first view of Chamonix. The approach was by car. Within half an hour after departure from the Italian resort town of Courmayeur, I had driven through the seven-mile-long international tunnel cut through the Alps's highest peak, cleared both Italian and French customs, and arrived in France's premier mountain resort, nestled in a breathtakingly beautiful valley.

Chamonix is framed by the snow-surfaced peaks that began luring intrepid English adventurers three and a half centuries back. What drew them was 15,781-foot Mont Blanc and a range of positively smashing satellite peaks. The year was 1741. Four decades later, a pair of Frenchmen—Balmat and Paccard, by name—reached the summit of Mont Blanc, to be followed, shortly afterward, by a third, Horace Saussure. They had pioneered French mountaineering, paving the way for development of what has become France's best-equipped and most scenically situated Alpine resort, hosting a million visitors each year.

This is the town that was the site of the first Winter Olympics—back in 1924. Still a second French Alpine point, Grenoble (chapter 18) hosted the Winter Olympics in 1968, and selection of the area for the 1992 Winter Olympics—with opening and closing ceremonies in Albertville and competitions in a number of resorts—refocused a world spotlight on this magnificent region, where a billion dollars went into new facilities—transportation, hotels, sports installations—in conjunction with the games. Still, despite competition from other resorts in the region—including elegant Courchevel, about which I write in this chapter—Chamonix has enough going for it, for nonskiers as well as winter-sports buffs, that it remains the No. 1 French Alpine destination.

ON SCENE

Lay of the Land: A pair of nearly contiguous squares—*Place de Saussure* and *Place Balmat* are the core of town; they're named for two of the three pioneer climbers of Mont Blanc, and the main street—*Rue Docteur Paccard,* extending south from Place Balmat—is named for the third member of that illustrious trio; it is lined with shops (Chamonix has no department stores), as is *Avenue Michel-Croz*—pedestrians-only at the point where it edges the main squares. It leads west to the town hall, tourist office, pretty, slim-steepled parish church, and the *railway station* at its eastern terminus. The town's fabulous *sports complex*—indoor ice skating (with rinks for ice hockey and curling), a three-pool swimming center, along with a clutch of adjacent tennis courts—is just north of the core, on *Avenue du Bouchet,* while the gracefully pedimented *casino* is on Place Balmat to the south, not far from departure points for major peaks and glaciers. The body of water flowing through town, north to south, is the *Arve River.* And even if you choose not to ascend to the peaks, you're already in the mountains; Chamonix's elevation is a respectable 3,000 feet.

Musée Alpin (Avenue Michel-Croz, heart of town) is the ideal introduction to Chamonix, a well-organized, three-level presentation that starts you off at the beginning—in the case of Chamonix, that was the eighteenth century—with furniture, clothes, maps, and documents of that period relating to historic early ascents; and prints, postcards, and photos of the ensuing century, along with exhibits of climbers' paraphernalia, early through contemporary, and some super antique posters for nostalgia buffs. Well done.

By cable car via Aiguille du Midi and/or tunnel to Italy: The 11-mile tunnel (opened in 1965) connecting Chamonix with Courmayeur (see *Italy at Its Best*) involves half an hour to 45 minutes' drive either way, to and from your Chamonix hotel; have your passport with you, for both French and Italian customs, going and returning. It's agreeable to depart after breakfast, arriving in *Courmayeur* in time for a visit to its *Museo Alpino* (on Piazza Abate Henry, just opposite the baroque *Parish Church* whose stone bell tower goes all the way back to 1392) and smart shops of *Via Roma,* stopping for coffee at that street's *Caffè della Posta,* staying on for lunch at *Le Vieux Pommier* (Piazzale Monte Bianco 25; phone 842-281; *First Class*), and returning by means of the tunnel.

Much more exciting would be to go one way—through Mont Blanc Massif—via a series of cable cars. First lap of the journey is easily the most extraordinary. You ride the highest cable car in the world to the peak called *Aiguille du Midi* (with an en-route stop at 6,900-foot *Plan des Aiguilles,* reached in 10 minutes from the Chamonix station). Twenty minutes later and you've arrived at Aiguille du Midi, wide-eyed while en route—views are trinational, of French, Italian, and Swiss peaks—for a pause at its restaurant-café, the while coming to grips with your situation: at an elevation of eleven and a half thousand feet, high above the vast region known, not inappropriately, as the *Vallée Blanche.* Aiguille du Midi is what the French term a *correspondance,* or transfer point (although, of course, you may opt to return from there to Chamonix), to an elevator taking you to still another cable car for a thrill-a-minute journey past Mont Blanc and other snowy peaks, as high as 13,000 feet, to *Pointe Helbronner*—through which the Franco-Italian frontier passes—and with a café and observation terrace. There you transfer to still another cable car for the final portion of the trip, descending to the terminal at *La Palud,* edging Courmayeur. You've arrived in Italy, ideally in time for lunch, returning later in the day the way you came or through the tunnel by means of either rented car or taxi.

Other Chamonix excursions include the summer-only scenic rail journey to *Montenvers,* at an altitude of 4,200 feet, descending to the grotto of the immense *Mer de Glace* glacier, through a tunnel into the so-called salon, a space in which a furnished living room—four easy chairs, coffee table, piano, and even a fireplace—have been carved from the ice; cable car trips to *La Flégère,* a few miles west of town, with an altitude of 5,700 feet, a restaurant and fabulous overhead views of Mer de Glace; and *Brévent* (farther west of town, at an altitude of some 7,700 feet), with a restaurant at the intermediate cable car station called *Planpraz,* and with a terrace—on Brévent—affording vistas of Mont Blanc.

Alpine golf is, to understate, unexpected and is, for that reason, called to your attention at this point. The Robert Trent Jones-designed course (18 holes, par 72) attached to *Golf Club de Chamonix,* in nearby Les Praz at the foot of Mont Blanc, is among the most beautifully situated on the planet. You may rent clubs and there's a restaurant.

Assy (a.k.a. Plateau d'Assy, 19 miles northwest of Chamonix) would be an unexceptional little mountain village were it not for the art of the architecturally undistinguished *Church of Notre Dame de Toute Grâce,* begun before World War II and finished a few years thereafter, which catches you up, first, with an enormous mosaic fresco occupying virtually its entire facade, by Fernand Léger, that is typically Léger in bold strokes and bright hues. Go on in to see works by such modern masters as Matisse (St. Dominick outlined in black on yellow tiles in the style of the Matisse-designed chapel at Vence, chapter 26), Rouault (or at least a stained-glass window based on a Rouault design, *Flagellation of Christ*), Bonnard (St.-François de Sales in a purple cape), Chagall, and Braque, with an extraordinary tapestry by an artist named Lurçat, covering the apse.

Albertville, a small mountain town cut through by the Arly River, had not been among the better-known Alpine resorts until it was designated as the venue for the 1992 Winter Olympics' opening and closing ceremonies, and for the games' speed- and figure-skating competitions. It then became a household word among snow-sports enthusiasts and spruced itself up accordingly. Its core is not difficult to take in. *Avenue Jean-Jaurès* cuts through it, from the train station to the river. The town's pride and joy is the 10,000-capacity *Ice Arena* constructed for the Olympic skating events, along with a 1,200-foot speed-skating track. Albertville is about midway between Chamonix, about 35 miles to the northeast, and Courchevel, about the same distance to the southeast. Moutiers, at whose station superspeed TGV trains (to and from Paris) stop, is a short distance to the south. (Venues for the overwhelming majority of 1992 Winter Olympics events were scheduled at places in the area other than Albertville—a dozen all told, the range Courchevel to Val d'Isère.)

Courchevel, easily the most grande-luxe of the French cluster of Alpine getaways, is not all that easy geographically. By that I mean it's divided in three, each segment at a different altitude, and each designated by its height in meters. You start from the top, in the toniest of the trio, Courchevel 1850, with the poshest hotels, most-difficult-to-reserve restaurants, trendiest après-ski action, smartest shops, and—not unimportant, this—closest access to the lifts (some three-score, all told) leading to and from the slopes. The neighborhood, Trois Vallées as it is called, is composed of half a dozen-plus additional villages—Val-Thorens and Les Menuires to the west, Méribel-Mottaret at midpoint, Brides-les-Bains to the east. The three Courchevel villages (*Courchevel 1650* and *Courchevel 1550* are the lower two) are linked by gondolas of a cleverly conceived aerial tramway, with *La Croisette* the core of the Courchevel 1850 action, with its tourist office and ski school, among much else. And you may rest assured that shops are at hand: La Croisette's extend over three levels.

SETTLING IN

Mont Blanc Hôtel (Place de l'Église, Chamonix; phone 5053-05-64) has a number of pluses: heart-of-town location, albeit in its own little park-cum-swimming pool, traditional with respect both to facade and interior that includes half a hundred cheerful rooms (some facing the peak for which the hotel is named), perky little bar, satisfactory restaurant, and pleasant staff. *Luxury.*

Auberge du Bois Prin (Les Moussoux, Chamonix; phone 5053-33-51) is a get-away-from-it-all choice. There are just under a dozen capacious, attractive, no-two-alike rooms, restaurant dominated by a stone fireplace that extends to the ceiling, congenial lounge, and marvelous mountain views. *First Class.*

Albert 1er Hôtel (Impasse du Montenvers, Chamonix; phone 5053-05-09), edging the core from which it is easily walkable, is set in a garden with swimming pool and tennis courts. There are 32 comfortable rooms, lounge-bar with a vast fireplace, agreeable restaurant. Same management as Auberge du Bois Prin (above). *First Class.*

Le Prieuré Hôtel (Allée du Recteur Payot, Chamonix; phone 5053-20-72) is not without the ambience of the mountains. All 90 of its mod-look, terraced rooms give onto Mont Blanc and have showers in their baths. There's a bar-lounge and *brasserie*-type restaurant, smartly rustic. Central. Same management as the Mont Blanc (above). *Moderate.*

La Sapinière-Montana Hôtel (Rue Mummέry, Chamonix; phone 5053-07-63) deserves credit for a situation just far enough from the center to be tranquil but still walkable. There are 30 terraced rooms, all facing south, with ravishing mountain views and inviting public spaces that include a reliable restaurant and lounge-bar. *Moderate.*

Alpina Hôtel (Place du Mont Blanc, Chamonix; phone 5053-47-77), formidably futuristic from without, blends a touch of the mountains with contemporary interiors. Those of the rooms I have inspected—there are 135, all told—are neat and functional. There are a rooftop restaurant-cum-panoramas and a lobby bar-lounge. Central. Best Western. *Moderate.*

Hermitage et Paccard Hôtel (Rue des Cristalliers, Chamonix; phone 5053-13-87)—a short drive (or a long walk) from the action—is an elderly chalet that has been brightly updated, with a pair of bar-lounges, each distinctive; picture-windowed restaurant; and 33 terraced rooms, most with their own baths. *Moderate.*

Million Hôtel (Place de la Liberté, Albertville; phone 7932-25-15) is an attractive house, with 28 comfortable rooms, a bar, and an exceptionally good restaurant you want to visit for a weekday lunch, when the menu is temptingly tabbed, with sautéed lobster a specialty of consequence. Both the hotel and the weekday lunch menu are *First Class;* the restaurant, otherwise, is *Luxury.*

Berjann Hôtel (33 Route de Tours, Albertville; phone 7932-47-88) is across the river from the center of town, but it's an attractive dozen-room house-cum-restaurant. *Moderate.*

Annapurna Hôtel (Courchevel 1850; phone 7908-04-60), like most of the Courchevel hotels, is small enough (70 rooms) to be able to maintain a high standard of service. This is a contemporary house with good looks, good views, a big indoor pool, and a terraced restaurant. *Luxury.*

Byblos des Neiges Hôtel (Courchevel 1850; phone 7908-12-12), arguably the most innovatively designed of the Courchevel hotels, puts one in mind of its St.-Tropez (chapter 33) counterpart. The novelty of the ambience begins with the porte-cochère at the entrance, extends through the woodsy lobby, restaurant, bar, and other public spaces, even to the big indoor pool. There are 69 rooms and suites, by and large good-sized with fine baths and picture windows. *Luxury.*

Bellecote Hôtel (Courchevel 1850; phone 7908-10-19) is the mountain chalet at its most luxurious. Its 55 terraced rooms afford spectacular views, the restaurant is a winner (lunches al fresco, on the deck, especially so), the dark-wood bar is cozy, and the ambience is engaging. *Luxury.*

Des Neiges Hôtel (Courchevel 1850; phone 7908-03-77) appears appropriately named if your first approach occurs at a time when there are a couple of feet of snow topping the porte-cochère. This is a delightful house, with—tony rustic look—restaurant, bar-lounge, just under 60 comfortable rooms with good baths, and buffet lunches on the terrace. Member, Relais et Châteaux. *First Class.*

Pralong 200 Hôtel (Courchevel 1850; phone 7908-24-82) is splendidly situated for collectors of memorable vistas. This is a modern house with 68 well-turned-out terraced rooms, two restaurants, bar, indoor swimming pool, golf driving range, and sauna-health center. Member, Relais et Châteaux. *First Class.*

Crystal 2000 Hôtel (Courchevel 1850; phone 7908-28-22) is both a neighbor and a relative of Pralong 200 (above), albeit with lower tabs; there are half a hundred bath- and terrace-equipped rooms, generous buffet breakfasts, lunch on the deck, and a piano bar following dinner in the restaurant. *Moderate/First Class.*

Ducs de Savoie Hôtel (Courchevel 1850; phone 7908-03-00) offers views from the terraces of all 60 rooms-cum-bath, no matter the side of the hotel. There's a big open deck for lunch, reliable restaurant and bar. *Moderate.*

Les Airelles Hôtel (Courchevel 1850; phone 7908-02-11) is a modern house with a reliable restaurant, terrace for lunches, and 43 bath- and balcony-equipped rooms. *Moderate.*

DAILY BREAD

La Tartiffle (Rue des Moulins, Chamonix; phone 5053-20-02) has the appropriate look of the Alps—woodsy and rustic—that one anticipates in Chamonix. This is a good spot for traditional specialties like the crêpes called matafans, chicken Savoyard style, and gratin Dauphinois—sliced potatoes baked in a creamy casserole. *First Class.*

Le Crochon (Rue des Moulins, Chamonix; phone 5053-41-78), a near neighbor of La Tartiffle (above), draws your eye from the street: It's a log cabin. Not unlike its neighbor, the look is *montagnarde.* Typical sausages of the region—open with an assorted platter—are delicious, the grilled trout, a pleasure. And the fondue—bits of bread dipped by all those at the table into a common cauldron of bubbly, hot melted cheese with kirsch—reminiscent of Switzerland. *First Class.*

Le Bartavel (26 Cours du Bartavel, Chamonix; phone 5053-26-51) is a delightful touch of the southwest, high in the Alps. By that, I mean you want to open with foie gras, continue with the bean-sausage-smoked-goose casserole called cassoulet and conclude with a light dessert. Wine is sold not only by bottles, but by the glass, which makes Bartavel an excellent place to become acquainted with Savoie vintages, opening, say, with a white Roussette and continuing with a red Gamay. *First Class.*

Le Coquelicot (88 Rue du Lyrat, Chamonix; phone 5055-93-40): You are so close to Italy that it would be a pity not to enjoy an Italian lunch or dinner. Open with antipasto, minestrone soup, or pasta before tackling a platter of carne mista—an assortment of beef, veal, and pork. *First Class.*

Eden (Praz-de-Chamonix, a mile and a half from Chamonix; phone 5053-06-40) makes a specialty of fish—trout prepared meunière style, amandine, or simply grilled, as well as half a dozen additional species from mountain lakes; seafood, too. (Eden is a 10-room hotel as well as a restaurant, so that you may overnight in this scenic area.) *First Class.*

Le Blanchot (at the foot of Aiguille du Midi cable car, Chamonix; phone 5053-30-80): Prix-fixe meals are good value (and include wine). If it's Monday, bear in mind that the plat du jour is the sauerkraut spectacular, choucroute garnie—especially good with local sausages substituted for those of Alsace, where the dish originated. *Moderate.*

La Taverne du Chamonix (69 Avenue de Michel-Croz) is at its best on a sunny day when you take a table on the terrace and watch the passing Chamonix parade, over coffee, a drink, or a casual lunch. If it's packed, consider next-door *Brasserie du Rond-Point;* both are *Moderate.*

Ligismond (in the Conflans quarter of Albertville, across the river from the center; phone 7932-53-50) makes a specialty of fish, which you do well to order as an entrée in the course of one of its multicourse menus, perhaps opening with foie gras and ending with pastry. Very nice, indeed, and with outdoor tables. *First Class.*

Bateau Ivre (Pomme de Pin Hôtel, Courchevel 1850; phone 7908-02-46) is indicated for a splurge meal—there are a choice of menus—in a setting that is at its most splendid on days when sunshine illuminates vistas. But you go principally for the cuisine, perhaps opening with the chef's crayfish tails, ordering the venison if it's in season, and concluding with poached pear–cum–ice cream under caramel sauce. Service is expert, wines fine. *Luxury.*

Chabichou Hôtel Restaurant (Courchevel 1850; phone 7908-00-55) invites with good looks and a cordial staff, and satisfies, in the course of tucking into one of its multicourse menus. The house's poultry and lobster specialties are delicious, no less so the crêpes at dessert. Savoie wines are well represented in the cave. Special. *Luxury.*

SOUND OF MUSIC

Centre d'Échanges Internationaux Auditorium (Jardin Alpin, Courchevel 1850) is put to use for concerts and other entertainments. A handsome hall.

INCIDENTAL INTELLIGENCE

Tour operators offer skiers a wide choice of French Alps packages that can be excellent value. Aspiring skiers do well to be aware of Chamonix's *École de Ski Français* (Place de l'Église)—with 200 instructors (they teach classes and privately, as well) and a reputation as one of Europe's best ski schools; and there are others in the region. Nearest transatlantic airport is Lyon—Air France flies nonstop between it and New York; high-speed TGV trains, besides linking Paris with Lyon, stop also at the Alpine resort of Moutiers. *Further information:* Office de Tourisme, Place Triangle de l'Amitié, Chamonix; Office de Tourisme, Place de la Gare, Albertville; Office de Tourisme, La Croisette, Courchevel 1850.

15

Colmar

and Alsace's Route du Vin

BACKGROUND BRIEFING

It is difficult to believe that this small, quiet town, a hop and a skip from the German frontier—whose contemporary political eminence is limited to serving as seat of one of France's 95 *départements*—was designated administrative center (in effect, capital) of Alsace by no less august a sovereign than Louis XIV in the third quarter of the seventeenth century.

By that time, Colmar had worn more than a few hats. At first Celtic, later Roman, then under the Germanic Allemani, who were succeeded by the Franks, Colmar became a Free City of the Holy Roman Empire in the thirteenth century. In the fourteenth, it joined nine other towns in the pan-Alsatian federation known as the Decapole. It was during the Revolution, in the late eighteenth century, that it became a departmental seat. The following century—in 1871—as a consequence of the Franco-Prussian War, Colmar, with the rest of Alsace, was annexed to the German Empire, of which it was a part for nearly half a century—until the Allied Victory in World War I. It was during the German period that Kaiser Wilhelm II designated the nearby medieval château, Haut Koenigsbourg, as an imperial residence. The Treaty of Versailles restored the castle to France in 1918. Precious contents of Alsatian museums were stored in it for safekeeping during World War II, toward the end of which it was occupied by American troops.

Though it lacks the animation and sophistication of considerably larger Strasbourg (chapter 35), some 40 miles to the north, enough remains of Colmar's earlier centuries—the Middle Ages when it became a spiritual center (an old convent houses one of Europe's most beautiful art museums), the Renaissance when it attracted painters, the Baroque era when builders came—to impel a visit. And its situation, at the southern edge of the Alsatian vineyards, which climb gentle slopes of the Vosges Mountains and are dotted with time-stood-still villages, makes Colmar a logical takeoff point for excursions into the Route du Vin, easily the most charming such in France. If you know German, speak it; virtually everyone you meet will be conversant in that language and in French, as well as in Alsace's own distinctive dialect.

ON SCENE

Lay of the Land: You can walk everywhere. Core of town revolves around *Rue des Clefs,* an east-west pedestrian street, off which *Rue des Unterlinden* leads to the museum whose name it takes. *Dames de France* and *Monoprix* department stores are on *Place des Unterlinden. Rue Rapp* leads a bit north to Hôtel de Ville; *Rue St.-Nicolas* leads a bit south to café-lined *Place de la Cathédrale* and the landmark *Church of St.-Martin.* Historic *Rue des Marchands,* site of several major monuments, is to the south. Two delightful quarters—each architecturally redolent of old Colmar, with half-timbered houses lining southeasterly streets—are *La Petite Venise,* so-called because it is cut through by the canallike, bridge-crossed *Lauch River,* with *Quai de la Poissonerie* its most scenic thoroughfare; and, contiguous with La Petite Venise to its north, relatively recently restored *Quartier des Tanneurs.* That district's principal streets are *Rue des Tanneurs* with the Renaissance *Ancienne Douane* (Customs House) on the square linking it with atmospheric *Grande Rue,* at whose northern terminus is the originally Franciscan, now Protestant *Temple St.-Mathieu,* treasure-filled. Westerly *Rue de la République* is the site of the railway station and several hotels; it's a 15-minute walk from the core.

Musée d'Unterlinden (1 Rue des Unterlinden) claims to be, with good reason, I am sure, the most visited museum in provincial France. What draws the crowds—and in the warm-weather months you must be prepared for congestion, allowing a solid half day in the museum—is the sixteenth-century altarpiece known as *Le Rétable d'Issenheim,* for the monastery from which it was taken at the time of the French Revolution and brought to Colmar, ironically at the same period that the building in which it now reposes was being closed after half a millennium as a Dominican convent. (It was not to reopen—as a museum—until 1852.) Mathias Grünewald, the Issenheim's creator, was the quintessential Renaissance artist, as skilled at perspective and color as at anatomy and architecture, not to mention theology and drama. The problem is to get close enough in, what with guides lecturing to tightly packed groups eager to hear every word of the commentary. You may want to allow for a return visit, to determine which of the numerous panels of Grünewald's masterpiece are for you the most memorable; *Concert of the Angels, The Annunciation,* and *The Nativity* are my favorites. See if you agree.

Then give the rest of the museum your attention. The high vaulted space in which the *Rétable* is exhibited, formerly the nuns' chapel, displays a number of other works as well. Gothic tracery in the arches of the gallery lining the cloister is reason enough for an Unterlinden visit. Medieval sculpture from Colmar churches fills the nuns' former cellar, sharing space with mammoth and ancient wine casks. Painters like Holbein and Cranach are on scene. Upstairs, take in the exquisite eighteenth-century drawing room, with its original ceiling fresco, wood carving, and superb Louis XV furniture. On that same floor are Strasbourg porcelain and furnished rooms, late-seventeenth-century Régence through nineteenth-century Charles X. Then the basement: It dazzles as much with its mint-condition Roman mosaic floor as with paintings of our era: Monet and Rouault, Dubuffet and Léger, Braque and Robert Delaunay, Picassos in profusion.

Church of the Dominicans (Rue des Serruriers) is fine thirteenth-century Gothic, well proportioned and vaulted, with excellent stained glass. Principal motivation for your visit, though, is the altarpiece—on the same aesthetic level as the Issenheim at Unterlinden (above)—painted in the fifteenth century by a Colmar-born master named Martin Schongauer. *La Vierge au Buisson des Roses* is, of course, *The Virgin of the Rosebush,* so called because roses climb a trellis forming the backdrop of a portrait of a red-robed Virgin, beautiful long auburn tresses covering her shoulders, a naked baby Jesus in her arms, a pair of protecting angels—black-robed—overhead. Have a look, too, at this church's cloister, entered through the Public Library, adjacent.

Collégiale of St.-Martin (Place de la Cathédrale) is Colmar's oldest Gothic house of worship, dating to the thirteenth century. Because it was the seat of a bishop—and therefore a cathedral—for a brief late-eighteenth-century period, it sometimes still is referred to as such. A rose by any other name. . . . St.-Martin is lovely, at its best in the splendidly sculpted portal (*The Last Judgment, Adoration of the Magi*) on its west side. Within, it is the exceptional height of the nave that is striking, along with stained glass that bears study.

Musée Bartholdi (30 Rue des Marchands): The ground floor of this building offers a bit of Colmar history in its exhibits. You go up a flight for displays celebrating the nineteenth-century career of Frédéric Bartholdi, the Colmar-born artist who designed New York harbor's *Statue de la Liberté;* there are sketches of Miss Liberty as M. Bartholdi conceived her, early on. Otherwise, pickings are mostly slim.

Route du Vin: There are easily half a hundred villages in the Wine Route extending north from Colmar, skirting the Rhine River and the Vosges Mountains, to its terminus in Strasbourg. Everywhere you go, vintners are happy to welcome you, show you through their wineries, invite you to taste their white wines (Riesling is the most popular; Sylvaner and Gewürztraminer follow), and even sell you a three-pack. Here is a quartet of villages that I have enjoyed exploring. Take them in en route to Strasbourg or as part of an excursion from Colmar, allowing extra time for others you'll pass through, which appeal. Order is south to north.

Kaysersberg is a piquant jumble of twin-gabled houses with a ruined castle, a fortified bridge, and two special treasures: a parish church, part Romanesque, part Gothic, with a luminous triptych over its altar; and an impressive *Mairie,* or town hall, dating to the Renaissance.

Riquewihr appears to have stopped building by the end of the Renaissance. With the exception of Rothenburg on Germany's Romantic Route (see *Germany at Its Best*), I don't ever recall being so captivated by half-timbered houses and elegant fountains in handsomely embellished squares. Pop into *Musée Postal* as much for its setting—an ancient castle—as for its contents. Dark-green pottery, typical of the region, is for sale at every turn. There are towers—one has a torture chamber—and drawbridges and fortifications. And you find yourself wanting to look at every courtyard you pass by.

Barr's La Folie Marco is an eighteenth-century house with a deceptively plain facade that shelters eighteenth-century furniture, as well as porcelain and pewter typical of the Alsatian countryside, all of which is charming. Strategically located almost next door is the cluster of structures—with vineyards climbing the hills just out back—of the A. Willm winery—as representative as any in the region. The Willms, third-generation owners, and their staff take you past meticulously tended vines into cool cellars where wine is stored in oaken casks, from fall through spring, when it is transferred to the green bottles that are an Alsace trademark. Hope that the rolls called *cressins*—part croissant, part salt-stick—will be served with the wines that you'll be invited to sample.

Obernai greets visitors with monuments of a venerable past, a fifteenth-century Marché du Blé—or wheat market—for starters, an opulently Renaissance council chamber in its *Mairie,* and atmospheric streets and squares, capacious Place du Marché most especially.

Château Haut Koenigsbourg (nine miles north of Colmar, near Kaysersberg, on the Route du Vin) is a Prince Valiant castle atop a misty mountain. It went up in the twelfth century and was restored at the turn of the present century, while Alsace was part of Germany, by Kaiser Wilhelm II. The ascent to its gate is made on a curvy road through wooded mountainside. At the top—2,266 feet up—is an elongated maze of towers, turrets, battlements, ramparts, and bastions, the lot connected by drawbridges and steep flights of crooked steps, interspersed by galleried courtyards and verdant gardens. Essentially—and, of course, originally—medieval and for long the home of a line of counts, the castle was burned by invading Swedes in the seventeenth century and lay in ruins until Wilhelm set it to rights, the better to let his Alsatian subjects understand what he perceived to be the glorious heritage of their empire. Work began in 1901, the job took seven years, and criticism of architect Bodo Emhardt's work has never quite stopped. There is no denying that liberties were taken with the original or that the interiors might not pass muster in today's Disneyland, the occasional piece of good furniture excepted. Still, credit where it is due: Koenigsbourg anticipated the Disney parks by three quarters of a century. And who would not opt for a mediocre re-creation of the genuine article than the fantasy castles that dominate contemporary funlands?

Mulhouse (27 miles south of Colmar and pronounced Mul-*ooze*) has almost twice Colmar's population (approximately 115,000). An Air France transatlantic gateway city, it is centered by *Place de la Réunion,* whose landmarks are the Gothic-origin *Temple St.-Étienne,* with fine stained glass, and *Hôtel de Ville,* with a handsome Renaissance facade and—inside—galleries of *Musée Historique,* as well as the viewable city council chambers. Pedestrian streets—*Rue Henriette, Rue des Boulangers,* and *Rue du Sauvage*—surround the square. Nearby, on *Place Guillaume Tell, Musée de Beaux-Arts* occupies a rococo mansion, with paintings by the likes of Boucher, Brueghel, Cranach, and Boudin. *Musée National de l'Automobile,* southwest of the center and gained by Avenue de Colmar, is packed with cars—more than 465 of them—representing 90 makes, foreign as well as French, antique through contemporary. *Musée Français du Chemin de Fer* (northwest of the center by way of Rue Franklin) vies with its English counterpart, the National Railroad Museum in York; biggest draws are cars created for Napoleon III's aides de camp, for a turn-of-century grand duchess of Luxembourg, and for presidents of France—this last Art Deco style and in use until 1971.

SETTLING IN

Mercure Hôtel (Rue Golbery; phone 8941-71-71) has the distinct advantage of edging the city center, with Musée Unterlinden a near-neighbor. This is a modern house with 72 well-equipped rooms, restaurant with tables in summer on its terrace, and the generous buffet breakfasts that are a favorite feature of links in this national chain. *Moderate.*

Turenne Hôtel (10 Route de Bâle; phone 8941-12-26) offers 72 contemporary rooms and breakfast only, with its plus a central location. *Moderate.*

Ville de Nancy Hôtel (48 Rue Vauban; phone 8941-23-14) pleases shoppers; you edge the pedestrian shopping area, core-of-town. Almost all 40 rooms have baths. Breakfast only. *Moderate.*

Arcade Hôtel (10 Rue St.-Éloi; phone 8941-30-14) is a five- or six-minute walk east of the heart of town, with 63 of the small, spotless, and utterly functional rooms with shower for which this national budget chain is known. Breakfast only. *Moderate.*

Terminus-Bristol Hôtel (7 Place de la Gare; phone 8923-59-59) is an elderly house, apparently refurbished in stages over the years, with little coordination of styles or decor. However, it works well enough. Some of its 70 rooms are quite attractive. There's a bar-café, as well as a restaurant (Rendez-vous de Chasse) evaluated in a later paragraph. Location is just opposite the railway station, a quarter-hour's walk from the center. *First Class.*

Altéa Champ de Mars Hôtel (2 Avenue de la Marne; phone 8941-54-54)—set back in a city park, 10 minutes' walk from the center—is modern, with 75 rooms and a bar-café that expands to an outdoor terrace in summer. *Moderate.*

Park Hôtel (52 Avenue de la République; phone 8941-34-80) is relatively contemporary, closer to the core than to the Terminus-Bristol or Champ de Mars (above), with 40 bath-equipped rooms, restaurant, bar. So-so. *Moderate.*

Colbert Hôtel (2 Rue des Trois-Épis; phone 8941-31-05) is between the railway station and the core of town—10 minutes by foot; 50 full-facility rooms. Breakfast only. *Moderate.*

Château d'Isenbourg Hôtel (Rouffach, eight miles south of Colmar; phone 8949-63-53) is indicated for a bit of relaxation in the course of Alsatian wandering. This romantic castle—high on its own vineyard-surrounded hill with a swimming pool and tennis court in the garden—has 37 no-two-alike, smartly styled suites and apartments; and a distinguished two-chamber restaurant (picture-window views from one part, vaults of a Renaissance wine cellar from the other) with hearty Alsatian specialties. *Luxury.*

Cour d'Alsace Hôtel (Rue de Gail, Obernai, on the Route du Vin; phone 8895-07-00) is originally seventeenth-century, still with architectural details from that era. The cobbled entry courtyard is impressive enough, but public spaces in traditional motifs are especially lovely; the dinner-only restaurant most definitely included. Not to mention the rooms—30 all told, the lot in low-key pastels. *First Class/Luxury.*

Résidence Chambard Hôtel (Rue du Général de Gaulle, Kaysersberg, on the Route du Vin; phone 8947-10-17) is modern (there are but 18 comfortable rooms with bath), albeit with its bar in the fifteenth-century cellar over which the hotel is built. The off-lobby restaurant, beamed and tapestried, merits a mealtime pause; its forte is cuisine at once distinctive (with Alsatian roots) and substantial. *First Class/Luxury.*

Les Alisiers Hôtel (Lapoutroie, Route du Vin; phone 8947-52-82) is nicely elevated so that the vistas are memorable. There are just 15 smallish rooms in this relatively recently refurbished farmhouse, along with an exemplary restaurant serving hearty Alsatian favorites. The restaurant is *First Class,* the hotel, *Moderate.*

Le Grand Hôtel (Trois-Épis, eight miles west of Colmar; phone 8949-80-65): Setting is a charming village up in the Vosges Mountains, with the panoramas memorable. The Grand is smart (there are 45 lovely rooms, each with a distinctive decor based on traditional mountain motifs) and well equipped. By that, I mean there's a picture-windowed restaurant that turns out as good a choucroute garnie as I've had anywhere in Alsace *and* a health club-cum-swimming pool—to work off all those calories. *Luxury.*

Du Parc Hôtel (126 Rue de la Sinne, Mulhouse; phone 8966-12-22) is Mulhouse's big surprise: a honey of a house behind a neoclassic facade facing Parc Steinbach from which it takes its name, with 83 rooms and super suites of varying sizes (ask to see the presidential, even if you do not hold that title), the exceptional Park Restaurant (go for the well-priced menu at lunch), and the amusing Charlie's, a piano bar; with Art Deco the style in public spaces, part of a relatively recent stem-to-stern renovation. And the bonus of a central location. Chaîne Concorde. *Luxury.*

Altéa Hôtel (4 Place Général-de-Gaulle, Mulhouse; phone 8946-01-23) has nearly a hundred full-facility rooms, convenient restaurant, and busy cocktail lounge, popular with locals. Near the railway station. *Moderate/First Class.*

Wir Hôtel (4 Porte Bâle, Mulhouse; phone 8956-13-22) is less luxurious than the Parc and Altéa but it's central; 40 rooms, restaurant, bar. *Moderate.*

DAILY BREAD

Au Fer Rouge (52 Grande Rue; phone 8941-37-24) occupies a landmark building of advanced age on one of Colmar's landmark-filled streets. There is a pair of intimate dining rooms, with tables set in yellow linen, beneath original beamed ceilings. And walls are hung with small but excellent paintings by contemporary Colmar artist Jean-Claude Allenbach. Choose from one of the four prix-fixe menus (there's an extensive à la carte, as well.) Fare is a mix of traditional Alsatian with just enough contemporary twists—*sensible* twists—to distinguish it. A typical meal might open with caviar-topped poached eggs in crayfish sauce, terrine de foie gras, or rich mushroom soup; and continue with such entrées as duckling roasted with wild mushrooms, the house's own filet of beef deliciously sauced, or médaillons of lamb sautéed in a basil sauce, accompanied by baby fresh vegetables. The cheese board is exceptional. No less so are desserts, one of which—a baked half apple doused with caramelized almond sauce and topped with coconut ice cream—is in and of itself worth the trip to Colmar. Delightful service. *Luxury.*

Schillinger (16 Rue Stanislaus; phone 8941-43-17) is at once central (at the western edge of the core), attractive (the look is very posh), welcoming, and delicious—with classic Alsatian specialties. Open with foie gras, consider roast duck or superbly prepared fish to follow. And don't skip a sweet. The menu at weekday lunches is your best value. *Luxury.*

Rendez-vous de Chasse (Terminus-Bristol Hôtel, 7 Place de la Gare; phone 8941-10-10) has an agreeable hum to it, especially at lunch when Colmar business types mix with the hotel's international clientele. Menu is essentially traditional, with Alsatian favorites—onion tart or snails to start, perhaps a sautéed trout to follow, with such entrées as coq au Riesling and filet of venison, this last the restaurant's most respected specialty. Super sweets. *First Class.*

Maison des Têtes (19 Rue des Têtes; phone 8924-43-43): If you haven't paused before this seventeenth-century house in the course of Colmar exploration, do so before entering. It's called House of Heads because of the plethora of busts that distinguish its facade. Hearty Alsatian grub is the name of the Têtes game—foie gras in a brioche frame or the day's soup as starters, followed by choucroute garnie—the sauerkraut and sausage specialty of the region—or, in season, roast pheasant. Apple pastries are indicated for dessert. *First Class.*

Au Trois Poissons (16 Quai de la Poissonnerie; phone 8941-25-21): Don't leave Colmar without having enjoyed a meal in the old Petite

Venise/Quartier des Tanneurs sectors. Here, the setting is a centuries-old house; the specialty is fish (I suggest the local trout, either amandine or meunière) with traditional openers and lavish desserts. *First Class.*

Helmstetter (7 Place des Dominicains) is a *pâtisserie* and *salon de thé;* pause for coffee with a slice of the yeast-dough confection called kugelhopf. *Moderate.*

Hostellerie du Cerf (Marlenheim, north of Colmar on Route du Vin; phone 8887-73-73) is an attractive and aged inn with eighteenth-century origins that is at one and the same time a 17-room hotel of no little charm and a restaurant of considerable repute, operated by the same family for several generations, featuring Alsatian specialties—with du Cerf touches as for example a choucroute with, among much else, foie gras. Consider the hotel *First Class,* the restaurant (best buy is the menu at lunch) *Luxury.*

Gilg (Mittelbergheim, a mile and a half outside of Barr on Route du Vin; phone 8808-91-37) is indicated for a festive lunch pause in the course of exploring the vineyards and villages north of Colmar. An ancient *weinstube* on scene since 1614, it serves up delicious victuals. Lunch might open with Monsieur Gilg's delicate fish soufflé or his also-celebrated pâté de foie gras en brioche; proceed with tournedos, Vieux Strasbourg style, or a poultry specialty. Distinguished desserts. And 10 rooms, should you want to overnight. *First Class.*

Auberge de l'Ill (Illhaeusern, near Ribeauville, 10 miles north of Colmar; phone 8971-83-23) is cool—very cool. Setting is a handsome house in a broad parklike garden, alongside the Ill River, with picture windows in the contiguous main-floor rooms constituting the restaurant. Reception, in my experience, is correct but distant; service, likewise; fare, competent, albeit—again, in my experience—unexciting. A meal might open with salmon soufflé, continue with filet of beef in a wine sauce, and conclude with a fruit-based sweet. Caveat: *Way*-in-advance bookings are usually required. *Luxury.*

Guillaume Tell (1 Rue Gillaume-Tell, Mulhouse; phone 8945-21-58): No bow, no arrow, no apple. Tasty Alsatian specialties, though, with a heart-of-town location. *First Class.*

Caves du Vieux Couvent (23 Rue Couvent, Mulhouse; phone 9846-28-79) is quite as atmospheric as its name suggests. Fare is hearty and traditional, not to mention temptingly tabbed. Central. *Moderate.*

La Tosca (6 Passage de l'Hôtel de Ville, Mulhouse) is just the *salon de thé* you're seeking, for a pause-cum-pastry between museums. *Moderate.*

Auberge de la Tonnelle (61 Rue Maréchal-Joffre, in the east-of-Mulhouse suburb of Riedisheim; phone 8954-25-77) makes for a super excursion from the core, ideally at night when you can relax over a delicious Alsatian meal that might open with the house's own duck-liver pâté, continue with game or salmon in season, concluding with a no-nonsense dessert. Interesting regional wines. *First Class/Luxury.*

SOUND OF MUSIC

Théâtre Municipal (Rue de la Sinne, Mulhouse) is the area's leading venue for opera, ballet, and concerts.

INCIDENTAL INTELLIGENCE

Aéroport de Bâle-Mulhouse is a remarkable example of Franco-Swiss cooperation, 17 miles from town, serving Switzerland's Basel, as well as Mulhouse. Air France links Mulhouse with New York, and there is service from Mulhouse to a number of French points. (Note also that Air France flies New York–Strasbourg—chapter 35.) Mulhouse is the area city with the swiftest train service to Paris. *Further information:* Office de Tourisme, 4 Rue des Unterlinden, Colmar; Office de Tourisme, 9 Avenue Foch, Mulhouse.

16

Deauville

Elegance on the Channel

BACKGROUND BRIEFING

Beach resorts develop either as a consequence of celebrated patronage, or they are deliberately created. Deauville's next-door neighbor on the English Channel coast that constitutes Normandy's northern flank, Trouville, is in the former category. Napoleon III's fashionable consort, Empress Eugénie, took a fancy to it in the middle years of the last century; the Imperial presence drew Imperial courtiers who in turn drew the bourgeoisie—and crowds packed Trouville.

Indeed, business was brisk enough to attract the attention of the canny Duc de Morny, who rounded up capital and partners and set to work creating Deauville, even erecting a racetrack as bait to draw holiday-makers. Period was the decade of the 1860s. It was a start. But the Second Empire fell in 1870, and Deauville limped along until the turn of the present century. By 1912, another entrepreneur, Eugène Cornuché, emboldened by the continued success of Trouville, where grand hotels encircled a casino edging the sea, put up a pair of luxury hotels—the Royal and the Normandy, both still Deauville leaders—and followed with the casino that remains, contemporarily, the smartest on the coast.

With the Roaring Twenties came cachet: Big names—the Dolly Sisters, the Rothschilds, the Cognac-producing Henesseys, Indian maharajas, Middle Eastern pashas, British and Spanish royals—became synonymous with Deauville. The beach-flanking boardwalk, Les Planches, became northern France's spiffiest promenade; new hotels went up. Alas, they were requisitioned by the Germans as officers' quarters during the World War II occupation. But post-World War II decades saw Deauville emerge as Paris's seaside suburb, with fast trains and new highways linking it with the capital to the south.

Irony of ironies, while Deauville prospered, Trouville became more plebeian. Movers and shakers ignored it—Imperial origins notwithstanding—to the point that today it has not a single luxury hotel. This is hardly to say, however, that Trouville is out of business. Its market is mass—the old casino remains in operation, though it's no longer big-league—while that of Deauville is classy. You'll want to compare the two.

ON SCENE

Lay of the Land: Deauville is delightfully easy to get about. *Boulevard de la Mer* flanks *Les Planches,* the celebrated boardwalk, which in turn borders the wide, white-sand beach. In season, the latter is massed with umbrellas and changing *cabines* and edged by cafés and restaurants. Area just inland from the beach's central sectors embraces such facilities as a giant, covered swimming pool complex (Maurice Chevalier came up from Paris to declare it officially open in 1964), tennis courts in abundance, mini-golf (which the French adore), a sailing club, and Club Enfants—with activities for kids. *Boulevard Eugène Cornuché,* named for the resort's turn-of-the-century developer, runs parallel to this beach area, framing it from the south. The casino fronts this boulevard, between *Avenue Général-de-Gaulle* and *Rue Gontaud. Rue Casino,* to the casino's rear, is lined with pricey boutiques. *Hippodrome de Clairefontaine*—the race-track dating to Deauville's origins a century and a quarter back—is at the western edge of town; still another track, *Hippodrome de la Touques* (with a polo field), is inland, to the south. The railway station is at Deauville's eastern edge, a hop and a skip from *La Touques,* the estuary separating Deauville from Trouville, with *Port Deauville,* a marina-yacht basin complex, at its northern flank.

Trouville's focal point remains its *casino,* on *Quai Albert 1er,* partially facing La Touques, partially open to the sea, and where fishermen still tie up their boats, as their ancestors did, over long centuries. Not unlike Deauville, its sands are framed by a boardwalk, *Promenade des Planches.* An enormous municipal *piscine,* or swimming pool, is just opposite the casino in the beach area, with tennis and other facilities nearby. Commercial Trouville begins at *Place du Maréchal Foch,* just west of the casino, spilling into adjacent *rues Paul Basson, Charles Mozin,* and *Victor Hugo.*

Casino de Deauville (Boulevard Eugène Cornuché)—immense, high-ceilinged, and crystal-chandeliered—shelters not only gaming rooms (slot machines in a room of their own, roulette, chemin de fer, trente-et-quarante, and blackjack), but also a theater, boîte, cinema, restaurants, and bars. Take your passport with you, and, gentlemen, wear a jacket in the evening.

Casino Municipal de Trouville (Promenade des Planches, Trouville) has, to be sure, seen better days, but its Second Empire facade—with a marvelous mansard roof—redeems it, and the Salle de Jeux, or gaming room, within—silk-shaded lamps over the tables—could be right out of an old movie.

Musée de Trouville (Villa Montbello, 64 Rue du Général Leclerc, Trouville) is a still-imposing town house dating to the mid-nineteenth century, when Empress Eugénie was a frequent visitor to Trouville and Impressionists painted it. Its eight galleries are a testament to the epoch, with photos and prints, ship models and Norman peasants' costumes, paintings and postcards. Evocative.

Aquarium Écologique (Promenade des Planches, Trouville): Don't let the pretentious title keep you away from what is probably the best-designed aquarium in France. Emphasis is on fish and shellfish from the Atlantic and the English Channel, but there are species from other regions of France and the tropics, not to mention a selection of crocodiles and giant snakes to scare the hell out of you.

Cabourg (11 miles west of Deauville) is a charming little resort with its core—a fabulous Belle Époque hotel and adjacent casino—the hub of a wheellike area from which a score of turn-of-century streets, the wheel's spokes, fan out. The hotel is the very same at which Marcel Proust wrote *Within a Budding Grove.* His room was reproduced in the 1970s film *Le Banc de la Désolation,* directed by Marcel Chabrol, and Cabourg's seafront boulevard is dubbed Promenade Marcel Proust. Go for lunch, perhaps taking in also the nearby town of *Dives-sur-Mer,* the historic point at which Guillaume le Conquérant—William the Conqueror—mustered the fleet with which he crossed the Channel to vanquish the English in 1066; William's officers' names are carved into a wall of Dives's venerable *Church of Notre-Dame.* There's an ancient *Halles,* or market, and an equally aged restaurant, later counseled.

SETTLING IN

Royal Hôtel (Boulevard Eugène Cornuché; phone 3188-16-41) is the very model of a grand seafront hotel of the old school, spanking white and colonnaded, with heroically proportioned public spaces—chandeliered lobby; rust-and-ivory Le Royal restaurant, later evaluated; à-la-carte-only grill; earth-toned bar-lounge, wherein there is always a choice of 25 brands of whiskey; a terrace on the lawn, its tables shielded with yellow umbrellas; and just over 300 suites and rooms, no two quite alike, the style, throughout, traditional. Those I have inspected are handsome and capacious and have excellent baths; terraced seafront accommodations are the choicest. The Royal is the flagship of the small but excellent

Chaîne Lucien Barrière, which has the top trio of Deauville hotels, among others. *Luxury.*

Normandy Hôtel (38 Rue Jean-Mermoz; phone 3188-09-21)—with mock-Norman facade, shingled, gabled, and half-timbered—is appropriately named. Inside, decor is more typical of the turn-of-century period of construction—high-ceilinged and neoclassic—with perhaps the handsomest dining room in town (later recommended), a clublike bar-lounge, and potted plants alongside easy chairs in the lobby. There are 332 suites and rooms—attractive, well equipped, capacious. Chaîne Lucien Barrière. *Luxury.*

Golf Hôtel (just off Route 278, two miles from Deauville; phone 3188-19-01): Given proclivities toward golf (there are 18 holes at the door) and seclusion (you are away from the fleshpots of town), you can be happy in this 165-room house. It's half-timbered without and traditional with respect to public spaces (a big porch, sprawling lobby, smart restaurant, and cozy bar). Those of the 165 rooms I've checked out are very pleasant. Chaîne Lucien Barrière. *Luxury.*

Helios Hôtel (19 Rue Fosserier; phone 3188-34-69) is one of the best-looking contemporary hotels I know in France—with a bar leading from its lobby and 44 rooms, eight of which are duplex and can accommodate families. Breakfast only; it's buffet style. With a little swimming pool as a bonus. And friendly management. Central. *Moderate.*

Altéa Hôtel (Boulevard Eugène Cornuché; phone 3888-62-62) is in Port-Deauville, the marina quarter that edges La Touques, with Trouville just opposite. There are 70 modern rooms, good restaurant, and bar-lounge. *Moderate.*

Beach Hôtel (1 Quai Albert 1er, Trouville; phone 3198-12-00) is Trouville's newest, with 125 neat rooms, restaurants, bar-lounge, and a super situation between the casino and La Touques, with the municipal pool and beach just opposite. Friendly. *First Class.*

Pullman Grand Hôtel (Promenade Marcel-Proust, Cabourg; phone 3191-01-79) dates to the Belle Époque period of the last century, whose flavor and look it retains, thorough refurbishing notwithstanding. The Pullman Grand looks bigger than it is; there are just 68 rooms and two lovely suites, the lot of them good-sized and—at least those I have inspected—charming. A tremendous crystal chandelier at the lobby entrance sets the tone of the public spaces, which include a red and gold bar-lounge and a duplex restaurant, later reviewed. The beach—wide and white-sand—is just out back.

And the hotel can make arrangements for guest privileges at the Sporting Club de Cabourg—with a pair of pools, five tennis courts, and a gym—nearby. *Luxury.*

DAILY BREAD

Ciro's (Promenade des Planches; phone 3188-18-10) occupies a seaside pavilion whose French doors give onto a warm-weather terrace and the sea. The specialty is seafood, and you could do worse than to order from the good-value prix-fixe, four-course menu, starting perhaps with filet of sole salad (served *tiède,* or warm) or rillettes of salmon and continuing with fish of the day simply sautéed or a platter of the day's assorted seafood catch. Norman cheeses in profusion are then offered from a wagon, with a choice of desserts—I counsel fondant chocolat au nectar d'orange—to conclude. Service is impeccable. *Luxury.*

Les Grands Ambassadeurs (Casino de Deauville, Boulevard Eugène Cornuché; phone 3188-29-55) is indicated for a gala evening in the see-and-be-seen casino, with the menu a contemporary-traditional mix and both seafood and beef entrées reliable. Dressy. *Luxury.*

Belle Époque (Normandy Hôtel, 38 Rue Jean-Mermoz; phone 3188-09-21): If it's cool, you lunch or dine in the best-looking of the town's restaurants—high-ceilinged, classically paneled and colonnaded, and superbly crystal-chandeliered. In warm weather, tables are set in the pretty courtyard, under boughs of a veritable orchard of apple trees. There's a good-value menu, which might run to soup, salad, or a fish specialty to start; roast lamb or a beef entrée; cheeses; and a sweet. Smiling service. *Luxury.*

Royal Hôtel Restaurant (Boulevard Eugène Cornuché; phone 3188-16-41): The town's poshest hotel offers a surprisingly good-value four-course meal—with choices ample—that might embrace fish soup to begin, roast lamb or a seafood entrée, cheeses from a great tray, and pastries *au choix. Luxury.*

Chez Marie (44 Rue Mirabeau; phone 3188-34-29) is indicated for hearty seafood specialties, the range soupe aux poissons through sole grillée. Central. *Moderate/First Class.*

Saratoga (8 Avenue Général-de-Gaulle; phone 3188-24-33) has the advantages of a central situation near the casino and super seafood—its classic sole Normande is a winner—from the à la carte; a prix-fixe menu as well. *First Class.*

Bar du Soleil (Promenade des Planches; phone 3188-04-74) is the favored spot for casual lunches on the beach, center of the action. Seafood and salads. *Moderate/First Class.*

Café Le Drakkar (77 Rue Eugène-Colas) is a heart-of-town stopping point for coffee or a cooling drink in the midst of a morning or afternoon in the shops. *Moderate.*

Petite Auberge (7 Rue Carnot, Trouville; phone 3188-11-07): a well-situated (near the casino), well-priced, and delicious source of seafood; fun for lunch. *Moderate.*

Pullman Grand Hôtel Restaurant (Promenade Marcel-Proust, Cabourg; phone 3191-01-79) is a compact duplex, with good-value prix-fixe menus at two prices; the less costly might include a shrimp appetizer, the house's own blanquette de poisson, a kind of fish stew, as well as cheese and dessert. *First Class.*

Guillaume le Conquérant (2 Rue Hastings, Dives-sur-Mer; phone 3191-07-26) is a four-century-old source of tasty fare, seafood-accented, in a lovely setting, ideal for lunch in connection with local exploration. *First Class.*

SHOPPER'S DEAUVILLE

Smart shops are in and about Rue du Casino, behind the casino, and include—to give you an idea—*Hermès* (men's and women's clothes and accessories, with their neckties and women's scarves celebrated), *Cartier* (jewelry), *Yves St.-Laurent* (women's haute couture), *Jean-Louis Scherrer* (women's haute couture), *Brummel* (men's clothes), *Jules-et-Julie* (kids' clothes), *La Gadgetière* (china and housewares), and a good-sized link of the *Printemps* department-store chain.

AFTER DARK

Deauville's Casino is the center of after-dark action, with restaurants (one is evaluated above) and cafés, theater, movies, and Regine's boîte, which keeps *very* late summer hours. The casino's gaming rooms admit only visitors with passports, and men, as I indicate on an earlier page, do well to wear jackets if not neckties as well—especially on weekends; at no time are sneakers permitted. For the casino's slot-machine room (and its Café de la Boule), no passport is required and the dress code is more relaxed. *Caveat:* there's a fairly stiff entrance fee for the gaming rooms. And don't neglect *Trouville's Casino;* its theater offers seasonal entertainment, and there are other diversions.

INCIDENTAL INTELLIGENCE

Further information: Office de Tourisme, Place de la Mairie, Deauville; Office de Tourisme, Place du Maréchal-Foch, Trouville; Office de Tourisme, Jardins du Casino, Cabourg.

17

Dijon

and the Beauties of Burgundy

BACKGROUND BRIEFING

If it is true that Dijon conveys the impression of basking in the reflected glory of its Golden Age as capital of the far-flung medieval Duchy of Burgundy—this is the least cordial of the principal provincial cities—it follows, too, that there is reason for its residue of arrogance. Burgundy, in its heydey, was a big deal, feared even by the crown of France. And its wealth and power emanated from Dijon, the seat of its dukes.

Still, there is no question but that this city's riches—archeological, architectural, artistic—warrant inspection; nor that Dijon's situation in the world-class wine region, Côte d'Or, makes of it a base for excursions to the vineyards and their villages, to which it shares access with smaller, friendlier Beaune (chapter 8), historic commercial center for Burgundy wine producers. It is from Dijon, too, that delightful day trips may be undertaken to beauty spots of western and northern Burgundy—Auxerre and Fontenay, Semur-en-Auxois and Bussy-Rabutin, Vézelay and St.-Thibault. And what its hotels lack in finesse (only Nantes [chapter 30] and Marseille [chapter 22] among the big French cities are as disappointing in this respect), Dijon compensates for with cuisine; the lavish Burgundian fare does justice to its celebrated wines.

Although it knew Romans as long ago as half a century before the birth of Christ (and assorted other governors, including fifth-century people from southerly Savoie whose name, *Burgundii,* was given to the region), it was not until the eleventh century—when rulers of Burgundy made it their seat—that Dijon came into its own. It was then that history began to celebrate dukes whose names were followed by qualifying adjectives—Philip the Bold, John the Fearless, Philip the Good. They developed a realm that extended into what is now Belgium, Luxembourg, the Netherlands, and northern France, the while maintaining a court in Dijon, whose art, music, and literature made it the talk of Europe. Alas, Duke Charles the Bold proved *too* bold, losing his life in a fifteenth-century battle against France's King Louis XI. The Duchy of Burgundy, shortly thereafter, was absorbed by the Kingdom of France. But Burgundian memories die hard.

ON SCENE

Lay of the Land: Two central squares anchor central Dijon. Westerly *Place Darcy* is identified by a triumphal arch, *Porte Guillaume.* From it, the principal shopping street, *Rue de la Liberté,* leads east to *Place de la Libération,* an elegant half-crescent that is dwarfed by multiwinged *Palais des Ducs de Bourgogne,* now housing both *Hôtel de Ville* (the city hall) and *Musée des Beaux-Arts* (below). *Place Rude,* north of Rue de la Liberté, at midpoint opens onto another shopping street, *Rue des Forges,* off which leads pedestrians-only *Rue Liégard.* Nearby *Rue Verrerie* is Antiques Row. The neighborhood's *Rue Chouette* is strollworthy because of its mansions—fifteenth through eighteenth century; so, for that matter, are *rues Berbisey, des Bons Enfants,* and *Chabot-Cherny.* The railway station is at the western edge of town on *Avenue Maréchal-Foch.*

Cathedral of St.-Bénigne (Place St.-Bénigne): Dijon's cathedral, chapel of a Benedictine monastery until the eighteenth century, is not nearly as exciting as big-city counterparts in Rouen, Lyon, or Bordeaux. Still, it does convey a sense of atmosphere, setting the mood for Dijon exploration. This is an upstairs-downstairs exercise. The cathedral proper is attractive Gothic, its facade framed by twin conical-topped towers backed by a slender steeple. After you've walked the nave, go below to the crypt, a Romanesque octagon that's a thousand years old, its surprisingly high ceiling supported by not one, but a pair of concentric rows of columns. Upon exiting, head next door to...

Musée Archéologique (Rue Docteur Maret) is an architecturally exceptional Gothic structure that served as living quarters of Benedictine monks whose chapel (above) is now the cathedral. You go as much for the main-floor space—a sumptuously vaulted room that was the monks' dormitory—as you do for exhibits that document Dijon's history, Bronze and Iron ages beyond to Roman, with both a bust and full-length statue of St.-Bénigne, for whom the cathedral is named.

Musée des Beaux-Arts (Place de la Ste.-Chapelle) is, as I indicate earlier on, a part of the onetime ducal palace, sharing space in its confines with the city hall (whose quite grand eighteenth-century reception rooms in the palace's central section are open to visitors upon application to its concierge). You want to have a look, too, at

Tour Bar, a veritable skyscraper of a medieval tower, and the high-ceilinged and adjacent palace kitchens. Then head for a collection of paintings, sculpture, and applied arts that is one of the best in the republic and in as felicitous a setting as any in the provinces, save Strasbourg (chapter 35). Elevated tombs, in Salles de Gardes, of Philip the Bold and John the Fearless—surrounded by hovering angels and with sculpted mourners on a lower level of each, created by a genius named Claus Sluter—is a tough act to follow. But as you carry on, you find the range—and the quality—of paintings remarkable. Specifics? Well, consider such canvases as Melchior Broederlam's fourteenth-century pair, with *Annunciation* and *Visitation* cleverly combined in one and *Presentation at the Temple* and the *Flight into Egypt* amazingly combined in the other; Van der Weyden's somber, black-robed *Philip the Good;* Luini's *Virgin and Child;* Colson's young lady, catnapping in *Le Répos;* and Nattier's much-reproduced *Marie Leczinska*—Louis XV's pretty, bonneted consort; with Bassano and Titian, Brueghel and Rubens, Brouwer and Hals, Greuze and Natoire, as well; and moderns—Millet through Monet—to add spice; not to mention furniture, ceramics, and objects fashioned of ivory, enamel, gold, and silver—Renaissance through rococo.

Musée Magnin (4 Rue des Bons Enfants, near Place de la Liberté) is a seventeenth-century town house, whose late owner turned it over to the French government with the proviso that it be operated as a museum, with paintings, other art objects, furniture, and accessories all left intact. It's fun to poke about on an expedition of discovery, coming upon canvases by Vouet and Le Nain, Bourdon and Géricault, Tiepolo and Boucher, the while taking in the interiors: a brilliant grand staircase, family sitting room, formal salon, the lot elaborately eighteenth-century.

Musée d'Art Sacré (15 Rue Ste.-Anne) is a desanctified church that brims with religious art—sculpture, most especially; an immense Baroque altar by Dijon-born Jean Dubois is star of the show. Should there be an exhibition—there are several each year—at nearby *Musée de la Vie Bourguignonne* in an ex-convent at 25 Rue Ste.-Anne, pop in.

Palais de Justice (Rue du Palais) is monumental Baroque. Apply to the concierge for permission to have a look at the lavish ceiling of the *Assises* courtroom and adjacent public spaces.

Church of Notre-Dame (Place Notre-Dame): Stand back on the square and look up—over the broad, triple-arched porch—to the clutch of gargoyles (by my count, seventeen) topping as many slim pillars on each of two galleries of the facade, with a third, or bottom, row for good measure. Inside, walk to the transept for another upward glance at inner walls of a tower framing the transept.

Church of St.-Michel (Place St.-Michel) is still another Dijon church requiring consideration from without. Its facade of five symmetric levels, topped by a pair of octagonal towers, is a Renaissance masterwork. The tympanum, or carved overdoor, of the central portal represents *The Last Judgment*—and beautifully—while the interior is graceful Gothic.

Wine country—south to Nuits St.-Georges: A tour of the southern tip of the Côte d'Or, touching Beaune, Mâcon, and Beaujolais—is outlined in chapter 8. From Dijon, a wine-country excursion, morning well into the afternoon, might follow the *Route des Grands Vins* that would include stops at *Fixin* (to visit an unexpected museum of Napoleonic memorabilia in Parc Noisot); *Gevrey-Chambertin* (for inspection of Château Gevrey-Chambertin, parts of it tenth-century, small, privately owned, and in a pathetic state of repair); *Clos de Vougeot* (for inspection of a medieval château set in a 225-acre vineyard that thrives on admissions charged of masses of tourists, fascinated at the sight of venerable wooden winepresses, casks, and the like, the lot explained in an excessive French-language commentary); and *Nuits St.-Georges* (surely the most euphoniously named of French wine villages, welcoming and with a small museum of Roman and medieval artifacts excavated locally). Throughout this pretty region—at such towns along the way as *Marsannay-la-Côte, Brochon, Morey St.-Denis, Chambolle-Musigny, Flagey-Echézeaux,* and *Vosne Romanée,* invariably friendly growers welcome you to their *caves*—you'll note signs as you move along—for gratis tastings, tours (upon occasion), and sales of their wines; but they do not high-pressure you to buy. Whether you do so or not is up to you.

Chablis and Auxerre (each about 80 miles northwest of Dijon) are near-neighbors (nine miles separate them). You'll be curious about Chablis because, no doubt, you drink its crisp white wine—the most globally famous French white—or California whites that have appropriated the Chablis name. Chablis is an unexceptional village with the Serein River to its northeast, vineyards with its celebrated grapes all about, and a friendly core, with Romanesque-origin *Church of St.-Martin* (Rue des Moulins) its major monument. *Auxerre* is something else again, a substantial town on the Yonne River that is based on *Place de l'Hôtel de Ville*—dead center and named for a bishop's palace that is now the city hall—with two visitable churches. The elder, *Church of St.-Germain* (Rue Docteur Labosse), attached to a venerable Benedictine monastery, is Gothic at street level, but it's the remarkable pair of Romanesque crypts that you want to inspect, one superimposed over the other, with their most striking features—capitals of columns supporting vaults excepted—frescoes relating scenes in the life of St. Stephen (for whom the town's cathedral, below, is named) that date to the ninth century, the oldest such in France. Move, then, to *Cathedral of St.-Étienne* (Place St.-Étienne), one of the most beautiful Gothic churches in the republic, with a lavishly sculpted facade—note *Christ in Majesty* and *The Last Judgment* in the tympanum of the central portal, *Coronation of the Virgin* over the left panel, *The Life of St. John the Baptist* over the right portal—and, inside, the thirteenth-century choir, stunning stained glass, and a frescoed crypt.

Vézelay (60 miles west of Dijon) is a tiny, walled village capping a hill and itself capped by a thirteenth-century church—*Basilica of Ste.-Madeleine,* so named for on-site presumed relics of St. Mary Magdalene—that just has to be the biggest village church in France and certainly one of its most magnificent, thanks not only to its original designers, but to a nineteenth-century restoration by Viollet-le-Duc that respects its Romanesque origins. The single-tower facade stands out because of an unusual pediment with statues filling its niches and framing its windows. There are three portals, with the tympanum of the central one, *Christ in Glory,* worthy of study, in preparation for still another tympanum—this one inside, infinitely more detailed, depicting *Christ and the Apostles.* The interior—principally because of Romanesque vaults patterned in black and white, which frame the high nave supplemented by sculpted capitals topping columns supporting the vaults—is one of the most outstanding in France.

Château de Bussy-Rabutin (40 miles southwest of Dijon) is the prototypical Renaissance castle: cylindrical towers delineating its extremities, moat leading to a courtyard galleried on either side, central section distinguished by a steep-pitched roof. Windows throughout—elegantly oblong in the style of the period—are superb. State rooms are, too. One, atop a tower, La Tour Dorée, is the most smashing; another, the bedroom of a Comte de Bussy, has walls and canopy of identical scarlet damask. All are distinguished by a plethora of portraits, as many of somberly suited gents as of ladies with generous bosoms, their necklines low and their foreheads ringed with the curls of elaborate coiffures.

Abbey of Fontenay (46 miles northwest of Dijon)—despite its cold severity, not surprising as it was inhabited by abstemious Cistercians—is an impeccably maintained Romanesque complex taken in by means of guided 45-minute tours. It is at its most likable in the twelfth-century cloister, centered by a manicured lawn, surrounded by a gallery, each of whose arches is supported by double columns. The church—more than 200 feet long—is virtually without embellishment, capitals of the columns flanking its nave and a statue of the Virgin Mary in the transept excepted. And the dormitory—wherein the monks slept on the floor on straw pallets—is even plainer, albeit with a superb barrel vault.

Semur-en-Auxois (38 miles northwest of Dijon) is, if visited in tandem with nearby, gloomy Fontenay (above), a barrel of laughs in contrast. This is a time-stood-still village, preserved quite as it was for centuries, amenities like electricity and plumbing excepted. All the ingredients of a medieval movie set are present: high-on-a-hill situation, the Armançon River flowing through the core, with a stone bridge traversing it, quartet of towers that date to when the village was defended by archers, walkable ramparts, *Musée Municipal* in a Baroque convent filled with medieval sculpture, and—frosting on the cake—single-steepled *Church of Notre-Dame,* a Gothic jewel that is a joy from without: elegant apse at the rear, tympanum over the central portal of a facade protected by an immense porch, exceptional sculpture, and good stained glass.

St.-Thibault (32 miles northwest of Dijon): If Semur (above) is a village, St.-Thibault is a hamlet. The only game in town is *Church of Notre-Dame*—unusual Gothic in that its designers made of its apse a veritable skyscraping tower, easily the equivalent of five or six stories and visible for miles around.

SETTLING IN

Châpeau Rouge Hôtel (5 Rue Michelet; phone 8030-28-10): There are 33 no-two-alike, traditional-style rooms, with those that I have seen tasteful, with respect to antique accents and interesting textiles, although some are, indeed, small. Public spaces, including a cocktail lounge and restaurant, later evaluated, are agreeable. And situation is central. Best Western. *First Class.*

Du Nord Hôtel (2 Rue de la Liberté at Place Darcy; phone 8030-55-20): In a city where hotels are not a strong point, the long-on-scene Nord—family-owned and operated, centrally situated, fairly comfortable—stands out. There are two dozen rooms—some bigger than others, all in unpretentious traditional style, with okay baths and soft mattresses, restaurant (Porte Guillaume) worthy of comment in a later paragraph, and kindly, caring, efficient management. *Moderate.*

Du Jura Hôtel (14 Avenue Maréchal-Foche; phone 8041-61-12) is an elderly house that has seen better days. But it's reasonably central—not far beyond Place Darcy—with a capacious lobby, a bar-lounge with a log-cabin look, 75 rooms, and a cordial reception staff. *Moderate.*

Wilson Hôtel (1 Rue de Longvic; phone 8066-82-50) makes its home in an originally seventeenth-century coaching inn. Beamed ceilings distinguish the interior—attractive lounge as well as those of the 27 bedrooms (all with bath) that I've inspected. They occupy the building's four wings, which enclose a courtyard. Restaurant Thibert (attractive and *First Class*) shares the premises but has its own phone (8067-74-64) and its own entrance on Place Wilson. The hotel is *Moderate.*

Montigny Hôtel (8 Rue de Montigny; phone 8030-96-86) is a small contemporary-look house that's reasonably central; 22 adequate rooms. Breakfast only. *Moderate.*

Altéa Château Bourgogne Hôtel (22 Boulevard de la Marne; phone 8072-31-13) would be at the top of my Dijon grouping if only it were central. You're a quarter-hour drive from the core here, opposite Palais des Congrès, but there are advantages: a modern house with 128 well-equipped rooms, convenient restaurant, relaxing cocktail lounge, swimming pool in the garden that's a pleasure in summer, and—hardly to be underestimated—a friendly welcoming staff. *First Class.*

De la Cloche Hôtel (14 Place Darcy; phone 8030-12-32) occupies only part of the interior of a Second Empire building fronting a major square. It was relatively recently refurbished with good-looking public spaces, including a crystal-chandeliered lounge, leather-chaired bar, breakfast room giving onto a garden, and independently operated luxury-category Jean-Pierre Billoux Restaurant. There are two problems: A majority of the 80 rooms are small and cramped (agreeable rattan-look decor notwithstanding). And service is mostly by youngsters at reception, whose principal qualification is language skills. The De la Cloche gives the unhappy impression of being operated without top-management supervision. *First Class.*

DAILY BREAD

La Toison d'Or (18 Rue Ste.-Anne; phone 8030-73-52)—a fairish but scenic walk from Rue de la Liberté, near Musée d'Art Sacré—is the handsomest restaurant in town, a Renaissance house with original beamed ceilings, flagstone floors, stone and paneled walls, Louis XIII chairs at flower-centered tables, and a half-timbered facade giving onto a courtyard. Not surprisingly, fare is traditional Burgundy. There are several well-priced prix-fixe menus. One of these opens with duck terrine, continues with filet of trout, proceeds to a cheese platter, and concludes with a house-baked pastry or a frozen coupe cassis. The à la carte includes a deliciously wine-sauced filet of beef. The cordial owning couple operates a wine museum on the premises and conducts tastings for groups that have booked accordingly. *First Class.*

Jean-Pierre Billoux (located in De la Cloche Hôtel, 14 Place d'Arcy, but operated independently of the hotel, with its own entrance and telephone—8030-11-00) occupies comfortable quarters, but your reason for going is chef-propriétaire Billoux's cooking. Time to go is midday for the multicourse menu—costlier in the evening. Look for house specialties like the warm filet-of-sole salad, interesting treatment of lobster, snail cassolette, and Monsieur Billoux's distinctive variations on Burgundian themes like coq au vin, roast Bresse duckling, and guinea-hen teamed with foie gras. Desserts are delicious and Burgundy wine buffs will appreciate the cellar. Member, Relais et Châteaux. *Luxury.*

Chapeau Rouge Hôtel Restaurant (5 Rue Michelet; phone 8030-28-10) is set in good-looking Louis XVI-style quarters, at once old-school and smart and, like the hotel in which it is situated, professionally staffed. There are traditional dishes—œufs en meurette (the Burgundian egg masterwork), foie gras, salmon rillettes, oysters on the half shell, truffled cream of seafood soup, roast lamb, and filet of beef, Calvados and other dessert soufflés. But if you order one of the multicourse menus, chances are your meal will be of a more contemporary bent albeit tasty. *First Class/ Luxury.*

La Porte Guillaume (Du Nord Hôtel, 2 Rue de la Liberté; phone 8030-55-20) has the look of old Burgundy—brass chandeliers, ladder-back chairs, candlelight at dinner—and the taste of old Burgundy. There are several menus, and even the cheapest is a winner; open with jambon persillé or half a dozen Burgundy-style snails and continue with Burgundy's own coq au vin or veal kidneys, Dijon-style, with dessert following. Everything I've had here is delicious, and service is super. *First Class.*

Le Pré aux Clercs/Trois Faisans (13 Place de la Libération; phone 8067-11-33): Considering its choice situation (just opposite the ducal palace, in heavily trod tourist territory), the Pré aux Clercs, over the sustained period that I have known it, maintains standards—fare is typically Burgundy-tasty—and a sense of decorum. You are welcomed cordially to this venerable stone-walled salon, and in the evening red candles in silver sticks illuminate tables. There are two prix-fixe menus—opening, for example, with smoked ham, a vegetable terrine, or Burgundy-style lamb brains, with entrées of pork filet, breast of chicken in tarragon-mushroom sauce, or filet of beef; with cheese and pastries following. The à la carte—including foie gras de canard, quenelles de brochet, kidneys flambés, to cite a trio of choices—is commendable, too. *First Class.*

Le Rallye (39 Rue Chabot-Charny; phone 8067-11-55) pleases both with appearance—pale green draperies contrast with ivory-hued walls and table linens—and with cuisine. Select the prix-fixe menu based on such entrées as filet of beef, fricassée of chicken with foie gras garlic-scented, or médaillon of pork prepared with prunes, in the manner of the region. And order meringues Chantilly to conclude. Very nice. *First Class.*

Bar Brasserie du Théâtre (1-bis Place du Théâtre; phone 8067-13-59) shares a square with the handsome municipal opera house (below) but is nothing like as grand. Therein lies its principal plus: tasty meals from either of two menus, based on entrées like roast pork and roast lamb, and with a bonus of outdoor tables that are a pleasure during warm-weather months. *Moderate.*

Chasse Royale (15 Place de la Libération; phone 8030-13-45) is a neighbor of Le Pré aux Clercs Restaurant (above). Asked to make a choice between it and Chasse Royale, I would opt without any question for Pré aux Clercs. Chasse Royale appears to have an out-front staff of two, at least in my experience, so that service can be coolly impersonal and painfully slow, and fare okay (jambon persillé) to downright disappointing (a chicken dish called poulet à la vigneronne). I can't recommend this one. *First Class.*

Rôtisserie (with its own entrance at the side of Central Urbis Hôtel, Place Grangier; phone 8030-44-00) is big and busy—locals pack it at lunch—and as good a place as any in town to try such Burgundian specialties as œufs en meurette (eggs poached in a red-wine sauce), soupe au vin (vegetable-flecked, wine-based bouillon) and bœuf Bourguignon—to name a few. Prix-fixe menus or à la carte. *First Class.*

La Chouette (1 Rue de la Chouette; phone 8030-18-10) occupies a smallish room in a half-timbered fifteenth-century house, sets a fussy-looking table—lace cloths over pink undercloths, with floral-patterned china and elaborately etched stemware—and offers a relatively skimpy prix-fixe—blanquette de veau (veal stew) and minced lamb casserole are typical entrées—which does not leave you especially content when you've concluded, no doubt because the cooking is competent but without flair; and service, though correct, is distinctly cool. *First Class.*

Nouvelles Galeries (41 Rue de la Liberté): The café-*salon de thé* of the Dijon link of a national department-store chain is convenient and central. *Moderate.*

Café de la Poste (43 Rue des Forges): Take an outdoor table and steep in the atmosphere of Old Dijon—and the passing pedestrian parade. *Moderate.*

Café le Glacier (19 Place Darcy): Ice cream, of course, but coffee or a drink are options in this smart café. *Moderate.*

Rôtisserie du Chambertin (Gevrey-Chambertin; phone 8034-33-20): I have lunched in this stone-walled, tapestry-hung restaurant in the course of two Gevrey-Chambertin visits, and on each I have enjoyed perfectly delicious traditional fare. Order foie gras frais, snails, œufs en meurette, or mussel soup as openers; grilled lobster, tournedos of beef topped with a trio of superb sauces, thyme-scented lamb chops, and an extraordinary coq au vin are among the hearty entrées. Opt for cheese to accompany the obviously excellent wine you're drinking. For dessert: the day's soufflé, floating island, or cassis sherbet doused with cassis. *Luxury.*

La Côte d'Or (Nuits St.-Georges; phone 8061-06-10)—red-walled, its windows smartly draped, Louis XV chairs at its tables—sets a super table. There is a trio of prix-fixe menus. Consider opening with the house's own pigeon pâté, snails in pastry, or smoked salmon. Fish dishes—a seafood platter, especially—are special here. But you are in Burgundy; beef is excellent. And desserts are rich. *Luxury.*

La Cambuse (8 Rue Fevret, Semur-en-Auxois; phone 8097-06-78): You're heart-of-town; come in for lunch after a visit to the neighboring Church of Notre-Dame, selecting a menu embracing snails or jambon persillé, coq au vin, or a beef entrée; pastry to conclude. *First Class.*

De la Poste et du Lion d'Or Hôtel Restaurant (Vézelay; phone 8633-21-23) is hardly as aged as nearby Basilique Ste.-Madeleine—your prime reason for a Vézelay visit. But it *is* a landmark. Open with a duck terrine or snails in a Chablis sauce, hoping that the chicken fricassee will be among the rib-sticking entrées. *First Class.*

L'Étoile Hôtel Restaurant (4 Rue des Moulins, Chablis; phone 8642-10-50): If you're motoring from the north or west, Chablis may well be your point of entry into Burgundy—and you may well be famished. This long-on-scene spot will fill the bill for a nourishing lunch, ideally based on an entrée of, say grilled trout, to be accompanied by a bottle of the celebrated wine bearing the village's name. *First Class.*

L'Espérance (St.-Père-sous-Vézelay, just east of Vézelay; phone 8633-20-45), in a manor house flanked by a lovely garden that's river-edged, is at once a hotel (there are 17 no-two-alike rooms and a quartet of suites) and a restaurant of national significance, with its cuisine based on that of Burgundy albeit with the chef-propriétaire's creative accents. You want to book for lunch—when the menu is considerably less pricey than in the evening—setting your sights on such specialties as truffled foie gras, oysters en gelée, and lobster as you have not previously encountered it. Special. Member, Relais et Châteaux. *Luxury.*

L'Abbaye St.-Michel (Tonnerre; phone 8655-05-99) is conveniently situated about midway between Chablis and Auxerre, making it a gala destination for lunch as you are going into or departing from eastern Burgundy; or as an overnight layover. Setting is a long-desanctified, medieval-origin Benedictine abbey set amid pretty rolling hills. There are 10 no-two-quite alike rooms and 5 suites. And the restaurant is one of considerable consequence. Order the multicourse menu, knowing that whatever that day's selections—appetizers, fish, lamb and other meats, luscious desserts—you are bound to be content. Member, Relais et Châteaux. *Luxury.*

SHOPPER'S DIJON

Wine and mustard—the big Dijon specialities—first: *La Cour au Vin* (3 Rue Jeannin), though hardly in a league with Marché au Vin in Beaune (chapter 8), conducts several daily tastings (at a charge), will ship wine it sells, and has a shop with accessories like glasses and *tastevins. Grey-Poupon,* a leading mustard manufacturer, maintains a retail shop at 32 Rue de la Liberté, which is elegant enough to be a *parfumerie,* and sells its product in ordinary jars and fancy pottery jugs as well. *Nouvelles Galeries* and the delightfully named *Au Pauvre Diable* department stores are on Rue de la Liberté, along with such shops as *Mulot & Petitjean* (chocolates and cassis-flavored candies typical of Dijon), and *Maille* (mustard). Place de la Libération's stores include *Duché de Bourgogne*—a source of wine, mustard, cassis, pain d'épices, and local crafts; Rue Verrerie abounds in antique shops, including *Las Crédence Buisson* (eighteenth-century pieces), and *Au Vieux-Dijon* (small objects).

SOUND OF MUSIC

Théâtre Municipal (Place du Théâtre, Dijon)—strikingly neoclassic, with tall Corinthian columns fronting its facade—is for opera, concerts, and ballet. Monthly calendars of events are available from the tourist office (address below).

INCIDENTAL INTELLIGENCE

Further information: Office de Tourisme, Place Darcy, Dijon; Office de Tourisme, 1 Quai de la République, Auxerre; Office de Tourisme, Place Gaveau, Semur-en-Auxois.

18

Grenoble

Edging the Alps

BACKGROUND BRIEFING

It is no wonder that Grenoble has served as a site of the Winter Olympics. This is a lively southeastern city flanking the French Alps, with a spectacular backdrop of always snowy peaks.

Grenoble's situation, at the foot of the Belledone massif, with the Isère River cutting through it, has been a magnet since Romans settled in, close to 2000 years back. The city they called *Gratianapolis* gradually became the more Gallic Grenoble, passing successively to rule from Burgundy to the north, Provence to the south, the area's own dauphins of Viennois (whose title eventually came into use as the name of the Dauphiné region, remaining so to this day) and, in the mid-fourteenth century—about the time the celebrated University of Grenoble was founded—the French crown.

Contemporarily, the university's sprawling suburban campus appears more successful at luring foreigners—it has more students from other countries than any other French university—than does the city proper, with respect to foreign tourists. This is a town that makes its money on industry generated by rich hydroelectric resources and on nuclear research. Wealth notwithstanding, there's not a single luxury hotel. Withal, the Grenoble restaurant and shopping scenes are substantial, and if the city's visitor attractions are relatively limited—the sole requisite, in my view, is an art museum that's one of France's best—an attractive core and the region surrounding compensate.

ON SCENE

Lay of the Land: Get to know Grenoble by starting at the top. Or, I should say, ascending to the top. Hie yourself to *Quai Stéphane-Jay,* adjacent to *Jardin de la Ville,* a square rather than a garden, just below the Isère River as it flows past the core of town. This is the site of the station for the *téléphérique,* or cable car, from which you may descend to *La Bastille,* a onetime fortress at an elevation of 1,400 feet, affording vistas of city, river, and assorted Alpine peaks. (Ideally, select a clear day and arrive in time for a summit lunch-cum-panorama at a restaurant below recommended.) Back in town, orient yourself from *Place Grenette,* heart of the old sector of the city, *Vieux-Grenoble,* with café tables spilling into it. Extending northeast from it, pedestrians-only *Grande Rue* proceeds to historic *Place St.-André,* dominated by the church whose name it takes. Take *Rue de la République* leading southeast from Place Grenette, and you'll soon arrive at *Place de Verdun,* site of the art museum. Go southwest from Place Grenette along pedestrians-only *Rue Félix Putlat,* and you arrive at *Place Victor Hugo,* entry point for *Avenue Alsace-Lorraine,* the street with the city's smartest shops, which terminates at *Place de la Gare* and the railway station.

Musée de Peinture et de Sculpture (Place de Verdun): The important French provincial cities all have substantial fine-arts museums; Lyon, Bordeaux, Dijon, Rouen, Toulouse, Marseille, Strasbourg, and Montpellier are all top class in this respect, and smaller spots like Pau, Colmar, and St.-Tropez have stellar collections, too. None of these, however, surpasses Grenoble. The beauty of this museum—I refer to the paintings rather than the nondescript setting—is that it is strong in several areas. European Old Masters, the French seventeenth century, and, most especially, modern work—the Impressionists, postimpressionists, and recent painters, as well. Consider such works as La Tour's kneeling *St. Jerome,* cross in hand; Vouet's *Rest on the Flight into Egypt;* Philippe du Champaigne's *Christ on the Cross* and his *St. John the Baptist,* direct and youthful; La Hure's *Supper at Emmaus,* oddly reminiscent of the work of Veronese; Le Brun's *St. Louis Praying for Christians Suffering from the Plague;* Jouvenet's multicharacter *Martyrdom of St. Ovid;* Largillière's portraits of a self-satisfied *Jean de Creponne* and of *Elizabeth de Beauharnais;* Desportes's opulent *Fruit, Flowers and Animals;* and the landmark painting of the group, Lorrain's *Roman Countryside: Morning.* Contemporaries of these Frenchmen are represented, too: Rubens and Jordaens, for example; a brilliant Zurbarán quartet; and a clutch of Dutch still-lifes and landscapes. Earlier Italians—Veronese, Tintoretto, Bassano—are present, as well. Later French painters are strong—Rigaud, Greuze, Vigrée-Lebrun, to name an eighteenth-century trio at random—with Italians of that epoch, like Canaletto, Tiepolo, and Guardi, to complement them. From the French nineteenth century, Ingres, Fantin-Latour, Courbet, and Corot are all on scene. You ascend a steep stairway to the top floor, then, for Impressionists and their successors: Monet, Sisley, Renoir, Utrillo. But it is the twentieth-century work that stuns: Chagall and Klee, Miró and Magritte, Cocteau and Tanguy, Van Dongen and Le Corbusier, Modigliani and Soutine, Léger and

Picasso, Gris and Braque, Vuillard and Bonnard, Matisse and Vlaminck. An all-Europe ranker.

Musée Dauphinois (Rue Maurice-Gignoux) is as good a reason as any to cross over to the Isère's North Bank. Indeed, the museum's quarters—a creatively converted seventeenth-century monastery perched atop a hill and affording fine perspectives of the river and the city—is at least as impressive as the exhibits. These fill a couple of floors that surround a grassy cloister. A mixed bag here: regional Roman mosaics, Merovingian soldiers' helmets, pottery running a range of centuries, prints and portraits and posters, furniture (some especially good eighteenth-century pieces) and frescoes, and an absorbing section on the life-style of people in the mountain villages and farms, labeled *Gens de Là-Haut.*

Vieux-Grenoble: A half-day's stroll might include visits to the *Cathedral of Notre-Dame* (Place Notre-Dame)—as old as the Romanesque tenth century, but with Gothic and Renaissance additions and later restoration, the lot adding up to a composite that is not a special esthetic treat; *Church of St.-André,* built by the dauphins, whose name the region takes, in the twelfth century and with a fine Gothic interior—choir, especially—and a graceful spire; *Palais de Justice* (Place St.-André), for long the dauphins' palace/parliament, with superb woodwork; and *Musée Stendhal* (Jardin de Ville), on the ground floor of the onetime city hall, with mementoes of the Grenoble-born author in and about a furnished-in-period eighteenth-century salon.

Musée de la Résistance (14 Rue Jean-Jacques Rousseau)—another single-room museum, not unlike the Stendhal (above) in that regard, but with its theme Grenoble's valiant Resistance movement during World War II. Pay your respects.

Parc Paul-Mistral, southeast of the center, is pilgrimage territory for sports and modern architecture buffs, with structures built for the 1968 Winter Olympics, including the futuristic *Palais des Sports* (seating 10,000) and *Stade de Glace,* the ice stadium.

La Grande Chartreuse (near Voiron, 14 miles north of Grenoble) is the headquarters monastery of the reclusive Carthusian monks (and of a companion group of somewhat less reclusive brothers). It's a magnificently facaded Renaissance complex spanning an isolated forest-encircled high valley. Because of the nature of this nine-century-old contemplative order, the monastery proper is not visitable. However, adjacent to the nearby—and visitable—distillery where the Carthusians still make their celebrated Chartreuse liqueur, they have created a museum in *La Corrèrie,* a complex used in the past by the order's brothers. Exhibits include a full-scale mockup of a typical cell, along with showcases of monks' habits, sacred art objects, and paintings, the lot of these alongside a Carthusian-built chapel, open to visitors. I was told, by distillery executives—who market and distribute the monks' liqueur—that there are fewer than 50 monks resident from countries around the world, that they speak only on Sundays in the course of communal walks lasting several hours, and that close family members may visit them, albeit very rarely. From the excellent Carthusian-written, English-language guidebook to the museum, one learns that because the monks live out entire lives in solitude (except for morning, evening, and middle-of-the-night communal worship and the Sunday walks) their cells—hermitages, actually—are relatively capacious duplexes where they sleep, eat (meals are brought to them by brothers), pray, study, work (chopping wood, for example, in winter), and garden (each cell has a little plot). And—again, I quote the guidebook: "The [monks'] food is simple, but adapted to the conditions of the life, and normally Carthusians reach the age of 80 and even beyond."

Château de Berenger (Sassenage, four miles west of Grenoble) is closest to the city of several eminently visitable castles. Berenger, backed by mountains, severely mansard-roofed, is a seventeenth-century house, with a suite of reception rooms—salon, library, dining room—mostly eighteenth-century in decor, shown on guided visits.

Château de Vizille (10 miles south of Grenoble), considerably more ambitious than Berenger—indeed, it is ranked as the premier Renaissance château of Dauphiné—dominates its own lake-centered park. State rooms—a magnificently paneled library, especially—are sumptuous. It was at Vizille that representatives of Dauphiné towns—450 strong—declared themselves in favor of the French Revolution in 1788. (Grenoble was strongly antiroyal during this period, and there's a *Museum of the French Revolution* in the castle.) For a period, the castle served as a summer residence of presidents, including Auriol, Coty, and de Gaulle.

Château de Touvet (18 miles north of Grenoble and the same distance south of Chambéry, chapter 5) goes back, originally, to medieval times. But it is, today, essentially eighteenth-century and very handsome, with a grand stairway dominating its entry hall, salons furnished with Louis XIV and Louis XV pieces, and formal gardens.

Crémieu (47 miles north of Grenoble) is a remarkably intact village that is a throwback to the days when dauphins ruled Dauphiné.

Visit *Château Delphinal,* high on a hill over town, and for long where the dauphins lived; *Cloître des Augustins*—an ancient monastery—one of a cluster of mellow structures on *Place de la Nation;* a superb covered market, or *Halles,* of the fourteenth century; and twelfth-century *Chapelle de St.-Antoine.*

Chemin de Fer Touristique de la Mure is just what it sounds like: a made-for-tourists mountain railway that runs from *St.-Georges-de-Commiers,* 12 miles east of Grenoble—through a roller-coaster-like maze of passes, tunnels, and bridges, past peaks as high as 10,000 feet, mirrorlike lakes, and jagged cliffs—to *La Mure,* journey's end. The line opened as long ago as 1888 and was electrified in the early years of this century, when the cars you will ride were built. Allow a day for the adventure, which may be booked through the Office de Tourisme in Grenoble (address below).

SETTLING IN

Mercure Alpotel (12 Boulevard Maréchal-Joffre; phone 7687-88-41) is a little closer to the center of town than the Park (below), but not all that much. Otherwise, it is commendable—with 90 modern, well-planned, and well-equipped rooms leading from its high-ceilinged lobby; a worth-knowing-about, good-value restaurant; generous buffet breakfasts and bar-lounge. Congenial. *Moderate.*

Angleterre Hôtel (5 Place Victor-Hugo; phone 7687-32-21): Happiness in Grenoble is a room at the Angleterre, with French doors giving onto a terrace and Place Victor-Hugo out front. The lobby-bar-lounge of this elderly but refurbished house is clean-lined contemporary; decor of the 70 rooms—which can be small but are equipped with satisfactory baths—is country-rustic. Central and friendly. Breakfast only. *Moderate.*

Ibis Hôtel (Îlot des Trois Dauphins; phone 7647-48-49) is heart-of-town and one of the more attractive links of this France-wide chain that I have encountered. Decor embraces blond woods, pale walls, primary-color textiles. One could wish for thicker mattresses, but there is an agreeable restaurant (later counseled) as compensation. *Moderate.*

Park Hôtel (10 Place Paul-Mistral; phone 7687-29-11) is contemporary. There are 50 rooms decorated in a mix of traditional and modern; bar-lounge and little limited-menu café that can be a convenience, given the away-from-center location of the hotel, whose combination reception-concierge-cashier desk is staffed by well-intentioned, albeit not necessarily professional, young people. *First Class.*

Grand Hôtel (5 Rue de la République; phone 7644-49-36): You must not be swayed by the name. The Grand's ace-in-the-hole is a central location and 75 clean rooms with baths. Corridors, when last I saw them, were gloomy; reception staff, in the course of that inspection, disagreeable. Breakfast only. *Moderate.*

DAILY BREAD

Chez la Mère Ticket (13 Rue Jean-Jacques Rousseau; phone 7645-44-40) typifies the unpretentious bistros, invariably with female owner-chefs, that dot southern cities. There is, to be sure, pink linen on the tables of this narrow, two-floor spot. It is otherwise quite plain—until you order. Start with a platter of charcuterie that is bound to include slices of ham and a variety of superb sausages, with coarse bread accompanying. Continue with truite meunière vivante—the fish plucked live from a tank and prepared to your order. Go on, then, to poulet aux écrevisses, chicken and shrimp served with gratin Dauphinois, the region's brilliant potato casserole. And desserts—if you're up to them—are very good. *Moderate.*

La Poularde Bressane (12 Place Paul-Mistral; phone 7687-08-90) is away from the center, but worth the taxi ride, with decor a successful mix of Belle Époque and contemporary and cuisine a blend of traditional and contemporary. Lean to the former, and there are such successful openers as crayfish-stuffed ravioli in a savory sauce, or mussel and shrimp salad. Entrées are more stick-to-the-ribs—navarin d'agneau (lamb stew with young vegetables), roast duck with mushrooms, filet of Charolais beef. Gracious service. *First Class.*

Le Pommerois (1 Place aux Herbes; phone 7644-30-02) has good looks as a major plus; it's quartered in a venerable house on a fine old square, with the ambience smartly rustic, a contrast to be sure, with the contemporary-influenced cuisine. Best buy is the prix-fixe menu, which opens with amuse-gueules, tiny slices of salami, radishes, puff pastry canapés; continue with a rich foie gras. Sliced breast of duck is a good entrée, served with a quartet of vegetables. Hot desserts—an apple and almond tarte, for example—are memorable. *First Class.*

Pique-Pierre (St.-Martin-le-Vinoux, two miles north of the center of Grenoble; phone 7646-12-88): Would that this lovely restaurant were closer in. Still, its regional specialties makes it worth visiting; a prix-fixe meal might run to gratin de moules Florentine—a spinach and mussels casserole—deliciously prepared veal or chicken entrées, and choices of cheese and dessert. Friendly. *First Class.*

À la Bastille (La Bastille, atop the *téléphérique;* phone 7642-09-74) is indicated for lunch on a clear, sunny day, say, soup and entrecôte aux frites, with fruit tart to conclude. No charge for the view. *Moderate/First Class.*

À la Table Ronde (7 Place St.-André; phone 7644-51-41): Forget about associations with King Arthur that the title might imply. This long-established restaurant on a long-established square specializes in Alsatian cuisine; go with an appetite for the copious choucroute garnie. Fun. *First Class.*

Ibis Hôtel Restaurant (Îlot des Trois Dauphins; phone 7647-48-49) is just the ticket for an unpretentious lunch. Omelets, salads, roast chicken are reliable; mousse au chocolat is a wise dessert choice. Attractive. *Moderate.*

Le Bœuf Mironton (9 Avenue Alsace-Lorraine; phone 7646-01-64): Given its location on Grenoble's classiest shopping street, this restaurant's three-course prix-fixe menus are good value. Open with house terrine, continue with escalope de veau, conclude with a sweet and, in fine weather, dine on the terrace. *Moderate.*

Café Le Grenette (Place Grenette): Seat yourself for coffee or a giant ice-cream concoction, to watch the passing parade on the city's handsomest square. *Moderate.*

Café du Tribunal (Place St.-André)—a coffee stop on a scenic square. *Moderate.*

Beau-Site Hôtel Restaurant (St.-Pierre-de-Chartreuse; phone 7688-61-34) is appropriate for lunch, in combination with an excursion to La Grande Chartreuse (above). Order one of the prix-fixe menus, with such options as crayfish mousse to start, jugged venison as an entrée, and cheese to follow, with the house's own black currant sherbet, vodka-laced, for dessert. *First Class.*

La Petite Auberge (Crémieu; phone 7690-75-45) appeals after a morning's exploration in this venerable village (above). Order the menu, making sure gratin Dauphinois is included. *First Class.*

SHOPPER'S GRENOBLE

Dames de France (Grande Rue, off Place Grenette) and *Prisunic* (Rue Lafayette) are leading department stores. The heart-of-town daily produce market is eminently visitable, on aptly named *Place du Marché.* Rue Bayard and Rue Voltaire constitute between them Antiques Row. Rue de Burdet has such fine shops as *Bally* (shoes), *Rodier* (women's clothes), and *Burdet* (porcelain). And chic Avenue

Alsace-Lorraine's boutiques include *Terrier* (men's accessories), *Paul* (women's duds), *Imperial House* (leather), *Robert Detraz* (men's and women's clothes), and *Rivoire* (chocolates, with a *salon de thé* in connection).

AFTER DARK

Maison de la Culture (Rue Paul Claudel) is Grenoble's architecturally innovative, ever-so-modern, multifunction cultural complex, with its several theaters (one of them features a revolving stage) venues for plays and other entertainment.

Théâtre Municipal (Rue Hector Berlioz) presents opera and ballet, and—just opposite—*Salles des Concerts* is the leading location for classical music.

INCIDENTAL INTELLIGENCE

Aéroport Grenoble-St.-Geoirs is a substantial 27 miles from town, but is served by buses that depart in time for principal flights to major French cities. *Further information:* Maison du Tourisme Dauphiné-Grenoble, 14 Rue de la République, Grenoble.

19

Honfleur

Normandy's Enchanted Village

BACKGROUND BRIEFING

Credit Honfleur with resilience. Everyone—from transoceanic explorers of half a millennium back to contemporary explorers, strolling its horseshoe-shaped inner harbor this very moment—has paid calls. And a clutch of the last century's Impressionist artists—headquartered in a farmhouse that is now a respected restaurant—interpreted the Honfleur scene in paintings that hang in museums from Chicago to Copenhagen. Withal, Honfleur has accepted celebrity with good grace and good sense. Summer congestion notwithstanding, it remains, season in and season out, Normandy's enchanted village.

It was during the sixteenth and seventeenth centuries that Honfleur knew its Golden Age—hardly less than it deserved after nearly three decades of English occupation in the course of the earlier Hundred Years War. Then came the captains and their crews. No question but that the most celebrated was Samuel de Champlain, who first visited Quebec as early as 1604. But there were other pioneer explorers: Dinot Paulmier de Gonneville, who journeyed to Brazil in 1503; Jean Denis, who, in 1506, made it to the coast of Newfoundland and the mouth of the St. Lawrence River; and Pierre Berthelot, an early-seventeenth-century wanderer in Asia.

As early as the start of the nineteenth century, descendants of the very same English who came as soldiers in the fifteenth century arrived to paint. Richard Bonington, better known in Britain today than in the United States, and J. M. W. Turner—challenged by the clarity of the light and the beauty of villages flanking the Channel shore—joined such French painter-pioneers of the region as Corot and Daubigny and others of the so-called Barbizon school (named for the village where they had congregated, near Paris). Later, at mid-century, Honfleur-born painter Eugène Boudin served as a kind of catalyst for a movement of painters—quartered at hospitable Mère Toutain's Ferme St.-Siméon, just outside of town—whose work of the period, as members of the so-called St.-Siméon school, influenced the paths of Impressionism. They included, besides the prolific Boudin (for whom an Honfleur museum is named and whose Norman harbor scenes are his trademark), such French talents as Claude Monet and Alfred Sisley, the American James McNeill Whistler, and the Dutchman Johann Jongkind. French writers came too—the poet Baudelaire the best known.

ON SCENE

Lay of the Land: This is a small town, easily and delightfully negotiable on foot. Inner harbors are four in number—*Bassin de Retenue* (largest and most distant from the core), *Bassin de l'Est,* and, the two most important, *Avant Port* (flanked by strategically situated *Quai de la Quarantine* and *Place de l'Hôtel de Ville,* named for the nineteenth-century City Hall dominating it) and, most significant, most painted, and most photographed *Vieux Bassin*—a rectangle formed by seventeenth-century houses on *Quais Ste.-Catherine* and *St.-Étienne,* along with the landmark *Lieutenance,* a Renaissance mansion that long served as the seat of the lieutenant of the port, and a charmer of a single-steeple, essentially fourteenth-century church, *St.-Étienne,* that's now a museum (below). *Rue des Logettes,* just west of Vieux Bassin, separates it from another landmark square, *Place Ste.-Catherine. Rue de la Ville,* a few blocks to the east, is the site of tiny *Grenière à Sel*—a salt warehouse dating to the seventeenth century. That street, in tandem with *Rue de la Prison,* constitutes the core of the pedestrian shopping area. Historic *Place Arthur-Boudin* is eminently inspectable, too, as are facades of venerable houses on such streets as *Rue Brûlée, Rue du Puits,* and *Rue de la Bavole.*

Musée Municipal Eugène Boudin (Rue de l'Homme de Bois) surprises, first off, with its modernity. It went up as recently as 1974, to honor the distinguished Honfleur-born Impressionist. Be assured that it displays works of his, including a pair of evocative cloudscapes of the beach at Trouville, with pastels and drawings as well. Boudin's fellow Ferme St.-Siméon colleague, Jongkind, is represented, and so is Honfleur-born Dubourg, a talented watercolorist. Monet's painting of the local Church of Ste.-Catherine (below) is a special treat. So is work by Dufy that includes a self-portrait and a blue-and-orange Normandy wheatfield. Paintings by lesser-known artists are hardly less appealing; especially those with local settings, including harbor scenes by André Hambourg and Gelso Lagar. On your way out, take in the gallery of amusing nineteenth-century posters and still another display—of traditional Norman applied arts, furniture and costumes particularly.

Church of Ste.-Catherine (Place Ste.-Catherine) is a one-of-a-kind wood structure, distinctive not so much for the material with which it was built, but because its Renaissance designer-constructors were shipwrights. Take a look at vaulting of the principal nave, and what you have is a downside-up hull of a venerable sailing vessel. Take your time as you stroll through; there is a second nave, lovely polychrome sculptures, an unexpected display of Renaissance musical instruments near the eighteenth-century organ, and in the detached, separately entered *Clocher de Ste.-Catherine*—the bell tower of the church—there's a mixed-bag exhibit of religious art, carved wood, and maritime regalia, which constitutes a branch of Musée Eugène Boudin (above).

Musée de la Marine (Quai St.-Étienne) has an inspired location: old St.-Stephen's Church (above). Model-ship buffs are happy here; but displays run to all manner of objects relating to maritime Honfleur—prints and paintings, documents and drawings.

Musée du Vieux-Honfleur (Rue de la Prison) reproduces—and with a striking sense of realism—interiors of Norman houses: sailor's kitchen through merchant's salon, along with a superb cache of antique furniture, porcelains, and clothing. Setting is special, too: several joined structures of yore; one is Honfleur's ex-prison.

Church of St.-Léonard (Rue Cachin) is as good an excuse as any to explore the St. Léonard quarter. The church has a disproportionately bulky but pleasing octagonal tower and is mellow Gothic within.

Mont Joli is an eminence just west of town that affords absolutely smashing panoramas not only of Honfleur but of the Seine Estuary and the port city of Le Havre. Nearby is the charming little seventeenth-century *Chapel of Notre-Dame-de-Grâce,* site of annual pilgrimages by Honfleur sailors. Do go up.

SETTLING IN

Ferme St.-Siméon Hôtel (Rue Adolphe Marais, a mile from the center of Honfleur; phone 3189-23-61) is the very same that gave its name to the last century's St.-Siméon school of painters headed by Eugène Boudin (above)—an intricately gabled, brick-facaded, seventeenth-century mansion, perhaps better known contemporarily as a restaurant (below). Its main building shelters a clutch of no-two-quite-alike double rooms, each traditionally decorated with marble baths, whose tubs are supplemented by proper showers. A second building—Le Manoir—is a few hundred yards away, in a garden overlooking the sea, and has similarly comfortable accommodations; there are 38 rooms and suites all told. Relaxing and friendly. Member, Relais et Châteaux. *First Class.*

Cheval Blanc Hôtel (2 Quai des Passagers; phone 3189-13-49) is agreeably situated, heart of town. Its lobby-lounge is half-timbered; its bar is cozy and offers ladder-back chairs; its restaurant is smartly Louis XIII. There are three dozen rooms; those I have inspected are brightly papered and agreeable, and you do well to insist upon one with a harbor view. *First Class.*

Lechat Hôtel (3 Place Ste.-Catherine; phone 3189-23-85): Ivy covers two of the three stories of this ancient stone structure. There are just over two dozen rooms with bath, as well as a commendable restaurant, later evaluated. Super situation. *First Class.*

Écrin Hôtel (away from the center, at 19 Rue Eugène-Boudin; phone 3189-32-39): Madame Blais, whose ebullient personality this immediately likable 20-room house reflects, is partial to the primary colors. No two rooms are alike—red-walled reception; main salon in blue and gold; emerald green-walled, coffered-ceiling library; bedrooms in a veritable rainbow of hues, with furnishings from sixteenth through nineteenth centuries. And yet it all comes together, thanks to Madame Blais's good humor and expertise. Breakfast only. Fun. *Moderate.*

Tour Hôtel (3 Quai de la Tour) is heart of the Honfleur action, with close to 50 functional rooms. Breakfast only. *Moderate.*

DAILY BREAD

Ferme St.-Siméon (Rue Adolphe Marais, a mile from the center of Honfleur; phone 3189-23-61) is both hotel (above) and restaurant. The latter occupies several connected rooms—each with beamed ceilings, antique prints, good paintings—taking up most of the space of the main floor, with a pretty terrace out front for warm-weather meals. Cuisine has for long been—and happily continues to be—authentic and traditional Norman, typical of this region, whose name is synonymous with superb cooking. At dinner, you order from an extensive à la carte menu (each dish, printed first in French, is accurately translated into English). Starters include a tasty fish soup, eggs scrambled in a shrimp sauce, and a refreshing seafood salad. Seafood entrées—grilled lobster with sauce Béarnaise, truffled escalope of salmon, classic sole Normande with mussels, mushrooms and shrimp in a cream sauce—are in themselves worth a Ferme visit, but roast duckling, saddle of lamb, and saddle of rabbit are tempting, too. Dessert choice is fabulous—there's a table full of tempters. What I counsel, though, is the house's celebrated hot apple tart served with a generous pitcher of heavy Norman cream. Bear in mind that there are solid-value prix-fixe menus weekdays at lunch. *Luxury.*

Lechat Hôtel Restaurant (3 Place Ste.-Catherine; phone 3189-23-85): Aged Norman apple presses are fashioned into lamps on the attractively laid tables of this heart-of-Honfleur eatery. Lobster, served in a number of ways, is the big specialty. But you do well, too, with such entrées as seafood au gratin and coq au vin. Prix-fixe menus are good value. *First Class.*

Deux Ponts Restaurant (20 Quai de la Quarantine; phone 3189-04-37) is enviably placed, heart of the harbor, and with seafood (including mussels and oysters) in abundance; sole Normande, of course, but the day's catch, simply grilled, if you so order. Temptingly tabbed menus. *Moderate.*

Au Bon Cidre (17 Quai de la Quarantine; phone 3189-04-24) is the ideal setting for an introduction to Norman cider; you'll find it cool, tart, and refreshing. And you do well to drink it in tandem with a savory crêpe or two; the species called Normande is filled with ham and cheese. *Moderate.*

Café de la Voile au Vent (Quai St.-Étienne) is indicated for close observation of the ambulatory Honfleur scene. *Moderate.*

INCIDENTAL INTELLIGENCE

Alas, trains do not serve Honfleur. Nearest railway stations are at Pont-l'Évêque (10 miles south) and Pont-Audemer (14 miles southeast), from both of which towns there is scheduled bus service to Honfleur. There is frequent bus service, as well, between Honfleur and points along the coast, including Deauville and Caen. *Further information:* Office de Tourisme, 33 Cours des Fossés, Honfleur.

20

Loire Valley Châteaux

Tours to Orléans

BACKGROUND BRIEFING

Beginnings were not all that different from beginnings elsewhere in France. The wooded hills that sloped to the shores of the Loire—the nation's longest river, swinging southwest at Orléans, past Tours to the port of Nantes (chapter 30) at its Atlantic estuary—knew early Romans, whose handiwork still is to be seen in regional museums. There were early Christians—St. Martin of Tours is surely the most celebrated—and the inevitable invading barbarians.

Then, with the advent of the Middle Ages, the Loire Valley's situation and terrain attracted feudal baronies, each with its own derring-do castle atop a riverview hillock. Counts of Blois opposed Counts of Anjou, and Plantagenets became so aggressive that one of them (Henry II) assumed the throne of the English enemy.

It was only the twelfth century. Some two hundred years later, the English were back again, a thorn deep in France's side for the long, difficult span of the Hundred Years War. Its end came about only when a woman still in her teens—who was to become patron saint of France—routed the English from the Loire Valley city of Orléans (which celebrates that occasion each spring).

Jeanne d'Arc's miraculous victory paved the way for a clutch of Italian-influenced kings—charming, well-educated, meticulously organized François I was the most brilliant of the group, which included Louis XI, Charles VIII, and Louis XII—to build a network of Loire Valley castles wherein, with courtiers—whose ranks included painters, writers, musicians, philosophers, architects, landscapists and, yes, chefs, as well as couturiers—they developed a life-style that saw the national culture reach a zenith that to this day evokes admiration and awe; they brought to fruition the French Renaissance.

ON SCENE

Lay of the Land: Nobles and wealthy merchants followed kings to the Loire Valley, building smaller, but not necessarily less beautiful, dwellings along the river. There are, today, some 300 eye-filling residences in the valley, and if you seek guidance on the lot of them at this point, you are reading the wrong book. My suggestion is that you settle for what I single out as the top 10—taking in two or three a day over a period of several days—in an area that stretches about 130 miles, from westerly Angers (chapter 4—and including five additional châteaux in its environs) to easterly Orléans, with the region's most engaging city, history-laden Tours, a geographical midships. Tours is the logical headquarters for exploration of a relatively compact region that has no equal anywhere in Europe and that draws more foreign visitors than any region of provincial France, save, of course, the Riviera; with good reason).

Tours, Roman-founded, was celebrated as early as the fourth century, when its Bishop Martin became St. Martin, and again in the sixth century, when its Bishop Gregory became St. Gregory. Two hundred years thereafter, its troops held off invading Moors in the course of what might have been a pan-European conquest. Renaissance kings, starting with Louis XI, used Tours as a supplemental meeting point beyond the confines of nearby châteaux. The proximity of those castles lured theologians and artists, sculptors and weavers to Tours. And, briefly, during the course of two much later wars—Franco-Prussian and World War II—it served as the French capital. It's well planned. The *Loire River,* its northern boundary, parallels busy *Boulevard Heurteloup,* its southern flank, with leading hotels and *Le Printemps* department store, as well as both *Palais de Justice* and *Hôtel de Ville,* at *Place Jean Jaurès,* from which *Rue Nationale* (with *Nouvelles Galeries* and *Monoprix* department stores, as well as many shops) cut north to *Place Anatole France* and a pair of nearby museums. Still another north-south thoroughfare is *Rue du Petit Roi,* connecting Boulevard Heurteloup with *Place de la Cathédrale,* around which are centered the cathedral, fine-arts museum, and *Château de Tours,* housing the relatively recent *Musée Historial.* Eminently walkable streets of *Vieux Tours*—gained by *Rue du Commerce,* leading west from *Rue Nationale*—include *rues Brettoneau, Grand Marché, Rôtisserie,* and *Châteauneuf,* based on *Place Plumereau,* with its lures splendid Renaissance mansions, many half-timbered.

Musée Historial de Touraine (Rue Lavoisier) gets you in the mood—in effect, sets the stage for Loire wanderings. Setting—Château de Tours—is the well-restored fifteenth-century castle that was inhabited by two kings—Charles VII and his son, Louis XI. Idea is to tell the story of the region by means of a series of marvelously detailed dioramas that bring the region's history to life, 31 all told, beginning with St. Martin of Tours blessing a young priest—he will become

St. Patrick—en route to Ireland; moving through the centuries with tableaux evoking the eighteenth-century Battle of Poitiers; the eleventh-century visit of King Richard Cœur de Lion to Château de Chinon; Jeanne d'Arc receiving the Tours-crafted breastplates she later wore in battle against the English; Charles VII, with his beautiful mistress, Agnès Sorel, at Château de Loches; Charles VIII marrying Anne of Brittany at Château de Langeais; Leonardo da Vinci with his patron, François I, at Clos-Luce; the writer Rabelais and the poet Ronsard in local settings; Diane de Poitiers with her lover, Henry II, at Chenonceau; and Mary Queen of Scots, while she was Queen of France, with the first of her three husbands, François II, and his mother, Catherine de Médicis at Amboise.

Tours's *Cathedral of St.-Gatien* is, like the city itself, underappreciated—a great Gothic beauty, with an intricately detailed facade embracing a trio of sculpted portals beneath a rose window, itself surmounted by twin belfries, each topped by an octagonal tower, or lantern. The scale of the interior staggers, with superior stained glass, art-filled chapels, and the adjacent Psalette Cloister, an unexpected treasure.

An utterly beautiful palace in its own garden, adjacent to the cathedral (it had been the archbishop's residence), serves with distinction as Tours's *Musée des Beaux-Arts*. Before you so much as glance at a painting, you envy long-ago clerics their opulent quarters in this building that was erected during the seventeenth and eighteenth centuries. Sculpture is exemplary, with works by Houdon and Bourdelle, among others. Precious eighteenth-century furniture is dotted about. Even the original floors are works of art. Then you observe paintings. There is a pair by Mantegna—a *Resurrection* and *Christ in the Garden*—that stick in your memory. But so many other artists are represented—Frenchmen like Largillière and Nattier, Boucher and Delacroix, and foreigners like Rembrandt and Rubens.

Make time for two more of a number of Tours museums. *Musée Archéologique* (Rue du Commerce) makes its home in an elegant town house; while the city's *Musée des Arts Décoratifs*—antique furniture is its forte—is located in another mansion on Rue Émile Zola.

The city surveyed, you're ready for country castles. Because you'll want to work out your own order of precedence according to the time you've available, my top 10 are presented alphabetically. Châteaux most popular with visitors are Chenonceau (800,000 per year) and Chambord (400,000 per year), with Cheverny, Bois, Villandry, Amboise, and Azay-le-Rideau following; in other words, plan on sharing the sights with crowds, especially in summer.

Amboise surmounts a plateau, surrounded by high walls, a complex dramatically dominating the agreeable riverfront village that takes its name. Quite the most interesting part of the interior is the suite of state rooms—this is one of the châteaux in which François I lived, but so did kings Charles VIII and Louis XI. The single most important element of the château remaining is the Chapel of St.-Hubert (honoring the patron saint of hunters and therefore of interest to Renaissance royals, virtually all of whom hunted avidly)—quite striking flamboyant Gothic. Note, too, a pair of towers, Tour Minimes and Tour Hurtault, one within the other, with an entry ramp—at first for horses, now for cars—to the château. Beyond, on Rue Victor-Hugo, is *Clos-Lucé,* the gracefully gabled, brick manor house where François I installed Leonardo da Vinci, his imported-from-Italy artist-in-residence. The most interesting interior is the room in which Leonardo died in 1519, but there is a lovely chapel and a fair sprinkling of Da Vinciana.

Azay-le-Rideau, detached from the charming village taking its name and—unlike Amboise—completely intact, is set, rather ingeniously, partially straddling the Indre River, partially alongside it. It is sublime in scale, restrained in ornamentation (turrets and chimneys are relatively limited in number; state rooms are dominated by splendid fireplaces), and handsomely furnished. Allow time for a walk about the grounds; Azay is a joy from every angle.

Beauregard went up originally as a hunting lodge for François I, but was later enlarged—and made a considerably more substantial mansion—by a minister of Henri II. It is one of the most serenely situated châteaux of our group of 10—in a vast, green park. You see a number of rooms in the course of a visit—paneled and beamed reception salons, the original kitchen. But you go particularly for the Galerie de Portraits, where attention was paid to ceiling (with exquisitely decorated beams), floor (paved in Delft tiles), and—most especially—walls, hung with 327 portraits of French luminaries, from early Valois dynasty kings and nobles to Louis XIII.

Blois—not unlike Amboise in that it is a town, as well as a castle—is a lesson in early architecture, part Gothic, part Renaissance, part baroque, the lot in four immense wings enclosing an also immense courtyard, where the *chef d'œuvre* is the so-called François I staircase, an inspired octagonal spiral that climbs five stories, on each of which it is intricately sculpted. The royal apartments' architecture compensates for the lack of furniture, with the room used by Catherine de Médicis—intricately paneled and with closets hidden behind some of those panels—the dazzler of the lot. And a museum of French paintings is a surprise. A pair of in-town destinations is noteworthy: *Cathedral of St.-Louis* (Place St.-Louis)—Gothic but with a Romanesque crypt—and, especially for chocoholics, *Chocolaterie Poulain,* for long a Blois institution.

Chambord —in a walled deer park of more than 13,000 acres adjacent to an oddly administered village that is government property (none of its houses is privately owned)—is the most painted, the most photographed, the most chronicled, the most romantic, and also the largest of the Loire châteaux, with well over 400 rooms. You need not enter to be enraptured. Chambord is François I's jewel—elongated, with a circular tower defining each end, its roof an extravagant jumble of pinnacles and turrets, chimneys and domes. Not unlike Blois, Chambord charms with a main staircase. One of but half a hundred, its kicker is a design whereby two spirals are superimposed, with each going its own way, so that if I am going up and you're en route down, we don't see each other. Chambord remained popular long after the Renaissance. All of François I's kingly successors made use of it, including Louis XIV, during whose residence Molière's *Le Bourgeois Gentilhomme* had its first performance; and Louis XV, whose father-in-law—a deposed king of Poland—lived in it until he became duke of Lorraine (chapter 25). Napoleon gave the castle to a courtier; it did not fare well thereafter, but was repurchased and restored by the French government in 1932. Have a walk around, taking in Chambord from a variety of exterior angles before you depart.

Chenonceau is No. 1 in the Château Sweepstakes because it is as beautiful without (it appears to float on the Cher River, and it is set off by formal gardens) as within, and because historical figures most associated with it (Catherine de Médicis, Diane de Poitiers, François I) are so well known. You enter on a drawbridge. Look right to Catherine de Médicis's garden; look left, and the garden is that of Diane de Poitiers. Look at the Cher, and you see it flowing under six exquisite arches that support the château's rectangular wing. The interiors—including bedrooms of both Catherine and François, chapel, library, salons affording river vistas—are unsurpassed in the valley, with furniture, paintings, and tapestries sublime throughout. Allow enough time.

Cheverny's Grand Salon—with the sumptuously worked panels of its walls and ceiling, its paintings and its Régence furniture—is reason enough for a visit. But this sixteenth-century mansion, set back in its own verdant park, pleases on other counts: the fine details of its facade, the breadth of its central stairway, the canopied state bed, the frescoed ceiling and tapestried walls of its Chambre du Roi, the sword collection of its armory, and the fine paintings—with a number by Clouet and Rigaud—throughout.

Chinon is as exciting from the Loire River—it dominates the village below it, taking its name—as from within. You go because it is the valley's most celebrated link with the Middle Ages. It is actually a trio of moated forts in partial ruins, with the central part, Château de Milleu, the site of a museum whose subject is the visit made to Chinon by Jeanne d'Arc; it was there that she met the dauphin—not yet Charles VII—in 1429. Chinon village is at its best in and around Grand Carroi, the core of the old quarter, with adjacent streets lined by aged houses; the house at 15 Rue de la Lamproie was inhabited by the monk-writer-physician Rabelais, whose patron for a time was François I.

Langeais is an appealing mix of moats and battlements and conical towers, set back from carefully tended flowerbeds. But what makes this castle special is the brevity of its period of construction. It went up in less than half a mid-fifteenth-century decade under the aegis of a minister of King Louis XI, in the center of the village that takes its name. A consequence is that it is of a piece, consistent in its architecture and decor and—significant, this—graced by splendid furnishings, in monumentally scaled state rooms, with high, wide, and handsome fireplaces and tapestried walls. Charles VIII and Anne of Brittany married here in 1491.

Villandry: If you've an interest in gardens, it seems to me there are three in France you don't miss: the Tuileries in Paris, to one of whose benches I repair for a tranquil pause in the course of every visit; Versailles, of course; and Villandry, in many ways the most spectacular of the trio. The château itself is interesting in that it was the last of the big ones to be built on the Loire shore. A minister of François I was first owner, but interiors are mostly eighteenth-century. The following century, the nineteenth, a gifted Spanish physician, Joachim Carvallo, and his American-born wife bought Villandry (which is why there are fine paintings by such Spaniards as Goya and Zurbarán within) and set about redesigning the vast garden, which had been allowed to deteriorate over a long period, to its original Renaissance style. Horticulturists now consider it an all-Europe ranker. Skip the house, if you insist, but not this extraordinary trio of vast terraces: kitchen garden, fragrant with jasmine and with giant decorative cabbages, lowest down; ornamental garden at mid-level—the most magnificent, with clipped box and yew trees, heart- and fan-shaped (the theme is love); and, at the top, a maze of moats fed from a central lake and by fountains interspersed throughout.

Other Loire Valley châteaux that you might want to inspect as you journey through the valley include *Chaumont-sur-Loire,* historically significant in that it belonged to Queen Catherine de Médicis in the mid-sixteenth century and was transferred by Catherine to Diane de Poitiers who turned over Chenonceau (above) to Catherine in its stead, with both medieval (crenelated walls) and Renaissance features (including a splendid circular staircase, both Catherine's and Diane's bedrooms, and the tapestried Chambre du Conseil); *Loches,* infamous as a royal prison in the Middle Ages, became a happier place during the Renaissance when Charles VII's mistress, Agnès Sorel, moved in, and which offers as its most noteworthy aspects Anne of Brittany's chapel in the Royal Apartments, a room where Jeanne d'Arc was received by Charles VII, and a pair of small museums; *Talcy,* reconstructed during the Renaissance, retains towers and other architectural aspects from earlier centuries, but is visitable primarily for a cache of superb Renaissance, Baroque, and rococo furniture, on display in a series of spaces, salons as well as bedrooms, with Louis XIV, Louis XV, and Louis XVI pieces stunners; and *Ussé,* as old as the fifteenth century, and as new as the seventeenth, with an interesting facade that mixes Renaissance detailing with Middle Ages proportions, and is visitable within for a smashing long gallery whose walls are surfaced with beautiful tapestries, dominated by a canopied bed fronted by Louis XVI furniture and with a lovely sixteenth-century chapel in the garden. Additional area châteaux—*Saumur, Brissac, Montgeoffrey, Montreuil-Bellay,* and *Plessis Bourré* are detailed in chapter 4.

Orléans—flanking the châteaux at its eastern edge—was badly bombed during World War II, not felicitously reconstructed, and nothing like as well equipped for visitors as Tours (above). Stay long enough, though, to have a look at *Cathedral of Ste.-Croix,* on central Place du Martroi, unusual in that it is essentially a reconstruction—begun in the seventeenth century but not finished until the nineteenth—of a Gothic structure substantially razed by seventeenth-century Protestants. Scale is stupendous, twin towers impressive, flying buttresses dazzling, nave high and long, decorative woodwork elaborate. This same square, with a statue of the city's beloved liberator, Jeanne d'Arc, is the site also of the relatively recent—and handsome—replacement quarters of a long-established *Musée des Beaux-Arts;* with fine portraits, including a Drouais of *Madame de Pompadour,* a Pourbus of *Anne of Austria,* and a de La Tour of *St. Sebastian,* as well as works by such Italians as Tintoretto, Correggio, and Carracci; Dutchmen including Van Goyen; Veláquez among the Spaniards; moderns including Orléans-born Gauguin; and earlier Frenchmen like de Champaigne, Boucher, Robert, Bourdon, Le Nain, and Nattier. Absorbing too, is *Musée Historique* (Rue Ste.-Catherine), located in a nineteenth-century mansion and brimming with sculpture and fragments from regional Roman ruins. And there are dioramas depicting events in her short but exciting life in *Maison de Jeanne d'Arc* (Place du Général de Gaulle).

SETTLING IN

De l'Univers Hôtel (5 Boulevard Heurteloup, Tours; phone 4705-37-12) is a Tours institution, easily dating back a century, with—I must caution at the outset—some of its 88 rooms by no means as nicely or anywhere as recently updated as others. You must specify accommodations that have been given new bathroom fixtures in recent seasons. That accomplished, you can be very happy indeed in this centrally situated, delightfully staffed house, with agreeable public spaces that include a restaurant and bar-lounge. *First Class.*

Jean Bardet Hôtel (57 Rue Groison, Tours; phone 4741-41-41): You're across the Loire, away from the center, here. But if you've a car, this hotel—set in a seven-and-a-half-acre garden, and with a truly outstanding restaurant (reviewed on a later page)—is a wise choice as your Tours headquarters. Monsieur Bardet, at once a creative chef and a skilled hotelier, along with his also-gifted, fluent-in-English wife, Sophie, opened this Napoleon III–style hotel-restaurant in the late 1980s, and I don't know of any latter-day enterprise that has brought Tours more distinction. The hotel—Sophie was chief decorator—is pale-walled in tones of beige and yellow, peach and pink, with a flower-massed lobby-lounge-cum-wickery terrace, the restaurant's French doors give onto the garden, and there are 15 no-two-alike suites (equipped with twin-sink marble baths) and rooms, each with a light and lovely look accented by zingy textiles and furnishings that marry contemporary and traditional. Special. *Luxury.*

De Groison Hôtel (10 Rue Groison, Tours; phone 4741-94-40) is, like the Jean Bardet (above) on the other side of the river from the core of town. This is an eighteenth-century house that has been tastefully transformed into a 10-room hotel and restaurant. Accommodations are no-two-alike; those I have inspected are delightful, with classic-design textiles on walls and as matching draperies and upholstery. All have baths, some twin-sinked. A fireplace dominates the cozy lounge edging the entry, owner-management is cordial, and I write about the good-looking restaurant (Jardin du Castel) on another page. *First Class.*

Central Hôtel (21 Rue Berthelot, Tours; phone 4705-46-44) is accurately titled—heart of town. This is a long-on-scene house with baths in 32 of its 42 rooms. Breakfast only. *Moderate.*

Bordeaux Hôtel (3 Place Maréchal-Leclerc, Tours; phone 4705-40-32) is quite as central as its near-neighbor, the Univers (above), though it's smaller (there are just over half a hundred full-facility rooms) and more modern. The restaurant is so good that I accord it space in a later paragraph. *First Class.*

Gambetta Hôtel (7 Rue Gambetta, Tours; phone 4705-08-35) is an agreeable old-timer, core of Vieux-Tours, with baths in almost all of its rooms of varying sizes (those I have inspected are pleasant; nearly all are traditional-style), many surrounding an ivy-walled courtyard. Breakfast only. *Moderate.*

Les Châteaux de la Loire Hôtel (12 Rue Gambetta, Tours; phone 4705-10-05) is a charming, old-school, Vieux-Tours house, with a handsome lobby-cum-bar and 32 rooms; those I have seen are delightful, and most have baths. Breakfast only. *Moderate.*

Les Hautes Roches Hôtel (86 Quai de la Loire, Rochecorbon, on the Loire near Tours; phone 4752-88-88) is hardly your run-of-the-mill country hotel. This one is quite literally hewn out of the rocks—high rocks—from which it takes its name. Eight of its 11 rooms—all that I have inspected are at once oversize and handsome, with double-sink baths, decor traditional, decorative accents smart—are ex-monastery cells in the cave that is the hotel's core, and there are three more rooms in a modern main building with a dilly of a restaurant. The staff is cordial and professional. Very nice indeed. *Luxury.*

Château d'Artigny Hôtel (Montbazon, 14 miles south of Tours; phone 4726-24-24) is, *sans doute,* grande dame of the region, an early-twentieth-century replacement—built by François Coty, of perfume fame—of a much older castle. Set in its own park and fronted by formal gardens, its high-ceilinged public spaces include the handsomest cocktail lounge in this part of France; oval-shaped restaurant, green-walled and with gilded paneling; and a smasher of a stairway that leads from the long gallery of a lobby to upper floors. Sizes and locations differ but all 33 rooms and suites are Louis XV style, with fine baths. There's a swimming pool in the garden, a pair of tennis courts, and nearby golf and fishing. Service is at once professional and cordial. Member, Relais et Châteaux. *Luxury.*

Le Grand Monarque Hôtel (Place de la République, Azay-le-Rideau; phone 4743-30-08): I can't imagine a more charming venue to overnight, in the course of exploring the valley, than this delightful old-timer, in the village adjacent to the château whose name it takes. Public spaces are welcoming. More than half of the 30 rooms—those I've inspected are very pleasant, indeed—have baths. There's a caged wild boar in the garden (who sleeps most of the time), and the restaurant is exemplary enough to warrant comment in a later paragraph. Friendly. *Moderate.*

Domaine de Beauvois Hôtel (Luynes, eight miles south of Tours; phone 4755-50-11)—set back in a forest-bordered park—is a Baroque château with handsome public spaces, 37 smartly furnished and accessorized rooms and suites, reliable restaurant, and diversion including swimming, tennis, and fishing. Member, Relais et Châteaux. *Luxury.*

Château de Pray Hôtel (Route 571, just outside of Amboise; phone 4757-23-67) is a small but choice château of respectable age, framed by a pair of circular towers, in its own garden, with splendid river views. There are 16 no-two-alike rooms, reliable restaurant, bar-lounge, welcoming staff. *First Class.*

Le Choiseul Hôtel (36 Quai Charles-Guinot, Amboise; phone 4730-45-45), on the banks of the Loire, just opposite Château d'Amboise, is special—a mini château embracing 23 Louis XV–style rooms of varying sizes and a spacious lounge, off which are a bar and picture-windowed restaurant that overlooks the Loire and moves to the garden in summer. *First Class.*

Novotel Amboise (17 Rue des Sablonnières, Amboise; phone 4757-42-07) is a fair distance from the center of Amboise, but so situated that there are panoramic views of the château from half of its 82 clean-lined rooms giving onto the town. This is a contemporary house, with restaurant, bar, swimming pool. *First Class.*

Château de Chissay Hôtel (Chissay, outside of Montrichard and just a few miles from Château de Chenonceau, above; phone 5432-32-01) is the genuine article—a Renaissance castle in the grand manner, set in its own 200-acre park, and with a lineup of former residents that numbers early kings through to General Charles de Gaulle. There are not quite 30 suites and rooms, a good terraced restaurant, and an outdoor pool. *First Class.*

Château de Danzay Hôtel (just outside Chinon; phone 4758-46-86) dates to the fifteenth century, with original furnishings dotted about in public spaces—and in the 7 good-sized rooms-cum-bath-and-fireplace. Breakfast is served in a period-piece room that could be a movie set, but there is no restaurant. *First Class.*

Domaine des Hautes-de-Loire Hôtel (Onzain, near Chaumont-sur-Loire, midway between Tours and Blois; phone 5420-72-57) is a honey of an ivy-walled manor house set in a spacious park, with swans paddling about in the pond out front; antique-furnished public spaces that include a congenial bar and an esteemed restaurant; and 30 rooms and suites, no two identical; each of those I have inspected, delightful. Member, Relais et Châteaux. *First Class.*

Du Château Hôtel (22 Rue Porte-Côte, Blois; phone 5478-20-24) is heart-of-town, just below the château. There are baths in 40 of its 45 rooms and a convenient restaurant. *Moderate.*

Château de Marcay Hôtel (outside of Marcay, just south and west of Chinon; phone 4793-03-47) is every stone and turret the country hotel you have wanted to stay at in the Loire Valley—a fortress château dating to the fifteenth century deftly converted into a honey of a 40-room hostelry. Traditional toile fabric accents decor, which varies in the suites, junior suites, and standard rooms, based on Louis XV, Louis XVI, and Empire styles. The most distinctive quarters are circular suites—in the towers. The restaurant warrants attention in a later paragraph, there's a cozy bar, and an outdoor pool that's a joy in summer. Member, Relais et Châteaux. *Luxury.*

Arcade Hôtel (4 Rue du Maréchal-Foch, Orléans; phone 3854-23-11) has a number of pluses. It's central, modern (there are 125 shower-equipped rooms, although beds can be narrow as in all links of this chain), and with a good-value restaurant and bar as well. *Moderate.*

D'Orléans Hôtel (6 Rue Adolphe Crespin, Orléans; phone 3853-35-34) has the advantage of a central situation in the shopping area, a hop and a skip from the cathedral. The look is agreeably contemporary, and there are 18 well-equipped rooms. Breakfast only. *Moderate.*

Les Cèdres Hôtel (17 Rue du Maréchal-Foch, Orléans; phone 3862-22-92) is closer to the railway station than to the core of town; 28 of its 32 rooms have baths. Breakfast only. *Moderate.*

Sofitel Orléans (44 Quai Barentin, Orléans; phone 3862-17-39) is considerably away from the center, in a nondescript—and by no means attractive—residential quarter. There are 110 functional rooms, smallish restaurant, bar and outdoor pool. Only so-so. *First Class.*

DAILY BREAD

Jean Bardet Hôtel Restaurant (57 Rue Groison, Tours; phone 4741-41-41): You will have read on an earlier page about the handsome hotel operated by Jean and Sophie Bardet. But Monsieur Bardet's restaurant (he is head chef) is at least as exemplary. Setting is a pale yellow space whose French windows are draped in textiles of the same hue, with tables surrounded by gilded English Regency-style chairs, and a staff as expert at serving as the boss is at cooking. Order from the multicourse menu or the à la carte, with the assurance, if my experience is an indicator, that you're not going to go wrong. The point to be made about the Bardet cuisine is that it's inventive but with strong enough roots in tradition to be delicious. Open with a salmon tartar with coulis, or sauce, based on fresh herbs, seafood minestrone, or oyster stew. Entrées—such as roast pigeon with figs and truffled guinea hen with fabulous mashed potatoes—rate A+. Bardet fans do not skip Bardet desserts like China-tea sorbet with a mite of mango, crème brûlée, the socko chocolatine bitter, or the ordered-in-advance, served-warm gratin of caramelized wild strawberries. Excellent cellar. *Luxury.*

Le Jardin du Castel (Hôtel de Groison, 10 Rue Groison, Tours; phone 4741-94-40) is an unlikely but successful mix of crystal chandeliers and ladder-back chairs, with big vases of flowers at strategic intervals. There are several menus, with that offered at weekday lunches—including wine and coffee—the best deal. It might include oysters on the half shell or a seafood platter as openers, continue with breast of chicken and Vouvray-infused cream sauce, or roast duck, concluding with the house's exemplary chocolate cake or floating island. *First Class.*

L'Odéon (10 Place de la Gare, Tours; phone 4720-12-65) is welcoming, pleasant of appearance, and central. And the price is right. A menu might open with cauliflower soup or green salad, continue with entrecôte in an exemplary wine sauce, or a poultry entrée, concluding with cheese or ice cream. Have the house red to accompany. *Moderate.*

La Table Compagnarde (90 Rue Colbert, Tours; phone 4720-38-73) is intimate and friendly and occupies a white-walled setting with red-and-white checked linen on tables. Good-value menus might run to vegetable soup, coq au vin, or a beef ragout, with standard sweets to conclude. *Moderate.*

Café le Vieux Tours (Place Plumérau, Tours) is just the spot for coffee or a drink, in the course of Vieux Tours exploration. *Moderate.*

Les Hautes Roches Hôtel Restaurant (86 Quai de la Loire, Rochecorbon, on the Loire near Tours; phone 4752-88-88)—in a hotel largely hewn from a rocky cliff, about which I write on an earlier page—offers a delicious three-course menu that might offer a sautéed salmon specialty as first course, the day's catch imaginatively prepared, or a meat entrée; with fig tarte to conclude. There are, as well, several plats du jour and a substantial à la carte. Attractive. *First Class* if you select the menu or a plat du jour; otherwise, *Luxury.*

Château de Marcay Hôtel Restaurant (outside of Marcay, just south and west of Chinon; phone 4793-03-47)—the dining room of an atmospheric hotel set in a turreted and towered Renaissance castle—offers candlelight at dinner or, if it's summer, a table on the terrace. The à la carte yields delicious dishes—a simple but superb tomato salad in a vinaigrette dressing or the day's soup among starters, the fish fingers known as goujonettes, or a deliciously sauced filet of beef, with irresistible warm fruit tartes favored dessert choices, and an excellent cellar. Service is at once expert and congenial. An ideal lunch stop in the course of a day's touring. *First Class/Luxury.*

Bordeaux Hôtel Restaurant (3 Place Maréchal-Leclerc, Tours; phone 4705-40-32): For long known as the "Garden of France," Tours is skilled at putting raw ingredients—produce, poultry, meats, cheeses—to expert use. Nowhere is this talent more evident than in this restaurant. Handsome—furniture is Louis XV–style, with sconces and chandeliers of crystal and murals on the walls—and with an expert staff, it offers one of the most delicious, and best-value, prix-fixe menus that I have come upon in France. Open with traditional saucisson chaud—sausages-cum-potatoes. Truite meunière, perfectly prepared, would follow. Entrée would be a hearty coq au vin. Then cheese from a platter, with a choice of tasty desserts to follow. *First Class.*

Les Tuffeaux (19 Rue Lavoisier, Tours; phone 4747-19-89) offers you either a very pricey prix-fixe or à la carte, with the cuisine a competent, if hardly exciting, mix of contemporary and traditional. I suggest sticking to such safe standbys as foie gras frais de canard, fileted fish of the day simply grilled, or filet de bœuf. Desserts are this house at its best; nougat glacé aux framboises—a frozen raspberry confection—is very good. The look is quietly antique. Central. *Luxury.*

Charles Barrier (101 Avenue de la Tranchée, Tours; phone 4754-20-39): You need a car for Barrier, located north of the center, across the Loire, and convenient if taken in tandem with a morning visiting area châteaux. Look is formal—crystal chandeliers, masses of flowers, marble floors, silver candelabra at tables. There are good things to eat, traditional with contemporary touches, from either a prix-fixe menu or à la carte. You might open with truffled eel terrine, consider Loire salmon in a beurre blanc sauce as a fish course, with either the house's special duck or pigeon entrées to follow, and frozen fruit soufflé as a sweet. *Luxury.*

La Rôtisserie Tourangelle (23 Rue du Commerce, Tours; phone 4705-71-21) edges the Vieux Tours quarter, is as good a place as any to open with rillettes—Touraine's own coarse pork pâté—

continuing with a freshwater fish or poultry entrée. Desserts are reliable; prix-fixe menus, good value. Congenial. *First Class.*

Château de Beaulieu (Route Villandry, Joué-les-Tours, two miles southwest of town; phone 4753-20-26) is an eighteenth-century manor house, set back in its own capacious garden, that is at once a country inn (there are 19 traditionally furnished rooms) and a restaurant worth knowing about, in the course of touring the châteaux. There are a couple of decently priced prix-fixe menus, with traditional specialties; local salmon, deliciously sauced, is a highlight, with the house's own cherry dessert counseled. *First Class.*

Le Grand Monarque Hôtel Restaurant (Place de la République, Azay-le-Rideau; phone 4745-40-08): Happiness in the Loire Valley is a sunny morning spent touring Château d'Azay-le-Rideau, with lunch following in the garden of Le Grand Monarque. Prix-fixe menus are good value, and fare is heartily traditional. Build your meal around duckling, Bigarade style, or fresh salmon expertly prepared. Don't skip the cheese course and conclude with a made-on-premises sweet. The owning Jacquet family are gracious hosts. *First Class.*

Monseigneur (12 Quai Charles Guinot, Amboise; phone 4757-08-09): You're just below the château, riverfront. Order the prix-fixe, commencing perhaps with pork rillettes or a game pâté, with an entrée of chicken and chanterelles mushrooms, and a fresh fruit tart to conclude. *Moderate.*

Chez Tantine (on the grounds of the Blois château) could not be more casual or more fun. Madame Tantine, *la patronne,* runs the show, darting about from table to table, barking orders to bar and kitchen. There are a couple of inexpensive prix-fixe menus—unpretentious but tasty. Open, for example, with crudités, a tasty sauce accompanying; continue with grilled pork chops; and conclude with a pastry. *Moderate.*

St.-Michel Hôtel Restaurant (opposite the château, Chambord; phone 5420-31-31) could not be more scenically situated, and it's nicely combined with a château visit. Well-priced prix-fixe menus, with local standbys like rillettes de porc to start, grilled trout or perhaps a game entrée; satisfying sweets. *First Class.* (With nearly 40 *Moderate* category rooms upstairs, should you want to stay the night.)

Au Plaisir Gourmand (2 Rue Parmentier, Chinon; phone 4793-20-48) is not misnamed. The multicourse menu abounds in local specialties, with such house favorites as foie gras teamed with rabbit, river fish interestingly prepared, and desserts embracing fruits and pastry. Service is sprightly, wines good. *First Class/Luxury.*

La Crémaillère (34 Rue Notre-Dame-de-Recouvrance, Orléans; phone 3853-49-17) has the old-fashioned look that becomes an ancient Loire Valley city—Louis XV armchairs in the cocktail area as you enter and a capacious dining room, beige-walled, luxuriantly draped, brass-chandelier-hung, with meticulously appointed tables illuminated at dinner by pink candles. You may order à la carte, but the prix-fixe menu is excellent value. Open with a terrine made from a trio of Loire River fish species or the smoked salmon specialty. Go on then to talented owner-chef Paul Hyart's crayfish-stuffed ravioli. As an entrée, choose pièce de bœuf, an unusual rice-and-veal kidney preparation, or breast of chicken, foie gras–garnished. Cheeses are served from an immense platter. M. Hyart's crème brûlée is indicated for dessert—one of a number of tempters. Sprightly, amicable service. *Luxury.*

L'Aviation (473 Faubourg Bannier, Orléans; phone 3888-71-92) entices with good-value prix-fixe menus. You want to make sure you have such house specialties as freshwater fish in a beurre blanc sauce, médaillions of lamb prepared with the mushrooms called cèpes, or the shrimp-sauced omelet. *Moderate.*

AFTER DARK

Son et Lumière—whereby historic monuments (châteaux in the case of the Loire Valley) are settings for evening entertainments in which piped actors' voices play out local history, while spotlights focus on architectural details—is a French invention; it had its birth in the decade following World War II in the Loire Valley's Château de Chambord. Contemporarily, a substantial number of châteaux present Sound and Light, traditionally June through August, with commentary usually alternating, one night to the other, between the French and English languages. At its best—when professionally staged and lighted, with ranking actors—Son et Lumière is at once good theater and an effortless lesson in history as well as architecture.

INCIDENTAL INTELLIGENCE

The Loire Valley is too often taken in by means of day-long bus excursions out of Paris. I am a firm believer in the maxim that half a loaf is better than none; still, day-tripping the Loire is the coward's way. Come and stay awhile. *Further information:* Office de Tourisme, Place Maréchal-Leclerc, Tours; Office de Tourisme, Quai Général-de-Gaulle, Amboise; Office de Tourisme, 3 Avenue Jean-Laigret, Blois; Office de Tourisme, Place Albert 1er, Orléans.

21

Lyon

France's Second City

BACKGROUND BRIEFING

Whatever Lyon has done, it has done well.

Roman Lyon—*Ludgunum,* founded in 43 B.C.—was more than a colony. It prospered so that the emperors decreed it capital of all Gaul. (And enough of it remains for contemporary Lyonnais to have created one of the great European archeological complexes.)

As early as 12 B.C., Lyon's leaders hosted chiefs of the Gallic tribes at a kind of parliament whose delegates discussed—for the first time—the idea of the confederation that would become France.

A century thereafter, Christians were martyred in Lyon, from where their religion was introduced into France; indeed, it was archbishops who ruled Lyon until 1308 when, during the reign of Philip IV, it became part of France. To this day, the Archbishop of Lyon is styled *Primat de Gaule*—Gaul's Primate.

As the Middle Ages became the Renaissance, Lyon pioneered with cultivation of silkworms, becoming the silk center of Europe, while its merchants and traders (who opened France's first stock exchange as early as 1506) dominated Continental finance, even providing funds for French kings like Henri IV and François I—among the era's visitors to a still-thriving Old Town that ranks with that of Rouen (chapter 31) as the most important such in today's republic.

Succeeding centuries saw the city expand eastward—from across the hills west of the Saône River, to the elongated strip between the Saône and the Rhône, thence eastward over the Rhône. This city, during the World War II Nazi occupation, was capital of the French Resistance movement. Contemporarily, it is a world-class innovator in scientific research, an extraordinarily rich cultural center, and with a cuisine tradition so fabulous that it's known to have visitors who come only to eat. But there are other reasons for a Lyon sojourn, as I try to make clear in the pages following.

ON SCENE

Lay of the Land: Lyon is a west-to-east city, historically as well as geographically. It began on the slopes of *Mont Fourvière,* east of the Saône, and still with Roman monuments. It moved down the hill, then, during medieval and Renaissance periods to the area now called *Vieux-Lyon,* dominated by a Gothic cathedral, with a principal street that takes the cathedral's name—*Rue St.-Jean.* Came the Baroque, rococo, and Second Empire centuries and the city expanded eastward across the Saône to the quarter that is now its core—dominated by *Place Bellecour* (Europe's largest traffic-free square). *Rue Victor-Hugo* leads south from the big square to Gare Perrache, one of the railway stations. (And *Rue Auguste-Comte,* running parallel to it, is Lyon's Antique Row.) Go north from Place Bellecour, along *Rue de la République*—through *Place de la République*—and you will be strolling one of the longest pedestrian shopping streets extant. Still another street leading from Place Bellecour, *Rue du Président Herriot,* is the venue of the city's smartest shops. These shopping streets lead to northerly squares edged by the *Opéra,* churches, and museums; *Place des Terreaux,* site of *Hôtel de Ville,* is the most important. Just as there are several bridges that traverse the Saône to Vieux-Lyon, so are there additional bridges that cross the Rhône to the biggest-in-area sector of the city—site of multipurpose *Palais des Sports* to the south—as well as the contemporary quarter called *Part-Dieu,* easily identified by a conical-topped cylindrical skyscraper, *Tour de la Part-Dieu* (part of which is a hotel), a shopping center that shelters a second railway station and a clutch of additional hotels.

Musée de la Civilisation Gallo-Romaine and Roman Lyon are reached by a funicular from Avenue Adolphe-Max. The museum (entered at 17 Rue Cléberg) is one of the best-looking and best-designed contemporary structures in France; it's built on a hillside with the entrance on an upper level and the collections below. Not that you go only for the architecture. Dramatically displayed exhibits are from Gallo-Roman Lyon: mosaic floor after mint-condition mosaic floor; a bust of a goddess, a tiara in her neatly coiffed hair; silver goblets and a bronze tablet—*La Table Claudienne*—on which is inscribed the Latin text of a speech by Lyon-born Emperor Claude, delivered in the year A.D. 48; sarcophagi and jewelry—the lot set against walls of poured concrete—with picture windows giving onto a complex embracing the still-used *Grand Théâtre Romain,* built in 15 B.C. by Emperor Caesar Augustus to seat 10,000 and enlarged a century later by Emperor Hadrian; with a second, smaller theater, *L'Odéon;* as well as remains of *Temple Cybèle* (dating to A.D. 160 and the largest of its kind, along with that of Ostia, outside Rome).

Cathedral of St.-Jean, Musée Historique, and Vieux-Lyon: The cathedral (Place St.-Jean)—with a Romanesque apse and transept, but which is otherwise essentially Gothic—was built over three centuries, twelfth through fifteenth, and has known its share of historic moments (it was the site of two medieval Catholic Church conclaves—the First and Second Councils of Lyon, the crowning of a pope (John XXII), and the marriage of a king (Henry IV, with Marie de Médicis). But it is, as well, a place of beauty, with a facade graced by superbly sculpted portals, a treasury of Limoges enamels and exquisitely carved ivories, outstanding stained glass in rose windows flanking the transept, an impressive bishop's throne, and an extraordinary astronomical clock—indicating feast days beginning with the fifteenth century through the year 2000—which goes into its act daily at noon, 1:00 P.M., 2:00 P.M., and 3:00 P.M.

Musée Historique de Lyon (Place du Petit-Collège)—as good a way as any to inspect the interior of a town house typical of the quarter (it went up between the fourteenth and sixteenth centuries)—and its courtyard, with four floors of galleries, is a stunner, the while taking in mementoes of the old city. Furniture-filled rooms, up one flight, constitute the museum at its handsomest, with canopied beds made for Napoleon and Josephine—they came to Lyon in 1805—the most spectacular exhibits. But eighteenth-century rooms are lovely, too. Collections of porcelain and medieval sculptures are top-rank, and there are antique marionettes as a bonus. Allow time to stroll Vieux-Lyon streets, noting especially their unique *traboules*—passages that cut through old houses, providing routes to streets that run parallel to each other; one such leads from 3 Place St.-Paul (the site of Romanesque-Gothic *Church of St.-Paul*) to 5 Rue Juiverie. You'll come across a number of others in the course of a stroll through this relatively compact quarter, which should embrace the facades of *Place du Change, Place de la Trinité,* and *Rue du Bœuf,* not to mention shops, restaurants, and cafés of *Rue St.-Jean,* Vieux-Lyon's Main Street.

Musée des Beaux-Arts (Place des Terreaux): An obviously wealthy order of nuns, Dames de St.-Pierre, built a convent toward the end of the seventeenth century that could have been an Italian Baroque palace, its rooms cavernous, its ceilings high, its staircases not for the easily short of breath. You enter through what was the cloister and is now a tranquil public park. If the main floor sculpture collection—most of it in what was the sisters' refectory—were not so outstanding, I would not suggest that you pause. But there are fine things—Greek heads, Roman sarcophagi, medieval fragments, polychrome saints, carved-wood biblical scenes, Baroque busts, and works by later sculptors, Canova through Maillol, with Chinard's *Madame Récamier*—isn't she winking her left eyelid?—surely the single most fetching of the lot. Upstairs, then, to the

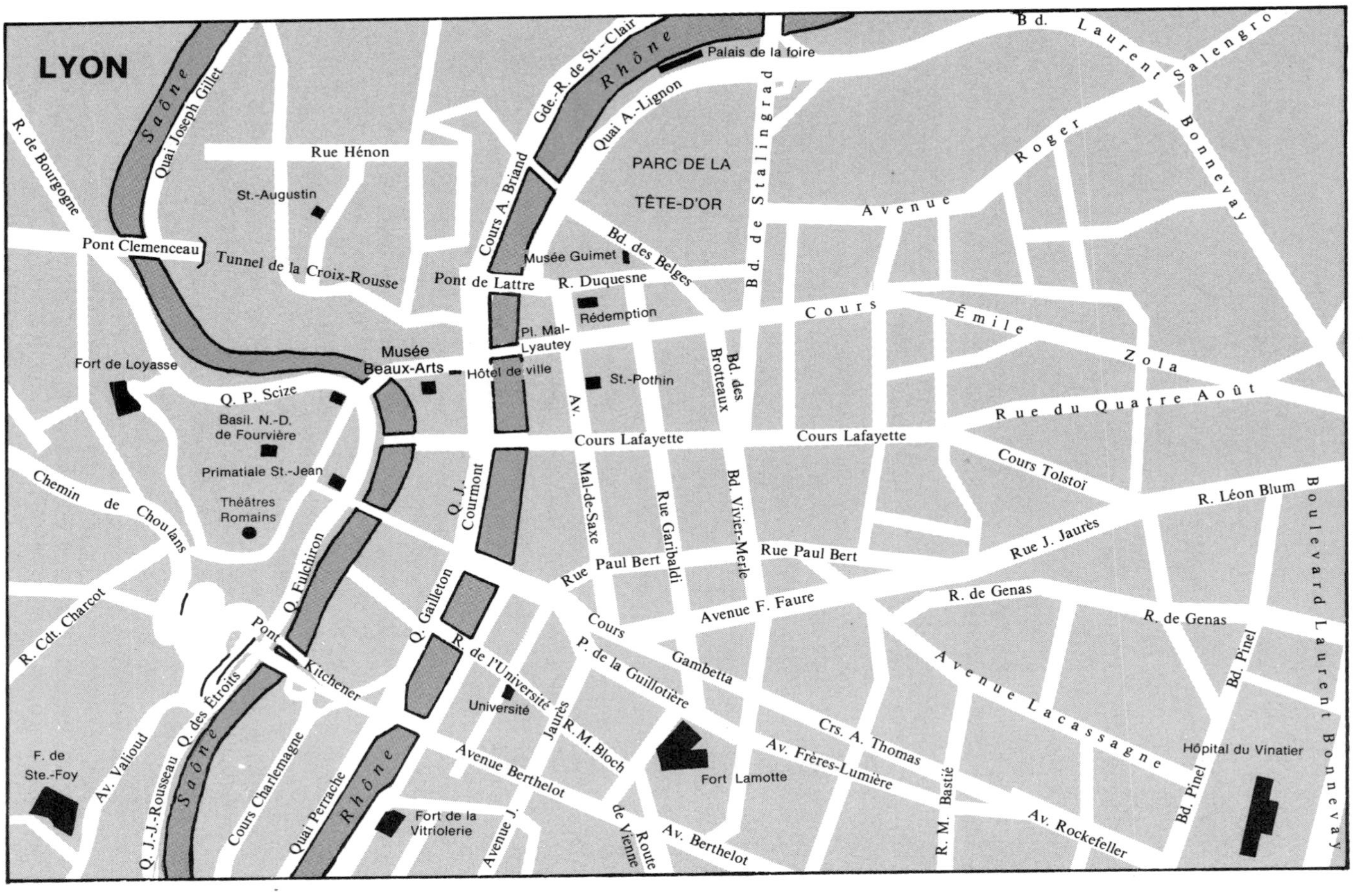

LYON
Saône
Quai Joseph Gillet
R. de Bourgogne
Pont Clemenceau
Tunnel de la Croix-Rousse
Rue Hénon
St.-Augustin
Fort de Loyasse
Musée Beaux-Arts
Hôtel de ville
Q. P. Scize
Basil. N.-D. de Fourvière
Primatiale St.-Jean
Théâtres Romains
Chemin de Choulans
R. Cdt. Charcot
Pont Kitchener
Q. Fulchiron
Q. J.-J.-Rousseau
Q. des Étroits
Av. Valioud
F. de Ste.-Foy
Cours Charlemagne
Quai Perrache
Rhône
Fort de la Vitriolerie
Avenue J.
Gde.-R. de St.-Clair
Cours A. Briand
Quai A.-Lignon
Palais de la foire
PARC DE LA TÊTE-D'OR
Bd. de Stalingrad
Musée Guimet
Bd. des Belges
Pont de Lattre
R. Duquesne
Rédemption
Pl. Mal-Lyautey
St.-Pothin
Cours Émile Zola
Bd. des Brotteaux
Av. Mal-de-Saxe
Cours Lafayette
Q. J.-Courmont
Q. Gailleton
R. de l'Université
Université
Jaurès
R. M. Bloch
Avenue Berthelot
Route de Vienne
Av. Berthelot
Rue Garibaldi
Bd. Vivier-Merle
Rue Paul Bert
Cours Gambetta
P. de la Guillotière
Fort Lamotte
Avenue F. Faure
Crs. A. Thomas
Av. Frères-Lumière
R. M. Bastié
Av. Rockefeller
Bd. Pinel
Hôpital du Vinatier
Avenue Lacassagne
R. de Genas
Rue J. Jaurès
R. Léon Blum
Cours Tolstoï
Rue du Quatre Août
Avenue Roger Bonnevay
Bd. Laurent Salengro
Boulevard Laurent Bonnevay

paintings, a brilliant survey of European art, Flemish Primitives through postimpressionists: a Quentin Matsys *Virgin*—in cloth of gold—*and Child*, Zurbarán's *St. Francis of Assisi*, Veronese's *Bathsheba at Her Bath*, and Rubens's *Adoration of the Magi;* with such other masters represented as David and Tintoretto, Van Cleve and Cranach, Bassano and Vouet; portraitists, French as well as English (Boucher and Lawrence, Lancret and Romney); preimpressionists like Corot, Millet, and Daumier; and beyond to Monet, Sisley, and Degas. Later work, too: Vuillard and Bonnard, Matisse and Picasso, Dufy and Van Dongen.

Musée des Arts Décoratifs (30 Rue de la Charité) is right up there with the best of its French counterparts—in Paris, Marseille, and Bordeaux. Setting is a garden-backed mansion designed by the same eighteenth-century architect, Soufflot, responsible for Paris's Panthéon. This museum celebrates the eighteenth century. There are, to be sure, galleries with display cases—of porcelain, glass, silver, clocks, and other small objects, But major excitements are period rooms, paneled and chandeliered and tapestried and exquisitely furnished with Louis XV and Louis XVI masterworks. Special.

Musée Historique des Tissus (34 Rue de la Charité), conveniently visited with neighboring Musée des Arts Décoratifs (above), pays tribute to Lyon's eminence as a silk center, with fine exhibits—in a jewel of a rococo house that was official residence of governors of Lyon—not only of luxurious local silk, but of foreign textiles as well. You'll see Coptic Egyptian tapestries, Islamic patterned cloth, Italian and Spanish silks from the Renaissance, and Turkish and Persian carpets, with the silk-savvy Orient represented, too.

Musée des Hospices Civils (Hôtel Dieu, Place de l'Hôpital): It is not often that public museums are located within the confines of working hospitals. But this museum—up a flight in the originally twelfth-century hospital known as Hôtel Dieu—is appropriately situated, given its theme: hospital care over the centuries. The exhibit that draws the most comment is a canopied bed that was shared by five patients until 1787—and was by no means atypical. Indeed, the museum catalogue points out that "often one was dead among them." There are, as well, surgical instruments covering a range of centuries, ancient syringes and urinals, a pill-making apparatus and microscopes, early patient ID bracelets, the costume and birdlike mask of a physician, worn during a plague epidemic, and even a padded cell used for mentally ill patients into the nineteenth century.

Musée de la Résistance (5 Rue Boileau) is, in effect, a tribute to France's anti-Nazi underground, as directed from Lyon during the World War II occupation: posters, blown-up photos, documents, newspapers, and other objects that chronicle the mission of a brave citizenry during a tragic period.

Hôtel de Ville (Place des Terreaux)—Lyon's magnificent city hall—went up originally at the height of the Baroque era, in the mid-seventeenth century. It was rebuilt, in period style, two centuries later and given a skilled 1980s refurbishing. If there are no attendants on hand to direct you, simply find your way to a stairway and ascend a flight to the high-ceilinged second floor. Then guide yourself through a series of unbelievably lavish reception rooms—each with coffered ceilings, gilded stucco, monumental murals, fireplaces tall enough to warm giants' hands, exquisitely patterned parquet floors, and crystal chandeliers of especial splendor. In one room, Salon de la Conversation, I counted a dozen of these mammoth chandeliers; in still another, Salon Louis XIII, there are 17. Have a look.

Musée d'l'Imprimerie et de la Banque (13 Rue de la Pouaillerie) may tell you more than you want to know about printing presses (the range is five centuries) and of the history of banks, especially those of Lyon. But there are stunning displays that delineate the evolution of typography, Gutenberg onward, with choice antique books, woodcuts, and engravings. And the setting is a honey of a house: Hôtel de la Couronne, built in the fifteenth century and headquarters of the city council during the first half of the sixteenth century.

Church of St.-Bonaventure (Place des Cordeliers) is a landmark, heart-of-town Gothic masterwork, with an immense—and immensely high—nave, a fine rose window gracing its facade, and an especially handsome apse.

Vienne —a charming, smallish Rhône River town 17 miles south of Lyon—rivals Arles (chapter 6), Nîmes (chapter 27), and Orange (chapter 7), with its remarkable Roman monuments. Go for a day's excursion, beginning your exploration in the core of town, at *Cathedral of St.-Maurice* (Place St.-Maurice), which impresses with the detail of its Gothic facade—the three portals' tympanums are splendidly carved—very grand nave, and exemplary stained glass. *Temple Romain d'Auguste et Livie* (Place du Palais) is the only remaining temple, except for similar-appearing Maison Carrée in Nîmes, built by the Romans in Gaul and still standing; it's a stunner, still with the original fifteen columns—topped by Corinthian capitals—framing its facade and sides. *Church of St.-Pierre* (Place St.-Pierre), parts of it dating to the fifth century (making it Gaul's oldest church), is now desanctified and a museum of Roman artifacts from Vienne and the neighborhood. Beautiful mosaic floors now surface what was the nave, with sarcophagi, sculptures, and fragments to either side. *Church of St.-André-le-Bas* (Rue des Clercs) is mellow Romanesque—dating to the twelfth century and eminently visitable in its own right, but with a cloister that is at once an architectural treasure and a repository of early Christian art. *Théâtre Romain* (Rue du Cirque) climbs Mont Pipet on the west side of town and was excavated only in 1938 after having been buried under heavy layers of soil for centuries. Its original capacity was 15,000, and it's still used for summer performances. *La Pyramide* (Route N-7, south of the center) is Vienne's trademark monument; it's actually a slim column—wider at its base than its summit and dating to the second century—that surmounts a fourth-century arch. *St.-Romain-en-Gal* (across the Rhône, on the Right Bank) is a relatively recently excavated Roman city; digs continue, but already a lot has been uncovered—foundations of houses and baths, market and artisans' quarter, with heating and drainage systems as well. And by the time of your arrival, there will no doubt be more.

Pérouges (23 miles north of Lyon) is an enchanter of a medieval fortified village, protected not only by the French government as a national monument, but by its own Comité de Défense. A few movie companies have discovered it—a version of *The Three Musketeers* was filmed on location—but far too many visitors give it short shrift. Based on central *Place du Tilleul,* it expands ovally, on radiating streets. Visitors who do nothing but stroll, planning their visit to coincide with an atmospheric restaurant (below) are happy enough. But there is a trio of visitable interiors: fortified *Church of Ste.-Marie-Madeleine* (Rue des Trois Rondes) is a Gothic marvel—its inner walls faced with flagstone, its principal embellishment the vaults of a narrow nave. *Musée Municipal* (Rue des Princes), in a galleried mansion (ivy climbs its stone walls) is filled with Pérougiana—furniture and weapons, looms and weathered documents, domestic implements and costumes, prints and paintings. Neighboring *Maison des Princes* (Rue des Princes) is a beauty of a minipalace in which long-ago princes of Savoy lived and is furnished in period. It's next door to the equally aged house sheltering a restaurant I recommend below for a lunch pause. After, it's fun to walk the ramparts along *Promenade des Terreaux,* past the series of towers that for long protected this anachronism of a village—quite unlike any other in this region of France.

SETTLING IN

Grand Hôtel Concord (11 Rue Grolée; phone 7842-56-21) is Lyon's grand dame, dating to the last century's Second Empire, but with all the comforts of the late twentieth century, including splendidly refurbished-in-marble public spaces that are among the handsomest in town, and—never to be underestimated in a city as big as this one—a superbly central situation. Although the entrance is on Rue Grolée—actually at the rear of the hotel—the Grand runs lengthwise out front, along Quai Jules-Courmont, fronting the Rhône. So, when you book for one of this hotel's 140 delightfully traditional-style rooms—many retaining original, albeit refurbished, Second Empire furnishings—you want to ask for a riverview room, so that upon waking, you may step onto your terrace and take in the splendid Lyon skyline. The Grand's Le Fiorelle Restaurant is worthy of evaluation on a later page. The welcoming lounge off the lobby doubles as a bar, and ace Directeur Général Gérard Minard's staff is one of the kindest and most efficient that I know of in France. Hôtels Concorde. *First Class.*

Royal Hôtel (20 Place Bellecour) is an agreeable old-timer that has wisely retained traditional ambience, the while tastefully updating facilities. There are 90 no-two-quite-alike rooms, a reliable restaurant, a friendly bar, and a core-of-town location. Very nice indeed. Best Western. *First Class.*

Pullman Perrache Hôtel (12 Cours de Verdun; phone 7837-58-11) is an uncommonly good-looking turn-of-century house that has been refurbished with considerable style. Public spaces are stunners—lobby with Art Nouveau capitals on columns supporting vaults of its high-ceilinged restaurant illuminated by original lighting fixtures, with murals in half-moon-shaped frames over doors punctuating paneled walls. The black-leather-upholstered bar is glass-ceilinged and there are 124 bedrooms, with varying styles of decor, often capacious, and with updated baths. Gare Perrache is adjacent, Place Bellecour and the core are a ten- or twelve-minute walk distant. *First Class.*

Sofitel Lyon (20 Quai Gailleton; phone 7842-72-50) is contemporary, with 196 full-facility, clean-lined rooms, a pair of restaurants and bars; centrally situated. *Luxury.*

Beaux-Arts Hôtel (73 Rue du Président Herriot; phone 7838-09-50) is enviably well located on the city's toniest shopping street. Marble-walled lobby is engaging Art Deco, and the 80 rooms are about half in that style, half conventionally traditional. Bar and breakfast only. Best Western. *First Class.*

Carlton Hôtel (Place de la République at Rue Jussieu; phone 7842-56-51) features 90 rooms remodeled in Art Deco style. Breakfast only. Central. Best Western. *Moderate.*

La Résidence Hôtel (18 Rue Victor-Hugo; phone 7842-63-28) is nicely placed on a principal shopping street. Most of its 63 rooms have baths or showers. Breakfast only. Friendly. *Moderate.*

Des Étrangers Hôtel (5 Rue Stella; phone 7842-01-55) offers half a hundred functional rooms, most with bath or shower, bar-lounge, breakfast, and the advantage of a central situation. *First Class.*

Globe et Cécil Hôtel (21 Rue Gasparin; phone 7842-58-95) is on a street parallel with cushy Rue du Président Herriot, heart-of-town. Lobby-lounge is contemporary, rooms traditional style; 45 rooms with bath or shower. *Moderate.*

Charlemagne Hôtel (23 Cours Charlemagne; phone 7892-81-61)—in the Gare Perrache area—is an inviting house relatively recently renovated and redecorated with a commendable sense of style. There are 119 bath-equipped rooms of varying sizes (some, I caution, can be small), a cozy bar off the lobby, and a convenient restaurant in the basement. *Moderate.*

Bayard Hôtel (23 Place Bellecour; phone 7837-39-95): You ascend a stairway to reach the lobby, but it's worth the climb, if a small, core-of-town hotel is what you seek. Look is Belle Époque; 15 bath- or shower-equipped rooms. Breakfast only. *Moderate.*

Des Terreaux Hôtel (16 Rue Lanterne; phone 7827-04-10) is named for a central square that's but a block distant. Though modest, its location is a plus; most of its 50 rooms have bath or shower. Breakfast only. *Moderate.*

La Maison de la Tour Hôtel (22 Rue du Bœuf in Vieux-Lyon; phone 7837-25-90) occupies an elaborately restored Renaissance mansion operated by the exemplary (and neighboring) Restaurant de la Tour Rose (below recommended). This is a small but smart operation: there are just 9 suites, with state-of-the-art video and other appliances, and a lovely garden. *Luxury.*

La Cour des Loges Hôtel (2 Rue du Bœuf in Vieux-Lyon; phone 7842-75-75) gets high marks for taking four contiguous Renaissance *hôtels-particuliers* in the Old Town and employing an inventive, color-drenched design motif in the course of their conversion into a 63-room hotel. The lobby and bar are striking, there's a small indoor pool-cum-sauna, and I like the sole big suite. Withal, management advised me, in the course of my inspection, that something like half of the accommodations (which in certain instances are duplex—on two floors) have their bathrooms split in two so that your sink can be on one level and your toilet on another. I observed, too, that beds can be narrow. Additionally, a true luxury hotel, in my view, has a proper restaurant, not just a half-dozen-seat counter where the specialty is Spanish-origin tapas—nibblies that are consumed with drinks at bars in Spain. Staff come and go in hotels, and ambience can change, but I was not taken with the Cour des Loges management's ever-so-grand attitude. Too impractically designed, too rich for my blood. *Luxury.*

La Part-Dieu—ultramod, multifunction complex well away from the center, on the east bank of the Rhône—has as much of the flavor of Lyon as would, say, a shopping mall in Carson City, Nevada. I say this despite its being the location both of the railway station, (named for it) used by TGV high-speed trains and of slews of stores, including Galeries Lafayette. You must take two subways, changing trains en route, to reach the heart of town. Withal, a number of chains have Part-Dieu hotels. If you're booking a room on your own and want to get to know Lyon, you're far better off core-of-town. If business is your mission and the city is of little interest or if you're part of a group using these hotels, well, so be it. They include: *Pullman Part-Dieu Hôtel* (129 Rue Servient; phone 7862-94-12), with 345 okay rooms (ask for one looking across the Rhône to the core of the city), good pair of restaurants and bar, the lot on top floors of the quarter's landmark skyscraping tower (*First Class*); *Mercure Part-Dieu Hôtel* (47 Boulevard Vivier Merle; phone 7853-40-69), a link of a good-value national chain with a restaurant serving all three meals including generous buffet breakfasts (*Moderate*); *Holiday Inns' Crowne Plaza* (29 Rue de Bonnel; phone 7261-90-90), a part of Holiday Inn's upscale Crowne Plaza group, with relatively recent tasteful redecoration and restaurant, bar-lounge, fitness center, 156 agreeable bath-and-shower-equipped rooms (some on a premium-category, extra-amenity Executive Floor), and, in my experience, a distinctly cool albeit correct ambience (*First Class/Luxury*); *Arcade Hôtel* (78 Rue de Bonnel; phone 7862-98-89), restaurant-equipped (meals are buffets), with 216 clean-lined, blond-furniture rooms with shower that are part of a successful no-frills chain (*Moderate*); and *Ibis Part-Dieu Hôtel* (Place Renaudel Sud; phone 7895-42-11), a link of still another no-frills chain, with 144 shower-equipped rooms and restaurant (*Moderate*).

Central Hôtel (7 Rue de l'Archevêché, Vienne; phone 7485-18-38) is, indeed, central—well placed for exploration of the core of Vienne—and is, as well, comfortable. There are 26 no-two-quite-alike rooms. Breakfast only. *Moderate.*

DAILY BREAD

Léon de Lyon (1 Rue Pleney; phone 7828-11-33): Restaurants with catchy names don't always live up to expectations. This one does. It *looks* like what we outlanders seek in Lyon: dark wood, stained glass, hanging copper pots, plentiful flowers, waiters in navy blue shirts and trousers protected by long navy aprons. And it *tastes* Lyonnais. Talented patron-chef Jean-Paul Lacombe splits his menu in two; the left is traditional cuisine; the right is M. Lacombe's. Or you may order from a prix-fixe. In either event, it's a good plan to sample both sides of the card. Saucisson chaud—hot sausage served with lentils and boiled potatoes; quenelle de brochet—fingers of minced pike—served with sauce Nantua; entrecôte accompanied by sauce marchand de vin; and blanquette de veau—veal stew—typify Lyonnais fare. And M. Lacombe does innovative things with salmon, foie gras, chicken, rabbit, and lamb. Chocolate mousse, presented in tandem with an orange salad in an orange sauce—along with house-baked madeleines served warm—is one of the masterful desserts. Expert, smiling service. Central. Member, Relais et Châteaux. *Luxury.*

Commanderie des Antonins (30 Quai St.-Antoine; phone 7837-19-21): Not for nothing has the Commanderie—situated in the arched, stone-walled *salle capitulaire* of a thirteenth-century monastery—been declared a *Monument Historique.* At dinner, when illumination is almost entirely by candles, I doubt there's a restaurant in town with a more evocative setting. And it tastes as good as it looks. Grills are the big thing here. I suggest opening with foie gras frais de canard—fresh duck liver served with hot toast, following with T-bone steak (which is what it's called on the menu) accompanied by sautéed mushrooms, a perfectly baked potato, and, perhaps, artichokes, with lemon tart rum-flamed, to conclude. *First Class.*

La Tour Rose (16 Rue du Bœuf; phone 7838-25-90) combines the best of two worlds: a Renaissance-origin, Vieux-Lyon house behind a pink tower—thus its name—as its setting and contemporary-influenced cuisine as its forte. Go at lunch for the good-value prix-fixe menu (not available at dinner), which might open with saffron-scented mussel soup or chicken and avocado salad and continue with filet mignon in a ginger sauce accompanied by honey-sauced turnips or a chicken and cabbage stew, with cheese and a choice of luscious desserts to conclude. Friendly. *Luxury.*

Nandron (26 Quai Jean-Moulin; phone 7842-10-26) is lovely and luxuriant—an up-a-flight room fronting the Rhône, with silk-shaded lamps illuminating exquisitely appointed tables. Skilled M. Nandron is in charge of the kitchen. Congenial Madame Nandron is in command out front. Fare is deliciously traditional. Madame Nandron is unhappy if you ask for mustard to accompany your saucisson chaud, but they're tasty without it; oysters on the half shell and quenelles de brochet are options. Entrées might be grilled filet of sole, chicken and sweetbread stew that comes off well, roast lamb, or the house's special tournedos. And desserts: crêpes flambées Grand Marnier and chocolate soufflé should be ordered at the start of the meal and do not disappoint; nor does chocolat glacé—mousse in a sponge crust slathered with whipped cream. Member, Relais et Châteaux. *Luxury.*

Hugon (12 Rue Pizay; phone 7828-10-94) is a typical Lyonnais *bouchon;* these are small, unpretentious restaurants with hearty Lyonnais fare. This one is operated by Monsieur Hugon. There are a few tables out front. You may be seated at one of three tables in the cramped, albeit impeccably organized, kitchen. Open with jambon persillé—a thick slice of parsley-flavored ham served with lentil salad; rillettes de porc, a coarsely ground pork pâté; or warm potato salad served with a filet of herring. Good entrées are bœuf Bourguignon or filet of veal with mushrooms. Cheese follows (a local St.-Marcelin, perhaps), with still-warm-from-the-oven chocolate cake to conclude. And a bottle of Beaujolais—Lyon's favorite wine. Central. *Moderate.*

Café des Fédérations (8 Rue du Major Martin; phone 7828-26-00) is still another *bouchon,* although it's larger than Hugon (above) and serves dinner as well as lunch. There's a reasonably tabbed menu or you may order à la carte, opening with such house specialties as sausages teamed with bacon or lentil salad, following with entrées including calf's liver accompanied by a delicious potato cake, or dishes beloved of Lyonnais like tripes, boudin, or andouillettes. The cheese board has such unusual species as St.-Marcelin and St.-Félicien. You skip apple tart at your peril. Beaujolais, Lyon's adopted wine, is a good accompaniment. Congenial. *Moderate.*

Orsi (3 Place Kléber; phone 7889-57-68) is rather grand: walls hung with good paintings, nineteenth-century chandeliers, and tables elaborately set and attended by waitresses in long gowns who look as though they might be trendy Smith College students spending their junior year abroad. And if you speak American-accented English—or, for that matter, American-accented French—a set of flags, one French, one the Stars and Stripes, is placed on your table, an unusual touch in France. You might open with potted snails or the house's own foie gras, follow with filet of beef, grilled confit of duck, or a fish dish. Cheese—you select from a generous-sized platter—might be next, with imaginatively prepared desserts to conclude. Member, Relais et Châteaux. *First Class.*

Christian Bourillot (8 Place des Célestins; phone 7837-38-64) occupies an attractive white house on a square not far north of Place Bellecour, where, at tables ringed by Louis XVI–style chairs in a paneled dining room, chef-propriétaire Bourillot adds his own accents to essentially traditional dishes. Order his multicourse menu (less costly at lunch), watching for specialties like fish of the day, Bourillot style, and veal kidneys, quenelle de brochet, or breast of chicken teamed with truffled potatoes, and frozen chocolate soufflée as an indicated dessert. Wine emphasis, wisely, is regional. Very nice, indeed. *First Class/Luxury.*

La Voûte (a.k.a. Chez Léa; 11 Place Antonin-Gourju; phone 7842-01-33) is a long-on-scene source of delicious Lyonnais cuisine, in a neat albeit unpretentious setting not far from Place Bellecour. The unsmiling, hardworking staff, at least on my last visit, appeared all-female. Service, I caution, can be very slow, but a meal—opening with a perfectly dressed salad of mesclun, continuing with macaroni au gratin or chicken in wine, with cheese from a platter or a substantial sweet—is, invariably, a good meal, and good value, with wine not expensive and bread exceptional. *Moderate.*

Brasserie Georges (30 Cours de Verdun; phone 7837-15-78) is nothing less than the prototypical Lyon brasserie: aged (it open in 1836, with Georges the first name of its founder, a Monsieur Hoffherr), generous of proportions, handsome to look upon (the most recent refurbishing is in Art Deco style), with an agile staff and a bill of fare embracing four multicourse menus and an enticing à la carte. The Menu du Jour, served only at lunch, is one of the best buys in town, opening with a salad, proceeding with the plat du jour, ending with cheese or crème caramel. But I don't want to infer that this is a barebones spot. The range—oysters on the half shell, mussels marinière, salads and foie gras, quiches and quenelles, steaks and sausages—is extensive. And best for last: there are five varieties of choucroutes garnies, the Alsatian-origin sauerkraut-based extravaganza. With omelette Norvégienne the specialty sweet. And a sound list of wines. Fun. Near Gare Perrache. *First Class.*

La Mère Vittet (26 Cours de Verdun; phone 7837-20-17): Brasserie George's immediate neighbor has the look of a more conventional restaurant, and the advantage of a never-close, 24-hours-per-day schedule. The red-jacketed waiters smile, the while delivering your order to pink-linen covered, rose-centered tables. There's a satisfactory menu that might commence with sausage and lentils or green salad flecked with croutons and lardons and topped with a poached egg; follow with bœuf Bourguignonne or Dijon-sauced grilled steak, with cheese or dessert to conclude. Satisfying. *First Class.*

Le Fiorelle (Grand Hôtel Concord, 11 Rue Grolée; phone 7842-56-21): In a city that glorifies the small restaurant, Fiorello Colatosti's compact albeit good-looking Le Fiorelle stands out. You sit on ladder-back chairs and order corking good Lyonnais fare from either of three excellent-value menus or à la carte. Vegetable and fish soups are hearty; duck terrine, exemplary; entrées like steak au poivre and médaillons of veal with sautéed mushrooms, excellent. And there's always a plat du jour to please neighborhood regulars who are patrons. Friendly. *First Class.*

Le Bistrot de Lyon (64 Rue Mercière; phone 7837-00-62) has the flavor of fin de siècle Lyon. Have a hearty meal of, say, the sausages called andouillettes, nicely prepared grenouilles (frog's legs), or a poulet aux morilles (chicken with mushrooms). Open until 1:30 A.M., with management the same as Léon de Lyon (above). *First Class.*

Le Savoy (50 Rue de la République at Place de la République; phone 7837-69-35) is as much outdoor café—go for coffee or a cold drink—as *brasserie,* with quenelles sauce Nantua and seafood as specialties. Central. *Moderate/First Class.*

Vettard (7 Place Bellecour; phone 7842-07-59) has as a major attribute its situation on Lyon's No. 1 square. It's small, with brown and ivory walls and Louis XVI–style chairs at tables with Limoges china. There are two prix-fixe menus and—considering this restaurant's steepish prices and exalted reputation—a surprisingly limited à la carte. Fare is uninspired contemporary, and portions tend to be small. One entrée specialty, to give you an idea, consists of modest slices of three grilled meats, each dabbed with a different sauce. But you may fall back on such standbys as quenelles de brochet. Disappointing. *Luxury.*

Les Adrets (38 Rue du Bœuf; phone 7838-24-30) is a less pricey alternative to La Tour Rose (above), when a Vieux-Lyon meal is your objective. Order from either of a pair of well-priced prix-fixe menus, both based on typically tasty Lyonnais entrées. Fun. *Moderate.*

L'Amphitryon (26 Rue St.-Jean; phone 7838-26-43) might prove okay when it's a casual setting you seek for an alfresco lunch at a table out in front, to watch Vieux Lyon pass in review. The three-course menu is a good deal, opening perhaps with saucisson chaud, preparatory to a beef entrée, with dessert included. *Moderate.*

Parfum de Tarte (17 Rue St.-Jean): How can you pass by a café-*salon de thé* whose name suggests that its pâtisserie will smell as good as you hope it will taste? Just the spot for an afternoon tea break in the course of Vieux-Lyon exploration. Sit outside. *Moderate.*

Paul Bocuse (Place de'Illaeusern, Collonges-au-Mont-d'Or, six miles north of Lyon; phone 7822-01-40): There is no denying that Paul Bocuse is a genius at self-promotion—surely the cleverest such among the celebrated French master chefs. He anticipates your arrival with giant directional markers and billboards with his likeness en route. His restaurant, a three-story white house with a giant sign bearing his name atop it, is unabasedly florid. There's a touch of kitsch and show-biz upon arrival; you're greeted first by a smiling page in a scarlet uniform, next by the maître d'hôtel in tails, who turns you over to a tuxedoed captain for the final lap of the escorted trip to your table. Depart the gents' after washing your hands, and pouff! There is M. Bocuse's shop—with cookbooks he has authored available for purchase in the French, German, Spanish, and English languages; Paul Bocuse-brand chocolates, Paul Bocuse-label tea, aprons with Paul Bocuse's name and face reproduced on them, and postcards of the restaurant. Back at the table, you remove your napkin from a disposable paper ring with M. Bocuse's toque-blanche-topped visage printed on it, sip water from a goblet bearing his name, and, when your meal arrives, eat from porcelain similarly identified. But there's a rub. M. Bocuse produces. His cuisine is, to be sure, innovative, but logically and sensibly. He is not afraid to cook with cream, butter, and wine. Nor to serve you more than you may be able to eat. With flair and with smiles. There are two prix-fixe menus. Under no circumstances would I counsel omitting soupe aux truffes noires—the pastry-topped, packed-with-truffles, Bocuse-created consommé, first served by the master for a 1975 dinner at Élysée Palace, the presidential residence in Paris. A typical Bocuse repast might continue with filet of sole presented on a bed of noodles in a light cream sauce, accompanied by mushrooms, peas, and carrots. Cassis-flavored sherbet, a palate cleanser, would arrive next. Médaillon of veal crisscrossed with vegetables, tarragon-flavored lamb chops, Charolais beef, and roast duckling are typical entrées. Vegetables, served in proper portions, include recognizable peas and spinach and a superb gratin Dauphinois, the potato casserole. Cheese? *Three* trolleys are rolled up for you to make a selection. And when you're ready, three *more* trolleys of desserts make their appearance: chocolate mousse, crème brûlée, œufs à la neige are among them, or you may order crêpes to be prepared at table. As if that were not enough, several plates of petits-fours and made-on-premises chocolates accompany coffee. If M. Bocuse is present—not always the case, as he travels a lot—chances are, he will come and say hello in the course of this extraordinary gastronomic adventure. *Luxury.*

La Pyramide (Boulevard Fernand Point, Vienne; phone 7453-01-96) originally opened in 1923. Its founder, the late Fernand Point, was a universally acknowledged pioneer chef. It is a measure of the admiration held for him that the street on which the restaurant—and an agreeable, relatively recently constructed, 26-room *First Class* hotel) is situated, edging Vienne—was renamed for him posthumously. La Pyramide was operated by Madame Point from the time her husband died in 1955 until she died in 1986—the period when I made her acquaintance and enjoyed a dinner served by her husband's successor as chef. A realty concern subsequently bought the place, turned the restaurant into the kitchen, built a new dining room (along with a hotel), and reopened in 1989, still with such beloved Point specialties as foie-gras and truffle-stuffed roast squab, but with an essentially contemporary—albeit *sensible* contemporary—bill of fare. *Luxury.*

Bec Fin (7 Place St.-Maurice, Vienne; phone 7485-76-72) is conveniently central and indicated for a well-priced lunch after a morning's rounds in Vienne. Select one of the prix-fixe menus. *Moderate/First Class.*

Ostellerie du Vieux-Pérouges (Rue des Princes, Pérouges; phone 7461-00-88)—a beautifully appointed thirteenth-century house in a village (above) that is, in toto, a protected national monument—makes a specialty of hearty regional cuisine; take your choice of entrées, making certain, though, that you open with panache Pérougien (mushrooms sautéed in a crayfish sauce) and that you conclude with galette Pérougienne, the village's celebrated dessert pancake. (You may overnight here; there are 15 bath-equipped rooms and an additional baker's dozen in an adjacent, less costly annex). *Luxury.*

SHOPPER'S LYON

Printemps, the big department store in the center of town, is on Place de la République. *Galeries Lafayette* is in Part-Dieu. *Grand Bazaar de Lyon,* a long-on-scene inexpensive department store, is on Rue de la République, the principal shopping street, with such other stores as *Voisin* (chocolates), *Bally* (shoes), *D. M. Passion* (Yves St.-Laurent and other women's haute couture, luggage), *Mister West* (men's clothing), and *Pimkie* (moderate-category women's clothing). Rue du Président Herriot has the smartest boutiques, including *Claire Belle* (women's haute couture), *Georges Rech* (women's haute couture), *Sugar* (moderate-category women's clothing), *Réciproque* (casual women's wear), *Caravel* (pricey men's duds), *De Fursac* (moderately priced men's wear), *Rodier* (the men's-wear chain), *Sephora* (cologne and perfume) and *Laser* (children's clothing). Rue

Auguste Comte has a concentration of antique shops and art galleries.

SOUND OF MUSIC

Opéra de Lyon (Place de la Comédie) is the city's Belle Époque opera house; look up from the square, at eight free-standing statues surmounting the facade. Its ranker of a resident troupe presents a varied repertory, ranging from Rossini's *Barber of Seville* through Weber's *Oberon,* with works, as well, by the highly regarded *Ballet de l'Opéra de Lyon* and visiting troupes.

Auditorium Maurice Ravel (Rue de Bonnel)—strikingly contemporary—is the city's principal concert hall for performances of *Orchestre de Lyon* and other musical groups. (The two major Lyon festivals—International every June, and Berlioz every September—take place in these venues, as well as at *Théâtre Romain,* the ancient amphitheater.)

INCIDENTAL INTELLIGENCE

Stations of Lyon's spanking modern *Métro,* or subway system, are recognized by orange signs. Method of operation is based on that of Paris (chapter 2), except, of course, that Lyon's network is infinitely smaller. There are two main railway stations—*Gare de Perrache,* adjacent to the center of town, and *Gare de la Part-Dieu,* considerably east of the center; ascertain in advance from which station your train will depart. *Aéroport International de Satolas,* 17 miles southeast of town—and connected with Gare de Perrache by frequently departing buses that make the journey in 45 minutes—is No. 2 in France after Paris's de Gaulle, serving more than 80 destinations: domestic, European, African, Middle Eastern, and transatlantic; Air France links Lyon with New York. *Further information:* Office de Tourisme, Place Bellecour, Lyon; Office de Tourisme, 3 Cours Brillier, Vienne.

22

Marseille

Mediterranean Metropolis

BACKGROUND BRIEFING

Credit where it is due: Ancient Greeks came upon a massive Mediterranean crescent of a beach—backed by high hills—some 2,600 years ago, and in establishing their colony of *Massilia,* they created what has come to be France's oldest city. And, I might add, its most beautifully situated.

It was the scheme of things for Romans to follow, and it was logical that, given its location, medieval Marseille would benefit from traffic between its port and the Middle East during the long Crusades period. Enough so, for it to have attracted attention in the ancient Kingdom of Provence, which vanquished it in the thirteenth century, only to be conquered two centuries later by a more powerful France.

Today's Marseille is a fascinating fusion of cultures and peoples and ideas. Call it what you will: metropolis of the south; premier city of Provence; major port of the Mediterranean. Marseille is good-looking, good fun, and a distinctive dimension of the French experience.

ON SCENE

Lay of the Land: Aptly named Vieux-Port—the old harbor whose fingerlike contours attracted the ancient Greeks—was the core of the original *Massilia.* It protruded from the Mediterranean into the heart of the city, protected by venerable *Forts St.-Jean* and *St.-Nicholas*—one on either side of its entrance—and is ringed by a café and restaurant-lined promenade variously called *Quai du Port, Quai des Belges,* and *Quai de Rive Neuve. Notre-Dame-de-la-Garde,* a nineteenth-century church that looks better from a distance than close up, straddles an eminence to the harbor's west, and with its high tower is a Marseille landmark. More easily visited *Hôtel de Ville*—the city hall—is a splendidly scaled Baroque palace at water's edge (you want to ascend its grand staircase for a view from the harborview reception room). Inland Marseille makes easy geographic sense, thanks to the broad boulevard, *La Canebière,* that proceeds north from Quai des Belges. *Rue St.-Ferréol,* perpendicular with it and jutting east, is Marseille's smartest shopping street; others in the neighborhood—*Rue du Paradis, Rue de la République, Rue de Rome, Cours Belsance*—are shop-lined, too. *Gare St.-Charles,* the railway station, is northwest of the center. The modern harbor, which has long since supplemented Vieux-Port, edges the western flank of town, while *Corniche J. F. Kennedy* follows the scenic coast east of town, eventually becoming *Promenade de la Plage*—lining the beaches where Marseille spends its summer leisure.

Exploring Vieux-Port: Marseille's geography is such that visitors tend to concentrate on the core, ignoring the Vieux-Port area, redolent of earlier centuries. Of the unexpected pair of *Cathédrales de la Major* (Quai de la Tourette), the elder (and no longer used) is lovely twelfth-century Romanesque, but you must ask for the key in the sacristy of its next-door, nineteenth-century successor. *Fort St.-Jean,* with a landmark fifteenth-century tower, is a hop and a skip distant. *Basilica of St.-Victor*—on the other side of the harbor, adjacent to seventeenth-century *Fort St.-Nicholas,* on Rue Neuve Ste.-Catherine—is a fabulously fortified church with a pair of crenelated towers replete with crypt and catacombs: It's nine hundred years old. Beyond Vieux-Port, out in the harbor, you can't help but admire the profile of the small, walled island atop which are battlements of the very same *Château d'If* you recall from Dumas's *The Count of Monte Cristo.* King François I built it in the sixteenth century and excursion boats make tours.

A Trio of Ancient-Marseille Museums: Newest of this extraordinary group is *Jardin des Vestiges* (Rue Barbuse), an area more or less the size of a stadium that was accidentally uncovered in the course of constructing the adjacent—and graceless—Centre Bourse shopping complex as recently as 1967. Amble about Greek/Roman Marseille in this pretty garden quite literally studded with fragments—bits of walls, ruined ramparts—of the ancient city. *Musée d'Histoire de Marseille* (Centre Bourse, Cours Belsance) adjoins Jardin des Vestiges and shelters treasures found in its confines during the 1960s excavations. They are presented chronologically, 600 B.C. (the Greek settlement) through A.D. 400 (the Romans), with quite the most amazing exhibit composed of the contents of a Roman ship wrecked in the third century. *Musée des Docks Romains* (Place Vivaux) is on the actual site of piers dating to the early Roman trader-settlers, with displays ranging from oil jars to boat fragments.

Musée du Vieux-Marseille (2 Rue de la Prison) makes its home in Maison des Diamants, so called because of the striking diamond design of its sixteenth-century facade. Two floors of galleries constitute one of the best—and most amusing—of French museums of municipal history, with the range high-caliber furniture and superb engravings through fetchingly displayed costumes and the carved-wood figures, typical of Provence, called *santons.*

La Vieille Charité (Rue de la Charité): Marseille has for long been proud of the Hospice La Vieille Charité because it was the creation of native-born Pierre Puget (whose portrait, by his son, François, is in the Louvre). But it has not always shown its regard. Erected in the seventeenth century as a hospital for prisoners and a residence for the impoverished, it knew varied uses over the centuries. Finally, a long-range rebuilding—exquisitely performed—was completed in 1986, and La Vieille Charité is today one of the most beautiful Baroque complexes in France. You go first to admire it architecturally. Its chapel, an elegant oval fronted by a frieze-surfaced portico supported by Corinthian columns, and topped by a superb dome, is in and of itself visitworthy. But there's more. The chapel is framed on three of its four sides by a graceful triple-level gallery, a number of whose spaces have become museums—Egyptian (including mummies, covered and open), archeological (with varied exhibits), and a gallery for often top-rank short-term exhibitions; on one of my visits, to give you an idea, the featured show included paintings loaned from such sources as New York's Museum of Modern Art, Washington's Smithsonian, Philadelphia's Fine Arts, and Paris's Picasso museums. Special.

Church of the Chartreux (Place des Chartreux) is, like la Vieille Charité, another seventeenth-century masterwork, with eight Ionic columns supporting an upper facade behind a quartet of Corinthian pilasters. The nave is long and severe but the church's high altar is art-embellished, in pleasing contrast.

Church of St.-Cannat (a.k.a. Les Prêcheurs, Rue du St.-Cannat) was put up by Dominican friars in the sixteenth and seventeenth centuries, with much of its rich Baroque facade original, a superbly sculpted, free-standing high altar, and side chapels with figures of saints, not to mention some good paintings, including several by eighteenth-century Marseille painter Michel Serre.

L'Hôtel Dieu (Place Daviel, just behind Vieux-Port's Hôtel de Ville, or city hall) is, like buildings throughout France similarly named, a hospital, with one of the great Marseille facades—double-winged, with two of its three stories galleried, both without and at the rear, giving onto an impressive courtyard. The eighteenth-century architect, Mansart by name, was a nephew of the architect of Versailles.

Musée de la Marine (Palais de la Bourse, Quai des Belges) is of interest not so much for its exhibits—models of sailing ships and early steamers—as for its setting: the very grand neoclassic hall of a onetime stock exchange erected at the peak of Marseille's nineteenth-century Golden Age, now the Chamber of Commerce and with occasional special shows.

Musée Cantini (19 Rue Grignan, in the shopping district) makes for a serene diversion in the course of a morning's exploration. The setting is felicitous, and the contents consist mostly of pottery and porcelain, seventeenth- and eighteenth-century—and quite beautiful.

Musée Grobet-Labadie (140 Boulevard Longchamp): I save this all-France ranker of a museum (and its neighbor—Musée des Beaux-Arts, below) for the end of this section only because they are farthest away from the center. Named for the woman who lived within—born Mlle. Labadie, later Madame Grobet, who, first with her industrialist father, later with M. Grobet, collected and arranged its contents—the Grobet-Labadie is a museum of decorative-arts on a level with counterparts in Paris, Bordeaux, and Lyon. But, possibly because its name does not signify its subject matter, it remains nothing like as celebrated. With the exception of certain of the collections—musical instruments, some decorative ironwork, a room full of sculptures—what you encounter is a series of rooms of a mid-nineteenth-century mansion, each furnished and accessorized in period by the onetime owners, the lot constituting a compendium of what was best in the decorative arts of the seventeenth and eighteenth centuries. There's not a room in the house you wouldn't want to live—or at least entertain—in: Louis XIV salon, with a spinet and Aubusson tapestries; Régence-furnished, paneled dining room; Louis XV bedroom, with paintings by Murillo and Nattier; upstairs sitting room, Louis XVI–furnished, its walls with paintings by Boucher, Fragonard, Watteau, and Greuze; music room, its ceiling coffered, with an eighteenth-century harp, needlepoint-covered furniture, art on its walls by England's Constable and France's Daubigny. For decorative arts buffs, the Grobet-Labadie alone can make a journey to Marseille worthwhile.

Musée des Beaux-Arts (Boulevard Longchamp) went up in the Napoleon III period, when museums were supposed to look palatial. This one is gained by flights of steps that frame a reflecting pool and sculpted fountains, with a colonnade at the summit and the *palais* beyond. It's worth the climb. Paintings most relevant to

Marseille are a pair by a local artist, Michel Serre, who lived through the city's eighteenth-century plague epidemic and recorded its suffering citizens—in one picture, before still-standing Hôtel de Ville, in the other, on a local boulevard. There are more celebrated works, as well. Simon Vouet's olive-complexioned *Virgin and Child* is surely the most memorable, but you are bound to be drawn, as well, to Rubens's exciting *Wild Boar Hunt*, Vigée-Lebrun's coquettish *Duchesse d'Orléans*, Signac's pointillist interpretation of the city's Vieux-Port. And so much else: Tintoretto and Perugino, Carracci and Bassano, Zurbarán and Anton Mor, Oudry and Panini, Fragonard and Tiepolo, David and Millet, Courbet and Corot.

Cassis (14 miles east of Marseille) was pretty enough for Dufy and Matisse to have painted it. Proximity to the big city notwithstanding, it remains so. The inner harbor—a still paintable mix of seafood restaurants and bobbing fishing boats—is indicated for an excursion-cum-lunch out of Marseille, after which it's fun to take a boat ride to *Les Calanques*, the coastal area just west of the village and bordered by dramatic high cliffs.

SETTLING IN

Pullman Beauveau Hôtel (4 Rue Beauveau; phone 9154-91-00) was built in 1781, became a hotel in 1815, was well enough known, in 1839, to have served as a Marseille home-away-from-home for George Sand and her lover, Chopin. Location is nothing less than the best in town: at the foot of La Canebière, the main thoroughfare, and overlooking Vieux-Port from its front rooms (one of which you want to specify when booking). Recent seasons have seen this 72-room hostelry refurbished throughout—and with charm. Louis-Phillippe and Napoleon III antiques are dotted about, with smart textiles draping windows and covering beds. There's a convenient restaurant open weekdays from 5 P.M. to 1 A.M., a congenial bar, and the first Lève-Tôt, or Early Riser, service of its type that I've come across in France: orange juice, pastry, and coffee are served, on the house, at reception, between 5:30 and 6:30 A.M.—a boon, believe me, if you must depart at such an inconvenient hour. This is a skillfully managed hotel and the views of Vieux-Port from front rooms are a memorable Marseille treat. *First Class.*

Novotel Marseille Centre (36 Boulevard Charles-Livon; phone 9959-22-22) edges Pharo Gardens to one side and Vieux-Port to the other, but I must make clear that it's near the far end of Vieux-Port, easily a ten-minute walk to the center. This relatively recent link of a reliable France-wide mid-level chain is unusual in that it occupies four floors of the building of the pricier and somewhat more elaborate (but I don't think as nice) Sofitel (below). This hotel is independent of its neighbor, with its own entrance, reception-lobby bar, good restaurant (worth knowing about it in that it's open nonstop 6 A.M. to midnight and later reviewed). Its 93 rooms are up to the minute, with new baths featuring rarely-encountered-in-France shower curtains, and separate toilets. This is a nicely managed, good-value hotel. *First Class.*

New Astoria Hôtel (10 Boulevard Garibaldi at the corner of La Canebière; phone 9133-33-50) is one of the grand old hotels of La Canebière thoroughly renewed and refurbished. It is no longer a luxury house as in former times (there's no restaurant and the 58 rooms, while spanking new and with okay baths or showers, are more functional than elaborate), but public spaces—especially including a glass-roofed, white-wicker-accented jardin d'hiver, or winter garden, edging reception—are zingy. Breakfast only, with room service for that meal, and drinks as well. Ask for a room with a little balcony overlooking La Canebière. Nice. *Moderate.*

Hermès Hôtel (2 Rue Bonneterie; phone 9190-34-51) is brought to your attention principally because it borders Vieux-Port and has been relatively recently updated. Though spanking clean and bright, its 28 rooms are small and its beds narrow, but all rooms have bath or shower, and some, terraces. *Moderate.*

Noailles Hôtel (68 La Canebière; phone 9154-91-48): The days when luxury hotels lined the boulevardlike Canebière are, alas, gone. But the Noailles—no longer with its Louis XV restaurant—carries on, contemporarily updated, with 56 full-facility rooms and a congenial bar-lounge. Breakfast only. *First Class.*

De Genève Hôtel (3-bis Rue Reine Elisabeth; phone 9190-51-42) has a convenient, near-Vieux-Port location and welcomes with an attractive and capacious lobby-lounge and half a hundred rooms, some traditional style (with brass beds), others plainly contemporary. Breakfast only. *Moderate.*

Grand Modern Hôtel (5 La Canebière; phone 9190-15-60) is more modern than grand, with a clean-lined lobby, friendly reception, and just under 50 neat rooms. Location is excellent—foot of La Canebière, facing Vieux-Port. Breakfast only. *Moderate.*

Résidence du Vieux-Port Hôtel (18 Quai du Port; phone 9191-91-22) could have done with a bit of sprucing up on my last inspection, but there is no denying the fabulous views from its front rooms. Some have terraces, and from all of them the Vieux-Port is just out front. Les Santonniers Restaurant is on the premises. *Moderate.*

Altéa Hôtel (Rue Neuve St.-Martin, in the massive Centre Bourse shopping center; phone 9191-91-29) has as its principal attribute a heart-of-town location. There are 200 minimalist-decor rooms, restaurant and bar. *First Class.*

Arcade Hôtel (Square Narvick at Gare St.-Charles; phone 9195-62-09): Hotels located near Marseille's train station are not all that central, although the Métro gets you to the Vieux-Port area quickly. With a lobby not as attractive as many in this national budget chain, the Arcade comes through with nice pastel-and-gray-toned rooms (including some big doubles), shower-equipped baths, and a restaurant featuring the generous buffet breakfasts typical of the chain, as well as inexpensive menus at lunch and dinner. *Moderate.*

New Select Hôtel (4 Allées Léon-Gambetta; phone 9150-65-50) is a neighbor of Gare St.-Charles, and therefore not all that central. Still, there are 60 modern rooms with bath (the hotel was relatively recently facelifted in toto). Breakfast only. *Moderate.*

Sofitel Vieux-Port (36 Boulevard Charles-Livon; phone 9152-90-19)—at the far end of Vieux-Port, easily a ten-minute walk from the center—relatively recently gave up four floors of its rooms (some 90 all told) to the separately operated, substantially less expensive and (in my opinion) far more agreeable Novotel (above). I found on my third and most recent Sofitel visit (the first two were downright nasty experiences) that the remaining 127 rooms are undergoing long-range refurbishing, and there are both restaurant and bar. But why pay more? If it's a choice between this house and its friendly same-building neighbor, I would select the latter. *First Class.*

Concorde Palm Beach Hôtel (2 Promenade de la Plage; phone 9176-20-20) was just as sprightly-modern and attractive on my most recent visit of inspection as on an earlier occasion when I stayed overnight. Indeed, it would head my list, were it central. Still, if you've a car, you can combine its beachfront locale with the city—a quarter-hour's drive distant. There are 161 good-sized, well-equipped, terraced rooms—you want to specify a front seaview one—as well as an excellent restaurant, cocktail lounge, and big, sundeck-surrounded swimming pool. Chaîne Concorde. *First Class.*

Le Petit Nice Hôtel (Anse de Maldormé, off Corniche Kennedy, a 20-minute drive from Marseille; phone 9152-14-39) is a country inn, with 16 vividly decorated suites and rooms—much orange, royal blue, and emerald green velvet—the lot of them antique-accented and with excellent baths, some with stall showers. There are, as well, swimming pool, bar, and restaurant. Vibrant-hued decor aside, the impression I am left with is ambience so chilling you could cut it with a knife. Indeed, no other Relais et Châteaux member-hotel has, in my experience, appeared so frigid in the course of inspection. Except in winter, lunch or dinner—*demi-pension*—is obligatory. *First Class.*

DAILY BREAD

Patalain (49 Rue Sainte; phone 9155-02-78): France remains a more sexist country than, say, the United States, and there are still, even as we approach the twenty-first century, not all that many female chefs, at least outside of Paris, which has a small cluster of women in command of restaurant kitchens, and of Lyons, where the owner-cooks of the modest but delicious *bouchons* are traditionally female. Which leads to Patalain. Chef-propriétaire Suzanne Quaglia greets customers, leaves them to oversee the preparation of their meal, and is invariably on hand to say au revoir. Her restaurant is stylishly handsome, a mix of Italian marble, inlaid woods and, for accent, a stained-glass window or two, with a barrel-vaulted private dining room adjacent to the cave, below. Madame Quaglia's à la carte includes the great regional dishes—this is an excellent source of daube Provençale and bourride; and, from other parts of France, coq au vin and pot au feu. In season, game birds and game—pheasant, partridge, grouse, hare, wild boar, venison—are a Quaglia specialty. But the time to go for a meal as good-value as it is delicious is weekday lunch for the three-dish menu, which might open with crudités, sea-snail salad, or the house's own chicken-liver appetizer; continue with the day's fish or chicken, beef or veal options among entrées—each of them Quaglia-accented—with cheese from an enormous platter or desserts from a trolley wheeled to table. A similar menu is available at dinner, when it's more expensive. This is an exceptional restaurant. Location is not far from Vieux-Port, between Place Thiars and Palais de Justice. *Luxury.*

Le Chaudron Provençal (48 Rue Caisserie; phone 9191-02-37) is small and plain as an old shoe, with Monsieur Paul the skilled chef and Madame Paul out in front, welcoming each customer and, preparatory to taking orders, carrying over an immense basket full of the day's catch, so that you know just what it is you're going to have for lunch or dinner. This is a super spot to sample bouillabaisse, the celebrated seafood soup/stew of Marseille. Its preparation and service has become so codified in recent years that a dozen-odd restaurants who make it a specialty have combined to publish a brochure indicating what its component parts should be. There must be four out of a possible eight coastal species of fish and either langouste or cigale de mer, of the crayfish family. There are ten additional ingredients—including saffron, garlic, potatoes, and olive oil; and the hot sauce called rouille should be an accompaniment. The restaurateurs are more permissive when it comes to service, although they make it clear they prefer that bouillabaisse be ladled out in two parts—the fish and shellfish separated from the soup. Try it here at Chaudron Provençal. Or order a seafood dinner embracing oysters on the half shell and a fish you've selected from Madame's basket. *First Class.*

Sauveur (4 Quai de Rive-Neuve; phone 9133-33-32) may not sound Italian, but the name of its game is pizza and pasta. In a capacious setting of blond wood and beige linen, you may tuck into a delicious pizza—cheese and sausage is tasty, but so is anchovy. And, to anticipate a question: The word *rella,* appearing frequently on the menu, is a local shortening of mozzarella; order a portion of it on a salad and it will come to you served on one of the metallic racks used in France for platters of oysters. Nice service. And Sauveur is directly on Vieux-Port. *First Class.*

Le Grill (Novotel Marseille Centre, 36 Boulevard Charles-Livon; phone 9159-22-22) is good to know about because it's open daily nonstop 6 A.M. to midnight, with the à la carte full of tasty choices, the range fish soup with rouille sauce and salade Niçoise among appetizers; a variety of steaks, lamb chops, and escalope of veal among entrées. With daily plats du jour and, of course, breakfast. *Moderate/First Class.*

Les Arceneaulx (25 Cours d'Estienne d'Orves) is the restaurant/ *salon-de-thé* area of what is essentially a bookshop and art gallery. It's popular for tea and pastry in the afternoon, or for a lunch of, say, tomato-mozzarella salad, poached egg with smoked salmon, grilled sole, or thyme-scented lamb chops. *Moderate/First Class.*

Des Mets de Provence (18 Quai de Rive-Neuve; phone 9133-35-38) can be off-putting from the moment of arrival. By that I mean you reach the entrance only after climbing two steep flights of steps in a venerable building where the stairwell, at least when I ascended, wanted brightening. There are antique pieces dotted about the unexceptional interior, where the menu—"Durée deux heures" it indicates, with accuracy: it does take two hours to get through it—opens with hors d'œuvre, a selection of which are served one at a time, in teensy portions plate by plate, with the chopped-olive tapenade and a slice of Arles sausage the best of the lot. Tasteless gray mullet, or possibly another fish, follows and is accompanied, in my experience, by an overcooked vegetable; with roast chicken—devoid of flavor—the next course, preparatory to a decent green salad, with cheese or nougat candy to conclude. Unless you order the house's best dish, an orange and lemon sorbet, for which a hefty extra charge is imposed. My party excepted, the place was devoid of customers on my visit, and the meal was constantly interrupted by the owner, hovering near the table and asking approbation for each dish served. I can't recommend this one. *Luxury.*

Le Jambon de Parme's (67 Rue de la Palud; phone 9154-37-98) setting is a neoclassic, quite formal room with brown suede walls, ivory paneling, crystal chandeliers, and a profusion of fresh flowers. It's staffed by tuxedoed waiters, smiling and cordial, and a chef who turns out pasta quite as delicious as any you are going to be served over the frontier to the east in Italy. Tortellini alla Modenese, tagliatelli ai pistou, and ravioli are masterful. So are entrées like piccata of veal, cassis-sauced duckling, and châteaubriand. For dessert: zuppa inglese, as you remember it from Rome or Florence. A delightful experience. *First Class.*

L'Oursin (14 Cours Jean-Ballard; phone 9133-34-85)—given its name, sea urchin—had just better serve seafood, and, of course, it does. Oysters and other crustaceans from a big ice-surfaced buffet are indicated as openers, with grilled fish of the day to follow. *Moderate.*

Miramar (12 Quai du Port; phone 9191-10-40): If it's a fine day, take a table on the terrace, with Vieux-Port a hop and a skip distant, and the profile of Notre-Dame-de-la-Garde in the background. Open with oysters or clams on the half shell, tuna tartar—a Miramar specialty—or the house's own fish terrine. Grilled lobster is always available, and there are reliable fish entrées—sole, salmon, and a seafood pot au feu among them. But Miramar's best-seller, not surprisingly, is bouillabaisse, available only if a minimum of two persons orders it. And the house white, in carafes, is good-value. Friendly. *First Class.*

L'Ami Fritz (17 Rue Euthymènes; phone 9154-23-26): Given its name, you should not be surprised to learn that Fritz is Alsatian and his bill of fare likewise. This is an agreeable venue—just off restaurant-filled Place Thiars—when you hanker after choucroute garnie, or perhaps, tournedos Strasbourgeois. The menu is well-priced. And there are Alsatian wines. *Moderate/First Class.*

Le Charpenterie (22 Rue de la Paix; phone 9154-22-89) is welcoming and central; Provençal specialties are tasty, and if you go on Friday or Saturday evening, ooh-la-la! The chef will have prepared a multicourse *menu gastronomique*. But the standard menus are good, too, and include coffee. *First Class.*

La Samaritaine (2 Quai du Port; phone 9199-31-41): Take an outdoor table, and watch ambulatory Marseille pass in review with

Vieux-Port just beyond, while you order an omelet or steak/frites lunch. In the afternoon: tea and pastries. *Moderate.*

La Boutique du Glacier (1 Place de la Bourse) is an ice-cream parlor *extraordinaire.* So long as you're prepared for a bit of congestion—all Marseilles seems intent on a boule fraise or a boule citron on a hot day—you can't help but be content. *Moderate.*

Liautaud (on the harbor in Cassis; phone 4201-75-37) is just the spot for lunch on a Cassis excursion; the bouillabaisse is celebrated, and there are other seafood options, as well. Take an outdoor table. *First Class.*

SHOPPER'S MARSEILLE

Le Marché aux Poissons (at the foot of La Canebière) is the daily seafood market, with more species of for-sale fish and seafood than I venture you'll have seen anywhere else in France. Best time to have a look is the morning; more fun than an aquarium. Major department stores—including *Galeries Lafayette* and *Nouvelles Galeries*—are all on Rue St.-Ferréol, a pedestrian street with such other stores as *Cacharel* (men's and women's clothes), *Le Must de Cartier* (jewelry), *Bally* (shoes), and *Burberry* (raincoats). Rue Grignan makes a point of men's-wear. The massive and confusing Centre Bourse has good stores. And Rue Crudère is dotted with antique shops.

SOUND OF MUSIC

Opéra de Marseille (Place Revyer): You'll have passed this neoclassic landmark. Book a seat, if you can, for the opera (which averages a dozen productions each winter season, ranging from Richard Strauss's *Salomé* to Joseph Strauss's *Vienna Waltzes,* Rossini's *Barber of Seville* to Milhaud's *Christophe Colomb*). This theater is home base, as well, to Roland Petit's *Ballet de Marseille;* concerts, too. (Office de Tourisme—address below—can advise you of programs in this and other theaters.)

INCIDENTAL INTELLIGENCE

Aéroport de Marseille-Marignane (18 miles north of town); both international (including Air France flights linking Marseille with New York in the U.S.) and domestic services. *Further information:* Office de Tourisme, 4 La Canebière; Office de Tourisme, Place Baragnon, Cassis.

23

Monaco

Profiling the Principality

BACKGROUND BRIEFING

There is something to be said for a ruling house that has been in business since the twelfth century. At the back of the little guidebook they used to sell at the Prince's Palace in the 390-acre Principality of Monaco, there is a genealogical table of the House of Grimaldi, which indicates that it was founded in 1133 by one Otto Canella, whose son gave his name, Grimaldi, to the clan. Rainier III, the current reigning prince, came along 30 Grimaldis later, Rainier II—according to that table—having concluded his reign in 1407.

Succession? Prince Rainier shared his throne with the late Princess Grace, who, as Philadelphia-born Grace Kelly, gave up a successful film career to marry Rainier in 1956; she died following a 1982 auto crash. They had three children. The youngest and eldest are princesses: Caroline (born 1957), and Stéphanie (born 1965). Their blond brother, Prince Albert (born 1958), educated in Europe and America and resembling his late mother more than do either of his sisters—is heir to this ancient, if hardly impoverished, throne.

The Monaco that the world knows today as a tiny enclave surrounded on three sides by France, on the fourth by the Mediterranean, with solid gold casinos as its trademark, was impoverished to the point of bankruptcy something over a century ago, during the reign of Prince Charles. The principality had to give up territory to France—the nearby towns of Menton and Roquebrune, with the small settlement atop the rocky promontory of Monaco constituting the bulk of the remaining territory.

But Prince Charles—a handsome, intelligent-looking man, if the portrait of him in the palace is a guide—had an idea. Better to say he adapted an idea—the scheme of the Duke of Baden, who had opened a profitable casino at Baden-Baden, his German spa (see

Germany at Its Best). Charles decided to do likewise. Success did not come overnight, so in 1860 he hired a pro to take over the enterprise. Before 1870 there was rail service from Nice, and business at the casino was so good that the prince did away with direct taxes (as have all of his successors).

Before long, the Riviera had its most fashionable resort. The rich English came over from older neighboring communities, to what they termed "Montie," and royalty made its way to the gaming tables, too. Although the Principality of Monaco retained its name, the area of the principality in which the new casino was situated had its name changed from hardly glamorous Les Spélugues to Monte Carlo, the Italian for Mount Charles, in honor of the enterprising man on the throne.

Until as recently as 1911, Monaco's princes were absolute rulers. A new constitution in that year set up a representative government, under a chief minister and an 18-member national council. Women were given the vote only in 1962 (an American-born princess may have had something to do with this). In the interim—in 1918—Monaco signed a treaty with France in which it agreed that the French government would have to approve succession to the throne; that with cessation of the monarchy, Monaco would become a part of France, and that its for long untaxed citizens would become subject to French taxation. Needless to say, there has never been a republican movement in Monaco, and so long as Monégasques enjoy the bliss of freedom from taxes, it is not expected that there will be moves in that direction.

Not everyone living in Monaco is Monégasque. By no means. Something like 4,500, out of an estimated population hovering at the 27,000 mark, are citizens. A great majority are French and must pay French taxes unless they were Monaco residents prior to 1957. And not a few other residents are successful foreign nationals come to live in the Riviera sunshine—and save paying high income taxes in their native lands. They populate seaview condominium apartments in an ever-increasing mass of skyscrapers; Monaco is the Riviera at its most decidedly vertical.

The buildings' construction reflects the aggressive development policy Prince Rainier adopted when, in 1967, his government bought out—for $8 million—Greek shipping tycoon Aristotle Onassis's controlling 52 percent of the Société des Bains de Mer, the euphemistically named company formed by Prince Charles in the last century to run the casino and which had become owner of hotels, clubs, restaurants, and cafés.

In control of their own ship, Monégasques charted a new course, constructing massive convention facilities to attract congresses, and making a strong bid for middle-income visitors to supplement a traditionally blue-chip gambling clientele, the while encouraging development of high-rise condos. Even allowing for some 75 additional acres gained by reclamation of land from the sea, it has not been possible to preclude congestion.

Monaco's situation—straddling an irregular Mediterranean shore, with rugged hills and distant snowy peaks as a backdrop—will always be a magnet. So will its feisty people, stubbornly clinging to the anachronistic form of government that allows them independence, even as they are hemmed in by a herculean neighbor. The Casino de Monte Carlo remains the most glamorous extant, and the long-on-scene leading hotels, De Paris and Hermitage, remain two of the most beautiful in Europe. The guard changes, day in and day out, at the palace, high on a rocky eminence over the blue-green sea. A white- or even black-tie gala at the Opéra or the Sporting Club, the thrust toward egalitarianism notwithstanding, remains as gala an evening as one is likely to come across along the coast. (It must be remembered that Monégasques take their Princely Family and its titles *very* seriously, indeed, as do the French.) Still, when all is said and done, a price is being paid for financial gains and burgeoning real estate. Monaco's charm quotient diminishes with the arrival on site of each new construction crew.

ON SCENE

Lay of the Land: Terminology first. The country—area is less than 500 acres—is termed *Principauté de Monaco,* the Principality of Monaco. Its oldest sector is called either *Monaco, Monaco Ville,* or *The Rock,* for it is an elevated stony peninsula that juts into the Mediterranean. It overlooks the principal harbor to its east, the Port of Monaco, which is flanked by a sea-level commercial and residential area, *La Condamine,* which separates Monaco from *Monte Carlo,* due east and site of the casinos, leading hotels, most shops, and beaches. The other harbor, *Port de Fontvieille,* is west of the Monaco promontory, flanking an area embracing the *Héliport* (from which scheduled helicopters connect Monaco with Nice) and the relatively recent *Louis II Stadium,* with a pair of French villages, each called *Èze,* not far distant. The Monte Carlo sector is based on *Place du casino,* named for the Casino dominating it, with *Centre des Congrès,* the principal convention complex due south, edging the sea; *Avenue des Beaux-Arts*—lined with classy shops—to its west; and a block-long green boulevard—*Allée des Boulingrins*—leading north to shops of *Boulevard des Moulins,* an east–west thoroughfare. Eastern Monaco's precincts are gained by *Avenue Princesse Grace,* which leads from the core to wide, white sands of *Plage de Larvotto, Monte Carlo Sporting Club* straddling a green peninsula just beyond, with the sands and cliffs of *Roquebrune* on France's *Cap Martin,* immediately to the east.

Casino de Monte Carlo (Place du Casino): Mock Baroque, in the best traditions of the Second Empire, the casino's portico—surmounted by a pair of minitowers backed by a glass dome framed by a pair of maxitowers—gives onto the carefully tended floral core of the square taking its name. Opened in 1863, and meticulously restored and refurbished (cost was 40 million francs) in the late 1980s, it retains original frescoes, sculpture, stained glass, gilded woodwork, and silk-shaded lamps hung from high ceilings over the gaming tables. It has, to be sure, reflected changes in gamblers' tastes: slot machines, for example, and more recently, an informal dress code for the onetime Salon de l'Europe, rechristened the American Room and with American roulette, blackjack, and craps—not to mention English-speaking croupiers. There is, as well, a slot-machine gallery at the entrance that is admission-free and where casual dress is allowed, as is the case in the American Room. Withal, though, the rest of casino remains the essence of Monte Carlo grandeur. The European Gaming Rooms—including Salon *Super*-Privé (where stakes are *very* high and whose open hours are by appointment only)—persist in requiring passports for admission and jackets and ties for gents. They concentrate, as has long been the case, on European roulette, trente et quarante, and baccarat; with quite good restaurants and bars in connection.

A part of the Casino's complex, Monte Carlo's opera house—called *Salle Garnier* in honor of its designer, the very same Charles Garnier who created the Opéra/Garnier in Paris—does not, more's the pity, keep daytime hours; it is open only for performances. I don't know of a small-space theater anywhere in Europe that is more beautiful; whatever the performance during your stay, go.

Let me, at this point, call to your attention Monte Carlo's other casinos. Unlike the European rooms of the Casino de Monte Carlo (above)—for which a really stiff admission fee is charged unless you present the Gold Card, a pass issued to guests of hotels that are a part of the SBM chain, below—*Loews Monte Carlo Hôtel Casino* on Avenue des Spélugues (American roulette, craps, blackjack, slots) is free and casual. There is a slot-machine room, as well as American roulette, craps, and blackjack tables, attached to *Café de Paris* (Place du Casino); and *Monte Carlo Sporting Club* (Avenue Princesse Grace) operates a casino (roulette, trente et quarante, chemin-de-fer) during July and August, traditionally opening at 10 P.M., and with an admission fee unless you present SBM's Gold Card.

Musée Océanographique (Avenue St.-Martin)—Monaco's premier museum—occupies quarters in a substantial neoclassic building, appropriately situated along the sea. It was established by a turn-of-century prince named Albert, and its ace-in-the-hole is a ranker of an aquarium occupying the basement—an all-Europe dazzler of its kind, with some 4,500 fish representing 350 species, exhibited in

90 tanks in settings similar to their natural environments in seawater around the planet. Before departing, take in the view—of the spectacular coastline and of the principality—from the elevated terrace. The Océanographique is the only museum of consequence in Monaco—the only requisite in its category, there being no art museum, an odd lack given the fabulous wealth of the reigning princes.

Palais Princier (Place du Palais) is essentially a Renaissance building with strong overtones of just-down-the-road Italy; the place gained some crenelated towers in the late nineteenth century during the rich Prince Charles era. Architecturally, it is at its best in a stunning galleried courtyard (wisely put to good use for summer concerts). I have no doubt the Princely Family's private living quarters in the palace are handsome and tasteful. But the Grands Appartements, or State Rooms—for regularly departing tours for which a fairly substantial admission fee is charged—come as a sad surprise. Indeed, no other interiors of mansions of substance of which I am aware, at least, anywhere in Europe, are as gaudily unattractive, lacking in style, good looks, and the sophistication and indeed brilliance to which such interiors so often aspire. I can't recommend that you spend your money or time (queues can be long, before you get in) on a Palais Princier tour, unless you are intent on being the first on your block to have observed the throne from which Grimaldis have long reigned. Traditionally, the *Changing of the Guard* takes place every morning at the palace; you must not—I caution—expect anything like the spit and polish of the ceremony at London's Buckingham Palace (see *Britain at Its Best*). *Musée du Souvenir Napoléonien* (in the Palace complex) exhibits uniforms, weapons, and documents of the Napoleonic era collected by a nineteenth-century prince.

Musée National Automates et Poupées d'Autrefois (Boulevard du Larvotto, above Larvotto Beach) may—or may not—be your cup of tea. It's a collection of dolls—400 all told—animated and otherwise, mostly eighteenth and nineteenth century.

Cathedral of Monaco (Rue de l'Église) is late nineteenth century, mock-Romanesque and hardly beautiful, albeit with a pair of altars painted by a respected area artist, Louis Brea, in the sixteenth century; and with tombs of Monaco princes.

Èze: There are two French villages called Èze, each about five miles west of Monte Carlo. Èze-Bord-de-Mer is a pleasant seaside village. But it's to just plain Èze—a onetime medieval fortress, on the summit of a mountain 1,200 feet above the sea—to which I now direct you, either for an excursion that would coincide with lunch or, better yet, an overnight stay. The views from on high—all along the coast—are spectacular. And it's fun to wander the narrow, hilly streets, flanked by ancient stone houses, poking about myriad shops in which are sold handmade jewelry, knitwear, leather, pottery, glass, Provençal cotton, and Riviera olives. But you want also to have a look at thirteenth-century *Chapelle de Ste.-Croix* (one of a number of charming churches), trek through pretty cactus-filled *Jardin Exotique,* and inspect locally created Renaissance paintings in *Musée d'Histoire et d'Art Religieux.*

SETTLING IN

De Paris Hôtel (Place du Casino, Monte Carlo; phone 9350-80-80) was a New Year's gift to the principality when it opened on January 1, 1864. Its original two stories have expanded to eight. But the ambience of this grande dame of the coast remains nineteenth-century. A crystal chandelier, affixed to a glass dome, illuminates the amber-toned lobby. The adjacent bar-lounge is a study in art nouveau. Louis XV, the principal restaurant, evaluated below, retains original massive murals, with gilded capitals on Corinthian columns supporting its high arched ceiling. The 271 rooms have been refurbished recently—and handsomely, with superb baths. Indeed, the refurbished suites—especially the one often frequented by Churchill and named in his memory—are among the most beautiful in France (if I may be permitted to so link Monaco with France at this point), along with those of the Crillon and Ritz in Paris. But less-exalted accommodations are hardly to be despised; and many rooms have balconies. When you book, specify seaview (priciest), Place du Casino (second priciest), or Avenue des Beaux-Arts (least pricey). A second restaurant, the rooftop-cum-view Grill, rates additional comment on a later page. And the hotel's Bar Américain is the principality's see-and-be-seen social center, becoming a buzzy piano-bar each evening. The de Paris is flagship of the SBM group—and deservedly so. *Luxury.*

Hermitage Hôtel (Square Beaumarchais, Monte Carlo; phone 9350-67-31) might better be called the Belle Époque. This is an enchanter of a turn-of-century period piece. The original gingerbread facade—with a painted frieze extending the length of the top of the building and with sculpted angels and bearded gents' heads supporting wrought-iron balconies—is impeccably maintained. Public spaces include a winter garden topped by a stained-glass dome and a restaurant (evaluated in a later paragraph) that is one of the handsomest in Europe. All 236 rooms have been refurbished in a smart art nouveau motif as part of a multimillion-franc renovation program; they're lovely. And the health-club-cum-pool, which the Hermitage shares with the de Paris (above) is café-equipped. Tabs are lower than those of Hôtel de Paris, but only somewhat. An SBM hotel. *Luxury.*

Beach Plaza Hôtel (22 Avenue Princesse Grace, Monte Carlo; phone 9330-98-80) went up a decade or so back as a Holiday Inn. A few seasons ago, Trusthouse Forte, a ranking British chain, took it over and did it over stylishly and tastefully, in a contemporary-traditional mix. The beauty part of the BP is that it's one of but two Monte Carlo hotels beachfront. (The other is farther-from-the-center Monte Carlo Beach Hôtel, below.) And it has a good-sized pool as well. The 300 rooms are capacious and terraced, with good baths; precisely half are seaview—the ones to aim for. There is a pair of restaurants (one of which I review on a later page) and a poolside café that's a pleasure for lunch. Cozy bar-lounge, too. Friendly. *Luxury.*

Mirabeau Hôtel (1 Avenue Princesse Grace, Monte Carlo; phone 9325-45-45), newest of the SBM hotels, is unprepossessing from without; the facade is almost too severe, and it's a bit tricky of access if you're a pedestrian, although it is conveniently central, below Place du Casino. Once inside, you perceive that the Mirabeau has a nice, intimate quality; modern, but not too big. There are 100 rooms (those I've inspected are immense, with super baths); seaview rooms are the most in demand. The pool is surrounded by a big sun deck, the bar-lounge congenial, the restaurant, Coupole, exceptional (it is reviewed in a subsequent paragraph), and the staff cordial. *Luxury.*

Loews Monte-Carlo Hôtel (Avenue Spélugues, Monte Carlo; phone 9350-65-00) is ingeniously designed. Only a really talented architect could have fitted this 636-room giant into the core of Monte Carlo—just below Place du Casino, adjacent to the Convention Center and straddling the sea—with a profile so low that it defers to (and does not conflict with) the nineteenth-century architecture of the square up the hill. The casino leading from the massive lobby is Yank-style (see above). The seaview swimming pool is good-sized, as are bedrooms, which have excellent baths. There are good restaurants, a cabaret, and a choice of bars, including one edging the lobby with a sea view. *Luxury.*

Métropole Hôtel (Avenue de la Madonne; phone 9315-15-15): Repeat visitors to Monte Carlo over the years will remember the heart-of-town Métropole. It opened in 1886 during the period when Monaco's Prince Charles was creating the casino-dominated area of Monte Carlo (see Background Briefing, above). Its initial owners were British, and it lured not only Brits (who adored Monte Carlo—*Montie,* as they termed it—from its beginnings) but assorted crowned heads. Nazi occupiers took it over during World War II, after which another British firm held control, selling to a Lebanese entrepreneur in the early 1980s. He tore down the old Métropole, painstakingly constructing a replacement in the original style, which opened as the eighties became the nineties. This is an elaborate—at times excessively elaborate—house, with a sprawling lobby doubling as a café, 170 rooms and suites whose decor is based on a Louis XVI motif, richly draped and accessorized, and with marble baths; several restaurants including a brasserie; swimming pool; business center; and an adjacent shopping center with some 130 boutiques, cafés, and restaurants. Although operated by its owner and his staff, the Métropole is affiliated with Conrad Hôtels, the overseas division of Los Angeles–based Hilton Hôtels Corporation. *Luxury.*

Abela Hôtel (23 Avenue de Papalins, in the Fontvieille quarter of Monaco, a bus or taxi ride from Monte Carlo; phone 9205-90-00) is a late 1980s house, with 192 blond-furnished rooms, most with terraces, and all with baths that are both tub- and shower-equipped. There are two restaurants and a bar. *First Class.*

Du Louvre Hôtel (16 Boulevard des Moulins, Monte Carlo; phone 9350-65-25) has the advantage of a location on a principal shopping street, core-of-town; 32 functional rooms with bath. Breakfast only. *Moderate.*

Balmoral Hôtel (12 Avenue de la Costa, Monte Carlo; phone 9350-62-37), elderly and central, with an agreeable lobby-lounge and 72 rooms; those I have inspected have soft mattresses. Chilly atmosphere. Restaurant. *Moderate.*

Alexandra Hôtel (35 Boulevard Princesse-Charlotte; phone 9350-63-13) occupies an elderly structure not far north of Place du Casino; most but not all of the 55 rooms have bath or shower. Breakfast only. *Moderate.*

Monte Carlo Beach Hôtel (Roquebrune/Cap-Martin, France; phone 9378-21-40): Though actually across the frontier in France—just barely—this hotel is one of the Monte Carlo–based SBM group; indeed, it's that company's elderly Old Beach Hôtel thoroughly refurbished and with a new name. This is the only hotel on the beach, other than the Beach Plaza (above), closer to town. There are just under half a hundred comfortable rooms—furniture is white rattan and every room is seaview, with a terrace—as well as a restaurant and bar-lounge. The Olympic-size swimming pool overlooks sand and sea and the hotel is within walking distance of the center. Closed in winter. *Luxury.*

Vista Palace Hôtel (Grande Corniche, Roquebrune/Cap-Martin, France, a four-mile drive from Monte Carlo; phone 9335-01-50): What happened was this: A hotel, Vistaero by name, had for some years been enviously situated atop a Grande Corniche cliff a thousand feet above the sea, with utterly enchanting views of Monaco and the Mediterranean. Recent seasons saw a small but exclusive German chain, Grundig Hotels, take over, replacing the old 25-room Vistaero with the quite splendid 75-suite-and-room Vista Palace. The old name was retained—a nice bit of nostalgia—for the picture-windowed main restaurant, which is one of the best on the coast (below evaluated). Accommodations—contemporary albeit with Louis XV and Louis XVI antecedents accented by pale-hued contemporary textiles and highlighted by state-of-the-art baths—are among the more eye-filling on the Côte d'Azur. There's a second restaurant, the casual La Corniche with tables spilling onto a terrace; a lively piano bar; what has to be the most spectacularly situated of swimming pools, high above the sea; and even a fabulous fitness center with heated pool, sauna, squash courts, and solarium. Not to mention kind and caring Grundig management. *Luxury.*

Château de la Chèvre d'Or Hôtel (Èze-Village, France; phone 9341-12-12)—of medieval origin—is stone-walled, with an antique-accented lounge, swimming pool hugging the edge of an eminence that affords smashing coastal views, pretty courtyard where breakfast is served, half a dozen rooms and 3 suites, no two alike, and an excellent restaurant—seafood is a specialty—that's enjoyable for a candlelit dinner, as well as for lunch in the course of an excursion from Monaco. An enchanter. Member, Relais et Châteaux. *First Class.*

Le Cap Estel Hôtel (Èze-Bord-de-Mer, France; phone 9301-50-44) straddles an elevated parklike promontory jutting into the Mediterranean and is so situated that there are sea views from all 37 terraced rooms. Public spaces are gracious and in traditional style. The restaurant—picture-windowed and Louis XVI-accented—moves either to a broad terrace or under trees on the lawn in warm weather. And there is a pair of big pools—one, enclosed for cool periods; the other, alfresco and with a sundeck. *Luxury.*

DAILY BREAD

Louis XV (De Paris Hôtel, Place du Casino, Monte Carlo; phone 9330-23-11) occupies an off-lobby space in the principality's premier hotel that is arguably among the handsomer restaurant environments within the confines of France. It's high-ceilinged and crystal-chandeliered, with gilded stuccowork, fine murals, exquisitely set tables, massed flowers, and a skilled staff. The meal you've ordered will be a meld of the Mediterranean's traditional dishes with contemporary flourishes. There are multicourse menus at two prices (I suggest choosing the less costly) and an à la carte. Open with mushroom risotto, pumpkin soup dotted with gnocchi, or the chef's version of salade Niçoise. Consider such entrées as grilled lamb chops stuffed with vegetables, any of the beef or fish specialties, and desserts in which wild strawberries, chocolate, and sorbet are among principal ingredients. This hotel's wine cellar shelters 200,000 bottles, so that your choice is wide. An exceptional experience. *Luxury.*

La Coupole (Mirabeau Hôtel, Avenue Princesse Grace, Monte Carlo; phone 9325-45-45) though low-ceilinged and in an unexceptional contemporary space, has, in a relatively recent rejuvenation, been made to look as engaging as possible, given its proportions, with muraled walls and Louis XVI–inspired chairs upholstered in a floral textile surrounding tables. The cooking is as contemporary as the hotel, albeit sensible—and tasty, with the best deal the three-course menu at midday, which might open with Scotch salmon, snails, or artichoke appetizers, all creations of the chef; offer filet of trout, lamb chops, sweetbreads, or a small steak among entrées, with half a dozen tempting dessert choices—or cheese, if you prefer. *Luxury.*

Le Grill (De Paris Hôtel, Place du Casino, Monte Carlo; phone 9350-80-80): What I categorize as top-of-the-world restaurants—those with wide-angle panoramic views—do not always come off so well with respect to cuisine. The Grill atop the de Paris is an exception. (And it has a retractable roof for under-the-stars dining on balmy evenings.) What the French call grillades—châteaubriand, served with a wine and shallot sauce, paillards of veal, filet of beef, lamb chops—are delicious. But there are other good bets—lobster in champagne and maigret de canard among them. Cream of watercress soup and seafood salad are good openers. And desserts deserve the separate card they are accorded. Be sure to peruse the wine list; the cellar of the de Paris (hewn out of rock in 1874 and open by appointment to guests) prides itself not only on quantity—bottle-total, as I mention above, is kept at 200,000—but quality as well. *Luxury.*

Belle Époque's (Hermitage Hôtel, Square Beaumarchais, Monte Carlo; phone 9350-67-31) ceiling frescoes are framed by gilded stucco. A marble colonnade—each pillar topped with a gilded Ionic capital—wraps itself around the room, illuminated by crystal chandeliers. Silver candelabra grace dinner tables. And fare remains traditional—truffled foie gras and smoked salmon, among appetizers; scallop-and-green-noodle casserole standing out among seafood entrées; with veal piccata, lamb filet with the chef's own sauce, and roast chicken with mushrooms other good bets. Warm desserts are a specialty; consider ordering a chocolate soufflé upon arrival, so that there will be time to prepare it. Or how about paper-thin crêpes combined with poached pears and then soaked with Poire William eau-de-vie? *Luxury.*

Le Gratin (Beach Plaza Hôtel, Avenue Princesse Grace, Monte Carlo; phone 9330-98-80): Le Gratin's beef is not American, but rather Black Angus imported from Scotland—hardly to be despised. An immense joint is roasted—rare and medium-rare, worry not—and wheeled to table for carving, with baked potatoes among accompaniments. You may substitute roast saddle of lamb for the beef. Open with avocado salad or turtle soup. Vacherin à la myrtille—a blueberry confection—is a favored sweet. Dinner only. *First Class.*

Chez Gianni (39 Avenue Princesse Grace, Monte Carlo; phone 9330-46-33): With Italy just a few miles down the road, it should come as no surprise that cuisine of the peninsula found its way to Monaco. There are easily a dozen reliable Italian restaurants; Chez Gianni is among the pioneers. What Gianni calls hors d'œuvres maison is assorted antipasto—an indicated opener—as might be a bowl of minestrone or the shredded raw beef specialty, carpaccio. There are a dozen pasta choices; spaghetti au vongole is, of course, alle vongole—in a clam sauce; penne aux quatre fromages is the classic quill-shaped pasta with a four-cheese—quattro formaggi—sauce. And saltimbocca alla Romana—the sliced veal and smoked ham specialty—is among entrées. *First Class.*

Giacomo (Galerie du Métropole, Avenue des Spélugues; phone 9325-20-30): You're not going to find a handsomer Italian restaurant in the principality. Giacomo Oliveri's quarters are tastefully contemporary in shades of pale gray and blue. Descamps linen covers flower-centered tables. Open with a generous assortment of antipasto, a platter of assorted Italian salamis, mozzarella-and-tomato salad, or the mushroom species known as porcini sautéed in oil and garlic. Giacomo makes pasta selection difficult; there are always 15 kinds, including fettucine ai formaggi misti, lasagna and spaghetti pomodoro e basilico. But there's risotto—with mushrooms or with saffron, Milanese style, if you prefer. The veal entrées—piccata, a giant grilled chop—are super; so is the Florentine beefsteak. There are two menus and a big à la carte. Swift and smiling Italian service. *Luxury.*

Rampoldi (3 Avenue des Spélugues, Monte Carlo; phone 9330-70-65): Like all Italian restaurants in France (including Monaco), there are French dishes on the menu, the principle being that Frenchmen esehew a restaurant completely devoid of Gallic fare. Still, Italian-operated and -staffed Rampoldi does well with food of the peninsula. You choose from an à la carte that might offer the day's soup or a variety of salads or antipasto selections as starters, excellent pastas (spaghetti Bolognese, tagliatelli Luciano, for example), reliable veal entrées, Italian wines. Location is heart-of-town. Nice. *First Class.*

Le Bistroquet (Galerie Charles III, Monte Carlo; phone 9350-71-68) is heart-of-town, with alfresco tables. Rillettes de porc—coarse pork pâté—is a good opener. Salade Niçoise goes down well on a hot day as a lunch entrée. So does entrecôte aux frites. Omelets are a specialty, too. Friendly. *Moderate/First Class.*

Café de Paris (Place du Casino, Monte Carlo) is the long-on-scene, stylishly redecorated center of the action, midday through midnight—and beyond. Go for coffee, a drink, a full meal, or a snack. Views from the outdoor tables are of the Casino, de Paris Hôtel, and Monte Carlo's ambulatory populace. The café is obligatory—at least once—in the course of a Monaco visit. *First Class.*

Roger Verge Café (Galerie du Sporting d'Hiver, Place du Casino, Monte Carlo; phone 9325-86-12): Established French restaurateurs rarely open branches; this café, taking the name of a near-Cannes luxury eatery's owner, is an exception. But it's not a clone of the original, where proper lunches and dinners are the name of the game. Monte Carlo's appendage is, rather, a source of breakfast, snacks, and afternoon tea as well as lunch and dinner, with both set menus and à la carte. *First Class.*

L'Estragon (6 Rue Émile de Loth, Monaco Ville; phone 9330-46-11) might be a good idea for lunch in the course of scouting the area around Place du Palais in Monaco Ville. Well-priced menus, tasty plats du jour. *Moderate.*

Prince's Tea (26 Avenue de la Costa, Monte Carlo) is nothing less than the principality's prime pâtisserie/tearoom, delightfully old-fashioned, with Louis XV–style chairs surrounding tables from which you may order scrumptious pastries with your tea, and a counter from which you may buy a bag. *First Class.*

Le Vistaero (Vista Palace Hôtel, Grande Corniche, Roquebrune/Cap Martin; phone 9335-01-50), in a hotel a thousand feet above the sea (see Settling In, above) has picture windows on two walls, the better for memorable panoramas of the Mediterranean and Monte

Carlo. This is a handsome room with unusually designed chairs upholstered in blue and pink, the latter the color of its table linen. Go at lunch on a clear sunny day for coastal views at their best. And delicious things to eat, starting with, say, crayfish salad in an orange-and-saffron-flavored vinaigrette or duck terrine, gin-infused; continuing with a trio of tiny lamb chops, thyme-seasoned, or the day's fish masterfully prepared; with pear tarte or rhubarb-filled pastry as sweets. There are a more elaborate *menu de dégustation* and an extensive à la carte as well. Lovely service. *Luxury.*

SHOPPER'S MONACO

Avenue des Beaux-Arts, leading from Place du Casino, is nothing if not blue chip. By that, I mean there are outlets of such firms as *Bulgari, Piaget,* and *Cartier* (jewelry). *Christian Dior* (women's clothes) is in the Hôtel de Paris. Boulevard des Moulins is another interesting street, with *Façonnable* (men's clothing), *Charles Jourdan* (costly women's shoes), *Salganik* (fabulous furs), *Souleïado* (Provençal cotton textiles), and *Tabbah* (jewelry). *Hermès,* the Paris leather, necktie, silk-scarf, and clothing chain, is on Avenue de Monte Carlo; *Puiforcat* (French silver) is on Avenue des Spélugues; *Chanel* and *Lanvin* (women's clothing) are in Le Sporting d'Hiver (Place du Casino). And there are a hundred-plus shops—*Yves St.-Laurent* (women's clothing) and *Manufacture de Monaco* (Monégasque porcelain, with crystal, silver, and table linen as well) are but a pair—in *Galérie du Métropole* (17 Avenue des Spélugues, adjoining Hôtel Métropole). Both of the major Britain-based auction houses have Monte Carlo branches—*Sotheby's* (Place du Casino) and *Christie's* (Park Palace).

SOUND OF MUSIC

As if to compensate for its lack of fine-arts museums, Monaco does very well indeed by the performing arts. I allude, with enthusiasm, on an earlier page to *Salle Garnier*—the treasure of an opera house that is attached to the Casino de Monte Carlo (Place du Casino); it's the principal venue for opera, *Orchestre Philharmonique de Monte-Carlo,* and the relatively recently formed *Ballet de Monte Carlo,* a latter-day successor to the pioneering Ballet Russe de Monte Carlo of Serge Diaghilev, from the early decades of this century. Such now-classic ballets as *L'Après-Midi d'un Faune, Le Spectre de la Rose,* and *Le Sacré du Printemps* had early performances in Salle Garnier; while operatic composers, including Berlioz, Massinet, Saint-Saëns, Ravel, and Puccini presented works there as well. *Auditorium Rainier III* (Centre de Congrès, Boulevard Louise II) sees Philharmonic and other performances, too. *Monte Carlo Sporting Club* (Avenue Princesse Grace) is the site of a variety of galas—black-tie dinners, floor shows with dancing and other special events, invariably dressy and pricey. In summer, the Philharmonic presents a season of concerts in the courtyard of *Palais Princier* (Place du Palais), and there are open-air concerts at *Théâtre du Fort Antoine* (Avenue de la Quarantine). *Théâtre Princesse Grace* (Avenue d'Ostende) is the leading venue for plays, all performed in the French language.

INCIDENTAL INTELLIGENCE

Monte Carlo Golf Club (La Turbie, France)—high over Monaco and the Mediterranean and, as you will note, over the border in France—is beautifully situated, with a restaurant-equipped clubhouse; 18 holes, par 70. Good *tennis,* too. Helicopter service, via *Heli Air Monaco,* is worth knowing about; it connects the principality with Nice; flying time is ten minutes, and there are frequent departures the day and evening long, so that you can easily spend the day, either in Monaco or Nice, returning to your hotel after a fairly early dinner. *Further information:* Monaco Government Tourist and Convention Bureau, 845 Third Avenue, New York, NY 10022. Direction du Tourisme et des Congrès de la Principauté de Monaco, 2 Boulevard des Moulins, Monte Carlo.

24

Montpellier

Ancient Languedoc Updated

BACKGROUND BRIEFING

If Montpellier is unusual among French cities in that it has absolutely no Roman roots—there was, also, no *Montpellierensis* or anything of the kind—it is almost as unusual in that it passed through a medieval period when it was the property, successively, of the Spanish kingdoms of Aragon and Majorca. It has been quite French, ever since, fear not. Indeed, it was strongly Huguenot-Protestant French until the early seventeenth century, when Louis XIII sent troops south and took control of this city—midway between Marseille and Toulouse—an ostensibly military tactic that spurred economic development.

That was the period that saw construction of a substantial clutch of *hôtels particuliers,* opulent mansions that remain landmarks of a city that became even richer when the next reigning Louis—the Fourteenth, in whose honor Montpellier's Arc de Triomphe went up in 1691—decreed it offical seat of the ancient province of Languedoc. To this day, dynamic Montpellier, as proud of a university that dates to the thirteenth century as of its contemporary flair for industry, persists in bilingual street signs. Every thoroughfare is labeled in Languedoc as well as in French—the better to remind its citizens and its visitors of an extraordinary heritage.

ON SCENE

Lay of the Land: *Place de la Comédie* is the nerve center of town, dominated by the mock-Baroque opera house whose name it takes and cafés that spill onto the pavement. *Rue de la Loge,* a principal commercial artery, extends northwest from this square until it reaches *Place des Martyrs de la Résistance,* off which another major thoroughfare, *Rue Foch,* extends west through the earlier mentioned seventeenth-century *Arc de Triomphe* into the capacious—and gracious—*Promenade du Peyrou,* an eighteenth-century mix of paths and pools. Its western edge is flanked by an utterly beautiful water tower—still another eighteenth-century souvenir called *Château d'Eau,* six-sided, double-tiered, and supported by Corinthian pillars. The tower flanks a reservoir that is the eastern terminus of yet one more manifestation of Montpellier's eighteenth-century golden age—fabulous *Aqueduc St.-Clément,* built to carry water from a source ten miles distant. The two principal pedestrian-shopping streets are *Rue de l'Ancien Courrier* and *Rue de l'Argenterie,* perpendicular to each other, core-of-town. Eastern precincts of the city are dominated by futuristic *Centre Commercial du Polygone,* a mix of hotels, department stores, and shops; with the also-recent *Antigone apartment complex,* wherein an innovative architect has deftly melded classic and contemporary motifs, nearby.

Musée Fabre (Boulevard Sarrail): If Montpellier is a sleeper of a city, Musée Fabre is likewise a sleeper of a museum, one of the most art-rich of the repositories of beaux-arts in the republic. My notes are punctuated with exclamation marks: Veronese's *Marriage of St. Catherine* and a Carracci *Pietà;* Reni's *St. Agnes in Agony* and Houdon's bust of a young Molière; Italian fantasy scenes—architecturally detailed, albeit ethereal—that typify Hugo Robert's work; Vernet landscapes and a still life of books by Oudry—departing from his usual animal scenes; a riveting study of hands and feet by Géricault; decorative portraits by Ingres and Delacroix; lovely landscapes as interpreted by Corot and Courbet (with a bonus of Courbet portraits—not usual subjects by that master); Rubens's *Martyrdom of a Saint* and Steen's *Traveler Resting;* and a host of other Baroque Dutch works by the likes of Van Ruysdael and Van Goyen, Ter Borch and Cuyp. Spaniards are present—Zurbarán and Sánchez Coello. More recent painters are on scene, too—an exquisite Bonnard landscape, a Matisse still life, Marquet and Degas, Robert Delauney and Utrillo; and the great sculptors of the last century—Canova, Bourdelle, Maillol, Carpeaux. Allow half a day.

Musée Atger (Faculté de Médecine, Rue École de Médecine): You need an advance appointment for the Atger; the city tourist office (address below) can arrange it for you. Setting in and of itself—the main building of the University of Montpellier's celebrated medical school—is noteworthy; a tablet in the lobby honors all of the school's deans and rectors starting in the year 1220. Up you go to the second-floor museum, where still another tablet advises that its collection of drawings was a gift from "Monsieur Xavier Atger, Amateur Montpelliérain." Once you are admitted, a curator takes you in hand, opening drawers of the cabinets in which prints are stored as a protective measure, commenting upon them (in French) as you move along. There are Renaissance Italians like Tiepolo (his *Head of an Old Man* is a star of the show). But most drawings are by such

French eighteenth-century masters as Fragonard (a bucolic landscape), Natoire *(Madonna and Child with Angels)*, Oudry *(The Birds' Christmas)*, and Fragonard *(Portrait de l'Abbé)*. A treat.

Musée de la Société Archéologique (5 Rue des Trésoriers-de-France)—just north of Place de la Comédie—is so central that it's a pity to miss. Its home is the seventeenth-century Hôtel des Trésoriers de France—the mansion that gave its name to the street—and is handsomely colonnaded. The Archeological Society's collections were assembled over the years since its founding in 1833. There's little they've missed, the range prehistoric stones called steles, Gallo-Roman domestic implements like vases and platters in bronze metalwork, bas-reliefs of the Middle Ages, and local ceramics—with paintings and enamel from other French regions.

Musée Sabatier-d'Éspeyran (6 Rue Montpelliéret) is a mammoth nineteenth-century *hôtel particulier* that was the home of the family for which it is named. This is Montpellier's repository of the decorative arts. It's operated by Musée Fabre (above), whose information desk arranges guided tours. There are two floors, and the contrast is nothing if not instructional. The second is a suite of reception rooms furnished locally in the last century, mostly ostentatious Second Empire. You ascend one more flight, then, to the top level, and it is as though you have moved to another house. These rooms comprise superb eighteenth-century—Louis XV and Louis XVI—furniture and accessories that were originally in the owning family's Paris home. Vive la différence!

Cathedral of St.-Pierre (Place St.-Pierre) is by no means one of the great ones. Withal, a visit to it by foot—through the core of town, perhaps with detours past courtyards of mansions on such atmospheric *Vieux-Montpellier* streets as *Rue Jacques-Cœur* and *Rue des Trésoriers de France*—makes for an agreeable excursion. The cathedral is at its best from without; its stone porch is flanked by two turreted towers out of the fourteenth century. The Gothic nave is of the same period, and rose windows flanking the transept are very old, too; but most of the rest of the building is a consequence of eighteenth- and nineteenth-century restoration.

Crypte Notre-Dame-des-Tables (Place Jean-Jaurès) occupies subterranean portions of a desanctified Gothic church whose exhibits relate the history of the city. Have a look.

Musée Fougau and Musée du Vieux-Montpellier (Hôtel de Varenne, Place Pétrarque, off Rue Embouque d'Or): Each occupies a separate floor in a town house, parts of which have original Gothic vaulting.

The building's architecture is at least as absorbing as the minimuseums' collections.

Château country: Earmark a good half day for a trio of châteaux north of town, checking open hours before departure with the Montpellier tourist office (address below). *Château de la Mogère* (two miles north) is a classic-style mansion set back from a formal garden whose rococo wall of shells frames a fountain. State rooms include a salon with stuccoed walls and ceiling and yellow and blue Louix XVI furnishings; a drawing room, dramatically scarlet-accented; and a dining room with original tables and chairs, not to mention a Rigaud portrait over the buffet. *Château Flaugergues* (five miles north) resembles nothing so much as a seventeenth-century Tuscan villa. The entrance hall is dominated by a tapestried stairway. The reception rooms' vaulted ceilings frame Louis XV and Louis XVI furnishings, with Aubusson rugs on the floors. The ex-chapel—neo-Gothic—is a library, and your hosts, Brigitte and Henri de Colbert, descendants of Louis XIV's finance minister, own a vineyard; you may buy their wines. *Château de Castries* (eight miles north) is the most important of our trio—and the oldest, essentially sixteenth-century, albeit with eighteenth-century refurbishing. Its magnificent park and formal garden were designed in 1666—and irrigated by water from a still-extant aqueduct four miles long—by the very same Le Nôtre whose work you know from Versailles. The still-resident Castries family has played a major role in regional history. And we are in its debt for opening the state rooms. A majestic stairway leads from the entrance hall to the second floor's Salon Bleu, Louis XVI–furnished, with a memento-filled library; the dining room, with family paintings on its half-paneled walls; Chambre Rouge, so called because of its red-upholstered canopied bed; and a ballroom-sized drawing room called Salle des États du Languedoc, with both historic and esthetic significance.

Palavas-les-Flots (8 miles south of Montpellier) is where Montpellier swims and suns, straddling a long, wide Mediterranean strand with beachfront hotels and restaurants, an amusing *Aquarium* (317 Avenue St.-Maurice), and even a casino. Spend the day.

Pézenas (29 miles southwest of Montpellier), where Molière lived and wrote, is a village whose core is a mass of tile-stone houses that constitute a medieval movie set. Position yourself at central *Place de la République,* wandering *Cours Jean-Jaurès* and adjacent streets, popping into *St.-Jean* and *St.-Ursule* churches, not missing *Musée du Vulliod St.-Germain* for its eighteenth-century furniture, tapestries, and porcelain; and the Gothic-Renaissance mansion known as Hôtel de Lacoste.

SETTLING IN

Métropole Hôtel (3 Rue Clos-René; phone 6758-11-22) is an attractively updated turn-of-century house, with 84 no-two-quite-alike rooms and suites (those I've inspected are delightful); smartly paneled breakfast room; delightful bar-lounge; and management that is at once congenial and professional. *First Class.*

Sofitel Montpellier (Le Triangle; phone 6758-45-45) occupies lower floors of an ungainly contemporary apartment house, midpoint between Place de la Comédie and the Polygone shopping complex. There are just under a hundred functional rooms, pair of suites, bar off the lobby and—the hotel at its best—a generous buffet at breakfast, the only meal served. *First Class.*

Noailles Hôtel (2 Rue des Écoles Centrales; phone 6760-49-80) charms with seventeenth-century ambience. The lounge is stone-walled, barrel-vaulted, with Louis XIII furniture. There are 30 rooms; all those I've inspected are charmers, with good baths. Location is Vieux-Montpellier. Friendly. *Moderate.*

Altéa Antigone Hôtel (218 Rue du Bastion-Ventadour, in the Polygone complex, east of the center; phone 6764-65-66) is of modern design, not unlike the shopping center of which it is a part. There are 116 full-facility rooms, restaurant, bar-lounge. *First Class.*

Arcade Hôtel (Boulevard d'Antigone; phone 6764-06-64)—contemporary and clean-lined not unlike sister-links of the Arcade chain—is east of the core, offers 125 neat rooms with showers rather than tubs in baths, and serves temptingly tabbed meals in its restaurant (breakfast is a generous buffet). Bar. *Moderate.*

Grand Hôtel du Midi (22 Boulevard Victor-Hugo; phone 6792-69-61) is an elderly house, centrally situated, with half a hundred rooms. Bar-café and breakfast. Okay. *Moderate.*

Palais Hôtel (3 Rue du Palais; phone 6760-47-38) thoroughly renovated its two dozen rooms relatively recently and is centrally situated. Breakfast only. Good value. *Moderate.*

Hôtel de l'Aéroport (Aéroport de Montpellier Fréjorgues; phone 6764-63-00) might prove useful if you've a connection to make after or before a transatlantic flight. There are 45 bath-equipped rooms, restaurant, and bar. *Moderate.*

DAILY BREAD

Chandelier (3 Rue Leenhardt; phone 6792-61-62) has the advantages of a central situation (south of Place de la Comédie) and of good things to eat. You might want to start with the house's celebrated tomato mousse, order its lamb-and-eggplant casserole therafter, and conclude with a skillfully prepared sweet. Go midday for the menu—pricier at dinner. Nice. *Luxury.*

Le Petit Landais (14 Rue du Palais; phone 6760-69-93) is small and friendly and operated by a delightful *patronne* who is at once hostess and chef. Cooking is regional, hearty, and delicious. Dinner might open with crab salad, followed by Madame's foie gras de canard, and continue with a superbly prepared maigret—or breast—of canard; order baked-on-premises chocolate cake or clafoutis aux cerises, a cherry confection, to conclude. *First Class.*

Le Louvre (2 Rue de la Veille; phone 6760-59-37) will remind you not at all of the Paris museum, but rather of 1940s movies you've enjoyed; decor is Art Deco. You do well to sample the house's own cassoulet—based on confit de canard and delicious—preceded by a light, but well-dressed, tomato salad. Or have the prix-fixe menu; select a veal entrée. *First Class.*

Isadora (6 Rue du Petit-Scel; phone 6766-25-23): You descend to the stone-walled cellar of an aged house to find Isadora (whose owner, to your surprise, is a gent) smartly styled and cheerily staffed, with a good-value menu that might open with shrimp-stuffed avocado, continue with a filet of beef or a poultry specialty, and conclude with a house-made sweet. *First Class.*

Le Ménestrel (Impasse Perrier, Place de la Préfecture; phone 6760-62-51) exudes ambience, given the high stone vaults of its medieval premises, a tremendous fireplace, red linen on the tables. The lower-priced of two menus features grilled lamb chops, with a hot Calvados-anointed apple tart to conclude. *Moderate/First Class.*

Chantegril (4 Rue Clos-René; phone 6758-14-15) is convenient to Place de la Comédie and a link of an attractive national chain—the lot with light, gardenlike ambience—that specializes in good-value prix-fixe *formules* that open with an appetizer followed by your choice of grill (steak, lamb chops, pork chops). *Moderate.*

Hôtel Montpelliérain des Vins du Languedoc (7 Rue Jacques Cœur; phone 6760-42-41) is operated by the Languedoc wine producers' promotion arm, primarily as a showcase for wines of the area. The menu, however, can read better than it tastes. Stick to simply broiled entrées, hoping for the best, while you sample regional whites, rosés, and reds. Service might be slow. *First Class.*

Viguier (56 Rue de l'Argenterie) is a *pâtisserie* that doubles as a *salon de thé;* order something scrumptious from the counter, to accompany coffee or tea. *Moderate.*

Café Riche (Place de la Comédie): While resting weary feet, observe ambulatory Montpellier; have coffee or a snack. *Moderate.*

Café de la Préfecture (Place Chabaneau) spills into a pretty square and is named for its next-door neighbor, the impressive structure housing the government of the *département. Moderate.*

SHOPPER'S MONTPELLIER

Galeries Lafayette, the No. 1 department store, is in the Polygone shopping center, along with *Prisunic* and *C & A* department stores and such clothing shops as *Daniel Hechter* and *Rodier.* There's a big *Monoprix* on Place de la Comédie. It's fun to take in the *daily market*—food, flowers, clothes, you name it—on Place Jean-Jaurès. Of the pedestrian streets, Rue de l'Argenterie is the smartest, with such boutiques as *Georges Rech, Patricia Oresaud,* and *Via Condotti* (women's clothes), *Daniel Crémieux* (men's clothes), *André Roch* (leather), *Spiral* (jewelry), and *Cacharel Junior* (kids' clothes). Two good bookstores are *English Books* (9 Rue de l'École de Pharmacie) and *Le Maître Soldeur* (art books, 39 Rue de l'Aiguillerie). Montpellier is an important city for antiques. *Galerie du Peyrou* and *Galerie M. de B.* are two of a number of shops along Rue du Palais; *Centaure/Emanuel de Sauvebœuf* (5 Rue de la Petite Loge) is another well-stocked shop.

SOUND OF MUSIC

Théâtre Municipal (Place de la Comédie) is elaborately Belle Époque and the setting for opera, ballet, and concerts.

Le Corum (Esplanade Charles de Gaulle), Montpellier's state-of-the-art congress center, includes 2000-seat *Opéra Berlioz,* and a pair of smaller auditoriums: 800-seat *Salle Pasteur* and 300-seat *Salle Einstein.*

L'Esplanade is a city park that's popular in summer for its day and evening concerts. Central.

INCIDENTAL INTELLIGENCE

Aéroport de Fréjorgues is five miles southwest of town, and is linked with New York via Air France; there are, as well, domestic flights throughout France. *Further information:* Office de Tourisme, Le Corum, Esplanade Charles de Gaulle, Montpellier; Office de Tourisme, Mairie, Palavas-les-Flots; Office de Tourisme, Marché au Bled, Pézenas.

25

Nancy

What Duke Stanislaus Hath Wrought

BACKGROUND BRIEFING

It is, of course, outrageous to be so corny as to declare that Nancy is fancy. But it is.

Even, I hasten to add, when pronounced properly—*Nahn*-SEE—in the French manner.

If you except Paris, whose Place de la Concorde is of the same era, no French city of which I am aware has a rococo square to equal that of northeastern Nancy—a hundred and seventy miles due east of the capital. For Place Stanislas—along with the palaces enclosing it and the monumental wrought-iron gates punctuating it—we must be grateful for what can only be termed the peculiar politics of the eighteenth century. What happened was that a man in need of a job, forced to step down as king of his native Poland, in the end settled for something less prestigious—the dukedom of Lorraine (of which Nancy has long been capital), which upon his death, and by terms of the deal he made with his father-in-law, King Louis XV, became a part of France.

Pre-Stanislaus Nancy had been seat of Lorraine's dukes since as early as the twelfth century. Neighboring Burgundians came from the south to annex it in a fifteenth-century battle, but Lorraine's Duke René II—a local hero to this day for valor—fended them off. The sixteenth century saw Duke Charles III lay out plans for a new city center. But the city did not blossom until, in the early eighteenth century, the ruling duke, François III, married Austrian Empress Maria Theresa and became an emperor. Imperial sleight-of-hand then saw François trade off Lorraine with Louis XV in exchange for Tuscany. At that point, King Louis, married to Polish-born Maria Leczinska, turned over Lorraine to his then-idle father-in-law, the deposed Polish king.

Stanislaus and Nancy hit it off beautifully. An educated and enlightened man with a sure sense of style, he set about creating a new core for his capital, commissioning the architect Hère and a designer of ornamental ironwork named Lamour to come up with a plan. Their square so enraptured Nancy that its citizens named it for Stanislaus, last of the Lorraine dukes. Nancy suffered in the nineteenth century (German troops occupied it during the Franco-Prussian War—and again during World War I). But its beloved square—exquisitely refurbished in recent years—remains both its symbol and its soul.

ON SCENE

Lay of the Land: It should go without saying that the core of the city is *Place Stanislas,* flanked by a clutch of palaces, not to mention cafés, spilling onto the pavement. Adjacent is *Place de la Carrière,* gained by a spectacular *Arc de Triomphe,* massed with trees in its center and bordered by handsome houses, and the colonnaded *Palais du Gouvernement. Grande Rue,* due north, is Nancy's Antique Row, and the site, as well, of the medieval *Palais Ducal,* now a museum complex. *Rue St.-Jean,* the main street, is a hop and a skip from Place Stanislas and becomes *Rue St.-Georges* in its easterly precincts. *Rue Stanislas,* parallel with Rue St.-Jean, leads west to *Place Thiers* and the railway station.

Place Stanislas palaces warrant inspection. *Hôtel de Ville,* the city hall, dazzles with a pair of second-story reception rooms, the bigger of which was refurbished in the nineteenth century for a state visit by Empress Eugénie. And getting to it is half the fun: The stairway's wrought-iron bannister is a 27-yard-long masterwork by Lamour. Do your best to have a look, too, at the elegant auditorium of the *Grand Théâtre,* by taking in a performance, perhaps of the Ballet de Nancy—one of France's top companies—or an opera. Another palace is occupied by *Musée des Beaux-Arts* (below), and still another by the *Grand Hôtel de la Reine* where—especially if you are not in residence—a meal and/or drink are certainly in order. Outside, amble about the square, taking in its gilded wrought-iron gates and its pair of fountains, Amphitrite and Neptune, and concluding your tour over coffee or a drink at one of the square's cafés.

Musée des Beaux-Arts (Place Stanislas): The setting is so beautiful that you half expect this museum's paintings to be anticlimactic; they are not. If you are wondering whether the Lorraine-born Renaissance master, Claude Lorrain (whose name was actually Claude Gelée), is represented, let me reassure you. By one ethereal landscape: *Paysage Pastoral.* His contemporaries, Poussin and Vouet, are on scene, as well. There are Old Master Italians, a Lorenzo Lotto *Gentleman's Portrait,* a Perugino *Virgin,* a Caravaggio *Annunciation,* Tintoretto, and Bassano—and later Frenchmen like Van Loo (with a likeness of Duke Stanislaus's father-in-law, Louis

XV) and Delacroix, with a massive interpretation of Lorraine Duke René's decisive victory over the Burgundian forces of Duke Charles the Bold in 1477. There is an enormous Rubens *Transfiguration* and more recent French work—Utrillo and Derain, Signac and Manet, Vuillard and Dufy—as well.

Musée de Lorraine (Palais Ducal, Grande Rue): What could be more appropriate a setting for a repository of Lorraine lore than the château in which its dukes lived? It dates to the sixteenth century and is a marvelous mix of Gothic and Renaissance, on two splendid levels. Downstairs is a maze of medieval sculpture, stained glass, and swords. And how about those immense fireplaces? Upstairs is even more spectacular. There are paintings of the dukes, a series of sumptuous tapestries, works by Lorraine artists, including Claude Lorrain and Georges de la Tour, a cache of Renaissance furniture and of eighteenth-century porcelain from nearby Luneville. You move along then to the adjacent building, *Couvent des Cordeliers*, long since abandoned by Franciscan nuns and now *Musée des Arts et Traditions Populaires;* head for the second floor, where the kicker is a series of rooms from houses in the Lorraine countryside, furnished—and superbly—in period.

Church of the Cordeliers (Grande Rue): Franciscans often are called *Cordeliers* in France because of the white cords they wear as belts. This Franciscan church is at its best in the adjacent chapel and is so similar to the Chapel of the Medici (see *Italy at Its Best*) that you could be in Florence, substituting stone-carved tombs of dukes of Lorraine for those of the ruling Medici.

Musée de l'École de Nancy (38 Rue du Sergent Blandan) wants its title explained, first off. It is called after the group, or movement, of celebrated turn-of-century Nancy artists and artisans—Majorelle (a cabinetmaker), Gruber (who designed stained-glass windows), and a number of others, whose specialties were tapestries, embroidery, jewelrymaking, bookbinding—who were brought together by glass-designer Émile Galle, the lot of them constituting the Art Nouveau period's École de Nancy. This museum is a onetime mansion with two floors of matchless Art Nouveau rooms—foyer, salon, music room, dining room below, bedrooms above; even an Art Nouveau-accented garden—that comprise a unique-in-the-world museum of an important period in the history of design. (The only other such that I know on the same esthetic level is Hamburg's Museum für Kunst und Gewerbe [see *Germany at Its Best*], whose Art Nouveau period rooms rank with these.)

Cathedral of Nancy (Rue St.-Georges) is by no means one of the great ones. Still, there are not many eighteenth-century cathedrals in France. Nancy's is monumentally scaled—and not surprisingly—with fine, wrought-iron grillwork typical of that period in this city.

Parc de La Pépinière, east of Grande Rue, contains a statue of Claude Lorrain by Rodin and *Church of Notre Dame de Bon Secours* (at the foot of Avenue de Strasbourg), designed by Hère, who also created Place Stanislas, contains the tomb of Duke Stanislaus—should you want to pay your respects at either or both.

SETTLING IN

Grand Hôtel de la Reine (2 Place Stanislas; phone 8335-03-01) is, as you've read above, one of the original eighteenth-century palaces of Place Stanislas. Hôtels Concorde, its owners, have sunk several million francs into an impeccable and very stylish restoration, with the consequence a hotel that is one of the most beautiful—and charming—in France. There are 60 suites and rooms, no two quite alike, the lot of them designed in period, with superb textiles, furniture, accessories, and, I might add, baths. The ones you want to aim for—always the first to go, not surprisingly—are those facing the square, with side rooms on which you can see the square by craning your neck, the next best. Public spaces are a pleasure. There's a lively bar—called Le Stan (what locals call the square)—and a restaurant worthy of additional comment in a later paragraph. And the staff is one of the best I've encountered in France. Along with the Crillon in Paris, this is the Concorde operation at its zenith. Member, Relais et Châteaux. *First Class.*

Altéa Thiers Hôtel (Place Thiers; phone 8336-61-01) is, as far as I can perceive, Nancy's only skyscraper, with 112 nicely furnished full-facility rooms, cocktail lounge, and reliable restaurant, Toison d'Or, with good-value menus. Central. *First Class.*

Europe Hôtel (5 Rue des Carmes; phone 8335-32-10) has the advantage of a central situation; 80 functional rooms. Breakfast only. *Moderate.*

Américain Hôtel (3 Place Maginot; phone 8332-28-53) is reasonably central, and with half a hundred bath-equipped rooms. Breakfast only. *Moderate.*

DAILY BREAD

Stanislaus (Grand Hôtel de la Reine, 2 Place Stanislas; phone 8335-03-01) is intimate (seating capacity is limited), handsome (you're in an authentic eighteenth-century setting), and delicious. Open with the local pike prepared Nancy style, a seafood salad, or the day's soup. Beef entrées—steak all poivre, especially—are tasty and nicely garnished. Desserts are wheeled on a trolley and memorable. And service is impeccable. *First Class.*

Le Capucin Gourmand (31 Rue Gambetta; phone 8335-26-98) extends a warm welcome in a luxurious setting. Open with foie gras prepared the house's way, consider a seafood or game-in-season specialty as an entrée, and on no account pass over desserts, ranging from made-on-premises ice cream doused with *eau-de-vie* to delicate pastries. *Luxury.*

Oxebon (85 Rue St-Georges; phone 8332-00-42): Of course, you want to try quiche lorraine in Lorraine's capital; Oxebon makes a specialty of it. There's a wide range of entrées; frog's legs among them. Central. *First Class.*

Nouveaux Abattoires (4 Boulevard d'Austrasie; phone 8335-46-25): Think what you will about calling a restaurant "New Slaughterhouses"; the fact remains that this is a long-established source of solid fare—filets of beef and steak au poivre, veal escalopes and veal chops, kidneys and sweetbreads. Chocolate mousse or crême caramel for dessert. *First Class.*

La Petite Marmite (8 Rue Gambetta; phone 8335-25-63) could not be more central—it's between Place Stanislas and Place Carnot—or better value. Go for the multicourse menu at lunch. *Moderate.*

Café Jean Lamour (Place Stanislas): Take a table on the square and remain as long as you like over a single drink. If Lamour is filled, move along to the same square's *Café du Commerce* or *Le Glacier;* all are *Moderate.*

INCIDENTAL INTELLIGENCE

Further information: Office de Tourisme, 14 Place Stanislas (where else?), Nancy.

26

Nice

and Riviera Satellites: Biot, Vence, St.-Paul, Cagnes

BACKGROUND BRIEFING

Nice has an image problem with a double causative: sunshine and situation. Contemporary visitors understandably associate its—dare I say "nice"?—name with neighboring Riviera points like Cannes (chapter 13), Monaco (chapter 23), and St.-Tropez (chapter 33), admire the action along the palm-lined crescent called Promenade des Anglais, deplore the pebbly strand edging the Baie des Anges, wonder what all the fuss was about—and move along.

They err. But it's neither their fault nor Nice's. With unabashed beach resorts—where the *raison d'être* is sun, sand, the spin of the roulette wheel, and the beat of the disco—flanking this city all along the Mediterranean shore, it's no wonder that today's traveler may be unaware that upon arrival he or she has reached a metropolis of a third of a million (only Paris, Lyon, Marseille, and Toulouse are larger) that was settled by the Greeks four centuries before Christ and was the scene of considerable activity—the lot contributing to Nice's vibrant life-style and underappreciated culture—between then and the middle of the last century, when the then-Italian city became a part of Napoleon III's Second Empire.

In between, there were few dull moments. Romans—whose name, *Nicaea,* has been changed little over the centuries—succeeded Greeks, making the still-visitable area called Cimiez (an amphitheater and ruined thermal baths remain) their town. Barbarians and assorted later invaders followed, by no means arresting this resilient city's development. Medieval Provence and then medieval Savoy were later landlords. François I's troops attacked Renaissance Nice. During the Revolution it was a haven for Royalists fleeing Paris, by which time it had also begun to lure wandering Britons partial to the mild climate and an idyllic location, with snowy mountains in the rear and the blue Mediterranean out front.

Indeed, it was a resident clutch of moneyed Englishmen who kicked in funds for the early-nineteenth-century construction of the appropriately named Promenade des Anglais, the pioneer shoreline artery that inspired others in sea-girdling communities planetwide.

Today's Nice is an amalgam of these disparate influences. Elegance came with the eighteenth-century Parisians. The tradition of the grand hotel is surely English in origin. The lusty cuisine as much as high houses hung with clotheslines flanking alleylike streets of Vieux-Nice are Italian. And much of the extraordinary art in the museums is a consequence of Nice's having lured such masters as Chagall, Matisse, and Picasso, their curiosity piqued by nineteenth-century enthusiasts like the painter Delacroix, the writer Maupassant, and the composer Berlioz. No question but that Nice beaches are narrow and pebbly. But there are compensations.

ON SCENE

Lay of the Land: Nice is big; you can't walk everywhere. The central city is fronted by crescent-shaped, hotel-lined *Promenade des Anglais,* which flanks a baker's dozen beaches—some private (with access gained through your hotel), some public (your concierge will direct you to the closest)—extending the length of the *Baie des Anges,* at its smartest in central precincts, in and about landmark Hôtel Negresco at the corner of north–south *Boulevard Gambetta,* which leads to *Rue de France,* running parallel with Promenade des Anglais and, as it works its way east, becoming pedestrians-only *Rue Masséna,* terminating at massive *Place Masséna,* edged by Hôtel de Ville. Directly east is the splendid fountain-filled parklike area successively called *Espace Masséna, Square Leclerc,* and *Promenade du Paillon.* It constitutes the northern border of *Vieux-Nice,* the medieval/Renaissance quarter dominated by the cathedral and Palais de Justice in its center, just above an immense public market that flanks *Cours Saleya,* a thoroughfare parallel with the sea that is lined with typically Niçoise seafood restaurants. What remains of the ancient Roman colony of Cimiez is in a quarter retaining that name, a fair distance north of the center, with a pair of museums. Still other museums are in other sectors. By no means all of Nice's hotels line the waterfront; many are on attractive inland streets in and about Rue Masséna, *Boulevard Victor-Hugo,* and *Avenue Médecin.* The railway station is north of the core on *Avenue Thiers,* while the international airport is southwest of town, on *Promenade Edouard Corniglion.*

Roman Nice: Why not start in ancient Cimiez—the Romans' *Cemenelum?* Poke about what remains of their city, including a still lovely *amphitheater* and *baths,* detouring to the adjacent *Church of*

Cimiez, whose treats are altars by the Renaissance-era Nice school's Louis and Antoine Brea. Both Dufy and Matisse are buried in an adjacent cemetery. But this is Matisse territory; by that, I mean the upper floor of nearby *Musée Matisse* (entered at 164 Avenue des Arènes-de-Cimiez) exhibits works that are a survey of that artist's long career, 1890s through designs for the chapel in nearby Vence (below), with scores of drawings and not a few paintings, the 1944 *Lectrice à la Table Jaune* among the more memorable. The same building houses the city's *Musée Archéologique,* whose special treasure is a first-century statue in marble of Antonia, a niece of the Emperor Augustus, but there are half a dozen galleries displaying excavated treasures of Roman Cemenelum—capitals, busts, sculpted fragments, and sarcophagi.

Vieux-Nice, nerve center of the city from the Middle Ages well into the eighteenth century and still vibrant and engaging, is a pleasant walk east from hotels of the core. *Cathedral of Ste.-Réparate* (Place Rossetti)—among the relatively few Baroque cathedrals in France and certainly among the loveliest—is strongly Italianate, with statues in niches of its classic-style green and yellow facade, a smashing tiled dome, a detached bell tower in the Italian manner, and an interior not overlarge, but lavishly stuccoed and sculpted, with a fine marble pulpit. *Musée du Palais Lascaria* (15 Rue Droite) went up in the mid-seventeenth century, deteriorated sadly until municipal authorities, having purchased it just before World War II, completed restoration in 1969. Its coat-of-arms-centered stone facade is impressive enough. But high-ceilinged, stone-walled interiors are not anticlimactic, especially the second floor's state rooms, at their most opulent in a sumptuous suite embracing a frescoed sitting room furnished with Louis XV pieces and an adjacent space centered by a bed canopied in scarlet and white damask, with both ballroom and chapel down the hall. If you haven't paid attention to the sculpture-embellished stairway going up, do so when you descend. While you're in the neighborhood, pop into whatever churches you pass by—a number are Baroque and charming—and amble about squares like *Place St.-François* (centered by a fish market), as well as shop-lined streets like *Rue Ste.-Réparate,* making sure that you have at least one meal in a raffish *restaurant du quartier* (see below) on *Cours Saleya.* Note, as you move about, that Vieux-Nice street signs are in both French and Nice dialect; *Rue de Jésus,* for example, is also *Carriera dou Jeuse.*

Belle Époque Nice is perhaps best exemplified by *Musée Masséna*—a mansion of the period (it was built about 1900) on Promenade des Anglais, entered at 65 Rue de France. For me, its most evocative exhibit is a painting, *La Promenade des Anglais,* executed in 1921 by Angelo Garino, with the tower of Hôtel Negresco at the upper left,

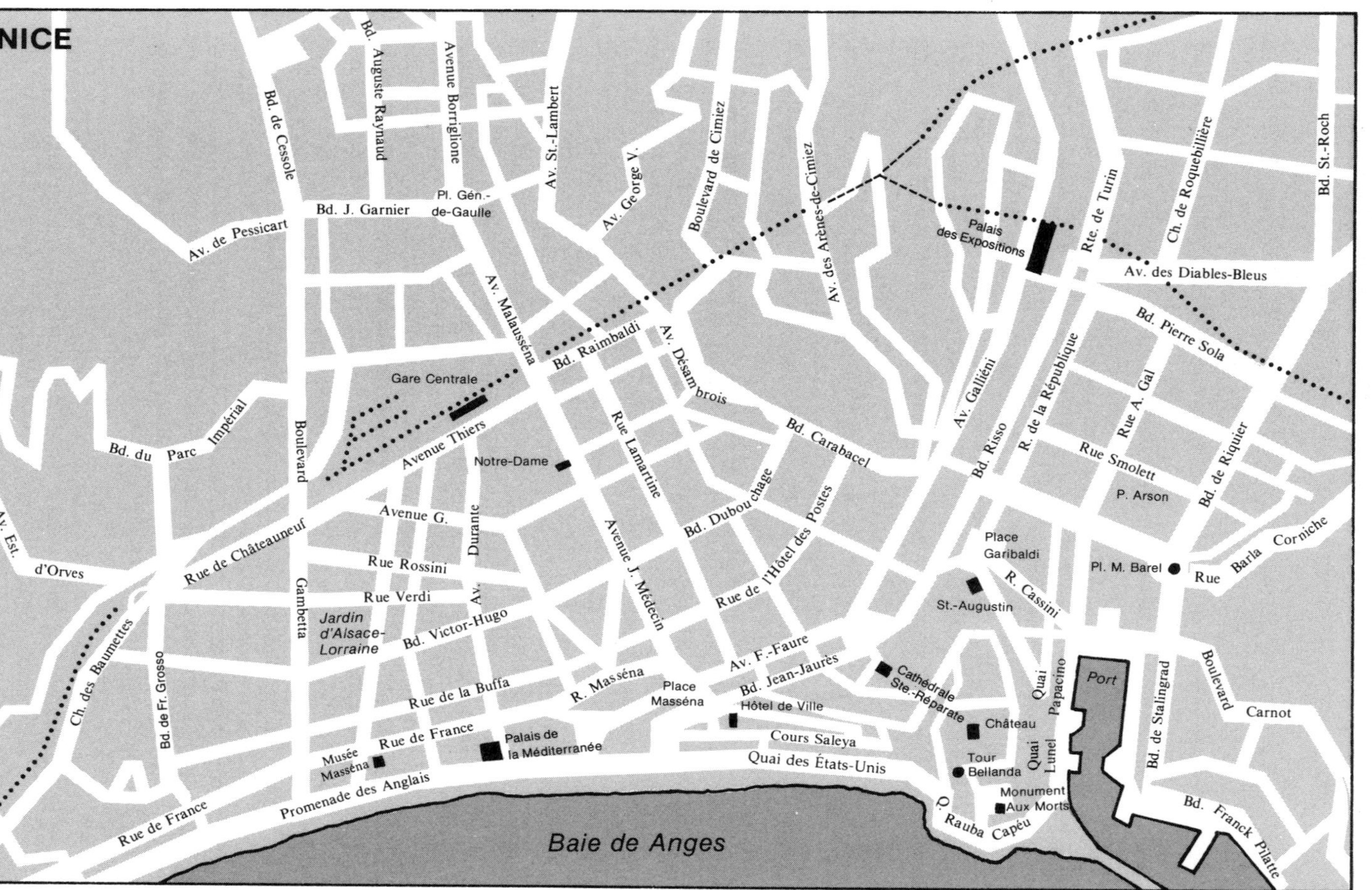
NICE
Bd. Auguste Raynaud
Avenue Borriglione
Av. St.-Lambert
Bd. de Cessole
Pl. Gén.-de-Gaulle
Bd. J. Garnier
Av. de Pessicart
Av. George V.
Boulevard de Cimiez
Av. des Arènes-de-Cimiez
Palais des Expositions
Rte. de Turin
Ch. de Roquebillière
Bd. St.-Roch
Av. des Diables-Bleus
Bd. Pierre Sola
Av. Malausséna
Bd. Raimbaldi
Av. Désambrois
Gare Centrale
Bd. du Parc Impérial
Boulevard Gambetta
Avenue Thiers
Notre-Dame
Rue Lamartine
Bd. Carabacel
Av. Galliéni
Bd. Risso
R. de la République
Rue A. Gal
Rue Smolett
P. Arson
Bd. de Riquier
Av. Est. d'Orves
Rue de Châteauneuf
Avenue G.
Av. Durante
Rue Rossini
Rue Verdi
Jardin d'Alsace-Lorraine
Bd. Victor-Hugo
Avenue J. Médecin
Bd. Dubouchage
Rue de l'Hôtel des Postes
Place Garibaldi
R. Cassini
St.-Augustin
Pl. M. Barel
Rue Barla
Corniche
Ch. des Baumettes
Bd. de Fr. Grosso
Rue de la Buffa
R. Masséna
Place Masséna
Av. F.-Faure
Bd. Jean-Jaurès
Hôtel de Ville
Cathédrale Ste.-Réparate
Château
Quai Papacino
Port
Bd. de Stalingrad
Boulevard Carnot
Rue de France
Musée Masséna
Palais de la Méditerranée
Cours Saleya
Quai des États-Unis
Tour Bellanda
Quai Lunel
Monument Aux Morts
Promenade des Anglais
Q. Rauba Capéu
Bd. Franck Pilatte
Baie de Anges

domed amusement pier (long since razed) on the right, and promenaders en masse (accompanied by leashed dogs, as, indeed, are successors today) *au centre.* But there's more in Musée Masséna. Its main-floor rooms are quite as opulent as they were in the early decades of the century (the city of Nice throws parties therein), and there's a mixed-bag collection of historical documents and drawings through regional folklore and antique jewelry.

Musée d'Art Moderne et d'Art Contemporain (Esplanade des Arts)—Nice's newest major museum—embraces an architecturally striking four-pavilion ensemble. The collection is an all-France leader of its category, with 160 works by the artist Dufy in the gallery taking his name. Great moderns from the first half of this century are represented—Braque and Bonnard, Chagall and Albert Marquet, Matisse and Max Ernst, Dubuffet and Giacometti. Schools of more recent decades—New Realism, Pop, Mimimal, to name three—have not been neglected either.

Musée Chagall (Avenue Docteur Ménard, just off Boulevard de Cimiez, about halfway between the center and the northerly Cimiez complex, above) constitutes a big dose of Chagall, the biggest extant, for that matter. The museum was erected to house a group of massive canvases—nearly a score—that Marc Chagall (1907–1985) painted to illustrate biblical themes. *Adam and Eve Chased from Paradise* draws the largest crowds, but others—*Paradise, Moses Receiving the Ten Commandments,* and *Abraham and the Three Angels*—are compelling, too, as is the museum's auditorium into whose walls are set a series of Chagall stained-glass windows depicting *The Seven Days of Creation* and a quite brilliant and massive mosaic of the master's over a reflecting pool.

Musée Jules-Chéret (33 Avenue Baumettes, a pleasant 10-minute walk east of the central hotels)—not unlike Musée Masséna (above), installed in a Belle Époque palace, with guards quite as friendly as those at the Masséna—is Nice's Beaux-Arts repository. If it is not in a league with those of, say, Dijon, Strasbourg, Grenoble, or Lyon, it does not disappoint. The collection's range is from Van Loo and Fragonard to the Impressionists. Especially memorable are Allen Ramsay's portraits of both George III and Queen Charlotte; other rococo works by a diverse group, Italy's Battoni through England's Lawrence; Renoir's nude *Bathers* and a solitary (and swimsuited) *Bather,* by onetime Nice resident Raoul Dufy.

Biot (15 miles southwest of Nice) is the pretty stone village in the hills to which art devotees gravitate. Their destination: *Musée National Fernand Léger,* a rectangular pavilion—whose facade in ceramic tile is based on a Léger composition—that opened in 1960, five years after Léger's death at the age of 74. Fans of Léger—who began as a cubist but whose later work became more representational and which is universally popular because it is immediately recognizable, boldly colorful, and not without wit—have a field day here. There are more than 300 Léger works, tapestries and mosaics, as well as paintings. It is the latter—most in the upper-floor gallery—that linger with us. *The Builders,* a 1950 work as busy with construction workers as with steel girders—typifies the Léger genre. But other paintings with people in them—*Party in the Countryside, Leisure, The Big Parade*—are delightful, and of the abstract pieces the red, white, and blue *July 14, 1914* stands out. Take time to stroll Biot's core, peeking into *Musée d'Histoire Locale* (Place de la Chapelle)—a jumble of village lore, aged kitchens through costumes of yore; and Romanesque-origin *Church of Ste.-Madeleine* (Place des Arcades).

Vence (15 miles northwest of Nice) is still another enchanter of a hill village to whose principal monument contemporary-art buffs beeline. It is *Chapelle du Rosaire* (Avenue Henri Matisse), and one has the feeling that nuns of the convent in which this chapel is situated regret that their order commissioned Matisse to decorate it over a period of several years, concluding in 1951, just a few years before he died at the age of 85 in 1954. Unless they have a change of heart—hardly likely—open hours are, to understate, minimal: 10:00 to 11:30 A.M. and 2:30 to 5:30 P.M., Tuesdays and Fridays. Guardlike sisters, on duty within, exclaim "Shush" if you so much as utter a whisper to a companion, the while marveling at what Matisse created: a series of striking semiabstract murals in stark black on equally stark white walls, painted tile edging the platform of the chapel's altar, stained-glass windows in joyous hues of blue and yellow; a wrought-iron cross—in effect the chapel's steeple, with a bell at its base—on the roof; even vestments for use by the priest celebrating mass.

The rest of Vence maintains civilized hours. Start in the core, on *Place Clemenceau,* in the multiepoch *Cathedral,* which is Romanesque, by and large, albeit with a fine Renaissance choir. Move along *Rue de la Place Vieille* to fountain-centered *Place du Peyra,* mellow and medieval. Proceed along *Avenue Henri Isnard* to admire tiles in the cupola of seventeenth-century *Chapelle des Pénitents Blancs.* Conclude with a café pause in *Place du Grand Jardin.* Unless you're settling in for a night or two—by no means a bad idea.

St.-Paul-de-Vence (a.k.a. just plain St.-Paul, 13 miles northwest of Nice and nicely combined with neighboring Vence on a day's outing) is proudly perched atop its own eminence—and fortified. The ramparts that surround it (commissioned by François I) afford wide-angle panoramas all the way to the Mediterranean. It is agreeable simply to stroll the street that cuts through the village—*Rue Grande*—pausing in craft shops, idling in a café, taking in squares and gardens. But you want especially to note Rue Grande's urn-shaped and ancient fountain; steplike streets, including *Montée du Casse-Cou;* and the pretty Gothic parish church, expertly vaulted. Even if you are not lunching or dining there (see below), make it a point to ask politely if you may wander through the restaurant—not at mealtime, when it's busy—of the *Colombe d'Or Hôtel* to peruse paintings on its walls contributed by their creators—St.-Paul was a magnet for celebrated artists in the 1920s—among whom were Braque, Chagall, Calder, Dufy, Léger, Matisse, and Picasso (according to my notes; I may have missed some). And allow time for a visit to *Fondation Maeght* (north of the village)—a striking, contemporary structure designed by the late Spanish artist/architect José María Sert (the pair of poured concrete semicylinders on the roof are its trademarks)—which is a gold mine of modern art, with alfresco sculpture by the likes of Arp, Calder, Miró, and Giacometti; paintings by Bonnard, Derain, Kandinsky, Léger, and Matisse; superb stained glass by Braque; even mosaics by Chagall.

St.-Jean-Cap-Ferrat (adjacent to Beaulieu-sur-Mer, six miles east of Nice) is a scenic finger of land jutting into the sea, dotted with mansions tucked behind impeccably manicured gardens. Your objective is one of those villas. It is styled *Fondation Ephrussi de Rothschild-Musée Île de France,* and is nothing less than the onetime Riviera home of a Rothschild baroness who had excellent taste in eighteenth-century furniture and made the collection thereof her hobby. There is furniture, as well, from the Renaissance and Middle Ages; superb antique carpets (Savonnerie) and tapestries (Aubusson and Beauvais); and—as a special treat—a ravishing clutch of eighteenth-century paintings by the likes of Hubert Robert, Lancret, Fragonard, and Boucher; not to mention works by such Impressionists as Renoir, Monet, and Sisley, along with French porcelain and Chinese lacquerware. When you've taken it all in, stroll the fountain-embellished, sculpture-filled gardens.

Cagnes-sur-Mer (nine miles west of Nice) comes in two installments: Cagnes-Ville, its lower-down sector, and elevated Haut-de-Cagnes, where, on Place du Château, is *Musée du Château,* a crenelated, originally fourteenth-century castle inhabited by Grimaldis related to the still-reigning Grimaldis of Monaco (chapter 23). State rooms of the two lower floors are impressive, but you want to head for the top floor *Musée d'Art Moderne,* brimming with works of this century by artists who worked in the neighborhood, including Chagall; and another group of paintings—all portraits of onetime resident Marquise de Grimaldi—by such masters as Dufy and Marie Laurencin. Cagnes's other destination of consequence is

Maison de Renoir (Avenue de Tuillères). Dubbed "Les Collettes" by the great Impressionist painter, it was his home for his last 12 years (he died at the age of 78 in 1919) and contains but two of his paintings (one is a charmer, of the house itself), along, however, with a number of his drawings and sculptures, including a bust of Madame Renoir, not to mention his workspace, furnishings in the rest of the house quite as they were when he died, and a pretty garden.

Other Rivieria points: For Cannes, Antibes/Juan-les-Pins, Vallauris, Grasse, and Mougins, see chapter 13; for Monaco (including Monte Carlo) and Èze, see chapter 23; for St.-Tropez, see chapter 33.

SETTLING IN

Negresco Hôtel (37 Promenade des Anglais; phone 9388-39-51): What happened was this: Rumanian-born Henri Negresco, after learning the hotel and restaurant trade in Paris, moved south to run the turn-of-century Casino Restaurant in Nice, decided that he wanted to house, as well as feed, the rich and the royal who were his customers at the casino, found a backer, and built this Promenade des Anglais house, immediately conferring upon it his own catchy, easily remembered family name. By the time the French government designated the Negresco a national monument in 1974, the hotel had become synonymous with Nice. The beauty part of its story is that success has not produced the kind of arrogance that can result from such situations. Credit veteran Directeur-Général Michel Palmer with this happy situation. His presence—cordial, efficient, caring—permeates the hotel; nothing happens that he doesn't know about. The doorman smiles when you enter. The reception staff smiles when you sign in. The concierge knows the location of any restaurant you name—and then some. The chambermaids are not chintzy with either soap or towels. The barman does not patronize you when you order a vodka martini with a twist, rather than a kir royale; he prepares it expertly. And the look of the Negresco—bold-hued, high-ceilinged, widely corridored, with even the singles good-sized—is a pleasure. Public spaces off the lobby—Salon Louis XIV, with its coffered ceiling and immense seventeenth-century fireplace, and Salon Royal, under a glass dome designed by Gustave Eiffel, with a crystal chandelier made by Baccarat for a czar of Russia—have, in recent seasons, been impeccably restored. All rooms are distinctively decorated with antique accents, many from the last century's Second Empire; seaview suites and doubles with terraces are sumptuous. There is a pair of restaurants, one amusingly casual (it emulates a carousel), the other (Chantecler) quite grand and evaluated in a later paragraph. In the city that, after Paris, is the best-equipped hotel town in France, the Negresco is a standout. Member, Leading Hotels of the World. *Luxury.*

Westminster Concorde Hôtel (27 Promenade des Anglais; phone 9388-29-44) is a lovely Belle Époque oldie deftly updated and smartly staffed, with capacious traditional-style public areas that include a pair of restaurants (one with an alfresco, seaview terrace) and a bar-lounge. Of the 110 rooms—sizes vary but they're all comfortable—it's the front ones, some with terraces, facing Promenade des Anglais and the sea, that you want to aim for. Very nice, indeed. Hôtels Concorde. *First Class.*

Meridien Hôtel (1 Promenade des Anglais; phone 9382-25-25) is among the better-located of this chain's hotels in France, with attractive public spaces including a restaurant giving onto Promenade des Anglais, a casual café as well as a bar-lounge and—special treat, this—a rooftop swimming pool from whose deck views are spectacular. There are 314 contemporary-decor rooms, the least expensive facing an inner courtyard. And the building is shared with the lesser-category Mercure Baie des Anges Hôtel (below). *First Class/Luxury.*

Mercure Baie des Anges Hôtel (12 Rue Halevy; phone 9382-30-88) occupies two floors (and its own separately entered lobby on a street leading off of Promenade des Anglais) of the building dominantly given over to the higher-priced Meridien Hôtel (above). The Mercure, part of a reliable moderate-category chain, has 124 good-sized and welcoming rooms with baths, only some of which face the outside; many—the least expensive—face an inner courtyard. Breakfast only, but it's the big buffet for which Mercure is noted. *Moderate.*

Beau Rivage Hôtel (24 Rue St.-François-de-Paule; phone 9380-80-70), though entered from a street inland from (and parallel with) Promenade des Anglais, the Beau Rivage is actually seafront. It's among the city's newer hotels, with tasteful public spaces, 120 pleasant rooms (the corner ones are especially nice) and suites with marble-accented baths, reliable restaurant, and—in emulation of the beaches operated by the leading Cannes hotels—a beach area just across the Promenade with restaurant, deck chairs, and beach mattresses on a wooden deck edging the pebbled shore. The Beau Rivage—a stem-to-stern rebuilding of an earlier hostelry of the same name—is a historic house. The artist Matisse was a permanent resident in 1917, and obviously liked where he was living well enough to have painted "My Room at the Beau Rivage"—now at the Philadelphia Museum of Art. *First Class.*

Élysée Palace Hôtel (59 Promenade des Anglais; phone 9386-06-06) shares ownership with the Beau Rivage (above) and, like it, is relatively recent. This is a good-looking house with smart public areas including a restaurant and bar, rooftop pool affording socko views, fitness center-sauna, and 140 comfortable rooms with well-fitted baths. *First Class.*

Altéa Masséna Hôtel (58 Rue Gioffredo; phone 9385-49-25) is centrally situated, a little inland from Place Masséna. It offers 116 agreeable rooms with bath. Breakfast only. *First Class.*

Suisse Hôtel (15 Quai Rauba Capeu; phone 9362-33-00) is among the better-equipped smaller houses, with 42 rooms with bath (some seaview) and a convenient restaurant. *Moderate.*

Mercure Hôtel Nice-Opéra (91 Quai des États-Unis; phone 9385-74-19) is a neighbor of the Nice Opéra for which it's partially named, in an interesting part of town. There are half a hundred rooms with bath, the more costly of which have sea views. As with all Chaîne Mercure hotels: buffet breakfast only. *Moderate.*

Plaza Concorde Hôtel (12 Avenue de Verdun; phone 9387-80-41) has 200 rooms, the nicest of which are good-sized, with terraces capacious enough for breakfast-cum-panoramas of nearby Place Masséna and the sea beyond. Restaurant, cocktail lounge. Central. *First Class.*

Aston Hôtel (12 Avenue Félix-Faure; phone 9380-62-52) has location—near Place Masséna and overlooking the fountain-centered gardens adjacent to it—and facilities in its favor; there are 160 modern-design, well-equipped rooms (those on the top floor have terraces), restaurant, and cocktail lounge. *First Class.*

Ambassador Hôtel (8 Avenue de Suède et Gustave V; phone 9387-90-19) is modestly sized—there are 45 full-facility rooms—but engaging, with a cordial staff, welcoming lobby, and super situation. Breakfast only. *Moderate.*

Park Hôtel (6 Avenue de Suède et Gustave V; phone 9387-80-25), like the neighboring Ambassador (above), is at once scenically and strategically situated. There are 135 full-facility rooms—all terraced, with the higher-up affording nice views—as well as a restaurant-bar. *First Class.*

Sofitel Splendid (50 Boulevard Victor-Hugo; phone 9388-69-54) is kingpin hotel among a considerable quantity of inland houses, four or five pleasantly walkable blocks north of Promenade des Anglais.

This is a rare—and most welcome—traditional-style link in the dominantly mod-look Sofitel chain. There are 128 tasteful rooms. Pluses include a rooftop pool/sundeck—views are fabulous—and an upper-floor bar, as well as a restaurant. Friendly, too. *First Class.*

La Malmaison Hôtel (48 Boulevard Victor-Hugo; phone 9387-62-56) welcomes you with a crystal-chandeliered lobby-lounge; a Louis XVI–style restaurant is adjacent, and there are 50 traditional-style rooms. Very nice, indeed. Best Western. *Moderate.*

Gounod Hôtel (3 Rue Gounod; phone 9388-26-20), a near-neighbor of Sofitel (above), charms with a smart decor that carries over from public spaces to half a hundred rooms. Breakfast only. *Moderate.*

Bedford Hôtel (45 Rue du Maréchal-Joffre; phone 9382-18-36) is contemporary and convenient; there are half a hundred full-facility rooms and a bar. Friendly. Breakfast only. *Moderate.*

Busby Hôtel (38 Rue du Maréchal-Joffre; phone 9388-19-41) is a neighbor of the Bedford (above) on a street parallel with busy Boulevard Victor-Hugo. There are 76 rooms, all well equipped, a restaurant, and a delightful lobby. *Moderate.*

Windsor Hôtel (11 Rue Dalpozzo at Rue du Maréchal-Joffre; phone 9388-59-35): You may or may not like the murals covering entire walls behind the beds of the Windsor's nearly 60 rooms; I think they're a nice touch. The big and welcoming lobby leads to a restaurant and bar-lounge; a swimming pool is in the garden. *Moderate.*

Brice Hôtel (44 Rue du Maréchal-Joffre; phone 9388-14-44)—just opposite the Windsor (above) is, alas, without a swimming pool like its neighbor, but does boast both a garden and a restaurant. There are 60 functional rooms. *Moderate.*

Napoléon Hôtel (6 Rue Grimaldi at Rue du Maréchal-Joffre; phone 9387-70-07) is agreeably traditional, with gracious lobby, cocktail lounge, and 80 rooms, the better of which are as good sized as they are well equipped. Breakfast only. *Moderate.*

Locarno Hôtel (4 Avenue des Baumettes; phone 9396-28-00) is nicely located in a quiet but easily gained quarter west of the business center. The lobby is welcoming, as, indeed, are those of the 50 traditional-look rooms I have inspected. Breakfast only. *Moderate.*

Carlone Hôtel (2 Boulevard François-Grosso, in the same western quarter as the Locarno, above, and but a block inland from Promenade des Anglais; phone 9344-71-61) has the look of a turn-of-century town house. The lobby-lounge is cozily Belle Époque, and 20 of the 23 traditional-style bedrooms have full baths. The hotel management is cordial. Sound value. *Moderate.*

Beach Regency Hôtel (223 Promenade des Anglais; phone 9383-91-51) opened a decade and a half back as the Hyatt Regency Nice, changing managements in the interim. It would be near the top of my Nice hotels grouping were it only closer in to the core of town. Despite a Promenade des Anglais address, it's *way* to the west, enough so that you want a car or taxi for excursions to the center. Withal, facilities are exemplary: 335 contemporary-design terraced rooms (seaview ones are, of course, preferred) with good baths; choice of restaurants; and two bars. *Luxury.*

Château St.-Martin Hôtel (Route de Coursegoules, Vence; phone 9358-02-02) is accurately named, a castlelike hostelry that went up as recently as the mid-1930s amidst atmospheric ruins of a medieval predecessor, in an elevated 35-acre park, just outside Vence village (above). There are just 25 rooms and suites; some of the latter are in cottages—*bastides* they're called—dotted about the grounds. Each is distinctively decorated with eighteenth-century antique accents, which are complemented by fine accessories and textiles. Public spaces are no less beautiful, the principal salon—giving onto a terrace affording splendid views—most especially, what with Flemish tapestries and medieval sculpture. Both swimming pool and tennis court are nestled among olive trees in the garden. And the picture-windowed restaurant is exceptional enough to warrant attention in a later paragraph. To sum up: one of France's most beautiful hotels. Member, Relais et Châteaux. *Luxury.*

Diana Hôtel (Avenue des Poilus, Vence; phone 9358-28-56) is adequate for a stay of a night or two in the heart of Vence village. This is an agreeable enough 25-room house, a five-minute walk from the core. Breakfast only. *Moderate.*

Mas d'Artigny Hôtel (Route de la Colle, two miles west of St.-Paul-de-Vence; phone 9332-84-54) straddles a hill in its own 20-acre park, with views of St.-Paul across the valley. This is a rambling complex embracing some 80 rooms and suites. There are nearly 30 suites, and each is fronted by a swimming pool of its own. Bedroom furnishings are wicker, while public spaces are more traditional. The restaurant is reputed, and there's a big central pool for the poor unfortunates who, alas, have none attached to their accommodations. You may well fall in love with Mas d'Artigny; I find it rather cold. Member, Relais et Châteaux. *Luxury.*

La Colombe d'Or Hôtel (St.-Paul-de-Vence; phone 9332-80-02) is intimate (there are but 16 rooms and 8 suites, the lot traditional style). There's a restaurant about whose extraordinary art I write (above) and about whose classic-style food I write (below), a swimming pool, and a casual, relaxing ambience. An interesting place to stay. Central. *First Class.*

Le St.-Paul Hôtel (St.-Paul-de-Vence; phone 9332-65-25) makes its home in a sixteenth-century *hôtel-particulier,* or mansion, that was, in the late 1980s, subjected to a stem-to-stern remake, with only significant architectural details retained. A consequence is this unusual hostelry, with 17 no-two-quite-alike rooms with fine modern baths and a trio of snazzy suites, as well as a classy restaurant, bar-lounge, and pretty garden. *Luxury.*

Le Métropole Hôtel (15 Boulevard Maréchal-Leclerc, Beaulieu-sur-Mer, adjacent to St.-Jean-Cap-Ferrat, six miles east of Nice; phone 9301-00-88) is a Riviera delight, situated in its own seaside park—flower-filled and with swaying palms—containing 50 no-two-alike rooms and suites and a generous-sized heated seawater pool on a fabulous sun-terrace just above the hotel's beach. Public spaces are smart, and the restaurant is as attractive as it is delicious—with seafood a specialty. A winner. Member, Relais et Châteaux. *Luxury.*

La Réserve Hôtel (5 Boulevard Maréchal-Leclerc, Beaulieu-sur-Mer, adjacent to St.-Jean-Cap-Ferrat, six miles east of Nice; phone 9301-00-01) is just next door to the Métropole (above), but a standout in its own right. There are just over 40 rooms; you want to specify a front one—the higher up, the better the view. The restaurant's picture windows overlook the great rectangle of a pool-cum-terrace and the beach. Smart, very smart. *Luxury.*

DAILY BREAD

Chantecler (Negresco Hôtel, 37 Promenade des Anglais; phone 9388-39-51): You're transported to the eighteenth century when you enter; antique crystal chandeliers, a marvelous rococo armoire, Louis XVI chairs covered in red velvet encircling tables centered with flowers—to supplement giant arrangements of gladiolas dotted about the room. The enormous staff—in tails, tuxes, or scarlet jackets—is as congenial as it is professional. Diners, predominantly French, are as dressy a crowd as you'll come across on the coast. There's an extensive à la carte, its range foie gras de canard and crayfish-stuffed ravioli through sautéed roast lamb. But you do very well indeed with the three-course menu, perhaps starting with smoked squab and lentil salad, or the house's imported-from-Scotland salmon specialty, going on to an entrée of roast guinea hen or a beef masterwork, with one of the chocolate desserts—

warm chocolate tart doused with almond-flecked cream or a trio of sherbets between thin leaves of bittersweet chocolate—to conclude. This is an exceptional enough restaurant for you to consider ordering the Menu de Dégustation—a veritable slew of courses in small-size portions, available only if everyone at the table wants to order it. Service is tip-top white-glove, wines outstanding. *Luxury.*

Maximin (12 Rue Sacha Guitry; phone 9380-70-10): You have to want to combine outrageous glitz with costly nourishment to appreciate Maximin, which headquarters in a late-nineteenth-century theater, with the kitchen on the stage (it's behind the curtain, which is opened—the better for you to applaud the chef-propriétaire whose name the restaurant takes—toward the end of each evening's dinner hour) and tables set among a forest of potted plants in what had been the orchestra. To be sampled are stuffed zucchini in a truffle sauce, and tian d'agneau—thin layered slices of lamb bound with a mélange of fresh vegetables. There are other zucchini specialties, along with the Riviera's favorite fish—loup (sea perch) and rouget (red mullet)—with fruit-based desserts the favorites and an extensive wine list. If the main restaurant's showbiz ambience sounds *de trop,* bear in mind Maximin's cheaper café next door. *Luxury.*

La Merenda (43 Rue de la Terrasse) is so popular with locals—who know that the only way to book a table is to stop in, and do so in person—that there's no telephone. Go early—at midday or in the evening—and hope that you'll be seated. Cuisine is traditional and hearty. Open with a plate of black olives served with coarse bread, the better to keep you occupied until a giant platter of assorted salamis arrives—and more of that marvelous bread. Next comes a Niçoise version of pizza (*pissaladière* is the local term), and it's superb. Or opt for pâtes au pistou, Nice's answer to not-far-distant Genoa's pasta, served with basil-flavored pesto sauce. But save space for bœuf en daube—a masterful beef stew—or any of several other entrées. Desserts are hearty, too. No credit cards. *Moderate.*

La Cambuse (5 Cours Saleya; phone 9380-12-31) is one of a number of congenial seafood restaurants in Vieux-Nice, opposite the big open market whose activity you may view from an outdoor table, at lunch. Open with the house's own tarte aux poireaux—a tasty leek tart—or a slice of pissaladière. I challenge you to eat, in its entirety, the gigantic mess of tiny fish that are a part of the friture de poissons, not to mention the assortment of local specialties that accompany the fish—including frites, deep-fried onions, Provençal-style tomatoes, and eggplant served several ways. An adventure. *Moderate.*

La Baieta (28 Cours Seleya; phone 9362-32-94) is a neighbor of La Cambuse (above) and, like it, specializes in seafood. Order one of the multicourse menus, perhaps opening with oysters on the half shell or shrimps, selecting a mixed grill of seafood—on an enormous platter and delicious—simply grilled fish of the day, a hearty serving of mussels marinière, or the plat du jour. End with one of the unpretentious desserts—crème caramel or ice cream. And do take an outdoor table, weather permitting. Friendly. *First Class.*

Le Grand Pavois (a.k.a. Chez Michel, 11 Rue Meyerbeer; phone 9388-77-42): Once you make up your mind not to let the dreadful paintings affect your meal, you can be happy here. You're in Nice, so it makes sense to open with a salade Niçoise—based, as you know from back home, on black olives and tuna; fish soup or stuffed mussels are options, and you continue with either fresh trout meunière or a filet of lotte (monkfish) grilled with fennel. Cordial and central. *First Class.*

Le Mac Mahon (50 Boulevard Jean-Jaurès; phone 9362-39-71) sounds oddly Irish to be on the Côte d'Azur. But when you hear its smiling staff pronounce its name (I will not attempt a phonetic imitation), you know you're in France. At any rate, oysters are the principal specialty, the half-dozen on the half shell that are the usual order, transatlantic, are only half a portion here, and you've several types to select from. Follow with a fish or seafood entrée. Central. *First Class.*

La Barale (39 Rue Beaumont; phone 9398-17-94) is appropriately located in Vieux-Nice—the Old Town, given that its specialties are Niçoise—and hearty. Base your meal, for example, on a stick-to-the-ribs ragoût Provençale, after having opened with assorted regional hors d'œuvres, olives and salami possibly among them. Rich sweets and Provençal wines. *First Class.*

Le Charolais (7 Promenade des Anglais; phone 9388-76-33) is strategically situated on the Promenade (take a terrace table if the day is fair) and accurately titled; specialties have to do with beef, primarily entrecôte and the pricier châteaubriand, served at tables set with pink and maroon linens, and with foie gras among openers, a range of pastas, and ice-cream coupes, or sundaes, to conclude. Agile service. *First Class.*

Le Chapon Fin (1 Rue du Moulin; phone 9380-56-92) is a Vieux-Nice favorite, atmospheric and delicious, salade Niçoise, seafood-stuffed ravioli, or, if you prefer, maigret de canard, the all-France duck-breast classic. The three-course menu, especially at lunch, is a good deal. Kindly staff. *First Class.*

Boccaccio (7 Rue Masséna; phone 9387-71-76) might be just the ticket if it's midday and shopping the neighborhood—Rue Masséna is pedestrians-only—has induced hunger. A table on the terrace is fun for crowd-watching, with the menu—specialties include seafood-sauced pastas, seafood platters, even a Spanish-influenced paella—good value. *First Class.*

St.-Moritz (5 Rue du Congrès; phone 9388-54-90) is a small spot, neat as a pin, enclosed by lacy curtains, and a wall surfaced with an Alpine mural the only Swiss feature of this restaurant other than its name. You're seated at red-leather upholstered chairs by a cordial hôtesse, but service can be very slow, albeit good-natured. Go with the menu—fish soup or cheese soufflé to start, roast lamb a tasty entrée, the day's sweet. Bread is good, wines fairly priced; location, central. *Moderate/First Class.*

Le Farniente (Westminster Concorde Hôtel, 27 Promenade des Anglais; phone 9388-29-44): Opt to lunch or dine inside, and the setting is pastel-shaded Louis XV, but warm-weather lunches or starlit dinners on the adjacent terrace are hardly to be despised. The prix-fixe menu—opening with a shellfish terrine and embracing a grilled fish of the day or sautéed lamb chops accompanied by Nice-origin ratatouille (a kind of vegetable casserole), as well as cheese and dessert—is good value, and good-tasting. *First Class.*

Café Tordo (Place Rossetti): I can't imagine a more picturesque setting for an alfresco cup of coffee or a cold drink than the Tordo, opposite the handsomely facaded cathedral in Vieux-Nice. *Moderate.*

Auberge du Jarrier (Biot; phone 9365-11-68) typifies this venerable village—and serves traditional dishes, expertly prepared. Have the prix-fixe menu, opening with the house's own duck tart, continuing with médaillon of lamb in a garlicky sauce, and concluding with any of Jarrier's house-made pastries. *First Class.*

Café des Acadias (Biot) is at the core of the village and a delightful spot to pause over a bit of refreshment and take in the scene. *Moderate.*

Hôtel du Château St.-Martin Restaurant (Route de Coursegoules, Vence; phone 9358-02-02): You're so preoccupied with the picture-window view of the garden and the sea way beyond that the unobtrusive captain is hesitant to interrupt. You order, though, beginning with an almost wickedly rich confit of foie gras frais de canard and following with goujonettes de sole—minifilets lightly breaded and deep-fried, with an entrée of mushroom-garnished veal médaillons. Assorted cheeses come next. Dessert is chocolate cake, chocolate-frosted, topped by delicately carved orange rind, with an orange filling between layers. Flawless service. *Luxury.*

La Colombe d'Or Hôtel Restaurant (St.-Paul-de-Vence; phone 9332-80-02): Paintings on the wall of this restaurant—by a mix of great artists of the era—are alluded to above. Herewith, I counsel the Colombe's traditional fare. Order your dessert—flaming Grand Marnier soufflé at the same time you select earlier courses, opening perhaps with vegetable soup or caviar and continuing with deliciously sauced pièce de bœuf, expertly prepared roast lamb, or a rich chicken fricassee. Green salads are a pride of the house. And there are other desserts, if you decide against the soufflé. Warm-weather terrace. *First Class.*

Café de la Place (Place du Général-de-Gaulle, St.-Paul-de-Vence) is a Vence institution. Nothing will do but that you pause here for coffee or a cold drink, the while watching villagers out front undertaking a game of bocci. *Moderate.*

SHOPPER'S NICE

Galeries Lafayette, the principal department store, is entered on Rue Jean-Médecin, just north of Place Masséna; it embraces six levels, with a supermarket/wine store in the basement and a bank on 4. Rue Masséna, leading west from Place Masséna, is the main pedestrian street, with such shops as *Daniel Hechter* (men's clothes), *Fil à Fil* (men's/women's accessories), *Les Must de Cartier* (jewelry), *Hédiard* (fancy foods and wine), and a number of women's clothing shops, including *Cacharel, New Man,* and *Alain Manoukian.* Rue de France, a westward extension of Rue Masséna, has a strong concentration of antique shops, including *St.-Michel, Occasions,* and *Récamier,* as well as a fabulous chocolate shop, *Ventadour*—which ships. Rue Paradis—still another pedestrian street—has such smart boutiques as *Chanel* (women's accessories), *Façonnable* (Yank-style men's clothes), and *Jacques Andréolis* (Baccarat, Daum, and Lalique crystal, as well as Christofle silver and several makes of Limoges china).

SOUND OF MUSIC

Opéra de Nice (Rue St.-François de Paule)—with a dignified neo-classic facade and a five-level auditorium—opened in 1885 and maintains a repertory company that is among the best in the south of France. Works presented run an interesting gamut, from Mozart's *Marriage of Figaro* and Wagner's *Die Meistersinger* through Richard Strauss's *Daphne* and Lerner and Lowe's *My Fair Lady.* There are, as well, seasons of ballet and symphonic and chamber music concerts.

Salle Apollon (in the Acropolis, Nice's extravagantly equipped Centre des Congrès), which opened just a century after the Opéra—in 1985—is one of Europe's most architecturally innovative theaters, embracing three irregularly contoured levels, with a seating capacity of 2,500 and a stage that's the largest in France. It serves as an alternative venue for presentations of concerts, classic and pop, opera, and other entertainments.

INCIDENTAL INTELLIGENCE

If you're driving about, via rented car, bear in mind that the Riviera has a trio of *corniches*—cross-country highways: *Grande* (or High), *Moyenne* (Middle), and *Basse* (Low); the top two are the most scenic. Nice is a major point of departure for bus excursions, both day and half-day, to such coastal points as St.-Paul-de-Vence, Grasse, Antibes, Cannes, Valauris, Èze, Monte Carlo, St.-Tropez, and even Genoa in Italy (see *Italy at Its Best*). Nice's annual *Carnaval* takes place the two weeks preceding Lent—and is an all-Europe leader of its type. *Aéroport de Nice–Côte d'Azur* (four miles southwest of town) is served by Air France, which flies nonstop to and from the United States; domestic service, too. *Further information:* Office de Tourisme, Avenue Thiers, Nice; Office de Tourisme, Place de la Chapelle, Biot; Office de Tourisme, Place du Grand Jardin, Vence; Office de Tourisme, Rue Grande, St.-Paul-de-Vence; Office de Tourisme, 59 Avenue Semeria, St.-Jean-Cap-Ferrat; Office de Tourisme, Boulevard Maréchal Juin, Cagnes-sur-Mer.

27

Nîmes

Ancient Rome in Provence

BACKGROUND BRIEFING

I thank Hubert Robert for first leading me to Nîmes. The prolific eighteenth-century artist, known more for interpretations in oil of idyllic Italian ruins than for works themed on his native France, quite obviously journeyed to Provence in order to paint two evocative works that now hang in Paris's Louvre—where, incidentally, he was an early curator. The one Robert to which I refer is of the Roman-built Maison Carré, in the core of Nîmes; the other is of the amazing Roman aqueduct, Pont du Gard, constructed 2000 years ago to provide Nîmes with water. Provoked by Robert into a visit, I was to learn that the subjects of both paintings not only still stand, but are eminently visitable—only two of a number of monuments of the ancient Roman presence.

It was location that drew the Romans to Nîmes. They liked its situation at a convenient stopping-off point between colonies in Spain and home base, to the east, in Italy. Originally *Colonia Augusta*—the Emperor Augustus was partial to it and lavish in his construction budgets—and later the French *Nismes,* it was, in the early centuries of our era, a showplace not only of the Romans' Gallic colonies, but of their empire. The empire's fall saw Nîmes decline. Starting in the early fifth century, a succession of invaders—Visigoths, Arabs, Normans—looted and plundered.

The Middle Ages saw it aligned with Languedoc and, eventually, the French Crown, gaining a university under François I and a disproportionately large Protestant populace. If the Huguenots thrived as a consequence of Henri IV's Edict of Nantes—protecting them—they suffered when his grandson, Louis XIV, revoked that edict. Later, they constituted the core of red-shirted guerrillas in the early-eighteenth-century Camisard Revolt—a case of Protestants quite literally protesting repression—against the royal army.

Still substantially Protestant—there are half a dozen-plus Protestant churches, a goodly number in a French city with a population of 140,000—Nîmes weaves textiles (the English word *denim* evolved from "Nîmes-origin cloth"—*de Nîmes*), and receives visitors curious to experience not only the vestiges of Rome painted by Hubert Robert, but others as well.

ON SCENE

Lay of the Land: Nîmes revolves around the greatest of the Roman constructions, *Les Arènes,* on the square taking its name, *Place des Arènes,* more or less in the center of town. Directly east is another square of consequence, *L'Esplanade,* from which the main shopping street, *Boulevard de l'Amiral Courbet,* leads north—passing the old quarter to its west, *Vieux Nîmes,* centered on the cathedral—to the Roman-built gate named for the city's builder-emperor, *Porte d'Auguste. Boulevard Victor-Hugo,* running north from the Arena to the *Maison Carré,* on the square taking its name, constitutes the western border of the city center. The railway station is east of the core on *Boulevard Sergent Triaire.*

Maison Carrée (Place de la Maison Carrée): Though it translates as Square House, this miraculously well-preserved rectangle of a Roman temple—built some 1,900 years ago—remains from without quite as exquisite as it must have been when new: the perfect pediment of its forward facade supported by half a dozen Corinthian columns, with still additional columns—10 at each extremity—flanking side walls. If the interior is not as it was, we cannot carp, given the wealth of objects on display, the lot of them from Roman Nîmes. Consider, for example, a perfectly preserved mosaic floor in tones of blue, brown, rust, and white; a sculpted Roman fisherman; a full-length *Apollo* in marble, discovered in the eighteenth century; and the equally superb *Vénus de Nîmes,* the city's single most celebrated work of sculpture.

Les Arènes (Place des Arènes): The amphitheater of Nîmes ranks easily, at least to this viewer of Roman-era amphitheaters—with the Colosseum in Rome, the Arena of Italy's Verona, the Roman-built colosseum of El Djem in Tunis, the Arena in Arles, and Théâtre Antique in Orange—as among the great ones of the onetime empire. Not unlike Maison Carrée, it is extraordinarily well preserved. Ideally, you want to see it in the course of a *corrida,* or bullfight, with the spectacle of the matador's entrance easily on a par with similar ceremonies in Spain. But, at any time, this masterwork impresses. In Roman days, spectators—come to marvel at feats of the gladiators or charioteers—were segregated by caste, their 20,000 seats on two dozen levels divided vertically into sections for various subdivisions of the citizenry, with a vast canopy shading the entire audience when the sun was strong.

Tour Magne (Chemin de Combret) quite accurately translates as Great Tower. Tallest of what had been a network of towers punctuating the city's walls, it straddles a substantial hill, Mont Cavalier, overlooking the city from the north. The tower, in three levels and octagonal at its base, is close to 150 feet high. If you're up to it, ascend its 140 steps by means of a contemporary stairwell; the view is spectacular.

Temple de Diane and Jardins de la Fontaine (Quai de la Fontaine) are a pair best taken in in the course of a descent from Mont Cavalier and Tour Magne (above). The temple, though in ruins and not actually dedicated to Diana when it was built in the second century A.D. (the name was appended in a later era), retains enough architectural detail—pedimented (albeit blocked up) windows, gracefully arched doorways, series of small but interestingly embellished side rooms, for example—to make it visitworthy. And surrounding Jardins de la Fontaine constitute a capacious eighteenth-century complex based on the town's ancient fountain, with an enormous reflecting pool—a perfect foil for the mix of sculpture, marble benches, and wrought-iron railings surrounding it.

Musée Archéologique (13 Boulevard Amiral Courbet) occupies a one-time Jesuit school. Its collection is considerably larger than the small group of Roman objects in Maison Carrée (above), if no less choice. Sculpture is first-rate, with the range busts of curly-headed youngsters to busts of bearded warriors. Medallions carved in terracotta record the life of the era. There are tombs and mosaics, capitals and toys, bronze lamps and glass jewelry, with a room full of Greek and Etruscan pottery as a bonus.

Musée des Beaux-Arts (Rue Cité Foulc) is more often than not ignored by short-term visitors intent on the city's Roman aspects. Its most spectacular exhibit is very Roman indeed: the largest and surely the handsomest of Nîmes-origin mosaics, called *Les Noces d'Admète,* embracing fifteen fabulous panels depicting scenes of a Roman wedding. Whip along, then, to the Renaissance—and later eras—for the hardly inconsiderable collection of paintings. Bassano, Giordano, Luini, and Panini are among the Italians, best represented of the foreign schools. And there are French works by Vernet and Moreau, Largillière and Rigaud, Natoire and Mignard, Boucher and Fragonard; not to mention sculpture by the likes of Rodin and Bourdelle.

Musée du Vieux Nîmes (Place de la Cathédrale) makes its home in a seventeenth-century mansion that was for long the palace of bishops of Nîmes. If, like me, you're partial to municipal historical collections, you'll have a good time here. Furniture alone is outstanding, chairs through chests, but there are, as well, paintings and prints, a wealth of ceramics, myriad assorted curios, and an extensive collection of objects—including toreadors' costumes—relating to Nîmes's bullfighting tradition.

Cathedral of St.-Castor (Place de la Cathédrale) is hardly among France's foremost. Still, its facade—top-heavy, with a formidable left-hand tower and a mix of epochs, Romanesque through rococo—is not unimpressive, and you want to give a few minutes to the frieze, busy with gargoyles and griffons. Then amble about the neighborhood; you are in *Vieux Nîmes,* and it's worthwhile strolling past medieval and Renaissance houses—some beautifully embellished—on *Rue de l'Aspic, Rue des Marchands, Rue de la Madeleine,* and *Place du Marché.*

Pont du Gard (23 miles northeast of Nîmes) represents both engineering and architectural skills of the ancient Romans at their most brilliant. They erected it in the nineteenth year of the first century A.D. to supply Nîmes with water from the Eure River, which it spans to this day. Even allowing for a nineteenth-century restoration commissioned by the government of Napoleon III (after a visit by the emperor), the resilience of this three-level construction is mind-boggling. To cite dimensions—three gracefully arched levels, 900 feet long by 160 feet high—is not to do the Pont du Gard justice. You'll appreciate the proportions of the aqueduct by having a look at it from either side of the river, ascending, then, for an ambulatory exploration, one side to the other.

SETTLING IN

Imperator Concorde Hôtel (Quai de la Fontaine; phone 6621-90-30) is a well-situated and handsome house of some years, kept nicely up to date, though in a traditional style, with its ace architectural feature a pretty inner courtyard. There are 62 well-equipped rooms, a restaurant later counseled, and a bar. Affiliated with Chaîne Concorde. *First Class.*

Cheval Blanc Hôtel (1 Place des Arènes; phone 6667-20-03) could not be more strategically situated—just opposite the Roman amphitheater, heart-of-town. This is an agreeable house with 50 rooms in the traditional manner, attractive restaurant, and friendly bar. Best Western. *First Class.*

Novotel Atria (5 Boulevard de Prague; phone 6676-56-56) is well situated just opposite the broad square called Esplanade, which edges Les Arènes. There are just under 120 well-equipped rooms with bath, and a convenient, reasonably tabbed restaurant. *Moderate/First Class.*

Les Tuileries Hôtel (22 Rue Roussy; phone 6621-31-15) is a small 11-room house that's reasonably central and comfortable. Breakfast only. *Moderate.*

Louvre Hôtel (2 Square de la Couronne; phone 6667-22-75) is central. There are 28 functional rooms, well-priced restaurant, and bar. *Moderate.*

Vieux Castillon Hôtel (Castillon du Gard, just opposite Rémoulins, a mile and a half from Pont du Gard and 15 miles northeast of Nîmes; phone 6637-00-77) is set in a charmer of a village and comprises a complex of typically Provençal stone buildings edged by an elevated garden-cum-swimming pool. The highly reputed restaurant (evaluated below), with copper lanterns extending from a beamed ceiling, moves outdoors in summer. Drinks are served in a clutch of lounges. And there are just under three dozen rooms, no two alike, each antique-accented and smartly wallpapered and accessorized, with excellent baths. Special. Member, Relais et Châteaux. *Luxury.*

Chemin de l'Hostellerie is the aptly named road a good quarter-hour's drive from town, to its south, on which are clustered a handful of relatively recently constructed hotels—functional, if hardly beautiful. On scene are *Mercure* and *Novotel* (both *Moderate/First Class*); as well as *Ibis, Nimotel,* and *Solotel* (all *Moderate*). All have restaurants and outdoor pools and they're okay for business travelers. But if your mission is to experience Nîmes, you want to be in town, especially if you're without a car.

DAILY BREAD

Imperator Hôtel Restaurant (Quai de la Fontaine; phone 6621-90-30) is a quiet but tasteful room—murallike pictures of ancient Nîmes adorn its mocha walls; flowers are everywhere—with a commendable kitchen. A multicourse dinner might include such specialties as scallop and foie gras salad, the house's own daube de sole with artichokes, lamb steak with a creamed tarragon sauce, and a warm multifruit tart enveloped in raspberry sauce. *First Class.*

Lisita (2 Boulevard des Arènes; phone 6667-29-15) is at once central, reliable, and delicious. This might be just the spot to try such local dishes as brandade de morue (the Provençal cod and olive oil blend that tastes much better than it sounds), and bœuf à la gardianne. Nice sweets. *First Class.*

Lou Mas (5 Rue de Sauve; phone 6623-24-71) is a wise choice for hearty specialties like filet of veal, Nîmes style; eels, garlic-sauced; preserved duck with beans. *First Class.*

Magister (5 Rue Nationale; phone 6676-11-00) has the virtue of a convenient situation, agreeable staff and ambience, and tasty Provençal specialties on its multicourse menus. *Luxury.*

Vieux Castillon Hôtel Restaurant (Castillon du Gard; phone 6637-00-77) is at its most romantic on a mild summer evening, when tables are set around the pool in the moonlight. Or go for lunch in connection with a visit to Pont du Gard. Consider a seafood salad or expertly prepared foie gras as openers; lamb chops, chervil-seasoned, and a platter of vegetables as an entrée; selection of cheeses; a sampling of, say, two of the house's celebrated sweets—poached whole fresh pears in a caramel sauce or a frozen soufflé scented with Poire William eau-de-vie. Expert service with a smile. *Luxury.*

INCIDENTAL INTELLIGENCE

Aéroport de Nîmes-Garons is five miles from town; scheduled domestic service. *Further information:* Office de Tourisme, 6 Rue Auguste, Nîmes.

28

Pau

Vive Henri IV!

BACKGROUND BRIEFING

It is not an Italian River, in the course of a diversion into France. It is not Edgar Allan's last name, misspelled. It is not the word *poor,* as an American southerner might pronounce it.

It is, rather, a medium-sized southwest city so close to snowy Pyrenees peaks that they appear almost touchable from the core of town. And it is the birthplace—his fabulous castle is a museum operated by the French government—of King Henri IV. Surely if a poll were to be taken today, four and a half centuries after his death, the likelihood is that Henri would come through, hands down, as France's favorite monarch. The very same Henri who wanted "a chicken in every pot" for all of his subjects was, as well, the very first of the dynasty of Bourbon monarchs that extended through his son, Louis XIII, beyond to Charles X in the post-Revolutionary period.

Given the complexity of his origins and, indeed, of his reign, Henri's kingly achievements are not always easy to appreciate. His father was, to be sure, a Bourbon duke, but his grandmother was the much-admired Queen Marguerite of Navarre, his great-uncle was French King François I, and his mother was Queen Jeanne d'Albret of Navarre, so that he became King Henri III of Navarre *before* becoming Henri IV of France.

His religion switches surely set some sort of record. He began as a Protestant, like his mother; became a Catholic after marrying his first wife (Marguerite of Valois); returned to Protestantism again during the Wars of Religion; leaned toward Catholicism later in the course of a conflict that translates as the War of the Three Henrys; reaffirmed his Catholicism—presumably by opining the oft-quoted "Paris is well worth a Mass" upon agreeing to enter the capital as king; and later came to the aid of Protestants with his proclamation of the Edict of Nantes, guaranteeing religious freedom. That edict was revoked by his grandson, Louis XIV, but Henri's reign saw other remarkable innovations.

Between the period of the annulment of his union with Marguerite of Valois and his second marriage—to Marie de Médicis—he achieved a reputation as a leader with a sense of organization, fostering commerce and agriculture, signing trade treaties with foreign countries, and manifesting a concern for the welfare of his commoner subjects—not usual with monarchs of that era—or, indeed, of succeeding eras. Henri was an interesting man who obviously inherited the wit and sharp intelligence of his grandmother, Marguerite—as well as her Pau castle.

Switch, then, to Napoleonic Pau. The emperor himself is said to have inspired the still extant central boulevard that affords smashing Pyrenees panoramas. Word of the mountain views and of the city's other charms—a salubrious climate, among these—spread north of the Channel to England. The British started coming as tourists in the post-Waterloo years, and, although their numbers are not strong contemporarily, Pau acknowledges its debt to them for racetracks, hunt clubs, and what is believed to have been the first golf course on the continent of Europe.

ON SCENE

Lay of the Land: The sector of Pau with which you want to become familiar is its southwest corner, lying north of the *Gave de Pau River. Place Clemenceau* and smart *Place Royale* are the central squares. The former lies amidships, with a wide street named for two military leaders cutting through it: *Rue Maréchal-Joffre* leads west into *Rue du Château* and the city's showplace castle, while *Rue Maréchal-Foch* lies to the east in the direction of an all-France sleeper of a fine-arts museum. Smart shops are clustered on *Rue Louis-Barthou* to the north of Place Royale. To that same square's south is *Boulevard des Pyrénées,* aptly named; it was designed to bring the mountains into glorious perspective.

Château de Pau (Rue du Château): The setting is out of a fairy tale. A river, first, low down and with a properly picturesque bridge traversing it. A hill, next, as the appropriate site. Then, the castle, behind a bulky keep dating to the fourteenth century, with most of the rest of the facade—towers and turrets and high, gabled windows set into severe, black-slate mansard roofs—two centuries younger. It is surely the supreme irony of this castle—which was the birthplace of Henri IV, first of a long line of Bourbon kings—that its restoration, after severe neglect that set in with the Revolution, was effected by a pair of non-Bourbon, nineteenth-century monarchs: King Louis-Philippe and Emperor Napoleon III. Credit them with a thorough and professional job. Using concepts of the nineteenth century, the two sovereigns' designers have given us a decidedly romantic series of Renaissance interiors, with furnishings an engaging mix of authentic pieces of the period, with reproductions made at the time of the restoration and magnificent Gobelin tapestries. It works very well, indeed.

You see it on guided tours that depart periodically, with commentary in French. I think the state bedrooms—Chambre de la Reine and Chambre des Souverains, both with opulently canopied beds, paneled walls, marble mantels, and coffered ceilings—are the most elegant. But the vast Grand Salon, in which Henry IV was baptized, and the bedroom—with an interminably long plaque embedded in the wall above its fireplace, affording presumed details—where Henri was, by tradition, born on December 13, 1553, are of interest, too. So is the bedroom of his mother, Queen Jeanne d'Albret, principally because of the splendid flight-of-angels tapestry on one of its walls. And every visitor oohs and ahs in the dining room, a Louis-Philippe creation, dubbed Salle aux Cent Couverts, its table comfortably seating a hundred for a regal meal.

Musée des Beaux-Arts (Rue Mathieu Lalanne) is nondescript architecturally, but you don't want its setting to discourage you from touring what is one of the most eye-popping of French provincial museums. You are engaged from the moment of entry. To your left is an open-to-visitors room that is hung with original works by *très jeunes Palois*—Pau youngsters, more or less kindergarten age, enrolled in museum classes. Then you make the rounds of the galleries, for the permanent collection. For Americans, surely the most unexpected painting is one labeled *Bureau du Coton à la Nouvelle-Orléans,* portraying top-hatted traders at the New Orleans Cotton Exchange and painted by none other than Edgar Degas in 1873. But there are other treats—a solemn religious procession by Juan de Juanès, whose works rarely are seen outside of his native Spain; other Spaniards, including El Greco, Zurbarán, Alfonso Cano, and Ribera—the lot attesting to the proximity of Spain to Pau; rich Italian representation—Bassano, Giordano, Guido Reni, to name a trio of painters from that country; Brueghel and Jordaens, Rubens (with an extraordinary *Last Judgment*) and David Teniers, among the Flemings; British portraitists like George Romney and Sir David Wilkie. And a wealth of French art: a Boudin of Bordeaux harbor; an unexpected self-portrait of the sculptor Carpeaux; a Corot landscape; a cluster of sailing ships by Daubigny; Largillière and Fantin-Latour; Marquet and Berthe Morisot; Nattier and Oudry, Rigaud and Robert; Van Loo and Vuillard. Wow!

Musée Bernadotte (8 Rue Tran): A funny thing happened in Pau on January 26, 1763: Jean-Baptiste Bernadotte was born in a middle-class Pau house. He went on to achieve distinction in Napoleon's army, becoming a general in 1794, married Désirée Clary in 1798, had a son named Oscar in 1799, and—through a chain of fortuitous political circumstances—was named Crown Prince of Sweden in 1810. He was officially adopted later that year by the childless Swedish king, Karl XIII, whom he succeeded as King Karl Johan XIV in 1818. His son by Désirée—who broke her engagement to Napoleon to marry Bernadotte—became King Oscar I upon his father's death in 1844; and the Bernadotte dynasty they established continues as Sweden's Royal Family. If you watch old movies on TV, you may recall the star-studded 1956 Hollywood film *Désirée,* which tells the Bernadotte story; Jean Simmons played the title role, Michael Rennie was Bernadotte, Marlon Brando was Napoleon, and Merle Oberon was Josephine. That background behind you, enjoy this charming house-museum, brimming with Bernadotte memorabilia, including the bedroom in which Karl Johan XIV was born. Visitors to the house have included the reigning Swedish monarch, King Karl Gustaf XVI.

Parc Beaumont (at the eastern end of Boulevard des Pyrénées) is the handsomest in town (Pau has three times been declared France's prettiest garden city in national competitions) with its ace-in-the-hole *Casino Municipal,* along with the requisite lake and waterfalls.

Cathedral of Lescar (Place Royale, Lescar) is a quarter-hour's drive from Pau. What makes the trip to the village of Lescar worthwhile is the cathedral's Romanesque apse and altar. Other parts of the multiperiod building—including a severe nave—are late Gothic, with the stained glass nineteenth century.

Parc National des Pyrénées—embracing much of the countryside south of town, in the beautiful mountainous region bordering Spain—makes for a pleasant excursion, given its mix of lures: dense forests, snowy peaks, mirrorlike lakes, and a wildlife population that includes bears and eagles.

Lourdes (25 miles east of Pau) is the town in which Bernadette Soubirous—later a nun and canonized in 1933—claimed to have witnessed the appearance of the Virgin Mary on 18 occasions, beginning February 11, 1858. Pilgrims, many of them incurable invalids, have not stopped going since, to pray at the grotto where Bernadette experienced her visions—*Grotte de Massabielle*—now the nucleus of a religious complex embracing hospitals as well as churches; most important of the latter is *Basilique Pie X,* built in 1958 on the hundredth anniversary of the visions and, to understate, massive, with a capacity of 20,000. The popularity of Lourdes is a phenomenon of France; there are some four million pilgrims each year, with Spain, Italy, and Ireland the heaviest represented countries, France following. Hotel capacity is extraordinary; room total is 17,000, with by far the majority in very simple hotels and pensions. And the souvenir shops appear limitless. Permanent reception centers—*Acceuil de Pèlerins* (Pilgrims' Registration) and *Halls des Malades* (Patients' Reception Rooms)—are at the railway station. Busiest times are at Easter, August, and October.

Sauveterre-de-Béarn (35 miles northwest of Pau), a pretty village flanking the Cave d'Oloron River, is indicated, perhaps, for a lunch stop combined with a visit to *Château de Gaston VII,* with a splendidly situated terrace, and *Church of Ste.-Marie*—twelfth-century Romanesque, with a massive tower and panoramas of the Pyrenees from the perspective of a romantic ruined bridge jutting into the river.

SETTLING IN

Continental Hôtel (2 Rue Maréchal-Foch; phone 5927-69-31) is an immediately likable turn-of-century house that has been efficiently updated, the while retaining a traditional look. The 85 rooms include some attractive and commodious quarters with good baths, and there are both a restaurant—seafood is the specialty—and a bar-lounge. Smiling service. Commendable. Best Western. *First Class.*

Grand Hôtel du Commerce (9 Rue Maréchal-Joffre; phone 5927-24-40) exaggerates, perhaps, with "grand" as part of its title, but it is agreeably traditional, with pleasant lobby, half a hundred rooms (accessories and wallpapers are tasteful; baths, modern), bar-lounge, and a Louis XIII–style restaurant recommended on a later page. *Moderate.*

Paris Hôtel (80 Rue Émile-Garet; phone 5927-34-39) is an elderly house whose management has modernized it: lobby bar-lounge as well as the 40 rooms, all bath-equipped. Breakfast only. *Moderate.*

Roncevaux Hôtel (25 Rue Louis-Barthou; phone 5927-08-44) is ideal for shoppers, given a situation on Pau's heart-of-town boutique street. There are just over 40 well-equipped rooms and a bar. Breakfast only. *Moderate.*

Gallia et Londres Hôtel (26 Avenue Bernadette-Soubirous, Lourdes; phone 6294-35-44) is No. 1 in Lourdes—with 90 full-facility rooms, restaurant, and bar. *First Class.*

Ste.-Rose Hôtel (2 Rue des Carrières Peyramale, Lourdes; phone 6294-30-96) is functional (there are nearly a hundred rooms, many with private bath, as well as a reasonably priced restaurant) and convenient to the religious complex. *Moderate.*

DAILY BREAD

L'Aragon (18 Boulevard des Pyrénées; phone 5927-12-34): Though it is more *brasserie* than proper restaurant, L'Aragon has big pluses, especially in the case of the visitor with time for but a single Pau meal. You see the mountains as you enjoy your meal, thanks to the Boulevard des Pyrénées location. And your meal can be composed of such regional specialties as the local and delicious hard sausage, the also-local rillettes (a coarse pâté) or—in cool weather—the celebrated Béarn soup, based on vegetables, with the added flavor of preserved goose and a hambone, as starters; and fresh local salmon simply grilled and served with sauce Béarnaise (you are, remember, in Béarn, although I'm told the sauce is not of local origin), caught-in-the-neighborhood trout sautéed with almonds, or confit de canard—preserved duck—accompanied by pommes persillées, as entrées. Delicious, made-on-premises fruit tarts and wines of the region—from across-the-river Jurançon. When last I checked, no credit cards. *Moderate.*

St.-Jacques (9 Rue du Parlement; phone 5927-58-97) welcomes with a smiling staff and an innlike interior with beamed ceilings, fireplace, and fresh flowers everywhere. The well-priced menu might embrace onion soup or smoked salmon, entrecôte served with a delicious sauce Béarnaise and crispy frites; or maigret de canard—sliced breast of duck—appropriately garnished. Near the château. *First Class.*

Les Pyrénées (Place Royale; phone 5927-07-75) attracts with a convivial Belle Époque ambience. There are tables out on the square in good weather and a downstairs bar-lounge, and the restaurant—up a flight—offers a prix-fixe menu that might be composed of salad as an opener, confit de canard as an entrée, and praliné mousse for dessert, with wine included. Friendly. *First Class.*

Louis XIII (Grand Hôtel du Commerce, 9 Rue du Maréchal-Joffre; phone 5927-24-40) is brick-walled and candlelit at dinner, with ladder-back chairs flanking tables, at which you might be served a menu of regional specialties, such as trout sautéed in Jurançon wine, confit de canard, and your choice of local cheeses or a made-on-premises sweet. *Moderate.*

Café de la Coupole (Place Clemenceau), an atmospheric locale for coffee-cum-people-watching on a central square; also a restaurant. *Moderate/First Class.*

A Boste (Sauveterre-de-Béarn; phone 5938-50-62) is part of a complex embracing an eleventh-century tower that is pleasant for a lunch pause—fare is traditional—in connection with village exploration; 10 hotel rooms, too. *Moderate.*

L'Ermitage (Place du Monsignor Laurence, Lourdes; phone 6294-08-42) is near the religious complex and offers a good-value menu in its upstairs dining room.

SHOPPER'S PAU

Department stores—*Nouvelles Galeries* and *Prisunic*—are on Place Clemenceau, and Rue Serviez is a busy pedestrians-only street, but you want to stroll Rue Louis-Barthou for its boutiques, which include—to give you an idea of how smart a small city can be—*Cacharel, Pierre Balmain, Chloë, Alain Manoukian, Natacha* (which features Kenzo), *Pérrineau* (with pricey jewelry), and *Olde England* (men's wear).

INCIDENTAL INTELLIGENCE

Further information: Office de Tourisme, Place Royale, Pau; Office de Tourisme, Mairie, Sauveterre-du-Béarn; Office de Tourisme, Place de Champ-Commun, Lourdes; Parc National des Pyrénées, Route de Pau, Pau. There is scheduled air service between Pau and Paris; Aéroport de Pau-Uzein is seven miles north of town.

29

Poitiers and La Rochelle

East-Central Neighbors

BACKGROUND BRIEFING

Geography and tourism? Of course there's a correlation. Consider these two east-central cities: Poitiers—respectably aged and with its fair share of architectural treasures; and not-far-distant La Rochelle—most monument-rich port of France's long stretch of Atlantic coast between Brittany and Biarritz. They are both far enough south to be ignored, more often than not, by inspectors of Loire Valley châteaux (chapter 20) to the northeast, and too far north to be considered visitable by travelers in more southerly Périgord (chapter 34).

Poitiers, by far the elder of the pair, is one of the rare French cities whose modern name is unrelated to what ancient Romans called it—*Limonum*. It had turned Christian even before the Romans left, and—under its first bishop, the sainted Hilaire (whose name was given to a still-standing Poitiers church)—was the venue of a considerable clutch of convents as early as the fourth century. Later, it was ruled by Germanic Visigoths, who were followed by the Franks and eventually by Normans.

Eleanor of Aquitaine, the consort first of a French king (Louis VII) and then of an English one (Henry II), established a court of her own—and a glittering one, at that—in twelfth-century Poitiers. Two centuries later, during the Hundred Years War, Poitiers knew both English rule, for a period, *and* Jeanne d'Arc, as well; she was interrogated about the divine "voices" exhorting her to aid the Crown in the still visitable Great Hall of the city's ducal palace prior to receiving a force of troops to battle the English enemy.

If you discount La Rochelle's contemporary eminence—among savvy French holiday-makers, for the most part—as a vacation destination, it has three claims to fame: as France's premier Atlantic fishing port; as departure point for many New World immigrants, especially the settlers of early Montreal; and as a focal point of

Huguenot (i.e., Protestant) strength, vanquished by troops under the command of Louis XIII and Cardinal Richelieu, after a near-interminable, 14-month siege.

Half a century after this bitter defeat, Louis XIV proclaimed the Revocation of the Edict of Nantes, which lost French Protestants their religious rights, but had one positive effect: establishment of America's Rochelle—New Rochelle, New York—by refugees fleeing to the New World from the original French Rochelle, in 1688.

ON SCENE

POITIERS

Lay of the Land: *Place du Maréchal-Leclerc* is dead center, site of Printemps department store, with such pedestrian streets as *Rue des Cordeliers* (with Monoprix department store), *Rue Gambetta,* and *Rue du Moulin à Vent* in its vicinity, as are such other central streets—these strollable because of Renaissance houses—*Grande Rue* and *Rue de la Chaîne.* Everything you'll want to visit is more or less central and reached by foot. The railway station is west of the core on *Boulevard du Grand-Cerf.*

Church of Notre-Dame-la-Grande (Place Charles-de-Gaulle), an all-France ranker, is one of the most beautiful Romanesque churches in the republic. The facade is an uninterrupted mass of carving—above the central portal and the arches flanking it and in two upper levels of sculpture-filled niches; look carefully and you'll recognize *The Annunciation, The Nativity, The Visitation,* Old Testament prophets, the dozen apostles. The interior is at its most sublime in the choir, surrounded by half a dozen columns—each with a magnificent capital—supporting a dome surfaced with a thirteenth-century fresco. And all of the chapels are art-filled.

Baptistry of St.-Jean (Rue St.-Jean) is a mind-boggler. You step down—descending half a flight—at its entrance to find yourself in a massive space that was constructed between the fourth and sixth centuries and is, not surprisingly, given this pedigree, among the oldest Christian monuments in France. The baptismal font in its center is simple and beautiful; so are the frescoes.

Cathedral of St.-Pierre (Place de la Cathédrale) is anticlimactic after Notre-Dame and the baptistry (above), its near neighbor. But richly ornamented Gothic is hardly to be despised, given the quality of the carving of the tympanum framing each of three portals. The nave is high, wide, and handsome, and the thirteenth-century stalls of the choir are among the oldest in France.

Church of St.-Hilaire (Rue du Doyenne) is named for Poitiers's first bishop and surely does his memory justice. It is sublime Romanesque, parts of it dating to the eleventh century. Start out back, taking in the graceful apse, before you move along in to admire a long, cool nave and a severe transept—these in contrast to ebullient capitals of pillars framing the choir.

Palais de Justice (Place du Palais) represents the handiwork of centuries, twelfth through nineteenth. A courthouse today, it was, in earlier centuries, the home of counts of Poitiers and of dukes of Aquitaine. Head for the *Grande Salle.* A triple-compartment fireplace, with an intricately carved mantel surmounted by a massive Gothic window, occupies the entire far wall. The carved-wood ceiling is worth a little neck strain. And you will want to pause a bit when reminded that it was in this room that the bishop of Poitiers quizzed Jeanne d'Arc about the visions that resulted in her leading French troops in battle against the English.

Musée Ste.-Croix (Rue Jean-Jaurès) goes on and on and on—high-ceilinged gallery after high-ceilinged gallery in rambling contemporary quarters, part archeological exhibits (bits and pieces of Roman Poitiers are the Ste.-Croix at its best) and with some paintings, none by celebrated masters or of any special distinction. Skippable.

LA ROCHELLE

Lay of the Land: Remember two words: *Vieux-Port.* The visitor's life in La Rochelle revolves around this romantic inlet of the sea, guarded these many centuries by a pair of battlements out of a fairy tale—*Tour St.-Nicolas,* fifteenth-century and the taller of the pair of towers; and somewhat older *Tour de la Chaîne,* so called because a chain was extended from it to its counterpart, as a way of closing the harbor. (Both of these towers are visitable; the Chaîne has a minimodel of medieval La Rochelle). Still a third tower—at times mistaken for a church because of the steeple topping it off—is *Tour de la Lanterne* nearby; take a walk up its spiral stairway to the summit for panoramas of town and sea. Cafés, restaurants, and hotels line Vieux-Port in and around *Cours des Dames, Quai de Carénage,* and *Quai Duperré.* The principal shopping street, *Rue St.-Yon*—perpendicular with Quai Duperré—passes a number of atmospheric thoroughfares intersecting it and lined with fine old houses. *Rue Gargoulleau,* at right angles to it, leads to *Place Verdun,* around which official La Rochelle is clustered, with its dominant monument *Cathedral of St.-Louis,* designed in the eighteenth century. The *Bourse* (now the chamber of commerce) and *Palais de Justice* (courthouse)—also classic style eighteenth-century—are nearby. Beaches? *Promenade du Mall,* a 10-minute drive from the center, is a wide, mile-long, white-sand strand, centered by a casino, with cafés and restaurants dotted about. Or take a ferry from *La Pallice,* three miles north of town, to *Île de Ré,* lunching and/or overnighting in the village of *La Flotte.*

Musée du Nouveau Monde (10 Rue Fleurieu)—the Museum of the New World—opened its elegant doors on May 15, 1982. I mention the date because of its significance: the three-hundredth anniversary of the founding of Louisiana. This museum, in this town with strong New World associations, was created as a cooperative venture of the City of La Rochelle, the Département of Charente-Maritime in which it is situated, and the French government. Setting is an extraordinarily beautiful eighteenth-century mansion, Hôtel Fleurieu, refurbished for museum use, but with decorative details—fireplaces surrounded with gilt-framed mirrors, superbly paneled walls, a marble stairway, with masterful wrought-iron bannister—left intact. Exhibits reflect the museum's theme: commerce between and relations with what had been Acadia (now Nova Scotia), Quebec, and other areas of Canada, Louisiana, the French West Indies, and Brazil. Displays are more a case of quality than quantity. Only a selection of objects from the permanent collection is shown at any given time: Walls of one room are covered with panels of antique wallpaper depicting Indian life in the New World; an early nineteenth-century clock made of gilded bronze, its dial surmounted with a spear-carrying Indian, is placed atop a mantel. A Mohawk brave, European-drawn in the eighteenth century, is framed on a wall opposite. The bronze bust of a fine-featured chief wearing a multihued feather headdress occupies the panel of another wall. Caches of moccasins and snowshoes, sleighs and jewelry, wampum and hatchets fill cases. And pieces with decorative interest—a spear fashioned like a fleur-de-lis, an exquisitely carved powder horn, a framed map of sixteenth-century *Floride Française,* a watercolor of a banana leaf—are displayed with an eye to aesthetics. There are, as well, fanciful painted interpretations of the New World and its people by artists who had never seen it. The only other comparable museum with which I am familiar—Museo de América, on the University of Madrid campus (see *Spain at Its Best*)—doesn't hold a candle to this one.

Hôtel de Ville (Place de la Mairie) is visitable by means of regularly departing guided tours; go along regardless of your fluency in French, to see this superb mansion, medieval without, elaborate Renaissance within, with one of its exhibits a plaque expressing the friendship of the people of New Rochelle, New York, toward the people of La Rochelle.

Musée d'Orbigny-Bernon (Rue St.-Côme) is a felicitous mix of history (exhibits that graphically portray the seventeenth-century Siege of La Rochelle) and the decorative arts (porcelain most especially), with the setting—an aged mansion—as appealing as the exhibits.

Musée des Beaux-Arts (Rue Gargoulleau) has a relative handful of known artists represented—Corot and Chassériau, out of the last century; Signac and Marquet, with postimpressionist paintings of La Rochelle's Vieux-Port; outstanding drawings; regional painters' works.

SETTLING IN

POITIERS

De France Hôtel (28 Rue Carnot; phone 4941-32-01) is your prototypical old-fashioned, small-city, French-traditional house. Public spaces are high-ceilinged and formal, the 86 rooms—no two quite the same—number some very agreeable accommodations among them, with good baths, and there are both congenial cocktail lounge and creditable restaurant. Core of town. *First Class.*

De l'Europe Hôtel (39 Rue Carnot; phone 4988-12-00) is quite as central as the De France (above)—just down the street. You enter through an aged courtyard, finding yourself in a pleasant lobby-lounge area. There are half a hundred full-facility rooms, and a restaurant that caters only to groups. For the rest of us, breakfast only. *Moderate.*

Domaine de Périgny Hôtel (Périgny, 18 miles northwest of town; phone 4951-80-43) is an isolated country complex, with lobby-bar and contemporary cuisine restaurant in the modern main building and 45 antique-accented rooms—differing in size and furnishings, some with little terraces—in a detached pavilion. Service is polite and professional, and the restaurant moves to the garden in warm weather. Swimming pool, tennis. Member, Relais et Châteaux. *First Class.*

Royal-Poitou Hôtel (Route de Paris, seven miles north of town; phone 4901-72-86) can be faulted (unless it's been redecorated since my last visit) for vivid-hued public spaces (lounge is a royal blue, bar is purple, restaurant and poolside terrace-café are red and white). But bedrooms—32 all told—are easy-to-live-with brown and beige, and staff is friendly. *First Class.*

Arcade Hôtel (15 Rue de Petit Bonneveau; phone 4988-30-42)—a link of the national chain known for its small but spotless and clean-lined rooms with showers rather than tubs in their baths. Room count is 75, location quite central. Breakfast only. *Moderate.*

LA ROCHELLE

Le Champlain Hôtel (20 Rue Rambaud; phone 4641-23-99) went up in the eighteenth century as the town house of a wealthy family and has retained much of its original decor—parquet floors and rococo furniture in lounges that are set off by gilded Ionic columns and illuminated by crystal chandeliers. Those of the 32 bedrooms I've inspected are not without antique pieces—armoire here, a chair there—and have good baths. Lovely. Breakfast only. Best Western. *First Class.*

De France et d'Angleterre Hôtel (22 Rue Gargoulleau; phone 4641-34-66) is an essentially contemporary house, with both mod-look and traditional-design rooms (76 all told), a congenial cocktail lounge, and a reliable restaurant that moves to the garden it overlooks in summer. Central. *First Class.*

Mercure Yachtsman Hôtel (23 Quai Valin; phone 4641-20-68) is nicely located near Vieux-Port, offers 44 agreeable rooms with bath and a restaurant that spills out to a terrace in good weather, and an outdoor pool. *Moderate/First Class.*

St.-Jean-d'Acre Hôtel (4 Place de la Chaîne; phone 4641-73-33) is heart of the La Rochelle action, by which I mean smack on the Vieux-Port. Public spaces and those of the 50 rooms I've looked at are contemporary and agreeable; you want, of course, to make sure your accommodations overlook the harbor. Au Vieux-Port Restaurant, a La Rochelle leader, is on the premises and later reviewed. *Moderate.*

Trianon et Plage Hôtel (6 Rue de la Monnaie; phone 4641-21-35)—a hop and a skip from Vieux-Port—is garden-bordered, with 25 okay rooms and a good-value restaurant. *Moderate.*

Le Richelieu Hôtel (La Flotte, Île de Ré; phone 4609-60-70) makes for an agreeable respite, in the course of either a day's outing from La Rochelle (in which case, I suggest a seafood lunch in its excellent restaurant) or for a relaxing night or two; there are 22 traditional-style rooms with terraces giving onto the garden; public spaces including a super bar-lounge; and a swimming pool, to complement the beach. *First Class.*

DAILY BREAD

POITIERS

Pierre Benoist (Route Nationale 10, Ligugé, a few miles southwest of town; phone 4957-11-52). A meal at Benoist may be likened to stopping by with friends in the country. Setting is a house in a garden: welcome is warm, cuisine traditional, service at tables on the terrace in warm weather. With the regional Poitou smoked ham, garlic-scented snails, or a lobster salad as openers, you may proceed with such entrées as steak au poivre, châteaubriand sauce Béarnaise, roast stuffed chicken, or a fish special. Desserts? Both mousse au chocolat and profiteroles au chocolat are special. *Luxury.*

Aux Armes d'Obernai (19 Rue Arthur Ranc; phone 4941-16-33) is relatively small, with the hearty cuisine of Alsace as its ace-in-the-hole. By that I mean you may have the sauerkraut-based choucroute garnie or poulet au Riesling—Alsace's answer to coq au vin—preceded by foie gras de canard and followed with cheese and house-baked pastry—from the prix-fixe menu. Service is both cordial and professional. Central. *First Class.*

Le Poitevin (76 Rue Carnot; phone 4988-35-04) is smartly rustic, makes a specialty of regional dishes. Build your meal around the house's own chicken casserole, roast kid, or unusually prepared duck with peaches in a sherry sauce. For dessert: frozen raspberry mousse. Central. *First Class.*

Taverne de Maître Kanter (24 Rue Carnot; phone 4941-07-74) is a *brasserie* with good salads, omelets, and steaks. Okay for a casual lunch. *Moderate.*

Crêperie Bretonne (51 Rue de la Cathédrale; phone 4988-81-74): The kind of crêpes you may remember from Brittany, both savory and sweet. *Moderate.*

Café Gambetta (Place du Palais): Take a table on the square and unwind in the midst of exploration, over coffee or something cold to drink. *Moderate.*

LA ROCHELLE

Au Vieux-Port (4 Place de la Chaîne; phone 4641-73-33): If it's cool, you'll be served indoors, at tables set with pink linen and flanked by country chairs. But hope for sunshine; an alfresco meal is what Vieux-Port is all about. The name of the game is seafood—a dozen oysters on the half-shell, crayfish with mayonnaise, half a cold lobster, or fish soup—among starters. Follow with sole grilled or prepared meunière style. Super sweets. *First Class.*

Claridge (1 Rue Admyrauld; phone 4650-64-19) is heart of Vieux La Rochelle, with antique chairs at tables set with beige linen. Open with the house's own smoked salmon or foie gras. Seafood is indicated as the entrée. *First Class.*

Serge (46 Cour des Dames; phone 4641-17-03) is a Vieux-Port favorite, and with good reason. It's all summed up in a single word, seafood: fresh-as-this-morning fish and shellfish traditionally—and deliciously—prepared, and with good-value menus. Nice. *First Class.*

Les Flots (1 Place de la Chaîne; phone 4641-32-51) is a Vieux-Port ranker, with bouillabaisse and grilled lobster among specialties. *First Class.*

Richard Coutenceau (Plage de la Concurrence; phone 4641-48-19): Restaurants named for individuals usually are called after young owner-chefs out to make reputations with creative cuisine. Such is the case with M. Coutenceau's establishment out at the beach; his fare has a solid seafood base. Open with this area's beloved mouclade—creamed mussels perked up with curry. And follow with a lobster specialty or fresh-caught fish, interestingly prepared. Good desserts and wines, whites especially. *Luxury.*

De La Chaîne (5 Place Verdun) is an agreeable café for people-watching on the town's main square. *Moderate.*

INCIDENTAL INTELLIGENCE

Further information: Office de Tourisme, 11 Rue Victor-Hugo, Poitiers; Office de Tourisme, 10 Rue Fleurieu, La Rochelle. There is scheduled air service between Aéroport La Rochelle-Laleu and Paris.

30

Rennes

And through Brittany to Nantes and La Baule

BACKGROUND BRIEFING

Relative proximity to the New World notwithstanding—France's westernmost point is in this region—Brittany and its cities remain relatively terra incognita. The cities, especially.

Nantes, for example, though the largest and most important urban center in western France (and seat of dukes of Brittany as long ago as the tenth century, yet not a part of France's contemporary Region of Brittany), has not been thought about by most of us since we learned about a proclamation protecting Protestants that was signed there by Henri IV nearly five centuries ago. (Unless, of course, you consider our familiarity also with its revocation by an even more famous king—Louis XIV—and the urgent consequences thereof.) Oddly enough, Nantes appears to appreciate that it is not celebrated; it has fewer good central-city hotels than any other major French city of which I am aware.

Then consider Rennes, smaller but today the principal Breton city, and hardly of less historic significance. There being no "Edict of Rennes" to afford it glory in the history books, much less a revocation, it is even less familiar—which is not as it should be. Rivalrous in earlier centuries with Nantes, Rennes emerges contemporarily still with vestiges of eminence as a consequence of the city's razor's edge location on the border with France, when Brittany was a separately governed duchy.

Developed by ancient Celts, later colonized by Rome, river-straddling Rennes (situated where the Ille converges with the Vilaine) achieved political power as long ago as the thirteenth century. Even after Brittany was united with France—as a consequence of the marriage in Rennes of French King Charles VIII and Duchess Anne of Brittany, in the late fifteenth century—the Bretons insisted upon retaining an appreciable measure of self-government. Later, they set up a legislature of their own—its meeting rooms are a principal reason for a visit to contemporary Rennes—with which they governed themselves until the Revolution. It was the century of the Revolution, the eighteenth, that was doubly significant for Rennes. With political changes came a rebuilding of much of the city's medieval/Renaissance core—following a disastrous fire—to designs by a neoclassicist architect named Gabriel, commissioned by Louis XV, as, indeed, was his better-known son, who created Paris's Place de la Concorde.

ON SCENE

Lay of the Land: Thank architect Gabriel for the essentially grid-design, eighteenth-century rebuilding of much of Rennes. The *Vilaine River,* running east-west, neatly separates northern from southern sectors, with the northern half the more visitworthy. A series of streets bearing different names—pedestrians-only, with shops lining them—run north of central, river-straddling *Place de la République* and are called, successively, *rues d'Orléans, d'Estrées,* and easy-to-remember *Le Bastard.* Walk, then, not only to window-shop and for café pauses, but to reach major monuments fronting such squares as *Place de la Mairie,* named for the eighteenth-century city hall fronting it (pop inside to see its very grand foyer), and even more significant *Place du Palais* (below), with medieval half-timbered houses on *Rue St.-Georges,* due east. But there's more to medieval Rennes: Walk west from Place du Palais to *Place St.-Sauveur,* and you're in *Vieux-Rennes,* dominated by multiepoch *Basilica of St.-Sauveur* and the nearby cathedral and indicated for strolls past landmark houses—mostly half-timbered—on *rues de la Psalette, St.-Sauveur,* and *du Chapitre.* If you've time to explore another district, walk east from Place du Palais along to *Square de la Motte.* The mansard-roofed palace with a masterful wrought-iron gate is the *Préfecture* of the department, and just north of it, on *Place Ste.-Melaine,* is the charmer of a cloistered church whose name it takes. The railway station is at the southern edge of Rennes's southern, more modern sector.

Parlement de Bretagne/Palais de Justice (Place du Palais) has served as the Brittany parliament from the time it went up in the early decades of the seventeenth century until the fall of the monarchy with the Revolution, with that function restored to it in the late 1980s; it doubles today as Rennes's principal courthouse. During final centuries of the ancien régime, kings of France within Brittany were styled dukes of Brittany and shared power with the duchy's legislature, which met in style, under coffered and frescoed ceilings, in the second-floor room still known—and hardly inappropriately—as *La Grande Chambre;* it constitutes one of France's more dazzling interiors. Credit a Paris *ébéniste* named Pierre Donis for wainscotting of the ceilings and walls that dates to 1680. Of the ceiling's baker's dozen frescoes, it's the center one—on the theme of justice—that bears study. Gobelin tapestries woven in this century take the place of wallpaper, but the room is at its most unusual—and charming—with its loggias (little balconies framed in carved, gilded wood) on three of four walls, for the benefit of Baroque-era VIPs intent on watching parliamentary debates from on high.

Cathedral of St.-Pierre (Rue de la Monnaie)—twin-towered and with an essentially classic-style facade—is among France's newest, completed toward the middle of the last century. Major lure is a Renaissance altarpiece, depicting scenes in the life of the Virgin, in a chapel edging the transept. A secondary lure is not in the cathedral, but rather in the neighborhood surrounding it—the core of Vieux Rennes and delightful strollers' territory—north to *Place des Lices,* south to *Rue des Dames,* east to *Basilica of St.-Sauveur,* parts of it a century newer than the cathedral.

Musée des Beaux Arts (20 Quai Émile-Zola, on the south side of the Vilaine River, not far east of Place de la République) shares a building—Palais des Musées—with a fellow museum (below), but is by far the more significant of the pair. You'll encounter works by such foreigners as Veronese, Rubens, Jordaens, Bassano, and Tiepolo; by such Renaissance Frenchmen as de la Tour, Philippe de Champaigne, and Simon Vouet; by their eighteenth-century successors, including Chardin, Natoire, Desportes, and Greuze; nineteenth-century masters like Corot and Chassériau; by Impressionists like Monet, Sisley, Boudin, and Gauguin to the more recent Vuillard, Dufy, and Picasso.

Musée de Bretagne (also in Palais des Musées, 20 Quai Émile-Zola) is a World's Fair-like mix of audiovisual displays and exhibits of Brittany objects going back to the Gallo-Roman period, with its Middle Ages sections—including tombs and sculpted capitals—the most successful, along with sections featuring nineteenth-century furniture. There's an immense hall of costumes; this is a good place to get an idea of the remarkable variety of the traditional Breton women's *coiffes*—high, white, and lacy headdresses. A special bravo to the management for legends throughout in English, as well as in French—a courtesy to non-French-reading visitors rarely encountered in French museums.

Fougères and Vitré are castle towns not far east of Rennes that, combined, constitute an enjoyable excursion into the past. Start with 30-mile distant Fougères. Its originally eleventh-century château—one of the biggest on the continent of Europe—is enclosed by a wall studded by no less than thirteen remaining towers. There were more, but not all have survived a history that saw the castle change hands often, especially during the Anglo-French Hundred Years War. Give yourself time enough to wander around this massive, multiacre complex—the walls are so thick that there's a sidewalk atop them—concluding your castle visit in a tower called Raoul, whose attraction is a museum exhibiting antique shoes, which is not as odd as it would appear after you learn that shoe manufacture has for long been a Fougères industry. Exit the castle for neighboring *Church of St.-Sulpice,* Gothic and with lovely altarpieces. There are fine old houses to be seen on nearby *Place du Manché.*

Pause, then, for lunch, continuing south to *Vitré* (22 miles from Rennes), smaller and better preserved than Fougères, as you can't help but notice on your approach from the north. You've a choice of castles. *Château de Vitré* is a fortified, multitowered triangle that evolved as the Middle Ages became the Renaissance. As at Fougères, you may walk atop the wall; do so, making your way to a trio of towers. *Tour de l'Argenterie* is skippable; it's a natural-history museum. But *Tour St.-Laurent* displays beautiful Renaissance sculpture, and *Tour de l'Oratoire* houses a charming chapel with a positively smashing altarpiece. Vitré's still-formidable ramparts enclose atmospheric streets flanked with fine old houses—*Rue Beaudrairie, Rue Notre-Dame, Rue d'Embas* are three such—and Gothic-era *Church of Notre-Dame* is a lure.

But even more so is *Château des Rochers-Sévigné,* four miles south and the seventeenth-century seat of the redoubtable Madame de Sévigné, whose 1,500 witty and detailed letters to her daughter constitute a rich lode of information on life in France of that era. Many of the letters were written from this essentially seventeenth-century castle; only a few rooms are inspectable. One crammed with objects belonging to this very interesting woman highlights a visit.

Quimper (112 miles west of Rennes, just inland from the Atlantic) is small, friendly, and attractive, with its core flanking the north shore of the Odet River, which cuts through it. *Rue St.-François* leading north from the river is one of a number of central, shop-lined streets. Passing east–west *Rue Kéréon,* it continues busily mercantile as *Rue des Boucheries.* Rue Kéréon's eastern terminus is *Place St.-Corentin,* named for the *Cathedral of St.-Corentin,* whose twin steeples date, surprisingly, only from the last century—appendages to an otherwise essentially Gothic structure with a long nave, exquisitely vaulted, an exuberant baroque pulpit, with side chapels at either end of the wide transept, and a lady chapel edging the apse.

The town's *Musée des Beaux-Arts* (Rue de la Mairie) stuns with the quality and diversity of its collection—extraordinary in a town with a population of 60,000. Its specialty is Pont Avon school of late-nineteenth- and early-twentieth-century paintings and similar to those of Gauguin, with a number by Émile Bernard. But there is so much more: Pannini and Piranesi, Giordano and Reni, among the Italians; Rubens and Jordaens, among the Flemings; Cuyp and Maes, among the Dutch; and a plethora of Frenchmen: Mignard and Vernet, Oudry and Fragonard, Boilly and Corot, Boudin and Marquet. A cache of drawings—by French masters like Vouet, Le Brun, Hubert Robert, Fragonard, and Watteau—is frosting on an already rich cake.

Musée Départemental Breton (Rue Ste.-Catherine) has quarters in the onetime Bishop's Palace, dating back four centuries. Certain of the exhibits—especially those from Roman Quimper—are considerably older, with a diverse range, wooden chests through peasant costumes. *Church of Notre-Dame-de-Locmaria* (Place Benandier) is exceptional: severely beautiful Romanesque, little changed since it was erected in the eleventh century—even to the tiny, nichelike windows of that era—with a splendid wooden *Crucifixion* suspended from a beam over the main altar. *Faïenceries de Quimper* (Route de Benodet) calls itself a museum (admission is charged) but is simply a showroom of hand-painted Quimper pottery.

Locronan (11 miles north of Quimper) is a requisite excursion destination, an enchanter of a hill town, built in the fifteenth and sixteenth centuries of the local granite—and little changed since. The village is based on its central—and sole—square, with a combination church-chapel dominant, within whose precincts is a tomb of the namesake saint, Ronan, along with polychrome sculptures, including a very moving Pietà. There's a little museum of local lore and a shop with weavers, potters, and other artisans at work on their wares.

Pont-l'Abbé (13 miles south of Quimper) is a tradition-bound village bordering a channel, just inland from the sea, with miles of wide, white-sand beaches adjacent, which make it agreeable for a day's outing in the sun. In town, visit the Renaissance château that houses not only town hall and tourist office, but also *Musée Bigouden*—with local lore.

Loctudy (18 miles south of Quimper) is smaller than Pont-l'Abbé, with which it may be combined on a day-long excursion. It's the site not only of extensive beaches, but of a striking parish church, twelfth-century Romanesque and in mint condition.

Pointe du Raz (25 miles west of Quimper) is to France what Land's End is to Britain; its westernmost point—and delineated by a little lighthouse on a rocky eminence just offshore. Visit it from the nearby resort-village of *Audierne,* like Loctudy and Pont-l'Abbé, with splendid beaches.

Nantes (65 miles south of Rennes, and actually not within the borders of today's Brittany, but a part of the adjacent Region known as Pays de la Loire) is big—population is a quarter-million—and sprawling; you can't walk everywhere. Zero in on what interests you. Main shopping street of this lively Loire River metropolis is *Rue Crébillon;* classy *Cours Cambronne,* mostly nineteenth century, and *Passage Pommeraye,* a shopping arcade that opened in 1843, are nearby. *Rue d'Orléans* leads to a pair of major monuments.

One, *Cathedral of Sts.-Pierre-et-Paul*—rededicated in 1985 following a long restoration after a tragic 1972 fire—is soaring albeit chilly-of-ambience Gothic, at its best out back, with flying buttresses framing a wide apse, and with the superbly sculpted early-sixteenth-century tomb of Duke François II of Brittany highlighting the elongated interior.

The other monument is the *Château des Ducs de Bretagne,* for centuries the ducal residence and an extraordinary Gothic-Renaissance meld with the facade of the sector called Grand Logis its most masterful architectural aspect. King Henri IV, come to promulgate the Edict of Nantes in 1598, was among its residents, and today it houses three small museums: *Arts Décoratifs* (mainly textiles), *Art Populaire Régional* (with superb Breton period rooms and fine old Breton furniture), and *Salorges* (matters maritime, including ship models).

There is a trio of away-from-the-center museums: *Jules Verne* (3 Rue de l'Hermitage, pertaining to the life and work of the Nantes-born author), *Thomas Dobrée* (a mix of art and history), and *Archéologique* (exhibits both domestic and imported, French and Greek through Egyptian and the New World); the latter two are both on Place Jean V.

Still, Nantes' No. 1 museum—indeed the No. 1 reason, at least for this traveler, to justify a Nantes visit—is *Beaux-Arts* (10 Rue Georges-Clemenceau, near the cathedral). Ingres's *Madame de Sennones* is the museum's mascot painting, but the range is wide, the quality superior—Rubens and Perugino, Tintoretto and de la Tour, Lancret and Courbet, Watteau and Delacroix, Corot and Oudry, Monet and Signac, Kandinsky and Van Dongen, Bronzino and Van Cleve.

Nantes is a shopping city of consequence. The department-store chains are exceptionally well represented—*Galeries Lafayette* and *Monoprix* (Rue du Calvaire), *Nouvelles Galeries* (Rue de la Marne), *Prisunic* (Rue Boileau). Rue Crébillon's boutiques include *Laura Ashley* (home furnishings), *Cartier* (jewelry), *Rodier* (women's clothing), *Polo Ralph Lauren* (men's clothing), and *Kenzo* (haute couture). Another pedestrian street, *Rue Scribe,* is the site of *Cacherel* (women's clothing), *Descamps* (the linen chain, also in New York), and *Chipie* (children's wear).

La Baule (40 miles west of Nantes, and like it in the Region of Pays de la Loire), though virtually terra incognita to New Worlders, is a justifiably popular summer resort with the French for two good reasons: It is inordinately well equipped with hotels and restaurants (below), and its beach—extraordinarily long white-sand crescent—is one of the great European strands. Other La Baule pluses include a snazzy *Casino* (Esplanade François-André) in whose pair of gaming rooms you may try your luck at roulette, blackjack, and baccarat, and with restaurants, boîtes, shops, and cinema in which to spend your winnings; 18-hole *St.-Denac golf course; Centre de Thalassothérapie Thalgo-La Baule* (a multifacility spa/health center on Avenue Marie Louise); *Tennis Country Club* (Avenue de Lattre de Tassigny), with 30 courts, restaurant, indoor swimming pool, and golf driving ranges; shop-lined *Avenue du Général de Gaulle*—the main business thoroughfare; and relatively recently opened *Atlanta* (Avenue de Lattre de Tassigny) a convention hall/performing arts center, with its auditorium event-packed the year long.

Guérande (four miles north of La Baule) is an extraordinary town that has managed to retain a tower-punctuated walled core. You may make a circuit of the wall and its network of nine towers (mostly fourteenth and fifteenth century). But the area within the walls is noteworthy, too. It's fun to amble along *Rue St.-Michel,* pausing at a café to watch passersby. And allow time for the principal church and the history museum. *Collégiale St.-Aubin* fronts Place St.-Aubin, smack in the center, at the end of Rue St.-Michel. It's a Romanesque-Gothic beauty constructed over a span of four centuries—twelfth through sixteenth. Take in the principal stained-glass window, La Grande Verrière, depicting the Assumption and the Coronation of the Virgin; the network of eight Romanesque columns of the nave, the side chapels, and if it's summer when it's open, the crypt. Nearby *Musée de Guérande* makes its home within the stone walls of the fifteenth-century Château de Guérande, whose twin towers are a town landmark. Exhibits embrace venerable weapons (battleaxes and crossbows among them) and porcelain dolls, antique furniture of the region and mannequins in folk-costumes, paintings and pottery, cooking cauldrons and butter churns. Apartments occupied by officialdom in centuries past are up a flight; and up still another—you ascend 29 steep stone steps—are windows affording views of the town and countryside.

SETTLING IN

Altéa Parc du Colombier Hôtel (Place du Colombier; phone 9979-54-54): I wish it were central—by that, I mean on the north side of Rennes' Vilaine River—but that reservation aside, this 140-room link of a national chain is agreeable enough. The bar-lounge is comfortable and the restaurant is popular with locals—always a good sign. *First Class.*

Mercure Rennes Centre Hôtel (Rue Paul Louis-Courier; phone 9978-32-32): Give credit to the well-operated Mercure chain. It took over the handsomely facaded early-twentieth-century printing plant of the newspaper *Ouest France* and deftly converted it into a good-looking, ever-so-contemporary hotel. Those of the 104 rooms I have inhabited or inspected are good-sized and good-looking with good baths, and the copious Mercure buffet is served at breakfast. Location is a plus, too: heart-of-town. And the staff is super. *Moderate.*

Central Hôtel (6 Rue Lanjuinais; phone 9979-12-36) has good-looking bedrooms—there are 44 all told—in smart traditional style as its strongest point. All have baths with showers (cheaper) or tubs. The lobby-lounge is attractive, and breakfast is buffet-style. Quite central. *Moderate.*

Anne de Bretagne Hôtel (12 Rue Tronjolly; phone 9931-49-49) is farther north than the Altéa (above), but still south of the Vilaine River. There are 42 neat-as-a-pin, contemporary-style rooms. Breakfast only. *Moderate.*

Novotel Rennes Alma (Avenue du Canada; phone 9950-61-32) is in the boonies, three miles from town, but there are just under a hundred well-planned, comfortable rooms, a no-frills restaurant at its best with a generous breakfast buffet, and a bar-lounge. *Moderate.*

La Tour d'Auvergne Hôtel (13 Rue des Régulaires, Quimper; phone 9895-08-70) is conveniently central, in traditional style, with 45 rooms—those I have seen are pleasantly papered and have nice baths—as well as a cozy bar where you sink into deep leather chairs and a looker of a restaurant with fare as agreeable as the hotel itself. Friendly. *Moderate.*

Dupleix Hôtel (34 Boulevard Dupleix, Quimper; phone 9890-53-35) is on the south bank of the Odet River, but it's a relatively easy walk to the core of this smallish city. Decor is contemporary—in tones of tan and pale pink, with just under 30 good-sized rooms with okay baths, including some duplexes for three persons. And in summer there's a seafood restaurant. *Moderate.*

Novotel Quimper (Route de Benodet, Quimper; phone 9890-46-26) is out of town—a 10-minute drive from the core. There are 92 good-sized, well-planned rooms, each with the same functional bath; swimming pool; excellent buffet breakfast; and an efficient staff. *Moderate.*

Le Griffon Hôtel (Route de Benoît, Quimper; phone 9890-33-33), a little farther from the center than the Novotel (above), has the look of an American motel from without and a pleasantly contemporary decor. There are 50 full-facility rooms, a swimming pool, cocktail lounge, restaurant operated by a concessionaire, and, attached to the friendly reception staff, a shaggy dog who greets guests carrying one of his toys. *Moderate.*

Manoir du Stang Hôtel (La Forêt-Fouesnan, nine miles south of Quimper; phone 9856-97-37) is a sixteenth-century château, its management descendants of a long-on-scene family. Its setting: formal gardens, to the front; to the rear, a large private park, dotted with pools, with the sea not far distant. There are just 26 no-two-alike rooms, restaurant, bar-lounge, tennis, and fishing. *First Class.*

De La Plage Hôtel (Ste.-Anne-La-Palud, eight miles northwest of Quimper; phone 9892-50-12) is ideal for seaside respite—on the beach, as its title implies, with a pool-cum-sundeck to boot, picture-windowed restaurant looking out to sea (seafood is among the specialties), bar-lounge with deep brown-leather chairs, and 27 cheerful Louis XV-style rooms. Member, Relais et Châteaux. *First Class.*

Les Moulins des Ducs Hôtel (Moëlin-sur-Mer, 28 miles southeast of Quimper; phone 9839-60-73): How about a sixteenth-century windmill complex—stone-walled, antique-accented, with handsome public spaces that include a cozy bar and a creditable restaurant, as well as just under two dozen no-two-alike, imaginatively decorated rooms? With an indoor swimming pool, whose open-up picture-window-wall gives onto a sun terrace. Member, Relais et Châteaux. *First Class.*

Kastelmoor and Kermoor Hôtels (Benodet, 9 miles south of Quimper; phone 9857-04-48) are a kind of Mutt-and-Jeff operation. Kastelmoor edges a wide, white-sand beach and has 23 rooms, a swimming pool, and five tennis courts; Kermoor, a five-minute walk inland from the sea, is bigger, with 70 rooms and a restaurant that specializes in seafood. Stay in one, and you may use the facilities of the other; same management for both. Fun. *First Class.*

De France Hôtel (24 Rue Crébillon, Nantes; phone 4073-57-91) is the long-on-scene winner in Nantes, located on its main shopping street; handsomely traditional style, with 80 no-two-alike rooms (those I have inspected are nice); bar-lounge; and a Belle Époque-style restaurant, later recommended. *First Class.*

Jules Verne Hôtel (3 Rue du Couëdic, Nantes; phone 4035-74-50) is a hop and skip from Rue d'Orléans and Place Royale—smack in the center. The look is clean-lined—lobby-lounge and breakfast-room, as well as those of the 65 rooms I've inspected (whose disadvantage is size; they tend to be small, but are otherwise pleasant), and all are with baths. Cordial management. Best Western. *Moderate.*

Amiral Hôtel (26-bis Rue Scribe, Nantes; phone 4069-20-21) is, like the somewhat pricier Jules Verne above, relatively recent, and central, on a principal shopping street. The smallish lobby is bright and welcoming, and those of the 46 rooms with bath that I've inspected are likewise small but cheerful, with okay baths. Breakfast only. Friendly. *Moderate.*

Arcade Hôtel (19 Rue Jean-Jaurès, Nantes; phone 4035-39-00)—modern of facade, with a restaurant and bar off its lobby—follows the Arcade chain's formula with respect to rooms: blond wood with clean lines, narrow beds, and showers rather than tubs in baths. There are 140 singles and doubles. Fairly central, north of Place Royale. *Moderate.*

L'Hôtel (6 Rue Henri IV, Nantes; phone 4029-30-31): A small reception area is backed by a lounge wherein breakfast and drinks are served. Those of the 32 rooms I have seen or inhabited are okay albeit with *very* soft mattresses. You are close to Musée des Beaux-Arts and the railway station. But you're not in the heart of town. *Moderate.*

Pullman Beaulieu Hôtel (3 Rue du Dr.-Zamenhof, in the Beaulieu district of Nantes, a modern shopping center a couple miles south of the center; phone 4047-10-58) is contemporary, with 150 full-facility rooms, restaurant, and bar-lounge. *First Class.*

Sofitel Nantes (Rue Alexandre-Millerand, in the same isolated Beaulieu quarter as the Pullman Beaulieu [above]; phone 4047-61-03) is contemporary, with a hundred rooms, restaurant, and bar. *First Class.*

Hermitage Hôtel (Esplanade François-André, La Baule; phone 4060-37-00) is separated from the great crescent beach of La Baule only by its well-manicured lawn. This is the prototypical Gallic seaside resort—red-jacketed pages darting through the impressive lobby, beige and brown leather seating in the contemporarily styled bar, crystal chandeliers dropped from the high-ceilinged restaurant, with a veritable army of white-jacketed waiters and tuxedoed captains. There are 230 balconied rooms with Louis XV–style decor and fine baths. Ask for one overlooking the swimming pool, garden, and cabana-lined beach, where, I should point out, if you are hungry and/or thirsty while on the sands, there's a restaurant-bar obviating a trek indoors. Operators are the same Lucien Barrière chain you may know from Deauville (chapter 16) or Cannes (chapter 13). *Luxury.*

Royal Hôtel (Esplanade François-André, La Baule; phone 4060-33-06) is inviting from without—it's a six-story graystone building, with white-painted wood trim—and does not disappoint within. Public spaces are grand and high-ceilinged, with a formal, stern-staffed restaurant; and in contrast, giving onto the lawn, an amusing, nautical-themed bar-lounge appropriately dubbed Le Yachting Club. Those of the 103 rooms I have inspected are wicker-accented, with up-to-the-minute baths, and, in many (but not all) cases, balconies. The heated saltwater pool punctuates broad lawns, and although the hotel is not directly on the beach, it's but a hop and skip distant, and operates a restaurant, Le Ponton, edging the sands. The casino is adjacent, and the hotel is linked to Centre Thalassothérapie Thalgo, the spa-health center, worth knowing if you'll be making use of that facility. A Lucien Barrière hotel. *First Class/ Luxury.*

Castel Marie-Louise Hôtel (1 Avenue Andrieu, La Baule; phone 4960-20-60) boasts the beach out front, the casino next door. This is a charming smaller house, with 31 no-two-quite-alike rooms—Louis XVI is a popular style—as well as an especially well-regarded restaurant (evaluated below), atmospheric bar, and pretty lawn separating the hotel from the sands. There's no pool, but guests are welcome at that of the Hermitage Hôtel (above), which shares Lucien Barrière management. *First Class.*

Flepen Hôtel (145 Avenue de Lattre de Tassigny, La Baule; phone 4060-29-30)—not far from the casino, the beach, and Avenue du Général, the top shopping street—is an agreeable smaller house, with just two dozen bath-equipped rooms (those I've inspected are of varying decors, wicker-accented and good-looking). The breakfast room, with paisley cloths on its tables, is engaging. And owner-manager Jean-Louis Pollitzer, among the more fluent English-speakers you'll meet in France, is a genial host. *Moderate.*

Alexandra Hôtel (3 Boulevard Dubois, La Baule; phone 4060-30-06) is at once central and beachfront, with three dozen okay rooms with bath, restaurant, and bar. *Moderate/First Class.*

Sud Bretagne Hôtel (42 Avenue de la République, Pornichet, at the southern tip of La Baule; phone 4061-02-68) is a pleasure: a hotel with a sense of style, smiling, welcoming management and staff, 30 no-two-alike rooms (those I've inspected have interesting textiles and color schemes and nice baths). There's a restaurant reviewed on a later page, pool in the garden, and tennis court with the beach nearby. *Moderate/First Class.*

Beau Rivage Hôtel (11 Rue Jules-Benoît, in Le Pouliguen, at the northern tip of La Baule; phone 4042-31-61) is a small house edging the beach, with bath-equipped rooms of varying sizes (some with balconies). Breakfast only. *Moderate.*

DAILY BREAD

Du Palais (7 Place du Parlement; phone 9979-45-01) borrows the name of Rennes' parliamentary palace across the square; it is distinctly unpalatial, but rather cozy, with tables in a pair of contiguous rooms and its best bets either of two prix-fixe menus. You might, with one of these, commence with *trois petites salads*—a trio of the house's special salades; continue with rosemary-scented lamb or duck crisply roasted and served with turnips. Lemon soufflé is among desserts. Caveat: Service, though kindly, can be painfully slow. *First Class.*

Le Corsaire (52 Rue d'Antrain; phone 9936-33-69): You're north of the center here, but the seafood is so good that it's worth the excursion. Open with fish soup. Proceed with simply—but deliciously—grilled sole, the house's delicate sole soufflé, or, if you would rather, chicken and mushroom fricassee, a Breton standby. Baked-on-premises desserts. Friendly. *First Class.*

Chouin (12 Rue de l'Isly; phone 9930-87-86) is a study in white—white walls, white draperies, white linen, with yellow accents including the flowers on the tables. Emphasis is seafood. Aim for a lunch, when the menu is exceptional value, commencing perhaps with a three-fish terrine, a dazzler of a seafood platter, or an order of nine oysters on the half shell. Entrée choice might be crayfish with melted butter, grilled salmon or the day's catch, prepared house-style. Cheese or a sweet is the conclusion, white-wine selection is excellent, and service a distinct pleasure. *First Class.*

L'Auberge St.-Sauveur (6 Rue St.-Sauveur; phone 9979-32-56) makes an opening statement with atmosphere: It occupies a half-timbered house out of the fifteenth century, with beamed ceilings, wrought-iron chandeliers, and fresh flowers gracing fastidiously set tables. Take advantage of good menus here. One might open with a platter of crispy crudités or the day's salad, perhaps served *tiède,* or warm, if its ingredients warrant. Entrecôte is a favored entrée, either with sauce Béarnaise (which I counsel) or sautéed mushrooms. Substantial sweets. Friendly. *First Class.*

Ti-Koz (3 Rue St.-Guillaume; phone 9979-33-89) occupies a landmark Rennes house—half-timbered, with its facade unchanged for something like half a millennium. Behind white organdy tiebacks on the front windows lies an atmospheric dining room, wherein are served good things to eat, the range—to give you an idea—smoked salmon or foie gras frais among openers; confit de canard or filet of beef—deliciously sauced—among entrées; made-on-premises desserts. There are three menus. *First Class.*

Piccadilly Tavern (15 Galerie du Théâtre; phone 9978-17-17) retains its Anglo name as an amusing come-on. Situation is central, look Belle Époque, fare *brasserie* style, with everything fresh and tasty. Open with warm Lyon sausage, onion soup—or oysters, mussels, or clams from the seafood bar. Entrées run to filet mignon, breast of chicken, Alsatian choucroute garnie. End, perhaps, with what the menu terms "L'Irish Coffee," made with whiskey Irlandais et crème fraîche. *First Class.*

Les Voyageurs Hôtel Restaurant (Place Gambetta, Fougères; phone 9999-14-17) is a good choice for a substantial lunch—Breton chicken and seafood entrées are featured—in connection with a day-long outing to Fougères and Vitré. *First Class.*

La Rotonde (36 Avenue de la France Libre, Quimper; phone 9895-09-26) is at once welcoming, cheerful, delicious, and—not unlike a number of restaurants you'll no doubt encounter in Brittany—with waiters who have practiced their trade at French restaurants in New York (which used to be largely staffed by Bretons). Open with a seafood terrine or the house's stuffed oysters and clams specialty. Confit de canard with a Breton cider sauce is a delicious entrée. House-made mousses—lemon and chocolate—are super. And so is fine de Bretagne—a Breton brandy taken at meal's end as a digestif. *First Class.*

Le Capucin Gourmand (29 Rue des Régulaires, Quimper; phone 9895-43-12) is intimate and inviting, with a pair of prix-fixe menus. The simpler might start you out with an oyster specialty, the kicker being a drop of fine de Bretagne brandy. Carry on, then, with veal médaillons in Breton cream and mushroom sauce, extravagantly vegetable-garnished. Dessert is warm apple tart—of course with cream, if you can handle it. *First Class.*

La Tour d'Auvergne Hôtel Restaurant (13 Rue des Régulaires, Quimper; phone 9895-08-70): Select from one of the pair of menus, concentrating perhaps on a mixed hors d'œuvres platter and following with roast chicken and rice or grilled fish of the day, with a caper-flavored sauce au beurre and choice of cheese or a sweet. The restaurant (not the hotel) is closed in winter. *Moderate/First Class.*

Crêperie Au Vieux Quimper (20 Rue Verdelet, Quimper; phone 9895-31-34) is as good a choice as you can make for a sampling of Brittany's celebrated pancakes. Setting is a stone-walled room in a venerable town house, with antique chairs at tables. Do as Bretons do: Open with a pair of crêpes with savory fillings—egg and sausage, for example, or ham and cheese (the menu offers scores of choices), and conclude with a sweet crêpe—hot banana is heartily counseled—as dessert, with Breton cider to accompany. At meal's end, move over to the open kitchen and watch pancakes being prepared. *Moderate.*

Holland (18 Rue Kéréon, Quimper) is at once a pâtisserie and *salon de thé;* stop in for pastry with tea or coffee. Near the cathedral. *Moderate.*

Café de l'Épée (29 Rue du Parc, Quimper) is riverfront and pleasant for a midmorning or midafternoon pause. *Moderate.*

Au Fer à Cheval Hôtel Restaurant (Place de l'Église, Locronan; phone 9891-70-74) is indicated for lunch in the course of an excursion from Quimper. There's a choice of prix-fixe menus embracing country pâté, smoked ham braised in port, and fruit tarts. Friendly. *Moderate/First Class.*

Les Petits Saints (1 Place St.-Vincent, Nantes; phone 4020-24-48): Nobody will giggle if you say you think you're in church, in the course of a visit to les Petits Saints. You are. Setting is the upper floor of an aged structure that had been an abbey—constructed in the sixteenth century. The Gothic vaulting is the real thing. Go for dinner and the space is illuminated by the light of antique pewter candlesticks. There are four menus, with the least expensive an indicated choice, opening with an unusual herb-flavored rabbit salad or only so-so filets of mackerel, preparatory to an excellent filet mignon—of pork, not beef. With such super sweets as baked apple under a caramel sauce, frozen nougat buried by coffee sauce, or the spectacular nectarines pochées et granité de Côteaux du Layon—

the stewed fresh fruit teamed with a liqueur-based sorbet. Special. *First Class.*

La Reine Margot (8 Rue de la Juiverie, Nantes; phone 4047-43-85)—one of a number of restaurants on a street that is a kind of restaurant row—is unpretentious but satisfactory, with its least pricey menu a solid value. It might open with pâté maison or rich but delicious rillettes—a coarse pork pâté out of the Touraine—offer lamb chops or a well-grilled entrecôte as entrées, terminating with cheese or dessert. Setting is a venerable stone-and-stucco-walled house, and the staff is cordial. *Moderate.*

Du Change (11 Rue de la Juiverie, Nantes; phone 4048-02-28): Monsieur and Madame Fresnet make you at home immediately here, while you're seated at a table dressed in pink linen in a room whose walls are papered in a floral pattern. The less costly of two menus is indicated, what with a whole grilled sole as entrée (coq au vin is an alternative), with fish soup preceding, and dessert. There are inexpensive wines, and this is as good a spot as any to down a snort of fine de Bretagne—the traditional digestif in this part of the world. *Moderate.*

Jamin (15 Rue Crébillon, Nantes; phone 4069-03-33): Don't allow yourself to be waylaid at pastry counters on the street floor. Make a purchase if you like, but ascend to the floor above, either for a casual lunch, or midmorning or midafternoon tea or coffee with baked goods from the kitchen, served at tables encircled by Provençal chairs. Nantes's favored *salon de thé. Moderate.*

La Gavroche (139 Rue des Hauts-Pavés, Nantes; phone 4076-22-49) is indicated for a candlelit dinner. Antique country chairs flank flower-centered tables. Open with foie gras en gelée, continuing with fish filet in the house's special sauce. Veal and poultry entrées are good alternatives. *First Class.*

L'Opéra (in Hôtel de France, with its own entrance at 4 Rue Molière, Nantes; phone 4073-57-91) is long-established, heart-of-town, and reliable, with three well-priced menus: even the least costly is satisfactory—terrine de canard or crudités to start, grilled sausage or the plat du jour, pastry or mousse au chocolat. *Moderate/First Class.*

La Cigale (Place Graslin, Nantes; phone 4089-34-84) looks better than it tastes. A National Historic Monument (it opened in 1895) with a marvelous Belle Époque look, its fabulous tiled walls bear inspection. *Brasserie*-style fare may or may not please; ditto the service. *Moderate.*

Castel Marie-Louise Hôtel Restaurant (Esplanade François-André, La Baule; phone 4060-20-60): Reserve a table edging a picture window, so that you look onto the lawn that separates this hotel from beach and sea. You're seated on Louis XV-style chairs by a courteous captain. The less pricey menu is a good choice. Crayfish and clam soup or quail salad are delicious openers. There's a palate-refreshing sorbet next, with either of two entrées: seafood mixed grill or the day's meat entrée, which might be an assortment of sliced roasts, with a chef-created sauce. Cheese board is exceptional, but so are pastries and profiteroles au chocolate chaud—the warm sauce makes a difference. Very nice, indeed. *First Class/ Luxury.*

Sud Bretagne Hôtel Restaurant (42 Avenue de la République, Pornichet, at the southern tip of La Baule; phone 4061-02-68): There's an extensive à la carte and several menus (one features six courses, each with its own wine). I suggest going with the least expensive, starting with a platter of fresh crayfish, or a salad teaming goose liver with crayfish. The chef's sole or duck specialties make good entrées, and you finish with a platter of assorted sherbets or chocolate cake. Attractive and congenial. *First Class.*

Chalet Suisse (114 Avenue du Général de Gaulle, La Baule; phone 4060-23-41) is nicely positioned on La Baule's main shopping thoroughfare, and is not a bad idea for lunch weekdays, when the menu pleases budgeters, and tastes good, too, with a soup or salad to open, a seafood or perhaps entrecôte as entrée, and a sweet. For this lunch special: *Moderate.*

Le Roc Maria (Rue St.-Michel, Guérande): A casual lunch of, say, a savory crêpe as entrée with a sweet crêpe to conclude is not a bad idea in the course of Guérande exploration. (*Chez Lucien,* Place St.-Aubin, opposite the Collégiale, is still another Guérande crêperie.) Both are *Moderate.*

SOUND OF MUSIC

Théâtre Municipal (Place de la Mairie, Rennes) is the city's principal venue for opera, concerts, and dance.

Théâtre Graslin (Place Graslin, Nantes)—an imposing colonnade supporting the pediment over its entrance—is very grand, indeed. It's home base for *Opéra de Nantes,* which traditionally stages a six-opera season, the repertory ranging from Wagner's *Tristan und Isolde* through Poulenc's *Dialogues des Carmelites;* there are operettas as well, not to mention the opera's ballet troupe.

Auditorium du Conservatoire (Rue Gaëtan Rondeau, Nantes) is the site of varied entertainments, including concerts of *Orchestre Philharmonique des Pays de la Loire,* which plays also in Angers (chapter 4).

INCIDENTAL INTELLIGENCE

There is scheduled service from airports of Rennes, Quimper, and Nantes to domestic points; and Air France links Nantes with New York's JFK. *Further information:* Office de Tourisme, Point de Nemours, Rennes; Office de Tourisme, Place Aristide-Briand, Fougères; Office de Tourisme, 3 Rue Roi-Gradlon, Quimper; Office de Tourisme, Place du Commerce, Nantes.

31

Rouen

Core of Normandy

BACKGROUND BRIEFING

Rouen's problem is Paris.

Contemporarily, that is. This ancient estuary port, not far inland from the mouth of the Seine on the English Channel, is, in effect, the port of Paris—a plus, of course, in the burgeoning economy of a city with a metropolitan population of half a million. At the same time, though, it is close enough to giant Paris—the 80-mile distance is bridged by fast and frequent trains and by motor on modern highways—so as to be considered by Parisians and visitors alike as little more than a town in exurbia. Rouen is not, in other words, taken seriously as would surely be the case if it were located where Bordeaux is, or Grenoble or Nice. (It is no doubt this promixity to Paris that has prevented if from becoming either a leading hotel or shopping city.)

It was not always thus. In centuries past, when communications were primitive and transport achingly slow, Rouen stood—and developed—quite on its own, to the point where, despite heavy destruction during the sixteenth-century Wars of Religion and this century's World War II, it remains an all-France showplace of Gothic and Renaissance monuments. (And not only churches and palaces. Eight hundred of Rouen's half-timbered houses have been restored—more than in any other French city—and 700 more are being restored.)

And Rouen's prominence in the evolution of France is hardly to be underestimated. The Romans' prosperous *Rotomagus* was the seat of a Catholic bishop as early as the fourth century. By the ninth, aggressive Viking raiders from the north—already called *Normands*—had become residents of the area surrounding Rouen, prosperous and powerful enough for the French king of the moment to declare their leader a duke, with jurisdiction over what has been known ever since as Normandy. It was, of course, one of this duke's successors, who, in 1066, as Guillaume le Conquérant, vanquished the English and became King William I. Increasingly rich Rouen itself became English in the course of the Hundred Years War—for almost three mid-fifteenth-century decades. Indeed, it was in Rouen that Jeanne d'Arc was captured by the enemy from across the Channel, eventually tried, and executed on the central Rouen square where a contemporary memorial honors her memory.

ON SCENE

Lay of the Land: Be grateful for early—very early—planners who devised Rouen's grid layout. The *Seine River,* running north and south, serves as the western edge of the *Rive Droite*—or principal—area. Three main thoroughfares run east from river-flanking streets: *Rue Jeanne d'Arc,* which extends past *Tour Jeanne d'Arc*—a circular medieval tower in which Joan was interrogated prior to imprisonment elsewhere in town—to *Gare Rive-Droite,* the main train station. (*Gare d'Orléans* is on the Rive Gauche.) Also on a west-east axis is central *Rue Grand-Pont,* which intersects *Place de la Cathédrale* (and Rouen's cathedral), continuing as shop-lined *Rue des Carmes* to Musée des Antiquités (below). The third major east-west street, *Rue de la République,* ends in massive *Place du Général-de-Gaulle,* site of the significant Church of St.-Ouen (below). Two other major museums, Beaux-Arts and Secq des Tournelles (below), flank the important north-south street, *Rue Thiers.* Even more trafficked is north-south *Rue du Gros-Horloge,* distinguished primarily because the landmark Renaissance clock—splendidly embellished, but with only a single hand to indicate time—is affixed to upper strata of buildings on either side of the street, one a Gothic bell tower, from which a nine o'clock curfew has been tolled nightly since 1389. Rue du Gros-Horloge has contemporary distinction, as well, as the first pedestrians-only street in France. Other central shopping streets are *Rue Damiette* (with antique shops), *Rue des Carmes,* and *Rue Croix-de-Fer.* Still other central streets—*Rue St.-Romain, Rue Malpalu,* and *Rue Eau-de-Robec,* to name three of many—make for meaningful strolls past medieval half-timbered houses (*maisons à colombage*) and no less handsome mansions of later eras.

Cathedral of Notre-Dame (Place de la Cathédrale): The Impressionist painter Monet chose well when he selected the cathedral of Rouen for the series of facade paintings that hang in a number of museums (Rouen's, below, included). It is an all-Europe Gothic ranker, built over four centuries, twelfth through sixteenth. Like Monet, you don't need to go inside. The west, or principal, facade—as wide as a generous-sized city block is long—is framed by a pair of irregular towers (the taller, the so-called Tour du Beurre, or Butter Tower, was named for a Lenten indulgence of the period of construction, permitting the consumption of butter) with a quartet of delicate pinnacles between them, these surmounting a rose window flanked by three rows of sculpted saints, above the church's three deeply recessed—and embellished—portals. Look at the cathedral from the rear, and your view is of a gracefully extended apse, with the *flèche,* or steeple, soaring into the sky. No cathedral in France, save Paris's Notre-Dame, has a more breathtaking nave. Two levels of arcades surmount floor-level arches and half a dozen columns with boldly carved capitals, which delineate the high altar. But tarry; the chapels and the tombs, dotted about, are works of art, each and every one.

Church of St.-Ouen (Place du Général-de-Gaulle) is quite as big as the cathedral and, again, like the cathedral, a Gothic jewel with a lovely, lacy facade dominated by a 242-foot-high tower, its outer walls braced by flying buttresses, a delicate pinnacle edging each buttress. Within, what appears most memorable is the perfect symmetry of the elongated nave.

Church of St.-Maclou (Rue Damiette) is No. 3—or No. 2, depending upon your preference—of Rouen's Big Three group of Gothic churches. It is distinguished by a disproportionately large steeple surmounting its transept and a fabulous west, or main, front, whose three intricately carved portals open into a nave flanked by a handsome chapel. But St.-Maclou's ace-in-the-hole is a carved-stone, circular stairway at the upper terminus of which is a rare Renaissance organ.

Âtre St.-Maclou (Rue Martainville, near the church) is a cloistered cemetery, part stone-carved, part half-timbered—and one of a kind.

Palais de Justice (Rue aux Juifs) is transitional—late Gothic/early Renaissance—with features like pinnacles and turrets of the former era and rectangular windows of the latter. The facade, as seen from the courtyard, is reason enough for a visit. The central sector was used as the Normandy parliament, starting with the reign of François I. The west wing contains courtrooms leading from Salles des Pas Perdus—the Room of Wasted Steps—so called because of the plethora of nervously pacing *avocats,* awaiting trial of their cases. Peep inside—interiors are elaborate—noting the area called *Cryptes Juifs,* remains of what is believed to be a twelfth-century Jewish seminary, discovered when a courtyard was excavated as recently as 1976.

Church of Ste.-Jeanne-d'Arc (Place du Vieux-Marché): To commemorate Joan's death on this very square, heart-of-town—she was burned alive and the year was 1431—this modern church, distinguished by irregularly sweeping roofs that extend to a *porte cochère* over the entrance, was opened in the early 1980s. It may or may not be to your taste: best part, for me, at least, is the stained glass, a clutch of beautiful windows that were salvaged from a sixteenth-century church that was otherwise destroyed by World War II bombs. A covered market and a waxworks themed on Joan's life are adjacent.

Musée des Beaux-Arts (Square Verdrel): Behind the undistinguished bulk of a late-nineteenth-century facade is a collection of paintings that is one of the finest in provincial France. Clouet's *Bath of Diane,* a Poussin *Venus,* Gérard David's *Virgin and Saints* are among the French Renaissance greats. There are Italians like Veronese (*St. Roch and St. Sebastian*) and Bassano (*Adoration of the Shepherds*) not to mention Bronzino and Caravaggio. There are also Dutchmen like Steen, Van Goyen, and Ruysdael, no less than a handful of works by Rubens, and a Velázquez of a portly gent called *Democrite.* The French eighteenth century is on hand in strength: Nattier, Fragonard, Oudry, Hubert Robert, Vigée-Lebrun. This country's nineteenth-century painters? Consider Ingres's lovely *Madame Aymon,* a stern-visaged Géricault army officer, a clutch of Corots, works by Daubigny, Delacroix, and Rosa Bonheur. Of the Impressionists, Monet (who lived and worked at nearby Giverny ["Excursionist's Paris," chapter 2]) and Sisley are the most heavily represented, but Renoir and Boudin (from not far distant Honfleur, chapter 19) are also present. And of later artists, Normandy-born Raoul Dufy figures heavily.

Musée des Antiquités (Rue Beauvoisine) is sheltered in an atmospheric old monastery, with its subject matter beautiful objects from no-longer-standing town houses and churches—furniture and tapestries; reliquaries and weapons, jewelry and bronzes, not to mention sculpted fragments and mosaics from Roman Rouen. Special.

Musée Secq des Tournelles (2 Rue Jacques-Villon) occupies a smasher of a desanctified Gothic church—a perfect foil for its collection of wrought iron. You may feel the subject matter somewhat limited, but as you move about you get hooked. How about a sixteenth-century doorknocker, a circular stairway from a nearby château, a tree-of-life created in the sixteenth century, amusing signs with the symbols of shoemakers, florists, and butchers? Lovely.

Musée des Céramiques (Rue Faucon) is indicated for china and porcelain buffs, with a collection totaling some 300 objects, the lot of them Rouen-crafted between the sixteenth and eighteenth centuries.

Musée Corneille (4 Rue de la Pie): You don't have to have read *Mélite, Médée, Le Menteur,* or any other of the comedies or tragedies of this seventeenth-century playwright to enjoy an inspection of the house where he was born, with both a salon and study furnished in period.

Musée Flaubert (in Hôtel Dieu, a hospital at 51 Rue de Lécat): It is more likely that you have read Gustave Flaubert's *Madame Bovary* than Corneille's plays. At any rate, the nineteenth-century novelist was born in this apartment that is a part of the Hôtel Dieu complex (both his father and grandfather were surgeons on the hospital's staff). Flaubert's birthplace-bedroom is charmingly furnished. Exhibits relate both to the author and his works and to matters medical.

Fécamp (40 miles northwest of Rouen) is the little seaside town that the Bénédictine liqueur people have put on the map. Still, its principal lure is a positively gigantic abbey-church, *Abbatiale de la Trinité* (Rue Couturier), whose square Gothic tower—soaring to more than 200 feet—is the town landmark. Not that the length of the nave, close to 411 feet, is modest. If its proportions are what make it a standout—this is one of France's biggest churches—you want also to hike through the interior. Stroll down the nave to the altar, going behind it to the charming Lady Chapel. *Musée Municipal* (Rue Alexandre-Legros) is a mixed bag, city-operated repository of local lore, fishing paraphernalia through some quite nice furniture. *Musée de la Bénédictine* (Rue Alexandre-le-Grand): What you're no doubt most curious about is the liqueur operation. It is a long time since the Benedictine order had anything to do with it. Unlike Chartreuse (chapter 18), the only liqueur still actually produced by monks, Bénédictine is a lay commercial operation. It is quartered in a mock-Renaissance horror of a building that went up in the last decade of the last century, with a museum whose exhibits relate to the founding of the distillery by a sixteenth-century monk and which includes some fine pieces from the old abbey—chalices and stained glass, ancient books and a sedan chair, a Renaissance carved-wood triptych and medieval sculptures. With tours of the distillery, if you like. (And note that there's a *casino* overlooking the public beach and next to the municipal swimming pool. *Rue Jacques-Huet* is the main pedestrian shopping street.)

SETTLING IN

Pullman Alban Hôtel (Rue Croix-de-Fer; phone 3598-06-98): Quietly contemporary in design, the Pullman Alban fits well into the core of Rouen city. If you are lucky, you will draw a room (there are 108, including several suites) facing the cathedral. There's a convenient restaurant and a pleasant cocktail lounge. *First Class.*

Nord Hôtel (91 Rue du Gros-Horloge; phone 3570-41-41) is a few yards—quite literally—from Gros Horloge. Rouen's landmark heart-of-town Renaissance clock. It has, in recent years, spruced itself up, to the point where all 60 rooms now have private baths. Friendly. Breakfast only. *Moderate.*

Colin's Hôtel (15 Rue de la Pie; phone 3571-00-88) is relatively recent, quite central, and with 48 bath-equipped rooms; standard doubles can be very small, but rooms with two beds are somewhat larger. Breakfast only. *Moderate.*

De la Cathédrale Hôtel (12 Rue St.-Romain; phone 3571-57-95) is heart-of-town, on a street lined with venerable houses. There are just 25 neat—but not elaborate—rooms with bath. Breakfast only. *Moderate.*

De Dieppe Hôtel (Place Bernard-Tissot; phone 3571-96-00) is an across-the-square neighbor of Gare Rive-Droite—a fairish walk away from the historic core, the only reason it's not right up there with the Pullman Alban at the top of my grouping. This is a professionally operated house—the same family has been running it since doors opened in 1880—with 44 rooms, some Louis XV–style, some modern; those I have seen recently renovated are pleasant, as well as a restaurant (Les Quatre Saisons—exemplary enough for me to evaluate it in a later paragraph) and a convivial bar. *First Class.*

Normandie Hôtel (19 Rue Bec; phone 3571-55-77) has location going for it—it's core-of-town and has just 23 neat rooms. Breakfast only. *Moderate.*

DAILY BREAD

Chez Dufour (67-bis Rue St.-Nicolas; phone 3571-90-62) epitomizes Vieux Rouen, given its location in a centuries-old house near the cathedral. Stone walls are hung with antique Rouen pottery and bits and pieces of medieval sculpture—including a likeness of St.-Nick, who figures in the restaurant's address. There are half a dozen meat entrées. (*Toutes nos grillades sont faites au charbon de bois*—they're all charcoal-broiled.) But this should be your destination for an old-style Norman seafood meal—butter-based and à la carte. (*Le beurre est à la base de notre cuisine.*) There are oysters in variety—Bretonnes, belons, or praires—served with fresh lemon, an herbed sauce, and the traditional accompaniment, buttered rye bread. The morning's market determines composition of the seafood platter. If available, crayfish are served with the house's own mayonnaise. Stuffed clams are tasty; ditto, mussels marinière. Entrées? I defy you to find a more deliciously grilled sole, accompanied by sauce Béarnaise. Brochette of charcoal-grilled scallops are super. Or go for broke with a lobster. And on no account omit apple-based tarte Normande as your sweet. Service is sprightly and attentive. *First Class.*

La Couronne (31 Place du Vieux-Marché; phone 3571-40-90) immodestly dubs itself "La Plus Vieille Auberge de France," indicating its opening date as 1345. Well, you can't quarrel with that pedigree—nor with a situation on the city's most historic square. Facade is appropriately half-timbered, interior mellow, service kindly. Order one of the three prix-fixe menus, each good value. The most ambitious, including Muscadet or Côtes de Bergerac wine, opens with half a melon, proceeds with a seafood terrine accompanied by a trio of sauces or with half a dozen oysters; and offers Calvados-flavored sherbet as a palate cleanser prior to a choice of entrées: entrecôte with Béarnaise sauce, port-sauced roast squab, or seafood casserole. But you're not finished; cheeses are next, with gratin de pommes et son sabayon—apple tarts deliciously sauced, to conclude. *First Class.*

Le Beffroy (15 Rue Beffroy; phone 3571-55-27): I have never *not* enjoyed a female-operated French restaurant, especially when Madame is chef as well as *patronne.* This restaurant is a charmer, in a traditional setting. Chilled scallop/crayfish/oyster soup is a refreshing starter. Fricassee of duck flavored with Norman cider is delicious; likewise, the house's own salmon, sole, and turbot specialties. Desserts deserve the separate card they are accorded, with marquise au chocolat, apples in puff pastry with a liqueur sauce, and caramel ice cream among the goodies. *First Class.*

Le Quatre Saisons (De Dieppe Hôtel, Place Bernard-Tissot; phone 3571-96-00): You will be seated, most likely at a rust-hued *banquette* illuminated by fringed silk lamps overhead. I don't know of a more appropriate place to experience the city's renowned duck specialty, caneton Rouennais—red burgundy, cognac, veal stock, butter, and a traditional quartet of seasonings are among its ingredients. Foie gras de canard is always among the appetizers, along with an unusual chicken-breast salad. Seafood platter is counseled, among entrées; so is rognon de veau à la moutarde—veal kidneys in mustard sauce. *First Class.*

Bertrand Warin (9 Rue de la Pie; phone 3589-26-69) is a smart spot—just off Place du Vieux-Marché—wherein the owner-chef presents a range of delicious comestibles, traditional, albeit upon occasion with Warin accents. First courses can be as classic as terrine de foie de canard, or novel—cream of watercress soup, pastry-topped, with mussels and vegetables. Continue with fish either simply grilled or with a Warin-created sauce. Roast rabbit, roast pigeon, chicken fricassee in a cider-based sauce, and grilled steak are entrée choices. I counsel Monsieur Warin's trois tartelettes en bouchée—a triple-threat dessert—to conclude. *First Class.*

Les Maraîchers (37 Place du Vieux-Marché; phone 3571-57-73) is a buzzy, busy, heart-of-town source of favorite bistro dishes, coq au vin through boeuf bourguignon, as well as super seafood, oysters on the half shell through grilled sole. There are two menus; cheaper of the pair is excellent value. *First Class.*

Auberge St.-Maclou (224 Rue Martainville; phone 3771-06-67) occupies a fine old half-timbered house but has more than atmosphere to recommend it—tasty well-priced menus, three all told, with the cheapest a solid buy; a meal might include goat cheese salad to start, trout meunière, tarte aux pommes or ice cream, as well as a quarter-carafe of wine or mineral water. *Moderate.*

Maison Périer (68 Rue du Gros-Horloge; phone 3571-44-88) opened as a bakery in 1822, and is still (in the front). It is, as well, a self-service restaurant out back and upstairs. Attractive and with good things to eat—salads, plats du jour, and desserts. Good for a casual lunch or snack. Central. *Moderate.*

La Cache Ribaud (10 Rue du Tambour; phone 3571-04-82) occupies half-timbered quarters on a street leading from Rue du Gros-Horloge and is worth knowing about for its bargain-priced menu *rapide*—based on poultry, lamb, or beef. Friendly. *Moderate.*

Pasoline (5 Rue de la Potérue; phone 3589-67-44) welcomes with its Belle Époque decor, congenial staff, and choice of several inexpensive prix-fixe menus. Central. *Moderate.*

Dame Tartine (52 Rue St.-Romain) combines a lovely location—on a landmark street—with lovely things to eat, pastries especially, combined with coffee or tea. *Moderate.*

La Mirabelle (3 Place du Vieux-Marché) is indicated for coffee or a drink, combined with people-watching, in this principal square. *Brasserie*-type food, too. *Moderate.*

La Marine (23 Quai Vicomte, Fécamp; phone 3528-15-94) is indicated for a seafood lunch in the course of a Fécamp excursion, with views of the beach as a bonus. *First Class.*

SHOPPER'S ROUEN

Printemps department store is opposite the cathedral on the Rue des Carmes; *Monoprix* is on Rue du Gros-Horloge, principal pedestrian thoroughfare, with such interesting shops as *Newman* (men's and women's clothes), *Jean Druet* (perfumes), *Aumusse* (leather and furs), and *Jambon de York* (a mouthwatering *charcuterie*). Rue Rollon, parallel with Gros-Horloge, is shopping territory, too; there's a branch of *Hédiard,* the Paris food emporium, and a branch, also, of *Descamps,* the linen chain. Rue de Croix-de-Fer, near the cathedral, has smart boutiques, including *Toiles* (women's haute couture) and *Artisanat* (hand-crafted pottery). And Rue St.-Romain, alongside the Cathedral, is trendy, too, with women's shops including *Garance* and such antique shops as *Galerie de l'Archevêché.*

SOUND OF MUSIC

Théâtre des Arts (Rue Jeanne-d'Arc, near the Seine) is Rouen's opera house and the venue also for concerts (especially of the Orchestre de Chambre de Rouen) and ballet. (This is a city for organ music, given a range of exceptional organs; watch for concerts in the *Church of St.-Ouen,* above, which has one of the best.)

INCIDENTAL INTELLIGENCE

There are about as many daily trains between Paris's Gare St.-Lazare and Rouen's Gare Rive-Droite as there are hours in the day; they take an hour and a half. *Further information:* Office de Tourisme, 25 Place de la Cathédrale, Rouen; Office de Tourisme, Place Bellet, Fécamp.

32

St.-Malo

and Eastward to Mont-St.-Michel

BACKGROUND BRIEFING

Canadians are familiar with St.-Malo because it was from this Breton port that Jacques Cartier sailed, in 1534, to discover their country. Englishmen and Channel Islanders know St.-Malo because they can—and do—sail to it from their shores, the summer long. The Welsh feel a bond with St.-Malo because it is named for a wandering seventh-century Welshman, sainted for miracles performed in the vicinity of the monastery he built in the neighborhood. Which leaves Americans, surely the last of the English-speakers to appreciate one of the most sparkling, and at the same time most monument-laden, of France's resort cities.

By the time St.-Malo became part of France in the late fifteenth century, bishops who doubled as its governors had moved it from what is now the quarter called St.-Servan to a nearby promontory that they proceeded to fortify with high walls topped with broad ramparts, punctuated at frequent intervals by defense towers and monumental gates. Its corsairs, thriving as early as the fifteenth century and continuing their raids into the eighteenth century, saw St.-Malo feared by neighboring maritime powers, the English especially.

Cartier was but one of many long-distance mariners. By the time he established the colony of New France on the Gaspé Peninsula, St.-Malo-based fishing vessels had reached the cod-rich waters off the coast of Newfoundland. Their mariner-successors went even farther in the seventeenth and eighteenth centuries—along coasts of South as well as North America, the West Indies, Africa, and even China.

Indeed, well into the fourth decade of the present century, St.-Malo's good fortune held. In 1944, World War II took its toll: 80 percent of the city within the walls was destroyed. But there was no stopping this valiant town. St.-Malo has been entirely rebuilt—

meticulously and lovingly. The city you see today—walkable ramps, keeps and towers, ceremonial gateways, stone-walled houses, even the cathedral with Cartier's tomb—appears quite as it did pre-World War II. And there remains the bonus of beaches: white-sand, hotel-backed, casino-equipped. St.-Malo is a winner.

ON SCENE

Lay of the Land: This town conveniently divides itself in two, with the aid of the Latin language. *Extra Muros* is the larger area, outside the walls. *Intra Muros*—within the walls—is what, elsewhere, might be called the Old Town. Its main entrance is through the walls at the splendid gateway called *Grande Porte,* into *Place du Poids-du-Roi,* which gives onto shop-lined *Grande Rue,* and extends north to the cathedral and *Place Châtillon.* This core-area is mercantile St.-Malo, with shops lining streets like *Rue Broussais,* west of the cathedral, and *Rue de la Vieille Boucherie* running parallel with it, to the south, and extending to the square called *Marché Légumes.* To the north—and beyond the wall—are two major beaches, *Plage du Mole* and contiguous *Plage de Bon Secours.* The beaches wind around the northern tip of the promontory to the eastern shore and *Grande Plage,* site of the casino. The southeast corner of Intra Muros is flanked by restaurant and café-filled *Rue Jacques-Cartier* and centered by *Place Châteaubriand,* site of the château (containing a pair of museums and the city hall as well), with the aquarium a near neighbor. Two additional quarters of interest are *St.-Servan,* with its beaches, restaurants, and a museum (below), and *Paramé,* southwest of Intra Muros, whose beaches are an extension of Grande Plage (above).

Les Remparts: Gain perspective by a walk along the ramparts, ascending them at the gate called Porte St.-Thomas. When the sun is shining, clouds billowy, tide in, and waves high, there is nothing else to compare with the experience in all France; when the tide is out, you may proceed to the offshore islands; there are guided tours of the historic fort on Petit Bé.

Le Château (Place Chateaubriand) shelters a pair of attractions. One, *Galerie Quic-en-Groigne,* consists of a series of wax-figure tableaux, portraying the history of St.-Malo, and is skippable. The second museum—*Musée d'Histoire de la Ville*—occupies part of several floors of the five-sided seventeenth-century castle, giving you an opportunity to appreciate its architecture (most exhibits are in the circular ex-dungeon) the while taking in objects relating to St.-Malo's history: an eighteenth-century globe, model ships, parchment documents, figureheads and drawings, paintings by moderns like Signac, and by unknowns, of early St.-Malo mariners. Go all the way up, for the view from the top-level terrace.

Cathedral of St.-Vincent (Place Châtillon): The cathedral's spire dominates the skyline of Intra Muros; within, it is essentially Gothic, the result of an extensive postwar restoration that was completed in 1972. The contemporary stained glass is first-rate. You do not want to miss the severe but simple tomb of Jacques Cartier; the Canadian ambassador came from Paris to attend the mass at which Cartier was reinterred when the cathedral reopened; the tomb's plaque indicates Cartier's name, followed by the dates of his birth and death, 1491–1557, and the legend *Découvreur du Canada.*

Musée International du Long-Cours Cap Hornier (Tour Solidor, in the St.-Servan section of town): The title is a mouthful but you go if only for the setting, a smashing skyscraper of a medieval château—it went up in 1382—that is half a dozen stories high, more vertical than horizontal, with a trio of graceful turrets topping it off. Stairs are steep, but exhibits—relating to explorers (Magellan is the best known) who rounded Cape Horn, from the sixteenth century through the nineteenth—are intriguing.

Aquarium (Place Vauban) concentrates on fish and other marine species native to Breton waters. You will no doubt be in the company of not a few loquacious youngsters.

Manoir de Limoë Lou (just outside the village of Rotheneuf, near St.-Malo) is the relatively recently restored home of the mariner-explorer Jacques Cartier, discoverer of Canada. This is a sixteenth-century stone house with an interestingly furnished interior, highlighted with Cartier mementoes. Open June–September.

Dinard is St.-Malo's next-door beach resort, due west, just across the estuary called La Rance. It was popularized a century ago by Britons (*Le Temple Anglicain,* on Rue du Temple, is a Church of England outpost) and remains popular today with their descendants. Dinard developed principally around crescent-shaped *Plage de l'Écluse*—a broad, white-sand beach dominated by a casino (whose facilities run a broad gamut, from gaming tables and restaurant to disco and café and modern convention center; backed by hotels and edged by *Pointe du Moulinet* at the edge of a rocky promontory, with memorable views). Another beach, *Plage de St.-Énogat,* is to the north, while *Plage du Prieuré* is to the south. An enormous indoor swimming pool, a regional maritime museum-aquarium, and pretentious villas—mostly from the last century—are dotted about the coast, while the mercantile core of town is based on *Rue de la Pionnière* and *Boulevard du Président-Wilson.* The 18-hole, par 68 *Dinard Golf Course,* with a restaurant-equipped clubhouse, is at St.-Briac, four miles west of town.

Cancale (nine miles east of St.-Malo) typifies north coast fishing villages in that it is small and simple and fronts a crescent-shaped bay with gaily painted boats at anchor. The only monument of consequence is the *Church of St.-Méen,* from whose tower there are good views of the scenic coastline. The name of the Cancale game is seafood restaurants. They flank its waterfront and are popular with visitors from St.-Malo and residents of Breton cities like Rennes, to the south. Cancale makes for a relaxing lunch stop in the course of a day's exploration; several restaurants are recommended below.

Dol de Bretagne (15 miles south of St.-Malo, a little more distant from Rennes) is a Breton surprise-package, an utterly charming village with its ace-in-the-hole *Cathédral St.-Samson,* which is as old as the ninth century—note Romanesque details of the facade—but is mostly thirteenth-century Gothic: the finest in Brittany. Indeed, the long, high, three-level nave is one of the loveliest such in France; it is lined by stained-glass windows that tell the story of Samson, and there is still more splendid glass in the apse, not to mention a fourteenth-century choir with interestingly carved misericords, or folding seats, and a bishop's throne. The village's mixed-bag *Musée Historique* is just opposite, in a house of advanced age. And you want to ascend the minimountain adjacent to Dol for a visit to its satellite village, *Mont-Dol,* and a landmark windmill.

Château de Combourg (21 miles south of St.-Malo, about the same distance from Rennes): Each of Combourg's four corners is defined by a fabulous circular tower-cum-turret. Windows are the kind of slits that archers used. The château's park is large enough to afford proper perspective; little Combourg village, adjacent, pales in contrast. You visit the castle's interior on guided tours taking less than an hour. It's essentially nineteenth-century, a comedown from outside.

Mont-St.-Michel (28 miles east of St.-Malo): The point worth making at the outset is that precisely because it is one of a kind, and with its compact area unexpandable, St.-Michel is packed—uncomfortably jampacked—spring through autumn, with the annual visitor count close to two million; May, July, and August are the peak months. Understandably, of course. How many other Gothic abbeys do you know that are constructed on a fortified rock of an island that was accessible only at low tide, until so recently as a century back, when a causeway was built, joining it to the mainland? Of course you want to visit St.-Michel. But because of the congestion, limited hotel space, and overpopulated restaurants, you may want to make it a day excursion from your St.-Malo base. Or come when you'll no doubt have the little island pretty much to yourself—but when hotels and restaurants are shuttered. My point is that you must take highly commercial Mont-St.-Michel on its own highly commercial terms.

With eighth-century origins, the Benedictine Abbey—mostly eleventh-century but with a nineteenth-century spire—rises more than 450 feet and warrants your highest priority. The 90-step ascent is effort well expended: sublime Romanesque nave, late Gothic altar, sumptuously colonnaded cloister, the entire complex topping a mass of granite and embracing such auxiliary spaces—*La Merveille* (The Marvel), they are called—as long since disused official guest quarters, barrel-vaulted refectory, capacious halls, crypt, and chapels.

If you've devoted much of the morning to the abbey, it will be time for a lunch pause. Afterwards, stroll souvenir-shop-lined *Grande Rue* and pop into the pair of museums (there's a single admission ticket for both, but neither is of earthshaking consequence), the lovely fifteenth-century *Église Paroissiale,* a handsome church with a silver statue of St. Michael, and *Logis Tiphaine,* a venerable house with also-venerable furniture.

SETTLING IN

Central Hôtel (6 Grande Rue; phone 9940-87-70) is—as far as I am concerned—No. 1, assuming you want to headquarter in the historic Intra Muros part of St.-Malo. There are 46 rooms, not all of them overlarge, but those that I have seen are attractive and full facility, the decor traditional. There's an on-premises restaurant (later recommended), bar where locals and guests mix, and the staff smiles. Best Western. *First Class.*

Des Thermes Hôtel (100 Boulevard Hébert, Grande Plage; phone 9956-02-56). If your prime St.-Malo mission is sun and sand, this turn-of-century beachfront house—tastefully updated—is indicated. There are 101 rooms, some really good-sized, with the seaview ones the nicest—along with an attractive restaurant, glass-roofed, and an indoor seawater pool: a health spa—Thermes Marina—is adjacent. *First Class.*

Mercure Hôtel (Chaussée du Sillon; phone 9956-84-84) hugs the seafront and is more attractive within than its severe facade suggests. The lobby, with its bar-lounge, is tastefully contemporary, as indeed are those of the 70 rooms and suites I've inspected; 11 have good baths. Breakfast is the generous buffet typical of this national chain. Very nice. *Moderate/First Class.*

De la Digue Hôtel (49 Chaussée du Sillon, Grande Plage; phone 9956-09-26) is a Grande Plage charmer: a delightful, 53-room house, with accommodations gracious, seafront bar and lounge congenial, and a honey of a terrace just above the sands, where breakfasts are a pleasure. No restaurant. *Moderate.*

La Villefromoy Hôtel (7 Boulevard Hébert; phone 9940-92-20): What happened was this: The owning La Villefromoy family bought this late-nineteenth-century house (not far from the Grande Plage) and, utilizing expertise in period decor and antique furniture, refurbished it, stem to stern. There are 25 no-two-alike rooms, accessorized with lovely old pieces and in varying color schemes. Main lounge and cocktail bar are quite the smartest public spaces of any hotel in town that I know. In a word: elegant. Breakfast only. *First Class.*

Le Valmarin Hôtel (7 Rue Jean XXIII; phone 9981-94-76) takes its guests back to eighteenth-century St.-Malo. Originally the home of a retired and wealthy corsair, it retains the ambience and furnishings of the period, with gracious public spaces and 10 thoughtfully equipped rooms. Near Grande Plage. Breakfast only. *Moderate.*

Alexandra Hôtel (138 Boulevard Hébert; phone 9956-11-12) welcomes guests with good-looking ground-floor lounges—popular for drinks and tea—that look out to sea and 15 smartly decorated rooms, the choicest those with terraces that overlook Grande Plage, an easy walk away. Congenial management. Breakfast only. *Moderate.*

Aux Ajoncs d'Or Hôtel (10 Rue des Forgeurs; phone 9940-85-03) is a handsome mansion, core of Intra Muros, that has been attractively converted into a two-dozen-room house that is friendly and comfortable. Breakfast only. *Moderate.*

Mascotte Hôtel (76 Chaussée du Sillon; phone 9940-36-36) is a relatively recent, bright-look house facing the Grande Plage, with a rattan-furnished lobby-cum-bar, 88 pleasant rooms with bath, and buffet breakfast. Friendly. *Moderate.*

Le Grand Hôtel (46 Avenue George V, Dinard; phone 9946-10-28)—on a street appropriately named for a British sovereign—evokes the Dinard of the last century, when Britons came south for respite in the sunshine. The Grand remains quite grand—with high-ceilinged public spaces, including a vast lounge and bar, restaurant with immense windows draped in scarlet, and 100 terraced rooms, just half of them seaview. Central. *Luxury.*

La Plage Hôtel (3 Boulevard Féart, Dinard; phone 9946-14-87) is not, despite its name, directly on the beach, but rather a short block distant. There are just under 20 well-equipped rooms, cozy bar, and a very good restaurant. *Moderate.*

La Mère Poulard Hôtel (Mont-St.-Michel; phone 3360-14-01): When you consider that this hotel—and its restaurant (evaluated below)—are named for Annette Poulard, the local lady globally honored for popularizing the omelet, it is hardly surprising that it can be hoity-toity, or that—for a hostelry that does not have an elevator, and with 5 of its 27 rooms lacking private baths—tabs are relatively steep. On my first visit, in the company of a French Government Tourist Office official, we were not only not allowed to inspect rooms, but asked to leave the premises posthaste. On my second, I was shown only the sole suite on the top floor (I walked four flights up, and again, down) but no ordinary rooms. There's a cocktail lounge to complement the restaurant, reviewed below. *Moderate.*

Les Terrasses Poulard Hôtel (Mont-St.-Michel; phone 3360-14-09) occupies a venerable Rue Principale house, not unlike La Mère Poulard (above), and the St.-Pierre and Mouton Blanc hotels (below). Les Terrasses shelters 30 bath-equipped rooms and a restaurant about which I write in a later paragraph. *Moderate.*

St.-Pierre Hôtel (Mont-St.-Michel; phone 3360-14-03) occupies a half-timbered fifteenth-century house that's a protected historic monument. Rooms have been engagingly refurbished in recent seasons but not all have bath. The restaurant is reviewed on a later page, and there's a bar-brasserie. *Moderate.*

Altéa Hôtel (Route du Mont-St.-Michel; phone 3360-14-18) is a modern, hundred-room-with-bath house on the mainland, edging the Mont-St.-Michel dike. All rooms are bath- and shower-equipped and comfortable, and there's a reliable restaurant. Okay. *Moderate.*

Mouton Blanc Hôtel (Mont-St.-Michel; phone 9960-14-08) is small (with just 20 rooms) and has a restaurant evaluated on a later page. *Moderate.*

DAILY BREAD

L'Âtre (7 Esplanade Cadet Menguy, in the St.-Servan quarter of St.-Malo; phone 9981-68-39) positively hums at lunch—and with good reason. Tables are, to be sure, tightly spaced. But the staff is cordial and the chef expert. The five-course menu yields memorable choices—a diverse platter of fresh seafood, oysters through mussels, to start; and grilled fish of the day, au beurre blanc, as the next plate. A smoked pork chop served with lentils and matchstick-thin frites might be the entrée. Then comes a salad dressed with a perfect vinaigrette. Desserts? You choose from a trolley—fresh strawberries in season, doused with Brittany cream, are among the possibilities. *First Class.*

À la Duchesse Anne (Place Guy La Chambre, Intra Muros; phone 9940-85-33) occupies quarters in a house of substantial age. Tables are dressed in red and white polka-dot linen, the wine waiter wears a sailor suit, serving staff is attentive, and fare is utterly delicious. You order from an extensive à la carte; a meal might embrace fish soup and filet of sole meunière, accompanied by sautéed mushrooms and a mound of crisp frites. Tarte Tatin, the house's dessert specialty, is superlative. *First Class.*

Central Hôtel Restaurant (6 Grande Rue, Intra Muros; phone 9940-87-70) tempts with daily specials; in asparagus season, open with that vegetable in tandem with a sublime sauce mousseline. Skewered broiled scallops, with beurre blanc sauce, are a treat. So is filet of beef in the company of sauce Béarnaise. *First Class.*

Jean-Paul Delaunay (6 Rue Ste.-Barbe, Intra Muros; phone 9940-92-46) bears the name of its talented chef-patron, and you could do worse than to order half a duckling, prepared by him with Calvados; or lobster in a variety of styles. Tempting desserts. Location is a street just off Rue Jacques-Cartier. *First Class.*

Tea-Time (4 Grande Rue, Intra Muros; phone 9940-89-12) could be across the Channel in England, with bacon-and-eggs breakfasts, salad-and-omelet lunches, and made-on-premises cakes served with afternoon tea. Fun. *Moderate.*

Chez Gaby (2 Rue de Dinan, Intra Muros) is a typically Breton *crêperie;* make a meal of several, starting with savory and ending with sweet. Delicious. *Moderate.*

Café de l'Ouest (Place Chateaubriand): Take a table, and watch the crowds pass in review, with the walls of the château just opposite. *Moderate.*

Bricourt (Cancale, 9 miles east of St.-Malo; phone 9989-67-14) might be termed the luxury leader in this restaurant-permeated coastal community. Seafood is the big specialty—open with the chef-propriétaire's spiced oysters, following with his lobster masterwork (it comes in two separate guises). Desserts and wines are rankers; the setting, attractive. *Luxury.*

Le Continental (Cancale, 9 miles east of St.-Malo; phone 9989-60-16) is, to be sure, an unpretentious 18-room, moderate-category hotel located on the waterfront of this fishing village, but it is called to your attention here primarily because of its excellent restaurant. There are two prix-fixe menus based on seafood; the pricier—worth the relative splurge—might embrace a dozen of the esteemed local oysters, half a grilled local lobster, cheese, and choice of sweets. (Also worth sampling: just-caught fish, mussels, scallops.) Congenial. *Luxury.*

Le Cancalais (Cancale, 9 miles east of St.-Malo; phone 9989-61-93) is still another of the many waterfront restaurants of this village—and an exemplary one. Order à la carte; mussels—either marinière, à la crème, or farcies (stuffed)—are a specialty; or pick one of four prix-fixe menus, on one of which blanquette de poisson—a fish stew—is always featured. *First Class.*

La Mère Poulard (Mont-St.-Michel; phone 3360-14-01): You will, of course, be curious about the best-known of the Mont's restaurants. It's attractive, with Gothic-era windowframes lining a rock-surfaced wall, an enlarged photo of Mère Poulard, the omelet whiz out of the last century, and a display of eggs, whisks, and copper omelet pans at the entrance. Prices for the two menus are by far the highest on the island; you can eat for a third or more less at other restaurants. The cheapest menu offers lamb terrine, crudités, or a fish dish as appetizers, with the presumably original Poulard omelet (accompanied by samplings of four house specialties), with a choice of house-made sherbets (each is spiked with alcohol—Calvados through Armagnac) to conclude. The costlier menu is more substantial, with the region's pre-salé lamb among entrées, and a flaming dessert omelet among sweets. *First Class/Luxury.*

St.-Pierre (Mont-St.-Michel; phone 3360-14-03) welcomes with good looks: red-and-white-checked cloths on tables surrounded by Provençal chairs; wrought-iron chandeliers suspended from a beamed ceiling. The well-priced menu might open with fish soup or mussels marinière, feature roast lamb or entrecôte as entrées, and conclude with cheese or a sweet. *Moderate.*

Mouton Blanc Hôtel Restaurant (Mont-St.-Michel; phone 9960-14-08) packs them in, especially at lunch, but never mind, the food is very good, indeed. Open your prix-fixe with a seafood platter packed with oysters, shrimp, clams, and sea snails; continue with a monster omelet—typically Mont-St.-Michel—which is preparatory to the entrée, gigot d'agneau (the lamb is pre-salé, fed on the salt marshes, adjacent) served with a minimountain of frites. *First Class.*

Terrasses Poulard (Mont-St.-Michel; phone 9960-14-09) presents a tempting prix-fixe menu with a variety of openers, the standard omelet as course No. 2, and—among entrées—sole prepared with Normandy cider. The *terrasses* of the title are the island's ramparts; no charge for the panoramic views. *First Class.*

SHOPPER'S ST.-MALO

Rue Broussais, in the Intra Muros section, is the main business street; *Aux Toiles de France* sells typical Breton lace. *Monoprix* department store is on nearby Rue St.-Vincent. *Jean Yves* (smart men's clothes) and *Guilbert* (linens) are among Rue Barbinais's many boutiques. *Au Marin Breton* (with typical Breton fishermen's sweaters) and *Richard Yachting* (women's haute couture) are both on Rue de la Vieille Boucherie. *Le Mazagran (white porcelain)* and *Hélène Noël* (nineteenth-century antiques) are among Grande Rue's grander shops. *Villefromoy* (Place Châtillon) is the quality antique shop owned by the family operating a hotel of the same name, recommended above.

AFTER DARK

Casino (Esplanade du Casino, Extra Muros) shares a contemporary, glass-fronted pavilion with a convention center. Assorted entertainments are presented in its theater; roulette and other games of chance, too; café-restaurant.

INCIDENTAL INTELLIGENCE

You may fly to the Channel Islands of Guernsey and Jersey, as well as London, Bournemouth, and Exeter (see *Britain at Its Best*), from nearby *Aéroport de Dinard,* from which there are flights to Paris as well. *Brittany Ferries* sail to Portsmouth from St.-Malo, and there is boat service, also, to the Channel Islands, provided by a number of companies. There is direct bus service in summer between Rennes (chapter 30) and Mont-St.-Michel, via Les Courriers Bretons. *Further information:* Office de Tourisme, Esplanade St.-Vincent, St.-Malo; Office de Tourisme, 2 Boulevard Féart, Dinard; Office de Tourisme, Port, Cancale; Office de Tourisme, 3 Grande Rue des Stuarts, Dol-de-Bretagne; Office de Tourisme, Corps de Garde des Bourgeois, Mont-St.-Michel.

33

St.-Tropez

Hedonism on the Côte d'Azur

BACKGROUND BRIEFING

It may not have seemed so when, many centuries back, this Roman-founded Mediterranean village—identified as much with the Riviera as with Provence—named itself after a Roman Christian martyr originally called *Torpes.* Nor, even later—in the Renaissance era—when it was virtually repopulated, after a period of decline, by a score of substantial Genoese families whose descendants constitute the nucleus of today's permanent populace.

No, it was not until much later—toward the turn of the present century—when long obscure St.-Tropez began to achieve celebrity. Maupassant exclaimed over its beauties in print. Signac followed, pioneering among the painters, to be followed by a star-studded cache of colleagues: Matisse, Bonnard, Henri Cross, and Marquet, to name a handful.

Colette joined this pre-World War I artistic contingent, following—by some decades, to be sure—Maupassant in printed praise. Pre-World War II St.-Tropez had become fashionable enough to attract the fashion and film worlds, innovating a casual, barefoot resort life-style on the French Mediterranean, nothing at all like more conventional fleshpots such as Cannes (chapter 13), Nice (chapter 26), and Monte Carlo (chapter 23) to the east.

It took only a handful of talented publicists, after World War II, to chronicle St.-Tropez's hedonism as manifested by such regular visitors as actress Brigitte Bardot and novelist Françoise Sagan and to place St.-Tropez on the world-class resort map. And with reason. It is one of a kind.

None of this is surprising when you consider the setting. St.-Tropez straddles the inner shore of an enormous sheltered gulf—with the distinction of facing north (the better for afternoon sun) rather than south, as is common in seaside resorts of the region. The village climbs a château-topped hill and is backed by formidable mountains. Combine its situation with limited means of access—trains do not reach St.-Tropez, nor is there an adjacent airport—and the special appeal of the place becomes apparent.

St.-Tropez does not receive massive tour groups flying in on jumbo jets. There are no grand-luxe hotels in the traditional sense where gents change to jacket and tie for dinner. Restaurants are adequate, rarely exceptional, and, in no case that I know, monumental. Sightseeing is not of the tour-bus variety. You shop in a way-out boutique rather than a department store. You dine very late and disco much, much later. The hotel social director is an unknown species; your daily schedule is of your own making. What I mean to say is that St.-Tropez is not for everyone. Still, if the dictionary definition of hedonism appeals—"The ethical doctrine that the seeking of pleasure is the primary good"—it may just be for you.

ON SCENE

Lay of the Land: St.-Tropez juts into the waters of a placid gulf, facing the contemporarily created vacation village of *Port Grimaud,* if you look north, and the village of *St.-Maxime,* across to the east. Core of town is the horseshoe-shaped *Vieux-Port,* with restaurants and cafés tightly packed, one after the other, on ground floors of handsome old houses. *Rue François Sibilli* is the more important of several streets leading inland from the harbor to a pair of atmospheric—and contiguous—squares: *Place des Lices* and *Place du XVᵉ Corps. Rue de la Citadelle* extends east from the harbor to *La Citadelle* (below), high over the village. *Rue Gambetta,* running parallel to Rue François Sibilli, is boutique-filled, as is *Rue Allard,* west of the harbor. Beaches are east of the center: *Plages des Graniers* is the closest; *Plages des Salins* is more distant. Hotels are dotted about, around the port, in hilly sectors overlooking the port, in the countryside, and in mountain villages. There is, of course, no railway station, but *Gare Routière,* the bus depot, is on *Place Blanqui,* west of the center.

Musée de l'Annonciade (Place Georges Grammont)—an all-France sleeper—is a St.-Tropez surprise package of the first order. Quartered in the early-sixteenth-century chapel whose name it takes, it is desanctified and beautifully adapted to its present function. It is the venue for exhibition of an extraordinary collection of postimpressionist paintings by artists who have worked in St.-Tropez, beginning with the pioneering Signac's *Le Port de St.-Tropez* (painted in 1899); Marquet's similarly titled work of 1905, and Matisse's barebreasted *La Gitane* of 1906. But there is so much more: a Braque mountain village, Seurat's twin-towered *L'Estaque,* a Dufy of northerly Honfleur, a Vlaminck *nature morte* (plums in a bowl alongside a blue pitcher), Van Dongen's *Femme à la Balustrade,* works by Derain and De La Fresnaye, Cross and Rouault, Bonnard and Vuillard.

Musée de la Marine (Rue de la Citadelle): The medieval hilltop stronghold of La Citadelle is St.-Tropez's most impressive monument of yore, a formidable sixteenth-century battlement, the views from which—of town and harbor—are at least as impressive as the collection within, of ship models and other souvenirs of the village's maritime past, including documentation relating to its liberation by valiant Resistance forces after World War II occupation.

Excursions into the mountains might center on visits to the villages of *Ramatuelle* and *Gassin,* each seven miles out of town and affording spectacular panoramas of St.-Tropez and the region. If I had to choose one, it would be higher-up Ramatuelle, centered about a charming Baroque church. Although lower-down Gassin, with its even older church, is hardly to be despised. Indeed, the two can be nicely combined in a day's outing.

SETTLING IN

Byblos Hôtel (Avenue Paul-Signac; phone 9497-00-04): You may get lost, but you won't be bored in this extraordinary complex, which attempts—and not without success—to emulate a traditional Provençal village in this series of irregularly contoured (but mostly connected) pavilions in an essentially U-shaped layout. Location is a promontory high above town, albeit an easy walk to the core. There are 107 rooms and suites, and when I say no two are alike, I understate. Decor theme is essentially traditional—natural woods, heavy beams, a proclivity toward beds and storage space built into nooks and crannies, with those rooms (the overwhelmingly majority) in the older part of the complex far handsomer, to me, at least, than the newer (which feature jacuzzi-equipped baths adjacent to beds, with toilets in enclosed compartments). There are a pair of exemplary restaurants, as many bar-lounges (one, out of the Arabian Nights), and two discos. Of these, the latter—Les Caves du Roy—illuminated by a quartet of giant, stylized, glass-leaved trees, can accommodate a thousand dancers. The swimming pool–terrace is inviting, and pricey shops are dotted about. As casual as Byblos appears—ambience is typically St.-Tropez-casual—this is a professional and skillfully operated hotel. *Luxury.*

Résidence de la Pinède Hôtel (Plage de la Bouillabaisse; phone 9497-04-21; a five-minute drive from town) is low-slung and more or less traditional in look, with 40 thoughtfully equipped rooms (the ones to aim for are seafront, with terraces), an attractive restaurant with an alfresco extension on which informal lunches are served, and swimming either from the beach or in the pool. Management is astute and kindly. *Luxury.*

Yaca Hôtel (1 Boulevard d'Aumale; phone 9497-11-79) is agreeably situated, halfway up the hill from the harbor, and pleases with its good looks—tile-floored lobby, 23 bedrooms whose beds and windows are covered in brown and white checks, and pretty pool flanked by a luxurious garden. Friendly staff. Breakfast only. *First Class.*

La Ponche Hôtel (Place du Revelin; phone 9497-02-53) attracts, first, with its situation on a landmark—and lively—square; then, with its agreeable ambience, clublike lobby, comfortable cocktail lounge, two dozen smartly styled rooms (the nicest those with seaview terrace), and a restaurant well known in its own right, later counseled. *First Class.*

Résidence des Lices Hôtel (Avenue Auguste-Grangeon; phone 9497-28-28) is at its most striking in a two-story, contemporarily designed lobby-lounge, fronting a big rectangle of a pool. There are 41 pleasant bedrooms, and you're central—just off Place des Lices. Breakfast only. *Moderate.*

Ermitage Hôtel (Avenue Paul-Signac; phone 9497-52-33) shares the same street—atop the hill overlooking the harbor—as the neighboring Byblos (above). Reception area/lounge are homelike, and there are 29 rooms, the most desirable those with views of town and sea. Friendly. *Moderate.*

La Maison Blanche Hôtel (Place des Lices; phone 9497-52-66) is not going to put you in mind of Washington's White House, which is hardly to say it is not worthy of consideration; this is an intimate house of but 8 no-two-alike rooms, with the location a principal square. Breakfast only. *Moderate.*

Sube Hôtel (Quai Suffren; phone 9497-30-04) is called to your attention should you desire a modest hotel—not all of its 26 rooms have bath—directly on the harbor, heart of the action. Breakfast only. *Moderate.*

DAILY BREAD

Le Chabichou (Byblos Hôtel; phone 9497-00-04) welcomes with white stucco walls and country Provençal chairs, their seats padded in regional fabrics, with interesting paintings and sculptures as accents. Menu is not without contemporary accents. You might open with lobster-chicken terrine served with a warm potato salad. Scalloped duck livers served on a bed of spinach and garnished with white onions and artichokes is a popular entrée. There's a traditional prix-fixe menu that might open with a truffled duck pâté, continue with sautéed lamb, and conclude with a choice of house-prepared sweets. Dinner only. *Luxury.*

La Ponche (Place du Revelin; phone 9497-09-29) is enjoyable on a mild summer evening, at a table set under the broad canopy in the square, elevated enough to afford seaviews. Order from the good-value menus, seafood-accented, ranging from fish soup through the day's catch simply grilled and beyond to the house's own desserts. *First Class.*

La Pesquière and Mazagran are a pair of restaurants contiguous to each other on Place du Revelin, with the same management, same phone (9497-05-92), similarly pleasant panoramas of the harbor, and same reliable fare. The prix-fixe menu—start with mussels marinière or pâté de campagne; continue with grilled fresh sardines or a steak, accompanied by frites and tomatoes Provence style; and end with a choice of sweets—is tasty and well priced. *First Class.*

Bistrot de la Marine (7 Quai Jean-Jaurès; phone 9497-04-07) is probably as satisfactory as any of the jumble of restaurants jam-packed into this street, directly on Vieux-Port. Do not count on space between tables in any of this group; the idea is sardinelike seating. Bistrot de la Marine makes some attempt at decor, however, with hurricane lamps on tables. The prix-fixe might include fish soup, filet of sole or gigot d'agneau, and dessert. *First Class.*

Leï Mouscardïns (Quai Jean-Jaurès; phone 9497-01-53) occupies fully enclosed quarters at the east end of Vieux-Port. There is, alas, no terrace, so that even on fine evenings, when all of St.-Tropez dines alfresco, you're indoors. There are some good local dishes—*anchoïade* (anchovy paste served on toast) as an appetizer is among them. Grilled fish is a satisfactory entrée. By and large, though—mediocre. *First Class.*

Chez Nano (Place de l'Hôtel de Ville; phone 9497-01-66)—with its central location and nice-looking quarters—packs in the crowds at dinner, which is à la carte only and minimally tasty, with simpler entrées like lamb chops the safest. Waiters are inexperienced youngsters. I can't recommend this one. *First Class.*

Café Senequier (11 Quai Suffren)—massive and hardly distinguished to look upon—is St.-Tropez's see-and-be-seen congregating spot; go for pastis or coffee and take in the crowds. *Moderate.*

Bello Visto (Gassin; phone 9456-17-30) is accurately named (if oddly spelled), affording fabulous views of the sea, way below, and indicated for a lunch break in the course of an excursion into the hills. *Moderate.*

SHOPPER'S ST.-TROPEZ

Modish, youthful sportswear appropriate to the barefoot St.-Tropez dress code typifies the shopping scene, with branches of pricey chains as options. For example, *Hermès* (men's and women's accessories) and *Les Must de Cartier* (watches, jewelry) are on Rue de la Ponche. *Porcelaine Blanche*—white housewares—is on Rue Gambetta. On Rue François Sibilli and adjacent Passage Gambetta, emphasis is on wearables—*Kansai, Lady Wilson, Claire l'Insolite, Kenzo, Gianni Versace, Accessoire Diffusion, Stéfane Kelian,* and *Gas* (this last with costume jewelry)—for women; *Façonnable, Uomo,* and *Daniel Crémieux* are for men. *Galerie Suffren* (eighteenth-century antique furniture) and *Souleiado* (Provence textiles) are among shops in the Byblos Hotel. And there's a branch of the *Jacques Dessange* hairdressing chain on Rue Allard.

INCIDENTAL INTELLIGENCE

Nearest train stations are St.-Raphaël (to the east) and Toulon (to the west); regularly scheduled buses serve St.-Tropez from each of these points. *Further information:* Office de Tourisme, Quai Jean-Jaurès, St.-Tropez.

34

Sarlat

By Huffle and Truffle through Périgord

BACKGROUND BRIEFING

Locate the southwesterly city of Bordeaux (chapter 10) on a map of France, fixing your eye in an easterly direction. The towns you'll note—Sarlat and Périgueux, especially—will be in small type. And it's not likely that, on an all-France map, many of the neighboring villages will appear at all. The point I make is that the region still termed Périgord, though lacking a single whizbang of a metropolis, compensates with a plethora of pretty towns where an overnight visitor is, to this day, an honored guest.

Périgord is a concentration of fortified castles on dramatic bluffs, elaborately facaded Renaissance mansions, and churches—more of them early, severe Romanesque than later Gothic—worshiped in over long centuries. And there is a pair of even more distinctive lures: caves in which Paleolithic man lived and painted, and an irresistibly rich cuisine—based on the truffle and the goose—that will never, *ever* come to terms with cholesterol.

Taking its name from ancient residents called *Petrocorii,* who date back to before the Roman occupation, Périgord evolved as a fiefdom of the dukes of Aquitaine and was English-held during the Hundred Years War, before becoming a part of Renaissance France. And although other parts of France have known quite as many battles and changes of landlord and allegiance as Périgord, appurtenances of its past appear in greater abundance—and with less celebrity—than is the case elsewhere. A cardinal rule of Périgord tourism is this two-word maxim: *Go inside.*

ON SCENE

Lay of the Land: Périgord is, by and large, a region of overnight layovers. Ideally, it is traversed by rented car—although trains serve larger towns; buses, smaller ones. There are no time-consuming metropolitan centers, but as many utterly charming small towns (including medieval fortified villages called *bastides*) and country castles as you have time and inclination for; not to mention visitable prehistoric caves, of which the most significant cluster is at *Les Éyzies.* Distances are not great. By that, I mean a journey of, say, 30, 40, or 50 miles between Point A and Point B is a long one. I open this chapter with *Sarlat* because—though small and with no outstanding hotels or landmark restaurants—it is nothing less than one of the best preserved Middle Ages/Renaissance towns in France. And it's delightful to walk about. *Rue de la République,* which cuts through it north to south, is virtually its sole claim to modernity—and pedestrians-only in summer. The bulk of the town lies to its west, based on venerable *Place de la Liberté* (dominated by seventeenth-century *Hôtel de Ville,* with outdoor cafés), from which *Rue de la Liberté* runs south to *Place de la Cathédrale* and a clutch of important structures (below). *Rue Fénelon, Rue Landry,* and *Rue de la Montaigne* are but a trio of central streets, lined by beautiful old houses. The railway station is south of the center on *Avenue Thiers.*

Cathedral of St.-Sacrédos (Place du Péyrou) was built as the chapel of a substantially endowed abbey between the twelfth and fourteenth centuries, with Renaissance additions. The tremendous height of its nave impresses, as does a Baroque choir and a rococo organ. The building is ingeniously tucked into a hill, with towering *Lanterne des Morts*—Lanterns of the Dead—out back, originally a chapel for funerals, with burials in the surrounding *Cimetière St.-Benoît,* and both a Romanesque chapel and tranquil cloister, adjacent. Just opposite is *Hôtel de la Boétie,* the house in which a noted writer whose name it takes was born, with the most celebrated Renaissance facade in town; note its carved-stone windowframes.

Musée de la Chapelle des Pénitents Blancs (Rue des Pénitents Blancs, just west of Rue de la République) is Sarlat's best-kept secret—a repository of sumptuous sacred art in an extraordinarily beautiful, desanctified seventeenth-century church. Every exhibit is handsome—gilded wooden angels, sculpted bishops, *Ste.-Claire* as the subject of an eighteenth-century painting, and a seventeenth-century *St.-Jerôme* in polychrome constitute but a handful—and the lot are framed by the church's dramatic barrel vault.

Marché aux Oies is Sarlat's centuries-old goose market, in the square whose name it takes. Regional wines (from Bergerac, below) may be sampled and are sold at this square's *Maison du Vin de Bergerac. Cellier du Périgord* (Place de la Liberté) is a delicious source of the region's celebrated foie gras, pâté, rillettes, tartines, and galantines. Antique shops—on rues Émile-Faure, Fénelon, and other streets—can yield quality objects. And the principal department store is *La Grande Fabrique* (Rue de la République).

Château de Puymartin (six miles north of Sarlat) is essentially Renaissance and sports a pair of turreted towers. Resident family members take you through; Grande Salle, with a gorgeous fireplace, Aubusson tapestries, and Louis XIII chairs, is the showplace room.

Périgueux (38 miles north of Sarlat and capital of Dordogne département, which approximates the area of old Périgord) is a town of considerable beauty, compact enough for ambulatory exploration. *Place Bugeaud* is the central square, with *Monoprix* department store and good shops; these continue on adjacent *Rue de la République* (site of *Nouvelles Galeries* department store) and on *Rue du Président-Wilson*. Nearby *Rue Limogeanne* is the core of the town's *Secteur Sauvegarde,* its meticulously restored old quarter, with Renaissance houses lining streets. Amble about for a bit to sense the flavor of Périgueux; then zero in on three interiors. *Cathedral of St.-Front* (Place Daumesnil) is one of the most curious such in France. It looks, as you approach it, for all the world like a southwest counterpart of Sacré-Cœur, above Montmartre in Paris—chock-filled with cupolas. These are nineteenth-century, not unlike Sacré-Cœur's, but other parts of this impressively immense pile go back nine hundred years. Don't miss the cloister. *Musée du Périgord* (Rue Barbecane) is a surprise package of no little interest, with exhibits at once prehistoric (the skeleton of a 35-million-year-old neighborhood gent), ancient (neighborhood Roman mosaics), medieval (a carved stone griffon from the cathedral belfry dating to the twelfth century), and relatively recent (rococo paintings and porcelain)—with later works by area artists. *Church of St.-Étienne de la Cité* (Place de la Cité) is severely Romanesque, a veritable fortress beneath an immense dome, with a lovely choir.

Bergerac (26 miles south of Périgueux and one of the region's Big Three towns, along with Périgueux and Sarlat): If, like me, you have read Rostand's classic *Cyrano de Bergerac* in French class or have seen it played, you want to pay your respects to the town of Cyrano and Roxanne, ringed by vineyards whose grapes are the basis of dry Bergerac and sweet Montbazillac wines. The town is centered by *Place de la République,* with shops on adjacent streets like *Rue Thiers* and *Avenue du Président-Wilson* and a pair of museums in *Hôtel de Ville* (Rue Neuve d'Argenson), one of which, *Musée Municipal,* has exhibits of local prehistoric finds, as well as later Bergerac art and artifacts. *Château de Montbazillac,* two miles south of town in the hilly vineyards, compensates with Renaissance architectural details—crenelated walls, a quartet of towers, elaborate entrance—

for what it lacks in size; museum exhibits within delineate, on the one hand, the story of the neighborhood's wines, and, on the other, the neighborhood's historic Protestant antecedents.

Les Éyzies (12 miles northeast of Sarlat): It is entirely possible to appreciate the global significance of the caves at Les Éyzies—and those nearby, as well as exhibits in the national museum here—without being able to relate to them as easily as to, say, a *paysage* by Poussin, a portrait by Largillière, or a pool of water lilies by Monet. It is a question of time frame. Prehistoric art and the science of prehistory can be difficult to come to grips with, even in southwest France, where the evidence of Cro-Magnon man—come upon only a century and a quarter back—is so startling. Withal, this 30,000-year-old handiwork wants to be experienced. First stop should be *Musée National de la Pré-histoire,* built into cliffs—in an originally medieval château, above the village. It is not big—there are but eight galleries—but it is significant, and what one most remembers is that its exhibits were the work of men who resembled the Neanderthal figure just outside the museum entrance: It was sculpted in 1930, using an actual Neanderthal skeleton as the basis of its design. From the museum, opt for as many as half a dozen caves in the neighborhood; those of *Font de Gaume*—but a third of a mile away—are quite the most fabulous, with some 200 designs, in still discernible color, of recognizable animals (bison, especially, but deer and horses, too). If you've time for more, those of *Les Combarelles* (two miles distant), some 300 extraordinary wall engravings, are important, too. If it's July or August, when this area, I must caution you, is packed with visitors, consider such alternatives as the *Caves of La Mouthe, Les Cent Mammouths, Bara-Bahau,* and *Du Sorcier.* (*Caveat:* Les Éyzies and surrounding caves traditionally close mid-October through mid-April.)

Lascaux II: But what, you are about to ask, about the famous paintings on walls of the prehistoric Cave of Lascaux? Alas, they have been closed since 1960, only 23 years after they were discovered, the better to protect them from destructive bacteria introduced by a plethora of visitors. But the mid-eighties saw the opening of Lascaux II—only a few hundred yards away from the original, outside of the village of *Montignac,* 14 miles north of Les Éyzies. This second Lascaux is a scientifically researched, carefully produced replica of the original; believe me, it is not a variation on a theme of Disneyland. You enter an unlighted cave whose contours are identical with the closed Lascaux, even to slippery terrain and surfaces worn by centuries. A team of painters, sculptors, engineers, and computer experts put it all together with amazing skill. You wait your turn to be taken through in a small group by a staff expert, watching your step as you move along in the dark, as the guide directs a flashlight at frescoes of animals—bulls and horses, bison and deer, delineated in earth tones of brown, beige, and goldish yellow—that were executed in candlelight to re-create the level of illumination available to painters who created the originals 15,000 years ago.

Château de Beynac, (in the Dordogne River village of Beynac-et-Cazenac, a few miles south of Sarlat, is a cliff-hanger—quite literally. It straddles an eminence at the river's edge, protected by formidably high, crenelated walls, part of a *re*building as long ago as the thirteenth century. You cross a courtyard to reach state rooms—a sumptuous salon and oratory are the top two. But it's views along the river that are most memorable, and it's agreeable to amble through the atmospheric adjacent village.

Château de Bourdeilles (10 miles north of Périgueux), not unlike Beynac (above), is dramatically elevated, but on the banks of another river—the Dronne. It's actually two châteaux: medieval fortress and Renaissance palace. The former's kicker is an octagonal keep. But it's the latter's Salle Dorée to which you beeline. This ravishingly decorated salon is the work of the same André le Nôtre who created Fontainebleau's interiors, a marvelous mix of fine furniture, splendid tapestries, paintings by the Fontainebleau school's Amboise Le Noble—and fabulously painted beamed ceilings.

Abbaye de Brantôme (seven miles north of Bourdeilles and nicely combined with it, edging the Dronne River, in a village whose name it takes) embraces a beautiful Gothic church, art-filled, with a detached bell tower, eighteenth-century abbey buildings, and a garden from which there are river views.

Domme (11 miles south of Sarlat) is the prototypical *bastide*—or fortified village; if you visit but one such in Périgord, this should be it. Tucked into a cliff high above the Dordogne River, it was built in the late thirteenth century and is little changed since then, turbulent Hundred Years War battles notwithstanding. A trio of original gates and still formidable ramparts—a tower at each extremity—enclose the town. It's fun to stroll *Grande Rue,* taking in *Maison du Gouverneur,* the old governor's mansion on *Place de la Halle,* along with the colonnaded market hall, and to view the river from *Promenade de Falaises,* on the cliff, as you depart.

Château de Hautefort (20 miles east of Périgueux) is an essentially seventeenth-century masterwork—elevated, massively scaled, and multitowered, with three of its sides enclosing a capacious court; classic-style Grande Galerie and domed chapel are the highlights of its interior, with terraced gardens a visitor bonus.

Trémolat (20 miles west of Sarlat) is one of Périgord's prettiest villages, affording fine views of the Dordogne, on which it is oddly positioned in a kind of horseshoe contour. Its ace-in-the-hole is an unusual fortified church, quite as forbiddingly plain as it was when erected in the ninth century.

Limoges (though not in Périgord, but at its northeastern extremity, with Périgueux 60 miles to the south) is an industrial city—its name is synonymous with fine French porcelain—albeit with a trio of visitable destinations. *Musée Adrien-Dubouchée* (Place du Champ-de-Foire) is a celebration of porcelain, housing some 10,000 objects, from ancient ceramics to patterns being produced this very week in Limoges factories, with displays of such other French china as Sèvres and St.-Cloud, as well as foreign porcelains, Ming through Wedgwood. *Musée Municipal* (Boulevard de la Corderie), occupying a onetime archepiscopal palace built in the eighteenth century, stands out because of its Limousin—regional—enamels, medieval through modern, with the former (work of the Middle Ages and Renaissance) the most outstanding. Directly next door is *Cathedral of St.-Étienne*—thirteenth-century Gothic, with an impressively vaulted nave, sculpted tombs, and a treasury highlighted by locally created enamels. If you've time, stroll around the center of town, in and about pedestrians-only *Rue du Consulat* and neighboring streets lined with half-timbered Renaissance houses.

SETTLING IN

Hostellerie de Maysset (Route D-67, less than two miles from Sarlat; phone 5359-08-29) is not, alas, central. But it's so pretty that I can't resist leading off with it. If you've a car, you'll be content in this contemporarily constructed but traditional-style inn. Public spaces—lounge, bar, nicely appointed restaurant—are delightful; ditto, the 22 no-two-alike rooms that look out into the Maysset's parklike garden. *First Class.*

St.-Albert Hôtel (Place Pasteur; phone 5359-01-09)—at the south edge of Sarlat and an easy walk to the center—is unpretentious but comfortable enough, with 61 adequate rooms, a cozy cocktail lounge, congenial staff, and a restaurant worthy of additional comment in a later paragraph. *Moderate.*

La Madeleine Hôtel (Place de la Petite-Rigaudie; phone 5359-12-40) is a centrally located Sarlat house. There are 22 traditional-style rooms, bar, and restaurant—an efficient operation that, alas, lacks spontaneity, warmth, even a smile. *Moderate.*

Salamandre Hôtel (Rue Abbé-Burguier; phone 5359-35-98) is a couple of blocks farther south of Sarlat's center than the St.-Albert (above), with which it shares the same management. There are 21 adequate rooms, as well as 5 vividly decorated duplex suites. Bar and breakfast only. *Moderate.*

Domino Hôtel (21 Place Francheville, Périgueux; phone 5308-25-80) is an old house whose owning family has taken care to modernize it without losing an iota of the charm that has accrued in the century of its operation. Most of the 37 rooms are bath-equipped, antique-accented—and delightful. There's a corking good restaurant that moves to umbrella-topped tables in the inner garden during warm weather, a bar whose clientele is a mix of locals and visitors, and skilled, congenial management. *Moderate.*

Bristol Hôtel (37 Rue Antoine Gadaud, Périgueux; phone 5308-75-90) is a relatively contemporary house, centrally situated and agreeable. There are 28 rooms. Bar and breakfast only. *Moderate.*

Ibis Hôtel (8 Boulevard Saumande, Périgueux; phone 5353-64-58) is conveniently central—a near-neighbor of the cathedral, with 86 neat rooms, bar, and restaurant. *Moderate.*

Manoir le Grand Vignoble Hôtel (St.-Julien-de-Crempse, six miles north of Bergerac; phone 5324-23-18) is indicated as a headquarters for the Bergerac area. It's a manor house that dates to the seventeenth century, with high-ceilinged public spaces that include a beamed lounge-bar and a paneled restaurant. There are 26 distinctively decorated rooms, a good-sized outdoor pool, tennis, and an unexpected surprise—riding—either on the backs of horses or in the hotel's antique buggy. *First Class.*

Royal Vézère Hôtel (Place de l'Hôtel de Ville, Le Bugue; phone 5307-20-01) is a clean-lined contemporary house edging the Vézère River in a pleasant village not far south of Les Éyzies—and worth knowing about in connection with a visit to that area. There are 53 well-equipped rooms, bar-lounge, and a restaurant featuring regional specialties. Best Western. *First Class.*

Cro-Magnon Hôtel (Les Éyzies; phone 5306-97-06) is among the more thoroughly likable of Périgord's hotels—small enough for service to be personal, owner-managed, handsomely traditional, and set in its own swimming-pool-equipped park. There are 20 no-two-alike rooms; each of those I have inspected is handsome. Bar-lounge, too, as well as an exceptional alfresco-in-summer restaurant featuring truffle-based Périgord specialties, that you do well to visit for the good-value—and delicious—menu at midday. Charming. *First Class.*

Les Glycines Hôtel (Les Éyzies; phone 5306-97-07) is an agreeable house, with a reliable restaurant, friendly bar, and 25 full-facility rooms. *Moderate.*

Du Centenaire Hôtel (Les Éyzies; phone 5306-97-18) makes a point of being stylish; has 27 comfortable rooms and a reputed restaurant with contemporary cuisine. Member, Relais et Châteaux. *First Class.*

Château de Puy Robert Hôtel (Montignac, near Lascaux; phone 5351-92-13) makes for an attractive stopover when you're in the neighborhood. Set in its own park, the château shelters nearly 40 no-two-quite alike suites and rooms with bath, welcoming public spaces, a swimming pool in the garden, and an estimable restaurant whose chef does delicious things with foie gras and truffles, not neglecting sweets, and with tables alfresco in summer. *First Class.*

Le Relais du Soleil d'Or Hôtel (Montignac, near Lascaux; phone 5351-80-22) is modern, to be sure, but with nearly 30 rooms traditional in style, as is the attractive restaurant. Bar-lounge, outdoor pool. Congenial. *First Class.*

Rush Hôtel (Terrasson, 20 miles north of Lascaux, 30 miles west of Périgueux; phone 5350-03-74) is stark modern without and graciously traditional within. There are 50 rooms, some Louis XV–style, some Louis XIV, and attractive public spaces that include restaurant and bar-lounge. *First Class.*

Les Îles Hôtel (Thonas, midway between Périgueux and Sarlat, near Lascaux and Les Éyzies; phone 5350-70-20) is well situated, rustic-attractive, with 10 rooms of differing sizes and facilities; and a stone-walled, beam-roofed restaurant featuring Périgord specialties, which moves outdoors in summer. *Moderate.*

Le Vieux Logis Hôtel (Trémolat, about midway between Sarlat and Bergerac, not far from Les Éyzies; phone 5322-80-06) is a long-on-scene, long-admired stone manor house of yore, with 20 antique-accented rooms, garden setting, and ranker of a restaurant with well-priced prix-fixe menus featuring Périgord classics. Member, Relais et Châteaux. *First Class.*

Le Panoramic Hôtel (Trémolat; phone 5322-80-42) is an unpretentious but comfortable 23-room house (not all rooms have baths); restaurant, bar. *Moderate.*

Les Bruyères Hôtel (Route de Cahors, Villefranche-du-Périgord; phone 5329-97-97) is strategically situated on Périgord's southern frontier, just outside an aged *bastide,* or fortified town. Setting is an originally thirteenth-century house in a garden, with 10 agreeable rooms and a stone-walled restaurant. *Moderate.*

DAILY BREAD

St.-Albert Hôtel Restaurant (Place Pasteur; phone 5359-01-09): I don't know of a better restaurant in Périgord in which to become acquainted with the rich cuisine of the region that's based on the goose, the goose's liver, and the delectable truffle than this Sarlat hotel dining room. Order à la carte or from a prix-fixe in this expertly operated restaurant. Open, perhaps, with foie gras frais served with an onion sauce or rillettes de confit de canard—pâté based on preserved duck; with confit de canard as an entrée accompanied by sautéed potatoes flecked with the mushroom species known as cèpes. Filet of beef, veal, and poultry are options. *First Class.*

Le Moulin du Roi (Passage Henri-de-Segogne, 7 Rue Albéric Cahuet; phone 5331-01-38) is typically Vieux Sarlat—beamed ceilings and silk-shaded lamps in the intimate interior, tables set outside against aged brick walls in warm weather. There are prix-fixe menus, one of which might embrace pâté de foie gras as an opener, a hearty cassoulet Périgourdin (truffle-flecked), a regional cheese, and a pastry dessert. Friendly. *First Class.*

La Rapière (17 Rue Tourny; phone 5359-45-38) is indicated for lunch in a scenic Sarlat quarter. The well-priced prix-fixe is based on confit de canard. Outdoor tables. *Moderate.*

Café de l'Hôtel de la Mairie (Place de la Liberté) is just the spot for coffee or a cold drink, the while you watch ambulatory Sarlat pass in review. *Moderate.*

La Flambée (Rue Montaigne, Périgueux; phone 5353-23-06) is small but smartly traditional, with tuxedoed waiters serving up tasty beef specialties grilled on an open-to-view fire. Open with the house's handsomely presented crudités or foie gras frais and continue, then, with filet de bœuf accompanied by sauce Périgueux—surely appropriate in the city of origin. Or select trout; the chef will come out and pluck a live one from La Flambée's tank, preparing it à la meunière thereafter. Luscious desserts. *First Class.*

L'Olson (31 Rue St.-Front, Périgueux; phone 5309-84-02): What it lacks in substantial size, this relatively intimate restaurant compensates for with tasty regional favorites, duck foie gras among the openers, delicious fish, hearty entrées. Try to make this one for the good-value menu at lunch. North of the cathedral. *First Class.*

Le Tournepiche (2 Rue de la Nation, Périgueux; phone 5308-90-36) is atmospheric—as well it might be, given a location close to the cathedral, heart-of-town. Prix-fixe menus are based on grilled lamb chops, filet of beef, and sliced smoked duck breasts and include wine. *First Class.*

De l'Univers Hôtel Restaurant (18 Cours Montaigne, Périgueux; phone 5353-34-79) is at its most tempting in summer, when tables are moved to the street-view garden, so that you watch the passing parade, the while enjoying a prix-fixe menu built around confit d'oie or a steak. Lots of locals. *Moderate.*

Le Cyrano (2 Boulevard Montaigne, Bergerac; phone 5357-02-76): No quarrel with this restaurant's appropriate title, nor, for that matter, with its fare. Order the prix-fixe menu, making sure that you open with warm foie gras and artichoke salad and follow with duck—also a Cyrano specialty. *First Class.*

Royal Limousin Hôtel (Boulevard Carnot, Limoges; phone 5534-65-30) is central, and a good Limoges headquarters, with 75 okay rooms. Breakfast only. *First Class.*

INCIDENTAL INTELLIGENCE

Further information: Office de Tourisme, Place de la Liberté, Sarlat; Office de Tourisme, 1 Avenue de l'Aquitaine, Périgueux; Office de Tourisme, 97 Rue Neuve d'Argenson, Bergerac; Office de Tourisme, Place de la Mairie, Les Éyzies; Office de Tourisme, Place de Born, Montignac (near Lascaux); Office de Tourisme, Pavilion Renaissance, Brantôme; Office de Tourisme, Boulevard Fleurus, Limoges.

35

Strasbourg

Showplace of Alsace

BACKGROUND BRIEFING

Border cities—cities that have dealt with political, cultural, and linguistic crosscurrents over long centuries—are invariably appealing. Find Strasbourg on the map—only the Rhine to separate it from Germany and Belgium, Luxembourg and Switzerland near-neighbors—this lot contrasted, of course, with the considerable territory of France to the west. Strasbourg's tale can be likened to a juggling act, practiced by experts over a 2000-year span. Little wonder that its people speak German as fluently as French, along with a dialect of their own, and that so many of them speak good English as well. Nor is it surprising, for that matter, that Strasbourg serves as seat of the European Parliament and the Council of Europe.

It was Celts who first settled Strasbourg at the dawn of the Christian era. Romans, who succeeded them, called it *Argentoratum*. Only with the influx of later Germanic settlers did the name change to *Strateburgum*. The tenth century saw Strasbourg part of the Holy Roman Empire. By the time it gained Free Imperial Status in the thirteenth century, it had become a medieval mercantile crossroads of consequence, with the German language dominant, to the point where it lured even Johann Gutenberg, who gave his name to a central Strasbourg street and square, remaining for a period in the fifteenth century before actually inventing the printing press in Mainz. (See *Germany at Its Best*.)

It was under Louis XIV's reign that Strasbourg became part of France in the seventeenth century, and it was after the French Revolution, in the late eighteenth century, that it became noticeably French, with respect to use of the language and adjustment to the culture.

There were, to be sure, two involuntary German relapses. As spoils of the nineteenth- century's Franco-Prussian War,

Strasbourg, along with the rest of Alsace (see Colmar, chapter 15) became German territory for nearly half a century, until the conclusion of World War I. The Second World War saw it German-occupied once again—and damaged. But Strasbourg has always bounced back. My only caveat with respect to a visit today is that you may not, at any given moment, be quite certain what country you're in. Strasbourg is by no means typical of urban France, nor of urban Germany, nor of rural Alsace. It is one of a kind, a city of extraordinary beauty that is comfortable with outlanders, knows how to have a good time, and—important, this—tastes as good as it looks.

ON SCENE

Lay of the Land: Strasbourg is old-fashioned enough to regard its palatial nineteenth-century railway station (*Place de la Gare*) as a focal point. Flanked by a clutch of hotels—including some very good ones—it's at the western edge of the city. *Rue du Maire Kuss* leads east to the core—crossing the *Ill River* just north of the scenic quarter, *La Petite France*—a delightful jumble of immaculately maintained medieval houses, half-timbered, their balconies giving onto the river and adjacent canals, with the view sublime from *Terrasse Panoramique* of the building known as *Barrage Vauban* on *Quai Mathias.* Area streets—*Rue des Moulins* (with the landmark *Maison des Tanneurs*), *Rue des Dentelles,* and *Grande Rue*—are lined with fine old houses, as is *Rue du Fosse des Tanneurs,* which leads to big and busy *Place Kléber,* Strasbourg's premier square. From it, via shop-lined *Rue des Grandes Arcades,* the city's towering cathedral is a hop and a skip, on *Place de la Cathédrale,* with *Château des Rohan*—housing several major museums—adjacent, on *Place du Château.* Walk everywhere; Strasbourg comes up with surprises at every turn.

Cathedral of Notre-Dame (Place de la Cathédrale): Be glad of the cathedral's central location; you can pop in every time you pass by—which will be often—to experience a facet of its complex interior missed on earlier visits. Built over five centuries—it is, of course, essentially Gothic, from the thirteenth and fourteenth centuries—the cathedral lacks nothing but a tower on its right side to match that on its left, which, incidentally, is ascendable, if you're up to 300-plus steps. Halt at the west, or principal, facade. Tympanums, or carved overdoors, of its three portals are busy with sculpted likenesses covering a range of subjects—Wise and Foolish Virgins through Old Testament Prophets. Look up at the exquisite rose window as you enter. Then move down the massively scaled nave to the transept, to pause between the unique-to-Strasbourg Angels' Pillar, with three rows of splendidly sculpted figures interpreting the Last Judgment. To be observed also in the transept is a plaque with this inscription: "In memory of American officers, non-commissioned officers and enlisted men who gave their lives to free Alsace 1944–45." Take in the pulpit, whose Gothic tracery makes it quite unlike any other. Enjoy the widely reputed stained glass. Note frescoes behind the high altar. Admire Romanesque capitals of the crypt—the remaining lower level of an earlier cathedral, over which this structure was built. Time your visit to conclude precisely at midday to watch the daily performance of the cathedral's Swiss-made, sixteenth-century astronomical clock, with Death—scythe in hand—striking the hour, while the twelve Apostles pass in review, beneath Christ blessing the audience, with a noisy cock crowing high in the background.

Musée de l'Œuvre Notre-Dame (Place de la Cathédrale) is a repository of art objects associated with the neighboring Cathedral of Notre-Dame, including the Romanesque structure that preceded the present one, *and* of Alsatian art, medieval through Renaissance. It embraces some two score galleries, several courtyards, and a number of art-filled corridors. It's brilliant, and you want to give it some time. Entire rooms—their original paneled walls and decorated ceilings—have been incorporated in the exhibits. There are a transplanted seventeenth-century spiral staircase, doorways from Strasbourg mansions, stained-glass windows and wrought-iron architectural elements, glassware and pottery, tapestries and sculpture—including, among the latter, an intact stonecutters' guild meeting room, with likenesses of saints in niches along four walls. There's also an entire cloister of a twelfth-century Alsatian monastery, scenes from the life of Christ carved into the capitals of its columns. You want not to overlook the courtyard designed as a medieval garden, with a stream winding through it. Paintings? You'll find several by Strasbourg-reared Hans Baldung Grien, with a complementary clutch by other artists of the same Renaissance period.

Château des Rohan museums (Place du Château) overwhelm with their treasures. Treasure No. 1 is the building itself, an all-France, early eighteenth-century masterwork, where Strasbourg's prince-bishops lived (Louis XV, Queen Marie Leczinska, Marie Antoinette, and Napoleon, on separate visits with each of his two empresses, were among its guests) in a setting of splendidly scaled, paneled, wainscotted, and furnished salons, themselves an integral part of a contemporary Rohan visit. Of the three actual Rohan museums, *Musée des Beaux-Arts* dominates, with a considerably larger collection than you might expect—in a single building housing several museums. There is, for example, a strong sprinkling of Spaniards—El Greco and Zurbarán, Ribera and Murillo; Italians like Lippi, Correggio, and the stellar portraitist Bronzino; the same

Hans Baldung Grien whose work we see in Musée de l'Œuvre Notre-Dame (above); Low Countries greats like Memling, Brueghel, Rubens, De Hooch, and Van Dyck; the early Renaissance Simon Marmion's moving *Pietà;* and a host of Frenchmen—Philippe de Champaigne through Renoir. *Musée des Arts Décoratifs* is a mix of Strasbourg-made furniture—mostly eighteenth century, but some older—and locally manufactured porcelain, much of it by a firm named Hannong, with antique clocks as a bonus. *Musée Archéologique* takes you back—*way* back—to prehistoric Strasbourg. Pottery, utensils, weapons—that sort of thing; with more interesting Roman pieces: sculpture, fragments, and later objects, as well.

Musée Alsacien (Quai Alsacien) is fun: a 20-gallery collection of folk art in a seventeenth-century building that wraps itself around three sides of a cobbled courtyard. Period rooms—paneled parlor with seventeenth-century tile stove and furnishings, all-purpose farmhouse room with bed in a cabinetlike frame, country kitchen lined with gleaming copper *kugelhopf* molds—are the standout exhibits; toys and costumes, pottery and paintings, too.

Musée Historique (Rue du Vieux Marché-aux-Poissons), though not as amusing as Musée Alsacien (above), brims with documentation that tells the Strasbourg story. Spiffy soldiers' uniforms, some with their original breastplates, are the most colorful exhibits. But there's stained glass galore, historical prints, and etchings, as well.

Musée d'Art Moderne (Quai St.-Nicolas) contrasts its quarters—an antique customs house unused for centuries—with its contents: a corking good clutch of contemporary paintings that make for a nice change of pace in this tradition-laden city. Impressionists represented include Degas, Pissarro, and Monet, with later painters like Braque and Dufy and master sculptors, Maillol through Arp.

Church of St.-Pierre-le-Vieux (Rue du 22 Novembre) is a Strasbourg contribution to ecumenism: Catholic and Protestant churches joined at right angles and dating to the Renaissance, with the Catholic part coming off with the more beautiful interior.

Palais de l'Europe (Avenue de l'Europe, a quarter-hour's drive northeast of the center) is a contemporary complex considerably younger (1977) and far less architecturally significant than the UN (1952) in New York—but reminiscent of it, with flags of the score-plus member European nations flying out front in the manner of the UN, and—again, like the UN—with a secretariat (headquarters of the Council of Europe) and an international legislature, the Parliament of Europe, which meets several times annually, with sessions usually lasting a week. Unlike the UN, which welcomes visitors without notice throughout the year, these chaps ask that you telephone (8861-49-61) first, to arrange a time for your tour.

SETTLING IN

Terminus Gruber Hôtel (10 Place de la Gare; phone 8832-87-00) is a lovely, old-fashioned house lining the vast square opposite the railway station—a seven- or eight-minute walk from Place Kléber. There are just a hundred no-two-quite-alike rooms, fussily but engagingly decorated, with good baths and—in some instances—good-sized. Leading from the lobby are a cozy cocktail lounge; a rather grand, two-story-high, beamed restaurant that serves up a mighty tasty dinner, even at a late hour; and—facing the square—a *brasserie* as popular with locals as with guests. Reception-concierge staff—cordial, kindly, and efficient—is one of the best such that I know in France, for which, three cheers. Best Western. *First Class.*

Sofitel Strasbourg (Place St.-Pierre-le-Jeune; phone 8832-99-30) is old enough—I suspect it goes back to the late sixties—to antedate the newer crop of Sofitels that dot the republic and tend to be less felicitous in appearance. This one is tastefully contemporary, with a big lobby, 180 rooms (some, to be sure, smaller than others), restaurant, cocktail lounge, and a super situation: steps from Place Kléber. Friendly. *First Class.*

Grand Hôtel (Place de la Gare; phone 8832-46-90) is a turn-of-century house that has been nicely refurbished. The lobby is bright, the elevator leading to upper floors is glass-walled, and there are 90 rooms; those that I have inspected are very comfortable, and no hotel of my acquaintance gives the impression of being more squeaky-spanking-sparkling clean. Breakfast only. *First Class.*

Bristol Hôtel (4 Place de la Gare; phone 8832-00-83) is an oldie, nicely updated, with 40 rooms, no two identical; restaurant, bar. *Moderate.*

Hôtel des Rohan (17 Rue du Maroquin; phone 8832-85-11)—a near-neighbor of the Cathedral—is a good-looking house with just three dozen no-two-alike rooms, many in Louis XV style, the others rustic-look, all with baths, either tubs or showers. Nice. Breakfast only. *Moderate.*

Hôtel Cathédrale (12 Place de la Cathédrale; phone 8822-12-12) is aptly named; the Cathedral is just opposite. This is a hotel with a sense of style in the lobby-bar-lounge, and in those of the 32 rooms (with counter-sink baths and shower curtains) I've inspected. *Moderate.*

Hôtel de l'Europe (38 Rue du Fossé des Tanneurs; phone 8832-17-88) edges the city's atmospheric Petite France quarter and is an ancient posthouse dating to the fifteenth century, still with a half-timbered facade and beamed ceilings. Breakfast only. *Moderate.*

Monopole-Métropole Hôtel (16 Rue Kuhn; phone 8832-11-94) is central, about midway between the train station and Place Kléber, with a traditional look employing regional motifs and 94 bath-equipped rooms. Breakfast only. *Moderate.*

Novotel Central (Quai Kléber; phone 8822-10-99) has just under a hundred functional rooms and agreeable public spaces that include a restaurant and bar. Generous buffet breakfasts. *Moderate.*

Ibis Hôtel (Quai Kléber; phone 8822-14-99) is a next-door neighbor of the Novotel (above), also with just under a hundred rooms, restaurant, and bar. Tabs are cheaper, rooms smaller, and mattresses a bit thinner than those of Novotel. *Moderate.*

Arcade Hôtel (7 Rue de Molsheim; phone 8822-30-00) is one of a chain of agreeably mod-look, budget-tabbed, full-facility houses. There are 245 rooms with showers (beds can be narrow), restaurant, and bar. Central. *Moderate.*

Le Pax Hôtel (24 Rue du Faubourg National; phone 8832-14-54) is no-frills but central, with baths in 86 of the 119 rooms, and a convenient inexpensive restaurant. *Moderate.*

Hilton International Strasbourg Hôtel (Avenue Herrenschmidt; phone 8837-10-10) would head my Strasbourg grouping were it central. Location, however, is northwest of the center, out in the modern Palais de l'Europe quarter, a quarter-hour's drive from the center. This is a looker of a contemporary house, with just under 260 rooms and suites, whose decor is a restful, modified-modern mix and whose baths—bless U.S.-founded Hilton International—have real, honest-to-goodness Yank-style showers over the tubs—a rarity, believe me, in provincial France. Smiles greet you as you reach reception in the high-ceilinged lobby, off which are the Bar Bugatti, hung with prints of vintage Bugatti cars, a piano bar that draws evening crowds, a pair of restaurants (Maison du Bœuf and Le Jardin, later evaluated), and a terrace for warm-weather drinks. *Luxury.*

DAILY BREAD

Le Crocodile (10 Rue l'Outre; phone 8832-13-02) is subdued but handsome: Brown-leather upholstered Louis XVI chairs surround tables dressed in white linen, lighted by white-shaded lamps, with comfortable booths to the side. You are welcomed graciously, attended to punctiliously, and served deliciously. Crocodile has made its reputation on cuisine that's a deft mix of old-time Alsatian with contemporary. You might, for example, open with a salad of foie gras—served warm—on a bed of endive, or cream of frog's legs soup. Seafood is exceptional—gratin d'homard, a lobster masterwork; a trio of sole filets in a truffled mushroom sauce, white-wine based. Chicken breasts are treated with skill; blanc de volaille et noix de St.-Jacques—the poultry melded with scallops, in a cream sauce laced with vermouth and Riesling—is a case in point. The house's duck and beef dishes are special, too. Cheeses are served in profusion, and œufs à la neige—gossamer but satisfying—is an indicated dessert. This is the restaurant selected to cater the civic lunch for President Reagan at Château des Rohan (above) in the course of an official Strasbourg visit. With good reason. Central. Member, Relais et Châteaux. *Luxury.*

Valentin Sorg (6 Place de l'Homme-de-Fer; phone 8832-12-16) is, like Le Crocodile (above), only steps from Place Kléber, but has the advantage of an elevated situation in a room lined with picture windows that give onto a cityscape dominated by the towering cathedral. Not that you come only for the view. Sorg cuisine is stubbornly—and satisfactorily—traditional. There are several prix-fixe menus, from one of which a meal might open with smoked trout served in tandem with celery rémoulade, continue with a médaillon of veal in a cream of mushroom sauce, and conclude with the house's own sherbet served with baked-on-premises petits-fours. Alternatives: Alsace's own poulet au Riesling served, as it should be, with broad noodles; canard à l'orange—duck in an orange-accented sauce; or roast lamb, Provençal style. Professional service. *Luxury.*

Maison Kammerzell (16 Place de la Cathédrale; phone 8832-42-14): You will have passed by this veritable skyscraper of a half-timbered medieval house—noting, particularly, the hand-carved wooden decorations between its windows—in the course of city strolls. It's a landmark, but it's also a corking good restaurant. There's no better spot to order the supreme Alsatian specialty, choucroute garnie—a vast platter with a generous base of sauerkraut, on which is piled pink cervelas sausage, white sausage, red Montbéliarde sausage, thick-cut slabs of bacon, the black "pudding" known as boudin noir, saucisse de Strasbourg (what we call knockwurst), sliced roast pork, liver dumplings, a ham shank, and—just so you won't leave the table famished—boiled potatoes. You don't attempt one of these every day, but you must have choucroute garnie at least once in the course of an Alsace visit. There are many other options here, grilled trout through roast pheasant among them. *First Class.*

Maison des Tanneurs (42 Rue Bain-aux-Plantes; phone 8832-79-70) is quite what its name indicates—a onetime tanner's house, wonderfully atmospheric, overlooking the Ill River in La Petite France, with Alsatian specialties. Open, perhaps, with onion tart or flammekueche, a variation thereof with bacon, served hot. Snails are good here, too, as are smoked shoulder of pork and coq au Riesling. *First Class.*

Maison du Bœuf (Hilton International Strasbourg Hôtel, Avenue Herrenschmidt; phone 8837-10-10) is a good choice for a festive lunch combined with a tour of neighboring Palais de l'Europe (above) or for a candlelit dinner. The beef of the title is roast prime rib, rolled to your table on a silver trolley. But seafood is special, too. If you're not going to have it as an entrée, open with the chef's assortment of three species of smoked fish (salmon is one of them). You might follow with filet of beef served with marrow, in sauce marchand de vin. And conclude with a chocolate or lemon soufflé. Super service. *Luxury.* (And bear in mind that the Hilton's casual restaurant, *Le Jardin,* makes a specialty of Alsatian favorites, including onion tart and coq au Riesling. *Moderate/First Class.)*

Buerehiesel (4 Parc de l'Orangerie, out in the Palais de l'Europe quarter; phone 8861-62-24) is quartered in a Hansel-and-Gretel cottage, garden-surrounded, with tables spilling into several small, primly decorated rooms. Welcome is chilly and service, likewise—at least in my experience. Cuisine is contemporary, with a prix-fixe menu that might open with lamb salad, continue with roast rabbit, and conclude with ice cream enveloped in a coffee-flavored sauce. Disappointing. Member, Relais et Châteaux. *Luxury.*

Du Dauphin (13 Place de la Cathédrale; phone 8832-86-95) is worth knowing about when you're in the core of town—and hungry. Hearty choices include choucroute garnie, tarte à l'oignon, and Riesling-sauced seafood stew. Outdoor tables. *Moderate.*

Pfifferbriader (9 Place de la Grande Boucherie, attached to Musée Historique; phone 8832-15-43): You want to sample at least one typically Strasbourg *winstub* while you're in town. Build your meal around bäckoffe—a pork, white wine, and potato casserole, tarte à l'oignon, or sausages, with a big pitcher of white wine to accompany. Everybody has a good time. *Moderate.*

Chez Yvonne (more properly known as s'Burjerstuewel, 10 Rue du Sanglier; phone 8832-84-15) is still another ranking weinstube, not far from the Cathedral, with hearty local favorites, including among entrées delicious langue de bœuf—beef tongue. Go for the menu, less pricey at lunch than dinner. Chez Yvonne, relatively small and with a considerable clientele of regulars, is fun. *Moderate/ First Class.*

Buffet de la Gare (in the train station, Place de la Gare; phone 8832-68-28) comprises a pair of restaurants, L'Assiette—less pricey and with good value *Moderate* menus—and L'Argentoratum, more expensive *Moderate/First Class.* Convenient and reliable.

Beyler (5 Place de la Cathédrale): Alsatians, I am told on good local authority, consume 25 percent more pastry than do Frenchmen in other regions of the republic and are, as well, the biggest ice-cream eaters in all France. If you want to understand why, select a plate of Beyler's baked goods, with or without frozen accompaniments. *Moderate.*

Café Tisza (14 Quai de la Bruche): It's a sunny day, and you could do with a cup of coffee alfresco; take it at Tisza. No finer views of La Petite France. *Moderate.*

Le Panoramic (Printemps, Rue de la Haute Montée): This café-cum-vistas—on the eighth floor of a department store—is accurately named. Have a casual lunch, snack, or coffee, bearing in mind that the store's excellent food—or *alimentation*—department is on five. *Moderate.*

Au Moulin (in the village of La Wantzenaus, Hotel du Moulin, northwest of the center; phone 8896-20-01) is indicated for a sunny lunch or a relaxing country dinner. Au Moulin is situated in its own garden-centered plot, hospitality is warm, fare is Alsatian—and exemplary. A meal might open with matelote aux nouilles—fish stew with noodles, continue with poussin—young chicken—prepared in the house's style, and proceed to cheese (local Muenster, most likely), with plum tart smothered in whipped cream for dessert. *First Class.*

SHOPPER'S STRASBOURG

Magmod, Strasbourg's big nonchain department store, is on Rue 22 du Novembre; *Printemps* is on Rue de la Haute Montée, and good, old, thrifty *Marks & Spencer,* out of Britain but also in Paris and several provincial French cities, is on Place Kléber, site also of links of the *Daniel Hechter* (clothing) and *Lancel* (gifts and accessories) chains. *Gillman,* a fabulous *pâtisserie,* is at 6 Place du Temple Neuf and 20 Quai des Batellers. *Frick-Lutz,* an also-fabulous *charcutier,* is at 10 Rue des Orfèvres. Both *Burberrys* (raincoats) and *Guy Laroche* (haute couture) are on Rue du Dôme. *Charles Jourdan* (shoes) and *Tedbury* (smart men's and women's duds) are on Rue des Grandes Arcades. Rue des Hallebardes is virtually lined with smart shops, including *D. Porthault* (linens), *Christofle* (crystal and silver), *Malbasa* (antiques), and *René* (classy men's shirts).

SOUND OF MUSIC

Théâtre Municipal (Place Broglie): If you collect theaters, this is one not to miss; early nineteenth century, handsome, and home of the regional Opéra du Rhin; concerts and ballet, too.

INCIDENTAL INTELLIGENCE

Aéroport de Strasbourg-Entzheim is seven miles west of town; scheduled transatlantic service via Air France, to New York, and to domestic points as well. *Further information:* Office de Tourisme, Palais des Congrès, Avenue Schutzenberger, Strasbourg.

36

Toulouse

Diversions to Albi, Carcassonne, and Auch

BACKGROUND BRIEFING

It is not so much that Toulouse is underappreciated abroad; it is more a case of its being unknown. I would not hazard even an informal poll among friends on its location, not to mention its significance. Still, this fourth-largest of the French cities—150 miles southeast of smaller but better-known Bordeaux and close both to the Mediterranean and to Spain—deserves more than passing acquaintance. It hums today as France's aircraft center (Caravelles and Airbuses you've flown were Toulouse-made). But it has always been busy at one sort of activity or another. Ever since Romans—calling it *Tolosa* and making of it one of the biggest of their Gallic colonies—set precedent, makers and doers have dominated the Toulouse scene.

Catholic bishops were present as early as the fourth century, following within but a hundred years the introduction of Christianity by the martyred St.-Sernin, whose name graces the city's all-Europe ranker of a Romanesque basilica. Germanic Visigoths came in the fifth century to make Toulouse capital of a kingdom that spread into neighboring Spain. The sixth century saw this city become seat of the wide-ranging kingdom of Aquitaine over a span of 300 years. In the mid-1100s, Toulouse was governed for the first time by the uniquely titled *capitoules* (from which the name of the current city hall, Le Capitole, derives).

By that time, counts of Toulouse ruled virtually all of Languedoc, competently and justly. They stood out because of their tolerance for Jews, many of whom settled in Toulouse, and they were hospitable to painters, writers, and philosophers, to the point where their court became a medieval culture hub celebrated throughout the continent. Simultaneously, Toulouse thrived as a spiritual center (Spanish-born St. Dominick established the Dominican order here) and as an educational center (the University of Toulouse opened in 1230 and is now the largest in France outside of Paris), as well as a mercantile *entrepôt* of no little significance. You have only to walk its core to observe still-standing mansions that bespeak medieval and Renaissance wealth.

Withal, treasures of Toulouse must be assiduously sought out. This city lacks the hill-backed Mediterranean setting of Marseille; a core dramatically cut through by two rivers, like Lyon; a backdrop of snowy peaks in the manner of Grenoble. And, contemporary commercial eminence notwithstanding, there's nary a luxury-category hotel. Still, it pays to tarry in La Ville Rose—so-called because red brick is the traditional building material—and to use it as a base for exploration of the nearby walled town of Carcassonne, Toulouse-Lautrec's native Albi, and the quiet little cathedral city of Auch.

ON SCENE

Lay of the Land: It's as though town planners knew we were coming and wanted to make it easy. Consider the *Garonne River* as Toulouse's southwest frontier. The bulk of the city to its west and north is what interests us. There are two central squares: northerly *Place du Capitole* (named for the eminently visitable city hall [below] overlooking it) and *Place du Président-Wilson,* with cafés spilling into its center. As if the latter square, named for a U.S. president, were not Yank association enough, the two squares are joined by *Rue Lafayette*—called after a French hero of the American Revolution. The principal shopping street, *Rue Alsace-Lorraine* runs through the two squares, concluding at southerly *Place Équirol,* through which the No. 2 street, *Rue Metz,* cuts, east to west. The neighborhood is crisscrossed by such pedestrian streets as *rues Filatiers, des Changes,* and *St.-Rome.* Beyond the core is a pair of concentric boulevards—each of which is multinamed—ringing it. The railway station is at the northwest of the center on one of these outer arteries, called, at that point, *Boulevard de la Gare.*

Basilica of St.-Sernin (Place St.-Sernin): The French are often more niggardly than the English in the space they reserve in front of their great churches, the better to afford perspective. St.-Sernin is a case in point; it deserves a considerably more generous Place St.-Sernin than is the case. Still, this nine-century-old beauty catches you up as you approach, its five-story tower not a whit overbearing for the massive structure beneath—housing a 350-foot-long nave leading to the transept and high altar, beneath a sublime, 60-foot-high barrel-vaulted ceiling. Looking inward as you enter is an esthetic experience in and of itself. But other aspects of St.-Sernin warrant attention; the saint whose name it takes lies buried beneath a baroque baldachine behind the eleventh-century marble high altar. Expressively carved capitals top columns in the transept; marble bas-reliefs of Christ and the Apostles grace the apse; below are a pair of crypts with half a dozen splendidly embellished chapels in the lower one.

Church of the Jacobins (Rue Gambetta) is like no other church you've seen before: a veritable Gothic tour-de-force, splendidly restored in the 1970s. The Jacobins is a successor to an earlier monastery complex established by St. Dominick and his black-and-white-robed preaching friars in the thirteenth century. It has three lures: pinnacle-like windows recessed into the facade of the church they ring; an utterly serene, poplar-planted cloister; and an abnormally high and elongated nave climaxed by a single pillar supporting the chancel, its vaults like the fronds of a palm tree.

Musée des Augustins (21 Rue de Metz) is a desanctified Augustinian monastery dating back seven centuries that was allowed to deteriorate pitifully—even after it became a museum in the last century—to the point where French government experts, with a multimillion-franc budget, stepped in during the mid 1970s. They closed the museum's doors for half a decade, restored the complex to its original Gothic splendor, remounted its exhibits—many of them world-class—with flair, and reopened Musée des Augustins in 1980. You go as much for the setting—the high-vaulted onetime chapel's massive space devoted to paintings by Rubens, Murillo, Van Dyck, and a host of French masters; Romanesque sculpture in the refectory and chapter room—as for the art. And that is hardly to be despised, given works by such other Frenchmen as Simon Vouet, Philippe de Champaigne, and Pierre Mignard, of the Baroque era; Largillière, Rigaud, and Oudry out of the eighteenth century; and the nineteenth century's Delacroix, Corot, and Courbet. With Italian Old Masters Perugino, Lorenzo Monaco, and Guercino on hand as well.

Cathedral of St.-Étienne (Rue Croix Baragnon): In a city without St.-Sernin, the Jacobins, and, for that matter, a cloistered monastery turned into an art museum (above), Toulouse's cathedral would be a stellar Gothic standout. As it is, even with the competition, you want to pop in, to see how it is actually two joined churches (built between the thirteenth and seventeenth centuries) with an oddly irregular but appealing facade, sublime tapestries, a rose window, and side chapels in near-limitless quantity.

Le Capitole (Place du Capitole) is city hall, eighteenth-century, with a dazzling classic-style facade stretching over some 400 feet. Pop through the courtyard to a grand staircase that will take you up a flight to the showplace reception room, *Galerie des Illustres*—it honors hometown lads who made good—lavishly frescoed with gilded capitals atop columns punctuating its walls.

Hôtel d'Assézat (Rue de Metz) is perhaps the most elaborate of a number of Renaissance town houses. It was built by a sixteenth-century *capitoul*—or municipal legislator. Go beyond its classic-style facade for a peep at its courtyard. Look, too, at *Hôtel de Bernuy* (Rue Gambetta), early sixteenth century, with a fabulous nine-level tower.

Musée St.-Raymond (Place St.-Sernin) is nicely combined with the Basilica of St.-Sernin, its neighbor. It comprises an oddball mix of collections, with Roman emperors' busts and medieval sculpture its standouts.

Musée du Vieux Toulouse (7 Rue de May) makes its home in Hôtel du May, a sixteenth-century merchant princes' mansion, that brims with Toulousiana—high-quality furniture, most especially, maps and prints, clothes and toys, domestic implements and pottery. Fun.

Albi (45 miles northwest of Toulouse) is surely the only city in France with a cathedral built to double as a fortress. Idea was to defend its bishop from communicants hostile to a kind of Inquisition he had instigated against believers in a peculiar medieval doctrine bearing Albi's name, called the Albigensian heresy. *Cathedral of Ste.-Cécile* (Place Ste.-Cécile) is severe and formidable without and lacks both flying buttresses and pinnacles. Yet its look is pleasing and distinctive—and could not contrast more with the interior than is the case, once one enters. Bolognese artists were imported from Italy to fresco virtually every conceivable available surface, except a mass of niches that frame polychrome likenesses of saints. The west wall contains an extraordinarily detailed interpretation of the Last Judgment, notable as much for content as for size. And the mammoth choir—carved-stone pinnacles behind its wooden stalls, exuberantly painted panels between the gilded vaults of its ceiling—is extraordinarily beautiful. Switch, then, to *Musée d'Albi,* but a hop and skip geographically, that represents a leap forward of half a millennium to the year 1864, when Henri de Toulouse-Lautrec was born to a local noble family and, despite impaired growth as a result of a rare kind of dwarfism called pyknodysostosis, achieved immortality in the 37-year span of his lifetime as one of the great postimpressionists. Toulouse-Lautrec is celebrated for penetrating studies, ranging from horses of his childhood to music hall habitués of later Paris years. He was as skilled at the brilliant-hued posters he pioneered as at drawings that reflected his gift for draftsmanship and at paintings—more formal but no less graphic.

Few small towns do as well by native-son artists of stature as does Albi, in the case of Toulouse-Lautrec, in this attractive repository of his work, overlooking the Turn River. There are, to be sure, other masters represented—Rigaud, Boucher, Georges de la Tour from an earlier era; a pair of Vuillards, with their subjects Toulouse-Lautrec. But you go for the Lautrecs—an early painting of his mother, sketches of the Moulin Rouge, Jane Avril—a favorite Lautrec subject—from the rear; studies of Paris types—train travelers, café-habitués, cabaret dancers, laundresses—in profusion; and interpretations you will not have seen before of Yvette Guilbert, La Goulue and—mascot of the collection—Bamboule, a bulldog drawn from life in 1897.

Carcassonne (53 miles southeast of Toulouse)—though extensively restored—remains nonetheless an originally thirteenth-century walled city that could be out of a fairy tale. There is a pair of concentric walls punctuated by towers and turrets, with entrance gained by a drawbridge over a moat. An overall view—in the course of your approach—is reason enough for a visit. But give this medieval marvel some time. Its *Musée Archéologique,* a part of the multiturreted château, brought to rights as part of the nineteenth-century ministrations of Viollet-le-Duc—the restoration wizard who worked France-wide—abounds in beautiful objects, the range busts and capitals and sarcophagi from the town's Roman period through murals, tombs, and bas-reliefs from Carcassonne's medieval Golden Age. Have a look, as well, at the stunning interior of *Basilica of St.-Nazaire*—noting especially capitals of columns flanking its Romanesque nave and its remaining, mostly Gothic, aspects, especially stained glass above stone choir stalls behind the high altar, and rose windows on either side of the transept. It's fun, then, to amble about, noting the dozen-plus towers that punctuate each of the city's two concentric rings of walls, by means of a stroll along the lists, between inner and outer walls.

Auch (46 miles west of Toulouse and pronounced *Ohsh*) is a tranquil cathedral town in the gently hilly heartland of ancient Gascony, celebrated as the legendary home of D'Artagnan, leader of Dumas's *Three Musketeers.* Auch's conveniently compact center is based on *Place de la Libération,* dominated by Hôtel de Ville, a lilting rococo palace of a town hall, from which lead a jumble of atmospheric streets, on one of which—*Rue Dessoles*—is located *Claude Laffitte,* a purveyor of the area's own brandy, Armagnac, along with food specialties, not to mention meals in his restaurant (below). Nearby, too, is *Musée des Jacobins* (Rue Daumesnil) named for the long-disused monastery it occupies, and a repository of Gascon lore—paintings, prints, and local furniture with the patina of centuries. Which leaves best for last. *Cathedral of Sainte-Marie* is Gothic-vaulted with Renaissance embellishments: a severe, twin-towered facade; massive sixteenth-century choir stalls that are masterworks of the woodcarver's art (ranking with those of Amiens Cathedral ["Excursionist's Paris," chapter 2] as France's finest); and just under a score of 400-year-old stained-glass windows by a beloved local called Arnaud de Moles; each is beautiful, but search out *The Nativity, The Crucifixion, Moses and the Burning Bush,* and *The Flight into Egypt*.

SETTLING IN

Grand Hôtel de l'Opéra (1 Place du Capitole; phone 6121-82-66): You walk through the courtyard of a mellow Place du Capitole complex to enter the Opéra, passing its garden-centered swimming pool en route. This relatively recently refurbished house emerges as one of the handsomest in southwest France. The lobby is small but handsome, in smart period style. No two of the not-quite half a hundred rooms are exactly alike, but each that I have inspected is imaginatively decorated in period style, with varying color schemes, textiles, wallpapers, and furniture and fabulous marble baths. The cocktail lounge has the look of a winter garden on an old transatlantic steamer, and the restaurant is worthy of comment on a later page. *First Class.*

Altéa Wilson Hôtel (7 Rue Labéda; phone 6121-21-75) is a core-of-the-city old-timer that has been agreeably updated. There are 95 rooms of varying sizes, with good baths, as well as a cozy cocktail lounge and a staff at once cordial and professional. Breakfast only. *First Class.*

Concorde Hôtel (16 Boulevard Bonrepos; phone 6162-48-60) is a ranker of a house—tastefully contemporary, with close to a hundred thoughtfully fitted-out rooms with fine baths, congenial cocktail lounge, and not one but a pair of restaurants—reviewed on a later page—and skilled management. Location is just opposite the railway station. Hôtels Concorde. *First Class.*

Mercure Hôtel (Rue St.-Jérome; phone 6123-11-77) is central and modern and equipped with 170 full-facility rooms, restaurant, and café. Chaîne Mercure. *First Class.*

Victoria Hôtel (76 Rue Bayard; phone 6162-50-90) is delightfully old-fashioned and refurbished relatively recently with a sense of style; there are 75 rooms, some more capacious than others. But you're closer to the railway station than the core. Breakfast only. *Moderate.*

Royal Hôtel (6 Rue Labéda; phone 6123-38-70) is worth knowing about: first, because it's central and second, because it's inviting; the lounge is decked out in comfortable rattan furniture. Most but not all of the 25 rooms have baths. Breakfast only. *Moderate.*

Arcade Hôtel (2 Rue Claire Pauilhac; phone 6163-61-63) follows the Arcade chain's formula: compact and clean-lined rooms (140 all told) with beds that can be narrow and showers in their baths, inexpensive buffets at breakfast, lunch, and dinner in the restaurant. Just north of the core at Place Jeanne-d'Arc. *Moderate.*

D'Occitanie Hôtel (5 Rue Labéda; phone 6121-15-92) would be higher up in my Toulouse ranking were it not closed during the extensive period when French schools observe summer vacation, as well as during other school holidays. Reason is that it's a hotel-school. Which is what makes it otherwise desirable: Student staff really toes the line, under constant professional supervision. The 20 rooms are positively shipshape, and, when you ask a question at reception, you half expect the youngster responding to stand at attention and salute in the course of his or her reply. Good restaurant in connection. *Moderate.*

Chiffre Hôtel (50 Rue Séré de Rivières, Albi; phone 6354-04-60) is a delightful, heart-of-town house operated by the third generation of its founding family, with 40 no-two-alike rooms in period style (Louis XVI dominates, with commendable attention to details like paneling, chandeliers, and coordination of wallpapers and textiles). There's a good-sized cocktail lounge and a restaurant evaluated on a later page. *First Class.*

Altéa Hôtel (41 Rue Porta, Albi; phone 6347-66-66) is, more's the pity, across the Tarn River from town, but there are super views of the cathedral from riverfront accommodations. There are 56 rooms all told, good restaurant and bar. *Moderate/First Class.*

Cité Hôtel (Place de l'Église, within the walls of Carcassonne; phone 6825-03-34) could not be more typical of Vieille Carcassonne, adjacent to the ramparts, with half a hundred well-equipped rooms, restaurant, bar, and pretty garden. *First Class.*

Du Donjon Hôtel (2 Rue du Comte Roger, within the walls of Carcassonne; phone 6871-08-80): Don't let its formidable name frighten you away; the Donjon has in recent seasons been completely refurbished with period-style public spaces, including a restaurant (breakfast and dinner but no lunch) and bar; and 36 okay rooms with bath. Best Western. *Moderate.*

De France Hôtel (Place de la Libération, Auch; phone 6205-00-44): The trim but simple lobby gives no promise of the smartness of this long-on-scene, 30-room hotel. Decor of each chamber differs, but count on Second Empire—or even older—furnishings, glazed chintz, antique prints on the walls, and marble-counter baths, some with stall showers, praise be. The cocktail lounge is charming; indeed, there is no better spot for a spot of the local Armagnac, served icy cold in heavy glasses designed so that they cannot be set down; idea is that, like it or not, you drink up in one fell swoop. The De France's restaurant is exemplary enough for comment in a later paragraph. *First Class.*

Lion d'Or Hôtel (7 Rue Pasteur, Auch; phone 6205-02-07) is, to be sure, modest and across the Gers River from the heart of town, but just might fill the bill—15 rooms with bath, restaurant. *Moderate.*

DAILY BREAD

Vanel (22 Rue Maurice-Fontvieille; phone 6121-51-82) is low-key; a generous-sized space, with contemporary chrome-accented chairs at tables set with immaculate white linen and the only touch of color a range of good-quality, recent paintings on the walls. Hospitable Lucien Vanel, the chef-patron, makes it a point to say hello to his customers at one point or other, in the course of a meal that cannot help but be extraordinary. Monsieur Vanel has for long championed southwest cuisine, and he stuck by it even during the height of the *nouvelle* vogue. You order à la carte from a full page of plats du jour or from among a group of standby favorites. Starters include truffled pâté de foie gras or foie gras au naturel, prepared in the house; or mushroom or truffled omelets and a scrumptious cassoulet of snails. Among entrées are confit de canard—served with Sarlat-style potatoes; tournedos in a pepper sauce, flamed with Armagnac; and stuffed goose neck. But M. Vanel's changed-each-day dishes are delicious, too. I recall, for example, opening with crayfish-flecked gazpacho, continuing with filet of beef with sauce Bordelaise, and concluding with a sweet from the separate dessert card—mille feuilles aux fraises des bois. And digestifs: M. Vanel's list includes a dozen eaux-de-vie and as many of the area's Armagnacs. Skilled, smiling, never-pretentious service. *Luxury.*

Les Jardins de l'Opéra (Grand Hôtel de l'Opéra, 1 Place du Capitole; phone 6123-07-76) is as handsome as it is delicious. There are two well-priced menus, of which the pricier is the more interesting; a meal might embrace avocado terrine, the house's duck or rabbit specialties; and your choice of sweets. The à la carte features cassoulet Toulousain, the region's hearty, baked bean-based casserole, as well as filet of beef, sauce Béarnaise. Super sweets. Smiling staff. *Luxury.*

Darroze (19 Rue Castellane; phone 6162-34-70): Once you resign yourself to the over-fussy, ever-so-grand ambience of this relatively small restaurant, you can enjoy the competent traditional fare. The cheaper of the two menus might open with the house's own terrine, garnished with a salad; continue with the day's fricassee, wine-sauced; and conclude with a designated frozen sweet. The more expensive menu—billed as a surprise—is just that: you take what pleases the chef to serve you that noon or evening. Far better to select from the à la carte, opening perhaps with scrambled eggs-cum-truffles or seafood salad. Proceed with filet of sole or médaillons of lamb, as an entrée, terminating with profiteroles au chocolat. *Luxury.*

Belle Époque (3 Rue Pargaminières; phone 6123-23-12)—a near-neighbor of the Church of St.-Pierre west of the center—bases its repertoire on dishes that were indeed popular during the turn-of-century Belle Époque, or variations thereof, with the range foie gras, poultry, and beef with delicious pastries and skilled selection of reds in the cellar. Pleasant. Go, if you can, for the menu at lunch. *First Class.*

La Pomme d'Amour (1 Rue de Gorse, opposite Church of La Dalbade; phone 6153-34-88) is indicated for a hearty dinner built around tranche de gigot grillée—grilled lamb steak—or confit d'oie—preserved goose—deliciously garnished. They're served as part of a three-course prix-fixe, with lemon tart or champagne sherbet among desserts. *First Class.*

Rôtisserie de l'Écluse (Concorde Hôtel, 16 Boulevard Bonrepos; phone 6162-48-60): Semiabstract, modern tapestries line the walls of this smart restaurant. The à la carte features tempters like smoked salmon, crudités presented with a dipping sauce, or hearty fish soup—to open; with such entrées as sole meunière, grilled lamb chops, and a cassoulet of which the chef is justifiably proud. Gracious service. *First Class.* (And bear in mind this same hotel's *Brasserie,* zeroing in on the well-priced plat du jour, or the daily prix-fixe, with an à la carte salade Niçoise or an omelet good bets, too. Snappy service. *Moderate.*)

Les Jardins de Li (9 Rue Croix-Baragnon; phone 6253-00-14) makes its home in a Renaissance mansion, but its look is sprightly—with modern art on bare brick walls. Stick-to-the-ribs regional fare is the specialty—stuffed goose neck or mussel soup to start, confit or maigret de canard among a number of entrées; the house's own tarte Tatin or Black Forest cake for dessert. *First Class.*

Pâtisserie Toulousaine (77 Rue Alsace-Lorraine) is, as well, a *salon de thé,* on the main shopping street. Stop in for pastry with coffee or a cup of tea. *Moderate.*

Le Cardinal (Place du Président-Wilson) is indicated for a pick-me-up—coffee or a drink, a casual lunch. Location is a principal Toulouse square. *Moderate.*

Chiffre Hôtel Restaurant (50 Rue Séré-de-Rivières, Albi; phone 6354-04-60) is a sensible choice for lunch, in the course of Albi exploration. The well-priced prix-fixe might be composed of foie gras-stuffed goose neck, salmon terrine, roast lamb generously garnished; and a choice of house-made desserts. Central. *First Class.*

Auberge du Pont-Levis (just outside the main gate, Carcassonne; phone 6825-55-23) is a two-story, multiroom restaurant. I suggest you take a table upstairs and tackle the delicious prix-fixe, which might commence with a fresh filet of salmon served with a piquant sauce, follow with confit de canard or a filet of beef, and conclude with one of the house's fabulous desserts—chocolate cake, mocha, or orange tart, for example. Friendly. *First Class.*

Crémade (1 Rue Plô, Carcassonne; phone 6825-16-64) is a sensible choice for a within-the-walls lunch while wandering, or dinner at day's end. The midday menu, usually based on a beef or poultry entrée, is a good buy. *Moderate.*

De France Hôtel Restaurant (Place de la Libération, Auch; phone 6205-00-44) is a formal room in brown and beige, with high, chandelier-hung ceilings and French windows giving onto the square. Fare is typically and traditionally Gascon; everything that I have sampled has been delicious, and presentation is flawless. Consider a meal that might open with foie gras d'oie et de canard *avec un verre de Sauternes*—braised goose *and* duck livers served according to local tradition, with a glass of Sauterne; proceed with cuisse de canard confits aux pommes Paillasson—preserved duck presented with straw potatoes, delicately deep-fried; and conclude with, for example, prune ice cream drenched with Armagnac or a trio of the house's own tart and grainy sherbets in primary colors, accompanied by petits-fours. *Luxury.*

Claude Laffitte (38 Rue Dessoles, Auch; phone 6205-26-81) made its reputation from the sale of a staggering assortment of Armagnacs and food specialties of Gascony. But it's also a restaurant with lovely local dishes the stars of its delicious menus, less pricey at lunch than dinner. Special. *First Class.*

SHOPPER'S TOULOUSE

Department stores are spread around: *Nouvelles Galeries* on Rue Laperouse, *Dames de France* on Place Jeanne d'Arc; and a whopping big, cafeteria-equipped *Monoprix* on Rue Alsace Lorraine, which has still another department store, *Parunis,* and such clothing shops as *Daniel Hechter, Armand Thierry,* and *Kopetzki,* where suede is a specialty, and *Bally* (shoes).

SOUND OF MUSIC

Théâtre du Capitole (Place du Capitole) is a part of the historic, eighteenth-century City Hall complex (above), with a traditional horseshoe-shaped interior that has, more's the pity, been modernized over the years. It's the setting for diverse presentations of opera, Beethoven's *Fidelio* through Richard Strauss's *Arabella;* the operettas still popular throughout France; ballet, with classics like *Petrouchka* through to modern works; and concerts. Musical events take place also at the modern *Halle aux Grains* (Place Dupuy).

INCIDENTAL INTELLIGENCE

There is scheduled air service to and from points throughout France from *Aéroport Toulouse-Blagnac,* west of the center; and Air France links Toulouse with New York's JFK. *Further information:* Office de Tourisme, Donjon du Capitole (a towering medieval fortress), Toulouse; Office de Tourisme, Palais Berbie, Albi; Office de Tourisme, 15 Boulevard Camille Pelletan, Carcassonne; Office de Tourisme, Place de la Cathédrale, Auch.

Acknowledgments

The pleasure of researching a considerably enlarged and revised edition of a book with a subject such as this—France and its increasingly contemporary façade, in the era of the builder-president, François Mitterrand—has been considerably enhanced by the cooperation and friendship extended by George L. Hern, Jr., public relations director of the French Government Tourist Office in the United States, with whom I have also been priveleged to work in connection with this book's earlier editions and its companion volume, *Paris at Its Best,* not to mention magazine and newspaper articles and columns over a sustained period. As I have said in this space on earlier occasions: It's always a pleasure. As indeed it is to work with other stars of the French travel and transportation galaxy based in New York, Air France's Jim Ferri and Bruce Haxthausen, and FrenchRail's Dagobert Scher, especially; they're never too busy to answer questions and offer counsel.

I am grateful, too, to George Hern's associates at the French Government Tourist Office, Marion Fourestier, and my longtime friend, Jacqueline Moinot-Schaff, as well as the crack press team at Maison de la France in Paris, with whom I have worked over the years, Nicole Garnier and Marie-Paule Bournonville. My research editor for the *World at Its Best* series, Max Drechsler, has been of inestimable help in on-scene exploration as we wandered France—Normandie to the Côte d'Azur—for this edition. And, as always, I appreciate the hard work on this book (as, indeed, on all volumes of this series, both new and revised, a score all told) of my editor, Michael Ross; and of my agent, Anita Diamant.

I want to extend, alphabetically, mes amitiés et mes remerciements to the following friends and colleagues in France and on this side of the Atlantic for their personal kindness and professional cooperation:

William Allen, Antonio Alonso, Dario dell'Antonia, Giuseppe Artolli, Catherine Audin, Susan Bang, Jacques Barache, Jean Bardet, Sophie Bardet, Deborah Bernstein, Nabil M. Boustany, Ann-Marie Carrière, Florence Ceneda, Claude Chapron, Enza Cirrincione, Michèle de la Clergerie, Shelley P. Cohen, Michel Couturier, Edward O. Douglas, Valérie Ducaud, Evelyn Dugast, Gilles Dumas.

Also Josiane Ermel, Dominique Fénelio, Franco Gentileschi, Elisabeth Gervais, Sophie Gimenez, Gabrielle Glickman, Fabienne le

Goff, Suzanne Gryner, Marie-Françoise Guichard, Linda C. Gwinn, Lou Rena Hammond, Olivier Lépine, Gilles Lesguer, Maguy Maccario-Doyle, Brigitte Maille, Jean-Paul Marro, Susan Martin, Josiane Merino, Gérard Minard.

Also David B. Mitchell, Franco Mora, Michel Palmer, William F. Peper, Eve Peterson, Georges-André Piat, Sylvie Picard, Jeannine Pierga, Carol D. Poister, Didier Rinck, André Rolfo-Fontana, Frederick J. deRoode, Nicolle Roques-Lagier, Philippe Reutsch, Georges and Marie-Thérèse Sauvayre, Rana Sahrai, Nadine Seul, Patrick Suba, Stéphane Thierry, Cécile Triballier, Murielle Velay, and Christine Vidal.

R.S.K.

Index

B

C

D

G

N

O

S

T

U

About the Author

Robert S. Kane's initial writing stint came about when, as an Eagle Scout, he was editor of the [Boy Scout] *Troop Two Bugle* in his native Albany, New York. After graduation from Syracuse University's noted journalism school, he did graduate work at England's Southampton University, first making notes as he explored in the course of class field trips through the Hampshire countryside. Back in the United States, he worked, successively, for the *Great Bend* (Kansas) *Daily Tribune, Staten Island Advance, New York Herald Tribune,* and *New York World-Telegram & Sun* before becoming travel editor of, first, *Playbill,* and later *Cue* and *50 Plus.* His byline has appeared in such leading magazines as *Travel & Leisure, Vogue, House & Garden, Atlantic, Harper's Bazaar, Family Circle, New York, Saturday Review,* and *Modern Bride;* and such newspapers as the *Newark Star-Ledger, New York Post, New York Daily News, New York Times, Los Angeles Times, Chicago Sun-Times, Boston Globe, San Diego Union, Dallas Morning News, San Francisco Examiner,* and *Toronto Globe & Mail.* And he guests frequently, with the subject travel, on TV and radio talk shows.

Africa A to Z, the first U.S.-published guide to largely independent, post–World War II Africa, was the progenitor of his acclaimed 14-book *A to Z* series, other pioneering volumes of which were *Eastern Europe A to Z,* the first guide to the USSR and the Soviet Bloc countries as seen through the eyes of a candid American author, and *Canada A to Z,* the first modern-day, province-by-province guide to the world's second-largest country. His current *World at Its Best* series includes two volumes (*Britain at Its Best* and *France at Its Best*) tapped by a pair of major book clubs, and a third (*Germany at Its Best*) that's a prize-winner.

Kane, the only American authoring an entire multivolume travel series, has the distinction of having served as president of both the Society of American Travel Writers and the New York Travel Writers' Association, and is a member, as well, of the National Press Club (Washington), P.E.N., Authors Guild, Society of Professional Journalists/Sigma Delta Chi, and American Society of Journalists and Authors. He makes his home on the Upper East Side of Manhattan.